Digital Image Processing - Latest Advances and Applications

Edited by Francisco Cuevas, Pier Luigi Mazzeo and Alessandro Bruno

Published in London, United Kingdom

Digital Image Processing - Latest Advances and Applications
http://dx.doi.org/10.5772/intechopen.1000363
Edited by Francisco Cuevas, Pier Luigi Mazzeo and Alessandro Bruno

Contributors
Anis BenHajyoussef, Asma Saidani, Dihao Ai, Eshwar Udhayakumar, Eunice Nduati, Fenja Ahrens, Francisco Cuevas, Jonathan Blackledge, José Felipe Hurtado Castaño, Juan Pablo Guerra, Manuel Garcia Salido, Manuel Rodríguez Villegas, Marlena Götza, Matthias Reuter, Max Mignotte, Miriam Rocha Navarro, Rakesh Rajegowda, Suganthi Srinivasan, Thomas Ngigi, Wei Xianhu

First published in London, United Kingdom, 2024 by IntechOpen
IntechOpen is the global imprint of INTECHOPEN LIMITED, registered in England and Wales, registration number: 11086078, 167-169 Great Portland Street, London, W1W 5PF, United Kingdom

British Library Cataloguing-in-Publication Data
A catalogue record for this book is available from the British Library

Additional hard and PDF copies can be obtained from orders@intechopen.com

Digital Image Processing - Latest Advances and Applications
Edited by Francisco Cuevas, Pier Luigi Mazzeo and Alessandro Bruno
p. cm.
Print ISBN 978-0-85466-491-7
Online ISBN 978-0-85466-490-0
eBook (PDF) ISBN 978-0-85466-492-4

For EU product safety concerns:
IN TECH d.o.o., Prolaz Marije Krucifikse Kozulić 3, 51000 Rijeka, Croatia,
info@intechopen.com or visit our website at intechopen.com.

Meet the editors

Francisco Javier Cuevas de la Rosa, computer systems engineer for the Tecnológico de Monterrey in 1984, completed his master of science in computer science with a specialty in artificial intelligence at the same institute in 1995, followed by a doctorate in sciences (optics) at the Centro de Investigaciones en Óptica (CIO) in 2000. With more than 80 publications in computer vision and artificial intelligence, he has participated in more than 60 national and international conferences. He has been a member of the Sistema Nacional de Investigadores del CONAHCYT since 1995 and has supervised more than 30 graduate students. As a senior researcher at the CIO, he has taught more than 90 courses in areas including optical metrology, computer vision, and artificial intelligence.

Pier Luigi Mazzeo (Institute of Applied Science Application and Intelligent Systems of the Italian Research Council in Lecce) received his MSc in computer science from the University of Salento in 2001. He joined the Italian National Research Council (CNR) as a researcher in 2002, and since then he has been working on several artificial intelligence and computer vision research topics. The projects in which he is currently involved include algorithms for video object tracking, face detection and recognition, facial expression recognition, deep neural networks (DNN), and machine learning. He has authored and co-authored a total of 100 publications, including more than 20 papers published in international journals and book chapters. He has also co-authored five national and international patents. He acts as a reviewer for several international journals and for some book publishers. Since 2004, Pier Luigi has been regularly invited to take part in the scientific committees of national and international conferences.

Alessandro Bruno (IULM University, Department of Business, Law, Economics, and Consumer Behaviour, 2014, Milan) earned a Ph.D. in computer engineering from DINFO (Department of Computer Engineering) at Palermo University. He is now a tenure-track assistant professor with the Department of Business, Law, Economics, and Consumer Behaviour at IULM University in Milan, Italy. Before joining IULM University, Alessandro was an assistant professor at Humanitas University (Milano, Italy); he worked as a lecturer in computing with the Department of Computing and Informatics, Bournemouth University, in 2021 and 2022. He covered postdoc positions at NCCA (National Centre for Computer Animation) in the UK and at INAF IASF (Italian National Institute for Astrophysics), University of Palermo, and IZS (Istituto Zooprofilattico Sperimentale della Sicilia). He was a research visitor at Mullard

Space Science Laboratory (MSSL), University College London (UCL), in the imaging group led by Professor Jan-Peter Muller. He is the author of more than 70 international articles and is an associate editor for international journals. Alessandro is currently the principal investigator of a project funded by the NGI-Search consortium named HeReFaNMi (Health-Related Fake News Mitigation). His research interests include computer vision, artificial intelligence, and image analysis. He has mostly dealt with visual attention and visual saliency, biomedical imaging, crowd behavior analysis, image and video forensics, remote sensing, and human-computer interaction.

Contents

Preface

The inspiration for this book project arose from a pressing need within the scientific and engineering community for a comprehensive review of new methods in digital image processing (DIP) across various disciplines. As technology advances at a rapid pace, it is imperative that specialists in computer science and related fields stay abreast of the latest developments to remain relevant and effective in their respective fields. Recognizing this need, we dedicated ourselves to the task of compiling different research works that would be useful references for scientists and technologists seeking to improve their knowledge and skills in DIP.

The main objective behind the creation of this book was to present a comprehensive review of the state-of-the-art methods in DPI, with a particular focus on its applications in various areas of science and engineering. By synthesizing and consolidating the latest research findings, we aimed to equip readers with insights into emerging trends and methodologies, empowering them to leverage these advances in their own work. The ultimate goal is to foster innovation and facilitate the development of more efficient and sustainable solutions to complex challenges in various fields.

In the field of agriculture, for example, the book delves into the exploration of recent techniques for pest detection, detection of nutritional deficiencies, and quality inspection. With the agricultural sector facing increasing pressure to improve productivity and minimize environmental impact, there is a growing demand for advanced tools and methodologies that can automate processes and optimize resource utilization. By providing a comprehensive review of state-of-the-art DIP methods adapted to agricultural applications, the book aims to empower agricultural technicians to adopt and implement these techniques to improve efficiency and sustainability in agricultural practices.

The book is structured into three distinct sections, each focusing on different aspects of DIP and its applications in contemporary research and industry. The first section, "Image Processing Techniques and Computer Vision", covers a wide range of innovative methods from image enhancement techniques to applications in agriculture and dentistry. By exploring these advances, readers gain valuable insights into the evolving landscape of image processing and computer vision, and how these technologies are shaping diverse fields.

The second section, "Image Perception and Analysis", delves into the complexities of image perception and analysis algorithms and their applications in advanced driver assistance systems and crack propagation trajectory prediction. Through in-depth discussion and analysis, this section highlights the critical role of perception and analysis algorithms in understanding and interpreting visual data, especially in contexts where accuracy and reliability are critical.

Finally, the third section, "Imaging Theory and Simulation", explores the theoretical foundations and practical applications of imaging theory, including bionic color theory and the simulation and analysis of synthetic aperture radar images. By exploring the theoretical foundations of images and their simulated representations, this section provides readers with a deeper understanding of the fundamental principles governing the generation and interpretation of visual data.

It is essential to express my deep gratitude to the people and institutions that have played a fundamental role in the editing and publication of this book. First of all, I would like to extend my sincere appreciation to the MC Juan Pablo Guerra for his dedication and unwavering support at every stage of this process. His commitment to editorial excellence and his tireless effort have been instrumental in successfully carrying out this project. Furthermore, I want to highlight his valuable contribution and support to the chapter dedicated to agricultural applications, which significantly enriches the content of this book. I want to express my most sincere gratitude to my wife, Marite Cuellar, for her unconditional support throughout the entire process of writing this book. Her constant encouragement, understanding, and patience were instrumental in overcoming the challenges and keeping me focused on achieving this goal. Likewise, I would like to express my gratitude to Elvira and the IntechOpen editorial team. Their professionalism and commitment to editorial quality have been invaluable in the development and completion of this project. Their constant support and ability to address editorial challenges effectively have been instrumental in ensuring the quality and consistency of content.

I want to thank the institutional support received from the Optical Research Center (CIO) of León, Guanajuato, Mexico. The infrastructure and resources provided by the CIO have been extremely important in carrying out the research and writing of this book. Your support has been a fundamental pillar in the completion of this work. Furthermore, I wish to express my deep gratitude to the National Council of Humanities, Sciences and Technologies of Mexico (CONAHCYT) for their financial and logistical support. Their commitment to the advancement of scientific and technological research in Mexico has been fundamental for the development of innovative projects like this one. Your contribution has allowed us to create this book and share knowledge that will benefit the academic and scientific community.

In summary, this project would not have been possible without the support and collaboration of all the people and institutions mentioned previously. Their commitment and dedication have been instrumental every step of the way, from initial conception to final publication. I sincerely appreciate your contribution and am deeply grateful for your invaluable support. This book represents a concerted effort to address the growing demand for comprehensive resources in the field of digital image processing.

By offering a comprehensive review of new methods and applications across diverse disciplines, we focus on empowering professionals to leverage the latest advances in DIP to drive innovation and effectively address real-world challenges.

Francisco Cuevas
Centro de Investigaciones en Óptica,
León, Guanajuato, México

Pier Luigi Mazzeo
Institute of Applied Science Application and Intelligent Systems
of the Italian Research Council,
Lecce, Italy

Alessandro Bruno
Department of Business, Law, Economics, and Consumer Behaviour,
IULM University,
Milan, Italy

Section 1

Image Processing Techniques and Computer Vision

Chapter 1

Perspective Chapter: Mix-Unmix Pan-Sharpener – Novel Pan-Sharpening Method Based on Mixing Constituent Multispectral Bands and Unmixing Panchromatic Band

Thomas Ngigi, Eunice Nduati, Wei Xianhu and Marlena Götza

Abstract

A panchromatic band (Pan-band) spectrally covers a number of the other bands (multispectral-bands, MS). The Pan-band is of higher spatial resolution than the MS. The respective advantages of the two are combined through pan-sharpening with the resultant image adopting the higher spatial resolution of the Pan-band and the colour information of the MS. Various techniques have evolved but most of them cannot pan-sharpen more than three MS, and none of them can pan-sharpen more than three MS at a go, nor pan-sharpen a multispectral image not geographically covered by the Pan-band. This novel concept overcomes the first problem. The sequel to this chapter will address the second problem through reverse pan-sharpening. The concept argues that for a given pixel in the Pan-band, the strata of digital numbers (DNs) in the MS combine to give rise to a panchromatic-DN. The concept estimates respective coefficients of strata of DNs in the encompassed bands corresponding to pure blocks of pixels in the Pan-band. On the basis of the coefficients, encompassed bands' DN contributions to the panchromatic-DN are computed from the Pan-band DN. The resultant DN contributions are regressed on the MS-DNs and one of the encompassed MS pan-sharpened on the basis of its model. The other multi-spectral bands are pan-sharpened through it.

Keywords: pan-sharpening, image fusion, mix-unmix classifier, geographical inadequacy of panchromatic band, multi-spectral imagery, hyper-spectral imagery

1. Introduction

All Earth observation satellites are multi-band. In most cases, there is a band that collectively covers some of the other bands. The band covering the collective spectral ranges covered by individual bands is called the panchromatic band. The

IntechOpen

other bands are collectively referred to as multi-spectral bands. The panchromatic band always has a higher spatial resolution than the multispectral bands it encompasses. For instance, for Geoeye-1, the panchromatic band covers the spectral range 450 nm–800 nm encompassing the blue (450 nm–510 nm), green (510 nm–580 nm), red (655 nm–690 nm), and partially near-infra red (780 nm–920 nm) bands. The spatial resolution of the panchromatic band is 0.41 m against 1.65 m for the multispectral bands.

A panchromatic band does not provide colour information as it cannot be viewed in combination with the other bands due to differing spatial resolution. The encompassed multispectral bands when viewed in combination, made possible by a common spatial resolution, provide colour information in the RGB colour space through colour combination. However, due to the higher spatial resolution, the panchromatic band provides greater spatial detail than the multispectral bands. For a variety of applications, an image with both high spatial and spectral resolutions would be desirable. The higher spatial detail of the panchromatic band and colour information of the multispectral bands can be combined through the process of image fusion by pan-sharpening [1], defined pan-sharpening as fusion of a multi-spectral image and panchromatic data aimed at generating an outcome with the same spatial resolution of the panchromatic data and the spectral resolution of the multispectral image [2], defined it as merging the spatial and spectral information of the source images into a fused one, which has a higher spatial and spectral resolution and is more reliable for downstream tasks compared with any of the source images.

Pan-sharpening may also be across multispectral imagery [3, 4], discussed fusion of hyperspectral and multispectral imagery, noting that: the latter has detailed spectral information for fine classification and identification of land-cover but the narrow bandwidths limit absorption of reflected surface energy; the former has limited representation of spectral information making it difficult to characterise the spectral features but the higher spatial resolution allows for more complete description of the morphology and distribution of land-cover. Fusion of the two provides high spatial resolution and detailed spectral information for value-addition to remotely sensed data.

There have been numerous studies on pan-sharpening and development of pan-sharpening algorithms with the aim of preserving spectral information while increasing the spatial resolution of low-resolution multispectral data. However, there seems to be no universal categorisation criteria of pan-sharpening techniques. For instance [1], categorises the techniques into (i) Component substitution, (ii) Multi-resolution analysis, and (iii) third generation techniques e.g. variational optimization and machine learning techniques; [2] has (i) Component substitution, (ii) Multi-resolution analysis, (iii) Degradation model, (iv) Deep neural network; [5] has (i) Component substitution-, (ii) Relative spectral contribution-, (iii) High-frequency injection-, (iv) Methods based on the statistics of the image-, (v) Multiresolution-family. Despite the disharmony, two classical techniques are common to all reviewers: component substitution and multi-resolution analysis. [6–12] give further detailed discussions on pan-sharpening techniques.

2. Classical pan-sharpening techniques

A need arises to harmonise the criteria for categorisation of pan-sharpening techniques. This chapter cannot cover all the uttered categories of pan-sharpening techniques.

2.1 Component substitution techniques

Component Substitution (CS) techniques include among others, The Brovey transform, Intensity-Hue-Saturation (IHS) and Principal Component Analysis (PCA) methods [13]. As a requirement for all the aforementioned methods, the images must be co-registered and resampled, the quality of which impacts on the results of pan-sharpening [13, 14]. The IHS method is the most popular of the three and involves conversion of a three-band image from the RGB colour space to the IHS colour space [15]. However, the technique has been shown to produce fused images with spectral and colour distortions [15, 16]. Modifications to the IHS method have included extension from three bands to four bands with the inclusion of near-infrared and the incorporation of weighting coefficients on the green and blue bands to minimise the difference between *I* and the panchromatic band [17]. Recent studies and developments have led to the development of other CS-based techniques and algorithms including the Fast Spectral Response Function (FSRF), the GIHS with Genetic Algorithm (GIHS-GA), the GIHS with Trade-off Parameter (GIHS-TP), University of New Brunswick (UNB)-Pan-sharpen and the Weighted Sum Image Sharpening (WSIS) techniques [16]. The aforementioned methods were evaluated using a uniform data set in the 2006 GRS-S Data-Fusion contest and were generally found to have various shortcomings including poor colour synthesis, missing colours and features, and blurred contours and shapes [16].

2.2 Multiresolution analysis techniques (MRA)

MRA methods, also referred to as wavelet-based fusion methods, include but are not limited to Generalised Laplacian Pyramid (GLP), Discrete Wavelet Transform (DWT), Contour-let transform, and Additive Wavelets Luminance Proportional (AWLP) techniques [6, 18]. These techniques employ the basic principle of extraction of spatial detail information from the high-resolution panchromatic image, which is not present in the low-resolution multispectral images and injecting it into the latter [6]. These methods preserve spectral characteristics of the multispectral image better than CS methods but tend to have less spatial information [15, 18].

Thus, depending on the application, it seems the trade-off is between the preservation of spectral information with limited increase in spatial resolution and distorted spectral information with increasing spatial resolution. Hybrid techniques aim to overcome the limitations of the CS- and MRA-based techniques, to preserve the spectral and spatial information content of the input images [16].

3. Materials and methods

This chapter introduces a novel pan-sharpening technique, the mix-unmix pan-sharpener, based on the Mix-unmix Classifier [19, 20]. The classifier was developed to overcome the problem of under-determinacy in linear spectral unmixing. Optical panchromatic and multispectral imagery are utilised in demonstration of the Mix-unmix Pan-sharpener.

3.1 Theory of the mix-unmix pan-sharpener

For a given sensor, a panchromatic band covers a number of multi-spectral bands. The former has a higher spatial resolution than the latter. One multispectral pixel covers an area of *n x n* (where n is at least 2) panchromatic pixels. If the *n x n* panchromatic pixels have the same DN, then the geographically corresponding multispectral pixel, ignoring any radiometric errors, can be taken to be spectrally pure. For instance, the panchromatic Band 8 (wavelength range = 0.50 nm–0.90 nm) of Landsat ETM+ has a spatial resolution of 14.25 m and spectrally covers the first four bands (spatial resolution of 28.5 m), namely: blue (0.45 nm–0.52 nm), green (0.52 nm–0.60 nm), red (0.63 nm–0.69 nm), and near-infra-red (0.76 nm–0.90 nm) of the sensor. This implies that the panchromatic band can be taken to be a mixture of reflectance from the other four bands. Therefore, it can be hypothesised that for a given pixel, the panchromatic DN can be decomposed into four multispectral DNs. In other words, the four multispectral DNs for the pixel mix result in the panchromatic DN. This begs the question: in what ratio do the four multispectral DNs mix to give rise to the panchromatic DN?

3.2 Study area, data, and determination of pure multispectral pixels

The study area is located in Kenya and Landsat ETM+ data is utilised for the research (**Figure 1**). The Mix-unmix pan-sharpener moves a 2×2 kernel over the panchromatic Band 8 and if all the four DNs in the kernel are the same, the value and also the multispectral DNs from bands one to four of the geographically corresponding pixels are retrieved. It is worth noting that the kernel does not cover any panchromatic pixel more than once nor does it skip any. The dimensions of the panchromatic band must be a multiple of *n*, and the band must, for this demonstration, geographically cover the multispectral bands. **Table 1** is an extract of DNs of pure pixels.

3.3 Determination of the most probable mixing ratios

The approach adopted in determination of mixing ratios in this research borrows from [19, 20]. In developing the Mix-unmix Classifier, they mixed all the DNs of all possible end-members in all possible complementary combinations to synthesise all possible hypothetical mixed DNs. Through back-propagation, they determined the most probable abundances of the initial end-members. In this research, the multi-spectral bands one to four are synonymous with end-members, the multispectral DNs in **Table 1** (columns two

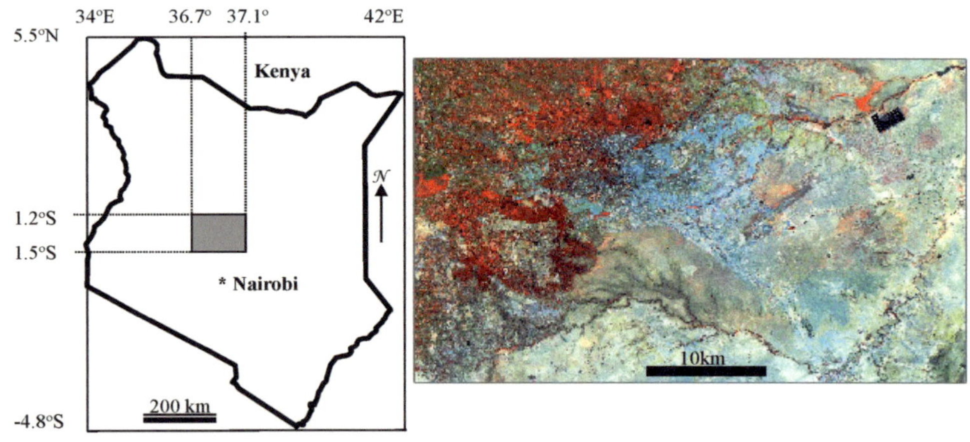

Figure 1.
Location of the study area (left), and 28.5 m spatial resolution Landsat ETM+ image of the study area; RGB = 431. Dimensions in pixels: Y = 993, X = 1639.

No.	Band 8	Band 1	Band 2	Band 3	Band 4
1	21	59	40	29	16
2	21	61	40	28	16
3	23	62	44	34	16
4	28	68	54	42	19
....					
909	95	99	98	149	102
910	98	106	112	148	103
911	98	134	131	160	79

Table 1.
DNs of pure blocks of pixels in the panchromatic band 8 and the corresponding multispectral DNs in bands 1 through 4. There are 911 such blocks comprising 59 (range 21–98) out of 192 different DNs (21–228).

to four) are synonymous with the DNs of end-members and the corresponding panchromatic DN (column 1) is synonymous with the DN of a mixture of the end-members. The mix-unmix pan-sharpening involves four steps: (1) determination of all possible mixture ratios of the multispectral DNs associated with a panchromatic DN; (2) determination of universal mixture ratios of multispectral DNs for the given panchromatic DN; (3) decomposition of the panchromatic DN, and; (4) pan-sharpening all the multi-spectral bands.

3.3.1 Determination of all possible mixture ratios

For simplicity, this research assumes that the multispectral DNs (**Table 1**, columns two to four) mix in a linear manner to give rise to the respective panchromatic DN (**Table 1**, column two). This is modelled as follows:

$$DN_P = f_1.DN_1 + f_2.DN_2 + f_3.DN_3 + f_4.DN_4 \tag{1}$$

Where:

DN_P = Digital number (DN) of a pure block of pixels in the panchromatic band.

DN_i = multi-spectral DN of a pixel in band i geographically corresponding to the above pure block of pixels.

f_i = coefficient of mixture of DN_i.

In Eq. (1), DN_P and DN_is are known (from **Table 1**) but the f_is are unknown. This under-determined system of equation cannot be solved by conventional mathematical principles including the method of least squares. Subsequently, the concept of the Mix-unmix Classifier is utilised here in solving for the f_is.

An f_i is varied from a minimum of x to a maximum of y, where x is greater than zero and it is equal to the mixture interval adopted and y is given by Eq. (2). It is worth noting that x must be greater than zero as the panchromatic signal contains all the constituent multispectral signals, and y cannot be greater than one as a single multispectral signal cannot be greater than the panchromatic signal (combination of all the multispectral signals).

$$y = \frac{DN_p - \sum_m^n (DN_m x)}{DN_i} \tag{2}$$

No.	Band 8	Band 1	Band 2	Band 3	Band 4
1	21	0.21186	0.26500	0.32759	0.51250
2	21	0.20656	0.26250	0.33214	0.50625
3	23	0.21936	0.26818	0.31765	0.56250
4	28	0.24265	0.27963	0.33095	0.61053
....					
909	95	0.60707	0.61225	0.43691	0.59216
910	98	0.58208	0.55625	0.44527	0.59611
911	98	0.45522	0.46336	0.39750	0.70253

Table 2.
Maximum coefficients of mixture of band 1 through 4 versus respective panchromatic DNs (band 8).

Where:

m varies from 1 to 4, skipping *i*.

For instance, assuming a mixture interval of 0.1, the maximum coefficient of mixture for Band 1 associated with the first panchromatic DN 21 is given by Eq. (3). **Table 2** gives the maximum coefficients of mixture associated with the panchromatic DNs in **Table 1**.

$$\frac{21-\{(40\,x\,0.1)+(29\,x\,0.1)+(16\,x\,0.1)\}}{59}=0.21186 \tag{3}$$

3.3.2 Determination of universal mixture ratios

All possible combinations of coefficients of mixture are applied on all the encompassed multispectral bands DNs associated with a particular panchromatic DN to generate hypothetical panchromatic DNs. For instance, for the panchromatic DN 21, assuming a mixture interval of 0.1, hypothetical panchromatic DNs are computed from the following combinations of the first set of coefficients of mixture (**Table 2** record 1) and the multispectral DNs associated with the panchromatic DNs 21 (**Table 1** records 1 and 2), as follows:

i. f_1, f_2, and f_3 are held at 0.1 each, and f_4 is varied from 0.1 to 0.5 with DN_P computed at each stage as follows:

a) $0.1x59+0.1x40+0.1x29+0.1x16=14$

b) $0.1x59+0.1x40+0.1x29+0.2x16=16$

c) $0.1x59+0.1x40+0.1x29+0.3x16=18$

d) $0.1x59+0.1x40+0.1x29+0.4x16=19$

e) $0.1x59+0.1x40+0.1x29+0.5x16=21$

$$f)\ 0.1x61 + 0.1x40 + 0.1x28 + 0.1x16 = 15$$

$$g)\ 0.1x61 + 0.1x40 + 0.1x28 + 0.2x16 = 16$$

$$h)\ 0.1x61 + 0.1x40 + 0.1x28 + 0.3x16 = 18$$

$$i)\ 0.1x61 + 0.1x40 + 0.1x28 + 0.4x16 = 19$$

$$j)\ 0.1x59 + 0.1x40 + 0.1x29 + 0.5x16 = 21$$

Note that the maximum f_4 from **Table 2** is 0.51250 but the maximum used above is 0.5 as a mixture interval of 0.1 is adopted. Going beyond 0.5 would give 0.6 which would exceed the computed maximum of 0.51250. To achieve this maximum exactly, a mixture interval of 0.00001 would have to be adopted;

ii. f_1 and f_2 are held at 0.1 each, f_3 changed to 0.2, and f_4 is varied from 0.1 to 0.5 with DN_P computed at each stage (steps *a-j*);

iii. Step (ii) is repeated with f_3 becoming 0.3 (the maximum coefficient of mixture for f_3 is 0.3);

iv. Steps (i) is repeated with f_2 changing to 0.2 (the maximum for f_2 is 0.2). Steps (ii) and (iii) are repeated with f_2 held as 0.2;

v. The above steps are repeated with f_1 changing to 0.2 (the maximum for f_1 is 0.2);

vi. All the above steps are repeated with the ranges of coefficients of mixture being drawn from the second set of coefficients of mixture (**Table 2** record 2).

The total number of possible hypothetical panchromatic DNs derived from the above combinations of coefficients of mixtures and multispectral DNs is 240. This is the product of 2 (possible number of fractions for Band 1), 2 (ditto band 2), 3 (ditto band 3), 5 (ditto band 4), and 2 (number of panchromatic DNs 21).

The universality of a combination of coefficients of mixture is based on the difference between the generated hypothetical panchromatic DN and the panchromatic DN whose multi-spectral DNs are subjected to the combinations of coefficients of mixture. For instance, adopting a threshold of 1 DN, out of the above 240 combinations, only 34 combinations are universal as given in **Table 3**.

3.4 Decomposition of panchromatic band pure DNs

As **Table 3** shows, a given pure panchromatic DN may be associated with several sets of universal coefficients of mixture e.g. 34 sets for the panchromatic DN 21. The 34 sets of universal coefficients are related to two sets of multispectral DNs through the panchromatic DN 21 (**Table 1** records 1 and 2). The average of the sets of multispectral DNs is adopted as the most probable combination of contributory multispectral DNs to the pure panchromatic DN 21. Likewise, the average of the sets of universal coefficients is adopted as the most probable set of universal coefficients for

No.	*f1*	*f2*	*f3*	*f4*	**Band 1**	**Band 2**	**Band 3**	**Band 4**	**Pan-DN**	**Generated Pan-DN**	**Difference**
1	0.1	0.1	0.1	0.5	59	40	29	16	21	20.8	−0.2
2	0.1	0.1	0.2	0.3	59	40	29	16	21	20.5	−0.5
3	0.1	0.1	0.3	0.1	59	40	29	16	21	20.2	−0.8
…											
33	0.1	0.2	0.2	0.1	61	40	28	16	21	21.3	0.3
34	0.2	0.1	0.1	0.1	61	40	28	16	21	20.6	−0.4

Table 3.
Universal coefficients of mixture associated with the panchromatic DN (pan-DN) 21.

the panchromatic DN. **Table 4** gives the most probable -contributory multispectral DNs and -universal coefficients of the respective pure panchromatic DNs in the study area. A pure panchromatic DN may not be associated with any universal coefficients, for instance, the panchromatic DN 98.

The product of a given most probable -contributory multispectral DN and its respective -universal coefficient gives its most probable DN contribution to the corresponding panchromatic DN. **Table 5** gives the most probable DN contributions of the multispectral bands to the panchromatic band DNs. Paraphrasing, the table shows decomposition of the panchromatic pure DNs into their most probable constituent multispectral DNs.

3.5 Decomposition models and constituent contributory multispectral DNs

Figure 2 is a plot of the panchromatic DNs in **Table 5** column 2 against their multispectral DN contributions (columns 3-6). The linear fit models and coefficients of determination are also given. Constituent contributory multispectral bands are generated by applying the above models on the panchromatic Band 8 DNs. **Figure 3** shows the generated constituent multispectral DNs (**Table 5** columns 3-6) versus the original multi-spectral DNs (**Table 1** columns 3-6, excluding the last two records associated with the panchromatic DN 98 for the reason in Section 3.4).

No.	Pan-DN	Contributory multispectral DNs				Universal coefficients			
		Band 1	Band 2	Band 3	Band 4	Band 1	Band 2	Band 3	Band 4
1	21	59.9	40.0	28.5	16.0	0.12	0.14	0.17	0.22
2	23	62.0	44.0	34.0	16.0	0.11	0.13	0.19	0.26
3	28	68.0	54.0	42.0	19.0	0.13	0.13	0.16	0.30
...									
57	93	93.0	93.0	129.0	106.0	0.24	0.24	0.16	0.25
58	95	99.7	99.5	149.6	101.1	0.23	0.21	0.15	0.29

Table 4.
Pure panchromatic DNs and corresponding most probable universal contributory multispectral DNs and their most probable universal coefficients of mixture.

No.	Pan-DN	Band 1	Band 2	Band 3	Band 4
1	21	7.1	5.4	4.9	3.6
2	23	7.0	5.5	6.4	4.2
3	28	8.7	6.9	6.6	5.7
...					
57	93	22.6	22.6	21.2	26.5
58	95	23.3	20.7	22.1	28.9

Table 5.
Most probable multispectral bands DN-contributions to the corresponding panchromatic DN, i.e. decomposition of pure panchromatic DN into its constituent multispectral DNs.

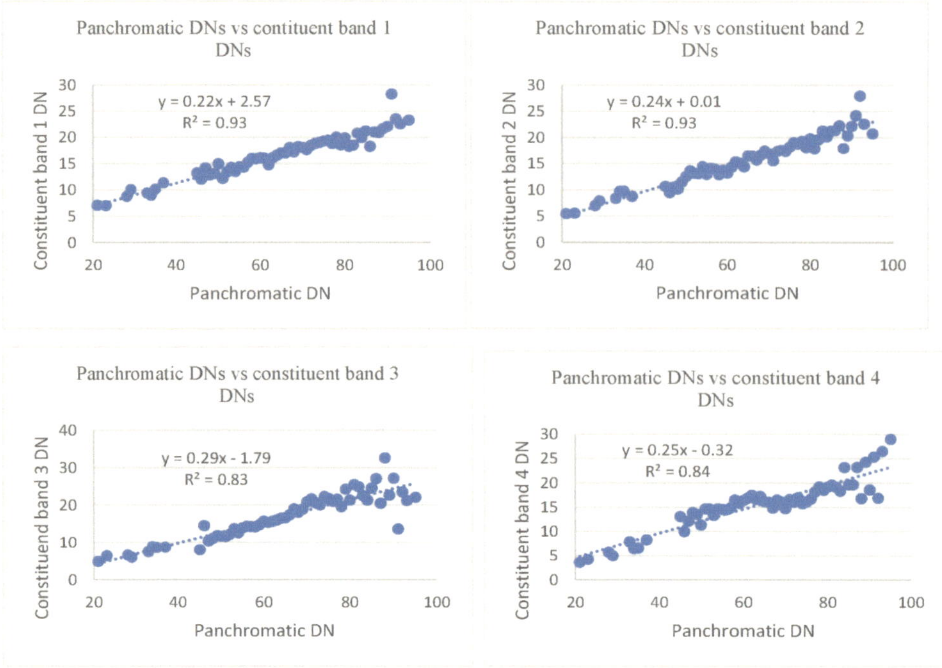

Figure 2.
Panchromatic band 8 pure blocks DNs versus constituent multispectral bands DNs.

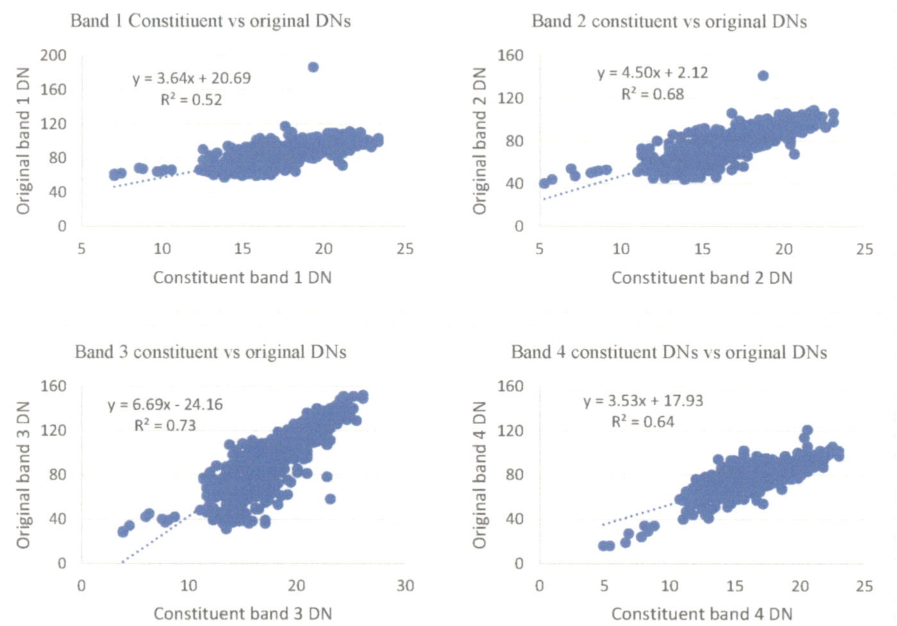

Figure 3.
Constituent multispectral DNs versus original multispectral bands DNs.

Band	CC1	CC2	Product
1	0.965	0.754	0.728
2	0.966	0.839	0.810
3	0.912	0.858	0.783
4	0.919	0.821	0.754

Table 6.
Products of correlation coefficients of universal panchromatic DNs versus constituent multispectral DNs (CC1) and correlation coefficients of constituent multispectral DNs versus original universal multispectral DNs (CC2).

Table 6 gives the respective products of the correlation coefficients in **Figures 2** and **3**. From the products, it can be taken that the descending order of correctly estimating the original multispectral bands from the panchromatic band via the constituent multispectral bands is Band -2, -3, -4, -1. Consequently, Band 2 is pan-sharpened first and used as a proxy to pan-sharpen the other bands as explained below.

3.6 Pan-sharpening original multispectral image

The model relating constituent Band 2 and original Band 2 is applied on the former to generate pan-sharpened band 2. The pan-sharpened Band 2 is used in pan-sharpening the other bands (Bands 1, 3, 4, 5, and 7) in the original image. At this stage, retaining the colour relationship (DNs relationship) between the original bands is critical. Tone ratio images (R_i) are computed for each original band ($band_i$) to the original Band 2 ($band_{proxy}$) as in Eq. (4). To generate pan-sharpened $band_i$, the ratio images R_i are applied on the pan-sharpened Band 2 as in Eq. (5). For instance, in the study area, the first pixel has the DN values 70, 62, 80, 62, 135, and 113 in Bands 1 through 7 (excluding Band 6) respectively. For the pixel, the ratios computed from Eq. (4) are 70:62, 80:62, 62:62, 135:62, and 113:62 for Bands 1, 3, 4, 5, and 7 respectively. The pan-sharpened Band 2 pixels of the same geographic coverage as the above original pixel have the DN values 61, 57, 61, and 64. Applying the ratio 70:62 on the pan-sharpened Band 2 pixels, Eq. (5), yields pan-sharpened-band 1 pixels with DN values 69, 64, 69, and 72, respectively. The pan-sharpened bands inherit the original colour/DN relationships of the original (non-pan-sharpened) bands through the tone ratio images. **Table 7** gives the mean DNs of the original and

Band	Original (1,627,527 pixels)	Pan-sharpened (6,510,108 pixels)
1	84.49 ± 12.30	84.15 ± 11.09
2	77.79 ± 14.40	77.72 ± 12.69
3	97.30 ± 25.28	96.34 ± 23.21
4	77.78 ± 11.26	79.05 ± 19.10
5	136.32 ± 32.55	136.38 ± 32.47
7	98.16 ± 27.08	97.18 ± 24.65
Tone ratio	1:0.9:1.2:0.9:1.6:1.2	1:0.9:1.1:0.9:1.6:1.2

Table 7.
DN means of original vs. pan-sharpened images.

pan-sharpened images. The means show that the original relative tone relationships are maintained.

$$R_i = \frac{band_i}{band_{proxy}} \tag{4}$$

$$PanB_i = Pan_{proxy} \times R_i \tag{5}$$

Where:
R_i = tone ratio image.
$PanB_i$ = pan-sharpened band i.
Pan_{proxy} = pan-sharpened proxy band.

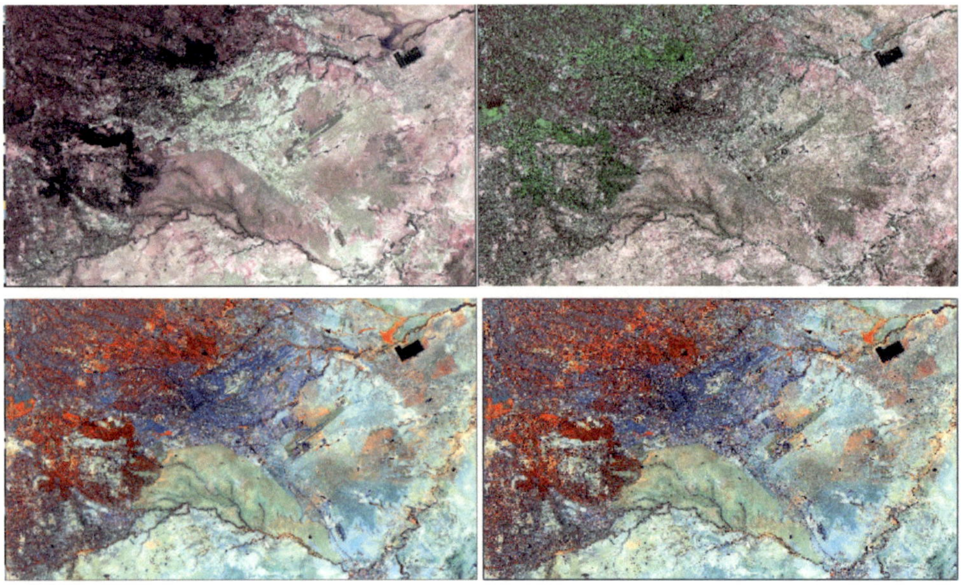

Figure 4.
Comparison of original and pan-sharpened multispectral images. (upper left) original bands: RGB = 321, (UR) pan-sharpened bands: RGB = 321, (LL) original bands: RGB = 457, (LR) pan-sharpened bands: RGB = 457. Dimensions in pixels; original: Y = 993, X = 1639; pan-sharpened: Y = 1986, X = 3278.

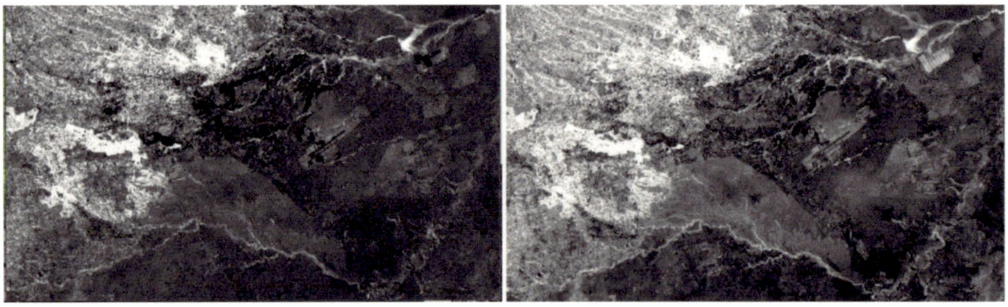

Figure 5.
NDVI image (left) and tasselled cap (greenness band) of the original image.

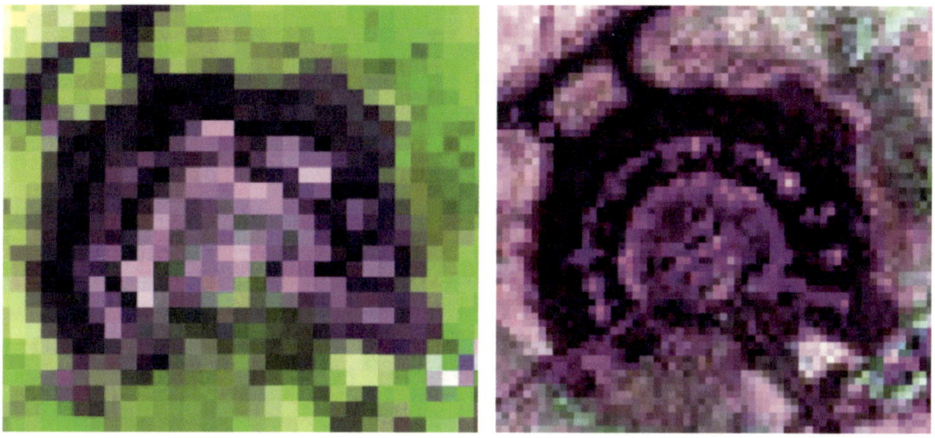

Figure 6.
Jomo Kenyatta international airport hangar – Left: Original image RGB = 342, right: Pan-sharpened image RGB = 342.

4. Results

Figure 4 compares the original and pan-sharpened images. **Figure 5** gives NDVI and Tasselled Cap (greenness band) images of the original image. The lighter the tone in the NDVI and greenness images, the denser the vegetation. The original image RGB = 321 captures dense vegetation as black and light vegetation as light green. This is an inconsistency. In the pan-sharpened image RGB = 321, dense and light vegetation appear as dark and light green, respectively, which is consistent with the NDVI and greenness images. The original image RGB = 457 and the pan-sharpened RGB = 457 are visually similar showing retention of colour relationship.

Figure 6 compares the Jomo Kenyatta International Airport hangar in the original and pan-sharpened images. In the former, the hangar appears as a blob but in the latter appears as rings as expected.

5. Discussion

The spectral range of a panchromatic band may not overlap with the spectral ranges of the encompassed bands. For the data used in this research, the panchromatic band starts at the wavelength 0.50 nm, and the collective range of the encompassed bands starts at 0.45 nm. Further, there are two spectral gaps (0.61 nm–0.62 nm, and 0.70 nm–0.75 nm) in the collective range. These gap ranges and the range 0.45 nm–0.49 nm are not accounted for in Eq. (1). This may explain the lack of perfect correlation coefficients between the panchromatic DNs and the constituent multispectral DNs (**Table 6**, CC1). Another source of error may be the assumption of linear combination of DNs, Eq. (1).

It is worth noting that constituent multispectral DNs versus original DNs correlation coefficients (CC2) may not be critically informative as the original DN has been split into four different DNs.

6. Recommendations

The Mix-unmix Pan-sharpener utilises a multispectral band as a proxy to pan-sharpen all the other multispectral bands after the proxy multispectral band has been pan-sharpened. The multispectral bands cover a common geographical extent. The panchromatic band of the particular sensor may not be of adequate spatial resolution depending on the end-use of the pan-sharpened image. This may call for an external finer spatial resolution panchromatic band which may not necessarily cover the entire geographical extent of the multispectral data. The problem of inadequate geographical coverage by a panchromatic band can be solved through the foregoing proxy pan-sharpening and it will be addressed in the sequel to this chapter - *Mix-unmix Pan-sharpener: overcoming geographical inadequacy of panchromatic band by reverse pan-sharpening.*

A mixture interval of 0.1 has been adopted for this demonstration – a comparison of different mixture intervals is necessary to establish any optimum mixture interval. The blue band has been considered as a constituent band despite it being largely not covered by the panchromatic band – does dropping it improve or worsen the results? This warrants further research. The Mix-unmix concept assumes a linear mixture of the constituent signals – there is a need for automatic determination of the mixture model. The concept needs to be assessed on hyperspectral-multispectral pan-sharpening [3, 4], optical-microwave pan-sharpening, and pan-sharpening by an external panchromatic band.

7. Conclusion

The proposed Mix-unmix Pan-sharpener can pan-sharpen any number of bands. The technique minimises colour distortion by incorporating the respective colour relationships between the original (non-pan-sharpened) bands and the proxy pan-sharpening band through tone ratio images, in the generation of respective pan-sharpened bands.

Acknowledgements

The data is downloaded from [21].

Author details

Thomas Ngigi[1*], Eunice Nduati[1], Wei Xianhu[2] and Marlena Götza[3]

1 Department of Geomatic Engineering and Geospatial Information System, Jomo Kenyatta University of Agriculture and Technology, Nairobi, Kenya

2 Aerospace Information Research Institute, Chinese Academy of Sciences, Beijing, P.R. China

3 Technische Universität Bergakademie Freiberg, Freiberg, Germany

*Address all correspondence to: tgngigi@gmail.com, tgngigi@jkuat.ac.ke

References

[1] Vivone G, Dalla Mura M, Garzelli A, Restaino R, Scarpa G, Ulfarsson MO, et al. A new benchmark based on recent advances in multispectral pansharpening: Revisiting pansharpening with classical and emerging pansharpening methods. IEEE Geoscience and Remote Sensing Magazine. 2020;**9**(1):53-81

[2] Zhang K, Zhang F, Wan W, Hui Y, Sun J, Del Ser J, et al. Panchromatic and multispectral image fusion for remote sensing and earth observation: Concepts, taxonomy, literature review, evaluation methodologies and challenges ahead. Information Fusion. 2023;**93**:227-242

[3] Zhu C, Gong L, Zhang Y, Chen S, Gao L, Ta N, et al. MGDIN: Detail injection network for HSI and MSI fusion based on multiscale and global contextual features. International Journal of Remote Sensing. 2023;**44**(18):5574-5596

[4] Sun W, Ren K, Meng X, Yang G, Xiao C, Peng J, et al. MLR-DBPFN: A multi-scale low rank deep back projection fusion network for anti-noise hyperspectral and multispectral image fusion. IEEE Transactions on Geoscience and Remote Sensing. 2022;**60**:1-14

[5] Israa A, Havier M, Miguel V, Rafael M, Aggelos K. A survey of classical methods and new trends in pan-sharpening of multispectral images. EURASIP Journal on Advances in Signal Processing. 2011;**2011**(79):1-22

[6] Amro I, Mateos J, Vega M, Molina R, Katsaggelos AK. A survey of classical methods and new trends in pan-sharpening of multispectral images. EURASIP Journal on Advances in Signal Processing. 2011;**1**:1-22

[7] Jinye Peng L, Liu JW, Zhang E, Zhu X, Zhang Y, Feng J, et al. PSMD-net: A novel pan-sharpening method based on a multiscale dense network. IEEE Transactions on Geoscience and Remote Sensing. 2020;**99**:1-15. DOI: 10.1109/TGRS.2020.3020162

[8] Li J, Hong D, Gao L, Yao J, Zheng K, Zhang B, et al. Deep learning in multimodal remote sensing data fusion: A comprehensive review. International Journal of Applied Earth Observation and Geoinformation. 2022;**112**:102926

[9] Qian D, Nicholas H, Roger K, Vijay P. On the performance evaluation of pan-sharpening techniques. IEEE Geoscience and Remote Sensing Letters. 2007;**4**(4):518-522

[10] Seema J, Baldeo S. Comparison of different pan-sharpening methods for spectral characteristic preservation: Multi-temporal CARTOSAT-1 and IRS-P6 LISS-IV imagery. International Journal of Remote Sensing. 2012:(33)5629-5643

[11] Xu S, Zhang J, Zhao Z, Sun K, Liu J, Zhang C. Deep gradient projection networks for pan-sharpening. In: Proceedings of the IEEE/CVF Conference on Computer Vision and Pattern Recognition (CVPR). 2021. pp. 1366-1375. Available from: https://openaccess.thecvf.com/content/CVPR2021/html/Xu_Deep_Gradient_Projection_Networks_for_Pan-sharpening_CVPR_2021_paper.html

[12] Tu TM, Su SC, Shyu HC, Huang P. S.: A new look at IHS-like image fusion methods. Information Fusion. 2001;**2**(3):177-186

[13] Ranchin T, Aiazzi B, Alparone L, Baronti S, Wald L. Image fusion—The

ARSIS concept and some successful implementation schemes. ISPRS Journal of Photogrammetry and Remote Sensing. 2003;**58**(1):4-18

[14] Wald L. Quality of high resolution synthesized images: Is there a simple criterion? Proceedings. 2000:99-103

[15] Choi M, Kim HC, Cho NI, Kim HO. An improved intensity-hue-saturation method for IKONOS image fusion. Pan. 2006;**1**:v2

[16] Javan FD, Samadzadegan F, Mehravar S, Toosi A, Khatami R, Stein A. A review of image fusion techniques for pan-sharpening of high-resolution satellite imagery. ISPRS Journal of Photogrammetry and Remote Sensing. 2021;**171**:101-117

[17] Rahmani S, Strait M, Merkurjev D, Moeller M, Wittman T. An adaptive IHS pan-sharpening method. IEEE Geoscience and Remote Sensing Letters. 2010;**7**(4):746-750. DOI: 10.1109/LGRS.2010.2046715

[18] Alparone L, Wald L, Chanussot J, Thomas C, Gamba P, Bruce LM. Comparison of pan-sharpening algorithms: Outcome of the 2006 GRS-S data-fusion contest. Geoscience and Remote Sensing, IEEE Transactions on. 2007;**45**(10):3012-3021

[19] Ngigi TG, Tateishi R. Solving under-determined models in linear spectral unmixing of satellite images: Mix-unmix concept (advance report). Journal of Imaging Science and Technology. 2007;**51**(4):360-367

[20] Ngigi TG, Tateishi R, Shalaby A, Soliman N, Ghar M. Comparison of a new classifier, mix-unmix classifier, with conventional hard and soft classifiers. International Journal of Remote Sensing. 2008;**29**(14):4111-4128

[21] GeoCover Landsat. Available from: https://zulu.ssc.nasa.gov/mrsid/

Chapter 2

Application of Digital Image Processing Techniques for Agriculture: A Review

Juan Pablo Guerra and Francisco Cuevas

Abstract

Agriculture plays a crucial role in human survival, necessitating the development of efficient methods for food production. This chapter reviews Digital Image Processing (DPI) methods that utilize various color models to segment elements like leaves, fruits, pests, and diseases, aiming to enhance agricultural crop production. Recent DPI research employs techniques such as image subtraction, binarization, color thresholding, statistics, and convolutional filtering to segment and identify crop elements with shared attributes. DPI algorithms have a broad impact on optimizing resources for increased food production through agriculture. This chapter provides an overview of DPI techniques and their applications in agricultural image segmentation, including methods for detecting fruit quality, pests, and plant nutritional status. The review's contribution lies in the selection and analysis of highly cited articles, offering readers a current perspective on DPI's application in agricultural processes.

Keywords: precision agriculture, computer vision, segmentation, binarization, color

1. Introduction

It is estimated that the human population will be 10 billion by 2050, this poses a challenge in the production of food for their livelihoods, particularly in agriculture. From 2010 to 2020, the cultivated area grew by 2,424,000 ha, and the use of fertilizers by 23,718,607 ha according to data from the Food and Agriculture Organization of the United Nations (FAO) [1].

The sense of sight is the principal source of information for humans. In agriculture, the observation of crops determines the state in which they are. Fatigue during a day's work, inexperience, and a lack of knowledge of the crop can influence the farmer's perception when making a judgment based on sight about the nutritional state of the crops, the presence of pests, and the quality of the fruit [2].

Science and technology support agricultural processes by increasing their efficiency [3–6], and among them are the research areas of computer vision (*CV*) [7–9] and artificial intelligence [10–12] (AI). Computer vision systems are composed of three elements: light sources, image acquisition devices, and *DPI* algorithms [6, 13].

There are two types of illumination sources, natural and artificial, each with particular characteristics. The natural sources are usually taken with indoor or outdoor sunlight on cloudy or sunny days [14, 15]. Artificial light sources can be incandescent, fluorescent, and LEDS [16], among others. In this type of lighting, you can control more variants, such as the angle of incidence and light power.

There are a wide variety of options to choose from the capture devices, depending on the features they have and the objective to be achieved. There are cameras with particular specifications, such as hyperspectral [17], for professional photography, and the most commonly used peripherals are scanners [18], mobile devices, and wireless and security cameras [19–21].

In order to increase control over the variables on which they are affected, metallic structures are developed in which the illumination sources and image capture devices are fixed; this allows experiments in laboratory environments.

The purpose of *DPI* algorithms is to analyze and process the information shown in images [22]. It is important to mention that an image is represented as a two-dimensional function $f(x,y)$, where x and y are spatial coordinates, and the amplitude of f at any pair of coordinates (x, y) is called the gray level of the image at that point. When x, y, and the intensity values are all finite, discrete quantities, we call the image a digital image [22]. There are several types of *DPI* algorithms, such as histogram operations, pixel neighborhood-base operations, morphological operations, binarization, edge detectors, Fourier methods, and other different classes of image transforms.

The *DPI* systems applied to agriculture were initially implemented in laboratory environments, food inspection lines, and real working conditions. The extension of their field of application is due to several factors, including the maturity reached by *DPI* algorithms, increased computational power, and the need for agriculture to become more efficient and sustainable from an environmental point of view.

In this review, an analysis of digital image processing methods applied to agriculture in recent years and reported in papers is made; these are emphasized in aspects such as the detection of pests and diseases (1), nutritional deficiencies (2), and inspection of fruit quality (3). The papers were selected based on the number of references that appear in Google Academic.

2. Digital image processing techniques applied to agriculture

2.1 Pest detection

Pests have always been present in nature. In modern agriculture, they are undesirable, as they affect the development and production of crops [23–25]. Because there is a wide variety of crops whose fruits are used for food, in the same way, the number of pests and diseases is equally diverse, which makes it difficult to detect, identify, and correct them in time [9, 26], especially if such detection is carried out exclusively by the farmer's experience. Among the most common pests, there are different types of insects, such as white flies, aphids, snails, and others.

Table 1 lists the papers on pest identification using *DPI*, which aims at the timely, effective, and non-invasive detection of pests.

2.2 Nutrition deficiencies detection

Crops need a series of nutrients that they naturally take from the air, water, and soil for their development. The elements that plants feed on are classified into macronutrients and micronutrients, depending on the amount required by crops.

Macronutrients Nitrogen (N), Phosphorus (P), and Potassium (K) are important for modern agriculture, as they are usually supplied to crops in different fertilization schemes [18, 47, 48].

Early detection of NPK excesses or deficiencies is important; *DPI* and *AI* algorithms represent an effective, non-invasive, and low-cost alternative for their detection.

Table 2 lists a selection of papers that make use of DPI algorithms to detect macronutrient deficiencies in different crops.

2.3 Inspection of quality detection

The final consumer of agricultural products seeks the highest quality in the items they will consume. It is important to mention that in order for farm products to reach their final destination, they have already passed through different filters for their classification, which is carried out by experts trained to detect characteristics such as color, shape, size, and weight, among others [75, 76]. The classification made by human beings is subject to conditions such as their state of health, mood, and fatigue, which can affect their judgment, and this can generate errors in the classification of the inspected products [77]. Researchers around the world have presented methods that support the task of determining attributes related to the quality of field products.

Table 3 shows a series of papers that make proposals based on *DPI* techniques for determining the quality of inspected field products.

Table of DPI algorithms applied to pest detection

DPI Topic	DPI Algorithm	Relevant aspects
Frequency Domain Processing and Image Transforms	Fourier [27, 28] Wavelt [23, 29]	Nansen et al. [28] Automatic detection method of caterpillar pests in mustard and broad bean crops, achieved results greater than 90% in detection. Asfarian et al. [27] Used Fourier transform spectra to carry out the detection of the most common pests in rice crops in Indonesia. The algorithms used show an accuracy of 83%. Luo et al. [29] Estimated by spectroscopy and Wavelt transform the number of aphids. Mentioned that the model developed with 5 characteristics is better than with 6 in wheat crop.
Spatial Domain Processing	Histogram transformation [30–32] Smoothening filter [7, 33, 34] AdaBoost [35] Saliency maps [36] Sobel Operators [26, 31]	Thenmozhi and Reddy [26] Detect and identify the shapes of insects in sugarcane crops. Use of MATLAB API. García et al. [31] Recognition of Lobesia botrana in vineyards by DPI and clustering, with 95% effectiveness. Rupesh and Mundada [33] Detection of aphids and whiteflies in greenhouse crops. Singh and Misra [7] Identifying and counting aphids on soybean plants grown in greenhouses. Yao et al. [35] Develop an image capture device for counting planthoppers in rice fields. Reported average of detection of 85.2% Nanni et al. [36] Automatic classifier insect pest in tea plants based on the fusion between Saliency methods. Uses a CNN as a classifier.

Table of DPI algorithms applied to pest detection		
DPI Topic	**DPI Algorithm**	**Relevant aspects**
Image Segmentation	RDI algorithm [37] Image subtraction [38] Threshold [7, 17, 30, 32, 34, 35, 39–41] K-Means classifier [9, 31] K-nearest neighbor classifier [42] Convolutional Neural Network [36, 43, 44]	Liu and Chahl [17] Detecting invertebrate insects on green leaves of several crops. It works in light spectra such as UV and NIR, allowing it to detect camouflaged pests. Singh and Misra [7] Identifying and counting aphids on soybean plants. Results are presented with several classifiers. Miranda et al. [34] Estimate the density of pest infestation in rice fields. Use of wireless technologies for image capture. Huddar et al. [37] Segment and identify whitefly in unstructured environments in various crops. Reports 96% with metric accuracy. Maharlooei et al. [38] Detect and count different-sized soybean aphids. Emphasizes the importance of lighting conditions, tries out different cameras. Nanehkaran et al. [40] Detection of diseases on leaves of plants of cucumber corn and rice. Presents time comparisons with different segmentation methods, qualitative comparisons of results. Barbedo [41] It uses classical DPI methods on images of soybean crops which makes it easy to replicate them in different contexts. Displays tables with the results obtained. Hossain et al. [42] Proposes a method for the detection and classification of leaf diseases. Generates results to detect and recognize selected diseases with an accuracy metrics of 96.76%. Sladojevic et al. [43] Developed convolutional neural networks for disease detection on leaves of different plants, obtaining a metric accuracy of 96% with the ImageNet and CaffeNet models.
Morphological Operators	Close operator [30] Dilation operator [26, 37, 39, 45, 46] Erosion operator [37, 39, 46]	Luo et al. [30] Automatically detect and classify weed in potato crops. Uses various color models, combines different *AI* techniques, and high efficiency. Chang and Lin [39] Detect and identify weeds in lettuce crops. Using fuzzy logic as a classifier to classify watering. Identification of lettuce and herbs is performed in real-time. Sabouri and Sajadi [45] Evaluated the relationship between leaf area and solar radiation in various crops.

Table 1.
Papers on pests detection applying digital image processing methods.

Table of DPI algorithms applied to nutrition deficit detection		
DPI Topic	**DPI Algorithm**	**Relevant aspects**
Frequency Domain Processing and Image Transforms	Fourier [49–51] Wavelt [52]	Nejati et al. [49] Proposed a method that uses the fast Fourier transform and leaf edges to classify between crop leaves and weed leaves in cornfields, obtained 92% accuracy metrics. da Silva Leite et al. [50] Characterized nitrogen uptake by fractions of plants, with different fertilization schedules, by means of Fourier Transform Attenuated Total Reflectance Analysis on leaves of Physalis peruviana and Physalis angulata. da Silva et al. [52] Measure the amount of Magnesium in corn leaves by transforms using the walvet transform in combination with other DPI algorithms. Reports an efficiency of 75%. Ray [51] Using the Fourier Transform to identify cell walls in leaves.

Table of DPI algorithms applied to nutrition deficit detection

DPI Topic	DPI Algorithm	Relevant aspects
Spatial Domain Processing	Histogram transformation [51, 53–56] Smoothening filter [57–59] Image subtraction [55] Color Index [53, 60–68] Canny Operator [58] SIFT [68] Convolutional Neural Network [44, 69]	Qi et al. [53] Relating foliar Nitrogen content to wheat crop development. Uses neural networks as classifier and displays statistical performance data. Larijani et al. [54] The timely and rapid diagnosis of rice blast based on the image processing technique in field conditions. The overall accuracy metrics was 94 Dhingra et al. [58] Determined the health status of the leaves by means of a neutrosophic technique in basil leaves, 3 groups are formed: healthy, unhealthy, and undetermined, reaching a classification accuracy metric of 98.4%. Wang et al. [60] Relate the intensity of the green color of the rice leaves with the amount of Nitrogen used to fertilize. Presents an analysis of the biomass of rice in relation to its green color with the use of Nitrogen. Wang et al. [64] Relationship between image color indexes and Nitrogen status in rice crops under natural light. Presents graphs contrasting green color versus Nitrogen and chlorophyll content. Lee and Lee [65] Construct a non-destructive method for monitoring rice crop growth and Nitrogen nutrition status with digital camera image analysis. Presents the relationship between Canopy cover and green color to determine the nutritional status. Vesali et al. [63] Develop an application for mobile devices for the estimation of chlorophyll in corn leaves using DPI algorithms. Use a commercial device to measure the amount of chlorophyll present in the leaves and validate the results obtained. Buchaillot et al. [66] Evaluate the adaptation of maize crops to limiting abiotic and biotic conditions using RGB images. Shows tables with data on the growth of corn varieties, showing their adaptation to growing conditions. Jia et al. [68] Detection of diseases and pests, monitoring of rice crop growth. Use the SIFT method to detect points of interest in the image mosaic. Kamelia et al. [58] Detecting plant nutrient deficits using a combination of DPI algorithms. Ponce et al. [69] Detected low nutrition in tomato crops by implementing the CNN + AHN model testing various configurations, delivering an accuracy metrics of 95 Fuentes et al. [47] Determined the most suitable architecture for pest and disease detection in tomato crops. Faster R-CNN, Region-based Fully Convolutional Network models were tested with average accuracy metrics of 82% and 85%, respectively.
Image Segmentation	Threshold [18, 19, 57, 58, 60–62, 64, 65, 70–72] Binarization [62, 73, 74] Otsu [54] K-Means [54, 57]	Sun et al. [18] Determine the changes in the characteristics of rice leaves under nutritional stress. Easy segmentation due to capture conditions. Story et al. [19] Detecting calcium deficiency and growth in greenhouse lettuces. Presents a simple segmentation, it is based on methods proven by other authors. Li et al. [70] Establishes the relationship between reflectivity and Nitrogen content in cereals. Report a mean squared error of less than 16% compared to other methods. Rorie et al. [71] Evaluating the Nitrogen content of maize in greenhouses by DGCI, used a simple segmentation. Makes use of color indexes to associate them with the amount of Nitrogen in the leaves. Chen et al. [73] Identifying NPK deficiencies in rice based on static scanning technology and hierarchical identification. Mao et al. [61] Develop a non-destructive method for Nitrogen estimation in lettuce using spectroscopy and *DPI*. Adopted different classifiers. Sun et al. [62] To analyze the temporal dynamics of the morphology and color of rice to evaluate their efficiency in identifying deficiencies of NPK. Makes use of morphological indexes for the identification of deficiencies in partially and fully developed leaves. Chen et al. [74] Identify Phosphorus stress in four stages of rice development. Using ANOVA to find differences in fertilization schedules. Aditini and Gupta [57] Generate a method for the identification of macronutrient deficits by means of DPI algorithms.

Table of DPI algorithms applied to nutrition deficit detection		
DPI Topic	**DPI Algorithm**	**Relevant aspects**
Morphological Operators	Close operator [59] Open operator [59] Erosion operator [42, 59] Dilatation operator [42]	Su et al. [59] Implemented a set of DPI algorithms for automatic location of soybean plants. Obtain results of 97% accuracy metrics.

Table 2.
Papers on nutrition deficiencies detection applying digital image processing methods.

Table of DPI algorithms applied to quality detection		
DPI Topic	**DPI Algorithm**	**Relevant aspects**
Frequency Domain Processing and Image Transforms	Fourier [78–80] Fast radial symmetry [81] Wavelet [82]	Ambrose et al. [78] Fourier transform near infrared spectroscopy and Raman spectroscopy techniques were used to evaluate the viability of corn seeds. It classifies seeds into viable and non-viable with an accuracy metrics of 100% and prediction of 95%, respectively. Bansal et al. [79] Proposed a technique for immature citrus from an outdoor color image and counting the number of fruits. It obtained results in correct detection of 82.2%. Xu and Katchova [80] Predicted soybean production using FFT and NDVI. Pérez-Zavala et al. [81] Recognition and detection of grape bunches. Shown a 96% accuracy metric. Dhakshina Kumar et al. [82] Proposed system performs classifications of tomatoes in 3 stages. Reports greater than 90% accuracy metrics.
Spatial Domain Processing	Smoothening filter [20, 77, 82–86] White Path [76] Decorrelation Stretch [87] Histogram equalization [81, 84] Image Subtraction [20] Sobel Operators [88] Color Index [80] SIFT [87, 89]	Nyalala et al. [20] Calculate tomato mass and volume using two and three-dimensional imaging, use a Kinect for image acquisition. Reports 97% in accuracy metrics. Sadeghi-Tehran et al. [87] Detect 3 stages of flowering and ear growth of wheat crops. Reports 95.21%, 97.29%, and 99.59% accuracy metrics of the 3 spike stages and 85.45% in the flowering. Ireri et al. [88] System for tomato grading based on RGB images. Shows an efficiency higher than 97% in tomato grading. Use ANN as classifier. Castro et al. [83] The combinations of machine learning techniques and three color spaces were evaluated to classify Cape gooseberry. Performs tests in controlled environments. The classifier with the best result was SVM with 70%. Zhu et al. [89] Identifying the ear in wheat plants during its development. Does not report a quantitative metric, defines its efficiency as acceptable. Wan et al. [86] Estimate tomato maturity at 3 levels, green, yellow, and red in roma and pear varieties. Reports 99.31% in accuracy metrics of the 3 maturity levels. Uses an ANN.

Table of DPI algorithms applied to quality detection		
DPI Topic	**DPI Algorithm**	**Relevant aspects**
Image Segmentation	Binarization [77, 82, 90] Otsu [20, 76, 88] Threshold [15, 20, 83, 86, 88–91] Contour tracking [86] K-Means [14, 92] Convolutional Neural Network [93–95]	Fan et al. [14] Segmenting apples in unstructured light conditions. Shown efficiency of 99.26% of accuracy metrics with various types of classifiers. Rico-Fernández et al. [15] Segmenting foliage of different crops. Reports 89% efficiency in 3 different crops. Arakeri and Lakshmana [77] Estimate tomato quality by detecting maturity and defects present in the fruit. Reports an 96.47% of accuracy metricsin identifying fruit maturity. Use a multilayer neural network for recognition. Villaseñor-Aguilar et al. [90] Estimating the maturity of the morron pepper. Report efficiency of 100% and 88% with two different classifiers. Uses fuzzy system and ANN as classifiers. Garcia et al. [91] Development of an automatic tomato maturity identification system. Obtains an accuracy metrics of 84%. Uses simple segregation by thresholds against a controlled background. Roy et al. [93] Work in classification of apples by means of the UNet and a proprietary model called En-UNet, obtaining in the IoU metric values above 90%. Majeed et al. [95] Segmented grape crops to determine the position and orientation of grape plant cordons using several CNN models such as SegNet-VGG16 obtaining up to 80% efficiency in determining the trajectory of the cordons.
Morphological Operators	Dilation operator [76, 84, 86] Erosion operator [76, 84] Closing operator [89]	Portugal-Zambrano et al. [76] Evaluating physical defects in green coffee beans. Reports an average of 98.48% accuracy metrics identification.

Table 3.
Papers on Inspection of quality detection applying digital image processing methods.

3. DPI techniques analysis

The literature documents different DPI techniques used for different purposes in fields ranging from agriculture to industrial applications [9, 96–98]. **Tables 1–3** are grouped papers according to the *DPI* techniques used; such classification is based on the following categories: filtering in the frequency domain, intensity and transformations spatial filtering, convolutions, image segmentation, morphological operators, and color image processing [22].

3.1 Frequency domain processing and image transforms

The concept of a transform introduces an alternative mathematical representation of an image, deviating from the conventional depiction based on two spatial variables. These tools wield substantial power, finding broad applications beyond digital image processing.

The integration of the Fourier transform has revolutionized digital image processing, offering an alternative mathematical representation that facilitates in-depth analysis in the frequency domain. This technique decomposes images into frequency components, revealing intricate patterns that are not always evident in the spatial domain. Fourier transform enhances image quality through frequency domain filtering, eliminating noise, improving contrast, and highlighting specific features. Its efficiency in compression ensures streamlined transmission and storage.

Asfarian [27] and Nasen [28] used the Fourier transformation for the purpose of detecting pests or diseases. The first one employed RGB images for the detection of caterpillars, and the second one used hyperspectral images for the detection of pesticide residues in corn. The application of frequency domain processing for the detection of nutrient deficiencies in crops, for example, in the identification of magnesium deficiency [52] or nitrogen utilized some variants, such as the application of filters [50]. An application and variant of this type of algorithm is the Fast Fourier transform, which was implemented to determine the viability of corn seeds [78] or for the detection of citrus fruits [79]. It can also be combined with the color index to estimate soybean yields [80].

Wavelet transforms and other image transforms excel in simultaneous frequency and spatial analysis. Unlike Fourier transforms, they offer localized assessments, proving effective for diverse image structures. Wavelets ensure efficient compression, preserving essential features while reducing the size of data. Their adaptability extends to applications like denoising and compression, with variants like discrete wavelet transform (DWT) and continuous wavelet transform (CWT) tailoring analytical approaches. Nagar [23] used the Wavelt transformation for the detection of caterpillars on crops in India, highlighting features such as ORB key points that can be extracted or utilized to estimate the density of aphids using spectroscopy and continuous wavelet analysis, as did Luo [29].

In agriculture, frequency domain processing and image transforms play an essential role. Fourier transforms reveal frequency patterns indicating variations in crop health or the presence of pests. Wavelet transforms offer advantages in capturing spatial and frequency information. These tools are fundamental for early disease detection, crop management, and optimizing agricultural practices, driving precise and sustainable decision-making.

3.2 Spatial domain processing

Spatial domain processing is a foundational aspect of image processing, distinct from transform domain processing. It involves directly manipulating pixel values in an image, allowing a nuanced understanding of intensity transformations. Essential techniques in spatial domain processing include intensity transformations and the manipulation of image histograms for enhancement. The mechanics of spatial filtering, encompassing the formation of filters, spatial convolution, and correlation, play an important role. Understanding various spatial filters, their applications, and the relationships between them, especially the fundamental role of lowpass filters, is integral. Additionally, awareness of combining enhancement methods is vital for addressing cases where a singular approach proves insufficient, highlighting the practical importance of spatial domain processing in refining and optimizing digital images. Spatial-domain image processing in color extends its significance to detailed imagery. This approach involves directly manipulating pixel values within the image space, offering nuanced adjustments for each color channel. From improving color contrast to refining object boundaries, spatial domain processing plays a crucial role in optimizing the visual appeal of color images. Techniques like spatial filtering and histogram manipulation have become powerful tools for tasks like color correction and feature enhancement. In the realm of color image processing, spatial domain techniques provide essential means for tailoring and refining the visual characteristics of intricate images. Spatial domain processing is pivotal in agriculture, driving precision and efficiency in crop management. By directly manipulating pixel values, it enables nuanced analysis of agricultural images. Understanding edge characteristics, employing spatial filtering for edge detection, and utilizing region-based segmentation refine identifications of crops, weeds, and soil conditions. Threshold and spatial filtering synergies enhance segmentation accuracy, while techniques like graph cuts and morphological watersheds further aid in analyzing complex agricultural landscapes.

Spatial domain processing algorithms are among the most widely used in agriculture. Image histogram manipulation is performed to improve brightness and contrast conditions mainly [30, 32, 76], and an adaptation of the histogram equalization is carried out to calculate a histogram of a given region by means of the K-means algorithm [31] for Lobesia botrana detection or in the grouping of bunches of grapes [81]. Other applications are used to adapt histograms to a certain pattern that is considered good for a certain purpose [84]. In the detection of nutrients such as nitrogen present in the leaves of different crops, histogram processing is applied, for example, by Qi [53]. Larijani [54] studied the use of histograms for the determination of thresholds, with the objective of removing background from rice crops. The calculation of histograms in images is a relatively simple process, and its contribution to DPI applications should not be underestimated.

The application of filters in the spatial domain is classified into low-pass and high-pass filters. Among the first ones, some of the most used are the mean, median, mode, and Gaussian filters, aimed at eliminating noise and smoothing the images. On the other hand, high-pass filters are used to detect sharp changes in contrasts, for example, edges. Among these types of filters are the Roberts, Sobel, and Prewitt operators. Arakeri [77] employed a median filter for noise removal following a segmentation process. Conversely, Rupesh [33] and Miranda [34] implemented low-pass filtering using mean, median, and mode with 3x3 and 9x9 kernels. This is done to eliminate “salt and pepper” noise, enabling the subsequent processes of pest detection and classification. Singh [7] utilized the media filter to remove unwanted elements in crops of beans, lemons, roses, and bananas with the intention of detecting pests and diseases. Edge detection is the counterpart of smoothing filters, which are used in order to highlight the borders of objects in the image. Thenmozhi [26] applied the Sobel filter for sugarcane pest detection, utilizing the absolute gradient. Garcia [31] uses the same filter to detect Lobesia botrana outline in Lobesia botrana trap images. Ireri [88] searched to extract the characteristics that describe the quality of a tomato by applying a Sobel operator. The detection of nutrient deficits is fundamental for modern agriculture. Kamelia [58] developed a method for the detection of macronutrients using a Canny detector for this purpose. Xu [56] applied a Roberts operator to extract characteristics; in his study, it showed better results than other operators used to detect nitrogen and potassium deficiencies.

The normalization of the color bands of the different models, mainly in RGB, allows to obtain a proportion of each band in a given pixel, in agriculture, this is used to relate a color to the nutritional status of the plant.

Wang [60] implemented NRI, NGI, and GMR to estimate the amount of nitrogen in rice crops, as well as complementing a separate threshold for the foliage background. Sun [62] provided and applied formulas to calculate different indexes such as dark green, excess green vegetation, excess green minus excess red, green-red vegetation, and Kawashima, which are basic elements to monitor NPK absorption. Another application of color indexes is to measure chlorophyll in crops. Vesali [63] utilized these indexes in a mobile application, where images are captured by coloring the corn leaf directly on the camera lens. Indexes such as GMR, GDR, and DGCI are among those employed by Vesali. Additionally, Lee [65] used color indexes to estimate rice crop growth by measuring leaf development. While color indexes are widely used for detecting nutritional deficiencies in crops, they can be used for other purposes as well. Xu [80] applied NDVI in conjunction with the Fourier transform to predict soybean yield in the United States.

Spatial domain processing, fundamental for decision-making, optimizes resource allocation, early disease detection, and sustainable agricultural practices, underscoring its significance in modern precision agriculture.

3.3 Image segmentation

Image segmentation is a foundational process in diverse applications, involving the partitioning of images for meaningful interpretation. It encompasses edge detection through spatial filtering, diverse thresholding approaches, and region-based segmentation. In agriculture, segmentation is pivotal for precision farming, distinguishing crops, weeds, and soil conditions. Spatial filtering and advanced edge detection refine these identifications. Thresholding becomes vital for discerning agricultural features, and the fusion of thresholding and spatial filtering enhances segmentation precision. Techniques like region-based segmentation, graph cuts, morphological watersheds, and motion-based segmentation prove invaluable for detailed crop and soil analysis.

One of the most used algorithms in image segmentation is bianrization, which can be carried out in several ways: the simplest ones, like thresholding, and others with more statistical bases, like OTSU. Within the segmentation by means of thresholds, the simplest way is to control the main variables such as illumination and background [19, 38, 86], which allows to define the threshold easily. Nanehkaran [40] implemented the use of thresholds in Lab color spaces; HSI in the first one used OTSU to divide the image into two classes, and HSI used a threshold to segment the green area in rice, corn, and cucumber crops. Larijani [54] used OTSU to perform an automatic threshold histogram of images of rice based on shape or to reduce the gray level in binary images. Finally, the binarization process can be applied to multispectral images. Liu [17] did it for invertebrate detection by manually setting the threshold for gamma. Barbedo [41] established trial-and-error thresholds in CMYK color space to achieve white fly segmentation and subsequent counting. Zhu [89] developed adaptive thresholds with RGB images to minimize noise and observe the wheat-gleaning phase.

Clustering algorithms are of importance for DPI, as they have the ability to label pixels into more than two groups. The k-means algorithm adds an element to the set to which its representative is closest. Fan [14] presented an apple segmentation algorithm in natural environments based on the K-means algorithm that uses blocks of pixels to determine the regions of the apple from the rest of the image. Garcia [31] performed a K-means algorithm for segmenting Lobesia botrana using decryptors in clustering. Sometimes a way to segment images is to have a base image and subsequent images. A pixel-by-pixel subtraction is carried out, and with this, it is possible to identify elements that are not in the base image, Maharlooei [38] used this algorithm with Sobeyian cultures for the detection of aphids. Perez-Zavala [81] used Density-based spatial clustering of applications with noise filters (DBSCAN) to reduce noise in images of grapes.

One of the algorithms of relatively recent emergence is deep learning, in particular, what is referred to as convolutional neural networks, which are based on an operation called convolution that uses a kernel as a base. Sladojevic [43] implemented a CNN model called CaffeNet that allows for the classification of diseases in various types of crops. Fuentes [44] explored the efficacy of various models of CNN Faster, R-CNN, R-FCN, VGG Net, and ResNet proposed by other authors in the detection of diseases and pests in tomato crops. The CNN has been tested to estimate the quality of fruits of various crops. Roy [93] proposed to perform a semantic segmentation and classification of apples by means of the UNet and a proprietary model called En-UNet, obtaining IoU metric values above 90%. Majeeda [95] processed images with grape crops to determine the position and orientation of grape plant cordons using the SegNet-VGG16, SegNet-VGG19, and FCN-AlexNet models, obtaining up to 80% efficiency in determining the trajectory of the cordons.

Image segmentation is integral for optimizing decision-making in agriculture, and fostering sustainability and efficiency in farming practices.

3.4 Morphological operators

Morphological operations in image processing are essential techniques for shape manipulation. By applying a structuring element to an input image, these operations generate an output image with identical dimensions. Initially designed for binary images, they have been adapted for grayscale applications. Key operations include dilation, expanding object boundaries, and erosion, contracting them. Closing, a two-step process of dilation followed by erosion, effectively closes gaps in objects. Opening, the complementary operation, involves initial erosion followed by dilation. These operations, fundamental for tasks like object detection and image enhancement, maintain original dimensions and contribute significantly to diverse fields, from medical imaging to computer vision, showcasing their importance as foundational tools in image processing. Morphological operations in image processing are pivotal for advancing precision agriculture. These techniques, such as dilation and erosion, refine crop analysis, weed detection, and soil assessment. The morphological operators play a crucial role in closing gaps, enhancing the identification of crops, and contributing to more accurate agricultural land evaluations. Portugal-Zambrano [76] carries out a dilation algorithm on images of trays with coffee beans to fill in any gaps that may exist in the contour, and then uses a dilation operator to reduce the thickness of these gaps in order to evaluate the quality of the coffee beans. Hamuda [84] proposed an automatic cauliflower crop detector using an erosion operator with a 3 x 3 structuring element to remove the remaining isolated white pixels from the binary image. Dilation with a 7 x 7 structuring element to recover the shape of the remaining objects. To estimate the freshness of tomato crops, Wan [86] applied erosion and expansion operators to improve fruit edges. In the detection of pests, the morphological operators have importance in the fact that it is necessary to identify perfectly where one insect or pest starts from another. Rajan [46] employed an erosion operator to eliminate elements that were not of interest and then implemented a dilation operator to close the outlines of whiteflies. Chang [39] used morphological operators applied to an image from a thresholding process to enclose the shape of the crop in a mask that shows its location within the image.

By optimizing decision-making, these operations contribute to sustainable farming practices, offering valuable tools for improved resource allocation and enhanced crop management in agriculture.

4. Conclusions

The algorithms discussed in the analyzed papers offer a glimpse into the future of the agricultural industry, indicating the growing presence and impact of various technologies. Computational algorithms, particularly those involving DPI and *AI*, have shown remarkable advancements in influencing the cultivation of diverse food types. Notably, prevalent DPI methods encompass color space transformation, binarization processes, morphological operators, edge detection, threshold segmentation, low-pass filters, and other techniques operating in the frequency domain.

In the analyzed papers, one notable aspect is the efficiency reflected in the results of the presented methods and algorithms. The most frequently employed metric was accuracy, consistently surpassing 90% and, in certain instances, achieving 100%. The high accuracy values underscore the significance and effectiveness of employing algorithms in agricultural processes, thereby supporting their development and the attainment of objectives.

Three elements influence the efficiency mentioned in the objectives of the different papers, such as the image acquisition conditions to work with, the features that can be extracted, and the classification algorithms used.

Image acquisition marks the inception of any *DPI* system. In the reviewed studies, images were captured under controlled conditions, encompassing controlled illumination sources, carefully chosen backgrounds to enhance contrast, and a specific arrangement of leaves and fruits—typically within a laboratory setting. Conversely, another category of image acquisition involved environments with less stringent controls, particularly concerning light and background; these images were directly captured in crop fields.

In addition to these features that are extracted from the images by applying the *DPI* algorithms, which were mentioned in the reviewed papers, there are those related to the color, shape of objects, and texture of these.

Once the images are processed and the features are defined and extracted, the subsequent step involves employing a classifier to ascertain the class to which the analyzed object belongs. Various classifier types exist; those outlined in the analyzed literature include minimum distances, SVM, simple and convolutional RNN, as well as linear regressions.

A challenge confronting the proposed methods lies in transitioning from the laboratory environment to the field, where the diverse algorithms need to contribute value to the agricultural production chain. Researchers are banking on technological advancements, particularly in terms of the mobility and accessibility of sensing devices, along with the natural increase in computing power, to effect changes in the field environment.

In conclusion, the utilization of DPI algorithms, is gaining prominence across diverse agricultural tasks and crops. The objective is to enhance productivity while concurrently reducing environmental impact, thereby ensuring that agriculture continues to serve as a fundamental pillar in the development of modern society.

Author details

Juan Pablo Guerra*† and Francisco Cuevas*†
Centro de Investigaciones en Óptica A.C., León Guanajuato, Mexico

*Address all correspondence to: juangi@cio.mx and fjcuevas@cio.mx

† These authors contributed equally.

References

[1] FAO. Our approach — Food Systems — Food and Agriculture Organization of the United Nations. 2023. Available from: http://www.fao.org/food-systems/our-approach/en/

[2] Shin J, Mahmud MS, Rehman TU, Ravichandran P, Heung B, Chang YK. Trends and prospect of machine vision technology for stresses and diseases detection in precision agriculture. AgriEngineering. 2023;**5**(1):20-39

[3] Gebbers R, Adamchuk VI. Precision agriculture and food security. Science. 2010;**327**(5967):828-831

[4] Smith R, Baillie J, McCarthy A, Raine S, Baillie C. Review of precision irrigation technologies and their application. In: National Centre for Engineering in Agriculture University of Southern Queensland Toowoomba Australia. 2010

[5] Tantalaki N, Souravlas S, Roumeliotis M. Data-driven decision making in precision agriculture: The rise of big data in agricultural systems. Journal of Agricultural and Food Information. 2019;**20**(4):344-380

[6] Gomes JFS, Leta FR. Applications of computer vision techniques in the agriculture and food industry: A review. European Food Research and Technology. 2012;**235**(6):989-1000

[7] Singh V, Misra AK. Detection of plant leaf diseases using image segmentation and soft computing techniques. Information Processing in Agriculture. 2017;**4**(1):41-49

[8] Mardanisamani S, Eramian M. Segmentation of vegetation and microplots in aerial agriculture images: A survey. The Plant Phenome Journal. 2022;**5**(1):1-32. Available from: https://acsess.onlinelibrary.wiley.com/doi/10.1002/ppj2.20042

[9] Tian H, Wang T, Liu Y, Qiao X, Li Y. Computer vision technology in agricultural automation —A review. Information Processing in Agriculture. 2020;**7**(1):1-19

[10] Awasthi Y. Press “a” for artificial intelligence in agriculture: A review. International Journal on Informatics Visualization. 2020;**4**(3):112-116

[11] Patrício DI, Rieder R. Computer vision and artificial intelligence in precision agriculture for grain crops: A systematic review. Computers and Electronics in Agriculture. 2018;**153**:69-81

[12] Jha K, Doshi A, Patel P, Shah M. A comprehensive review on automation in agriculture using artificial intelligence. Artificial Intelligence in Agriculture. 2019;**2**:1-12

[13] Jaiswal S, Pandey MK. A review on image segmentation. Advances in Intelligent Systems and Computing. 2021;**1187**:233-240

[14] Fan P, Lang G, Yan B, Lei X, Guo P, Liu Z, et al. A method of segmenting apples based on gray-centered rgb color space. Remote Sensing. 2021;**13**(6):1-17. Available from: https://www.mdpi.com/2072-4292/13/6/1211

[15] Rico-Fernández MP, Rios-Cabrera R, Castelán M, Guerrero-Reyes HI, Juarez-Maldonado A. A contextualized approach for segmentation of foliage in different crop species. Computers and Electronics in Agriculture. 2019;**156**(February):378-386

[16] Villaseñor-Aguilar MJ, Botello-Álvarez JE, Pérez-Pinal FJ, Cano-Lara M, León-Galván MF, Bravo-Sánchez MG, et al. Fuzzy classification of the maturity of the tomato using a vision system. Journal of Sensors. 2019;**2019**:1-12. Available from: https://www.hindawi.com/journals/js/2019/3175848/

[17] Liu H, Chahl JS. A multispectral machine vision system for invertebrate detection on green leaves. Computers and Electronics in Agriculture. 2018;**150**(May):279-288

[18] Sun Y, Tong C, He S, Wang K, Chen L. Identification of nitrogen, phosphorus, and potassium deficiencies based on temporal dynamics of leaf morphology and color. Sustainability. 2018;**10**(3):1-14. Available from: http://www.mdpi.com/2071-1050/10/3/762

[19] Story D, Kacira M, Kubota C, Akoglu A, An L. Lettuce calcium deficiency detection with machine vision computed plant features in controlled environments. Computers and Electronics in Agriculture. 2010;**74**(2):238-243

[20] Nyalala I, Okinda C, Nyalala L, Makange N, Chao Q, Chao L, et al. Tomato volume and mass estimation using computer vision and machine learning algorithms: Cherry tomato model. Journal of Food Engineering. 2019;**263**(July):288-298

[21] Reyns P, Missotten B, Ramon H, De Baerdemaeker J. A review of combine sensors for precision farming. Precision Agriculture. 2002;**3**(2):169-182

[22] Gonzalez R, Woods R. Digital Image Processing. 4th ed. New York, NY: Pearson education; 2018

[23] Nagar H, Sharma RS. Pest detection on leaf using image processing. In: 2021 International Conference on Computer Communication and Informatics (ICCCI). Coimbatore, India: IEEE; 2021. pp. 1-5. Available from: https://ieeexplore.ieee.org/document/9402606/

[24] Punithavathi R, Rani ADC, Sughashini KR, Kurangi C, Nirmala M, Ahmed HFT, et al. Application of computer vision in assessing crop abiotic stress: A systematic review. Procedia Computer Science. 2023;**216**(2022):e0290383

[25] Mccartney L, Lefsrud MG. Protected agriculture in extreme environments: A review of controlled environment agriculture in tropical, arid, polar, and urban locations. Applied Engineering in Agriculture. 2018;**34**(2):455-473

[26] Thenmozhi K, Reddy US. Image processing techniques for insect shape detection in field crops. In: 2017 International Conference on Inventive Computing and Informatics (ICICI). Coimbatore, India: IEEE; 2017. pp. 699-704. Available from: https://ieeexplore.ieee.org/document/8365226/

[27] Asfarian A, Herdiyeni Y, Rauf A, Mutaqin KH. Paddy diseases identification with texture analysis using fractal descriptors based on fourier spectrum. In: 2013 International Conference on Computer, Control, Informatics and its Applications (IC3INA). Bogor, Indonesia: IEEE; 2013. 2013. pp. 77-81. Available from: http://ieeexplore.ieee.org/document/6819152/

[28] Nansen C, Abidi N, Sidumo AJ, Gharalari AH. Using spatial structure analysis of hyperspectral imaging data and fourier transformed infrared analysis to determine bioactivity of surface pesticide treatment. Remote Sensing. 2010;**2**(4):908-925

[29] Luo J, Huang W, Yuan L, Zhao C, Du S, Zhang J, et al. Evaluation of spectral indices and continuous

wavelet analysis to quantify aphid infestation in wheat. Precision Agriculture. 2013;**14**(2):151-161

[30] Sabzi S, Abbaspour-Gilandeh Y, García-Mateos G. A fast and accurate expert system for weed identification in potato crops using metaheuristic algorithms. Computers in Industry. 2018;**98**:80-89

[31] García J, Pope C, Altimiras F. A distributed K-means segmentation algorithm applied to Lobesia botrana recognition. Complexity. 2017;**2017**:1-14. Available from: https://www.hindawi.com/journals/complexity/2017/5137317/

[32] Espinoza K, Valera DL, Torres JA, López A, Molina-Aiz FD. Combination of image processing and artificial neural networks as a novel approach for the identification of Bemisia tabaci and Frankliniella occidentalis on sticky traps in greenhouse agriculture. Computers and Electronics in Agriculture. 2016;**127**(3):495-505

[33] Rupesh RGM, Mundada G. Detection and classification of pests in greenhouse Using image processing. IOSR Journal of Electronics and Communication Engineering. 2013;**5**(6):57-63

[34] Miranda JL, Gerardo BD, Tanguilig BT III. Pest detection and extraction Using image processing techniques. International Journal of Computer and Communication Engineering. 2014;**3**(3):189-192

[35] Yao Q, Xian DX, Liu QJ, Yang BJ, Diao GQ, Tang J. Automated counting of rice planthoppers in paddy fields based on image processing. Journal of Integrative Agriculture. 2014;**13**(8):1736-1745

[36] Nanni L, Maguolo G, Pancino F. Insect pest image detection and recognition based on bio-inspired methods. Ecological Informatics. 2020;**57**(April):101089

[37] Huddar SR, Gowri S, Keerthana K, Vasanthi S, Rupanagudi SR. Novel algorithm for segmentation and automatic identification of pests on plants using image processing. In: 2012 3rd International Conference on Computing, Communication and Networking Technologies (ICCCNT'12), July. Coimbatore, India: IEEE; 2012. pp. 1-5. Available from: http://ieeexplore.ieee.org/document/6396012/

[38] Maharlooei M, Sivarajan S, Bajwa SG, Harmon JP, Nowatzki J. Detection of soybean aphids in a greenhouse using an image processing technique. Computers and Electronics in Agriculture. 2017;**132**(May):63-70

[39] Chang CL, Lin KM. Smart agricultural machine with a computer vision-based weeding and variable-rate irrigation scheme. Robotics. 2018;**7**(3):1-17. Available from: http://www.mdpi.com/2218-6581/7/3/38

[40] Nanehkaran YA, Zhang D, Chen J, Tian Y, Al-Nabhan N. Recognition of plant leaf diseases based on computer vision. Journal of Ambient Intelligence and Humanized Computing. 2020;**1**(0123456789):1-18. Available from: https://link.springer.com/10.1007/s12652-020-02505-x

[41] Barbedo JGA. Using digital image processing for counting whiteflies on soybean leaves. Journal of Asia-Pacific Entomology. 2014;**17**(4):685-694

[42] Hossain E, Hossain MF, Rahaman MA. A color and texture based approach for the detection and classification of plant leaf disease Using KNN classifier. In: 2019 International Conference on Electrical, Computer

and Communication Engineering (ECCE). Chittagong, Bangladesh: IEEE; 2019. pp. 1-6. Available from: https://ieeexplore.ieee.org/document/8679247/

[43] Sladojevic S, Arsenovic M, Anderla A, Culibrk D, Stefanovic D. Deep neural networks based recognition of plant diseases by leaf image classification. Computational Intelligence and Neuroscience. 2016;**2016**:1-11. Available from: http://www.hindawi.com/journals/cin/2016/3289801/

[44] Fuentes A, Yoon S, Kim S, Park D. A robust deep-learning-based detector for real-time tomato plant diseases and pests recognition. Sensors. 2017;**17**(9):1-21. Available from: http://www.mdpi.com/1424-8220/17/9/2022

[45] Sabouri H, Sajadi SJ. Image processing and area estimation of chia (Salvia hispanica L.), quinoa (Chenopodium quinoa Willd.), and bitter melon (Momordica charantia L.) leaves based on statistical and intelligent methods. Journal of Applied Research on Medicinal and Aromatic Plants. 2022;**30**(March):1-21. Available from: https://linkinghub.elsevier.com/retrieve/pii/S2214786122000146

[46] Rajan P, Radhakrishnan B, Suresh LP. Detection and classification of pests from crop images using support vector machine. 2016 International Conference on Emerging Technological Trends (ICETT). Kollam, India: IEEE; 2016. pp. 1-6. Available from: http://ieeexplore.ieee.org/document/7873750/

[47] Muñoz-Huerta RF, Guevara-Gonzalez RG, Contreras-Medina LM, Torres-Pacheco I, Prado-Olivarez J, Ocampo-Velazquez RV. A review of methods for sensing the nitrogen status in plants: Advantages, disadvantages and recent advances. Sensors (Switzerland). 2013;**13**(8):10823-10843

[48] Meiqing L, Jinyang L, Hanping M, Yanyou W. Diagnosis and detection of phosphorus nutrition level for Solanum lycopersicum based on electrical impedance spectroscopy. Biosystems Engineering. 2016;**143**:108-118

[49] Nejati H, Azimifar Z, Zamani M. Using fast fourier transform for weed detection in corn fields. In: 2008 IEEE International Conference on Systems, Man and Cybernetics. Singapore: IEEE; 2008. pp. 1215-1219. Available from: http://ieeexplore.ieee.org/document/4811448/

[50] da Silva Leite R, Hernandéz-Navarro S, do Nascimento MN, Potosme NMR, Carrión-Prieto P, dos Santos Souza E. Nitrogen fertilization affects Fourier transform infrared spectra (FTIR) in Physalis L. species. Computers and Electronics in Agriculture. 2018;**150**(May):411-417

[51] Ray A. Characterization of biochars from various agricultural by-products Using FTIR spectroscopy, SEM focused with image processing. International Journal of Agriculture Environment and Biotechnology. 2020;**13**(4):423-430

[52] da Silva FDF, Luz PHC, Romualdo LM, Marin MA, Zúñiga AMG, Herling VR, et al. A diagnostic tool for magnesium nutrition in maize based on image analysis of different leaf sections. Crop Science. 2014;**54**(2):738-745

[53] Qi X, Zhao Y, Huang Y, Wang Y, Qin W, Fu W, et al. A novel approach for nitrogen diagnosis of wheat canopies digital images by mobile phones based on histogram. Scientific Reports. 2021;**11**(1):1-15

[54] Larijani MR, Asli-Ardeh EA, Kozegar E, Loni R. Evaluation of image processing technique in identifying rice blast disease in field conditions based

on KNN algorithm improvement by K-means. Food Science and Nutrition. 2019;**7**(12):3922-3930

[55] Dhingra G, Kumar V, Joshi HD. A novel computer vision based neutrosophic approach for leaf disease identification and classification. Measurement: Journal of the International Measurement Confederation. 2019;**135**:782-794

[56] Xu G, Zhang F, Ghafoor Shah S, Ye Y, Mao H, Shah SG, et al. Use of leaf color images to identify nitrogen and potassium deficient tomatoes. Pattern Recognition Letters. 2011;**32**(11):1584-1590

[57] Shah A, Gupta P, Ajgar YM. Macro-nutrient deficiency identification in plants using image processing and machine learning. In: 2018 3rd International Conference for Convergence in Technology (I2CT). Vol. 1. Pune, India: IEEE; 2018. pp. 1-4. Available from: https://ieeexplore.ieee.org/document/8529789/

[58] Kamelia L, Rahman TKBA, Saragih H, Haerani R. The comprehensive review on detection of macro nutrients deficiency in plants based on the image processing technique. In: 2020 6th International Conference on Wireless and Telematics (ICWT). Yogyakarta, Indonesia: IEEE; 2020. pp. 1-4. Available from: https://ieeexplore.ieee.org/document/9243623/

[59] Su WH, Sheng J, Huang QY. Development of a three-dimensional plant localization technique for automatic differentiation of soybean from intra-row weeds. Agriculture. 2022;**12**(2):1-16. Available from: https://www.mdpi.com/2077-0472/12/2/195

[60] Wang Y, Wang D, Zhang G, Wang J. Estimating nitrogen status of rice using the image segmentation of G-R thresholding method. Field Crops Research. 2013;**149**:33-39

[61] Mao H, Gao H, Zhang X, Kumi F. Nondestructive measurement of total nitrogen in lettuce by integrating spectroscopy and computer vision. Scientia Horticulturae. 2015;**184**:1-7

[62] Sun Y, Gao J, Wang K, Shen Z, Chen L. Utilization of machine vision to monitor the dynamic responses of rice leaf morphology and colour to nitrogen, phosphorus, and potassium deficiencies. Journal of Spectroscopy. 2018;**2018**:16-18

[63] Vesali F, Omid M, Kaleita A, Mobli H. Development of an android app to estimate chlorophyll content of corn leaves based on contact imaging. Computers and Electronics in Agriculture. 2015;**116**:211-220

[64] Wang Y, Wang D, Shi P, Omasa K. Estimating rice chlorophyll content and leaf nitrogen concentration with a digital still color camera under natural light. Plant Methods. 2014;**10**:11

[65] Lee KJ, Lee BW. Estimation of rice growth and nitrogen nutrition status using color digital camera image analysis. European Journal of Agronomy. 2013;**48**:57-65

[66] Buchaillot ML, Gracia-Romero A, Vergara-Diaz O, Zaman-Allah MA, Tarekegne A, Cairns JE, et al. Evaluating maize genotype performance under low nitrogen conditions using RGB UAV phenotyping techniques. Sensors. 2019;**19**(8):1-27. Available from: https://www.mdpi.com/1424-8220/19/8/1815

[67] Chiu MT, Xu X, Wei Y, Huang Z, Schwing A, Brunner R, et al. Agriculture-vision: A large aerial image database for agricultural pattern analysis. In: 2020 IEEE/CVF Conference on Computer Vision and Pattern Recognition (CVPR).

Seattle, WA, USA: IEEE; 2020. pp. 2825-2835. Available from: https://ieeexplore.ieee.org/document/9157397/

[68] Jia Y, Su Z, Shen W, Yuan J, Xu Z. UAV remote sensing image mosaic and its application in agriculture. International Journal of Smart Home. 2016;**10**(5):159-170

[69] Ponce H, Cevallos C, Espinosa R, Gutiérrez S. Estimation of low nutrients in tomato crops through the analysis of leaf images Using machine learning. Journal of Artificial Intelligence and Technology. 2021;**1**(2):131-137

[70] Li Y, Chen D, Walker CN, Angus JF. Estimating the nitrogen status of crops using a digital camera. Field Crops Research. 2010;**118**(3):221-227

[71] Rorie RL, Purcell LC, Karcher DE, King CA. The assessment of leaf nitrogen in corn from digital images. Crop Science. 2011;**51**(5):2174-2180

[72] Sari YA, Maligan JM, Prakoso AF. Improving the elementary leftover food estimation algorithm by using clustering image segmentation in nutrition intake problem. In: 2020 International Conference on Computer Engineering, Network, and Intelligent Multimedia (CENIM). Cenim. Surabaya, Indonesia: IEEE; 2020. pp. 435-439. Available from: https://ieeexplore.ieee.org/document/9298005/

[73] Chen L, Lin L, Cai G, Sun Y, Huang T, Wang K, et al. Identification of nitrogen, phosphorus, and potassium deficiencies in rice based on static scanning technology and hierarchical identification method. PLoS One. 2014;**9**(11):1-17

[74] Chen LS, Zhang SJ, Wang K, Shen ZQ, Deng JS. Identifying of rice phosphorus stress based on machine vision technology. Life Science Journal. 2013;**10**(2):2655-2663. Available from: https://www.lifesciencesite.com/lsj/life1002/368_B01259life_1002_2655_2663.pdf

[75] Bhargava A, Bansal A. Fruits and vegetables quality evaluation using computer vision: A review. Journal of King Saud University - Computer and Information Sciences. 2021;**33**(3):243-257

[76] Portugal-Zambrano CE, Gutierrez-Caceres JC, Ramirez-Ticona J, Beltran-Castanon CA. Computer vision grading system for physical quality evaluation of green coffee beans. In: 2016 XLII Latin American Computing Conference (CLEI). Valparaiso, Chile: IEEE; 2016. pp. 1-11. Available from: https://ieeexplore.ieee.org/document/7833383/

[77] Arakeri MP, Lakshmana B. Computer vision based fruit grading system for quality evaluation of tomato in agriculture industry. Procedia Computer Science. 2016;**79**:426-433. DOI: 10.1016/j.procs.2016.03.055. Available from: https://linkinghub.elsevier.com/retrieve/pii/S1877050916001861

[78] Ambrose A, Lohumi S, Lee WH, Cho BK. Comparative nondestructive measurement of corn seed viability using Fourier transform near-infrared (FT-NIR) and Raman spectroscopy. Sensors and Actuators, B: Chemical. 2016;**224**:500-506

[79] Bansal R, Lee WS, Satish S. Green citrus detection using fast Fourier transform (FFT) leakage. Precision Agriculture. 2013;**14**(1):59-70

[80] Xu C, Katchova AL. Predicting soybean yield with NDVI using a flexible Fourier transform model. Journal of Agricultural and Applied Economics. 2019;**51**(3):402-416

[81] Pérez-Zavala R, Torres-Torriti M, Cheein FA, Troni G. A pattern recognition strategy for visual grape bunch detection in vineyards. Computers and Electronics in Agriculture. 2018;**151**(August):136-149

[82] Dhakshina Kumar S, Esakkirajan S, Bama S, Keerthiveena B. A microcontroller based machine vision approach for tomato grading and sorting using SVM classifier. Microprocessors and Microsystems. 2020;**76**:103090

[83] Castro W, Oblitas J, De-La-Torre M, Cotrina C, Bazan K, Avila-George H. Classification of cape gooseberry fruit according to its level of ripeness using machine learning techniques and different color spaces. IEEE Access. 2019;**7**:27389-27400

[84] Hamuda E, Mc Ginley B, Glavin M, Jones E. Automatic crop detection under field conditions using the HSV colour space and morphological operations. Computers and Electronics in Agriculture. 2017;**133**:97-107

[85] Hemamalini V, Rajarajeswari S, Nachiyappan S, Sambath M, Devi T, Singh BK, et al. Food quality inspection and grading using efficient image segmentation and machine learning-based system. Journal of Food Quality. 2022;**2022**:1-6. Available from: https://www.hindawi.com/journals/jfq/2022/5262294/

[86] Wan P, Toudeshki A, Tan H, Ehsani R. A methodology for fresh tomato maturity detection using computer vision. Computers and Electronics in Agriculture. 2018;**146**(January):43-50

[87] Sadeghi-Tehran P, Sabermanesh K, Virlet N, Hawkesford MJ. Automated method to determine two critical growth stages of wheat: Heading and flowering. Frontiers in Plant Science. 2017;**8**(February):1-14

[88] Ireri D, Belal E, Okinda C, Makange N, Ji C. A computer vision system for defect discrimination and grading in tomatoes using machine learning and image processing. Artificial Intelligence in Agriculture. 2019;**2**:28-37

[89] Zhu Y, Cao Z, Lu H, Li Y, Xiao Y. In-field automatic observation of wheat heading stage using computer vision. Biosystems Engineering. 2016;**143**(April):28-41

[90] Villaseñor-Aguilar MJ, Bravo-Sánchez MG, Padilla-Medina JA, Vázquez-Vera JL, Guevara-González RG, García-Rodríguez FJ, et al. A maturity estimation of bell pepper (Capsicum annuum L.) by artificial vision system for quality control. Applied Sciences. 2020;**10**(15):1-18. Available from: https://www.mdpi.com/2076-3417/10/15/5097

[91] Garcia MB, Ambat S, Adao RT. Tomayto, Tomahto: A machine learning approach for tomato ripening stage identification using pixel-based color image classification. In: 2019 IEEE 11th International Conference on Humanoid, Nanotechnology, Information Technology, Communication and Control, Environment, and Management (HNICEM). Laoag, Philippines: IEEE; 2019. pp. 1-6. Available from: https://ieeexplore.ieee.org/document/9072892/

[92] Giménez-Gallego J, González-Teruel JD, Jiménez-Buendía M, Toledo-Moreo AB, Soto-Valles F, Torres-Sánchez R. Segmentation of multiple tree leaves pictures with natural backgrounds using deep learning for image-based agriculture applications. Applied Sciences. 2019;**10**(1):1-15. Available from: https://www.mdpi.com/2076-3417/10/1/202

[93] Roy K, Chaudhuri SS, Pramanik S. Deep learning based real-time industrial framework for rotten and fresh fruit

detection using semantic segmentation. Microsystem Technologies. 2021;**27**(9):3365-3375

[94] Cevallos C, Ponce H, Moya-Albor E, Brieva J. Vision-based analysis on leaves of tomato crops for classifying nutrient deficiency using convolutional neural networks. In: 2020 International Joint Conference on Neural Networks (IJCNN). CDMX, Mexico: IEEE; 2020. pp. 1-7. Available from: https://ieeexplore.ieee.org/document/9207615/

[95] Majeed Y, Karkee M, Zhang Q, Fu L, Whiting MD. Determining grapevine cordon shape for automated green shoot thinning using semantic segmentation-based deep learning networks. Computers and Electronics in Agriculture. 2020;**171**:105308

[96] Barbedo JGA. A review on the main challenges in automatic plant disease identification based on visible range images. Biosystems Engineering. 2016;**144**:52-60

[97] Njoroge BM, Fei TK, Thiruchelvam V. A research review of precision farming techniques and technology. Journal of Applied Technology and Innovation. 2018;**2**(1):22-30

[98] Gao J, Yang Y, Lin P, Park DS. Computer vision in healthcare applications. Journal of Healthcare Engineering. 2018;**2018**:1-4. Available from: https://www.hindawi.com/journals/jhe/2018/5157020/

Chapter 3

Recent Advances on Image Edge Detection

Anis BenHajyoussef and Asma Saidani

Abstract

This chapter delves into the intricate field of image edge detection, a pivotal aspect of computer vision and image processing. It provides a comprehensive exploration of the underlying principles, methodologies, and algorithms employed in the identification and extraction of significant contours in digital images. Traditional edge detection techniques, as well as advanced approaches that are based deep learning, are thoroughly examined.

Keywords: image processing, edge detection, gradient, deep learning, neural networks

1. Introduction

In the world of computer vision and image processing, edge detection plays a fundamental role. Edge detection techniques enable computers to identify and extract important boundaries and contours from digital images, leading to numerous applications such as object recognition, image segmentation, and feature extraction.

Many research works have been conducted on this sense. In Ref [1], Ziou and tabbone proposed an edge detection algorithm based on the Robert operator introduced by Lawrence Roberts in 1963—a rudimentary yet pioneering step in the field. In Ref [2], Shrivakshan and Chandrasekar used the Prewitt operator, tailored for scenarios with high noise and fading pixel values. Then, Sobel operator [3]-based algorithm was proposed [4] and have given the differentiation algorithms a particular popularity. Xin Wang used then the Laplacian operator [5], leveraging second-order differentiation for more precise edge identification. In a significant milestone, John Canny introduced the optimal Canny operator [6]. This method continuously improved image contour information through a series of filtering, enhancement, and detection steps, ushering in a new era and establishing higher standards in the field of edge detection.

The previous mentioned differentiation approaches are now considered as traditional. In fact, with the progress of artificial intelligence, a lot of recent research has focused on edge detection and proposed deep learning-based approaches. In Ref. [7], Bertasius proposed (DeepEdge), a two branches-based deep network for edge detection. In the first one, a classification solution is applied to predict the edge likelihood. In the second one, regression criteria to predict edges based on training data. By combining multi-scale levels, Xie and Tu proposed the HED, a holistic nested edge detection [8] that can predict hierarchical representations. In Ref. [9], Deng et al. enhanced the HED using the VGG16 [10] as a backbone network and implementing a full convolution architecture. The solution named, LPCB, avoids some prediction ambiguities as thick edges allowing better detection performance. In Ref. [11], Yang et al. proposed a full convolution codec network ECDN. Such network includes a decoder through deconvolution steps aiming at resizing the encoder output map to the original image size. The decoder allows better edge localization performance. Since complexity is also a key point, Su et al. have proposed lightweight architecture named Pixel Difference Network (PiDinet) [12]. In this proposal, the authors integrate a differential operator into the network to perform a novel pixel difference convolution. In Ref. [13], Xavier Soria differentiates between edges, contours, and boundaries and consider them as three distinct visual features and propose two sub-networks: Extremely Dense initial network and an Up-sampling part. In Ref. [14], Elharrouss propose the (CHRNet) network where he maintains the high-resolution of the edge map during the network stage overcoming the down-sampling of pooling and connect consecutive scales through sub-blocks. Due to the complexity of the proposed networks, some research proposed a light-weighted solutions as in Ref. [15].

The rest of the chapter is organized as follows. First, we present in basics of image detection, edge types, applications, used dataset, and evaluation criteria in Section 2. Then, we discuss the traditional edge detection methods in Section 3. In Section 4, we describe the basics of recent deep learning-based approaches and present our conclusions in Section 5.

2. Basis of image edge detection

2.1 Definition of image edges

In the domain of digital imagery, an edge encapsulates a fundamental concept embodying the transition between contrasting regions within an image. Specifically, an edge marks the boundary where intensity or color values undergo significant and rapid changes. These variations might indicate shifts in texture, object boundaries, or underlying structures in texture area. Mathematically, an edge can be seen as a locus of points where the derivative of spatial intensity (Luminance) or color (chrominance) experiences a pronounced variation. **Figure 1** illustrates the edge lines in white color.

Figure 1.
Detected edges.

2.2 Types of edges

Edges in images exhibit diverse characteristics based on the nature of the underlying transitions in intensity or color. These variations lead to the classification of edges into several distinct types as presented in **Figure 2**, each conveying different information about the image content.

2.2.1 Step edges

Step edges are perhaps the most fundamental type of edge, characterized by a sudden and significant change in intensity across neighboring pixels. These transitions often correspond to object boundaries or abrupt changes in surface orientation. Step edges manifest as sharp transitions, representing a rapid shift from one color or brightness level to another.

2.2.2 Ramp edges

Ramp edges denote a smoother transition in intensity, typically resembling a linear change across adjacent pixels. This type of edge can arise from gradual shifts in illumination or material properties, such as the transition from a shadowed region to a well-lit area.

2.2.3 Ridge edges

Ridge edges represent situations where the intensity undergoes a gradual decrease before experiencing a sudden increase. This type of edge is prominent in scenarios where a transition from a brightly illuminated region to a shadowed area takes place, creating a ridge-like intensity profile.

2.2.4 Roof edges

Roof edges are characterized by a transitional phase that exhibits a gradual increase in intensity followed by an abrupt decrease. These edges often occur in images with highlight reflections or transition from shadow to highlight regions.

Understanding the different types of edges is essential, as they provide insights into the underlying content of an image. Recognizing the specific type of edge can aid in accurately interpreting the objects, materials, or lighting conditions present within the image. This categorization forms the basis for subsequent edge detection methodologies, enabling the development of techniques tailored to different edge types.

This pixel based classification based is mainly significant for traditional edge detection approaches, which will be addressed in next sections.

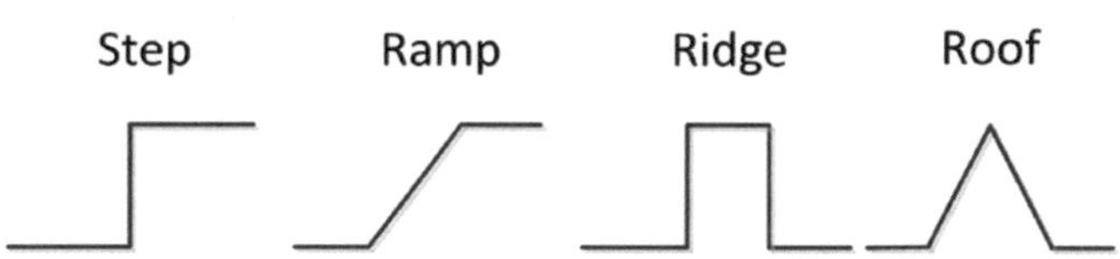

Figure 2.
Types of edges.

2.3 Applications of edge detection

Edge detection, a foundational technique in image processing and computer vision, demonstrates its significance through various applications and disciplines:

1. Image Segmentation: Edge detection frequently precedes image segmentation, delineating images into coherent regions. Edges play a pivotal role in distinguishing objects and structures.

2. Object Detection and Recognition: In identifying and recognizing objects, edge detection defines their contours, enabling subsequent classification and analysis.

3. Medical Imaging: Edge detection finds utility in medical imaging, delineating organs, vessels, and anomalies within X-rays, MRI scans, and CT images, augmenting diagnostic accuracy.

4. Robotics and Autonomous Systems: Essential for real-time processing, edge detection empowers robots and autonomous vehicles to navigate, discern obstacles, and interpret visual inputs.

5. Biometrics: In biometrics, edge detection distinguishes intricate patterns in fingerprint recognition and retinal scans, allowing better identification accuracy.

6. Document Analysis: Edge detection helps analyze documents, character recognition, processes forms, and extracts textual content.

7. Satellite Image Processing: In satellite imagery, edge detection aids in landform assessment, urban monitoring, and environmental analysis.

8. These diverse applications underscore edge detection's pivotal role in extracting crucial insights from images, underpinning sophisticated image analysis across an array of scholarly disciplines.

3. Traditional edge detection techniques

Gradient-based edge detection techniques are cornerstone approaches in identifying abrupt changes in intensity across an image. These methods exploit the concept of gradient, which represents the variation of intensity at each pixel position. By locating areas with high gradient values, gradient-based methods can effectively locate edges.

3.1 Roberts operator

The Roberts operator [1] uses a pair of simple 2x2 kernels to compute the gradients along the diagonals. It is relatively simple to implement in comparison with other operators. However, it is sensitive to noise due to its small kernel size.

3.2 Prewitt operator

Similar to the Roberts operator, the Prewitt operator [2] employs convolution but with specific 3x3 kernels to calculate gradients along both horizontal and vertical directions. The absolute magnitude of these gradients helps detect edges.

3.3 Sobel operator

The Sobel operator [3] is a widely employed gradient-based technique for edge detection. Like the Prewitt operator, it utilizes convolution with two 3x3 kernels, one for detecting horizontal edges and the other for vertical edges. The resultant gradient magnitude and direction provide insights into the edge's strength and orientation.

3.4 Laplacian of Gaussian (LoG)

The Laplacian of Gaussian (LoG) [5] is a prominent edge detection technique that combines the benefits of smoothing and gradient-based approaches. This method involves two key steps: applying Gaussian smoothing and then calculating the Laplacian operator.

Gaussian smoothing: The first step of LoG is to convolve the image with a Gaussian kernel. Gaussian smoothing reduces noise and emphasizes areas with significant intensity changes, effectively highlighting potential edges.

Laplacian operator: The Laplacian operator is then applied to the Gaussian-smoothed image. It computes the second derivative of intensity, highlighting regions where the intensity changes rapidly. This operation enhances edges while suppressing gradual intensity variations. Combining Gaussian smoothing and the Laplacian operator helps LoG overcome noise-related issues in gradient-based methods. However, LoG may also lead to over-detection of edges and generate multiple responses for a single edge due to the nature of the Laplacian operator. Consequently, techniques like zero-crossing detection are employed to refine the edge map and extract accurate edges from the enhanced image.

3.5 Canny edge detection

Canny edge detection [6] is a multi-step algorithm widely recognized for its effectiveness in accurately identifying edges while suppressing noise. Developed by John F. Canny in 1986, this method aims to optimize edge detection by addressing the disadvantages of earlier techniques.

Gaussian smoothing: Canny edge detection begins with applying Gaussian smoothing to the image. The Gaussian filter reduces noise and creates a smoothed representation of the image, which is crucial for accurate edge detection.

Gradient calculation: This step involves computing the derivatives of the smoothed image in both the horizontal and vertical directions. The gradient magnitude highlights regions with significant intensity changes, indicative of edges, while the gradient direction provides the edge orientation.

Non-maximum suppression: Non-maximum suppression eliminates false detection in the gradient magnitude image by thinning edges. It consist in preserving only the local maxima along the direction of the gradient.

Hysteresis thresholding: Hysteresis thresholding is the final step, classifying pixels into strong, weak, or non-edges. This step employs two threshold values: a high threshold to identify strong edges and a low threshold to detect weak edges. Weak edges are retained only if they are connected to strong edges.

The Canny edge detection algorithm produces sharp, well-defined edges while also handling noise effectively. Its adaptability through parameter tuning makes it suitable for various image types and conditions. However, setting appropriate thresholds can be challenging, and the algorithm's multi-step nature may impact its computational efficiency. Despite these considerations, Canny edge detection remains an effective technique in image processing due to its balance between accuracy and noise robustness.

4. Deep learning-based edge detection

Deep learning represents a significant progression within machine learning, especially in image processing.

The key point is its foundation in neural networks—layered algorithms inspired by the human brain's neural structure. This emulation empowers machines to learn more effectively than traditional machine learning models. Many deep learning-based research works rely on backbone networks, a kind of network architectures. Then, elucidating theses essential concepts is pivotal for comprehending primary approaches within edge detection.

4.1 Concept of neural network

A neural network is a computational model inspired by the structure and function of the human brain's interconnected neurons.

It consists of interconnected nodes, or "neurons," organized into layers. These networks are designed to process and interpret complex patterns and relationships in data.

A typical neural network includes an input layer, one or more hidden layers, and an output layer. Neurons in each layer are connected to neurons in adjacent layers through weighted connections. These weights determine the strength of the connections, enabling the network to learn from data and adjust its internal parameters during a training process. Neural networks excel in tasks such as pattern recognition, classification, regression, and feature extraction. Their capacity to learn from large amounts of data and discover intricate patterns makes them especially suitable for complex problems in fields like image.

4.2 Convolutional neural network

Convolutional Neural Network (CNN) is the main key point in deep learning-based edge detection. A CNN is a type of neural network specifically designed for processing and analyzing visual data, such as images and videos.

Indeed, CNNs play a central role in the field of computer vision by revolutionizing how machines perceive and analyze images.

Some of the main roles of CNNs are as follows:

- Feature Extraction
- Image Classification

- Object Detection
- Image Segmentation

At its core, a CNN is composed of multiple layers that perform various operations on the input data. A typical CNN architecture is exposed in **Figure 3**.

The CNN components include the following:

1. Input Layer: This is the raw image data, considered as the input into the network. Images are represented as a grid of pixel values.

2. Convolutional Layer: This layer applies filters (also called kernels) to the input image. It aims to extract specific features such as edges, corners, or textures. The filters slide across the image, performing convolutions and generating feature maps.

3. Pooling Layer: Also known as subsampling or downsampling, this layer reduces the spatial dimensions of the feature maps. It helps reduce computational complexity and makes the network more invariant to small variations in position.

4. Fully Connected Layer: Toward the end of the network, one or more fully connected layers aggregate the extracted features and make decisions. In image classification, these layers connect to the output neurons representing different classes.

5. Flattening: Before the fully connected layer, the 3D feature maps are flattened into a 1D vector. This allows them to be connected to the fully connected layer.

6. Output Layer: The final layer produces the network's output. In image classification, this might be a softmax layer that assigns probabilities to different classes.

7. Loss Function: The loss function quantifies the difference between the predicted output and the true labels. It serves as a guide for adjusting the network's weights during training.

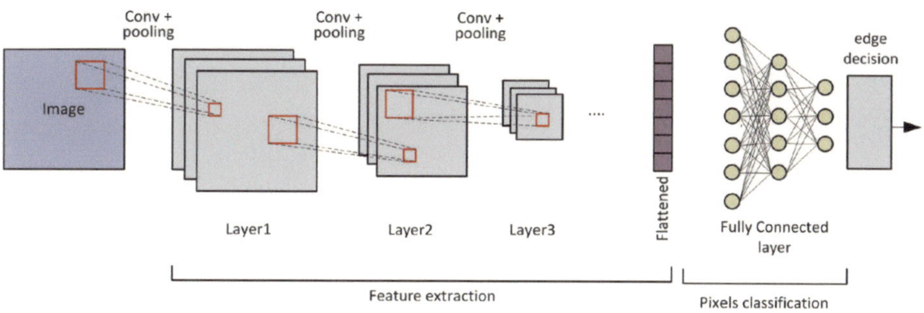

Figure 3.
A typical CNN architecture.

8. Backpropagation: The network adjusts its internal parameters (weights and biases) using backpropagation. The gradients of the loss with respect to the weights are calculated and used to update the weights through optimization algorithms like Stochastic Gradient Descent (SGD).

9. Training: The network is trained using labeled data, where it iteratively adjusts its parameters to minimize the loss function. The training data help the network learn to recognize features and patterns.

10. Prediction: After training, the network is evaluated on unseen data to assess its performance. It is then used to make predictions on new, unseen images.

11. The above steps constitute a basic overview of how a CNN operates. Depending on the architecture and specific task, the network's structure and the number of layers may vary.

4.3 Backbone networks

In image processing, backbone networks refer to the foundational architectures that serve as the initial configurations of deep neural networks designed for tasks such as image analysis, object recognition, and segmentation.

They serve as the foundation upon which more specialized architectures and algorithms are built to perform various image processing tasks effectively. The most popular backbone are VGGs, ResNets, and Inception v1—GoogleNet.

4.3.1 AlexNet

AlexNet [16] is a pioneering CNN architecture that achieved remarkable success in the ImageNet Large Scale Visual Recognition Challenge (ILSVRC) competition in 2012. Developed by Alex Krizhevsky, Ilya Sutskever, and Geoffrey Hinton, AlexNet marked a significant breakthrough by employing deep learning techniques for image classification tasks. Notably, AlexNet consisted of eight layers, including five convolutional layers and three fully connected layers. This design was substantially deeper than previous models and facilitated the recognition of intricate features in images. AlexNet's success was further propelled by the utilization of Rectified Linear Units (ReLU) as activation functions, dropout for regularization, and the novel implementation of Graphics Processing Units (GPUs) for accelerated training. It demonstrated the potential of deep neural networks in image classification tasks, inspiring subsequent developments of more high-performing architectures.

4.3.2 VGGs

VGG16, denoting the VGGNet model [10], represents a convolutional neural network (CNN) architecture comprising 16 layers. Its appellation originates from "Visual Geometry Group." Proposed by K. Simonyan and A. Zisserman from Oxford University, this model has notably excelled in the ImageNet dataset, achieving a remarkable test accuracy of 92.7%. Positioned prominently in the ILSVRC-2014 competition, VGG16 stands as a remarkable achievement.

4.3.3 ResNet

In 2015, the deep residual network (ResNet) [17] emerged as an important contribution in the domain of computer vision and deep learning.

It is particularly recognized for the ability to facilitate training of networks encompassing hundreds, or even thousands, of layers while sustaining compelling performance.

ResNet introduced the innovative concept of an "identity shortcut connection." This mechanism enables the model to bypass one or more layers, facilitating training on extensive layer configurations without compromising performance. ResNet has gained prominence as a leading architecture in diverse computer vision tasks beyond image classification, including object detection and facial recognition, owing to its robust representational capacity.

4.4 Supervised learning-based edge detection

Supervised learning in image edge detection is a machine learning approach where algorithms are trained to identify and classify the boundaries or edges. The key point in such approach is the rely on a labeled dataset used to train the model. A process flow of supervised learning edge detection is presented in **Figure 4**.

This approach involves the following key steps:

1. Labeled Edge Data: In supervised edge detection, we have a dataset consisting of images as input data and corresponding labels or annotations that indicate the locations of edges or boundaries within these images. The labels specify which pixels or regions in the images are part of an edge. In general, the labelling process is done manually and its output is the called ground truth. This ground-truth information serves as a reference for evaluating the performance of edge detection algorithms.

2. Training Phase: During the training phase, the algorithm uses this labeled image data to learn the relationships between the visual features in the images and the locations of edges. It aims to create a model that can accurately identify these edges within new, unlabeled images.

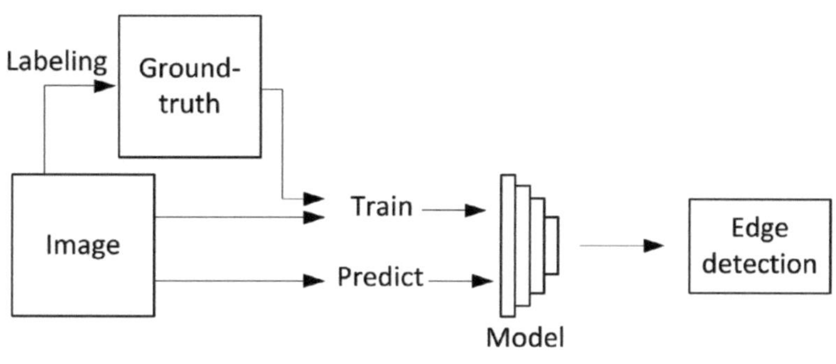

Figure 4.
Supervised learning approach.

3. Feature Extraction: Image features, such as gradients, intensity changes, or other relevant characteristics, are extracted from the input images. These features serve as the basis for the algorithm to make edge predictions.

4. Prediction of Edges: Once the model is trained, it can be used to analyze and predict the edges on new images.

The CNN-based supervised learning approaches are hardly categorizable, as many works combine many techniques. We separate here the approaches based on two main techniques: codec-based and multi-scale fusion-based techniques. But it is not impossible to find a research work that combines these techniques for refinement purpose.

The codec-based technique is quite related to the property of the CNN itself. In fact, due to the downscaling effects of convolutional networks through successive convolutions and pooling, the ultimate output does not correspond to each pixel in the initial image. To address this, a decoder is added after the encoding. A representative process of the codec-based edge detection is presented in **Figure 5**.

While the encoder network's role is to generate semantic-rich feature images, the decoder task is to up-sample these low-resolution feature images through deconvolutions. The goal is to remap feature images, to match the input image's dimensions for pixel-level matching.

Among the research works in this context, we can mention CEDN [11], CASENet [18], REDN [19], and RINDNet [20].

The multi-scale fusion-based technique presented in **Figure 6** is related to another property of CNN. In fact, this later operates in a layer-by-layer extraction of target features, a process in which the concept of perceptual field assumes critical importance. Notably, higher layers exhibit an expanded perceptual field, facilitating robust semantic characterization, while lower layers, with a smaller perceptual scope, excel in extracting geometric details.

Then fusing multi-scale features enables it to capture both fine-grained details and broader contextual information simultaneously.

This approach, consisting in the integration of features across divergent scales, emerges as a pivotal modality for substantial enhancement in the research work on edge detection. Among the works in this sense, we can find DeepEdge [7], HED [8], LPCB [9], PidiNet [12], DexiNed [13], RCN [21], and DSCD [22].

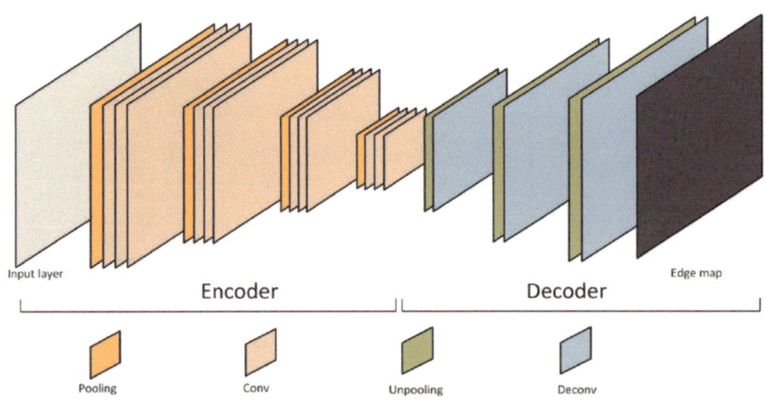

Figure 5.
The architecture of the codec-based edge detection.

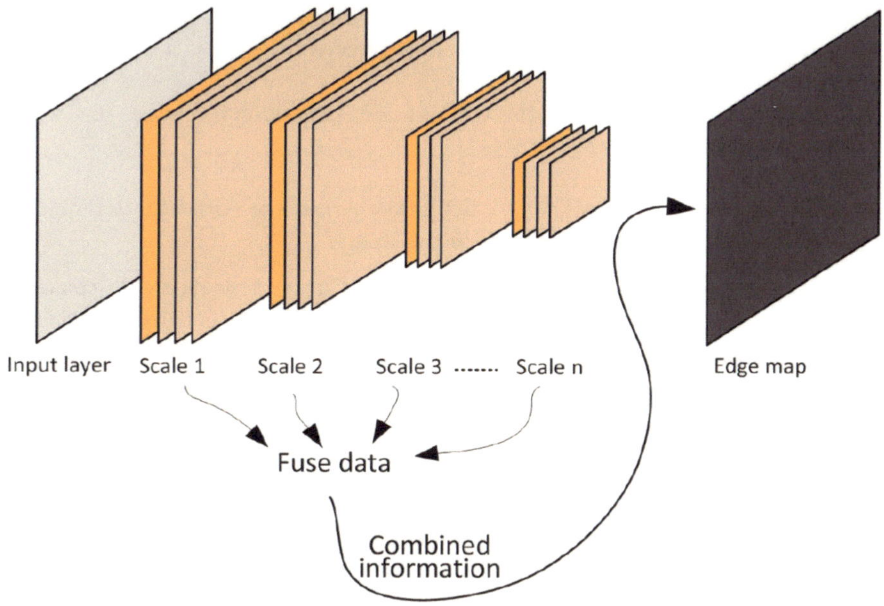

Figure 6.
Multi-scale typical architecture-based edge detection.

We can summarize a comparison between the two approaches as follows:

- Codec-based algorithms:
    - Advantage: Better edge pixel-to-pixel localization on the output map avoiding the low resolution of pooling process.
    - Disadvantages: The decoder approximately doubles the complexity of the network
- Multi-scale fusion-based algorithms:
    - Advantage: Better combination of semantic information extracted from higher layers and the geometric details extracted from lower layers.
    - Disadvantages: Processing of many inter-layers parameters can increase complexity

5. Edge detection performance evaluation

5.1 Evaluation criteria

Evaluation criteria for edge detection techniques serve as benchmarks to assess the performance and efficacy of various algorithms. The most common metrics in recent research works are Optimal Dataset Scale (ODS) and Optimal Image Scale (OIS). But there are many other related metrics that should be considered. We present here the main common evaluation metrics used in edge detection:

1. Precision: Precision measures the ratio of correctly detected edges to the total number of detected edges.

2. Recall, also known as sensitivity, calculates the ratio of correctly detected edges to the total number of actual edges in the image.

   It is common to present a Precision-Recall Curve. This curve illustrates the relationship between precision and recall across various threshold values, offering information into an algorithm's performance across different operating parameters.

3. F-score: This F-score [23] is a combination of precision and recall, providing a balanced assessment of algorithms performance in terms of both false positives (false-detected edges) and false negatives (non-detected edges).

$$F - scrore = \left(1 + p^2\right) \times \frac{Pr \times R}{p^2 \times Pr \times R} \tag{1}$$

Where p is a threshold value, Pr being the precision and R is the recall. Adjusting the threshold allows us to refine on the impact of precision and recall.

1. ODS (Optimal Dataset Scale): This metric represents the optimal F-score obtained at a fixed threshold for the whole dataset.

2. OIS (Optimal Image Scale): OIS is obtained from the F-score by finding the best threshold for each image in the dataset.

3. Accuracy: Accuracy evaluates the overall correctness of edge detection results, considering both true positives (correct detected edges) and true negatives (correct detected non-edges).

4. Mean Squared Error (MSE): MSE computes the average squared difference between the detected edges and the ground truth edges (The ground truth is a contours generally drawn by humans and used to evaluate the edge detection algorithms. Lower MSE values indicate better edge detection accuracy.

5. Mean Absolute Error (MAE): MAE calculates the average absolute difference between detected and ground truth edges. Similar to MSE, lower MAE values signify more accurate edge detection.

6. Receiver Operating Characteristic (ROC) Curve: The ROC [24] curve plots the true positive rate against the false-positive rate at different detection threshold levels, helping to assess the trade-off between sensitivity and specificity (true detected edges).

7. Pratt FOM: The Figure of Merit (FOM) introduced by Pratt [25] is an evaluation metric commonly used in image processing and edge detection to assess the quality of detected edges in a binary image. The main property of FOM is that it

does not need the ground truth. This metric aims to provide a comprehensive measurement that takes into account both the sensitivity (true positive rate) and selectivity (false-positive rate) of an edge detection algorithm. Mathematically, the FOM is calculated as:

$$FOM = \frac{1}{max\,(n_o, n_d)} \times \sum \frac{1}{1 + k.d(e^i)^2} \quad (2)$$

where n_o is the optimal edge number and n_d is the number of detected edges. k is a constant and $d(e^i)$ is the distance between the ith edge noted here as e^i and the optimal edge point.

5.2 Datasets

Numerous datasets are prevalent for appraising the efficacy of edge detection algorithms. These datasets encompass a spectrum of image characteristics, complexities, and applications, facilitating the assessment of algorithmic performance across diverse scenarios. Some prominent datasets for edge detection assessment are listed in **Table 1**.

5.3 Performance evaluation

We present, in **Table 2**, the performance evaluation on BSDS500 dataset of the latest state-of-the-art algorithms. We can find in some surveys the performance on others datasets such Pascal or NYUD [36, 37].

From this table, we can conclude that deep learning-based edge detection far surpass the traditional methods such Canny. It should also be noted that the performances presented are in relation to a defined learning stage. In fact, their learning capacity makes their performance still improvable for certain cases such as noise cases.

In **Figure 7**, we present a visual comparison between a recent algorithm (HED) and a traditional one (Canny). The HED represents deep learning algorithms well. It has gained a lot of success and has been integrated into the Opencv library. Canny, for its part, is the most recognized traditional algorithm, especially for its ability to cope with noise. From this figure, we can see the evolution of the HED output map through layers. We can see the performance limit of Canny algorithm, with three sigma parameter values. In terms of detection, HED presents very clear contours that are very close to the ground truth.

Dataset	Images	Download
BSDS500 [26]	500	[27]
NYUD [28]	1449	[29]
PASCAL-VOC [30]	11,530	[31]
Multi-cue [32]	100 scenes each (10-frame)	[33]
BIPED [34]	250	[35]

Table 1.
Main dataset list.

Algorithm	ODS	OIS
Canny	0.600	0.640
DeepEdge	0.753	0.772
DexiNed	0.728	0.745
N4Fields	0.753	0.769
CEDN	0.788	0.804
COB	0.793	0.820
HED	0.788	0.808
PiDiNet	0.707	0.823
RINDNet	0.800	0.811
DSCD	0.822	0.859
RCN	0.823	0.838
EDTER	0.824	0.841
CHRNet	0.830	0.853

Table 2.
Performance evaluation of the latest deep learning edge detection algorithms on BSDS500 dataset.

Figure 7.
Comparison of HED vs. Canny algorithms. (a) Image from the BSD500 dataset; (b) its corresponding annotated image; (c) the HED output. (d), (e), and (f), respectively, show side edge responses from layers 2, 3, and 4 of HED. (g), (h), and (i), show edge responses from the Canny detector respectively at the scales σ = 2.0, σ = 4.0, and σ = 8.0.

6. Conclusions

Edge detection techniques have evolved significantly over the years, providing valuable tools for extracting important information from digital images. This chapter covered the basics of image edges, traditional edge detection algorithms, advanced techniques, challenges, and real-world applications. As technology continues to advance, especially in deep learning area, edge detection methods will continue to play a crucial role in various fields, paving the way for further research and innovation.

Despite these significant advancements, edge detection is still facing some challenges:

- Complexity: While network-based algorithms have significantly improved detection performance, they often come at the cost of increased computational complexity. In scenarios such as real-time video processing and embedded applications, the performance of these algorithms remains a limiting factor, preventing their full utilization.

- Variations in illumination conditions: Modern algorithms exhibit varying performance when applied to the same images under different lighting conditions, such as day and night. Such lack of performance underlines the challenges in achieving a consistent semantic understanding of image edges.

- Ambiguous edges: Some edges can be particularly challenging to interpret. For example, in the case of thick edges or in the case of zoomed images, some algorithms could predict these edges as two adjacent edges. This ambiguity underscores again the need for further refinement on semantic understanding of edges.

It is important to mention that the while presence of noise is a big challenge for traditional methods, supervised learning-based methods operates better in this case. This is related to the fact that these algorithms can be trained with augmented images with any kind of noise.

In light of these challenges, there is still ample room for research and improvement to enhance edge detection performance that affects other important applications that rely on edge detection such as image segmentation or object recognition.

Acknowledgements

This work was supported in part by the Imagin research team of Ecole Supérieur Privée d'Ingénierie et de Technologies. The authors would like to thank this research team for the valuable support and provided resources.

Conflict of interest

The authors declare no conflict of interest.

Abbreviations

CNN	convolutional neural network
ODS	optimal dataset scale
OIS	optimal image scale
ResNet	deep residual network
ROC	receiver operating characteristic
FOM	the figure of merit
SGD	stochastic gradient descent
ILSVRC	imagenet large scale visual recognition challenge competition

Author details

Anis BenHajyoussef* and Asma Saidani
Ecole Supérieur Privée d'Ingénierie et de Technologies (ESPRIT), Ariana, Tunisia

*Address all correspondence to: anis.hajyoussef@esprit.tn

References

[1] Ziou D, Tabbone S. Edge detection techniques - an overview. Pattern Recognition and Image Analysis C/C Raspoznavaniye Obrazov I Analiz Izobrazhenii. 1998;**8**:537-559

[2] Shrivakshan GT, Chandrasekar C. A comparison of various edge detection techniques used in image processing. International Journal of Computer Science Issues (Ijcsi). 2012;**9**(5):269

[3] Marr D, Hildreth E. Theory of edge detection. Proceedings of the Royal Society of London - Series B: Biological Sciences. 1980;**207**(1167):187-217. DOI: 10.1098/rspb.1980.0020

[4] Sobel IE. Camera Models and Machine Perception [thesis]. Stanford: Stanford University; 1970

[5] Xin Wang X. Laplacian operator-based edge detectors. IEEE Transactions on Pattern Analysis and Machine Intelligence. 2007;**29**(5):886-890. DOI: 10.1109/tpami.2007.1027

[6] Canny J. A computational approach to edge detection. IEEE Transactions on Pattern Analysis and Machine Intelligence. 1986;**PAMI-8**:679-698. DOI: 10.1109/tpami.1986.4767851

[7] Bertasius G, Shi J, Torresani L. Deepedge: A multi-scale bifurcated deep network for top-down contour detection. In: Proceedings of the IEEE Conference on Computer Vision and Pattern Recognition. Vol. 2015. Boston: IEEE; 2015a. pp. 4380-4389. DOI: 10.1109/cvpr.2015.7299067

[8] Xie S, Tu Z. Holistically-nested edge detection. In: Proceedings of the IEEE International Conference on Computer Vision. Santiago: IEEE; 2015. pp. 1395-1403. DOI: 10.1109/iccv.2015.164

[9] Deng R, Shen C, Liu S. Learning to predict crisp boundaries. In: Proceedings of the European Conference on Computer Vision (ECCV). Munich: Springer; 2018. pp. 562-578. DOI: 10.1007/978-3-030-01231-1-35

[10] Simonyan K, Zisserman A. Very deep convolutional networks for large-scale image recognition. arXiv preprint. arXiv:1409.1556. 2014

[11] Yang J, Price B, Cohen S. Object contour detection with a fully convolutional encoder-decoder network. In: Proceedings of the IEEE Conference on Computer Vision and Pattern Recognition. Las Vegas: IEEE; 2016. pp. 193-202. DOI: 10.1109/cvpr.2016.28

[12] Su Z, Liu W, Yu Z. Pixel difference networks for efficient edge detection. arXiv preprint arXiv. 07009. 2021

[13] Soria X, Sappa A, Humanante P, Akbarinia A. Dense extreme inception network for edge detection. Pattern Recognition. 2023;**139**:109461

[14] Elharrouss O, Hmamouche Y, Idrissi AK, El Khamlichi B, El Fallah-Seghrouchni A. Refined edge detection with cascaded and high-resolution convolutional network. Pattern Recognition. 2023;**138**:109361

[15] Soria X, Pomboza-Junez G, Sappa AD. LDC: Lightweight dense CNN for edge detection. IEEE Access. 2022;**10**: 68281-68290

[16] Krizhevsky A, Sutskever I, Hinton GE. Imagenet classification with deep convolutional neural networks. In: Advances in Neural Information Processing Systems 25. Vol. 25. San

Francisco: Morgan Kaufmann Publishers Inc.; 2012. pp. 1097-1105

[17] He K, Zhang X, Ren S. Deep residual learning for image recognition. In: Proceedings of the IEEE Conference on Computer Vision and Pattern Recognition. Las Vegas: IEEE; 2016. pp. 770-778. DOI: 10.1109/cvpr.2016.90

[18] Yu Z, Feng C, Liu MY. Casenet: Deep category-aware semantic Edge Detection. In: Proceedings of the IEEE Conference on Computer Vision and Pattern Recognition. Honolulu: IEEE; 2017. pp. 5964-5973. DOI: 10.1109/cvpr.2017.191

[19] Le T, Duan YE. REDN: A recursive encoder-decoder network for edge detection. IEEE Access. 2020;**8**: 90153-90164. DOI: 10.1109/access.2020.2994160 Epub 2020 May 12

[20] Pu M, Huang Y, Guan Q. RINDNet: Edge detection for discontinuity in reflectance. illumination, normal depth. arxiv Preprint arxiv. 00616. 2021

[21] Kelm AP, Rao VS, Zolzer U. Object contour and edge detection with RefineContourNet. In: International Conference on Computer Analysis of Images and Patterns. Salerno: Springer; 2019. pp. 246-258. DOI: 10.1007/978-3-030-29888-3-20

[22] Deng R, Liu S. Deep structural contour detection. In: Proceedings of the 28th ACM International Conference on Multimedia. New York: ACM; 2020. pp. 304-312

[23] Martin DR, Fowlkes CC, Malik J. Learning to detect natural image boundaries using local brightness, color, and texture cues. IEEE Transactions on Pattern Analysis and Machine Intelligence. 2004;**26**:530-549

[24] Bowyer K, Kranenburg C, Dougherty S. Edge detector evaluation using empirical ROC curves. Computer Vision and Image Understanding. 2001; **84**:77-103

[25] Pratt WK, Wiley J. Digital Image Processing. New York: Citeseer; 1978

[26] Arbelaez P, Maire M, Fowlkes C, Malik J. Contour detection and hierarchical image segmentation. IEEE Transactions on Pattern Analysis and Machine Intelligence. 2010;**33**:898-916

[27] Berkeley Segmentation Dataset (BSDS500) download link. Available from: https://www2.eecs.berkeley.edu/Research/Projects/CS/vision/bsds/ [Accessed: September 01, 2023]

[28] Silberman N, Hoiem D, Kohli P, Fergus R. Indoor segmentation and support inference from RGB-D images. In: European Conference on Computer Vision. Berlin: Springer; 2012. pp. 746-760

[29] NYUD Datset download link. Available from: https://cs.nyu.edu/~silberman/datasets/nyu_depth_v2.html [Accessed: September 01, 2023]

[30] Everingham M, Eslami SA, Van Gool L, Williams CK, Winn J, Zisserman A. The pascal visual object classes challenge: A retrospective. International Journal of Computer Vision. 2015;**111**:98-136

[31] Pascal-VOC dataset download link. Available from: http://host.robots.ox.ac.uk/pascal/VOC/voc2012/index.html [Accessed: September 01, 2023]

[32] Mely DA, Kim J, McGill M, Guo Y, Serre T. A systematic comparison between visual cues for boundary detection. Vision Research. 2016;**120**: 93-107

[33] Multicue dataset download link. Available from: https://serre-lab.clps.brown.edu/resource/multicue/

[34] Chollet F. Xception: Deep learning with Depthwise separable convolutions. In: Proceedings of the IEEE Conference on Computer Vision and Pattern Recognition. Las Vegas: IEEE; 2017. pp. 1251-1258. DOI: 10.1109/cvpr.2017.195

[35] BIPED download link. Available from: https://xavysp.github.io/MBIPED/

[36] Sun R, Lei T, Chen Q, Wang Z, Du X, Zhao W, et al. Survey of image edge detection. Frontiers in Signal Processing. 2022;**2**:826967

[37] Jing J, Liu S, Wang G, Zhang W, Sun C. Recent advances on image edge detection: A comprehensive review. Neurocomputing. Vol. 503, No. C. 2022. pp. 259-271. DOI: 10.1016/j.neucom.2022.06.083

Chapter 4

Fusion of Color-Based Multi-Dimensional Scaling Maps For Saliency Estimation

Max Mignotte

Abstract

This work presents an original energy-based model, using a pixel pair modeling combined with a fusion procedure, to the saliency map estimation problem. More precisely, we formulate the saliency map segmentation issue as the solution of an energy-based model involving pixel pairwise constraints, in terms of color features, to which are then added constraints of higher levels of abstraction given by a preliminary over-segmentation whose location of regions but also contour information are exploited. Finally, this segmentation-driven saliency measure solution is then expressed in different color spaces which are combined together in order to take into account the specific properties of each of these color models with a outlier rejection scheme. Experimental results show that the proposed algorithm is both simple, efficient by performing favorably against state-of-the-art methods and also perfectible.

Keywords: color spaces, energy-based model, fusion procedure regions of interest, saliency map estimation, salient object detection, FastMap optimization, outlier rejection scheme, image partition, modeling with pixel pairs or constraints, tracking

1. Introduction

Saliency detection (SD) is generally defined as the detection and segmentation of the most important or interesting objects or visual elements in the image scene which immediately and naturally attract and hold the attention of the viewer.

This algorithm basically attempts to imitate the natural *eye-fixations* process of human visual system (HVS) which has the amazing capability to rapidly detect and precisely localize the most noticeably visible and informative object or region within a (potentially very) cluttered image. In fast, this mechanism, which has developed during the evolutionary process, allows the human (and most mammals) to quickly and efficiently analyze the scene and focus its attention, on the important objects or regions of this one, with a minimal allocated processing (visual) resources.

SD is a low-level image processing task which is important in a variety of vision or image processing applications, especially for those where there is a need to reduce the information overload. This kind of problems can be commonly encountered in content-based image/video retrieval, summarization, categorization, compression, or browsing, automatic resizing, image cropping, advertising design or adaptive image display on small devices to name a few.

A significant number of methods have used (with some variations) the same principle proposed by the pioneer work of Itti and Koch [1] based on local contrast concepts and modeling the fact that a salient object/region presents a strong contrast with respect to its existing spatial neighborhood [2–12]. Another class of algorithmic procedures is rather based on the hypothesis that the salient element is remarkably distinct; *i.e.*, it exhibits a (or a mixture) of unique and discriminating colors (eventually combined with textural features) compared to the rest of the image [6, 10, 13–20].

Nevertheless, local contrast-based algorithms tend to produce over-estimated saliency values close to the edges and contours of objects while producing too low saliency values inside objects instead of highlighting them uniformly and are also affected by high-frequency spatial signals in the image, while techniques based on global contrast can not differentiate regions precisely and are often altered by the presence of cluttered background [21, 22].

That is why some SD models propose to combine local and global contrast-based techniques either by combining local and global features [23] or by combining local contrast cues *via* a multi-layer or multi-scale approach [19, 21], or a tree structure [18] or have based their saliency estimation on a multi-level segmentation [17].

Other approaches are modeled within the conceptual framework of quantum mechanics [22], bag-of-features [24], matrix decomposition [25] or have been developed in the regression (or equivalently energy-based) framework [17, 21, 26] sometimes guided by the Gestalt-laws [27]. Other approaches are based on graph theory [28] or image statistics possibly obtained in advance from a database of natural images [29] or modeled within the Bayes statistical framework and only based on the statistics of the input image [30, 31] or eventually by using conditional random field (CRF) [23, 32–36], Bayesian model [37] or Markov random field (MRF) [38] generally by formulating the saliency estimation as a random walk problem [4, 39–49] or *via* an absorbing Markov chain [50] possibly guided by depth information [51].

Contrary to the above-mentioned strategies, our saliency model is based on the combination of three contributions:

- The first one relies on a generic energy-based model involving pixel pairwise constraints or using an original modeling by pair of pixels, giving a first and rough saliency map (based on the color cue) whose solution is then efficiently and quickly obtained with a linear computational complexity (in terms of number of pixels in the image).

- The second one is a set of original and efficient constraints based on a preliminary over-segmentation whose location of regions but also contour information are exploited as constraints to improve the previous saliency map result.

- Finally, the third contribution is the use of a simple but efficient fusion procedure combining the saliency result expressed in several color systems with a robust outlier rejection scheme.

The remainder of this paper is organized as follows: Section 2 describes the proposed model. Section 3 reports and evaluates the performances achieved by our model by comparing them with state-of-the-art methods and then discuss the reliability, strengths and interest of the proposed approach and the quantification (in terms of classification gain) of each component of the proposed model. Finally, Section 4 concludes the paper.

2. Proposed model for the saliency map estimation problem

2.1 Color-based multidimensional scaling saliency map

Our saliency model is first based on the hypothesis that the salient region or element to be detected is remarkably distinct; that is to say that it has discriminating colors compared to its surrounding spatial neighborhood. To this end and in order to provide a rough but meaningful first *soft* saliency measure map $\hat{x}$ (with values varying from 0 to 1 representing the saliency probability of each pixel in the sense of a given criterion), we can search the solution map $\hat{x}$ that will translate the distance between the mean color existing between each pair of pixels in the input image by an identical gray-scale distance between each pair of pixels in the resulting saliency map to be estimated (or otherwise said by estimating $\hat{x}$ that preserves, as much as possible, the color or gray-scale distance between respectively each pair of pixels of the input image and the soft saliency map). Mathematically speaking, this can be efficiently done by searching the map $\hat{x}$ that minimizes the following energy-based or cost function (which is also commonly called the *stress* function):

$$\hat{x} = \arg\min_{x} \sum_{i \neq j=1, \dots, N} \left(\left(\|y_i^w - y_j^w\|_2 - \|x_i - x_j\|_2 \right)^2 \right)^{1/2} \tag{1}$$

where N is the number of pixels of the input and the saliency images and the summation $\sum_{i \neq j=1, \dots, N}$ is on all pixel pairs (*i.e.*, for all pixels i and for all pairs of pixels involving i) being within the image. x_i corresponds to the gray level at pixel location i and y_i^w is a three-dimensional (3D) vector coding the three mean color channel values computed within a local squared region of size $N_c \times N_c$ centered on the pixel at location i (of the input color image y). The notation $\|.\|_2$ refers to the Euclidean distance.

This stress function given in Eq. (1) is often minimized using procedures called stress majorization. This class of techniques act as an efficient global minimizer of this loss function consisting of residual sum of squares by integrating all the pairwise constraints. Conceptually, this kind of optimizers treats each distance or constraints between a pair of pixels (in terms of gray level difference in our application) like a *rubber band* between the couple of pixels, and searched to reorganize the gray-scale value of each pixel of $\hat{x}$ to minimize the tension or the stress of the rubber bands (hence the name of *stress* measure) or in an equivalent way, to fulfill all constraints in a least-squares (LSQ) problem formulation. Multidimensional scaling (MDS) is the most known stress majorization procedure allowing to minimize such a stress function with pairwise constraints and this optimizer has proven to be particularly effective in its ability to solve certain image processing problems requiring a modeling by pair of pixels (*e.g.*, such as color image segmentation [52, 53], hyperspectral compression [54, 55], asymmetry detection [56], human action recognition [57], fusion procedures [58], histogram specification algorithms [59] high dynamic range compression (HDR) [60], multimodal change detection [61] and database browsing and visualization [62] to name a few).

However, the MDS algorithm which is initially proposed (and named *metric* MDS [63, 64]) is not ideally suited to our application (as well as for all large scale applications) due to its computational and memory load. Indeed, it requires a $O(N^2)$ computational complexity and an entire $N \times N$ distance matrix to be stored in memory. Instead, we have resorted to a faster (and near-optimal) variant here, named FastMap [65] whose major benefit lies in its linear computational complexity (through an efficient Nyström [66, 67] approximation[1]). In addition, it worths mentioning that the efficiency of the FastMap is all the more important as the dimension of the final mapping is low [67]. That's also why this optimizer is particularly well suited to our application since the final (saliency) mapping has to be estimated at very low dimensions (i.e., one dimension since we finally want to obtain a 1-channel gray-scale saliency map[2]).

Let us now recall that a configuration $\hat{x}$ that minimizes Eq. (1) will give us a gray-scale map in which the pixel pairs that are close in terms of mean color in the input image y will also give us pixel pairs, in the saliency map $\hat{x}$, with gray-scales that are faithfully close (in the LSQ sense). Nevertheless, the configuration, given by the FastMap technique, may optionally generate an image with an inverted gray-scale scale (negative of an image or/positive inversion) (*i.e.*, with values of gray levels all the lower as the regions are estimated as salient and vice versa). In order to rearrange this gray-scale mapping in the appropriate direction (with correspondingly higher gray-scale values for the most salient regions), we simply assume that a salient element/region is a priori more likely to appear in the image center [17, 21, 26, 29] (or conversely unlikely at the edges of the square image frame). To do this, we calculate the Pearson correlation coefficient between the $\hat{x}$ saliency map estimated by the FastMap and a rectangle, with maximum intensity value and about half the image size, and located in the center of the image, more precisely, a rectangle beginning and ending respectively at the row $lgth/4$ and $lgth - lgth/4$ and respectively at the column $wdth/4$ and $wdth - wdth/4$ where $lgth$ and $wdth$ represents the length and the width of the image. If the correlation coefficient is negative (anti-correlation), we must then associate to each pixel (of $\hat{x}$) its complementary gray value.

2.2 Segmentation-based adaptive central location constraint

In order to improve the saliency map result $\hat{x}$, we decide to incorporate an adaptive location constraint favoring the fact that salient objects are more likely to appear in the segmented regions locating in the center of the image. To this end, we first exploit an over-segmentation of the input image and more precisely the concept of super-pixel which has already been successfully used, in different ways, in several saliency SD models [17, 18, 26, 30, 68–70]. An over-segmented region or super-pixel brings together a group of pixels (forming a perceptually meaningful atomic region allowing

---

[1] The basic idea of the Nyström method can be deemed as choosing a subset of samples to obtain a rough non-linear mapping (or embedding) and then by estimating the solution obtained to the complete set of remaining samples (using a technique similar to extrapolation from the original data).

[2] The first step of the FastMap procedure consists in selecting two feature vectors (or objects) the most different to build the projection line. These two feature vectors are estimated by using a deterministic algorithm named *choose-distant-objects* [65]. The second step consists in projecting any other object onto this orthogonal axis (named a pivot line) by using the cosine law to the angle (see Algorithm 1). The FastMap C++ code is openly accessible online.

to preserve the important structures in the image) which can be exploited to replace the rigid pixel grid structure in images. Herein, we use the super-pixel technique introduced by Felzenswal [71] with the settings (default values) proposed by the authors (see **Figure 1c**).

In addition to the location of the different regions, this segmentation allows us to estimate the strength of the contour of each region relatively to the other regions. In our application, this visual cue is simply expressed as the average magnitude of the gradient per pixel of the contour of the concerned region divided by the average gradient (per pixel) of all the contour points given by the segmentation (thus giving a positive number ξ all the greater as the region is prominent in the sense of the strength of its outline). This visual cue allows us to incorporate in our model the fact that a saliency region is more likely to appear with a strong contour (see **Figure 1f**).

Finally, in our model, the set of pixels belonging to each segmented region R_i is assigned the mean the initial saliency measure (within this region) firstly estimated by $\hat{x}$ and the mean of the potential favoring saliency regions in the center of the image (see **Figure 1e**) and finally weighted by ξ_{R_i}, the relative strength of the boundary of R_i (**Figure 1f**):

$$\text{saliency}(R_i) = \xi_{R_i} \cdot \frac{1}{|R_i|} \sum_{s \in R_i} (\hat{x}_s \cdot c_s) \tag{2}$$

Figure 1.
Refinement of the MDS-based saliency map $\hat{x}$ [see Eq. (1)] with the two segmentation-based constraints favoring the fact that salient objects are 1—more likely to appear both in the segmented regions locating in the center of the image and 2—with a strong contour (see Section 2.2) in the RGB color space. (a) Input ECSSD image (b) Ground truth binary salient mask (c) Segmentation into regions given by the FH algorithm (d) Potential c favoring the central regions of the image (e) Potential c favoring the central regions of the image (f) Relative strength (in terms of average gradient magnitude) of the boundary of each region (g) Potential c combined with the segmentation into regions and weighted by the relative strength of the boundary of each region (h) Initial saliency map (i) Saliency map combined with the map obtained at step (g).

with c_s the potential at site s of coordinates (row,col) favoring saliency regions in the center of the image (and disfavoring them on the edges of the image) defined in the following way:

$$c_{\text{row,col}} = 2 - 2\max\left(\left|\frac{\text{row} - \text{lgth}/2}{\text{lgth}/2}\right|, \left|\frac{\text{col} - \text{wdth}/2}{\text{wdth}/2}\right|\right) \quad (3)$$

where lgth and wdth represents the length and the width of the image and $c_{\text{row,col}}$ is the pixel gray-scale value of the map c at coordinates (row, col). The refinement of the MDS-based saliency map $\hat{x}$ with these two constraints (see **Figure 1i**) is noted in the following $\hat{x}_c$. One of the undeniable advantages of these two types of constraints is that they both do not depend on any internal parameter to be adjusted or tuned afterwards (thanks to their inherent adaptation to each image). The effectiveness of these two constraints will be quantified individually in Section 3.3.Algorithm 1. FastMap.

Algorithm 1: FastMap

Input:
k: Target space dimension
N_p: Object (vector) number in database $\mathcal{O}$
Output:
$X_{[N_p,k]}$: Array of objects in target space
Initialization:
$d \leftarrow 0$
FASTMAP ALGORITHM (k, D(),$\mathcal{O}$)

- **if** $k \leq 0$ **then** return X
- $d \leftarrow d + 1$
- Choose *pivot* objects O_a and O_b so that the metric $D(O_a, O_b)$ is maximal

foreach *object i from* $\mathcal{O}$ **do**

- Project O_i on the line (O_a, O_b)

  Compute: $X_{[i,d]} = x_i$
  $x_i = \frac{D^2(O_a, O_i) + D^2(O_a, O_b) - D^2(O_b, O_i)}{2D^2(O_a, O_b)}$

end
foreach *object i from* $\mathcal{O}$ **do**

- Project O_i on an hyper-plane perpendicular to the line (O_a, O_b)

  $(D')^2\left(O_i', O_j'\right) = D^2(O_i.O_j) - \left(x_i - x_j\right)^2$

end
call FASTMAP($k - 1, D'(), \mathcal{O}$)

2.3 Fusion in different color spaces

In order to further improve our final saliency estimation, the segmentation-driven saliency map obtained by the two previous steps (cf. Sections 2.1 and 2.2) is repeated for different and non-linearly related color spaces which are then combined with a fusion method. Let us note that this strategy has already proven its efficiency to improve the accuracy of an image segmentation with different fusion methods optimal in a particular criterion sense [58, 72, 73]. Let us recall that a color space is just an arbitrary model that combines three numbers (or tristimulus values) to describe a sensation of color that our vision system can possibly perceive. In a fusion model combining several color systems, each color space can be in fact regarded as different image channels provided by different sensors or as different complementary filters. In our application, we use N_s saliency maps provided by the $N_s = 8$ following non-linearly related color spaces; $C = \{\text{LUV}, \text{HSV}, \text{LAB}, \text{RGB}, \text{YIQ}, \text{XYZ}, \text{HSL}, \text{TSL}\}$. Each color space has a specific and interesting property[3] [74–79], which can efficiently be taken into account and makes the fusion process very efficient (and whose effectiveness will be quantified in Section 3.3).

In our application, the fusion model is simply performed by averaging the $N_s - 1$ more reliable saliency maps achieved in these different color spaces (after their individual normalization in order that all values are between 0 and 255). In order to eliminate the less reliable saliency map which is identified in our fusion model as an isolated outlier, we just calculate the one that is least correlated with all the others in the Pearson's correlation sense (see **Figure 2**). This fusion strategy will be quantified in terms of F-measure gain in Section 3.3.

3. Experimental results

3.1 Set-up and dataset description

First, to limit the computational load, we decided to resize all the images so that the maximum (height, width) of the image is 200 pixels. In the following, all parameters are defined relative to this new base image size.

The only internal parameter of our model is the size of the squared window N_c (introduced in the initial MDS-based saliency map, see Eq. 1). In our experiment, we have tuned this internal parameter in order to maximize the F measure on a subset of 10 images randomly extracted from the ECSSD dataset. This was done by applying a fixed step-size grid search method to select the best parameter (over the space of parameters) and in possible ranges of parameter values (namely $N_c \in [3-25]$ [step-

---

[3] For example, RGB is an additive color system based on tri-chromatic theory and non-linear with visual perception. HSV is noteworthy because it allows chromatic information to be decoupled from shading effects. YIQ color channels have the interesting property of separately encoding chrominance and luminance information (which can be interesting in the field of compression). In addition, this color space is intended to take advantage of human color characteristics. XYZ has the benefit of being more linear from a psycho-visual point of view, although they are non-linear when it comes to mixing colors of linear components. LAB color is designed to approximate human vision. It aspires to perceptual uniformity, and its L component closely matches human perception of lightness. Finally, The LUV components give an Euclidean color space and provide a perceptually uniform spacing of color quite close to a Riemannian space.

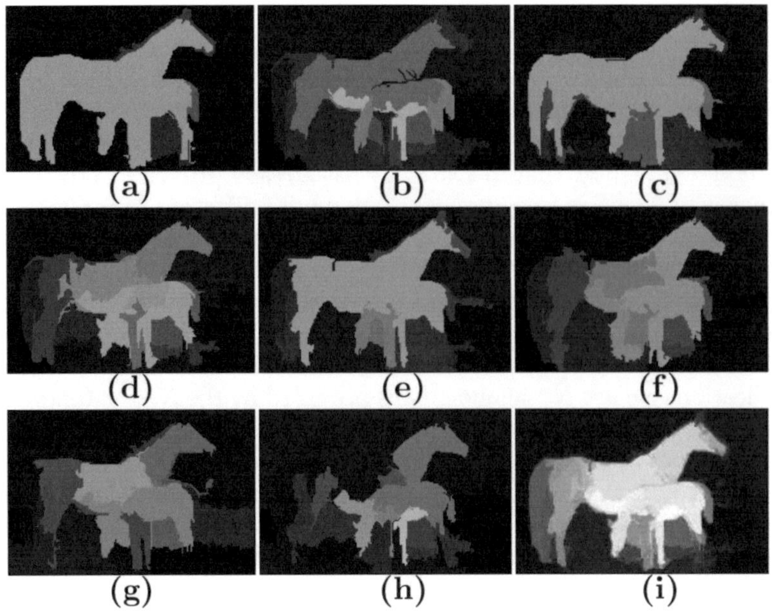

Figure 2.
Saliency map $\hat{x}_c$ obtained by the two previous steps (cf. Sections 2.1 and 2.2) estimated respectively in the (a) RGB (b) HSV (c) LAB (d) LUV (e) YIQ (f) XYZ (g) HSL and (h) TSL color spaces and (i) final saliency map obtained by our fusion model [averaging of the seven more reliable saliency maps. For this ECSSD image, the outlier which is automatically eliminated is the saliency map estimated in the TSL (h) color space].

size: 2]). We have found $N_c = 19$ and a quiet relative insensitivity of our model if this size parameter is held within plus or minus 30% of this value. We recall that the internal parameters of the super-pixel algorithm used in our model is set with the default values suggested by the authors [71]. In addition, it is worth also recalling that the two segmentation-based constraints applied on the initial MDS-based saliency map do not depend on any internal parameter (since these two constraints adapt to each image (see Section 2.2).

We have validated our algorithm on the extended complex scene saliency dataset (ECSSD) (see **Figures 3** and **4**) which was built by Yan et al. [21] and Shi et al. [80]. This database is composed of 1000 images containing various categories (natural or man-made objects) and different backgrounds (sometimes non uniform with possible change in illumination intensity and/or composed of several parts or including

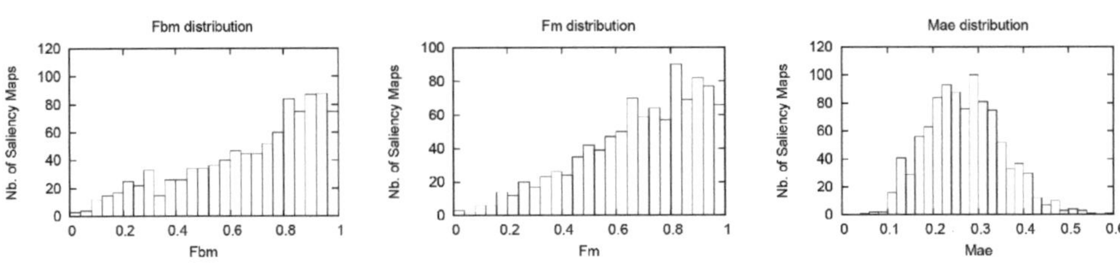

Figure 3.
From lexicographic order, distribution of respectively the F_β, F and mean absolute error (MAE) measures given by our MDSSME (multidimensional scaling map-based saliency map estimation) model on the 1000 images of the ECSSD dataset.

Figure 4.
Visual comparison between our model and the SOTA CHS saliency model presented in [80] on the first eight images of the ECSSD dataset. From left to right, ECSSD image, ground truth salient mask, CHS saliency map [80], our MDSSME saliency result.

small-scale structures). In addition, multiple salient objects possibly exist in one image, while part of or all of them are sometimes transparent (or do not have a sharply clear boundary and/or obvious difference with the background) and are regarded, all the same, as salient decided by an expert. The binary mask or ground truths have been synthetically generated for each image with a well-defined and reliable protocol (more precisely, for each image, several experts have manually drawn a saliency map which was finally combined in one ground truth binary mask that minimizes the inter-subject label consistency in the majority vote sense. (see [80] for additional details). We have also tested our method on the 5000 images of the commonly used MSRA-5000 (or MSRA-5K) saliency dataset [23]. Images of MSRA-5000 are relatively less complex (with less variability) and therefore are therefore rightly considered as less challenging to process than those of the ECSSD image database [80]. Examples of visual comparison between our model and the state-of-the art (SOTA) CHS saliency model presented in [80] (and also the designer/constructor of the ECSSD dataset) on the first 8 images of this image database is shown in **Figure 4**.

3.2 Quantitative measure

Our quantitative assessments and experiments follow the framework presented in [10, 14, 68, 80]. First, the precision-recall curve, associated with the set of saliency measures achieved by our model is plotted. and then compared with other methods (see **Figure 5a**). In addition, since in many applications, high precision is preferable to high recall, we thus also estimate the F_β-measure proposed in [68, 80], as a function of each possible threshold:

$$F_\beta = \frac{\left(1+\beta^2\right)\cdot \text{precision} \cdot \text{recall}}{\beta^2 \cdot \text{precision} + \text{recall}} \tag{4}$$

in which thresholding (within range [0,255]) are applied, β^2 is set to 0.3 as suggested in [10, 68, 80][4] and the obtained F_β-measure is shown and compared to other methods (see **Figure 5b**).

Besides, we studied as a performance metric, the *mean absolute error* (MAE) [68, 80] which actually measures the quality of the weighted continuous saliency map (which could turn out to be, for some applications, more important information than the binary mask itself). Mathematically, the MAE measures the MAE between the soft saliency measurement map x and the binary ground truth x_G (both normalized in the interval $[0,1]$). The MAE metric is given by:

$$\text{MAE} = \frac{1}{(\text{hgth} \times \text{wdth})} \sum_{i=1}^{\text{hgth}} \sum_{j=1}^{\text{wdth}} |x(i,j) - x_G(i,j)| \tag{5}$$

with i and j designating respectively the row and column coordinates of x or x_G.

The precision-recall curve along with the F_β-measure as a function of the threshold and the MAE distance are complementary measures to each other and help interpreting the global or the local behavior (for a given or optimal threshold) of a SD model.

[4] The major reason for over-weighting precision over recall is that recall rate is an error metric that is not as important as precision [23, 68] (since 100% recall can be easily achieved by labeling the entire image as a saliency region).

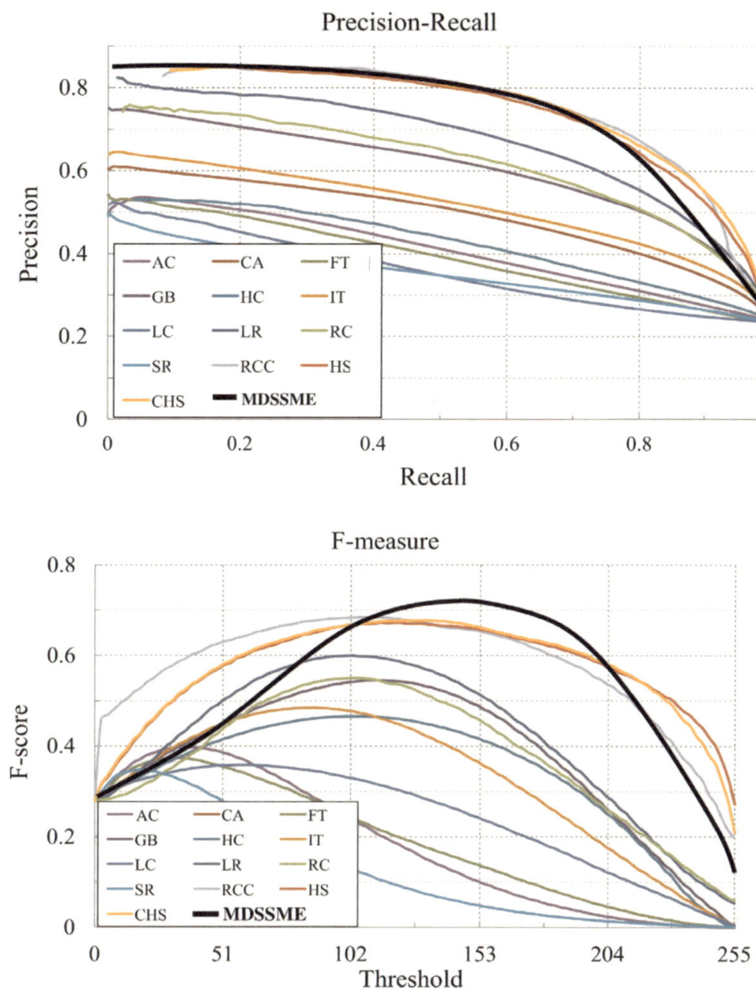

Figure 5.
Qualitative comparison on ECSSD. From top to bottom. Precision-recall curve for each possible threshold (within range [0,255]) and F_β-measure (see Eq. (4) and [80]) with $\beta^2 = 0.3$ as a function of the threshold.

3.3 Results and discussion

First of all, we have tested (see **Figure 6**) the efficiency (in terms of precision-recall curves) of the different main characteristics of our MDSSME model on ECSSD dataset. More precisely, **Figure 5** shows the plot of the precision recall curve obtained by our model for respectively, for the first four curves; (1) a fusion process (see Section 2.3) involving one, two, four or eight space colors; thus quantifying the efficiency of our fusion strategy through different color spaces (while the other characteristics of our model being optimal and remain unchanged), (2) for the last three curves; our model without the *a priori* constraint that a saliency region is more likely to appear with a strong contour (gradient prior), or without the *a priori* constraint of the central location (see Section 2.2) or without any constraint, i.e. without the two previous constraint and the over-segmentation process (just the MDS estimation expressed and averaged over the eight color spaces).

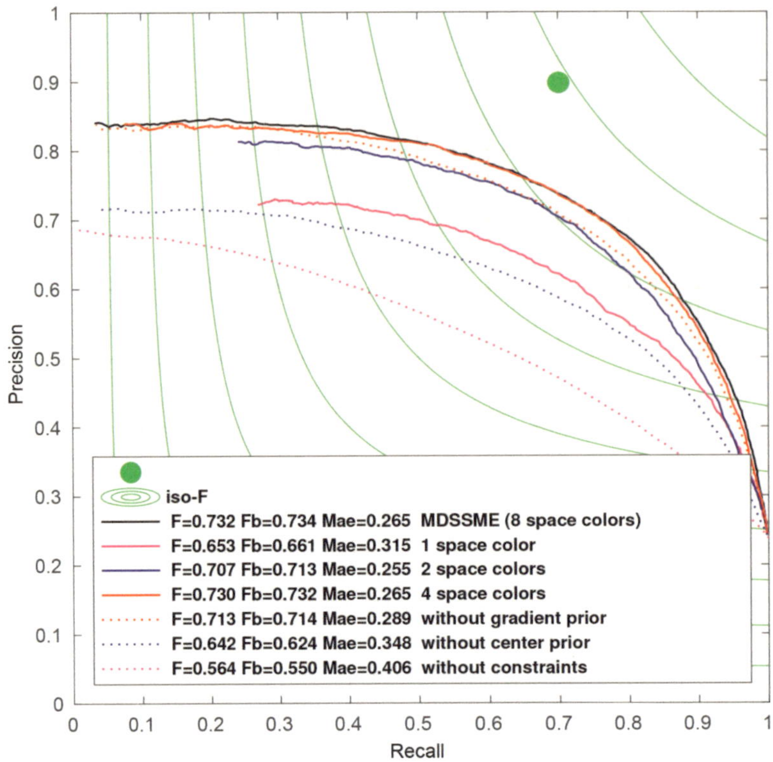

Figure 6.
Precision-recall curves (and optimal F and F_β-measures [see Eq. (4)]) for different variations of our MDSSME model on ECSSD [80] dataset.

We can notice that the fusion process through different color spaces is efficient and allows an interesting gain of approximately 12% (on average) on the results but beyond four color spaces, the improvement gain is negligible. Let us recall that the color spaces must be chosen different and as uncorrelated as possible; this guarantees both, an over-segmentation (and a set of constraints based on it), which are different but complementary. We also notice that the gradient-based constraint brings a slight 3% gain compared to the full model. Nevertheless, this constraint (combined with the over-segmentation constraint) remains interesting when one does not consider the commonly used central location constraint.

We have first evaluated our SD model on the ECSSD dataset and compare our results with local methods; IT [2], GB [4], AC [8], and global methods; LC [13], SR [6], FT [10], HC [14], RC [14], CA [15], LR [16], RCC [19], and CHS [80]. **Figure 5** shows the plot of the precision recall curves and the F_β curve [see Eq. (4)] as a function of threshold, and **Table 1** lists the MAE distances achieved by these different SD methods compared to our model, on the ECSSD dataset.

For the MSRA-5K dataset, the optimal F_β measure we can achieve is $F_\beta = 0.791$, (for the particular threshold 136) and $F = 0.786$ ($\beta = 1$ for the threshold 106) and MAE=0.218 (see **Table 1**).

Overall, we obtain a competitive precision-recall or F_β measure curve with a correct MAE when compared with existing state-of-the-art algorithms. Nevertheless, in terms of performance, the strong point of our method remains the very competitive optimal F_β-measure (for a given optimal threshold) which is reflected graphically by

AC [8]	CA [15]	FT [10]	GB [4]	HC [14]	IT [2]	LC [13]	LR [16]	SR [6]	RC [14]	RCC [19]	HS [80]	CHS [80]	MDSSME
0.264	0.310	0.270	0.282	0.326	0.290	0.294	0.267	0.264	0.301	0.187	0.224	0.227	**0.265**
0.228	0.250	0.230	0.243	0.239	0.248	0.245	0.215	0.225	0.264	0.140	0.153	0.150	**0.218**

Table 1.
Quantitative comparison with [2, 4, 6, 8, 10, 13–16, 19, 80] in terms of MAE measurement on the ECSSD [80] (first column) and MSRA-5000 (second column) databases.

	PPMRF [38]	LTPSD [20]	MDSSME
ECSSD	$F_\beta = 0.727$ MAE = 0.150	$F_\beta = 0.729$ MAE = 0.257	$F_\beta = 0.734$ MAE = 0.265
bf MSRA	$F_\beta = 0.790$ MAE = 0.108	$F_\beta = 0.781$ MAE = 0.215	$F_\beta = 0.791$ MAE = 0.218

Table 2.
Quantitative comparison with two recent salient detection energy-based models [20, 38] in terms of MAE and F_β measurements on the ECSSD (first line) and MSRA (second line) databases.

the fact that the F_β curve associated to our model reaches a maximum above all other curves (see **Figure 6b**) with a plateau wide enough for an estimation of the optimal threshold to be possible (this plateau is also centered around the mean value of the gray scale range, i.e. between [100–170]).

We have also compared our model with two very recent salient detection energy-based models, very recently published in the literature [20, 38]. These two energy-based models are based, for the first, on LTP (local ternary patterns) texture based features [20] and, for the second, on pairwise pixel based features [38] to capture the notion of saliency in a scene (and these two energy-based models operate both of them within a single specific color space). We have compared our model on the ECSSD and MSRA-5K datasets in terms of the optimal F-beta and MAE efficiency measures (see **Table 2**) which shows that our model is very competitive, in terms of these two highly complementary efficiency measures.

Our current implementation takes on average 0.6 seconds to process one image with resolution 400×300 on a 8 GB and 3.33 GHz Intel i7 CPU (6675.25 bogomips) with an un-optimized C++ code running under Linux (or about 10 minutes for the processing of the entire ECSSD dataset composed of 1000 images). In the proposed algorithm, each MDS maps is calculated very quickly, in approximately 0.05 second due to the linear computational complexity (in terms of the number of pixels) of the FastMap algorithm and this, we recall, despite the fact that this algorithm will model and take into account a quadratic number of pairs of pixels [see Eq. (1)]. Let us also mention that our SD model can be easily parallelized by using an OpenMP implementation on several CPU cores (each MDS map estimated on each CPU core) or even better, by using a GPU implementation of the FastMap algorithm as proposed in [81], in order to reduce the computation time by a factor of 1000 (on a mid-range GPU card) and to allow the processing of the entire ECSSD dataset in less than 1 second.

Let us note that, in addition to being perfectible (by adding more color spaces) and possibly faster (by using GPU programming), our unsupervised energy-based model also has the property of depending on very few parameters. This defines a low complexity model, ensuring no over-fitting and good generalization properties and consequently, this allows our algorithm to have the advantage of performing well on other datasets.

In addition, and this also complements what has been stated previously, since our algorithm exploits the notion of colors in different (non-linear between them) color spaces, our algorithm is perfectible by combining (or fusing) our model with those using as features; the LTP texture [20] or the notion of pixel pairs [38] (or possibly different other features).

4. Conclusion

In this paper, we have proposed a novel and simple saliency measure and segmentation method. The proposed method is based on an energy-based model, involving a pixel pair modeling using color features and segmentation-based constraints finally combined with a fusion procedure taking into account the specific property and the complementarity of several color space models. The proposed model has very few internal parameters and is designed to be highly adaptive to the image content. Qualitative and quantitative results show that the proposed method is effective and performs particularly well against state-of-the-art methods, especially in terms of optimal F-measure (for a given optimal threshold). In addition to its efficiency, the proposed model achieves a good compromise between simplicity and accuracy while being fast enough, easily parallelizable (in different ways), and also perfectible if more color spaces or more constraints are added to the fusion procedure.

Acknowledgements

This research was funded by individual discovery grant RGPIN-2022-03654. The data supporting the results of this study are freely available at:

HTTP://WWW.IRO.UMONTREAL.CA/MIGNOTTE/RESEARCHMATERIAL/INDEX.HTML

The author wishes to acknowledge the NSERC (Natural Sciences and Engineering Research Council of Canada) for having funded this study under the individual discovery grant program (RGPIN-2022-03654). The author certifies no potential conflicts of interest influencing this study.

Data availability statement

The data (C++ code under Linux OS, makefile, image databases, etc.) supporting the results of this article are freely accessible at:

http://www.iro.umontreal.ca/~mignotte/ResearchMaterial/index.html.

Author details

Max Mignotte
Vision Lab. of the Département d'Informatique et de Recherche Opérationnelle (DIRO), Université de Montréal, Faculté des Arts et des Sciences, Montréal, QC, Canada

*Address all correspondence to: mignotte@iro.umontreal.ca

References

[1] Itti L, Koch C. Computational modelling of visual attention. Nature Reviews Neuroscience. 2001;**2**(3): 194-203

[2] Itti L, Koch C, Niebur E. A model of saliency-based visual attention for rapid scene analysis. IEEE Transactions on Pattern Analysis and Machine Intelligence. 1998;**20**(11):1254-1259

[3] Ma Y-F, Zhang H-J. Contrast-based image attention analysis by using fuzzy growing. In: Proceedings of the Eleventh ACM International Conference on Multimedia, ser. MULTIMEDIA '03. New York, NY, USA: ACM. 2003. pp. 374-381

[4] Harel J, Koch CC, Perona P. Graph-based visual saliency. In: Proceedings of the 19th International Conference on Neural Information Processing Systems. ser. NIPS'06. Cambridge, MA, USA: MIT Press. 2006. pp. 545-552

[5] Harel J, Koch C, Perona P. Graph-based visual saliency. In: Schölkopf B, Platt JC, Hoffman T, editors. Advances in Neural Information Processing Systems 19. Vancouver, British Columbia, Canada: MIT Press; 2007. pp. 545-552

[6] Hou X, Zhang L. Saliency detection: A spectral residual approach. In: Computer Vision and Pattern Recognition, 2007. CVPR'07. IEEE Conference on. IEEE. 2007, pp. 1-8

[7] Achanta RR, Estrada F, Wils P, Susstrunk S. Salient region detection and segmentation. Gasteratos A, Vincze M, Tsotsos JK, editors. In: Computer Vision Systems. Berlin, Heidelberg: Springer Berlin Heidelberg; 2008. pp. 66-75

[8] Achanta R, Estrada F, Wils P, Susstrunk S. Salient region detection and segmentation. In: Proceedings of the 6th International Conference on Computer Vision Systems, ser. ICVS'08. Berlin, Heidelberg: Springer-Verlag; 2008. pp. 66-75

[9] Guo C, Ma Q, Zhang L. Spatio-temporal saliency detection using phase spectrum of quaternion fourier transform. In: IEEE, Conf. Computer Vision and Pattern Recognition. 2008

[10] Achanta R, Hemami SS, Estrada FJ, Susstrunk S. Frequency-tuned salient region detection. In: CVPR. IEEE Computer Society. 2009. pp. 1597-1604

[11] Klein D, Frintrop S. Center-surround divergence of feature statistics for salient object detection. In: IEEE International Conference on Computer Vision, ICCV 2011, Barcelona, Spain, November 6-13, 2011. 2011. pp. 2214-2219

[12] Zhang J, Ma S, Sameki M, Sclaroff S, Betke M, Lin Z, et al. Salient object subitizing. International Journal of Computer Vision. 2017;**124**(2):169-186

[13] Zhai Y, Shah M. Visual attention detection in video sequences using spatiotemporal cues. In: Proceedings of the 14th ACM International Conference on Multimedia, ser. MM '06. New York, NY, USA: ACM. 2006. pp. 815-824

[14] Cheng M-M, Zhang G-X, Mitra NJ, Huang X, Hu S-M. Global contrast based salient region detection. In: Proceedings of the 2011 IEEE Conference on Computer Vision and Pattern Recognition, ser. CVPR '11. Washington, DC, USA: IEEE Computer Society. 2011. pp. 409-416

[15] Tal A, Zelnik-Manor L, Goferman S. Context-aware saliency detection. IEEE

Transactions on Pattern Analysis and Machine Intelligence. 2012;**34**(10): 1915-1926

[16] Shen X, Wu Y. A unified approach to salient object detection via low rank matrix recovery. In: Proceedings of the 2012 IEEE Conference on Computer Vision and Pattern Recognition (CVPR), ser. CVPR '12. Washington, DC, USA: IEEE Computer Society. 2012. pp. 853-860

[17] Jiang H, Wang J, Yuan Z, Wu Y, Zheng N, Li S. Salient object detection: A discriminative regional feature integration approach. In: The IEEE Conference on Computer Vision and Pattern Recognition (CVPR). June 2013

[18] Liu Z, Zou W, Le Meur O. Saliency tree: A novel saliency detection framework. IEEE Transactions on Image Processing. 2014;**23**(5):1937-1952

[19] Cheng M, Mitra NJ, Huang X, Torr PHS, Hu S. Global contrast based salient region detection. IEEE Transactions on Pattern Analysis and Machine Intelligence. 2015;**37**(3): 569-582

[20] Ndayikengurukiye D, Mignotte M. Salient object detection by ltp texture characterization on opposing color pairs under slico superpixel constraint. Journal Imaging (JI), Special Issue: Advances in Color Imaging. 2022;**8**(4):11. Available from: https://www.mdpi.com/2313-433X/8/4/110

[21] Yan Q, Xu L, Shi J, Jia J. Hierarchical saliency detection. In: Proceedings of the 2013 IEEE Conference on Computer Vision and Pattern Recognition, ser. CVPR '13. Washington, DC, USA: IEEE Computer Society. 2013. pp. 1155-1162

[22] Aytekin C, Kiranyaz S, Gabbouj M. Automatic object segmentation by quantum cuts. In: 2014 22nd International Conference on Pattern Recognition. Aug 2014, pp. 112-117

[23] Liu T, Yuan Z, Sun J, Wang J, Zheng N, Tang X, et al. Learning to detect a salient object. IEEE Transactions on Pattern Analysis and Machine Intelligence. 2011;**33**(2):353-367

[24] Huang F, Qi J, Lu H, Zhang L, Ruan X. Salient object detection via multiple instance learning. IEEE Transactions on Image Processing. 2017; **26**(4):1911-1922

[25] Peng H, Li B, Ling H, Hu W, Xiong W, Maybank SJ. Salient object detection via structured matrix decomposition. IEEE Transactions on Pattern Analysis and Machine Intelligence. 2017;**39**(4):818-832

[26] Zhu W, Liang S, Wei Y, Sun J. Saliency optimization from robust background detection. In: The IEEE Conference on Computer Vision and Pattern Recognition (CVPR). June 2014

[27] Yan Y, Ren J, Sun G, Zhao H, Han J, Li X, et al. Unsupervised image saliency detection with gestalt-laws guided optimization and visual attention based refinement. Pattern Recognition. 2018; **79**:65-78

[28] Ye L, Liu Z, Li L, Shen L, Bai C, Wang Y. Salient object segmentation via effective integration of saliency and objectness. IEEE Transactions on Multimedia. 2017;**19**(8):1742-1756

[29] Zhang L, Tong MH, Marks TK, Shan H, Cottrell GW. Sun: A bayesian framework for saliency using natural statistics. Journal of Vision. 2008;**8**(7): 32.1-20. Available from: https://jov.arvojournals.org/article.aspx?articleid=2297284

[30] Li X, Lu H, Zhang L, Ruan X, Yang M-H. Saliency detection via dense and sparse reconstruction. In: The IEEE International Conference on Computer Vision (ICCV). December 2013

[31] Xie Y, Lu H, Yang M. Bayesian saliency via low and mid level cues. IEEE Transactions on Image Processing. 2013; **22**(5):1689-1698

[32] Mai L, Niu Y, Liu F. Saliency aggregation: A data-driven approach. In: The IEEE Conference on Computer Vision and Pattern Recognition (CVPR). June 2013

[33] Rahtu E, Kannala J, Salo M, Heikkilä J. Segmenting salient objects from images and videos. In: Daniilidis K, Maragos P, Paragios N, editors. Computer Vision - ECCV 2010. Berlin, Heidelberg: Springer Berlin Heidelberg; 2010. pp. 366-379

[34] Fu K, Gu IY, Yang J. Saliency detection by fully learning a continuous conditional random field. IEEE Transactions on Multimedia. 2017;**19**(7): 1531-1544

[35] Qiu W, Gao X, Han B. A superpixel-based crf saliency detection approach. Neurocomputing. 2017;**244**:19-32

[36] Yang J, Yang M. Top-down visual saliency via joint crf and dictionary learning. IEEE Transactions on Pattern Analysis and Machine Intelligence. 2017; **39**(3):576-588

[37] Feng L, Li H, Cheng D, Zhang W, Xiao C. An improved saliency detection algorithm based on edge boxes and bayesian model. Traitement du Signal. 2022;**39**:59-70

[38] Mignotte M. Saliency map estimation using an unsupervised pairwise pixel-based MRF model. MDPI (Multidisciplinary Digital Publishing Institute), Mathematics (-2156922), Section: Probability and Statistics, Special Issue: Bayesian Inference Modeling Applications (open access). 2023;**11**(4):986

[39] Junwei H, Ngi NK, Mingjing L, HongJiang Z. Unsupervised extraction of visual attention objects in color images. IEEE Transactions on Circuits and Systems for Video Technology. 2006; **16**(1):141-145

[40] da Fontoura Costa L. Visual Saliency and Attention as Random Walks on Complex Networks. arXiv. physics/0603025. 2007

[41] Gopalakrishnan V, Hu Y, Rajan D. Random walks on graphs for salient object detection in images. IEEE Transactions on Image Processing. 2010; **19**:3232-3242

[42] Wang W, Wang Y, Huang Q, Gao W. Measuring visual saliency by site entropy rate. In: The Twenty-Third IEEE Conference on Computer Vision and Pattern Recognition, CVPR 2010, San Francisco, CA, USA, 13-18 June 2010. 2010. pp. 2368-2375

[43] Jiang B, Zhang L, Lu H, Yang C, Yang M-H. Saliency detection via absorbing markov chain. In: The IEEE International Conference on Computer Vision (ICCV), December 2013

[44] Yuan Y, Li C, Kim J, Cai W, Feng DD. Reversion correction and regularized random walk ranking for saliency detection. IEEE Transactions on Image Processing. 2018;**27**(3): 1311-1322

[45] Zhang L, Ai J, Jiang B, Lu H, Li X. Saliency detection via absorbing markov chain with learnt transition probability.

IEEE Transactions on Image Processing. 2018;**27**(2):987-998

[46] Tang W, Wang Z, Zhai J, Yang Z. Salient object detection via two-stage absorbing markov chain based on background and foreground. Journal of Visual Communication and Image Representation. 2019;**71**:102727. DOI: 10.1016/j.jvcir.2019.102727

[47] Xia C, Li X, Zhao L. Infrared small target detection via modified random walks. Remote Sensing. 2018;**10**(12). Available from: https://www.mdpi.com/2072-4292/10/12/2004

[48] Singh V, Kumar N. Cobra: Convex hull based random walks for salient object detection. Multimedia Tools and Applications. 2022;**81**(21):30283-30303

[49] Jiang F, Kong B, Li J, Dashtipour K, Gogate M. Robust visual saliency optimization based on bidirectional Markov chains. Cognitive Computation. 2021;**13**(1):69-80

[50] Pengfei L, Xiaosheng Y, Jianning C, Chengdong W. Saliency detection via absorbing markov chain with multi-level cues. In: IEICE Transactions on Fundamentals of Electronics, Communications and Computer Sciences, vol. advpub, p. 2021EAL2071. 2021

[51] Wu J, Han G, Liu P, Yang H, Luo H, Li Q. Saliency detection with bilateral absorbing markov chain guided by depth information. Sensors. 2021;**21**(3)

[52] Mignotte M. MDS-based multiresolution nonlinear dimensionality reduction model for color image segmentation. IEEE Transactions on Neural Networks. 2011;**22**(3):447-460

[53] Mignotte M. MDS-based segmentation model for the fusion of contour and texture cues in natural images. Computer Vision and Image Understanding. 2012;**116**(9):981-990

[54] Mignotte M. A multiresolution markovian fusion model for the color visualization of hyperspectral images. IEEE Transactions on Geoscience and Remote Sensing. 2010;**48**(12):4236-4247

[55] Mignotte M. A bi-criteria optimization approach based dimensionality reduction model for the color display of hyperspectral images. IEEE Transactions on Geoscience and Remote Sensing. 2012;**50**(2):501-513

[56] Moevus A, Mignotte M, de Guise J, Meunier J. A perceptual map for gait symmetry quantification and pathology detection. BioMedical Engineering OnLine (BMEO). 2015;**14**(1):99. Available from: https://www.ncbi.nlm.nih.gov/pmc/articles/PMC4659413/

[57] Touati R, Mignotte M. MDS-based multi-axial dimensionality reduction model for human action recognition. In: Eleventh conference on Computer and Robot Vision, CRV'2014, Montréal, Quebec, Canada. May 2014. pp. 262-267

[58] Mignotte M. A label field fusion bayesian model and its penalized maximum rand estimator for image segmentation. IEEE Transactions on Image Processing. 2010;**19**(6):1610-1624

[59] Mignotte M. An energy based model for the image edge histogram specification problem. IEEE Transactions on Image Processing. 2012; **21**(1):379-386

[60] Mignotte M. Non-local pairwise energy based model for the HDR image compression problem. Journal of Electronic Imaging. 2012;**21**(1):013016

[61] Touati R, Mignotte M, Dahmane M. Multimodal change detection in remote sensing images using an unsupervised pixel pairwise-based markov random field model. IEEE Transactions on Image Processing. 2019;**29**(1):757-767

[62] Khlif A, Mignotte M. Segmentation data visualizing and clustering. Multimedia Tools and Applications. 2016;**76**(1):1-22

[63] Torgerson W. Multidimensional scaling: I. theory and method. Psychometrika. 1952;**17**:401-419

[64] Cox T, Cox M. Multidimensional Scaling. London: Chapman & Hall; 1994

[65] Faloutsos C, Lin K-I. FastMap: A fast algorithm for indexing, data-mining and visualization of traditional and multimedia datasets. In: Proceedings of the ACM SIGMOD International Conference on Management of Data, San Jose, California. June 1995, pp. 163-174

[66] Nyström EJ. Über die praktische auflösung von integralgleichungen mit anwendungen auf randwertaufgaben. Acta Mathematica. 1930;**54**(1):185-204

[67] Platt JC. Fastmap, metricmap, and landmark mds are all nystrom algorithms. In: Proceedings of 10th International Workshop on Artificial Intelligence and Statistics (AISTATS). 2005. pp. 261-268

[68] Borji A, Cheng M, Jiang H, Li J. Salient object detection: A benchmark. IEEE Transactions on Image Processing. 2015;**24**(12):5706-5722

[69] Wang J, Jiang H, Yuan Z, Cheng M-M, Hu X, Zheng N. Salient object detection: A discriminative regional feature integration approach. International Journal of Computer Vision. 2017;**123**(2):251-268

[70] Liu G, Yang J. Exploiting color volume and color difference for salient region detection. IEEE Transactions on Image Processing. 2019;**28**(1):6-16

[71] Felzenszwalb P, Huttenlocher D. Efficient graph-based image segmentation. International Journal of Computer Vision. 2004;**59**(2):167-181

[72] Mignotte M. Segmentation by fusion of histogram-based k-means clusters in different color spaces. IEEE Transactions on Image Processing. 2008; **17**(5):780-787

[73] Mignotte M. A label field fusion model with a variation of information estimator for image segmentation. Information Fusion. 2014;**20**:7-20

[74] Banks S. Signal Processing, Image Processing and Pattern Recognition. Upper Saddle River, NJ: Pearson Prentice Hall; 1990

[75] Martinkauppi JB, Soriano MN, Laaksonen MH. Behavior of skin color under varying illumination seen by different cameras at different color spaces. In: Proc. SPIE, Machine Vision Applications in Industrial Inspection IX, San Jose California. January 2001. pp. 102-113

[76] Braquelaire J-P, Brun L. Comparison and optimization of methods of color image quantization. IEEE Transactions on Image Processing. 1997;**6**:1048-1952

[77] Stokman H, Gevers T. Selection and fusion of color models for image feature detection," IEEE Transactions on Image Processing. 2007;**29**:371-381

[78] Kato Z. A Markov Random Field image segmentation model for color textured images. Image and Vision Computing. 2006;**24**(10): 1103-1114

[79] Perez P, Hue C, Vermaak J, Gangnet M. Color-based probabilistic tracking. In: Eur. Conf. on Computer Vision, ECCV'2002, LNCS 2350, Copenhaguen, Denmark. June 2002. pp. 661-675

[80] Shi J, Yan Q, Xu L, Jia J. Hierarchical image saliency detection on extended CSSD. IEEE Transactions on Pattern Analysis and Machine Intelligence. 2016;**38**(4): 717-729

[81] Reina G, Ertl T. Implementing fastmap on the GPU: Considerations on general-purpose computation on graphics hardware. Eurographics UK Theory and Practice of Computer Graphics. 2005;**01**:51-58

Chapter 5

Data Acquisition System for Calibration of Handheld Digital Multimeters through Digital Image Processing

José Felipe Hurtado Castaño

Abstract

The purpose of the project was to develop an automatic system for the acquisition and recognition of measurements taken by handheld digital multimeters through the use of images; this was proposed in order to improve their calibration process in the magnitudes of direct and alternating current, direct and alternating voltage, and electrical resistance. Thus, a system was developed to automatically capture, process, and recognize the values associated with multimeter readings in its calibration process, divided into three stages: The first stage consisted of creating a database with information of the multimeter models to be calibrated, the standard instrument (evaluating the feasibility of using it in the process), and the calibration points. In the second stage, an algorithm was developed to identify and classify the values displayed on the under-test multimeter. In the third stage, the process of uncertainty estimation, reporting, and evaluation of the validity of the results was carried out. From this last subprocess, it was determined that the capture and uncertainty estimation system is adequate to perform the calibration of the evaluated handheld digital multimeters.

Keywords: digital handheld multimeter, multimeter calibration, image processing, uncertainty estimation, validity of results

1. Introduction

The concept of metrology, as expressed by Marbán et al. [1], has been present in human life since the establishment of the firsts comparisons. To measure is, on a basic way, an action of comparing a something unknown (a quantification of a magnitude that we do not know), with something with a known value (reference quantification that we know). The calibration process of any measurement instrument represents a significantly important component to validate the indication given by equipment. International vocabulary of metrology [2] defines calibration as:

> *operation that, under specified conditions, in a first step, establishes a relation between the quantity values with measurement uncertainties provided by measurement standards and corresponding indications with associated measurement uncertainties and, in a second step, uses this information to establish a relation for obtaining a measurement result from an indication. (p. 28)*

To give conformity to their measurement processes or following the guidelines of specific procedures, companies in the industrial sector and laboratories that perform work related to metrology require to calibrate their instruments periodically. The whole process involves both administrative and technical tasks that require specific times for its execution, and any human process is prone to incur in any type of error. However, it has the possibility of being automated, even if it is partially, reducing the duration and the possibilities of error of the process, guaranteeing in the same way the quality of the obtained results.

Particularly in electricity, electrical current intensity represents the base unit from which important units such as electrical voltage, electrical resistance, and capacitance, among others, are derived. An alternative to measuring these physical phenomena is by the use of digital multimeter which, according to Fluke Corporation [3], is an "electronic meter for making electrical measurements," which has a wide range of special measurement functions.

Digital technology is increasingly present in human life, and as a result, the industry has been involved in a digital transformation, which leads to the use of new techniques that help to provide greater reliability and accuracy in the various production processes, reducing time, probability of error occurrence, and, likewise, costs per process. The use of this technology in metrology is particularly convenient since it not only allows the improvement of the internal processes of each laboratory but also opens the way to a substantial improvement in the communication and information management of customers, laboratories, regulatory bodies, national institutes, and other entities related to metrology. As mentioned by Bauer et al. [4], the technological growth curves of both automation and metrology have increased significantly fast and are increasingly influenced by micro, nano, and even femto technologies.

2. Database of multimeters and measurement standards

For the construction of the database, information related to the accuracy of the instruments to be calibrated, the accuracy of a generating instrument, and the relationship between both parts was taken into account, to determine the feasibility of using such calibrator as a working standard, in each of the calibration points.

2.1 Test multimeters and information of interest

For the project, three different models of handheld digital multimeters were used: Fluke 87-V, Fluke 112, and Fluke 179.

The three models do not have a communication protocol and, therefore, are suitable for the development of the recognition of its indication by image processing. Additionally, other influencing factors are considered to evaluate whether the proposed standard instrument (Fluke 5500A calibrator) is suitable for the work.

2.1.1 Maximum allowable error of the models

The user's manuals of digital multimeters refer to information corresponding to the accuracy of the instrument or, in other words, its maximum permissible error of measurement or accuracy. This characteristic is commonly given as the sum between a percentage of the measurement and a predetermined number of counts and is calculated as follows:

$$EMP = \pm[\%of\ reading \cdot V_n + Counts \cdot Resolution] \quad (1)$$

2.2 Calibration procedure

Laboratories must have methods or procedures for calibration activities, verifying that they can be adequately developed before putting them into operation (ISO/IEC 17025:2017 numeral 7.2.1 [5]). Thus, the document written jointly by the National Metrology Institute of Colombia—INM, members of the Colombian Metrology Network—RCM, and the National Accreditation Body of Colombia—ONAC is used. This is called "GUÍA PARA LA CALIBRACIÓN DE MULTÍMERTOS DIGITALES 4 5/6 (50000 CUENTAS) – INM\GTM EM-CCA\01" [6] and was published in July 2019, in its version number 1.

The purpose of the document is to provide recommendations for calibrating digital multimeters with resolution not greater than 4 5/6 digits (50,000 counts). It covers

Measurement function: D.C. voltage					
Test points		**Accuracy**		**Traceability assessment**	
Range	**Test point**	**Standard**	**Multimeter**	**TAR**	**State**
Model: Fluke 179					
600 mV	0 mV	***0.003000 mV***	***0.200000 mV***	66.67	**Pass**
600 mV	60 mV	***0.006600 mV***	***0.254000 mV***	38.48	**Pass**
1000 V	100 V	***0.0060 V***	***2.1500 V***	358.33	**Pass**
1000 V	900 V	***0.0510 V***	***3.3500 V***	65.69	**Pass**
Model: Fluke 87-V					
600 mV	0 mV	***0.003000 mV***	***0.100000 mV***	33.33	**Pass**
600 mV	60 mV	***0.006600 mV***	***0.160000 mV***	24.24	**Pass**
1000 V	100 V	***0.0060 V***	***1.0500 V***	175.00	**Pass**
1000 V	900 V	***0.0510 V***	***1.4500 V***	28.43	**Pass**
Model: Fluke 112					
600 mV	0 mV	***0.003000 mV***	***0.200000 mV***	66.67	**Pass**
600 mV	60 mV	***0.006600 mV***	***0.230000 mV***	34.85	**Pass**
600 V	60 V	***0.0038 V***	***0.2300 V***	60.53	**Pass**
600 V	540 V	***0.0312 V***	***0.4700 V***	15.06	**Pass**
Where italic and bold numbers are used to assess the state of traceability.					

Table 1.
Traceability accuracy ratio (TAR) assessment for D.C. voltage.

the required quantities and estimates the measurement uncertainties, based on the guide to the expression of uncertainty in measurement (GUM) [7].

2.3 Accuracy ratio

For each of the functions to be evaluated, the corresponding calibration points and relation of specifications were established. For each of the points, the Fluke 5500A calibrator has sufficient accuracy to perform the process, allowing the use of the multimeters mentioned as sample for the development of the data acquisition system from images. **Table 1** shows the evaluation of the maximum and minimum points considered by the procedure in the D.C. voltage function; however, this exercise was performed for each of the points to be calibrated for each multimeter.

According to the accuracy evaluation, it is concluded that the Fluke 5500A calibrator is suitable for calibrating the three multimeters under test.

3. Recognition of multimeter readings

3.1 Initial conditions for processing

Before implementing the algorithm for digit recognition, a compartment with internal illumination was created, where the multimeters are positioned, such that the illumination conditions for image processing are standardized, without the presence of exogenous disturbances given by external illumination sources.

The side holes of the compartment (see **Figure 1**) are intended to allow the movement of the multimeter's fastening element and the connection cables between the standard equipment and the instrument under calibration. The front hole, on the other hand, is used to locate the camera that captures the photos of the multimeter display.

The image acquisition of the multimeter to be calibrated was performed with a mobile device camera of 108 megapixels. The communication between the camera and the image processing system is done through an application that allows using the camera of the mobile device as a complement to the computer that will be used for the processing.

Figure 1.
Multimeter location compartment.

3.2 Recognition algorithm

The digit recognition system of the digital multimeters was made from four subsystems or processing subsequences shown in the diagram of **Figure 2**. The first stage is responsible for making a first cleaning and thresholding of the image; in the second stage, the segmentation or partitioning of the display is performed, with respect to the rest of the image; followed by, in the third section, the recognition and separation of each of the digits shown by the multimeter is performed to finally recognize and locate the decimal point of the value shown on the display.

3.2.1 Initial processing

Initial processing on the captured image is divided into standardizing the size of the original image, changing its color scale to gray scale, applying filters that remove some unwanted information for processing, and thresholding the image from edge recognition.

Initially, in order to ensure that the display recognition parameters do not vary in the event of a change in the acquisition camera, the image size was standardized and set to a width of 1280 pixels by 720 pixels high. Additionally, the photos captured by the camera are color images, an aspect that does not provide relevant information to the proposed recognition process. Thus, in order to reduce the size of the images to improve the processing speed, a gray space transformation is performed as shown in **Table 2**.

Once the gray scale image is obtained, it is smoothed or blurred from a normalized matrix (kernel), which follows the form:

$$k_{Blur} = \frac{1}{9} \cdot \begin{bmatrix} 1 & 1 & 1 \\ 1 & 1 & 1 \\ 1 & 1 & 1 \end{bmatrix} \tag{2}$$

The purpose of this smoothing is to reduce information related to possible scratches or other minor conditions of the multimeter and the environment that may alter the subsequent thresholding as presented in **Table 3**.

For binarization or thresholding, the Canny edge detector was used, which makes use of the intensity gradients of the image and, according to established upper and lower limits, detects the edges of the processed figure. In this way, the edges will be colored in white and the rest of the pixels will be black.

As an additional process to binarization, it was necessary to implement a morphological operation of dilation (as exemplified in **Figures 3** and **4**), which was performed with the purpose of closing the edges of the display.

3.2.2 Segmentación del display

With the image already binarized, we proceed to find the existing contours and extract the associated information so that the section of the display can be

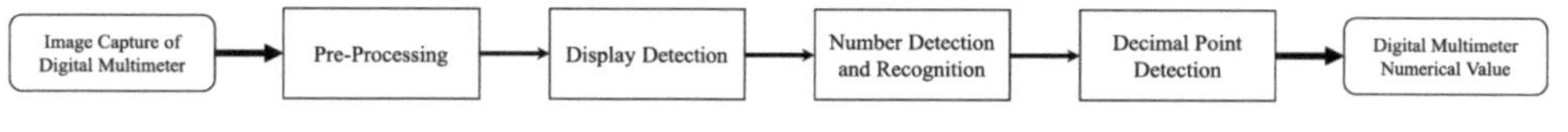

Figure 2.
General processing block diagram.

Fluke 112 capture	
Color scale	Gray scale

Size: 835 kB	Size: 313 kB
Fluke 179 capture	
Color scale	Gray scale
	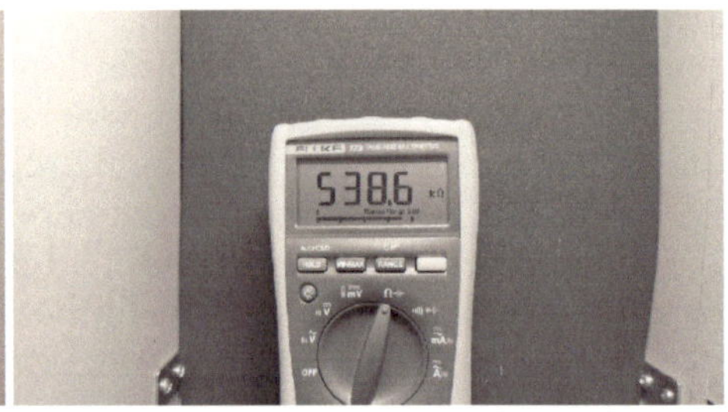
Size: 1439 kB	Size: 494 kB
Fluke 87-V capture	
Color scale	Gray scale
	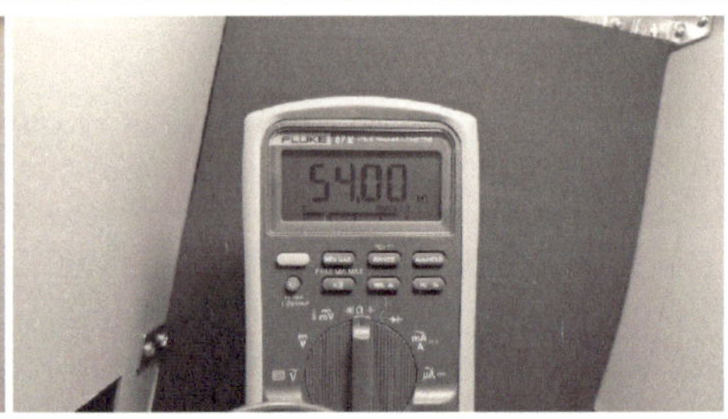
Size: 1286 kB	Size: 447 kB

Table 2.
Size difference due to the color transformation.

discriminated from the rest of the capture. Five values of interest are extracted from the contours. The first one corresponds to the area of the contour found that will be compared with two reference thresholds, with which it is determined if the area found can be attributed to the multimeter display, or if it is part of another element of the image; the following two parameters correspond to both the width and the height of the contour and will be used to determine a variable of interest called "aspect ratio" that corresponds to the existing proportion between the width and the height, which is given as follows:

Fluke 179 thresholding	
Without smoothing	With smoothing

Fluke 87-V thresholding	
Without smoothing	With smoothing
	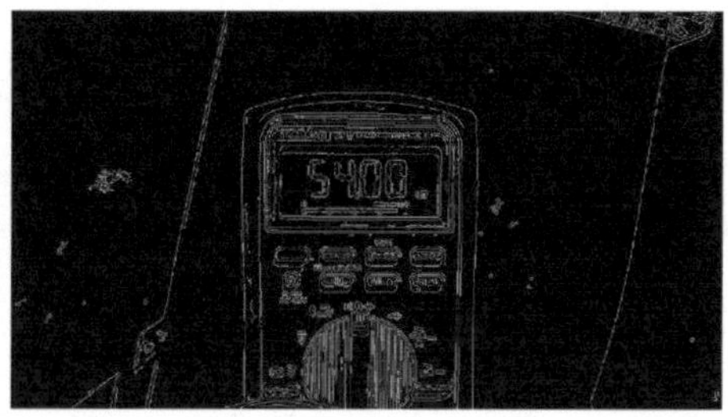
Fluke 112 thresholding	
Without smoothing	With smoothing
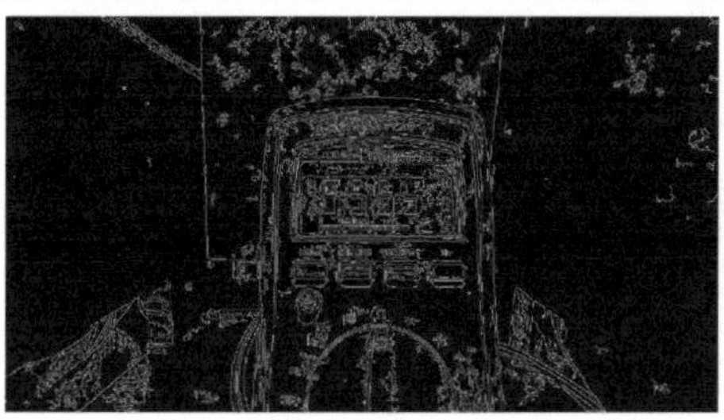	

Table 3.
Importance of image smoothing.

Figure 3.
Model 87-V dilatation.

Figure 4.
Model 179 dilatation.

$$R_{Aspecto} = \frac{Width\ of\ Contour}{Height\ of\ Contour} \tag{3}$$

Measurements were made of both the width and height of the displays of the three selected multimeters, with these approximate values the corresponding aspect ratio associated with each model was calculated, the three values were averaged and experimentally a tolerance associated with that average value was determined, such that in most cases it detects the display outline satisfactorily. The dimensions of the three displays are shown in **Table 4**.

From experimental tests performed on the selected multimeters and taking into account the calculated aspect ratio, an allowable tolerance of ± 0.4 was established, which determined that the upper and lower limits with which the experimental aspect ratio will be compared are 2.6 and 1.8, respectively.

Once these comparison conditions are established, each of the contours found by the algorithm is evaluated and the one that complies with both the area and the aspect ratio will correspond to the digital multimeter display and this area will be demarcated by the algorithm, as shown in **Figures 5–7**.

Subsequently, the selection associated with the display is segmented from the rest of the image, resulting in the clipping of the multimeter display (see **Figures 8–10**).

3.2.3 Segmentation of numerical values

Once the multimeter display has been segmented, each of the numerical values corresponding to the measurements of the various functions to be calibrated is recognized. Thanks to the fact that the selected models present their values from seven

Model	**Width**	**Height**	**Aspect ratio**
Fluke 87-V	64 mm	28 mm	2.286
Fluke 112	51 mm	24 mm	2.125
Fluke 179	61 mm	28 mm	2.179
Mean			2.197

Table 4.
Aspect ratio of evaluated displays.

Figure 5.
Model 87-V contour of interest.

Figure 6.
Model 179 contour of interest.

Figure 7.
Model 112 contour of interest.

segments that follow the shape of the **Figure 11**, a detection algorithm is proposed in which initially each segment is separated from the rest and it is evaluated if it is on or not, making use of the intensity of the pixels.

A labeling of the numbers from zero to nine that will be treated as reference to be later compared with the display to be evaluated is performed. Values of one (1) correspond to segments that are on; on the contrary, values of zero (0) indicate that the value of the segment is off. The labeling of each one of the numbers was established as presented in the **Table 5**.

Figure 8.
Model 87-V segmented display.

Figure 9.
Model 179 segmented display.

Figure 10.
Model 112 segmented display.

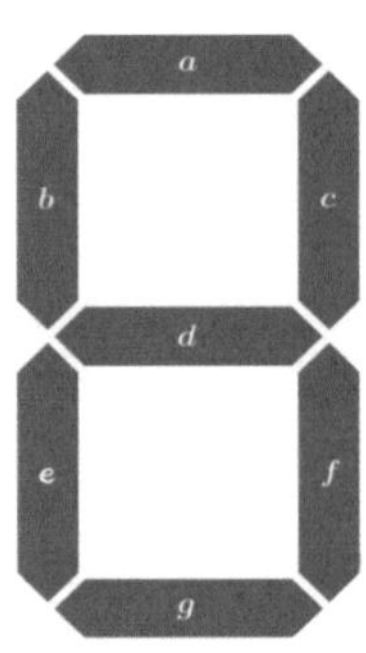

Figure 11.
Seven segments display.

	Location						
Number	***a***	***b***	***c***	***d***	***e***	***f***	***g***
0	1	1	1	0	1	1	1
1	0	0	1	0	0	1	0
2	1	0	1	1	1	0	1
3	1	0	1	1	0	1	1
4	0	1	1	1	0	1	0
5	1	1	0	1	0	1	1
6	1	1	0	1	1	1	1
7	1	0	1	0	0	1	0
8	1	1	1	1	1	1	1
9	1	1	1	1	0	1	1

Table 5.
Reference label.

When the reference vectors representing each of the numbers have been constructed, we continue with the processing of each of the digits of the display separately.

The display cutout is subjected to thresholding and subsequent morphological operations to highlight the geometric characteristics of the digits in the image (as shown in the **Figure 12**).

Then, a second cropping is performed within the display so that only the numerical values to be evaluated and the point are shown (see **Figure 13**). For this, a second

Figure 12.
Display thresholding.

Figure 13.
First cut of the display.

contour search is performed to extract information such as height, width, and the corresponding aspect ratio (determined from the Eq. (3)) of each of the detected objects. From estimates made experimentally, it was determined that the height of the digits ranges between 200 and 600 pixels, the width has an approximate value of less than 300 pixels, and the aspect ratio is less than 0.5 (ranging between 0.1 and 0.2 for the representation of the number 1).

With the mentioned conditions, the numerical values corresponding to the measurement are enclosed in rectangles (see **Figure 14**) and separated as shown in **Figures 15–18**. Finally, the last sequence is initialized for number recognition.

3.2.4 Number recognition

After each numerical value of the display associated with the measurement has been segmented, the images are divided into seven subsections corresponding to the seven segments of each display. Afterward, the number of white pixels and the number of black pixels in each division are counted, which evaluates whether the segment is on or off (a record of 1 is kept if it is on, or 0 if it is off) as presented in the **Table 6**; a vector or label is obtained that will represent the number and this value will be compared with the references presented in the **Table 5**.

Figure 14.
Digits location.

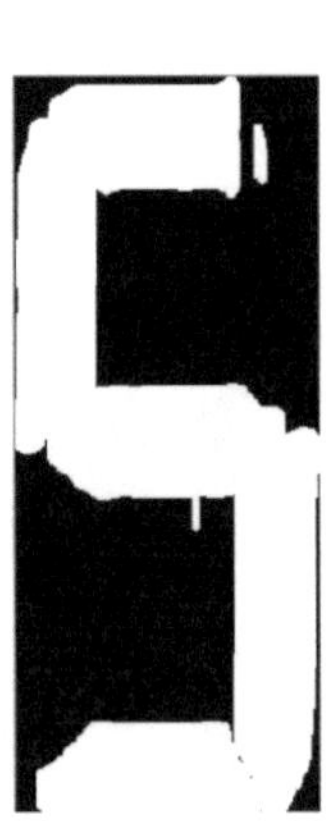

Figure 15.
First digit separation.

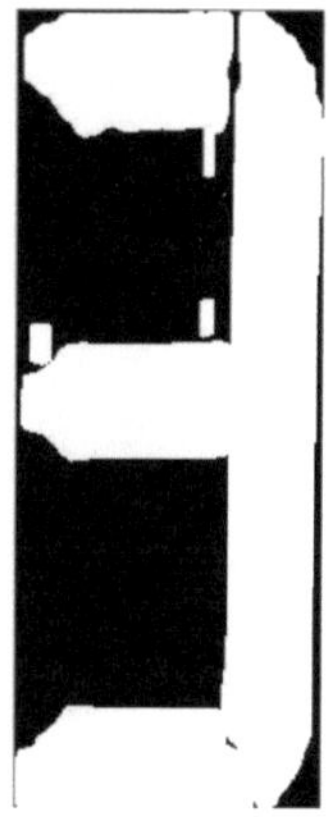

Figure 16.
Second digit separation.

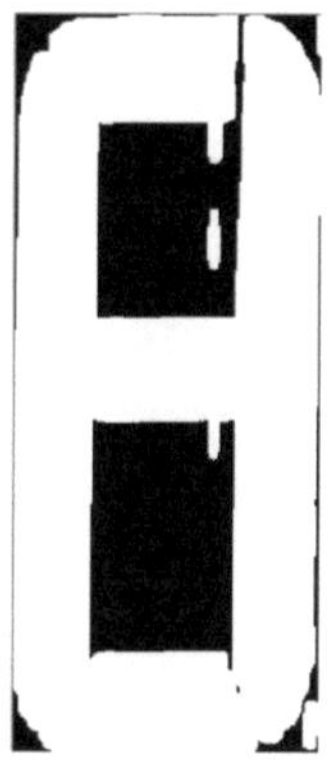

Figure 17.
Third digit separation.

Figure 18.
Fourth digit separation.

White pixel count	
Segment *a*	Segment *d*

White pixel percentage: 65.38%	White pixel percentage: 91.38%
Segment *b*	Segment *c*

White pixel percentage: 85.68%	White pixel percentage: 16.11%
Segment *e*	Segment *f*
	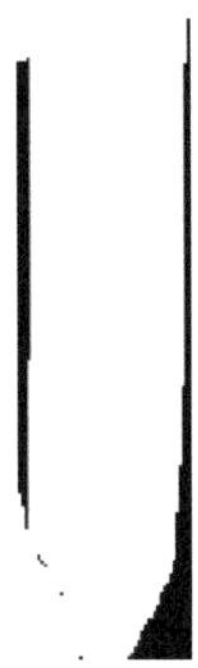
White pixel percentage: 23.39%	White pixel percentage: 88.87%
Segment *g*	Label value
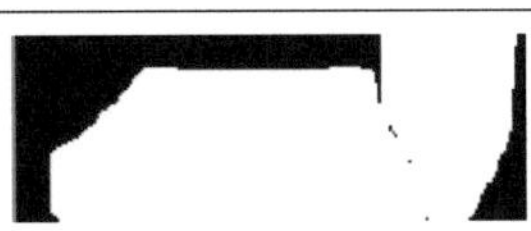	1101011
White pixel percentage: 72.37%	

Table 6.
Pixel count in each segment of number five.

This process is repeated with each of the values found and thus the numerical value associated with the photo of the digital multimeter indication will be determined.

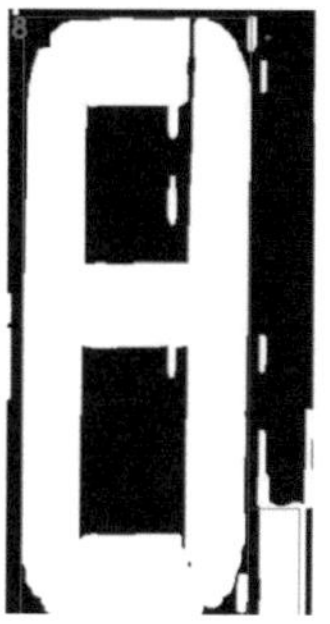

Figure 19.
Decimal point location.

Figure 20.
Value recognized by the algorithm.

3.2.5 Recognition and decimal point location

A rectangular area ($80x40$ *Pixels*) for evaluation is associated to each segmentation in which the number of white pixels will be counted as well. If the count exceeds half of the total pixels, then the decimal point is considered to be located in that space (as illustrated in the **Figure 19**).

With the recognition of both the numerical values and the decimal point, the numerical value displayed on the digital multimeter is obtained. **Figure 20** illustrates the recognition performed by the algorithm.

4. Data acquisition and estimation of uncertainties

The purpose of the data acquisition system is to capture the following data: Nominal value to be generated by the standard instrument and 12 readings corresponding to the instrument under calibration. These will be sent to an Excel sheet in charge of making the respective calculations necessary for the process.

The scheme proposed in **Figure 21** represents the proposed step-by-step approach for reporting measurement errors and their associated uncertainties in the calibration of digital multimeters.

From the data captured from the digital multimeter, the average value and the associated standard deviation are calculated; from the calculated average and the nominal value, the bias of the measurement corresponding to the mathematical model associated with the calibration is established [6]:

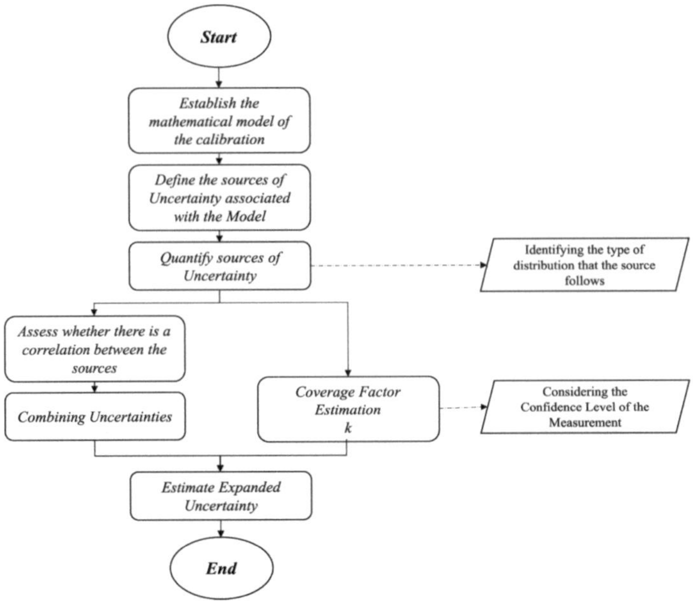

Figure 21.
Scheme to establish the measurement result.

$$E = \overline{V}_x - V_s \tag{4}$$

where E refers to the measuring bias, $\overline{V}_x$ corresponds to the mean value of the multimeter indications and V_s corresponds to the nominal value of the standard instrument. Taking into account the possible deviations due to the standard system and the instrument under calibration, the model is complemented as presented in Eq. (4).

$$E = \left(\overline{V}_x + \delta V_x\right) - \left(V_s + \delta V_s\right) \tag{5}$$

where δV_x corresponds to the correction due to the resolution of the multimeter and δV_s corresponds to the corrections of the standard system due to different effects. The corrections due to the zero measurement were not taken into account in the exposed model because this was taken as an independent measurement point. In summary and taking into account the reference document for calibration, a representation of the sources of uncertainties involved in the process is shown in **Figure 22**.

By means of the propagation of uncertainties for uncorrelated input variables established by (BIPM/JCGM) Bureau International de Pois et Measure Joint Committee for Guides in Metrology [7], the corresponding uncertainty associated with the measurement is obtained, such that:

$$u^2(E_x) = \sum_{i=1}^{n} \left(u_i(E_x)\right)^2 = \sum_{i=1}^{n} \left(C_i \cdot u(x_i)\right)^2 \tag{6}$$

After identifying the input quantities and their corresponding typical uncertainties, the law of propagation of uncertainties was applied, such that:

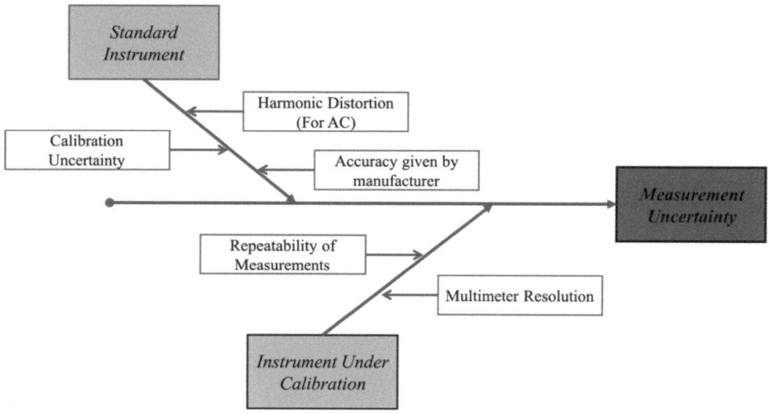

Figure 22.
Representation of process error sources.

$$u_c(E) = \sqrt{\sum_{i=1}^{n} \frac{\partial E}{\partial x_i}^2 \cdot u^2(x_i)} \tag{7}$$

where $\frac{\partial E}{\partial x_i}$ corresponds to each of the sensitivity coefficients of the input variables.

Finally, we determine the factor k that ensures a coverage probability of 95.45% in the results, such that the expanded uncertainty can be determined as follows:

$$U_{exp}(E) = k \cdot u_c(E) \tag{8}$$

4.1 Presence of atypical data

From the results obtained by the recognition system, it was determined if there was presence of atypical data, which was done graphically from a box plot. In general, it was evidenced that in the data capture, there was no presence of atypical data, product of the bad recognition of the images, but by the natural behavior of the equipment under calibration. **Figures 23–27** show some of the diagrams obtained at specific calibration points:

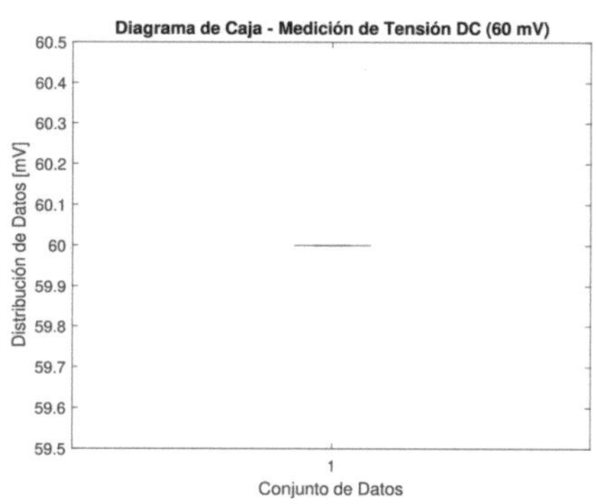

Figure 23.
Box plot 60 mV_{DC}.

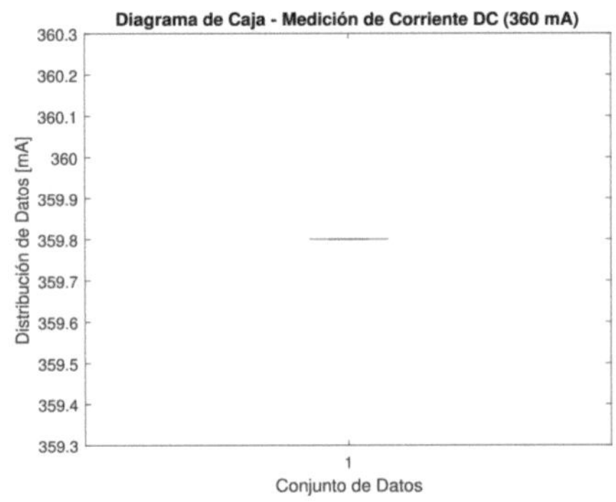

Figure 24.
Box plot 360 mA_{DC}.

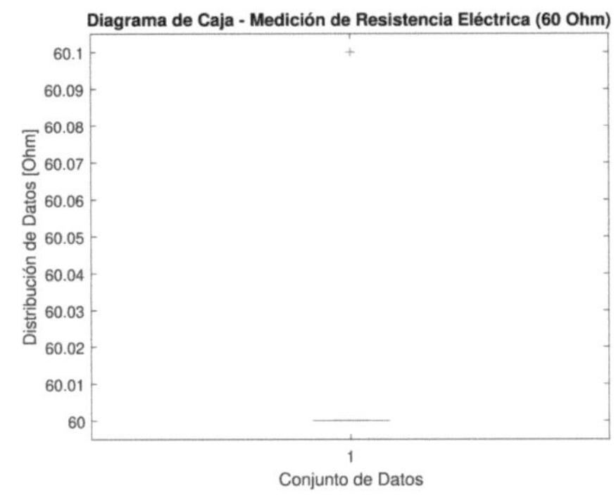

Figure 25.
Box plot 60 Ω.

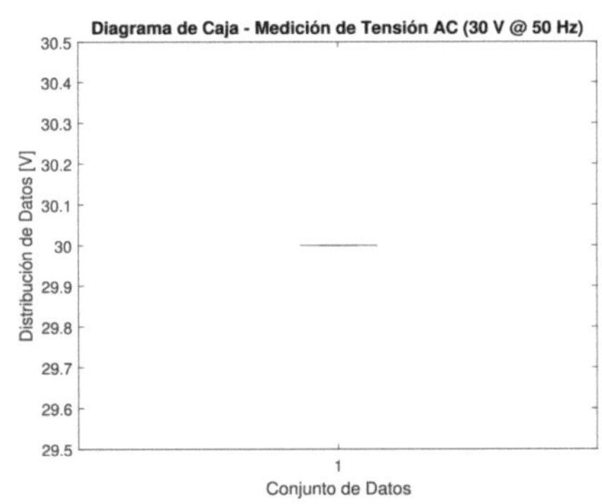

Figure 26.
Box plot 30 V_{AC}.

4.2 Normalized error

The statistic called normalized error, in association with the box plots, was one of the parameters used to evaluate the validity of the results obtained from the calibration performed by the system. To perform the evaluation, the reference and processing system errors and uncertainties are used.

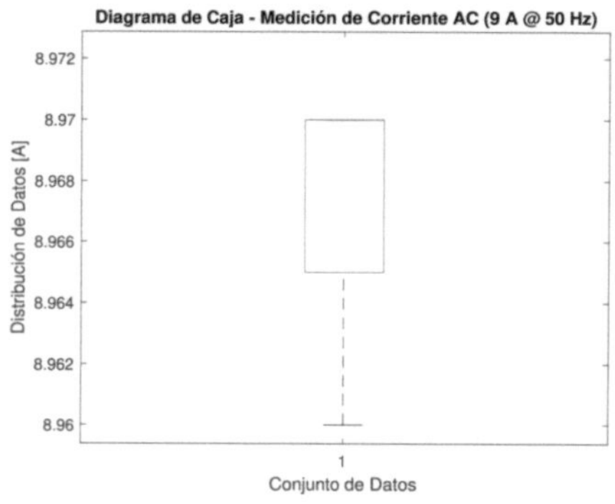

Figure 27.
Box plot 9 A_{AC}.

Nominal value	Test values		Reference values		E_n
	Error	U_{exp}	Error	U_{exp}	
60 mV	0.000 mV	0.058 mV	0.000 mV	0.057 mV	**0.0000**
54 mA	−0.02 mA	0.015 mA	−0.026 mA	0.011 mA	**−0.3217**
6 $k\Omega$	0.0020 $k\Omega$	0.0019 $k\Omega$	0.0000 $k\Omega$	0.0058 $k\Omega$	**−0.3274**
540 V @ 1 kHz	0.2 V	1.1 V	0.56 V	0.41 V	**0.3046**
9 A @ 50 Hz	−0.032 A	0.027 A	−0.030 A	0.033 A	**0.0467**

Table 7.
Error normalizado para funciones de medición.

Table 7 shows some of the results obtained from the *normalized error*.

Given that there is no evidence of outliers produced by the recognition system and that the normalized error values remained in the range of 1 and −1, it is possible to conclude that the system results are satisfactory and therefore, at the metrological level, the system is capable of reporting reliable results.

5. Conclusions

The purpose of this work was to improve the data acquisition system in the calibration of handheld digital multimeters that do not have communication protocols other than their display. Therefore, a system was developed to automatically capture, process, and recognize the values associated with multimeter readings.

In order to achieve this objective, three fundamental subprocesses were developed:

In the first stage, an initial database was created with the multimeter models to work with. The information associated to the required measurement points was related, considering the normative procedure used. Information on the instrument to be calibrated was associated to each of the points, such as ranges and specifications; for the standard instrument, information on the specifications or maximum error allowed by the manufacturer was also related.

In the second stage, an algorithm was developed that, based on the geometry of each segment, identifies and classifies in an ordered way each number of the display of the instrument under calibration. It started with a first trimming of the display with respect to the rest of the image, where a second stage of trimming is then performed where the position of each digit is identified and, based on a count of black and white pixels, it is determined which segments are on or off. With the information obtained, the displayed values are labeled and compared with reference labels to associate numerical values to what is displayed by the acquisition system. From the tests performed, an overall system accuracy (600 samples) of 99.33% was obtained; where, particularly for the Fluke 112, 179, and 87-V models, the percentage of correct recognition was 98.5%, 99.5%, and 100.0%, respectively. As an alternative to mitigate processing errors, a verification process was implemented to discard the processed values whose amplitude is not within the maximum and minimum limits established on the median value of the data vector.

The third stage included the reporting of the results and the metrological assurance of the implemented system. The measurement uncertainties associated with the process were established, taking into account the normative procedure, which, in turn, follows the guidelines of the guide for the expression of uncertainty in measurement [2]. Finally, the quality of the results was evaluated metrologically, comparing them with reference values reported by external suppliers for the same items.

Based on the percentage of successes obtained by the data capture system, the strategies implemented to mitigate processing errors and the proposed metrological evaluation metric, it was determined that the capture and uncertainty estimation system is adequate to perform the calibration process of digital multimeters. In general terms, the automatic data acquisition system for the calibration of digital multimeters through digital image processing has sufficient accuracy and metrological support to perform the calibration process of handheld digital multimeters that do not have a communication protocol that facilitates the automation of the process.

6. Recommendations

For future works related to the presented project, it is recommended to improve the physical compartment and the illumination system since they are highly relevant components to perform a correct task of recognition of the values displayed on the display.

Likewise, it is recommended to strengthen the numerical recognition algorithm to allow a greater variation in the input conditions that affect the process such as illumination, inclination, and distance, among others.

Acknowledgements

This chapter summarizes the published master thesis in Spanish by the same author: Hurtado Castaño [8].

Note

To see the detailed development of the project, please refer to the repository of the Universidad Nacional de Colombia, through the following link: https://repositorio.unal.edu.co/bitstream/handle/unal/82929/1016074514.2022.pdf?sequence=2&isAllowed=y.

Thanks

I am infinitely grateful to my family and friends, for supporting me throughout this process, making special mention of my parents Luis Enrique and Amparo, who were always present to give me their unconditional support and words of encouragement, even in the most difficult moments. Thank you for being the best example for me to follow.

Thanks immensely to my directors Jesús María Quintero Quintero Ph.D. and Angélica Vargas Chavarro M.Sc., who with their experience, knowledge, and patience guided and supported me firmly and generously in each of the stages of the project. Finally, I would like to thank engineer Alexis García for his collaboration and unconditional friendship. I would not have achieved the results obtained if it had not been for his help.

Author details

José Felipe Hurtado Castaño
Independent Researcher, Bogotá, Colombia

*Address all correspondence to: jfhurtado514@hotmail.com

References

[1] Marbán R, Pellecer J. Metrología para No-Metrólogos. 2002

[2] Joint Committee for Guides in Metrology. Vocabulario Internacional de Metrología—Conceptos Fundamentales y Generales, y Términos Asociados (VIM). 3rd ed2012

[3] Fluke Corporation. Conceptos Básicos de los Multímetros Digitales. 2014

[4] Bauer JM, Bas G, Durakbasa NM, Kopacek P. Development trends in automation and metrology. IFAC-PapersOnLine. 2015;**48**(24):168-172. DOI: 10.1016/j.ifacol.2015.12.077

[5] Organización Internacional de Normalización and Comisión Electrotécnica Internacional. General Requirements for the Competence of Testing and Calibration Laboratories (ISO 17025). 2017. Available from: https://www.iso.org/obp/ui/#iso:std:iso-iec:17025:ed-3:v1:en

[6] Martínez López A, Sáchica Avellaneda M, Vargas Sáenz NV. Guía para la calibración de multimetros digitales 4 5/6 (50 000 cuentas). Instituto Nacional de Metrología, according to the current published document 2022. p. 2. Available from: https://inm.gov.co/web/wp-content/uploads/2022/11/1_2022_Guia-para-la-Calibracion-de-MULTIMETROS-DIGITALES-4-5_6-50-000-CUENTAS-min.pdf

[7] (BIPM/JCGM) Bureau International de Pois et Measure Joint Committee for Guides in Metrology. Evaluation of measurement data —Guide to the expression of uncertainty in measurement. International Organization for Standardization Geneva ISBN. 2008;**50**:134

[8] Hurtado Castaño J. Sistema Automático de toma de Datos en la Calibración de Multímetros Digitales a Través de Procesamiento Digital de Imágenes. Colombia: Universidad Nacional de Colombia; 2022

Chapter 6

Metrology and Digital Image Processing in Dentistry

Francisco Cuevas, Miriam Rocha Navarro, Manuel Garcia Salido and Manuel Rodríguez Villegas

Abstract

Metrological techniques using digital image processing techniques have been extended into different fields of science such as optics, meteorology, mineralogy, agriculture, and medicine, among others. In the field of medicine, particularly in dentistry, it is important to perform different dental measurements to support the biometric work of specialists using panoramic radiographic images. Due to the poor capturing of these radiographic images, several problems, such as poor contrast and quality, are generally present. As the detection of the dental area must be done using these images, this chapter presents an algorithm that will assist in bettering image quality and make the dental measurements needed. This is done by binarizing using the histogram statistics of the image for the determination of threshold in order to establish sections of the teeth and the detection of the intramaxillary section by fitting a nonlinear function. The proposed method is applied to panoramic digital radiographs of subjects with permanent dentition ($\geq$12 years and $<$30 years). The algorithm achieved an adjustment of 96% of the processed radiographs as a result from patients of the School of Dentistry of the Universidad de la Salle Bajío.

Keywords: medical imaging, segmentation, panoramic X-ray images, biometrics, digital image processing, dental X-ray segmentation, polynomial regression, image thresholding

1. Introduction

Medical specialists in dentistry often use image analysis, most commonly using radiographs, to assist in making diagnoses and as support for planning out major and minor surgeries for a patient's treatment [1–14]. For this task, dentists and other specialists have relied on computational algorithms of Digital Image Processing and Optical Metrology to carry out the recognition of benign and malignant structures in bone tissue, delimit organs, and determine biometric characteristics that can be used in forensic tasks [15–18]. Unfortunately, due to problems in capturing radiographic images, such as noise, quality of film, inadequate adjustments of X-ray equipment parameters, and inexperience of radiological technicians, it is possible that medical specialist may incur errors during diagnosis.

Every day, dental pathologies in patients continue to increase, while the number of dentists worldwide is increasingly inadequate for the number of patients who require treatment in such a way that the development of automatic techniques for biometrics and dental metrology using Digital Image Processing and Artificial Intelligence is becoming of great importance. These techniques that carry out dental measurements are very useful to specialists because they assist in making diagnoses quicker and the follow-up after treatment easier [19–38]. Some of the most common ailments are periodontal disease, cavities, bone loss, chronic periapical abscess, periapical granuloma, radicular cyst, and malignant or benign tumors. Several of these conditions are monitored through dental biometric analysis using different X-ray images taken from different perspectives. The different perspectives used most frequently by dentists are periapical, bitewing and panoramic, or orthopantomograms. The panoramic perspective shows all the patient's teeth in one image making it possible to perform different measurements. Within the biometric process that must be done, there is the automatic detection and division of the intradental region and jaw (denture), since it is the starting point for performing dental segmentation and the detection of diastemas (intradental spacing).

It is also important to mention that there are other types of biometric applications using panoramic dental images where these algorithms can be applied. One alternative is using these dental images to identify people instead of using traditional methods such as face, iris, or fingerprint recognition in a forensic setting. Most often than not, the traditional methods mentioned can be damaged in serious incidents such as car and air accidents to the point where they cannot be used for biometric identification, so analysis and recognition from dental images is an excellent alternative for these forensic cases [15–18, 23].

Several researchers have worked on the development of manual and semiautomatic methods to detect and segment the jaw using different digital image processing algorithmic techniques. Several of the proposed methods require manual marking [15], which generates a disadvantage. Jain et al. [16, 17] proposed a method that uses an integral projection process of the image and Bayes rule to carry out the segmentation of the jaws and later an integration method for diastema detection. In [18], Wanat improved the method of Jain et al. by using splines to divide the jaws. The Jain and Chen algorithm [16] has continued to be improved and semiautomatic methods have been proposed; Harandi et al. [19] show a method for the segmentation of the intramaxillary region (IMR) through the use of modified geodesic active contour and different morphological operations on the X-ray image but it has some drawbacks due to the use of a cropped manually and that it works only with periapical images, in addition to the fact that the active detection of contours is an iterative process that can take up to 200 iterations. In [20], Hasan uses information from the gradient vector flow for the automatic adjustment of snakes in the image and the k-means method to perform the segmentation process. This method has the drawback that it is necessary to set the number of classes and the thresholding conditions manually. On the other hand, in [21], Haghanifar uses evolutionary computation and the Sauvola binarization algorithm to perform mandibular segmentation and separation; the jaw was divided using two steps: the calculation of the midpoints of the intradental zone and the use of snakes, which is computationally expensive. Recently, artificial intelligence and metaheuristic techniques have been used to carry out segmentation. In [22], Kong et al. propose a method that uses deep learning to carry out the detection of the maxillary region through an encoder and decoder network (EED-Net). This method has the disadvantage that a marking and annotating process must be carried out by dental experts, which consumes the specialists' time and must be carried out manually, which complicates its application. Additionally, considerable time must be spent on training the EED-Net. On the other hand, in [23], an adjustment function is calculated with Particle Swarm Optimization as a metaheuristic process. This requires the manual selection of a series of points in the intramaxillary region, and a high-order polynomial is passed whose biggest problem is the oscillations it suffers due to this.

In this chapter, a method of segmentation using a polynomial function adjustment with coefficient estimation by the least squares approximation of the intramaxillary region (IMR) is proposed. The steps of the procedure are the following: (a) low-pass filter, (b) binarization using the gray-level frequency histogram, (c) calculation of centroids, (d) detection of the intramaxillary region (IMR), (e) detection of random points in the intramaxillary region, and (f) polynomial adjustment of parameters using least squares. The proposed method is applied to panoramic digital radiographs of subjects with permanent dentition ($\geq$ 12 years and $<$ 30 years). The following sections show the operation of each procedure of the proposed method, the experiments carried out, and the conclusions of the work.

2. Automatic intramaxillary region detection method

During the automatic biometric dental process, to give a diagnosis or treatment, it is essential to locate the intramaxillary region and detect the teeth of both jaws. To achieve this, an algorithm that performs the following steps is proposed: (a) smoothing by median filtering, (b) binarized with thresholding from the histogram, (c) detection of centroids, and (d) determination of the intramaxillary region. Each step of the proposed method is detailed below.

2.1 Image smoothed

Before starting with the IMR detection in the panoramic dental X-ray images, it is adequate to use spatial masks to perform spatial filtering processing. It is also possible to perform this same filtering but in the frequency domain by using the Fourier transform, although this is more laborious. In the case of panoramic dental X-ray images, it is prudent to carry out low-pass filtering that can reduce the noise effects related to high frequencies that are present in the Fourier domain because high-frequency components are related to the edges of objects, fine structures, and noise contained in images. Carrying out this process will result in an unfocused or blurred image due to the removal of this information by low-pass filtering. For these purposes, a Gaussian-type kernel or an averaging filter (statistical mean) can be used to remove high frequencies, but unfortunately in most cases they leave traces of noise and destroy important edges of the image. For this reason, for dental applications, it is preferred to work with the statistical method of the median since this method preserves the edges of the important dental pieces for segmentation tasks and dental biometry. In this method, the central pixel of the subimage mask around the (odd-sized) pixel is replaced by the statistical median instead of the value of the means or the application of the Gaussian spatial filter.

For IMR detection, it must be segmented into bright and dark regions. Given the *a priori* information of the images obtained from an X-ray process, the brightest regions of the image will be related to both compact and spongy bone tissue; on the other hand, the dark information is related to the other regions of the image among which is the IMR region of interest. It is important to eliminate high-frequency structures prior to the binarization process in order to improve its performance and avoid undesirable structures generated by spongy and compact bone tissue and additive noise contained in the image that prevent good IMR segmentation. To avoid this, a low-pass filter is applied beforehand using the statistical median of a neighborhood of pixels of size 11×11. Using the set of values of the established neighborhood, we obtain the element that leaves half of the smaller elements below it and the other half above it, in such a way that the high-frequency elements in the region remain on the shores. This filter is applied because it better maintains the contours of the regions when binarizing, including the IMR zone of interest.

2.2 Thresholding

After having applied the filter to eliminate high frequencies of the X-ray image that interfere in the detection of the regions, the next step is to carry out the binarization process by thresholding to start the segmentation of dark regions where the IMR region is located. It is important and very common to use a thresholding method to be able to carry out a process of segmentation and partitioning of the image in binary form from the gray intensity levels of the image in this dental panoramic X-ray case. For this case, the global information of the X-ray image is used depending on the value of the pixel. The intent of these methods is to allow starting from the pixel value $I(x,y)$ at the spatial position of the digital dental panoramic X-ray image (x,y), where each l-bit pixel can contain values in the range of $G \varepsilon [0,2^l\text{-}1]$ representing the gray levels of the image. The idea of thresholding procedures is to map each pixel from an original value $I: M \times N \rightarrow G$ to a function of only two possible values B: $M \times N \rightarrow \{0,2^l\text{-}1\}$ from a threshold value T such that the thresholding image can be represented as

$$B(x,y) = \begin{cases} 0, \text{if } I(x,y) < T \\ 2^l - 1, \text{if } I(x,y) \geq T \end{cases}. \tag{1}$$

The intention is to find and design a robust criterion that can perform and be applied in a repeatable way the IMR segmentation to find an adequate threshold value T that can be used and ensure the detection of the region of interest depending on the value of each pixel in the original X-ray image $I(x,y)$. To carry out the segmentation for the initial detection of the IMR, the thresholding procedure is applied to the entire dental X-ray image with a single threshold value to generate the partition into dark and bright regions.

The IMR has the attributes of having a large area compared to the average of the regions in addition to having a centroid close to the center of the image because the dentist focuses the area of interest (teeth) in the capture process of the X-ray image. For this, we perform a binarization considering the *a priori* knowledge related to the fact that the concentration of bone tissue information is located in the bright section of the image and, therefore, recorded in the gray-level frequency histogram and that the remaining regions including the region of interest (IMR) are located in the region related to the frequency of dark gray levels.

Carrying out experimentation, a threshold was located that correctly segments the intradental region. To do this, we determine the probability distribution function of gray levels from the calculation of the histogram using the following expression:

$$p_i = \frac{h_i}{MN}, \tag{2}$$

where h_i is the frequency of occurrence of the gray level i, $M \times N$ is the resolution of the radiographic image, and p_i represents the probability of occurrence of the gray level; then, we determine the cumulative probability function using the following expression:

$$P_k = \sum_{i=0}^{k} p_i. \tag{3}$$

The optimal threshold detected by experimentation to determine the threshold T in the range of $[0{,}255]$, where the IMR is adequately separated, is when the cumulative probability function reaches 0.3, that is, the histogram represents 30% of the total resolution of the image; this can be expressed as

$$\begin{aligned} &T\epsilon \operatorname{ArgMin}\left(\sum_{i=0}^{T} p_i > 0.3\right) \\ &T\epsilon G\forall G = 0, 1, 2, \ldots, 255. \end{aligned} \tag{4}$$

From this threshold, the binarization of the image is carried out, from which several regions of different sizes related to the dark and bright information of the image are obtained. In the case of the IMR region of interest, it has the attribute of having an area with a larger dimension than the average of the other regions. To carry out the identification of this region, we eliminate the regions with a smaller area than the average of the total dark regions in order to speed up the detection process.

2.3 Calculation of centroids and IMR detection

After the binarized segmentation process of the dental X-ray images, it is important to determine some properties that can characterize them in order to discern the IMR region of interest in relation to the other partitions related to the dark regions of the X-ray image. One of the properties of the regions that are useful to carry out the IMR detection is undoubtedly the geometric information of the image and particularly its location of the centroids of the region. For this, it is necessary to calculate the areas of each region in the dark sections of the X-ray dental image and add the coordinates of these regions in rows and columns (x,y) so as to average the location of the pixels in the k region $R_k(x,y)$. From these images, the centroids $(\bar{X}_k, \bar{Y}_k)$ of each region k $(R_k(.))$ with area A_k are determined by calculating the following mathematical expressions:

$$\bar{X}_k = \frac{\sum_{x=0}^{M}\sum_{y=0}^{N} x R_k(x,y)}{A_k}, \bar{Y}_k = \frac{\sum_{x=0}^{M}\sum_{y=0}^{N} y R_k(x,y)}{A_k}. \tag{5}$$

Due to the fact that, when performing the capture, the dental specialist centers the patient's teeth on the X-ray plate, we can determine the IMR region from that region whose centroid is closest to the center of the image in such a way that the IMR region will be the region k with the minimum indicated distance, that is,

$$k = \min_k \left(\sqrt{\left(\bar{X}_k - \frac{M}{2}\right)^2 + \left(\bar{Y}_k - \frac{M}{2}\right)^2} \right). \tag{6}$$

2.4 Polynomial fit to the intramaxillary region

Once the IMR intramaxillary region has been determined using the procedure outlined in the last process, the next step in the procedure consists of fitting a polynomial function expressed by

$$P_m(x) = a_o x^0 + a_1 x^1 + a_2 x^2 + \cdots + a_m x^m, \tag{7}$$

that fits the patient's teeth from this region by fitting a smooth curve that minimizes the squared error Q of a sample of points from this region given by

$$Q = \sum_i^P \left[P_m(x_i) - y_i\right]^2. \tag{8}$$

For this, at least a sample of 2% of the points of the IMR region is used, that is, the number of points P will be greater than 0.2 of $M \times N$. Then, the following system of equations is solved to minimize the quadratic error related to the points of the region and the fit polynomial

$$\begin{bmatrix} n+1 & \sum x_i & \sum x_i^2 & \cdots & \sum x_i^m \\ \sum x_i & \sum x_i^2 & \sum x_i^3 & \cdots & \sum x_i^{m+1} \\ \vdots & \vdots & \vdots & \vdots & \vdots \\ \sum x_i^m & \sum x_i^{m+1} & \sum x_i^{m+2} & \cdots & \sum x_i^{2m} \end{bmatrix} \begin{bmatrix} a_0 \\ a_1 \\ \vdots \\ a_m \end{bmatrix} = \begin{bmatrix} \sum y_i \\ \sum x_i y_i \\ \vdots \\ \sum x_i^m y_i \end{bmatrix}, \tag{9}$$

where (x_i, y_i) represent the sampled points of the IMR region and the vector $\mathbf{a} = (a_0, a_1, a_2, \dots, a_m)$ represents the coefficients of the fitted polynomial. A complete flowchart of the IMR region polynomial detection and fitting process is shown in **Figure 1**.

3. Experiments

This section shows examples of the segmentation process carried out on images of patients from the School of dentistry, Universidad La Salle, León, Mexico. The equipment with which the images were captured is Morita Veraview X800 X-ray equipment. The captured panoramic dental X-ray images have a resolution of 1935 × 1024 pixels. **Figure 2(a)** shows the panoramic image obtained by the X-ray equipment. To evaluate the performance of the method, the established process was carried out on 50 panoramic radiographic images of patients with age range between 12 and 30 years from the School of Dentistry, Universidad de La Salle Bajío, León, Guanajuato, Mexico, with the following inclusion and exclusion criteria:

DOI: http://dx.doi.org/10.5772/intechopen.108375

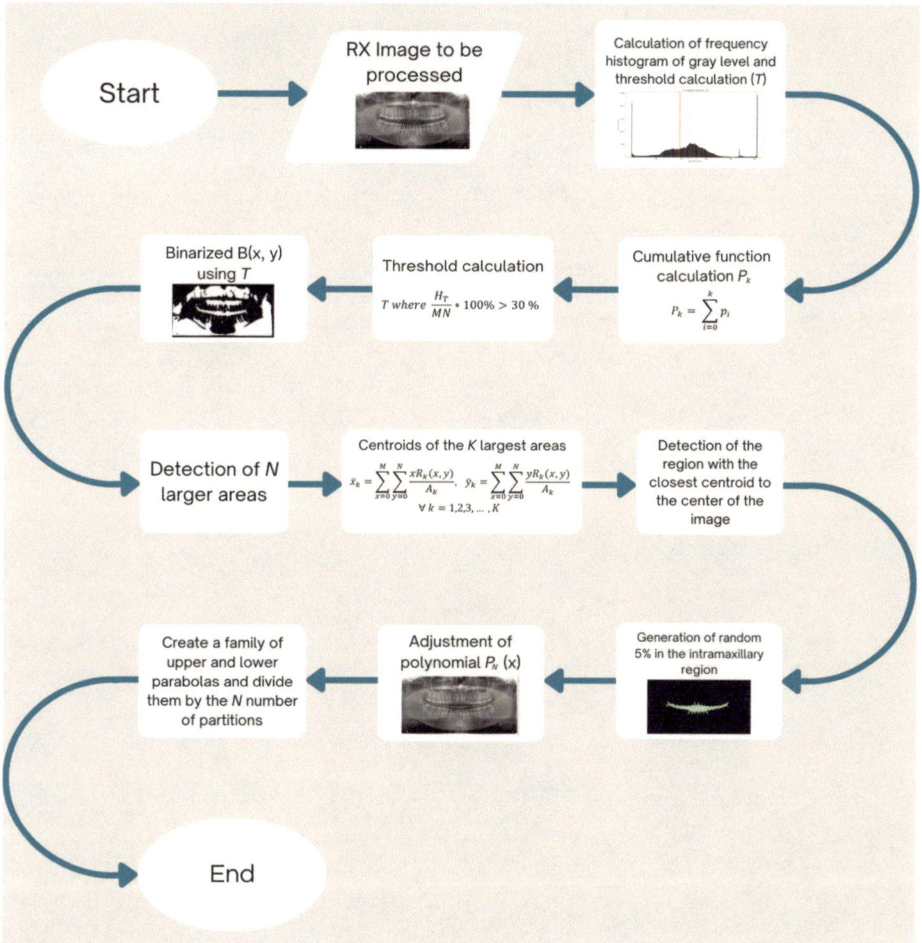

Figure 1.
Flowchart of the IMR denture and jaw segmentation process.

a. *Inclusion Criteria*

- Panoramic digital radiographs of subjects with permanent dentition (≥ 12 years and < 30 years).
- Subjects of both genres.

b. *Exclusion criteria*

- Panoramic digital radiographs of subjects with teeth showing evidence of incisal or occlusal edge with restorative intervention, traumatic injury, or occlusal wear from bruxism.
- Radiographs showing mixed dentition or edentulism.

The first step in the procedure consists of filtering out high-frequency structures such as mandibular spongy and compact tissue and capture noise using a kernel that

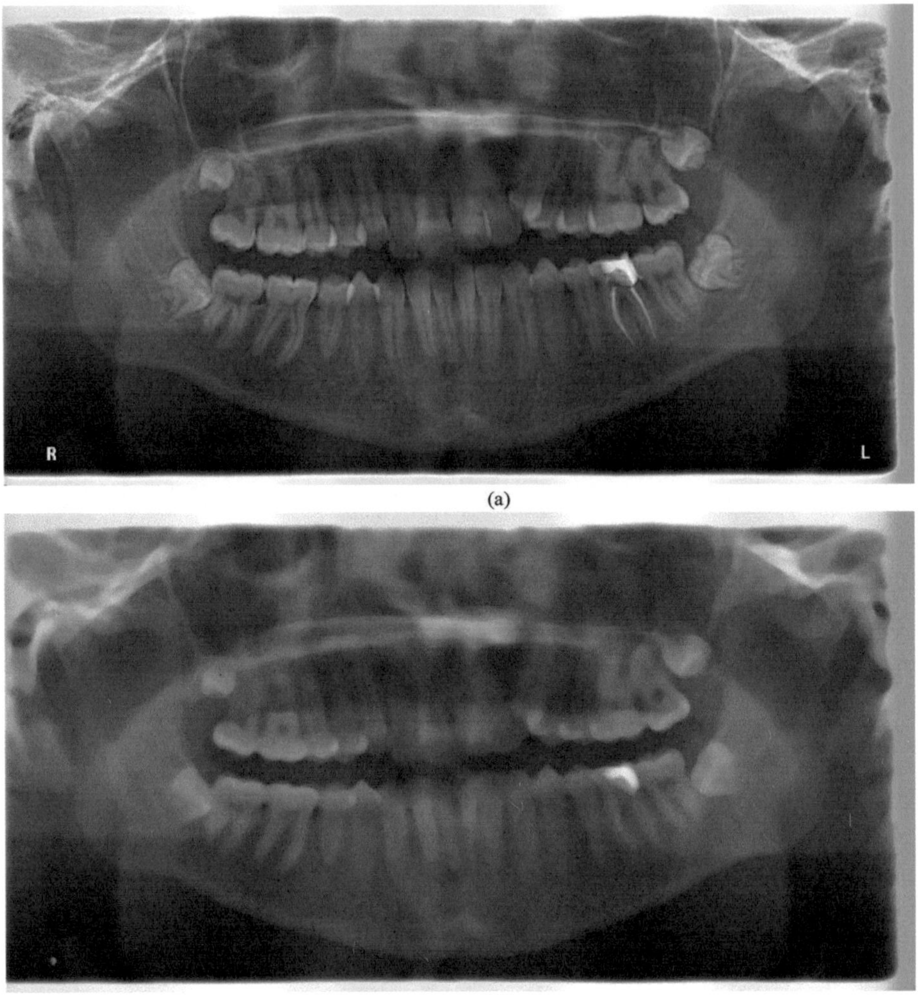

(a)

(b)

Figure 2.
(a) Original image. (b) Smoothed image using median filter size 11×11 where high-frequency structures (spongy and compact bone tissue) are removed.

calculates the median of a window of size 11×11, the result of which is shown in **Figure 2(b)**.

After applying the low-pass filter (median), we calculated the gray-level frequency histogram of the panoramic dental image. From the generation of the histogram, we determine the probability distribution function using Eq. (2) and determine the value of the threshold T when the cumulative probability function reaches or exceeds 0.3. The histogram of the image of **Figure 1** and the detected threshold value (red line) is shown in **Figure 3**, and the binarized image with the threshold value T is shown in **Figure 4**.

The next step is to extract the centroids of the K largest regions and determine which of them is located closest to the center of the image, which is related to the IMR region of interest. **Figure 5** shows the largest areas from **Figure 4**, and **Figure 6** shows the related centroids. Finally, **Figure 7** shows the selected IMR region. Once the IMR region has been determined, the next step in the procedure necessary to carry out the

DOI: http://dx.doi.org/10.5772/intechopen.108375

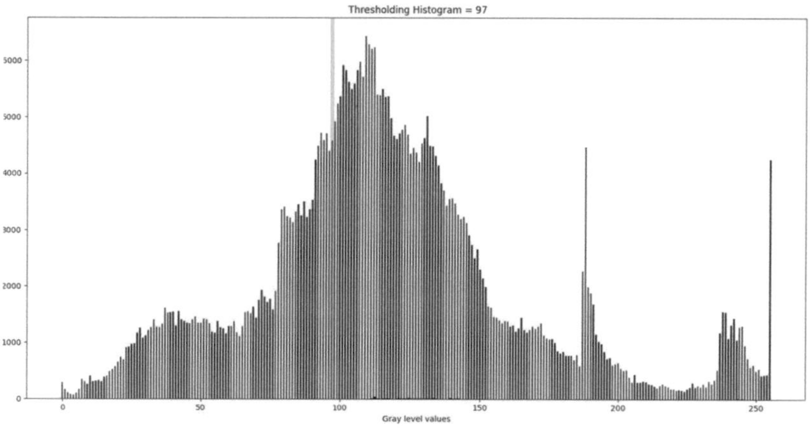

Figure 3.
*Histogram with the frequency of occurrence of the gray levels of the image in **Figure 1**.*

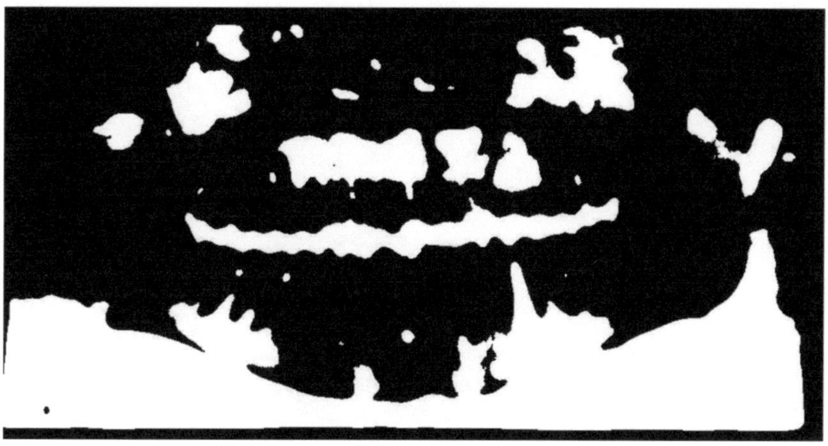

Figure 4.
Binarized image using a threshold of 30% from the cumulative function of the histogram of gray levels.

Figure 5.
*Selection of the regions with the largest area from the binarized image in **Figure 4**.*

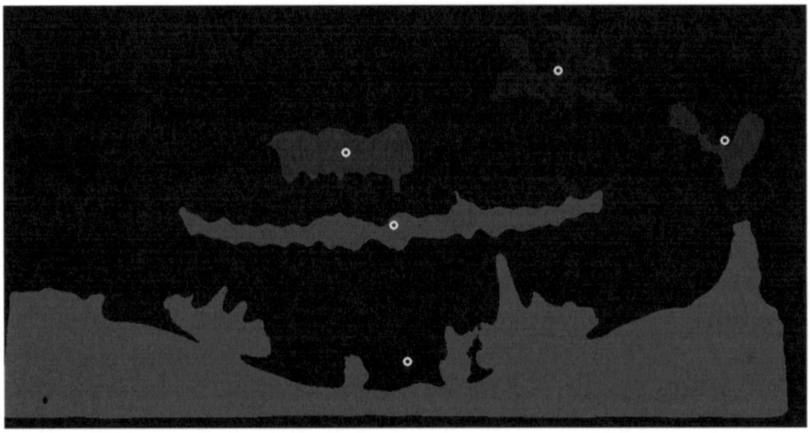

Figure 6.
Centroids of the dark regions of the original image.

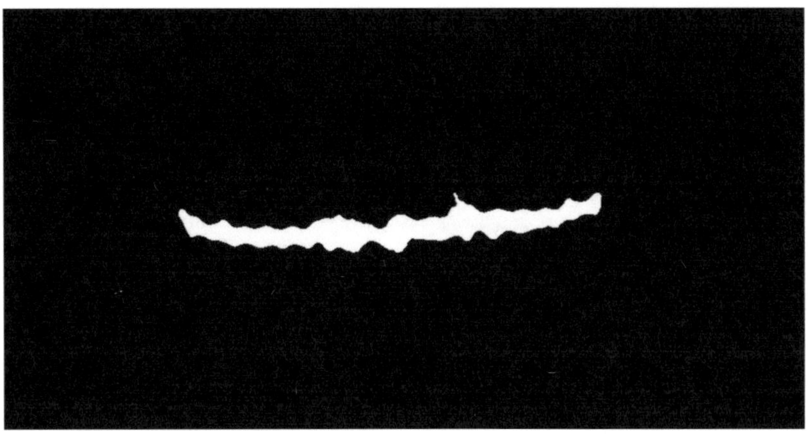

Figure 7.
Detection of the IMR region with centroid closest to the center of the image.

intramaxillary partition is to fit a polynomial (order 2) that smoothly divides the IMR. This is useful to carry out a subsequent process of dental biometric analysis. The fit is carried out by taking a sample of IMR points (2% of the points) and applying the optimization process to them to calculate the polynomial coefficients by estimating and reducing the mean square error by least squares. **Figure 8** shows the selected points and the fit of the curve (quadratic polynomial) that minimizes the error. **Figures 9** and **10** show the detection of the denture in both the lower and upper jaws on the original image. **Figure 11** shows eight additional results with images of different patients by using of the proposed method.

The efficiency of the method was calculated based on the total number of regions IMR divided correctly according to the established manual marking and qualified by dental specialists and the one that did not meet the established segmentation requirements. Then, the efficiency eq. E used for the proposed segmentation process was

$$E = \frac{C}{N} * 100\% \tag{10}$$

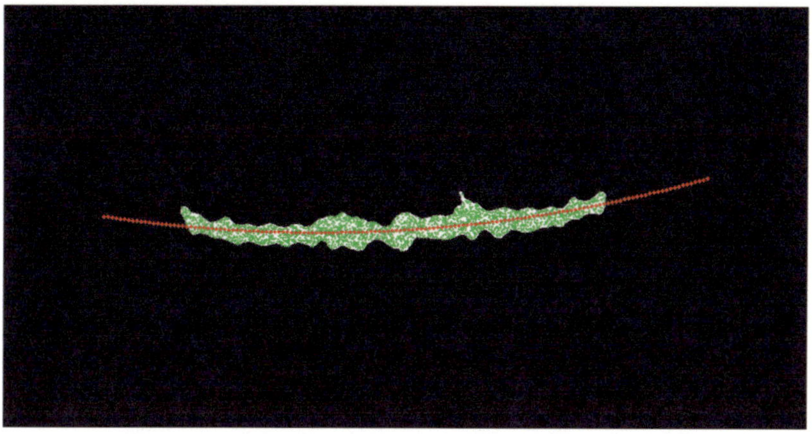

Figure 8.
Parabolic adjustment by point sampling in the binarized IMR region.

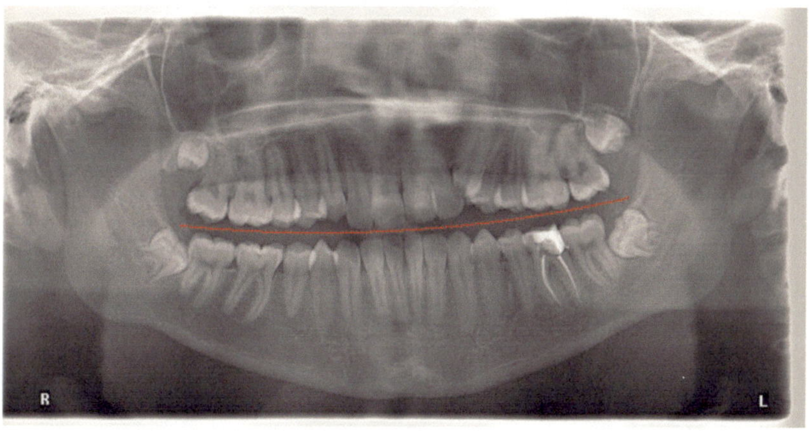

Figure 9.
Original image with a parabolic polynomial adjusted for division of the IMR section.

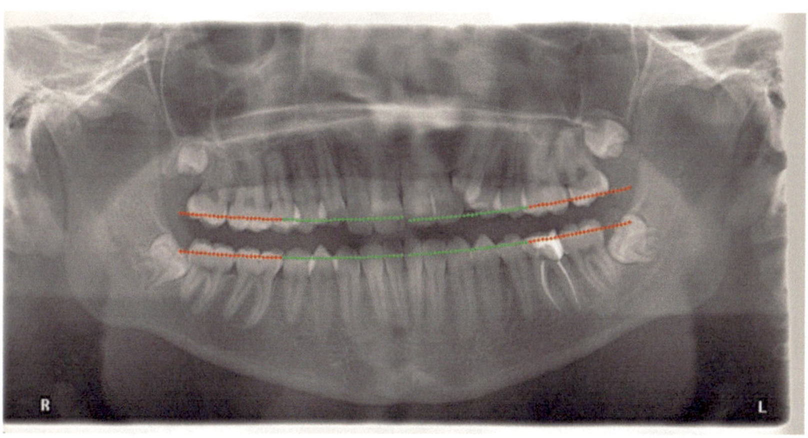

Figure 10.
Detection of the jaw in the lower and upper jaws.

where C is the number of X-ray panoramic dental images well segmented according to dental specialists and N is the total number of processed X-ray panoramic dental images. Using the previous equation, the efficiency of the method to detect the mandible and IMR was calculated, which turned out to be 96%.

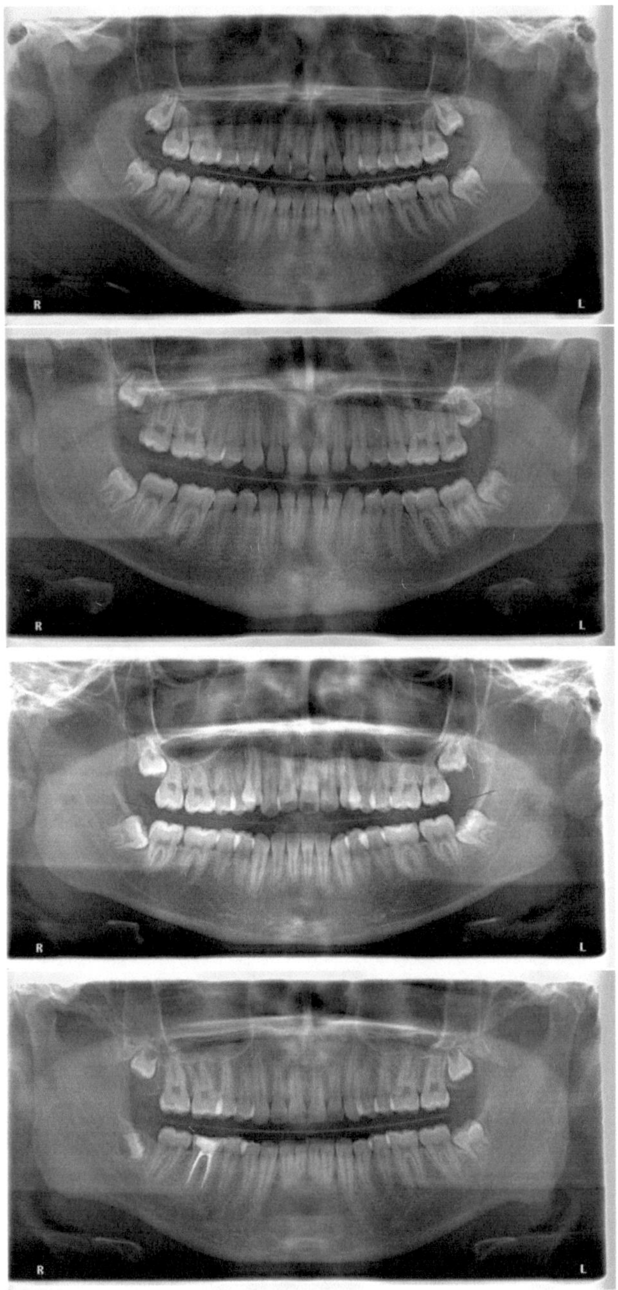

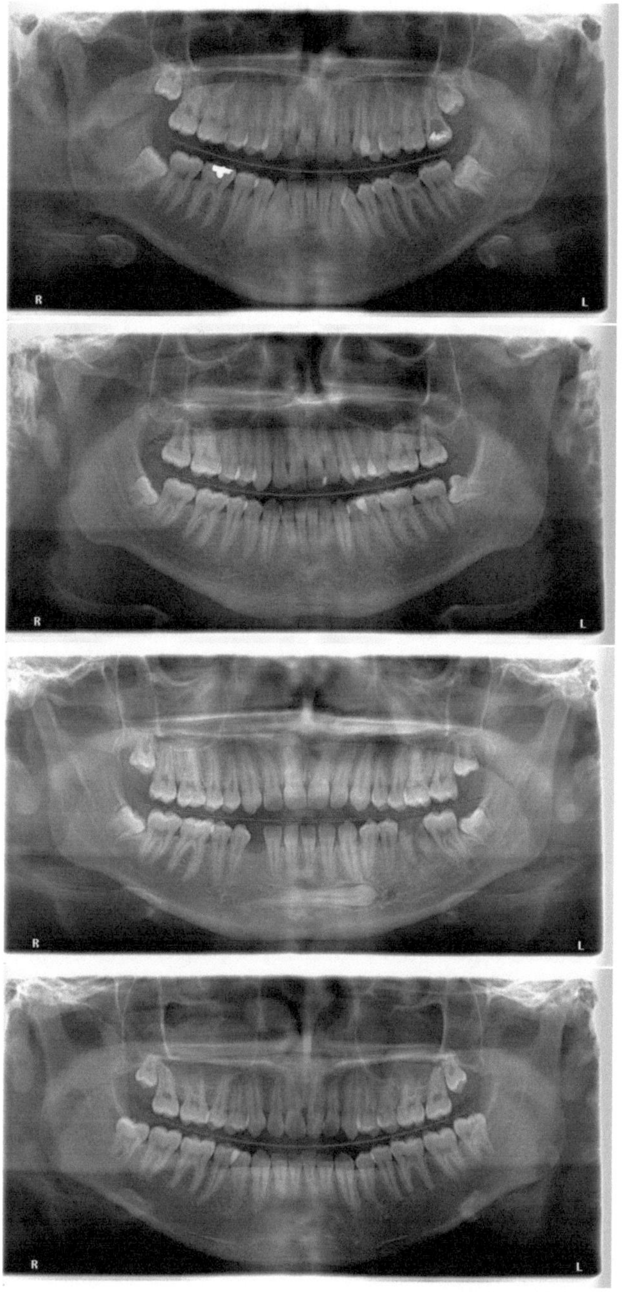

Figure 11.
Results using the proposed method applied to X-ray images from database with a curve fitting.

4. Conclusion

It is shown that it is possible to use the proposed method to carry out the division and recognition of the intramaxillary region automatically from panoramic X-ray images without requiring the assistance of a dental specialist. Among the improvements proposed in this chapter is the establishment of a thresholding method that adapts to the gray-level statistics of the dental X-ray image of the patient in order to determine the area of interest to be detected (IMR). The established method calculates the density and cumulative probability functions to determine the region of bone tissue and absent regions of this tissue where the IMR is located. Likewise, a function is proposed that minimizes the distance from the centroids of the dark regions related to the intramaxillary space, eliminating the bright regions related to the spongy and compact bone tissue for IMR detection. Then, a random sample of points from the IMR region is used to fit a quadratic polynomial that fits this region and the teeth. This procedure is carried out without requiring the assistance of a dental specialist. This detection method is useful for biometric measurements of teeth. The method was tested with 50 images and had an efficiency greater than 96%. Future work includes diastema detection and automatic segmentation of teeth for diagnostic and biometric tasks to monitor treatment and forensic applications, as well as a biometric dental support application for the daily work of dentists.

Acknowledgements

The authors wish to thank the Government of the state of Guanajuato in Mexico for supporting this research work under the fund IDEAGTO/CONV/079/2021-Ciencia Productiva- I + D Sociales y Humanidades en Sectores Estrategicos. The authors would like to thank the following people for their support: Martha Eugenia Fajardo Araujo, Juan Manuel Lopez, Fatima Hernandez Alvarez, Kenya Garcia Garcia, Hector Eduardo Gomez Perez, Alessio Sanchez Blasutti, and Karina Guerrero Abrgo who were a fundamental part of the development of the work. The authors also thank the following institutions whose facilities and financial support were important in the development of the research: Centro de Investigaciones en Óptica, A.C, Universidad de la Salle Bajio and Instituto Tecnologico y de Estudios Superiores de Monterrey, CONACYT, and Universidad de Guanajuato.

DOI: http://dx.doi.org/10.5772/intechopen.108375

Author details

Francisco Cuevas[1*], Miriam Rocha Navarro[2], Manuel Garcia Salido[3] and Manuel Rodríguez Villegas[4]

1 Centro de Investigaciones en Óptica, A.C, México

2 Faculty of Dentistry, Universidad de la Salle Bajio, A.C, México

3 UNITEC Campus Leon, México

4 Universidad De La Salle Bajío, A.C, México

*Address all correspondence to: miriamrocha@yahoo.com

References

[1] Iannucci JM, Howerton LJ. Dental Radiography: Principles and Techniques. 5th ed. St. Louis, MO: Elsevier/Saunders; 2017

[2] Whaites E, Drage N. Essentials of Dental Radiography and Radiology. 5th ed. Edinburgh: Elsevier; 2013

[3] Gonzalez RC, Woods RE. Digital Image Processing. 4th ed. Upper Saddle River, NJ: Pearson; 2017

[4] Sonka M, Fitzpatrick JM, editors. Handbook of Medical Imaging. Medical Image Processing and Analysis. Vol.2. Bellingham: SPIE Press; 2000. DOI: 10.1117/3.831079

[5] Risnes S, Segura JJ, Casado A, Jiménez-Rubio A. Enamel pearls and cervical enamel projections on 2 maxillary molars with localized periodontal disease: Case report and histologic study. Oral Surgery, Oral Medicine, Oral Pathology, Oral Radiology, and Endodontology. 2000; **89**(4):493-497. DOI: 10.1016/s1079-2104(00)70131-4

[6] Hellén-Halme K, Nilsson M, Petersson A. Digital radiography in general dental practice: A field study. Dentomaxillofacial Radiol. 2007;**36**(5): 249-255. DOI: 10.1259/dmfr/95125494

[7] Ennes J, Lara V. Comparative morphological analysis of the root developmental groove with the palato-gingival groove. Oral Diseases. 2004; **10**(6):378-382. DOI: 10.1111/j.1601-0825.2004.01009.x

[8] Anjna E, Kaur ER. Review of image segmentation technique. International Journal of Advanced Research in Computer Science. 2017;**8**(4):36-39. DOI: 10.26483/IJARCS.V8I4.3691

[9] Bansal GJ. Digital radiography. A comparison with modern conventional imaging. Postgraduate Medical Journal. 2006;**82**(969):425-428. DOI: 10.1136/pgmj.2005.038448

[10] Fujita M, Kodera Y, Ogawa M, Wada T, Doi K. Digital image processing of periapical radiographs. Oral Surgery, Oral Medicine, and Oral Pathology. 1988;**65**(4):490-494. DOI: 10.1016/0030-4220(88)90365-9

[11] Gormez O, Yilmaz HH. Image post-processing in dental practice. European Journal of Dentistry. 2009;**3**(4):343-347

[12] Goldstein AR. Enamel pearls as contributing factor in periodontal breakdown. The Journal of the American Dental Association. 1979;**99**(2):210-211. DOI: 10.14219/jada.archive.1979.0258

[13] Said E, Fahmy GF, Nassar D, Ammar H. Dental X-ray image segmentation. Biometric Technology for Human Identification. 2004;**25**:409-417. DOI: 10.1117/12.541658

[14] Stolojescu-Crisan C, Holban S. A comparison of X-ray image segmentation techniques. Advances in Electrical and Computer Engineering. 2013;**13**(3):85-92. DOI: 10.4316/aece.2013.03014

[15] Omanovic M, Orchard JJ. Image registration-based approach to ranking dental x-ray images for human forensic identification. Canadian Society of Forensic Science Journal. 2008;**41**(3): 125-134. DOI: 10.1080/00085030.2008.10757170

[16] Jain AK, Chen H, Minut S. Dental biometrics: Human identification using dental radiographs. In: Lecture Notes in

Computer Science. Berlin Heidelberg: Springer-Verlag; 2003. pp. 429-437. DOI: 10.1007/3-540-44887-x_51

[17] Jain AK, Chen H. Matching of dental X-ray images for human identification. Pattern Recognition. 2004;**37**(7): 1519-1532. DOI: 10.1016/j.patcog.2003.12.016

[18] Wanat R. A problem of automatic segmentation of digital dental panoramic x-ray images for forensic human identification. In: Proceedings of CESCG: The 15th Central European Seminar on Computer Graphics. Slovakia: Vinicné; 2011

[19] Harandi AA, Pourghassem H, Mahmoodian H. Upper and lower jaw segmentation in dental X-ray image using modified active contour. In: 2011 international conference on intelligent computation and biomedical instrumentation. Wuhan, Hubei, China: IEEE; 2011

[20] Hasan MM, et al. Automatic segmentation of jaw from panoramic dental X-ray images using GVF snakes. In: 2016 World Automation Congress (WAC). Rio Grande, Puerto Rico: IEEE; 2016. DOI: 10.1109/wac.2016.7583022

[21] Haghanifar A, Majdabadi MM, Ko SB. Automated teeth extraction from dental panoramic x-ray images using genetic algorithm. In: 2020 IEEE International Symposium on Circuits and Systems (ISCAS). Sevilla, Spain: IEEE; 2020. DOI: 10.1109/iscas45731.2020.9180937

[22] Kong Z, Xiong F, Zhang C, et al. Automated maxillofacial segmentation in panoramic dental x-ray images using an efficient encoder-decoder network. IEEE Access. 2020;**8**:207822-207833. DOI: 10.1109/access.2020.3037677

[23] Bozkurt MH, Karagol S. Jaw and teeth segmentation on the panoramic x-ray images for dental human identification. Journal of Digital Imaging. 2020;**33**(6):1410-1427. DOI: 10.1007/s10278-020-00380-8

[24] Sezgin M, Sankur B. Survey over image thresholding techniques and quantitative performance evaluation. Journal of Electronic Imaging. 2004; **13**(1):146. DOI: 10.1117/1.1631315

[25] Gayathri V, Menon HP. Challenges in edge extraction of dental x-ray images using image processing algorithms – A review. International Journal of Computer Science and Information Technologies. 2014;**5**(4):5355-5357

[26] Amer YY, Aqel MJ. An efficient segmentation algorithm for panoramic dental images. Procedia Computer Science. 2015;**65**:718-725. DOI: 10.1016/j.procs.2015.09.016

[27] Pham DL, Xu C, Prince JL. Current methods in medical image segmentation. Annual Review of Biomedical Engineering. 2000;**2**(1):315-337. DOI: 10.1146/annurev.bioeng.2.1.315

[28] Liao P, Fan Y, Nathanson D. Evaluation of maxillary anterior teeth width: A systematic review. The Journal of Prosthetic Dentistry. 2019;**122**(3):275-281.e7. DOI: 10.1016/j.prosdent.2018.10.015

[29] McGowan S. Characteristics of teeth: A review of size, shape, composition, and appearance of maxillary anterior teeth. Compendium of Continuing Education in Dentistry. 2016;**37**(3):164-quiz172

[30] Tsukiyama T, Marcushamer E, Griffin TJ, Arguello E, Magne P, Gallucci GO. Comparison of the anatomic crown width/length ratios of unworn and worn maxillary teeth in

Asian and white subjects. The Journal of Prosthetic Dentistry. 2012;**107**(1):11-16. DOI: 10.1016/S0022-3913(12)60009-2

[31] Orozco-Varo A, Arroyo-Cruz G, Martínez-de-Fuentes R, Jiménez-Castellanos E. Biometric analysis of the clinical crown and the width/length ratio in the maxillary anterior region. The Journal of Prosthetic Dentistry. 2015; **113**(6):565-70.e2. DOI: 10.1016/j.prosdent.2014.11.006

[32] Al-Khatib AR, Rajion ZA, Masudi SM, Hassan R, Anderson PJ, Townsend GC. Tooth size and dental arch dimensions: A stereophotogrammetric study in southeast Asian Malays. Orthodontics & Craniofacial Research. 2011;**14**(4):243-253. DOI: 10.1111/j.1601-6343.2011.01529.x

[33] Fernandes TM, Sathler R, Natalício GL, Henriques JF, Pinzan A. Comparison of mesiodistal tooth widths in Caucasian, African and Japanese individuals with Brazilian ancestry and normal occlusion. Dental Press Journal of Orthodontics. 2013;**18**(3):130-135. DOI: 10.1590/s2176-94512013000300021

[34] Reynoso Rodríguez JL. Segmentation of molars in noisy pantomograms using digital image processing techniques. In: Master in Optomechatronics [thesis]. León, Mexico: Centro de Investigaciones en Óptica; 2017

[35] Garcia-Alcala LM. Segmentation of X-Ray Dental Panoramic Images by Using of Digital Image Processing, Computer Sciences Engineering [Bachelor Thesis]. León, México: Instituto Tecnológico de Zamora; 2020

[36] Gomez HE. Algortihm for the Automatic Segmentation of Panoramic Dental X-Ray Images by Using of Techniques of Digital Image Processing and Artificial Intelligence, Technical Report on Professional Residence of Computer Science Engineering at CIO. León, México: Instituto Tecnológico de Leon; 2021

[37] Hutter F, Kotthoff L, Vanschoren J. Automated Machine Learning: Methods, Systems, Challenges. 1st ed. Cham, Switzerland: Springer International Publishing; 2019

[38] Engelbrecht AP. Computational intelligence: an introduction. The Atrium, Southern Gate, Chichester, West Sussex, England: John Wiley & Sons Ltd; 2007

Section 2

Image Perception and Analysis

Chapter 7

Latest Advancements in Perception Algorithms for ADAS and AV Systems Using Infrared Images and Deep Learning

Suganthi Srinivasan, Rakesh Rajegowda and Eshwar Udhayakumar

Abstract

Perception system plays an important role in Advanced driver assistance systems (ADAS) & Autonomous vehicles (AV) to understand the surrounding environment and further navigation. It is highly challenging to achieve the accurate perception of ego vehicle mimicking human vision. The available ADAS and AV solutions could able to perceive the environment to some extent using multiple sensors like Lidars, Radars and Cameras. National Highway Traffic Safety Administration Crash reports of ADAS and AV systems shows that the complete autonomy is challenging to achieve using the existing sensor suite. Particularly, in extreme weather, low light and night scenarios, there is a need for additional perception sensors. Infrared camera seems to be one of the potential sensors to address such extreme and corner cases. This chapter aimed to discuss the advantage of adding infrared sensors to perceive the environment accurately. The advancements in deep learning approaches further leverages to enhance ADAS features. Also, the limitations of current sensors, the need for infrared sensors and technology, artificial intelligence and current research focus using IR images are discussed in detail. Literature shows that by adding IR sensor to existing sensor suite may lead a way to achieve level 3 and above autonomous driving precisely.

Keywords: perception, ADAS, autonomous vehicle, visible image, infrared image, automotive sensors, deep learning, object detection

1. Introduction

Recent development in sensor technology, processors and computer vision algorithms used for processing the captured data lead to rapid development of perception solutions for Advanced driver assistance systems (ADAS) and autonomous vehicles (AV). The drive for autonomous vehicles was triggered due to the DARPA grand challenge. The US Armed Forces and Defense Advanced Research Projects Agency (DARPA) conducted a Robotic challenge towards the development of unmanned autonomous systems which could eventually replace human drivers in

IntechOpen

combat zones and hazardous areas without remote operators. Many DARPA Grand Challenges were organized in order to come up with the technology for fully autonomous ground vehicles with collaboration across diverse fields. The first challenge took place in 2004 when 15 self-driving vehicles were competing to navigate around 228 km across the desert in Primm, Nevada. None of the team was able to succeed due to the technological hurdles involved. The second event was held in 2005 in southern Nevada were 5 teams competed to navigate 212 km. With limited and better technology, this time, Stanford University's Stanley managed to complete the distance and won the prize money. In 2007, third event took place in an urban environment commonly known as DARPA Urban Challenge. Here, the team need to showcase the autonomous driving capability in the driving traffic scenarios and needs to perform complete maneuvering that includes braking and parking events. The boss vehicle from Carnegie Mellon University won the first prize and the Junior vehicle from Standford University claimed the second prize [1]. Since after DARPA, the grand challenges for autonomous driving solutions, the accurate perception and navigation of the vehicle more autonomously became one of the hottest fields for research and industry. There are 6 levels of Society of Automotive Engineers (SAE) international standards to achieve fully autonomous driving from ADAS as shown in **Figure 1**. Upto level 3, the presence of driver is mandatory to take control of the vehicle whenever needed. Levels 4 and 5 allow for fully autonomous driving with and without driver, respectively [3].

Worldwide, major accidents were reported due to human error which might have resulted in fatal incidents. Considering the safety of the drivers and passengers, ADAS systems have indeed been targeted by top manufactures to support the drivers during unpredicted circumstances. The most common ADAS systems that are available include lane departure warning, forward collision warning, high beam safety system, traffic signals recognition, adaptive cruise control and so on. ADAS systems are semi-autonomous driving concepts that assist drivers during driving. The objective is to automate, adapt, and enhance safety by reducing human errors. The fully autonomous vehicle is capable of sensing the environment and navigating without human intervention under all environment circumstances. Here, the vehicle is capable of perceiving the environment, thinking and reasoning to take a decision and control the vehicle autonomously similar to a human driver [4]. The major

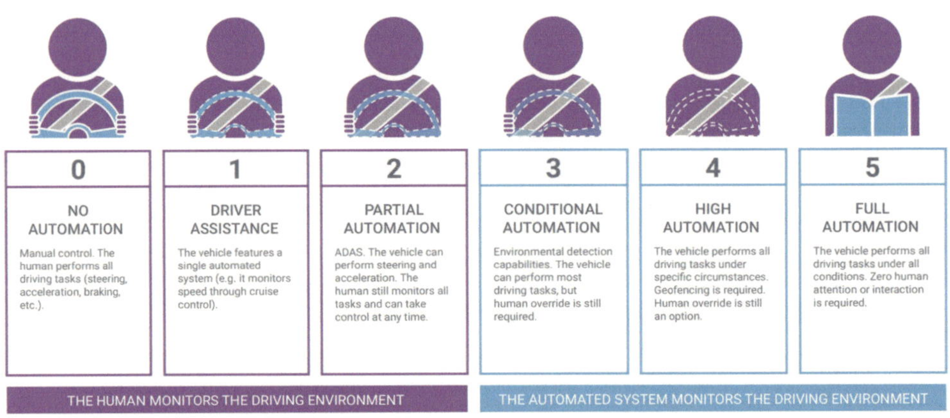

Figure 1.
Levels of automation according to SAE standards [2].

components of autonomous vehicles include sensing, perception, decision making such as path and motion planning and actuating by generating controls for steering and braking.

Like human driver, ADAS and AV systems aim to perceive the environment using various sensors which help them to navigate autonomously. Passive sensors such as visible cameras and active sensors such as Lidars, Radars and ultrasonic are the most commonly preferred sensors to perceive the surrounding environment. Multiple sensors of different types are configured in such a way that the complete 360° surrounding environment can be perceived.

Figure 2 shows the state-of-the-art ADAS solution and sensors used to perceive and derive the information from environment. This article focuses mainly on the accurate perception of environment using various sensors. It includes vision, lidar, radar and ultrasonic sensors. Vision sensors are used either as monocular and/or stereo cameras. They are mostly used for 2D/3D object & pedestrian detection, lane, parking slots, traffic signs and signal detection and recognition. Both 2D and 3D Laser scanners (Lidar) are precise in determining the object's position, orientation and object dimension. All moving and static objects that include buildings and surroundings along with road markings and kerbs can be detected using laser scanners. Automotive lidars are capable of scanning the environment both vertically and horizontally covering from certain field of view to 360° view. On the other hand, Radars generate the object position and relative velocity information more accurately for the detected objects. Each sensor exhibits its own advantages and disadvantages [3, 4]. For example, in adverse weather conditions, the performance of camera sensor may not be accurately compared to radar sensor to some extent. Similarly, camera sensor lacks in-depth estimation whereas, radars and lidars estimate depth more accurately. Individual sensors may not help to achieve level 2 and above ADAS solutions. Hence, to achieve the goal of level 3 and above autonomy, multiple sensor modalities in different configurations shall be beneficial [3–5]. The fusion of complementary and redundant information from various sensors helps to generate the complete perception of the ADAS and AV systems [4, 6]. In the automotive industry, many original equipment manufacturers (OEM)s and Tier-1 s are extensively concentrating on the research and development of successful autonomous driving concepts and Level 3 & above ADAS. Waymo, Uber, Tesla, Zoox etc., are a few OEMs into this autonomous vehicle research and development. Every autonomous vehicle is equipped with one or more automotive sensors that include cameras, lidars and radars in order to sense the environment as a perception system, supported by guidance and navigation systems. Manufacturers and operates of ADAS (Level 2 and above) and AV systems

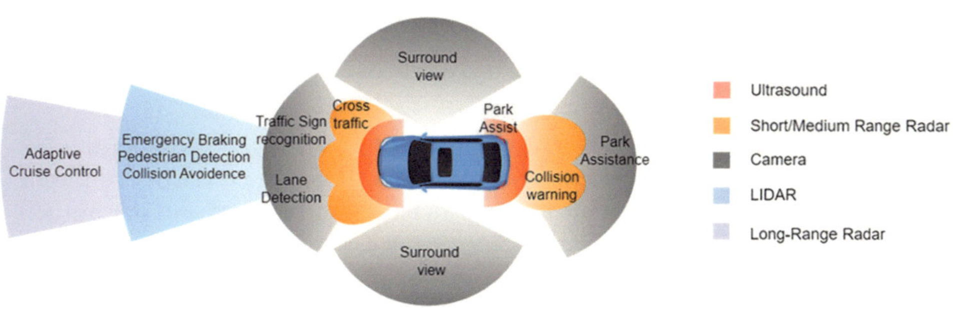

Figure 2.
State-of-the art-ADAS sensors.

need to report crashes to the US agency as per a general standing order issued by NAtional Highway Traffic Safety Administration (NHTSA) in 2021 [2]. An average of 14 accidents were reported since July 2021 with the maximum of 22 and minimum of 8 crashes reported in a month by AV (level 3 and above) equipped vehicles still in development. Similarly, an average of 44 crashes were reported since July 2021 with maximum of 62 and minimum of 26 crashes reported in a month by level 2 ADAS equipped vehicles. Autonomous vehicle collision reports shows that the on road experience of such to be claimed as matured ADAS & autonomous driving technology still needs improvement to match with human driver perception. Numerous incidents as major and minor crashes are reported by self-driving cars on the road for test drive. This shows that the existing sensor suite that are claimed to achieve level 4 autonomous driving are lacking with the performance especially during extreme weather conditions, dark/night scenarios, glare and so on. This demands for more robust sensors to achieve full autonomous driving irrespective of environment conditions.

The recent advancements in artificial intelligence (AI) have a significant impact on the fast development and deployment of level 3 and above ADAS and AV solutions. Especially, in order to generate precise information from surrounding environment, high data from different sensing modalities and advanced computing resources play a key role in enabling AI as an essential component for ADAS and AV perception system [7]. Extensive research and development activities are currently invested to analyze the effective use of AIs in various functionalities of AVs such as perception, planning and control, localization and mapping and decision making.

In this article, the limitations and challenges of the existing sensor suite, need for infrared camera, infrared technology, applications of AI in the development of perception systems and the need for multiple sensor fusion strategy are presented in detail. Also, some latest research in the field of infrared sensors and deep learning approaches for ADAS and AV systems are discussed in detail.

2. Perception sensors for ADAS and AV systems

In ADAS and AV systems, sensors are considered equivalent to eyes and ears of the human driver to sense and perceive the environment. Different aspects of the environment are sensed and monitored using various types of sensors and the information will be shared with the driver or Electronic control unit. This section introduces commonly used automotive sensors and their functionality in achieving level 2 and above ADAS and AV solutions. **Figure 3** shows the representative image of a vehicle equipped with perception sensors for one or more ADAS and AV solutions [9].

2.1 Vision sensors

RGB or visible cameras are most commonly used in any ADAS and AV systems due to their low cost and easy installation. Normally, more than one camera is used to capture/sense the complete environment. Images captured by vision sensors are processed by an embedded system to detect, analyze, understand and track various objects in the environment. Captured images are rich in information such as color, contrast, texture and details which are more unique features over other sensors. Visible cameras are used as a single lens camera called as monocular camera and two lens camera called as stereo setup. Monocular cameras are low-cost and require less

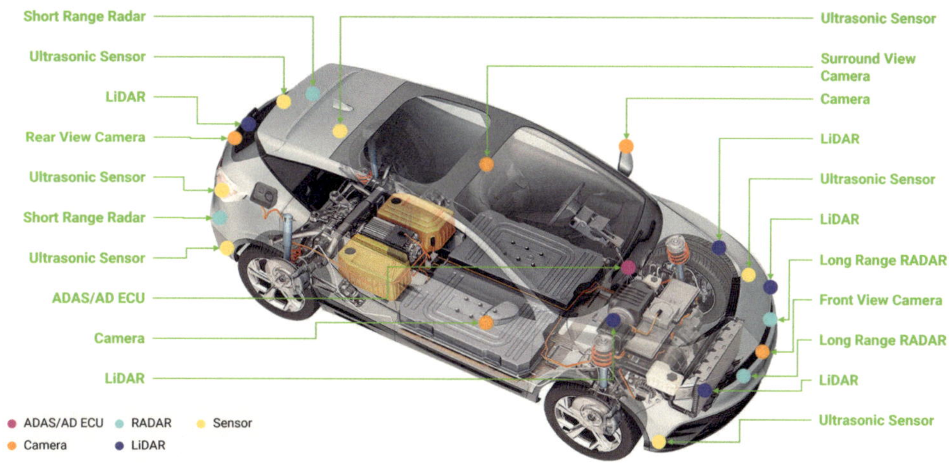

Figure 3.
Representative figure of AV/ADAS vehicle with various perception sensors. Figure from [8].

processing power. They are commonly used for object detection and classification, lanes and parking lines detection, traffic sign recognition etc., Monocular cameras lack distance/depth information compared to other active sensors. There are a few techniques used to estimate the distance information but not as accurate as expected by ADAS and AV systems for maneuvering autonomously. On the other hand, stereo cameras are useful in extracting depth or distance information as the system consists of two lenses separated by a distance resembling two eyes of the human. Such systems are highly beneficial to detect and classify the objects in the environment along with depth/distance information with better accuracy compared to monocular cameras. When compared to the other automotive sensors, the depth estimation using stereo cameras is reliable up to 30 m over a short distance [10]. Autonomous vehicles demand accurate distance estimation at far distances, especially in high ways (**Figure 4**) [3, 10].

Figure 4.
Common adverse scenarios where current ADAS/AV sensor suite struggles to perform.

2.1.1 Lidar

LiDAR stands for Light Detection and Ranging. This is an active sensor that works by emitting a laser beam which gets reflected by any object. The time taken between the emitted laser beam and its reflection measures the distance of the object. These sensors are capable of generating high-resolution 3D point clouds and operate at longer ranges when compared to vision sensors. Also, it can generate 360° 3-D images surrounding the ego vehicle with accurate depth information. In recent autonomous vehicles, LiDAR sensor plays a major role in driving the vehicle autonomously by generating accurate and precise environment perception. ADAS systems such as autonomous braking, parking solutions, collision avoidance, object detection etc., can be achieved with more accuracy using Lidar sensors. A major setback of Lidars is the bulky size and expensive. Also, extreme weather conditions such as rain and fog can impact the performance of Lidar sensors. Due to the latest advancements in semiconductor technology, significantly smaller and inexpensive Lidars may be possible in future [3, 10].

2.1.2 Radar

Radar stands for radio detection and ranging. This is an active sensor that works on the principle of the Doppler effect. Radars emit microwave energy and measure the frequency difference between emitted and reflected beams in order to estimate the speed and distance of the object from which the energy gets reflected. It is capable of detecting objects at a longer distance compared to lidar and vision sensors. Radar performs equally in all weather conditions, including extreme conditions such as rain and fog. Radars are classified as short, medium and long-range sensors. Short and medium-range sensors are mostly used in blind spot detection, cross traffic alert and they will mounted in the corners of the vehicle. Long-range radars are mostly used for adaptive cruise control and are mounted near front/rear bumpers [3, 10].

2.1.3 Ultrasonic sensors

Ultrasonic sensors are active sensors which use sound waves in order to measure the distance between ego vehicle and objects. Such sensors are most commonly used to detect nearby objects to the vehicle such as kerbs, especially in parking spaces [3, 10].

Other sensors such as GPSs and IMUs are also used in most of the ADAS and AV use cases. These sensors are used to measure the position and for localization of the ego vehicle. **Table 1** shows the consolidated summary of the advantages and disadvantages of various sensors for ADAS and AV systems.

2.1.4 Challenges with existing sensor suite

Human-perceivable sunshine is a small part of the spectrum of solar irradiance, which approximately contains 5% ultraviolet, 43% visible, and 52% infrared wavelengths [12]. Whereas at night, streetlamps and headlamps are the primary sources of light. However, the lighting pattern of the vehicle headlamps is strictly regulated for safety reasons: the range of low and high beams can only vary from 60 m to 150 m. The visibility of the targets of interest may vary based on the light reflections from their surfaces. Diffuse reflection is observed when the surface is rough like asphalt, clothing, wood etc. and specular reflection is observed when the surface is mirror-like, wet, epoxy, metallic etc. However, as shown in **Figure 5**, adverse conditions, such as direct

Sensor	Advantages	Disadvantages
Radar	Long range	Low accuracy and resolution
	Works in poor visibility	Mutual interference of Radar
	Consumes less power	Poor azimuthal and elevation resolution
	Robust to Failure	Error-prone object classification
	Small, lightweight and affordable	No surround view perception
Lidar	Long range	Expensive and high-maintenance
	Surround-view perception	Transmission is sparse
	Good accuracy and resolution	Affected by varying climatic conditions
	No significant interferences	Poor small object detection
Ultrasonic	Low in cost	Only short-range distances
	Low in cost and small in dimensions	Sensitive to temperatures
	At short ranges, higher resolution	Prone to interference and reverberation
	Overcome pedestrian occlusion problems	Pick noise from environments
Camera	High-resolution and color scales	Requires a powerful computation
	Surround-view and 3D information	Poor distance estimation
	Low cost and maintenance	Sensitive to adverse conditions
	Small size and Easy to deploy	Inaccurate during low light
Infrared	Works at all light conditions	Demanding computation sources
	The sensing range can cover up to 200 m	Classification issues in cold conditions
	Better vision through dust, fog, and snow	Challenging to detect and classify

Table 1.
List of advantages and disadvantages of various sensors for ADAS/AV perception systems [11].

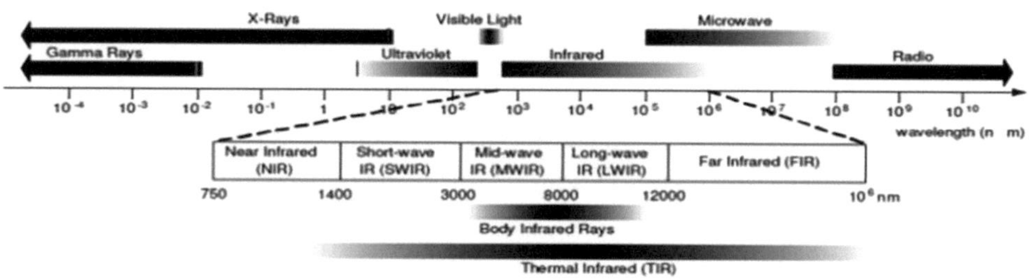

Figure 5.
Electromagnetic Spectrum-representation of IR range

sun glare, dense fog, heavy rain, high beam glare, surface reflections and low light, would cause light reflections that result in the reduction of visibility for RGB Cameras.

Existing ADAS solution in the market uses vision & ultrasonic sensors predominantly to achieve level 1 features such as warning and alert signals for traffic lights, and detecting obstacles while reversing the vehicle etc., To achieve level 2 and above ADAS features, vision, radar and ultrasonic sensors are used either as individual sensor modality or combination of these sensors. For example, a vision sensor is capable of generating accurate detection and classification of on-road objects, static objects etc., whereas radar sensor is capable of generating accurate position and velocity, distance of the objects from a vehicle. Hence, these two pieces of information will be fused to generate the combined representation of the detected objects with their position, velocity and class. Here, each object can be represented with more rich information so that the guidance and navigation module can make proper decisions and planning for the vehicle to move autonomously. Fusion of the information from multiple sensors modality implies the combined representation of complementary and redundant information in order to represent the environment more precisely. Also, this enables theextension the feasibility of ADAS and AV systems to function in all weather/lighting conditions [6]. However, above said sensor fusion is best suited to address the challenges during daylight and not fully compliance during night time. The sensors combination in the latest ADAS and AV solutions are still not able to precisely generate the environment perception as human driver perceives. The latest standing general order crash report [2] available on the National Highway Traffic Safety Administration web page, clearly shows that the existing sensor suite is not sufficient to achieve level 4 & above autonomous driving. The system fails especially during adverse weather conditions, low light and dark scenarios, extreme sun glare and so on. After the accident of the autonomous Uber car in 2018 [13], the research community started considering including the infrared sensor in the ADAS sensor fusion suite. This shows that there is a need for another sensor which can complement the information, especially during extreme weather and lighting conditions. To enable level 4 or 5 ADAS functionalities with zero human intervention, it is necessary to make the system more robust to various weather and lighting conditions [11, 14].

2.1.5 Need for infrared sensors for ADAS and AV

The most state-of-the-art approaches constitute camera and lidar sensors as the major sensory modality for detecting the object, mostly due to the fact that these sensors will have dense image pixel information/high-density point cloud data. Whereas, these lidar and radar sensors are costly and computationally expensive. Vision sensor-based perception algorithms depend on the brightness and contrast of the images captured. They are cost-effective sensors and use either image processing or deep learning-based techniques for object detection. Due to limited image features, CNN-based algorithms are able to detect the objects only with good lighting conditions or with minimum lux level. Moreover, vision sensor-based approaches often fail at daylight glare, night-time glare, fog, rain, and strong light/direct sun situations. The performance may be degraded in poor lighting conditions such as dark scenarios, dams, tunnels, parking garages, etc.,. Similarly, when there is contamination in the camera lens and increased complexity of the scenes such as the detection of pedestrians in crowded environment are always challenging for any vision-based perception algorithms [15].

Apart from the mentioned challenges, the vision sensors are also limited to the distance of the objects. Reasonable performance can be expected up to 20 meters using visible images and hence, recognition of long-distance objects is limited. It has limitations in low light conditions, fog and rain weather conditions to sense the environment precisely. The limitations and challenges can be overcome by adding additional sensors such as lidars and radars that can detect objects at a long distance even in fog and rain.. Recent accidents by Uber and Tesla autonomous vehicles indicate that the sensors suite comprising vision sensors, lidars and radars are not sufficient, especially in the detection of cars and pedestrians during extreme weather and lighting conditions The robust perception algorithm is expected to work in all lighting and adverse weather conditions as shown in **Figure 5**. Hence, the ADAS/autonomous driving sensor suite should require a night vision-compliant data-capturing sensor, such as infrared or thermal imagery. Infrared (IR) sensors look promising, especially in extreme conditions such as poor lighting, night, bright sun glare and inclement weather. IR sensors are capable of classifying vehicles, pedestrians, animals and all objects in common driving conditions. They are capable of performing equally in daylight and dark scenarios. It outperforms in low light and dark lighting conditions compared to other sensors used for ADAS and AV applications [15].

3. Infrared sensor technology

Infrared falls within electromagnetic radiation with wavelengths longer than the visible spectrum and shorter than radio waves. IR ranges from 0.75 μm to 1000 μm. Any object with an absolute temperature over 0 K is capable of radiating infrared energy. Generally, it is a measure of internal energy due to the acceleration of electrically charged particles. Hotter objects radiate more energy. It is invisible to human eyes but sensed as a warmth on the skin. The electromagnetic spectrum and IR range are shown in **Figure 5**. Infrared sensor is an electronic device which is capable of emitting and detecting Infrared radiations within the IR range. It works on three basic laws of physics [16–18]:

1. *Planck's law of radiation*—It states that any object whose temperature is not equal to absolute zero Kelvin (O K) emits radiation
2. *Stephan Boltzmann's law*—It states that the total energy emitted by a black body at all wavelengths is related to the absolute temperature
3. *Wein's law of displacement*—It states that objects at different temperatures emit spectra whose peak is at different wavelengths that are inversely proportional to the temperature.

Figure 6 shows the radiant existence of a perfect black body according to Planck law and the maximum peak is inversely proportional to the temperature as per Wein's displacement law.

Based on the operating principles, IR sensors are broadly classified into thermal and photonic detectors. Infrared rays emitted by any objects are captured by thermal sensors and then converted into heat which is then transformed into a change in resistance. Thermo electromotive force extracts the output. Quantum sensors use the photo conductive effect and photovoltaic effect in semiconductors and PN junctions. For ADAS and AV applications, thermal sensors are most widely accepted. Another classification of IR detectors into cooled and non-cooled detectors based on operating temperature is often used at initial stages. Based on the detector's construction, it can be further classified into single and linear or array detectors. The commonly used detector arrangement is the FPA, focal plane array sensor which consists of multiple single detectors placed as array of matrices [16–18]. Further classification of IR sensor type is based on the operating frequency band as IR detectors operate in the bank where maximum transmission with minimal absorption is possible [16–18]. It is generally classified as:

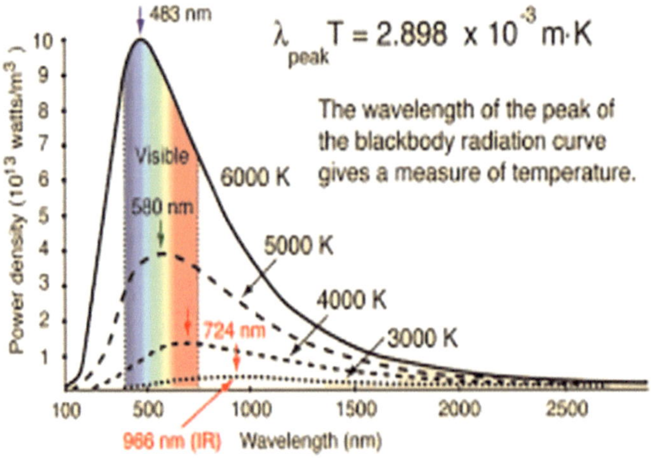

Figure 6.
Radiant existence of a black body according to Planck law [16].

1. *NIR*—Near infrared radiation falls in the range from 0.75 μm to 1 μm

2. *SWIR*—Short wave Infrared Radiation falls in the range between 1 μm and 2.5 μm

3. *MWIR*—Mid-wave infared radiation falls in the range between 3 μm and 5 μm

4. *LWIR*—Long Wave Infrared Radiation falls in the range between 8 μm and 12 μm

A pictorial representation of the IR sensor types based on the operational frequency band is shown in **Figure 7** and **Table 2** summarizes the various specifications of IR sensor types. NIR and SWIR cameras are known as 'reflective infrared' like RGB cameras, which require an external light source for illumination. NIR is mainly used in the in-cabin applications for Driver monitoring systems. Whereas, SWIR provide

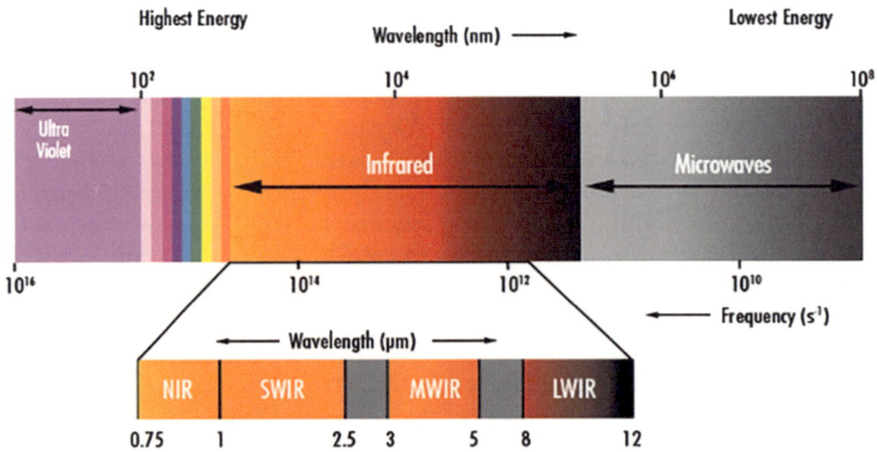

Figure 7.
Infrared sensor types based on operational frequency bands.

	NIR	SWIR	LWIR
Known as	Reflected IR	Reflected IR	Thermal IR
Wavelength, μ m	0.7–1.4	1.4–3	8–14
Imager	Silicon-based	InGaAs detectors	Photon detectors
Detection range	Short	Short	Long (165 m)
Usage	Night vision	Feature extraction	Heat detection
Applications	Driver monitoring	Road marking detection	Pedestrian and object detection

Table 2.
Details of various types of infrared images used in automotive industry.

more context information, like lane markings, traffic signs, etc. Unfortunately, SWIR camera applications are uncommon due to the high cost of indium gallium arsenide (InGaAs) detectors [19]. LWIRs are commonly referred to as 'thermal infrared' as they operate solely through thermal emissions and do not require any external sources for illumination [20].

Representative images for visible camera (RGB), near infrared (NIR), short-wavelength infrared (SWIR), mid-wavelength infrared and long-wavelength infrared (LWIR) cameras are shown in **Figure 8** [16–18].

The basic components of the Infrared imaging system are shown in **Figure 9**. It measures the IR radiations emitted from the objects and then converts them into electrical impulses using an IR detector. The converted signal is transformed into temperature map considering the ambience and atmospheric effects. A temperature map is displayed as an image which can be color-coded to represent thermograms thermal images or IR images using an imaging algorithm. IR detector acts as a transducer, which converts radiation into electrical signals. Microbolometric detectors are the most widely used IR detectors as they can operate at room temperature. It is basically a resistor with a very small heat capacity and a high negative temperature coefficient of resistivity. IR radiations received by detectors change the resistance of the microbolometers and produce the corresponding electrical outputs. Considering the ambient and atmospheric effects between the object and IR detector, an infrared measurement model is used to represent the detected heat map to temperature map. The measurement model depends on the emissivity of the object, atmospheric and ambient temperature, relative humidity and distance between the object and detector as per

Figure 8.
Representative images for visible camera (RGB), near-infrared (NIR), short-wavelength infrared (SWIR), mid-wavelength infrared and long-wavelength infrared (LWIR) cameras [20].

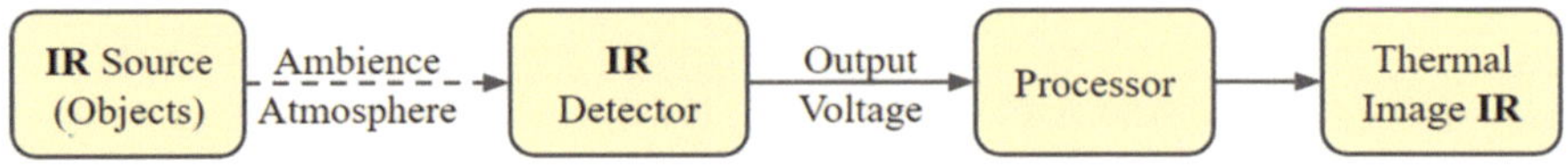

Figure 9.
Basic components of IR imaging system.

Figure 10.
Representative RGB and IR images used in ADAS and AV applications from Kaist multispectral pedestrian detection dataset [21].

the FLIR thermal camera. It varies between different manufacturers and IR detector characteristics. The measured temperature map is visually represented as grayscale images. For industrial applications, pseudo color-coded images named as thermograms can also be generated by the thermal imaging system for easy representation of the difference in temperature distribution. **Figure 10** shows a representative RGB and the corresponding IR thermal images used in ADAS and AV applications [17].

4. Role of infrared sensors in ADAS and AV applications

In automotive domain, it is a highly challenging requirement to achieve level 3 and above autonomous driving under all weather and lighting conditions and deliver an environment perception. ADAS and AV systems are expected to support all driving conditions, in high complex roads, totally unpredictable situations and vehicles must be mounted with cost-effective sensor suites that are capable of extracting maximum information possible to make an accurate decision. It is also expected that the perceived environment to represent the scene information adequately such that computer vision algorithms can detect and classify the objects. This will ensure precise autonomous navigation and control and provide safe advanced ADAS and AV systems. SAE automation level 2 systems in commercial market already have vision sensors, ultrasonics and radar sensors. The next level of SAE automation can be achieved by adding multiple sensors and lidar sensors to the existing sensor suite. Each sensor has their own limitations and advantages [16–18]. Thus, sensor fusion will come into play where the advantages of different sensor modalities can be utilized to address the various limitations. Even though, NHTSA shows that the existing ADAS and AV solutions are lacking in achieving the expected performance as there were crashes reported by every vehicle supported with ADAS and AV features [2]. Also, the Uber and Tesla accidents clearly show that the current SAE automation level 2 and 3 sensors suite do not provide accurate detection of cars and pedestrians. In particular, vulnerable road users (VRUs) such as pedestrians, animals and bicyclists are challenging to detect and classify accurately. Classification of these objects are challenging in poor lighting condition, low light and dark scenarios, direct sunlight in driving direction and extreme weather conditions such as fog, rain and snow. The performance of vision sensors does not meet the requirement of autonomous driving in such conditions. Other sensors performance was also more or less affected and failed to provide the complete environment perception for autonomous navigation. A combination of low light vision sensors, lidar and radar can help to some extent to perform night scenarios up to 50 meters. Beyond that, it will be challenging to drive the vehicle autonomously [15]. Infrared sensor technology overcomes the aforementioned challenges and reliably detects, classifies cars, vehicles, pedestrians, animals and other objects that are common in driving scenarios. Also, IR sensors are capable of performing equally in daylight conditions thereby they can provide redundant information for the existing sensor suite thereby increasing confidence in detection and classification algorithms. IR sensors can be used effectively to address the limitations of vision and other sensors. The real-time performance of IR camera is not affected by low light and dark scenarios, sun glare or vehicle headlight and brake light reflections. It can be considered as a potential solution in extreme weather conditions such as snow, fog and rain. Un-cooled thermal imaging systems that are available in the market are the most affordable low-cost IR sensors due to advancements in microbolometer technology. These sensors are capable of generating the temperature map as an image to visually analyze and further process the environmental information. In existing automotive sensor suites, these sensors can supplement or even replace existing technology due to the advantages of sensing the infrared emission of the objects, and operates independently of illumination conditions, thereby providing a promising and consistent technology in order to achieve more precise environment perception systems [15].

As per the NTSB report, the fatal incident of a pedestrian by Uber vehicle which is a level 3 autonomous car in Tempe, Arizona. This vehicle uses lidar, radar and vision sensors. The report shows that the incident happened at night time when there were only street lights lit. The system is first classified as an unknown object, after some time as a car, then as a bicycle and finally as a person. This scenario was recreated and tested by FLIR using a wide field of view thermal camera using a basic classifier. The system was capable of detecting the person at a distance of approximately 85.4 m which is twice the required stopping distance for a vehicle at 43 mph. When performed using narrow FOV cameras, FLIR IR cameras have demonstrated the performance of pedestrian detection even at a distance four times greater than the required by decision algorithms in autonomous vehicles [15].

The vehicle currently on the road with ADAS systems that support SAE level 2 with partial automation and level 3 with conditional automation does not include an IR sensor in the sensor suite. AWARE (All Weather All Roads Enhanced) vision project was executed in 2016 to test the potential of sensors operating in four different bands on the electromagnetic spectrum such as Visible RGB, near infared (NIR), short wave Infrared (SWIR) and long wave infared (LWIR), especially in challenging conditions such as fog, snow and rain. It was reported that LWIR camera performed well in detecting pedestrians in extreme fog (visibility range = 15 ± 4 m) compared to NIR and SWIR whereas the vision sensor reported with lowest detection performance comparatively. Similarly, LWIR camera was capable of detecting pedestrians in extreme dark scenarios and when reflections were present due to other vehicles headlights in the fog conditions whereas the other sensors failed to detect pedestrians as they were not seen due to headlight glare/reflections [15, 22]. Also, as per Wien's displacement law, the peak radiation for the human skin with emissivity 0.99 is 9.8 μm at room temperature which falls in LWIR camera operating range. Therefore, being completely passive sensors, LWIR cameras take advantage of sensing the emitted IR radiations from objects irrespective of extreme weather conditions and illuminations [16]. The distance at which the IR sensor can detect and classify an object depends on the field of view (FOV) of the camera. Narrow FOV cameras are capable of detecting objects at far distances whereas wide FOV cameras are capable of detecting objects in the greater angle of view. Also, IR sensors require the target object of 20 x 8 pixels to reliably detect and classify the object. IR sensor with a narrow FOV lens is capable of detecting and classifying an object of 20 x 8 pixel size at a distance greater than 186 meters. Therefore, IR sensors with narrow FOV can be used on highways to detect far objects whereas wide FOV cameras can be used in urban or city driving scenarios [15]. In the automotive domain, IR sensors can be effectively used in both in-cabin sensing and driving applications. In cabin sensing applications, IR sensors will be mounted inside the vehicle in order to understand the driver's drowsiness and fatigue detection, eye gaze localisation, face recognition, occupant gender classification. Facial expression, emotion detection etc. In ADAS and AV systems, IR sensors can be efficiently used to generate precise and accurate perception of the surrounding environment by providing one or more cameras mounted in the vehicle. It is commonly used to generate object detection, classification and semantic segmentation [23].

5. AI applications in the development of ADAS and AV systems

In the automotive domain, the challenges to achieve full level 5 autonomous driving seem to be possible due to the advancements in sensing technologies and artificial intelligence (AI). Advancements in AI advancements lead to achieving the requirement of AV systems such as perceiving, thinking and reasoning. In addition to that, advanced computing resources to process the huge amount of data sensed through multiple sensors of different modalities also play an important role for the research and development community to move towards autonomous vehicles. In ADAS and AV systems, AI becomes the gold standard approach in order to perceive the surrounding environment so that proper planning and vehicle motion can be achieved. In Level 3 and above ADAS and AV systems, AI is used primarily in perception, localization and mapping and decision-making. There is a need to understand the various aspects of AI applied in AV development and the current practices in bringing the AI system for autonomous driving. In particular, deep learning (DL) based algorithms are capable of handling various challenging issues such as accurate and precise object detection and classification, appropriate control of steering wheel, acceleration and deceleration etc., AI research field focuses on DL approaches including convolutional neural networks, LSTM and deep belief network for vehicle perception, motion planning, path planning and decision making [4, 7]. Generally, DL-based approaches are used to recognize the objects on the road that includes a perception module and localization and mapping module. On-road objects are detected, classified, fused and tracked in the perception module. It receives input from multiple sensors of different modalities such as lidars, radars, vision and IR cameras. In addition to on-road objects, vision sensor-based traffic sign detection, lane detection and parking lines detection are also achieved using DL approaches. It can also be used to

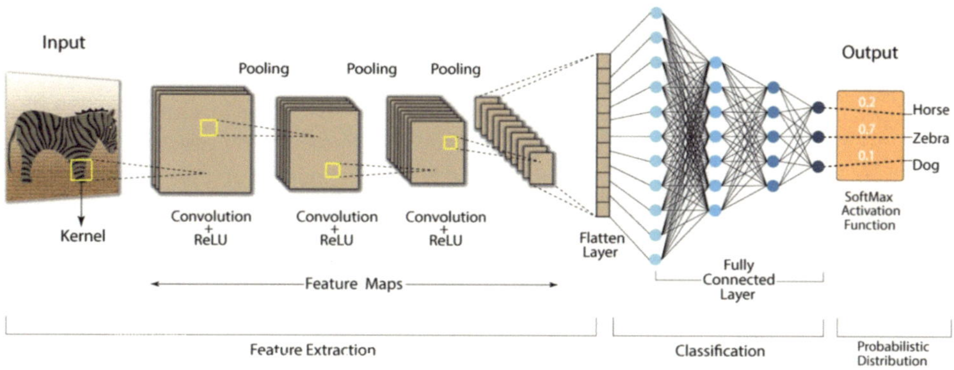

Figure 11.
Representative convolutional neural network and its components.

generate the object-level information such as object position, size, class, distance, and orientation from ego vehicle and also as semantic information which generates pixel-wise object class. Mostly commonly convolutional neural networks (CNN) are used for object detection and classification tasks. A more generic representation of convolutional neural network and its components are shown in **Figure 11**. Any deep learning model has an input layer, few hidden layers and a final fully connected layer called an output layer. Input layer takes an image as input and final output layer define the detected objects along with their confidence score. A combination of the convolution layer, pooling and activation layer represents one hidden layer whereas in deep networks, multiple layers of these feature extraction layers are added to extract the coarse to detailed information. At last softmax function is used to classify more than one object detected with the corresponding confidence score based on the feature similarity. The object with the highest confidence score is recognized as the object class with the detected bounding box information [24]. CNN, RCNN, fast RCNN, faster R-CNN, SSD, Yolo, Yolov2, Yolov3 etc., are a few DL approaches that are most commonly used for the recognition of road objects. In case level 3 and above ADAS and AV systems, multi-task networks are predominantly used where a common network architecture will be trained to perform multiple tasks. End-to-end AI system can also be used to generate the complete perception of ADAS and AV systems that include perception, localization and mapping algorithms [7].

6. Survey on deep learning approaches using infrared images for ADAS and AV applications

Training, testing and validation are the most important steps to be considered for any deep learning-based perception algorithms. After proper training of the networks, it can deployed in real time to perceive the environment successfully. The captured dataset and its size used for training the model play a critical role while deploying the model in real time. Convolutional neural networks (CNN) have significantly improved the performance of many ADAS and AV applications, whereas it requires significant amounts of training data to obtain optimum performance and reliable validation outcomes. Fortunately, there are multiple large-scale publicly available thermal datasets with annotations which can be used for training CNN. However, when compared to visible imaging data, there are not many 2 dimensional thermal datasets available for automotive applications on the open internet. In **Table 3**, a list of available datasets captured by various types of thermal sensors in different environmental conditions is provided. These datasets are widely used in building various pre-trained CNN models for several applications like Pedestrian detection, Vehicle detection and classification and small object detection in the thermal spectrum on GPU/edge-GPU devices for the automotive sensor suite [31]. Whereas there are inherent challenges also associated with the training and validation of the thermal data for CNN models are as follows: A limited number of publicly available datasets, little variability in the scenes such as weather, lighting and heat conditions, difficulties while using RGB pre-trained CNN models for thermal data.

6.1 Object detection in the thermal spectrum

Object detection is an important part of autonomous driving, which is expected to accurately and rapidly detect vulnerable road users (VRUs) like pedestrians and cyclists, vehicles, traffic signals, sign boards, animals etc. during all lighting and weather conditions. These detection results are used for motion tracking and pose estimation of the objects and subsequently utilized to take appropriate actions while ADAS technologies like Cruise control, Lane departure systems and Emergency breaking are in action.

6.1.1 Classical detection techniques

The acquisition of frames, selection of region of Interest, feature extractions and classification are the generic steps followed for VRUs detection. Identifying the Region of Interest (ROI) [32] is the the first instance of detection of the desired objects and then feature extraction takes place such as edges, shapes, curvature etc. These extracted features are further used for object classification. Background subtraction is the most commonly used technique for detecting the moving objects, whereas there are more advanced techniques such as sliding window, objectiveness and selective search to counter adverse conditions. The Histogram of Oriented Gradients (HOG) features [33] and Local Binary Patterns (LBP) [34] are basic hand-crafted image processing techniques to extract features and classify objects, but they are limited when we have complex features are need to be extracted. Whereas deep learning-based techniques allow the network to extract the features, which can provide a higher level of information. Then support vector machine, a decision tree or

Dataset	Size	Resolution	Thermal Images	Content
C3I [25]	0.5 GB	640×480	39,000	Person, Vehicles, Bicycles, Bikes
LITIV [26]	0.7 GB	320×430	6000	Person
CVC [27]	5 GB	640×480	11,000	Person, Vehicles, Bicycles, Bikes, Poles
TIV [28]	5.4 GB	1024×1024	63,000	Person, Vehicles, Bicycles
FLIR [29]	16 GB	640×512	14,000	Person, Vehicles, Bicycles, Bikes, Poles, Dogs
KAIST [30]	37 GB	320×256	95,000	Person, Vehicles, Bicycles, Bikes, Poles

Table 3.
Details of various open access infrared datasets available related to ADAS applications.

a deep neural network are used to classify the object. DL-based techniques are found to be the out performing the traditional methods [35].

6.1.2 Deep learning approach for object detection

The two commonly used deep learning approaches for VRUs detection are two-stage detector (region proposal approach) and single-stage detector (non-region proposal approach). Two-stage or regional proposed approach is the hand-crafted technique that uses HOG, LBP or similar for feature extraction in the first stage and includes CNN networks for classification in the second stage such as region-CNN (R-CNN) [36], regional-fast convolution network (R-FCN) [37] and faster R-CNN [38]. Whereas single-stage detector is able to perform region proposal, feature extraction as well as classification in a single step. Some of the non-region proposal-based approaches include single shot detector (SSD) [39] and you only look once (YOLO) [40]. The advantages and disadvantages of two and single-stage detectors are presented in **Table 4**.

6.1.3 Deep learning based sensor fusion techniques

Many studies are conducted around the most reliable approach to using both color and thermal information from visible cameras and thermal cameras [41–43]. Commonly, these studies highlight the illumination dependency of visible cameras as well as their limitations during adverse weather conditions and the benefits of including the thermal data for better performance. The fusion of visible and thermal cameras aids in reducing the inaccuracies of object detection mainly during nighttime. The fusion of this sensor information can be possible at various levels like pixel level, feature level or decision level. For pixel-level fusion, the thermal images that are intensity values, which can be fused with the visible images in the intensity (I) component and fused images can be reconstructed with the new I value. In general, the pixel-level fusion is done through the following methods: Wavelet-based transform, curvelet transform and laplacian pyramid transform fusion. Typically pixel level fusion is not used with deep learning-based sensor fusion as it takes place outside the neural network.

The typical architectures for deep learning-based sensor fusion are early fusion, late fusion and halfway fusion, as shown in **Figure 12**. Early fusion is also called feature-level fusion, in which visible and thermal images are combined together as a 4-channel (Red, Green, Blue, Intensity (RGBI)) input for the deep learning network to learn the relationship between the image sources. The late fusion is also called decision-level, in which feature extraction of visible and thermal images happens separately into subnetworks and fused just before the object classification layer. Halfway fusion is another approach which involves feeding the visible and thermal information separately into the same network and the fusion happens inside the network itself. There are various studies which demonstrated the benefits of using multispectral detection techniques,

Type	Examples	Advantages	Trade-Offs
Single stage	SSD, YOLO	Higher speeds	Information loss, Large number of False Positives
Two-stage	R-CNN, R-FCN	Increased Accuracy	Slower Speeds
	Faster R-CNN	Information rich	Complex computation

Table 4.
Deep learning-based object detection types.

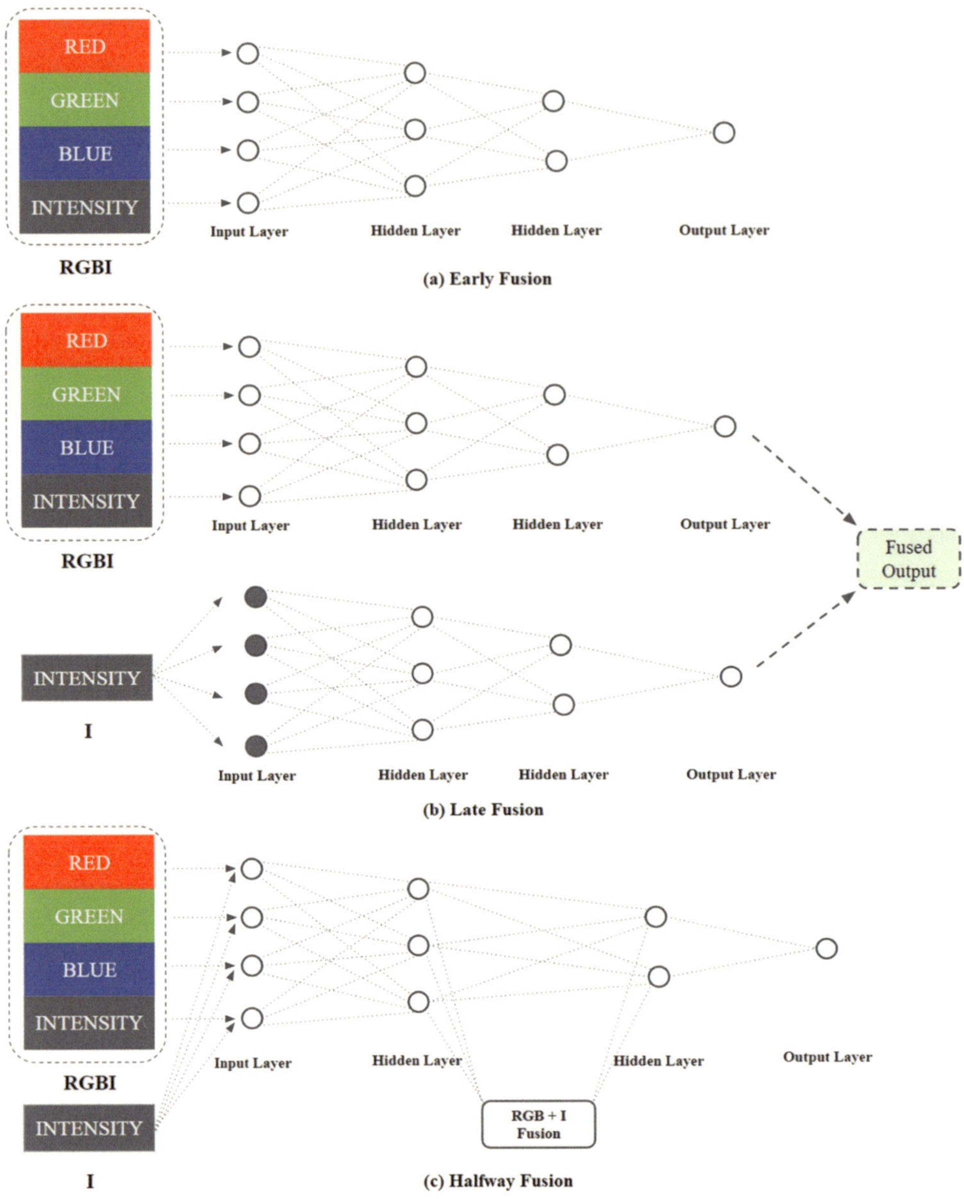

Figure 12.
Sensor fusion techniques [35].

which produced the best results while combining the visible and thermal images. However, during night conditions thermal cameras performed much better than the fusion data. At low light conditions, fused data performed worse with an Average Miss rate of 3% and an overall decrease of 5% during daytime is observed. Also, the usage of multiple sensors causes an increase in system complexity due to differences in sensor positions, alignment, synchronisations and resolutions of the cameras used [35].

By far, the halfway fusion is considered the most effective of the other two techniques with 3.5% lower miss rate. Also, using the stand-alone visible and thermal information was shown to be performing much worse than halfway fusion by 11% [44].

Wagner et al. [45] investigated finding the optimal fusion techniques for pedestrian detection using Faster R-CNN and KAIST datasets and found that the multispectral information with single-stage and halfway fusion can achieve better performance. Similarly, there are various studies conducted highlighting the importance of detection stages and sensor fusion techniques at various lighting conditions to draw similar conclusions [46]. However, these deep learning models should estimate the bounding box of the object appropriately and calculate the probability of the class it belongs *via* neural networks, which makes them unsuitable for real-time applications [40].

DenseFuse, a deep learning architecture to extract more useful features proposed by Li et al. [47] uses a combination of CNN, fusion layers and dense blocks, which creates a reconstructed fused image that outperforms all the existing fusion methods. SeAFusion network combines the image and semantic segmentation information and uses gradient residual blocks to enhance image fusion process [48]. An unsupervised fusion network called U2Fusion was proposed by Xu et al. [49] to best estimate the fusion process considering the source image importance. Similarly, multiple image fusion networks were proposed such as end-to-end fusion network (RFN-Net), the effective biletaral mechanism (BAM), bilateral ReLU residual network (BRRLNet), etc. [50, 51]. Despite so much progress in deep learning-based fusion architectures, they are no lightweight real-time running application, they are all limited by appropriate hyper-parameter selection and significant memory utilization. The advantages and disadvantages of image fusion model-related literatures are summarized in **Table 5**.

6.1.4 Real-time object detection

In YOLO framework [40], both creating the bounding box and classification of image are dealt as a single regressive problem to enhance the inference speed and train the neural network as a whole task. YOLO creates a grid of *mxn* of the input image then predicts the N number of bounding boxes and estimates the confidence score on each Bounding Boxes (BB) using the CNN. Each BB consists of *(x,y)* central coordinates, *(w,h)* is its width and height along with class probability value. The intersection of union (IOU) is calculated based on the overlap of the detected BB and the actual ground truth (GT). The width of the IOU indicates how accurately the BB is predicted. The probability of the BB is expressed as the multiplication of probability of the object and the width of the IOU. The central coordinates of the predicted BB and the GT exist in the IOU then it is assumed that successful detection and *Pr(Object)* is set to 1, else it is set to 0. If there are *i* number of classes that could be classified as *Pr(Class | object*. The BB with the highest probability of the classified object among all possible N numbers of BBs is considered as the best fit BB of the concerned object.

Literature	Advantages	Disadvantages
DenseFuse [47]	Extract useful features	Loss of contrast and brightness
SeAfuseion [48]	Combines fusion and semantic segmentation	Cannot handle complex scenes
U2Fusion [49]	Adapts to new fusion tasks	Not robust to noise
Y-shaped net [50]	Extracts local features and context info	Introduce artifacts or blur
RFN-Net [51]	Two-stage training strategy	Large amount of training data and time

Table 5.
Summary of image fusion model-related literature.

Yoon and Cho [52] have proposed a multimodel YOLO-based object detection method based on late fusion using non-maximum suppression to efficiently extract the features of an object using color information from visible cameras and boundary information from thermal cameras. The architectural block diagram is shown in **Figure 13**. The non-maximum suppression is generally employed towards the second half of the detection model to improve the object detection performance of models like YOLO and SSD.

Further, they have also proposed an improved deep multimodel object detection strategy by introducing dehazing network to enhance the performance of the model during reduced visibility. The dehaze network constitutes evaluation of haze level classification, light scattering coefficient estimation from visible images and depth estimation from thermal images. Detailed performance metrics for dense haze condition results from Yoon and Cho [52] are presented in **Table 6** based on YOLO trained for (a) visible (b) IR/thermal (c) visible and IR and (d) visible, IR and dehaze network. Examples of output images from Yoon and Cho [52] of the vehicle detection results based on YOLO model trained for visible alone, IR/thermal alone, fused visible and IR and fused visible, IR and dehaze model are shown in **Figure 14**. Missed detection is marked as red box and correct detection is marked as blue box. The performance of vehicle detection model improved from 81.11% to 84.02% of accuracy from fusion model, but badly impacted by the run time, hence dehaze model is unfit for real-time applications.

6.1.5 Real-time pedestrian detection

Chen et al. [53] proposed a thermal based R-CNN model for pedestrian detection using VGG-16 as a backbone network as it has good network stability which enables the integration of any new branch network. To address the pedestrian occlusion problem, they have proposed a part model architecture with new aspect ratio and block model to strengthen the network's generalization. The presence and resemblance of pedestrian will be completely lost if the occlusion rate is over 80%, henceforth, training pedestrians occlusion <80% only be considered. **Figure 15** represents the possible types of pedestrian occlusion and the ground truth labelling and possible detection are represented as green and red rectangle boxes, respectively. **Figure 16** shows the

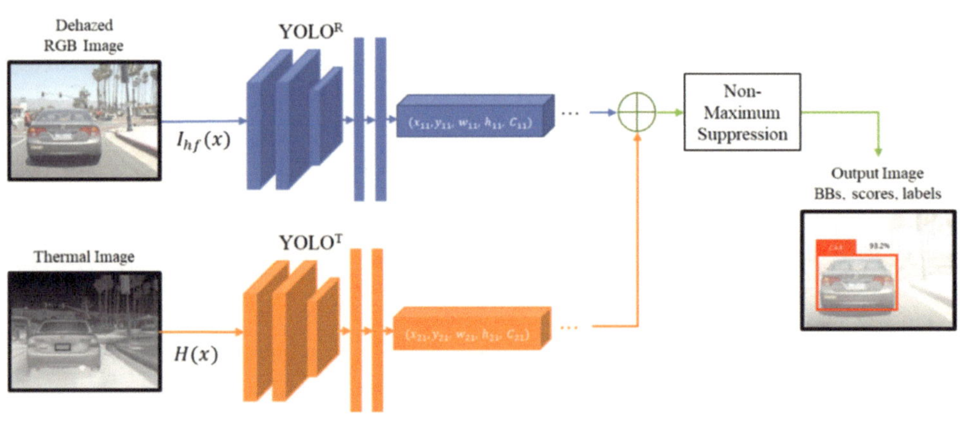

Figure 13.
Block diagram of the multimodal YOLO-based object detection method based on late fusion [52].

Metrics	Visible	IR/Thermal	Visible+IR	Visible+IR + Dehaze
Accuracy	61.55	78.6	81.11	84.02
TP	1264	1626	1683	1747
FP	30	182	238	269
Precision	0.97	0.90	0.87	0.86
Recall	0.61	0.79	0.82	0.85
Run time (ms)	27.82	27.82	27.89	686.99

Table 6.
Performance of vehicle detection model during dense haze condition based on YOLO trained for (a) visible (b) IR/thermal (c) visible and IR and (d) visible, IR and dehaze network. Results from [52].

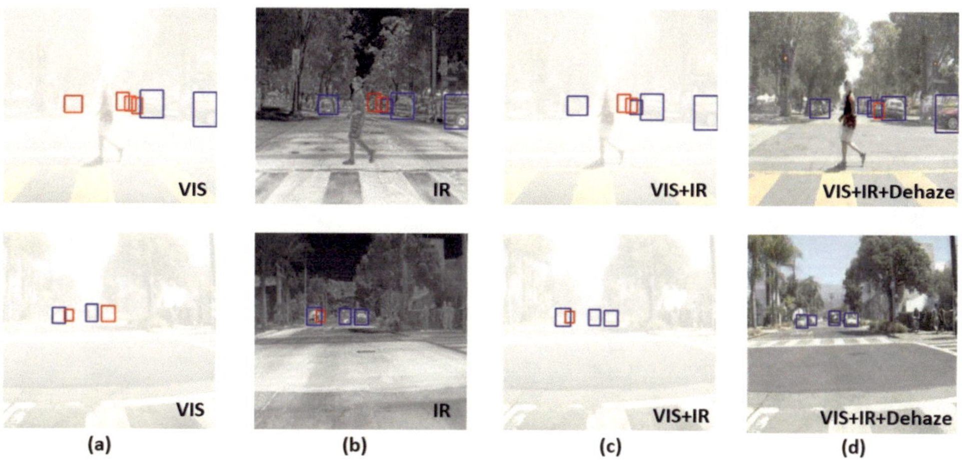

Figure 14.
Examples of vehicle detection results based on YOLO model trained for (a) visible (b) IR/thermal (c) visible and IR and (d) visible, IR and dehaze network. Missed detection is marked in red box and correct detection is marked in blue box. Results from [52].

architecture of the thermal R-CNN fusion model for improved Pedestrian detection proposed by [53], which constitutes a full body and region decomposition branch to extract the full body features of pedestrian and segmentation head branch to extract the individual pedestrian from the crowded scenes. The loss function is defined considering five loss components such as BB loss, classification loss, segmentation loss, pixel level loss and fusion loss.

In **Table 7**, the performance comparison results from [53] for thermal R-CNN fusion pedestrian detection model with state-of-the-art deep learning models found that the thermal R-CNN fusion model is effective and performing better. The thermal R-CNN fusion model is sensitive to regional features which may easily tend to misjudge the images, however, the semantic segmentation feature enhances the information of the complete pedestrian bounding box and the final output is accurate resulting in higher precision. **Figure 17** shows the results from [53], the example images to demonstrate the improved pedestrian detection by the thermal R-CNN fusion model compared to ground truth and benchmarked modified R-CNN model. It is evident from the results that modified R-CNN results partially detect the occluded pedestrians and in some cases, double partial bounding boxes are created for single

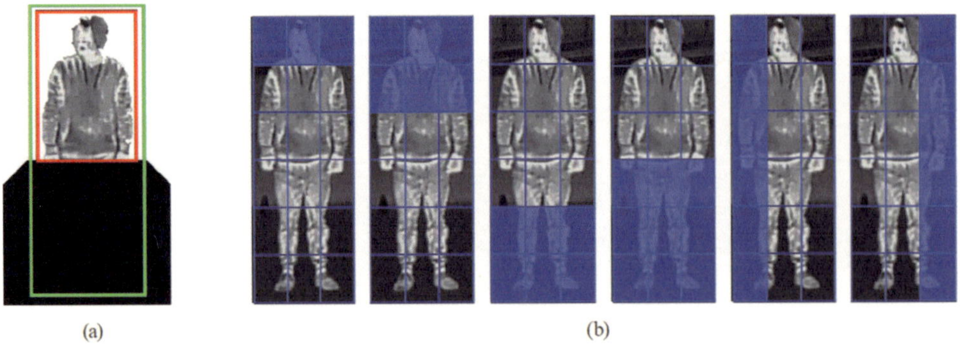

Figure 15.
Illustration of types of pedestrian occlusion. (a) the green BB rectangle represents full pedestrian and red BB rectangle represents detectable pedestrians. (b) Top six types of pedestrian occlusion types [53].

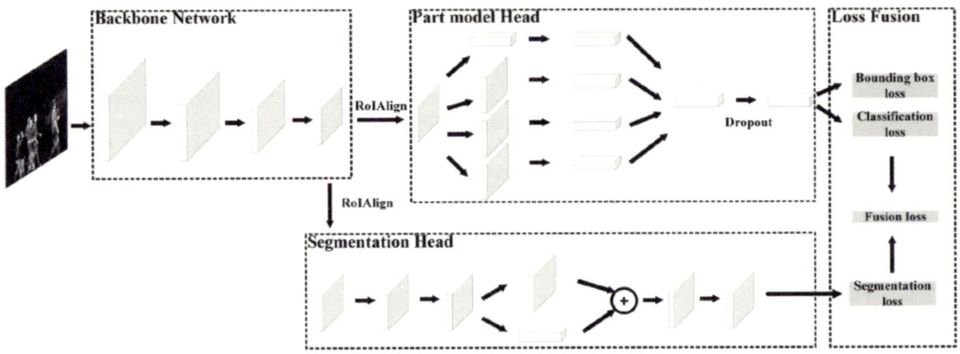

Figure 16.
The architecture of the thermal R-CNN fusion model for improved pedestrian detection [53].

Metrics	Faster R-CNN	Mask R-CNNl	YOLO	Thermal R-CNN fusion
TP	992	1050	1250	1317
FP	740	720	954	334
FN	995	937	734	670
Precision	0.572	0.593	0.567	0.797
Recall	0.499	0.528	0.630	0.662
F1-score	0.533	0.558	0.661	0.724

Table 7.
Performance comparison of various pedestrian detection models. Results from [53].

pedestrians, whereas this issue is addressed and the pedestrian detection is improved in the thermal R-CNN fusion results.

6.1.6 Knowledge distillation

Knowledge distillation is widely known as a student-teacher approach for model compression where a student network is trained to match a large pre-trained teacher

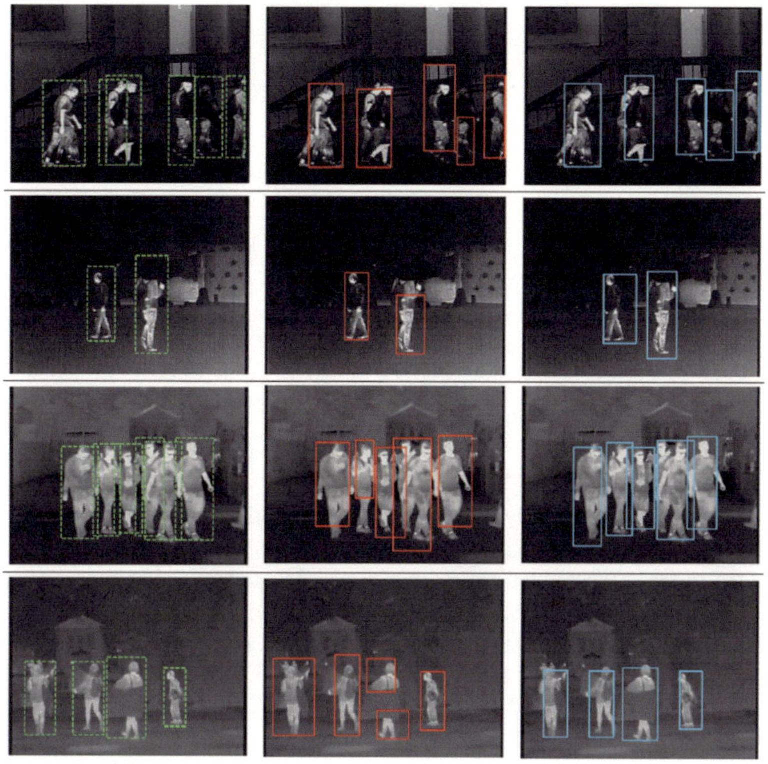

Figure 17.
Example images to demonstrate the improved pedestrian detection by (c) the thermal R-CNN fusion model compared to (a) ground truth and (b) modified R-CNN. Results from [53].

network. Here, the information is transferred from teacher network to the student network by reducing the loss function as well as GT labels. Chen et al. [54] proposed to use the low-level feature from the teacher network to supervise and train the deeper features for the student network resulting in improved performance. To address the low-resolution issues of IR-visible fused images, Xiao et al. [55] introduced a heterogeneous knowledge distillation network with multi-layer attention embedding. This technique consists of teacher network with high resolution fusion and a student network with low-resolution and super-resolution fusion. The perceptual distillation method used to train the image fusion neural networks without GTs is proposed by Liu et al. [56] to train the teacher network and a multi-autoencoder with self-supervision for a student network. Furthermore, there are multiple such studies conducted in recent times summarized in **Table 8**.

6.1.7 Adaptive mechanism

Over the years, many researchers proposed to incorporate adaptive mechanisms for image fusion networks as they enable the system to adjust its behavior according to varying environmental or operating conditions. For a better fusion effect, Xia et al. [59] introduced a parameter adaptive pulse coupled neural network, and Kong et al. [60] proposed an adaptive normalization mechanism-based fusion method. To extract features and to estimate similarity Leu et al. [61] integrated a new strategy

Literature	Advantages	Disadvantages
Original knowledge distillation [54]	Compresses a large model	Loses information
Cross-stage connection path [55]	Uses low-level features to supervise deeper features	Increases the complexity
Heterogeneous [56]	Joint fusion and Super-resolution	Depends on Teacher network quality
Perceptual distillation [57]	Trains image fusion networks without ground truths	depends on teacher network quality
Depth-distilled multi-focus [58] image fusion	Transfers depth knowledge to improve fusion accuracy	Depends on accuracy of depth knowledge

Table 8.
Summary of knowledge-distillation network-related literature [57].

for image retrieval using adaptive features. In brief, this adaptive feature mechanism blends the effectiveness of multiple features and outperforms the single feature retrieval techniques. This can enhance the image fusion precision, reduce the noise interference and enhance the real-time performance of the network. Conversely, there have been various adaptive mechanisms such as adaptive selection loss function, activation and sampling functions proposed to optimize the deep learning neural networks. The advantages and disadvantages of adaptive mechanism-related literature are summarized in **Table 9**.

6.1.8 Generative adversarial network

Ma et al. [65] introduced the generative adversarial network (GAN) based generation countermeasure network to the field of image fusion, making the generators synthesize the fused images from visible and thermal cameras with good textures using discriminators. A typical GAN-based image fusion framework is represented as shown in **Figure 18**. They have also proposed loss of detail and edge enhancement loss to enhance the quality of the minute details and sharpen the

Literature	Advantages	Disadvantages
Parameter adaptive pulse-coupled neural network [59]	Better image fusion	Sensitive to Parameter settings
Adaptive features and information entropy [60]	Effective feature extraction good similarity estimation	Poor complex scene handling
Adaptive normalization mechanism-based fusion [61]	Injects detailed features into structured fusion	Introduces artifacts or distortion
Adaptive loss, activation and sampling functions [62]	Optimizes the performance	More computational resources
Global group sparse coding [63]	Automatic network depth estimation by learning inter-layer connections	Suffer from sparsity or redundancy issues
Novel network structures [64]	Outperforms traditional ones	Difficulty to design

Table 9.
Summary of adaptive mechanism network-related literature.

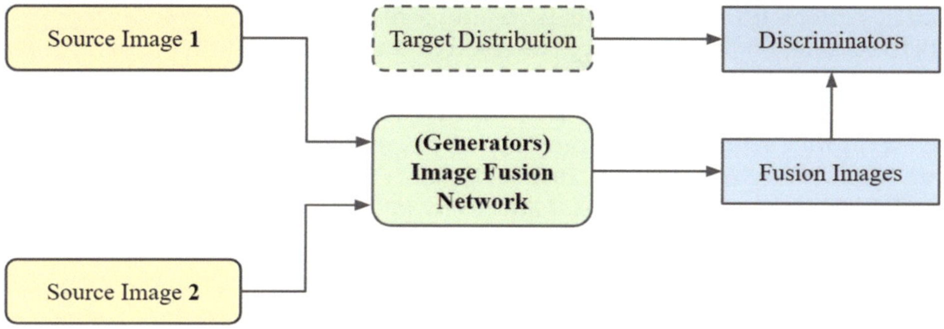

Figure 18.
Generative adversarial network based image fusion framework.

edges and features in the target images. Further, they have attempted to improve the GAN-based framework by including the double discriminator conditional generation countermeasure network. Li et al. [66] showcased improvement in capturing the interested region through integrating a multi-scale attention mechanism branch into the GAN-based Image fusion framework. These networks generate fused images with excellent quality, which are useful for entertainment and human perception, However, these networks are not suitable for demanding visual processing tasks like in automotive applications.

6.1.9 Hybrid model

Hybrid models [67] are created by combining the high-performing models in specific scenarios to enhance the performance in generic situations. Hybrid models generally include multi-scale transformation with expression detection, saliency detection, sparse representation or pulse-coupled neural networks. These hybrid models effectively improve the performance of fused models by enhancing the clarity and texture features of the fused images, whereas the model complexity and computational cost should be majorly considered while designing such models.

7. Conclusions

Level 3 and above ADAS and AV systems demand accurate and precise perception of the surrounding environment in order to drive the vehicle autonomously. This can be achieved using multiple sensors of different modalities such as vision, lidars and radars. ADAS and AV systems provided by various OEMs and Tier 1 companies show a lack of performance in extreme weather and lighting conditions, especially dark scenarios, sun glare, rain, fog and snow. The performance can be improved by adding another sensor to existing sensor suite that can provide complementary and redundant information during the extreme environments. The properties and characteristics of Infrared sensors look promising as it is capable of detecting the natural emission of IR radiations and representing that as an image which indicates relative temperature map. Recent advancements in AI paved the way to establish efficient algorithms that can detect and classify objects more accurately irrespective of weather and lighting conditions. Also, it is capable of detecting objects at long distances compared to other sensors. Literature shows that fusing the information from IR sensor with other sensor data results more precisely thereby ensuring the path towards autonomous driving. The research community looks for more datasets available for RGB images for quick and easy deployment of IR in ADAS and AV applications. Integration in the automotive domain is challenging currently as IR camera needs a separate setup for calibration and is an expensive technology due to sensor array. More intense research in IR technology and deep learning models may be highly beneficial to make use of IR cameras effectively in ADAS and AV systems.

Abbreviations

ADAS	advanced driver assistance system
AV	autonomous vehicle
AD	autonomous driving
NHTSA	National Highway Traffic Safety Administration
OEM	original equipment manufacturer
SAE	society of automotive engineers
2D/3D	two dimenional/3 dimensional
GPS	global positioning system
IMU	inertial measurement unit
IR	infrared
NIR	near infrared
SWIR	short wave infrared
FLIR	forward looking infrared
MWIR	mid wave infrared
LWIR	long wave infrared
Lidar	light detection and ranging
Radar	radio wave detection and ranging
FOV	field of view
AI	artificial intelligence
VRU	vulnerable road user
ROI	region of interest
BB	bounding box
GT	ground truth
IoU	intersection over union
CNN	convolutional neural network
DL	deep learning
GAN	generative adversarial network
RGBI	red, green, blue, intensity
VRU	vulnerable road user
HOG	histogram of oriented gradients
LBP	local binary patterns
R-CNN	region-CNN
R-FCN	regional-fast convolution network
SSD	single shot detector
YOLO	you only look once

Author details

Suganthi Srinivasan*†, Rakesh Rajegowda† and Eshwar Udhayakumar
Software Products and Services Product Line (DSW), Driving Assistance Product Group, Valeo India Private Limited, Chennai, India

*Address all correspondence to: suganthiss@gmail.com

†These authors contributed equally

References

[1] Williams M. The drive for autonomous vehicles: The DARPA grand challenge. Available from: https://www.herox.com/blog/159-the-drive-for-autonomous-vehicles-the-darpa-grand

[2] US Department of Transportation. Standing general order on crash reporting: For incidents involving ADS and level 2 ADAS. Jun 2022. Available from: https://www.nhtsa.gov/laws-regulations/standing-general-order-crash-reporting

[3] Kukkala VK, Tunnell J, Pasricha S, Bradley T. Advanced driver-assistance systems: A path toward autonomous vehicles. IEEE Consumer Electronics Magazine. 2018;7(5):18-25

[4] Moller DP, Haas RE. Advanced driver assistance systems and autonomous driving. In: Guide to Automotive Connectivity and Cybersecurity: Trends, Technologies, Innovations and Applications. Cham: Springer; 2019. pp. 513-580

[5] Rosique F, Navarro PJ, Fernãndez C, Padilla A. A systematic review of perception system and simulators for autonomous vehicles research. Sensors. 2019;**19**(3):648

[6] Odukha O. How sensor fusion for autonomous cars helps avoid deaths on the road. Intellias; Aug 2023. Available from: https://intellias.com/sensor-fusion-autonomous-cars-helps-avoid-deaths-road/

[7] Ma Y, Wang Z, Yang H, Yang L. Artificial intelligence applications in the development of autonomous vehicles: A survey. IEEE/CAA Journal of Automatica Sinica. 2020;7(2):315-329

[8] Website blog. Available from: https://interplex.com/trends/proliferation-of-sensors-in-next-gen-automobiles-is-raising-the-b [Accessed: September 28, 2023]

[9] Ondrus J, Kolla E, Vertaä P, Åaric Å. How do autonomous cars work? Transportation Research Procedia. 2020;**44**:226-233

[10] Thakur R. Infrared sensors for autonomous vehicles. Recent Development in Optoelectronic Devices. 29 Aug 2018;**84**

[11] Mohammed AS, Amamou A, Ayevide FK, Kelouwani S, Agbossou K, Zioui N. The perception system of intelligent ground vehicles in all weather conditions: A systematic literature review. Sensors. 2020;**20**:6532. DOI: 10.3390/s20226532

[12] ASTM G173-03. Standard Tables for Reference Solar Spectral Irradiances: Direct Normal and Hemispherical on 37deg Tilted Surface. American Society for Testing Materials; 2012. Available from: https://www.astm.org/g0173-03r20.html

[13] Uber Accident. 2018. Available from: https://en.wikipedia.org/wiki/Death_of_Elaine_Herzberg

[14] Image Engineering. Challenges for cameras in automotive applications. Feb 2022. Available from: https://www.image-engineering.de/library/blog/articles/1157-challenges-for-cameras-in-automotive-applications

[15] Why ADAS and autonomous vehicles need thermal infrared cameras. 2018. Available from: https://www.flir.com/ [Accessed: September 25, 2023]

[16] Minkina W, Dudzik S. Infrared Thermography: Errors and Uncertainties.

Hoboken, New Jersey, United States: John Wiley & Sons; 2009

[17] Vollmer M. Infrared thermal imaging. In: Computer Vision: A Reference Guide. Cham: Springer International Publishing; 2021. pp. 666-670

[18] Teledyne FLIR commercial System. The Ultimate Infrared Handbook for R & D Professionals. 2018. Available from: https://www.flir.com/ [Accessed: September 25, 2023]

[19] Li Y, Moreau J, Ibanez-Guzman J. Emergent visual sensors for autonomous vehicles. IEEE Transactions on Intelligent Transportation Systems. 2023;**24**(5):4716-4737. Available from: https://ieeexplore.ieee.org/document/10092278

[20] Nicolas Pinchon M, Ibn-Khedher OC, Nicolas A, Bernardin F, et al. All-weather vision for automotive safety: Which spectral band?. SIA Vision 2016. In: International Conference Night Drive Tests and Exhibition, Oct 2016, Paris, France.

[21] Hwang S, Park J, Kim N, Choi Y, So Kweon I. Multispectral pedestrian detection: Benchmark dataset and baseline. In: Proceedings of the IEEE Conference on Computer Vision and Pattern Recognition. 2015. pp. 1037-1045. Available from: https://soonminhwang.github.io/rgbt-ped-detection/

[22] Nicolas Pinchon M, Ibn-Khedher OC, Nicolas A, Bernardin F, et al. All-weather vision for automotive safety: Which spectral band? In: SIA Vision 2016 - International Conference Night Drive Tests and Exhibition, Paris, France. 2016. p. 7. Available from: https://hal.science/hal-01406023/document

[23] Farooq MA, Shariff W, O'Callaghan D, Merla A, Corcoran P. On the Role of Thermal Imaging in Automotive Applications: A Critical Review. IEEE Access; 2023

[24] Shahriar N. What is convolutional neural network – CNN (Deep Learning). Available from: https://nafizshahriar.medium.com/what-is-convolutional-neural-network-cnn-deep-learning-b3921bdd82d5

[25] Farooq MA, Shariff W, Khan F, Corcoran P, Rotariu C. C3I thermal automotive dataset. IEEE Dataport; 2022. DOI: 10.21227/jf21-rt22. Available from: https://ieee-dataport.org/documents/c3i-thermal-automotivedataset

[26] Torabi A, Masse G, Bilodeau G-A. An iterative integrated framework for thermal visible image registration, sensor fusion, and people tracking for video surveillance applications. Computer Vision and Image Understanding. 2021;**116**(2):210-221

[27] Chen Y, Shin H. Pedestrian detection at night in infrared images using an attention-guided encoder-decoder convolutional neural network. Applied Sciences. 23 Jan 2020;**10**(3):809

[28] Wu Z et al. A thermal infrared video benchmark for visual analysis. In: Proceedings of the IEEE Conference on Computer Vision and Pattern Recognition Workshops. Columbus, Ohio: IEEE; 2014. pp. 201-208

[29] Krišto M, Ivašić-Kos M. Thermal imaging dataset for person detection. In: 2019 42nd International Convention on Information and Communication Technology, Electronics and Microelectronics (MIPRO). FLIR thermal dataset; 20 May 2019. pp. 1126-1131. Available from: https://www.flir.com/oem/adas/adas-dataset-form/

[30] Hwang S, Park J, Kim N, Choi Y, Kweon IS. Multispectral pedestrian detection: Benchmark dataset and baseline. In: Proceedings of the IEEE Conference on Computer Vision and Pattern Recognition. Boston, MA, USA: IEEE; 2015. pp. 1037-1045

[31] Farooq MA, Shariff W, Ocallaghan D, Merla A, Corcoran P. On the Role of Thermal Imaging in Automotive Applications: A critical Review. Vol.11. IEEE Access; 2023. pp. 25152-25173. Available from: https://ieeexplore.ieee.org/document/10064306

[32] Solichin A, Harjoko A, Eko A. A survey of pedestrian detection in video. International Journal of Advanced Computer Science and Applications. 2014:5. DOI: 10.14569/IJACSA.2014.051007. Available from: https://thesai.org/Publications/ViewPaper?Volume=5&Issue=10&Code=ijacsa&SerialNo=7

[33] Chavez-Garcia RO, Aycard O. Multiple sensor fusion and classification for moving object detection and tracking. IEEE Transactions on Intelligent Transportation Systems. 2016;**17**:525-534. Available from: https://ieeexplore.ieee.org/document/7283636

[34] Wang X, Han TX, Yan S. An HOG-LBP human detector with partial occlusion handling. In: Proceedings of the IEEE 12th International Conference on Computer Vision, Kyoto, Japan, 29 September-2 October 2009. Japan: IEEE; 2009. pp. 32-39. Available from: https://ieeexplore.ieee.org/document/5459207

[35] Ahmed S, Huda MN, Rajbhandari S, Saha C, Elshaw M, Kanarachos S. Pedestrian and cyclist detection and intent estimation for autonomous vehicles: A survey. Applied Sciences. 2019;**9**:2335. DOI: 10.3390/app9112335

[36] Girshick R, Donahue J, Darrell T, Malik J. Rich feature hierarchies for accurate object detection and semantic segmentation. In: Proceedings of the EEE Conference on Computer Vision and Pattern Recognition (CVPR), Columbus, OH, USA, 24-27 June 2014. Columbus, Ohio: IEEE; 2014. pp. 580-587

[37] Dai J, Li Y, He K, Sun J. R-FCN: Object detection via region-based fully convolutional networks. In: Proceedings of the IEEE conference on Advances in Neural Information Processing, Barcelona, Spain. Spain: IEEE; 2016. pp. 379-387

[38] Ren S, He K, Girshick R, Sun J. Faster R-CNN: Towards real-time object detection with region proposal networks. Advances in Neural Information Processing Systems. 2015;**39**:1137-1149

[39] Liu W, Anguelov D, Erhan D, Szegedy C, Reed S, Fu CY, et al. SSD: Single shot multibox detector. In: European Conference on Computer Vision. Cham, Switzerland: Springer; 2016. pp. 21-37

[40] Redmon J, Divvala S, Girshick R, Farhadi A. You only look once: Unified, real-time object detection. arXiv 2015, arXiv:1506.02640

[41] Geronimo D, Lopez AM, Sappa AD, Graf T. Survey of pedestrian detection for advanced driver assistance systems. IEEE Transactions on Pattern Analysis and Machine Intelligence. 2010;**32**:1239-1258

[42] Enzweiler M, Gavrila DM. Monocular pedestrian detection: Survey and experiments. IEEE Transactions on Pattern Analysis and Machine Intelligence. 2009;**31**:2179-2195

[43] Dolã P, Wojek C, Schiele B, Perona P. Pedestrian detection: An evaluation of the state of the art. IEEE Transactions

on Pattern Analysis and Machine Intelligence. 2011

[44] Hou YL, Song Y, Hao X, Shen Y, Qian M. Multispectral Pedestrian Detection Based on Deep Convolutional Neural Networks. In: Proceedings of the IEEE International Conference on Signal Processing, Communications and Computing (ICSPCC), Xiamen, China. 2017. pp. 22-25

[45] Wagner J, Fischer V, Herman M. Multispectral pedestrian detection using deep fusion convolutional neural networks. In: Proceedings of the European Symposium on Artificial Neural Networks, Bruges, Belgium. Belgium: ESANN; 2016. pp. 27-29

[46] Du X, El-Khamy M, Lee J, Davis L. Fused DNN: A deep neural network fusion approach to fast and robust pedestrian detection. In: Proceedings of the 2017 IEEE Winter Conference on Applications of Computer Vision, WACV 2017, Santa Rosa, CA, USA. CA, USA: IEEE; 2017. pp. 953-961

[47] Li H, Wu XJ. DenseFuse: A fusion approach to infrared and visible images. IEEE Transactions on Image Processing. 2018;**28**:2614-2623

[48] Tang L, Yuan J, Ma J. Image fusion in the loop of high-level vision tasks: A semantic-aware real-time infrared and visible image fusion network. Information Fusion. 2022;**82**:28-42

[49] Xu H, Ma J, Jiang J, Guo X, Ling H. U2Fusion: A unified unsupervised image fusion network. IEEE Transactions on Pattern Analysis and Machine Intelligence. 2020;**44**:502-518

[50] Tang W, He F, Liu Y. YDTR: Infrared and visible image fusion via Y-shape dynamic transformer. IEEE Transactions on Multimedia. 2023;**25**:5413-5428. DOI: 10.1109/TMM.2022.3192661

[51] Hui L, Xjw A, Jk B. RFN-Nest: An end-to-end residual fusion network for infrared and visible images. Information Fusion. 2021;**73**:72-86

[52] Yoon S, Cho J. Deep multimodal detection in reduced visibility using thermal depth estimation for autonomous driving. Sensors. 2022;**22**:5084. DOI: 10.3390/s22145084

[53] Chen Y, Shin H. Pedestrian detection at night in infrared images using an attention-guided encoder-decoder convolutional neural network. Applied Sciences. 2020;**10**:809. DOI: 10.3390/app10030809

[54] Chen P, Liu S, Zhao H, Jia J. Distilling knowledge via knowledge review. In: Proceedings of the IEEE/CVF Conference on Computer Vision and Pattern Recognition (CVPR), Nashville, TN, USA. IEEE; 2021. pp. 5006-5015

[55] Xiao W, Zhang Y, Wang H, Li F, Jin H. Heterogeneous knowledge distillation for simultaneous infrared-visible image fusion and super-resolution. IEEE Transactions on Instrumentation and Measurement. 2022;**71**:1-15

[56] Liu X, Hirota K, Jia Z, Dai Y. A multi-autoencoder fusion network guided by perceptual distillation. Information Sciences. 2022;**606**:1-20

[57] Zhao Z, Su S, Wei J, Tong X, Gao W. Lightweight infrared and visible image fusion via adaptive DenseNet with knowledge distillation. Electronics. 2023;**12**:2773. DOI: 10.3390/electronics12132773

[58] Mi J, Wang L, Liu Y, Zhang J. KDE-GAN: A multimodal medical image-fusion model based on knowledge distillation and explainable AI modules. Computers in Biology and Medicine. 2022;**151**:106273

[59] Xia J, Lu Y, Tan L. Research of multimodal medical image fusion based on parameter-adaptive pulse-coupled neural network and convolutional sparse representation. Computational and Mathematical Methods in Medicine. 2020;**2020**:3290136

[60] Lu X, Zhang L, Niu L, Chen Q, Wang J. A novel adaptive feature fusion strategy for image retrieval. Entropy. 2021;**23**:1670

[61] Wang L, Hu Z, Kong Q, Qi Q, Liao Q. Infrared and visible image fusion via attention-based adaptive feature fusion. Entropy. 2023;**25**:407

[62] Zeng S, Zhang Z, Zou Q. Adaptive deep neural networks methods for high-dimensional partial differential equations. Journal of Computational Physics. 2022;**463**:111232

[63] Yuan J, Pan F, Zhou C, Qin T, Liu TY. Learning Structures for deep neural networks. 27 May 2021. arXiv arXiv:2105.13905

[64] Li H, Yang Y, Chen D, Lin Z. Optimization algorithm inspired deep neural network structure design. In: Asian Conference on Machine Learning. PMLR; 4 Nov 2018. pp. 614-629. arXiv 2018, arXiv:1810.01638

[65] Ma J, Yu W, Liang P, Li C, Jiang J. FusionGAN: A generative adversarial network for infrared and visible image fusion. Information Fusion. 2019;**48**:11-26

[66] Li J, Huo H, Li C, Wang R, Feng Q. AttentionFGAN: Infrared and visible image fusion using attention-based generative adversarial networks. IEEE Transactions on Multimedia. 2021;**23**:1383-1396

[67] Ma W, Wang K, Li J, Yang SX, Li J, Song L, et al. Infrared and visible image fusion technology and application: A review. Sensors. 2023;**23**:599. DOI: 10.3390/s23020599

Chapter 8

Visual Recognition and Prediction of Crack Propagation Trajectories

Dihao Ai

Abstract

Accurately detecting and tracking cracks on construction materials, such as concrete and rock surfaces, is of paramount importance in the field of structural engineering and materials science. The presence and propagation of cracks in these materials can have significant implications for structural integrity and safety, making it crucial to develop robust methods for crack detection and tracking. This work explores the application of computer vision and deep learning algorithms in the visual recognition and prediction of crack propagation trajectories in construction materials. Specifically, a Split Hopkinson Pressure Bar system and a static compression loading platform were constructed to simulate fracture processes in concrete and rock materials. The high-speed camera was used to capture the fracture process as a video or image sequence. An automatic pixel-level crack segmentation method was proposed to extract cracks at critical moments within the fracture video. Subsequently, the Long Short-Term Memory network was employed to learn temporal patterns and dependencies within the crack segmentation masks across consecutive frames. By leveraging the learned temporal patterns, the network can estimate how cracks will evolve and propagate in subsequent frames. The proposed method has potential applications in assessing structural integrity, understanding fracture mechanisms, and informing maintenance and repair decisions.

Keywords: crack detection, crack propagation trajectories, computer vision, static-dynamic loading, construction materials

1. Introduction

Timely and accurate inspection and assessment of civil infrastructure, including buildings, roads, and underground tunnels, is crucial to ensure their continued safety and functionality. After years of operation, these structures may experience deterioration and damage, making it essential to identify and address potential issues promptly. Among the various types of distress, cracks are particularly significant as they can indicate severe structural integrity problems, posing risks to both the structure itself and the people in its vicinity. Therefore, the development of accurate, fast, and automated crack detection methods is of utmost importance in various civil engineering applications.

In recent decades, substantial advancements have been made in the automatic detection and quantification of cracks, thanks to the progress in hardware data acquisition systems. These advancements have enabled the implementation of sophisticated techniques for crack detection and analysis. By leveraging state-of-the-art sensors and imaging technologies, such as high-resolution cameras, LiDAR, or ground-penetrating radar (GPR), it is now possible to capture detailed information about the surface conditions of civil structures [1]. Automatic crack detection algorithms can utilize these acquired data to identify and locate cracks on structure surfaces. Computer vision techniques, including image processing and pattern recognition methods, play a vital role in analyzing the captured images or point cloud data and extracting relevant crack features [2, 3]. Machine learning algorithms, such as deep neural networks, can be trained on large datasets of annotated crack images to learn the characteristic patterns and textures associated with cracks. These models can then be deployed to accurately and efficiently detect cracks in real time or during post-processing.

Furthermore, advancements in data processing and computing capabilities have facilitated the development of efficient algorithms for crack quantification. Once cracks are detected, various parameters such as crack length, width, orientation, and depth can be measured to assess the severity and extent of the damage. These quantitative measurements are crucial for making informed decisions regarding maintenance, repair, or rehabilitation strategies.

The integration of remote sensing techniques, such as aerial or satellite imagery, with ground-based data acquisition systems has further enhanced the capabilities of crack detection and monitoring. By combining data from multiple sources, it becomes possible to obtain a comprehensive understanding of the structural health and performance of civil infrastructure over large areas.

In this study, we propose an automatic pixel-level crack segmentation method to extract cracks at critical moments within the fracture videos. This method leverages image processing techniques and deep learning models to identify crack regions accurately. By segmenting cracks at the pixel level, we can obtain detailed information about crack geometry, size, and orientation, which are essential for subsequent analysis and prediction. Furthermore, we employ a Long Short-Term Memory (LSTM) network, a type of recurrent neural network (RNN), to learn temporal patterns and dependencies within the crack segmentation masks across consecutive frames. The LSTM network is capable of capturing long-term dependencies and sequential information, making it suitable for modeling crack evolution over time. By leveraging the learned temporal patterns, the network can estimate how cracks will evolve and propagate in subsequent frames, enabling us to predict crack trajectories accurately.

The paper is structured as follows. Section 2 provides an overview of the related work on automatic crack detection and segmentation algorithms. Section 3 outlines the methodology employed in this study. Details regarding the experiments, specimens, and dataset preparation are presented in Section 4. Section 5 presents the results and discussions. Finally, Section 6 concludes the paper and discusses potential extensions of the work.

2. Related works

In the field of crack visual detection, significant research efforts have been devoted to developing effective methods for crack segmentation and analysis.

This section presents a comprehensive review of the related work, focusing on four key categories: threshold-based, filter-based, machine learning, and deep learning methods.

Threshold-based methods involve setting a threshold value to distinguish crack and non-crack regions based on intensity or gradient information. Chen et al. [4] proposed a real-time image thresholding method for pavement crack detection. They calculated the mean and standard deviation of the pixel intensities in a gray-level pavement image to determine the threshold value. By comparing the pixel intensities with the threshold, cracks could be accurately segmented from the background. The method demonstrated the effectiveness of utilizing statistical measures for threshold determination in real-time crack detection scenarios.

Filter-based methods utilize various image filters to enhance crack features and improve segmentation results. These filters can be designed to capture specific crack characteristics such as texture or shape. Abdel-Qader et al. [5] conducted early research on visual detection of surface crack defects in bridges. They implemented and compared four crack detection image operator techniques, namely, Haar, Fast Harr Transform (FHT), Fast Fourier Transform (FFT), Sobel, and Canny, in the context of bridge monitoring and maintenance. The results indicated that FHT demonstrated higher reliability than the other three edge detection techniques in crack identification. Apart from above filters, Gabor filters offer selectivity for both scale and orientation, making them a valuable tool for crack detection. In numerous studies, researchers have utilized Gabor filters to detect cracks in images of pavements and bridges [6, 7].

Machine learning techniques have been widely applied to crack detection and segmentation tasks. These methods involve training a classifier or regression model on annotated crack images to automatically identify cracks. For example, the work in [8] explored the application of Support Vector Machines (SVM) for concrete crack detection. The training process involved feeding the SVM algorithm with a labeled dataset, where each sample was labeled as either "crack" or "non-crack." The SVM algorithm learned to separate the two classes by finding an optimal hyperplane in a high-dimensional feature space. This hyperplane maximizes the margin between the two classes, allowing for accurate classification of new, unseen images. The results of the study demonstrated the feasibility and effectiveness of using SVM for concrete crack detection, achieving high detection accuracy and providing a reliable approach for crack identification in concrete structures. An example of employing a pavement crack detection framework based on random forests (RF) is presented in the work by Shi et al. [9]. They proposed a framework called CrackForest, specifically designed to identify complex cracks in pavement images. The CrackForest framework utilized random structured forests along with integral channel features to define crack tokens that incorporate structural information. These crack tokens represented crack regions within image patches, with each patch measuring 16x16 pixels and containing labeled crack edges. The CrackForest method demonstrated its capability to extract complex cracks with arbitrary topologies, including corners, curves, and lines, on the road crack dataset known as CFD. By leveraging the RF technique and incorporating integral channel features, the framework exhibited robust crack detection performance. It provided an effective approach for automated identification of complex cracks in pavement images, offering potential benefits in road inspection and maintenance. Kim et al. [10] proposed a machine learning-based method for concrete crack recognition, which aids in identifying the presence and location of cracks from surface images.

In recent years, with the increase in hardware computing power and data scale, deep learning algorithms have been widely applied to high-level feature learning in crack defect images. They have achieved remarkable results in the precise identification of complex crack defects in scenarios with complex background noise. Deep learning techniques, particularly convolutional neural networks (CNNs), have revolutionized crack detection and segmentation. These methods leverage the hierarchical representation learning capabilities of CNNs to automatically extract discriminative crack features. For instance, Zhang et al. [11] introduced a novel approach called CrackNet, which is based on Convolutional Neural Networks (CNN), for 3D asphalt pavement crack detection. In their studies, Zhang et al. compared the performance of CNN with other methods, including SVM and a 3D shadow modeling method. The results demonstrated the superiority of CNN over these alternative approaches. CNNs have the advantage of automatically learning discriminative features from raw data, allowing for more accurate and efficient crack detection in pavement images. Dung et al. [12] presented an algorithm for crack detection on concrete materials utilizing Fully Convolutional Networks (FCN). Their approach involved employing various CNN architectures, including VGG16, Inception-V3, and ResNet, as encoders to extract features. To evaluate the performance of the algorithm, Dung et al. conducted experiments on the Concrete-Crack-Ozgene dataset, which is a publicly available dataset commonly used for concrete crack analysis. The results of their study revealed that VGG16 outperformed Inception-V3 and ResNet in terms of crack image classification. Zhang et al. [13] proposed a novel context-aware deep convolutional semantic segmentation network for the effective detection of concrete surface cracks under various conditions.

3. Methodology

3.1 Overview

Figure 1 illustrates the framework overview of the visual recognition and prediction of crack propagation trajectories in this study. Firstly, we established static and dynamic loading experimental systems using a hydraulic machine and SHPB (Split Hopkinson Pressure Bar), respectively. Concrete, rock, and coal standard specimens were subjected to destructive tests at different loading rates. The crack propagation process of different materials under various loading conditions was recorded using a high-speed camera. Subsequently, the FPN (Feature Pyramid Network) was employed to identify and extract cracks, while ConvLSTM (Convolutional Long Short-Term Memory) was used for spatiotemporal modeling and analysis of the extracted cracks. Ultimately, predictive analysis of crack propagation in building materials was conducted.

3.2 FPN for crack segmentation

Pixel-level crack segmentation plays a crucial role in accurately identifying and delineating crack regions within construction materials. To tackle this task, we used the Feature Pyramid Network (FPN), a popular architecture that has shown remarkable performance in various semantic segmentation tasks, including crack detection [14].

The FPN architecture is designed to address the challenge of effectively utilizing multi-scale features for pixel-level segmentation. It leverages a top-down pathway

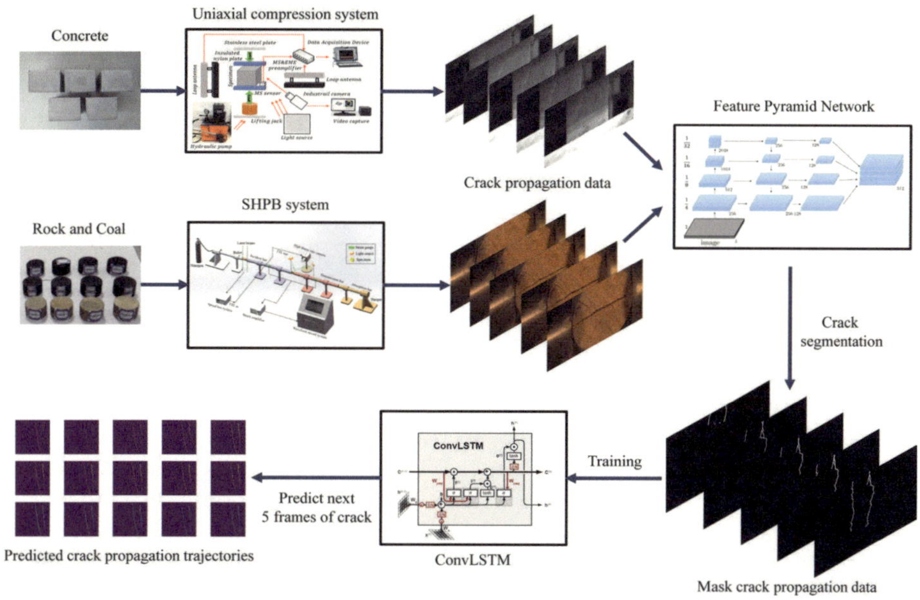

Figure 1.
An overview of this work.

and lateral connections to create a feature pyramid with multiple levels of abstraction. This allows the network to capture both local and global contextual information, enabling accurate and precise segmentation. The FPN module consists of two main components: the top-down pathway and the lateral connections. The top-down pathway involves upsampling the higher-resolution feature maps to match the dimensions of the lower-resolution feature maps. This process allows the network to propagate fine-grained details from higher levels to lower levels, enhancing the ability to capture small-scale crack features. The lateral connections, on the other hand, involve the fusion of feature maps from different levels of the pyramid. This fusion operation helps to preserve both local and global contextual information by combining features at different scales. By integrating multi-scale features, the FPN can effectively handle cracks of varying sizes and complexities, improving the accuracy of pixel-level segmentation.

In this work, we employ ResNet as a pre-trained backbone network to extract high-level features from the input crack images. These features are then fed into the FPN module, which generates a set of feature maps at different resolutions, each corresponding to a specific scale of the input image. To perform pixel-level crack segmentation, we employ a segmentation head on top of the FPN module. This head typically consists of convolutional layers followed by upsampling and downsampling operations. The convolutional layers further refine the features obtained from the FPN, while the upsampling and downsampling operations adjust the resolution of the features to match the input image size and the desired output segmentation map.

During the training phase, we optimize the FPN network by minimizing the binary the Dice loss, and Intersection over Union (IoU) score. This loss function measures the discrepancy between the predicted crack segmentation map and the ground truth map at each pixel location. By backpropagating the error through the network, the FPN adjusts its parameters to improve the accuracy of crack segmentation.

The FPN-based pixel-level crack segmentation method offers several advantages. Firstly, the multi-scale feature fusion enables the network to capture crack details at different resolutions, improving the segmentation accuracy for cracks of varying sizes. Secondly, the top-down pathway facilitates the propagation of fine-grained details, enhancing the network's ability to capture small-scale crack features. Lastly, the FPN architecture is flexible and can be easily integrated with different backbone networks, making it adaptable to various crack detection scenarios.

3.3 ConvLSTM for crack propagation prediction

The ConvLSTM [15] architecture extends the traditional LSTM by replacing fully connected layers with convolutional layers. This modification enables the network to process spatially structured data, such as images or video frames, directly. By integrating convolutional operations into the LSTM framework, the ConvLSTM can learn spatial patterns and temporal dependencies simultaneously. Specially, ConvLSTM layer consists of a grid of LSTM cells, where each cell maintains a hidden state and a cell state. The hidden state captures the learned representation of the crack segmentation masks, while the cell state retains the long-term memory of the temporal sequence. By processing each input frame sequentially, the ConvLSTM network can learn and update its hidden and cell states, capturing the evolution of cracks over time.

In other words, the CNN component enables the network to extract spatial features from crack segmentation masks, effectively capturing the local patterns and structural characteristics of cracks. This is particularly important when dealing with heterogeneous materials or complex crack networks. On the other hand, the LSTM component enables the network to learn long-term temporal dependencies and dynamics in crack evolution. By analyzing the sequential nature of crack segmentation masks, the LSTM can capture the temporal patterns and propagate information across frames, allowing the network to make accurate predictions about future crack configurations.

In this framework, the crack segmentation masks from consecutive frames are treated as input sequences to the ConvLSTM network. Each crack segmentation mask is first passed through a series of convolutional layers, which extract spatial features and encode local patterns. The output of the convolutional layers is then fed into the ConvLSTM layer, which models the temporal dynamics and dependencies between crack segmentation masks.

During the training phase, we optimize the ConvLSTM network by minimizing the prediction error between the predicted crack segmentation mask and the ground truth mask for each frame. We employ a suitable loss function, such as binary cross-entropy, to measure the discrepancy between the predicted and ground truth masks. By backpropagating the error through time, the network adjusts its parameters to improve the accuracy of crack propagation prediction. Once trained, the ConvLSTM network can be used for crack propagation prediction in unseen frames. Given the crack segmentation mask at time t, the network predicts the mask at time t + 1, representing the expected crack configuration in the subsequent frame. By iteratively applying this prediction process, we can forecast the crack propagation trajectories over multiple future frames.

In the subsequent sections, we will present the experimental setup, dataset acquisition, and training procedure in detail. We will also show the results to demonstrate the effectiveness and robustness of the ConvLSTM-based crack propagation prediction approach.

4. Experimental details

4.1 Experimental system

Figures 2 and **3** show the uniaxial compression loading and SHPB experimental setup used in this work, respectively. In **Figure 2**, the uniaxial compression loading experimental setup is depicted. This setup is typically used to apply a unidirectional compressive force to a specimen. It consists of a hydraulic machine that generates the compressive force and a load cell to measure the applied load. A manual servo-hydraulic machine with a maximum capacity of 80 MPa and a loading rate of 1.00 mm/s was used in the experiments. This machine allows for controlled application of compressive forces to the specimens. A high-resolution and high-frame-rate camera (GS3-U3-23S6M-C) was used in the experiment. It captures images at a resolution of 1920 × 1200 pixels and a frame rate of 163 fps. This camera effectively recorded the fracture behaviors of the specimens under uniaxial compressive loading.

Figure 3 illustrates the Split Hopkinson Pressure Bar (SHPB) experimental setup. The SHPB is commonly used to generate high-strain-rate loading conditions for dynamic material testing [16]. The experimental system is composed of four main components: SHPB bars, impact control system, stress pulse recorder, and video capture. To capture the images of the failure process, a full-color high-frame camera, specifically the Fastcam-SA5(16G) developed by PHOTRON corporation, was utilized. This camera is equipped with a Gigabit Ethernet high-speed communication interface, enabling it to capture images at a frame rate of up to 50,000 Frames Per Second (FPS). The camera has a resolution of 512 × 272 pixels, allowing for detailed and high-quality image capture of the crack propagation and failure process in the specimens.

4.2 Sample preparation

The study focused on conducting experiments on commonly used materials such as concrete, rock, and coal, as shown in **Figure 4**. To prepare the

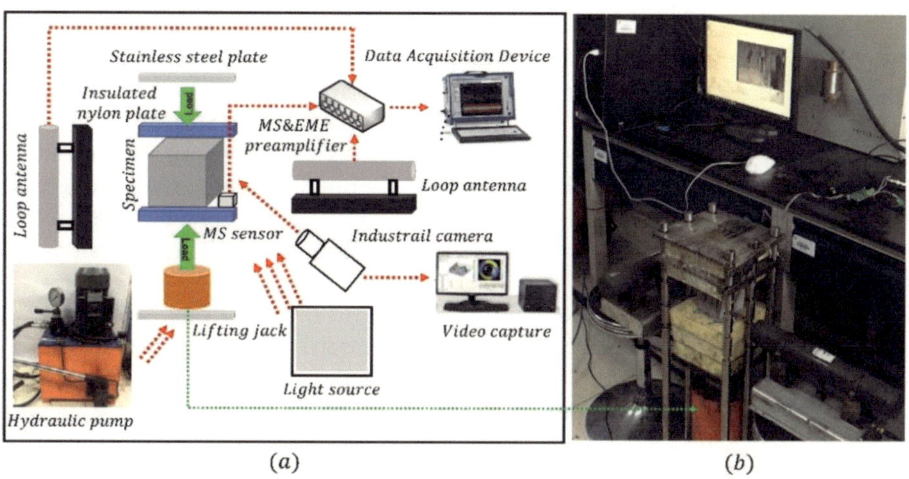

Figure 2.
An illustration of the uniaxial compression loading system: (a) the schematic diagram; (b) the physical map.

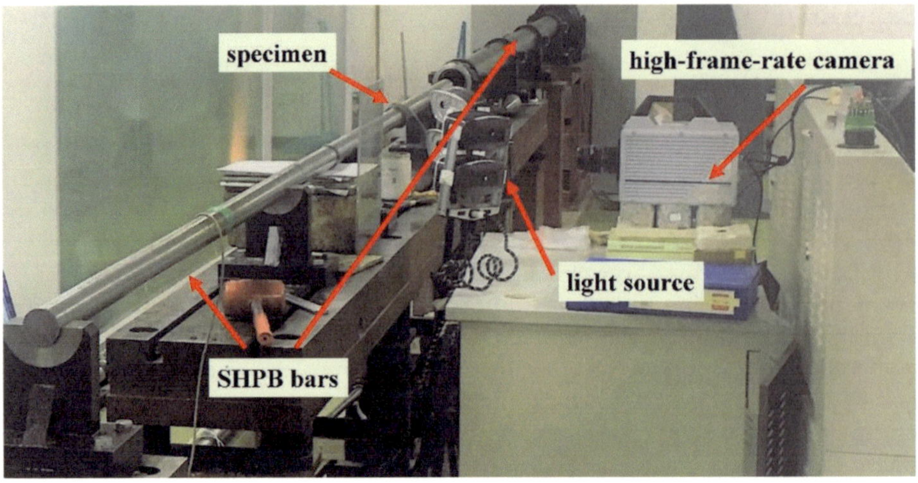

Figure 3.
An illustration of the dynamic SHPB loading system.

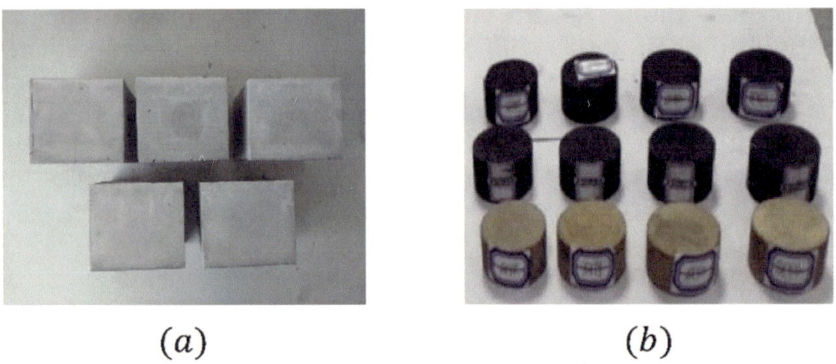

Figure 4.
An illustration of the specimens: (a) concrete; (b) coal and rock.

concrete specimens, cuboid shapes were used with approximate dimensions of 100 mm × 100 mm × 80 mm. In the case of concrete specimen preparation, a suitable concrete mix was formulated by combining cement, aggregates, and water in specific proportions. The mix was thoroughly blended to ensure uniformity and poured into molds designed to achieve the desired dimensions of approximately 100 mm × 100 mm × 80 mm. The specimens were then allowed to cure and harden under controlled conditions, ensuring proper hydration for the development of desired strength and properties.

Similarly, the rock and coal specimens were shaped into cylinders with a diameter of 50 mm and a height of 25 mm, following the recommendations of the International Society for Rock Mechanics (ISRM) for indirect tensile strength tests. The surfaces of the specimens were prepared to ensure flatness and smoothness, which are essential for accurate testing and analysis.

By adhering to the recommended dimensions specified by the ISRM for indirect tensile strength tests, the study ensured standardization and comparability of the specimens. This standardized sample preparation approach enables consistent and reliable evaluation of the mechanical properties and fracture behavior of concrete, rock, and coal materials.

4.3 Dataset preparation

In order to train the FPN (Feature Pyramid Network) network, a dataset was prepared by randomly selecting 30% of the data, which included 20 sets of crack propagation processes, consisting of nearly 300 images. The dataset was meticulously annotated to accurately label the crack propagation processes for different materials. Each frame in the dataset was carefully annotated, specifically focusing on annotating the cracks. **Figures 5** and **6** illustrate the original images and extracted crack images of different materials under various loading conditions.

The primary objective of annotating this dataset was to create a comprehensive training set that would enable the FPN network to effectively learn and understand the crack propagation processes across various materials. Through meticulous manual

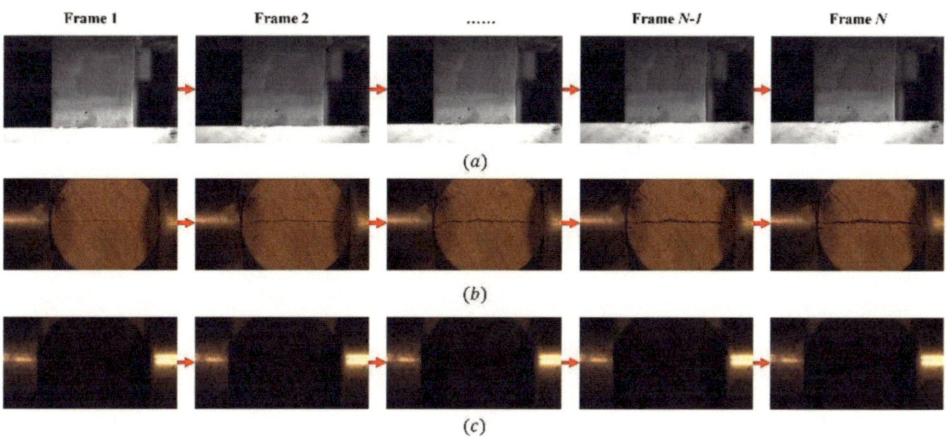

Figure 5.
An illustration of the original crack propagation data: (a) concrete material; (b) rock material; and coal material.

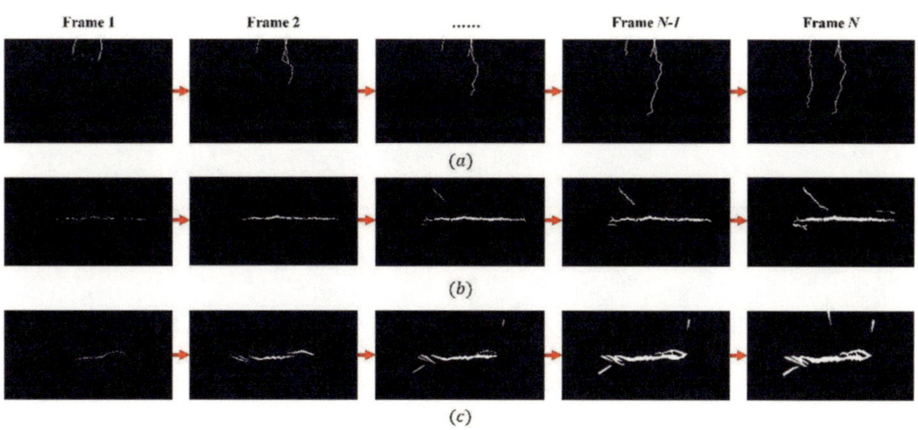

Figure 6.
An illustration of the annotated crack propagation data: (a) concrete material; (b) rock material; and coal material.

annotation, professional annotators marked the cracks visible in each frame, ensuring precise identification and characterization of the cracks.

This meticulous annotation approach ensured the dataset's high quality, providing valuable information for subsequent network training. By incorporating diverse crack propagation scenarios and materials, the dataset offers a robust and representative collection of crack images.

5. Results and discussion

5.1 Crack segmentation

Figure 7 illustrates the Dice loss and IoU score curves obtained during the training process of the FPN, as **Figures 8–11** are the segmented crack images using trained FPN. The results demonstrate that the FPN network performs well in identifying and segmenting cracks in concrete, rock, and coal materials, under both static and dynamic loading conditions. These findings provide valuable data for the subsequent training of the ConvLSTM network.

The Dice loss and IoU score curves indicate the network's performance in terms of segmentation accuracy and overlap with ground truth annotations. The curves show consistent improvement during the training process, demonstrating the network's ability to effectively capture the intricate details of cracks in different materials.

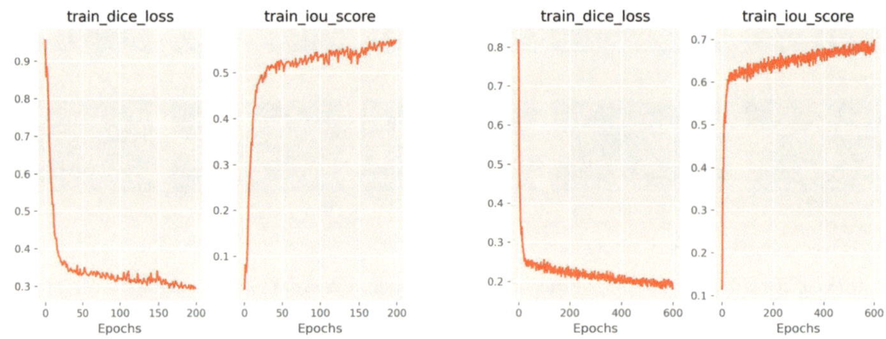

Figure 7.
Training dice loss and IoU score of FPN model.

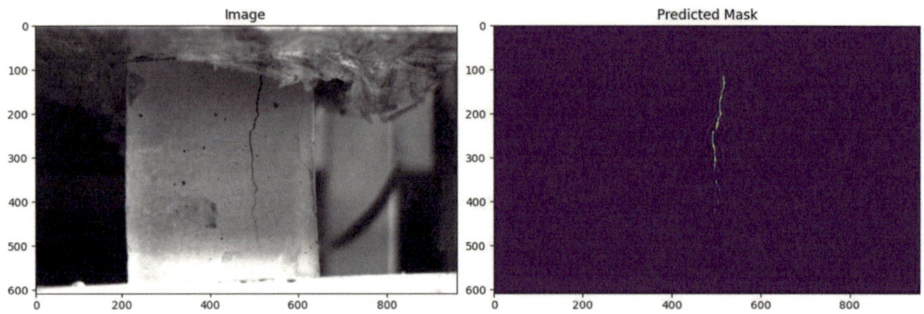

Figure 8.
An illustration of crack segmentation results of concrete specimen.

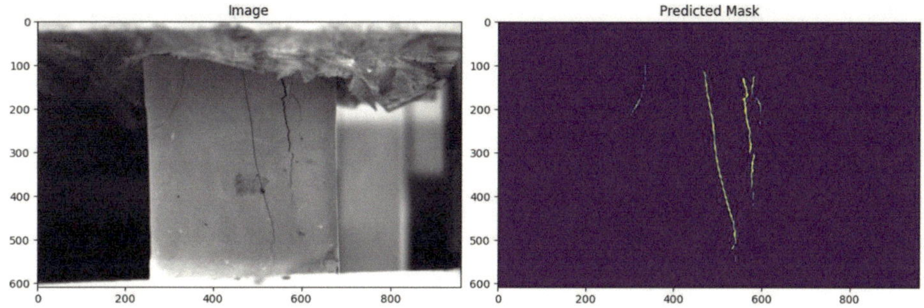

Figure 9.
An illustration of crack segmentation results of concrete specimen.

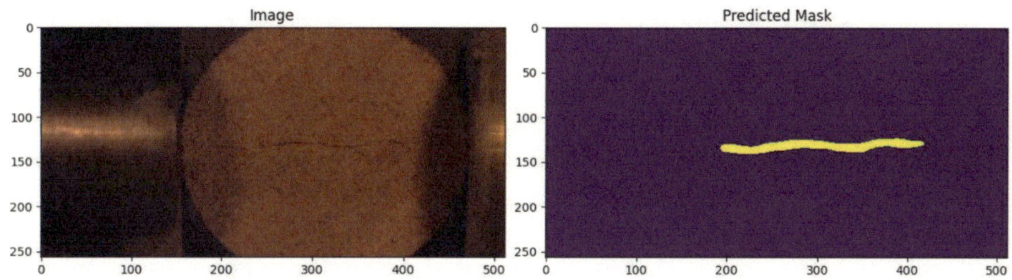

Figure 10.
An illustration of crack segmentation results of rock specimen.

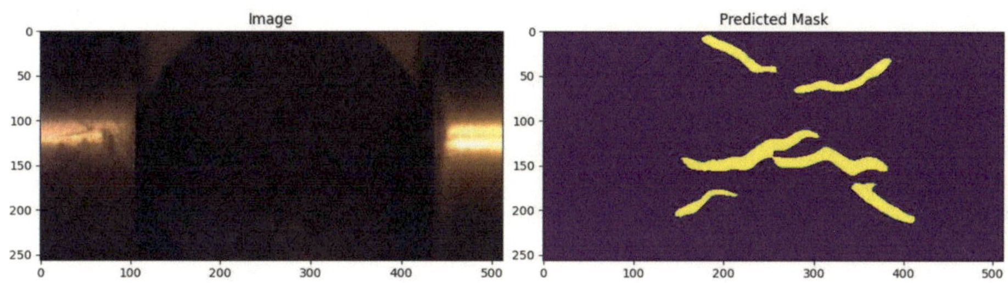

Figure 11.
An illustration of crack segmentation results of coal specimen.

The segmented crack images reveal that the FPN network successfully identifies and delineates cracks in concrete, rock, and coal materials. The network demonstrates robust performance in recognizing cracks of varying shapes and sizes, enabling accurate segmentation. This capability is crucial for further analysis and characterization of crack propagation behavior. The FPN network, with its multi-scale feature fusion and top-down pathway, proves to be a powerful architecture for pixel-level crack segmentation in construction materials. By effectively utilizing contextual information and capturing crack details at different scales, the FPN enables accurate and precise identification of crack regions.

However, despite the overall success, there are some limitations observed in the crack segmentation results. For instance, in static loading scenarios, the network occasionally fails to accurately identify the full length of cracks, resulting in incomplete segmentation. Additionally, in dynamic loading cases, the network tends to overestimate the width of cracks, leading to slightly broader segmentation than the ground truth annotations. These limitations could be addressed through further fine-tuning of the network architecture and augmentation techniques or by incorporating additional training data. Future improvements in the network's performance would enhance its ability to accurately segment cracks in both static and dynamic loading scenarios, facilitating more comprehensive analysis and prediction of crack behavior.

5.2 Crack propagation trajectories prediction

To accurately predict crack propagation trajectories, we employ a Convolutional Long Short-Term Memory (ConvLSTM) network. Based on experimental data and crack information extracted using the FPN network, we constructed a dataset comprising 217 sets of crack propagation videos. This dataset consisted of 73 sets of static loading-induced concrete crack videos, 74 sets of dynamic loading-induced rock crack videos, and 70 sets of dynamic loading-induced coal crack videos. Each video sequence included 10 frames depicting the progression of cracks. To train the ConvLSTM network, we utilized the first 5 frames as input data and the remaining 5 frames for crack propagation trajectory prediction.

Figure 12 illustrates the training and validation loss curves of the ConvLSTM network for both static and dynamic loading-induced crack propagation. These curves provide insights into the network's learning process, showing the convergence of the training loss and indicating the network's ability to capture the complex relationships between consecutive frames. **Figures 13–15** present the predicted crack propagation trajectories for different materials, showcasing the ConvLSTM network's capabilities for crack trajectories generation. The network successfully predicts the paths along which cracks propagate in concrete, rock, and coal materials. This demonstrates its ability to capture the underlying patterns and tendencies of crack growth under various loading conditions.

However, alongside its achievements, the ConvLSTM network faces certain challenges and limitations. For example, inaccurate Prediction of Complex Crack Patterns: The ConvLSTM network may struggle to accurately predict crack propagation trajectories in cases where cracks exhibit complex and intricate patterns. This limitation may arise due to the network's difficulty in capturing the subtle details and variations in such scenarios.

The accuracy of the LSTM network can also be evaluated qualitatively by visually inspecting the predicted crack masks and comparing them with the ground truth masks. If the predicted crack masks closely resemble the actual crack boundaries and capture the overall crack propagation trends, it indicates a higher level of accuracy in predicting crack propagation. However, it is important to note

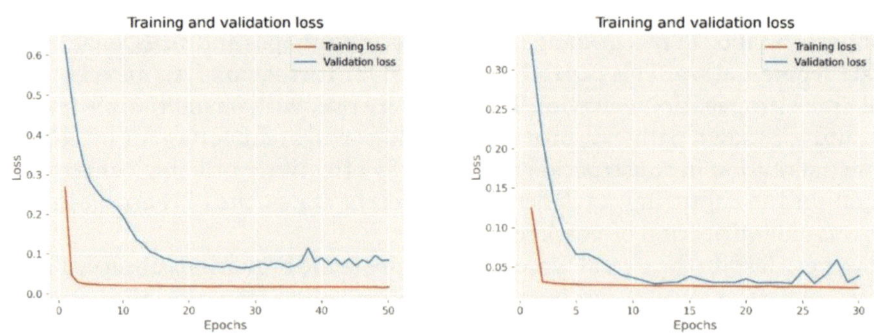

Figure 12.
Training and validation loss of ConvLSTM model.

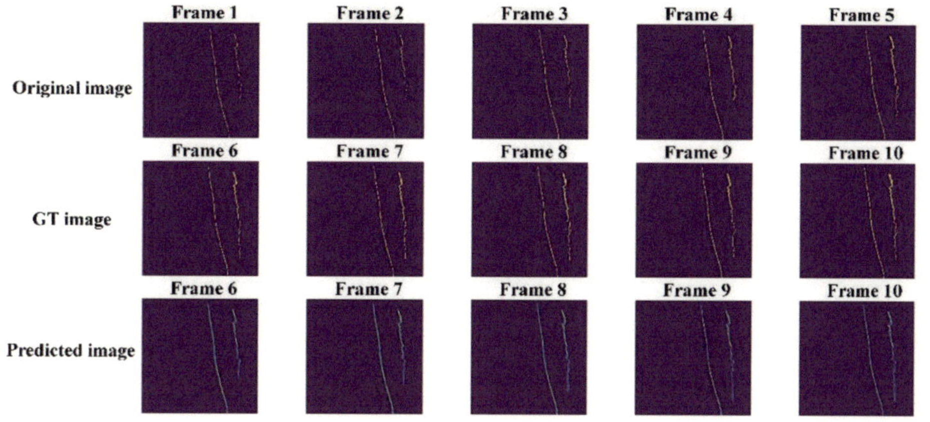

Figure 13.
An illustration of crack propagation trajectories prediction of concrete specimen under uniaxial compression loading.

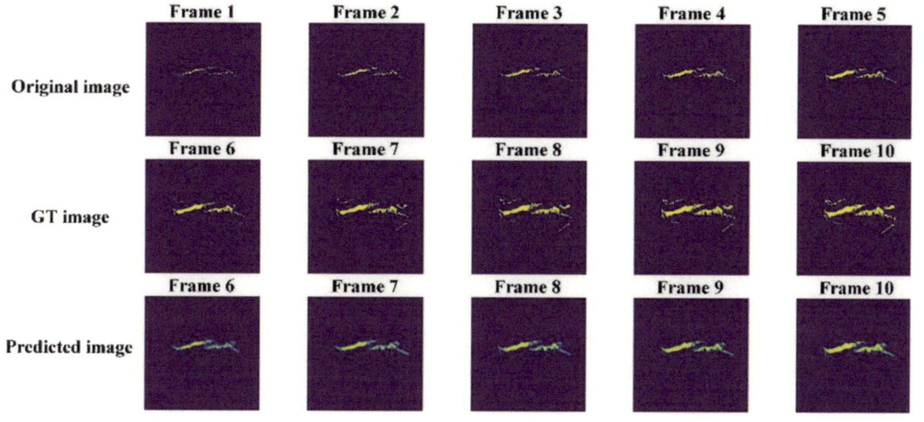

Figure 14.
An illustration of crack propagation trajectories prediction of rock specimen under dynamic SHPB loading.

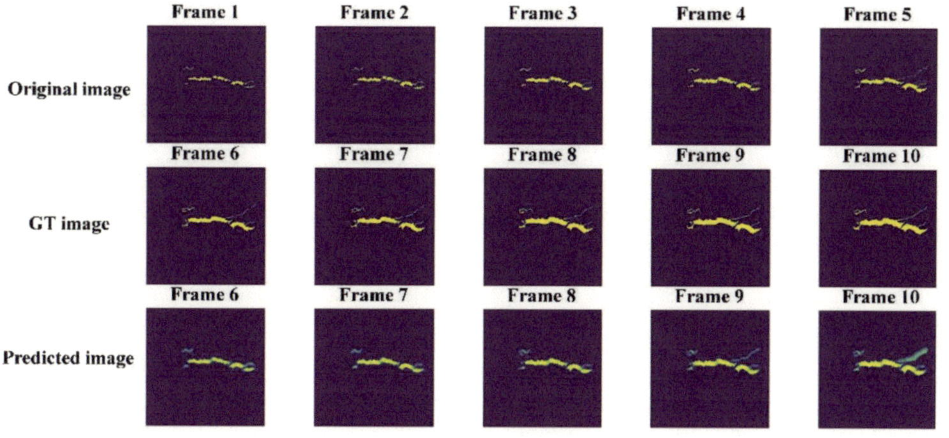

Figure 15.
An illustration of crack propagation trajectories prediction of coal specimen under dynamic SHPB loading.

that crack propagation prediction is a challenging task due to the complex nature of crack behavior. Factors such as crack branching, merging, and irregular patterns can make accurate prediction difficult, especially in dynamic and complex fracture scenarios. To improve the accuracy of crack propagation prediction, several approaches can be considered: (1) High-quality Training Data: A large and diverse dataset of fracture videos with accurately annotated crack masks can enhance the training process and improve prediction accuracy. (2) Network Architecture Design: Optimizing the architecture of the LSTM network, such as adjusting the number of layers, hidden units, or incorporating attention mechanisms, can potentially enhance the network's ability to capture temporal dependencies and improve prediction accuracy. (3) Data Augmentation: Applying data augmentation techniques, such as rotation, scaling, or adding noise, can help increase the robustness of the LSTM network and improve its generalization capability. (4) Ensemble Methods: Employing ensemble methods, such as combining predictions from multiple LSTM networks or incorporating other prediction models, can potentially improve the overall accuracy by leveraging diverse perspectives. It is worth noting that achieving high accuracy in crack propagation prediction is an ongoing research area, and the performance of the LSTM network can vary depending on the specific dataset and experimental conditions.

6. Conclusions

Accurate detection and tracking of cracks on construction materials are essential for understanding crack evolution and fracture mechanisms. By leveraging computer vision and deep learning techniques, we can develop automated systems that provide reliable crack detection, boundary tracking, and even predictive capabilities. These advancements contribute to enhancing structural integrity, safety, and durability in the field of construction materials.

This paper proposes the application of computer vision and deep learning techniques for the visual recognition and prediction of crack propagation trajectories in construction materials. By leveraging the power of these technologies, we can enhance crack analysis capabilities, improve structural health assessment, and enable proactive maintenance and repair strategies. The work combines experimental techniques, computer vision, and deep learning to advance crack detection and prediction in construction materials.

Further research can focus on enhancing the method's robustness to complex crack patterns, improving generalization to unseen materials, and exploring the integration of additional contextual information to enhance crack prediction accuracy. The development of advanced network architectures and the utilization of larger and more diverse datasets can also contribute to improving the overall performance of the crack detection and prediction system.

Acknowledgements

This work is supported by the National Natural Science Foundation of China (Grant No. 52004292), Shenzhen Polytechnic (Grant Nos. 6021310002K, 6022312015K and LHRC20220405), Shenzhen Science and Technology Program (ZDSYS20210929115800001).

Conflict of interest

The authors declare no conflict of interest.

Author details

Dihao Ai[1,2,3]

1 School of Construction Engineering, Shenzhen Polytechnic, Shenzhen, China

2 Shenzhen Technology Institute of Urban Public Safety, and Key Laboratory of Urban Safety Risk Monitoring and Early Warning, Ministry of Emergency Management, Shenzhen, Guangdong, China

3 Shenzhen Key Laboratory of Urban Disasters Digital Twin, Shenzhen, China

*Address all correspondence to: aixi1020@szpt.edu.cn

References

[1] Taheri S. A review on five key sensors for monitoring of concrete structures. Construction and Building Materials. 2019;**204**:492-509

[2] Kasireddy, Varun, Fieguth, et al. A review on computer vision based defect detection and condition assessment of concrete and asphalt civil infrastructure. Advanced Engineering Informatics, 2016, 30(2):208-210.

[3] Deng J, Singh A, Zhou Y, et al. Review on computer vision-based crack detection and quantification methodologies for civil structures. Construction and Building Materials. 2022;**356**:129238

[4] Cheng HD, Shi XJ, Glazier C. Real-time image thresholding based on sample space reduction and interpolation approach. Journal of Computing in Civil Engineering. 2003;**17**(4):264-272

[5] Abdel-Qader I, Abudayyeh O, Kelly ME. Analysis of edge-detection techniques for crack identification in bridges. Journal of Computing in Civil Engineering. 2003;**17**(4):255-263

[6] Chanda S, Bu G, Guan H, et al. Automatic bridge crack detection–a texture analysis-based approach. In: Artificial Neural Networks in Pattern Recognition: 6th IAPR TC 3 International Workshop, ANNPR 2014, Montreal, QC, Canada, October 6-8, 2014. Proceedings 6. Midtown Manhattan, New York City: Springer International Publishing; 2014. pp. 193-203

[7] Zalama E, Gómez-García-Bermejo J, Medina R, et al. Road crack detection using visual features extracted by Gabor filters. Computer-Aided Civil and Infrastructure Engineering. 2014;**29**(5):342-358

[8] Liang S, Jianchun X, Xun Z. An algorithm for concrete crack extraction and identification based on machine vision. IEEE Access. 2018;**6**:28993-29002

[9] Shi Y, Cui L, Qi Z, et al. Automatic road crack detection using random structured forests. IEEE Transactions on Intelligent Transportation Systems. 2016;**17**(12):3434-3445

[10] Kim H. Crack and noncrack classification from concrete surface images using machine learning. Structural Health Monitoring. 2018;**18**(3):725-738

[11] Zhang A, Wang KCP, Li B, et al. Automated pixel-level pavement crack detection on 3D asphalt surfaces using a deep-learning network. Computer-Aided Civil and Infrastructure Engineering. 2017;**32**(10):805-819

[12] Dung CV. Autonomous concrete crack detection using deep fully convolutional neural network. Automation in Construction. 2019;**99**:52-58

[13] Zhang X. Concrete crack detection using context-aware deep semantic segmentation network. Computer-Aided Civil and Infrastructure Engineering. 2019;**34**(11):951-971

[14] Lin TY, Dollár P, Girshick R, et al. Feature pyramid networks for object detection. In: Proceedings of the IEEE Conference on Computer Vision and Pattern Recognition. New York City, United States: Institute for Electrical and Electronics Engineers (IEEE). 2017. pp. 2117-2125

[15] Shi X, Chen Z, Wang H, et al. Convolutional LSTM network:

A machine learning approach for precipitation nowcasting. Advances in Neural Information Processing Systems. 2015;**28**:802-810

[16] Khosravani MR, Weinberg K. A review on split Hopkinson bar experiments on the dynamic characterisation of concrete. Construction and Building Materials. 2018;**190**:1264-1283

Section 3

Image Theory and Simulation

Chapter 9

Perspective Chapter: Bionic Color Theory

Matthias Reuter and Fenja Ahrens

Abstract

Despite a lot of research, the actual methodology of how the vertebrate retina encodes the final color experience from its 3 color-sensitive sensory cells in such a way that it allows us to experience the world as we see it through the visual brain centers is still far from completely clear. Two phenomena in particular have shaped our research in recent years: the first was that, despite complex technical filter chains, the colors we see never looked the way we see them, and the second was the phenomenon that we experience the world more vividly, as it appears in photographs. The latest generation of cell phone images today show quasi-plastic scenes, but we only have two eyes that create this impression independently of each other. But that can only mean that the retina processes images differently than we have previously technically implemented. The following paper therefore discusses a new image processing chain that leads to "eye-like" images, without complex filter architectures, by one eye only and process in a bionic way at the first layer of picture analysis, the retina.

Keywords: bionic models of retinal information processing, color restauration, robotic vision control, opponent color theory, 3-compartment model for On–Off-pathways

1. Introduction

Bionic applications mean at first that some preconditions have to been taken into account, these are:

- Nature cannot count, means do not know numbers at all.
- Nature tries to minimize information to find a solution as fast as possible
- Nature systems in living systems can be divided in two structural components: genetic structured subparts, unable to "learn" and adaptive structured subparts, enabling an individuum to adapt in its habitat as good as possible.
- Information processing in an individuum is done either by a chemical, electrical or a combination of both way
- Information will be ruled excitatory or inhibitory information processing or a combination of both

Mostly information processing in living organism is realized by neurons of different types which are surrounded either by other kinds of "helping and supporting" cells or liquid. The information flow and the types of interacting neurons can be organized either in a genetic preconditioned way, or interacting neurons can learn, whereby this adaption to the information flow of the surrounding habitat is defined by a hand of learning rules.

Furthermore, we have learned that neurons are not responding to an input signal with a "on/off signal" but in so called spike trains, which can be interpreted as a kind of "singing" or melody of them, it is this item which empower them to have an almost unlimited amount of information capacity.

And: neurons have a threshold which means, that they only can "sing" if:

- the its soma wears a positive potential
- all dendritic input information just arrives at the soma in a manner that for a short time a stable potential is realized enabling the "construction" of an information wearing spike train
- if the form and structure of this spike train can be understood by the downstream neuronal structures, special if we are taking about genetical preconditions neural structures.
- Neurons – even for genetic structures - cannot differentiate to which kind of information sources they are (momentary) connected

Even so here only a rudimentary list of preconditions of bionic principals – means preconditions for imitating nature – are listed here, these are still enough to understand and to simulate the way how vertebrate's eyes information capture, code and transmit it in a retinotopic to brain.

Next, we have to take or list to formulate some basic assumptions, which will lead to an unconventional tool to realize an artificial algorithm to come a little bit closer to the way nature do visual based information processing, even so we will at least will show that – sorry to say - a lot of still common theories and methods are led to adsurdum.

First let us look at some weak points to common theories/methods how visual processing like nature runs:

- Yellow is the counterpart of blue
- White is the arithmetic sum of the colors: red blue and green

Why these two theoretical assumptions are weak?

Well, we just have only sensory for red, green and blue and yellow is the color where the contributions of red and green are equal, but that's one and only one value of 19.000.000 possible colors we can differentiate. Why we can detect otherwise light red yellow colors or light green yellow colors?

And, when white is the arithmetic sum of the red, green and blue, then red = 200, green = 100 and blue = 150 would lead to the same impression of white as if red = 100, green = 150 and blue = 200, what definitely is wrong.

Beneath the questions, why we can without any problems in a lightning independent way contours and colors it has been exact these two "small" contradictions which pushed us some years ago the start again from the beginning to define a more exacter bionic theory how vertebrate's optical system processes a robust contour- and color-processing.

2. Theoretical part

Let us start simple: As known we have four lightning sensitive receptors: one kind, which most sensitive for red light, one which is most sensitive for green light, one which is most sensitive blue light and one which between the blue and green band detects a kind of white, means a kind of illumination dimension, when we have day vision. Furthermore, we have one kind of white/grew receptor as a kind of illumination sensor when it becomes too dark for the first four types of sensors.

Next, we have to take into account, that these receptors– or their downstream cells - are connected to all kinds of other receptors in the retina, as more or less the nascent eye build connection to every other neuron of the to the different bipolar cells. Bipolar cells are constructed in such a way that Bipolar Cells are structured in such a way that they are realizing a Center-Surround-Architecture in the following way: Horizontal cells - located immediately behind the photoreceptors - collect the activities of one class of photoreceptors and form a mixed potential from these contributions. This forms the surround component, which is supplied to the bipolar cell as the first contribution. The second contribution, which is supplied to the bipolar cells, consists of a mixed potential, which lies in the middle of the surround area and is formed by only a few photoreceptors of one of the other color receptor types. By this architecture the following color pairs of different bipolar cells are formed:

- Red-Green
- Red-Blue
- Green-Blue

This means that the individual primary colors (red, green, and blue) do not exist alone in the bipolar cells as an information unit, but rather only in combinations that modulate the other color, with the color impressions of yellow, purple and turquoise representing exactly the colors where this modulation is zero. In addition, here lies the crux of the opposite color theory. Blue as the opposite color to yellow would assume that the red-green component would be exactly yellow, which is extremely rarely the case. Or in short: we would only be able to see blue sometimes. At this point, common misconception in the literature needs to be corrected, which nis that the opposite color of blue is yellow. Rather, it is true that on the one hand red and blue and on the other hand green and blue modulate each other, which ultimately leads to the three modulation oaths in the field of the color-coding receptors and another three modulation paths in the area of cones and white sensors. If we put all this together, we come to the fist, the basic building blocks of our theory, shown in **Figure 1**.

Next, we take the mechanism of the opponent color theory for all the possible color-receptor-types into account, means have to explain, in which way all 1.7 million colors and 160 "steps" of white we Can detect (see) are defined.

First this sounds easy, but: nature cannot count, so at least we have only chemical/physical potentials and for the interaction symmetry operations only. And as if

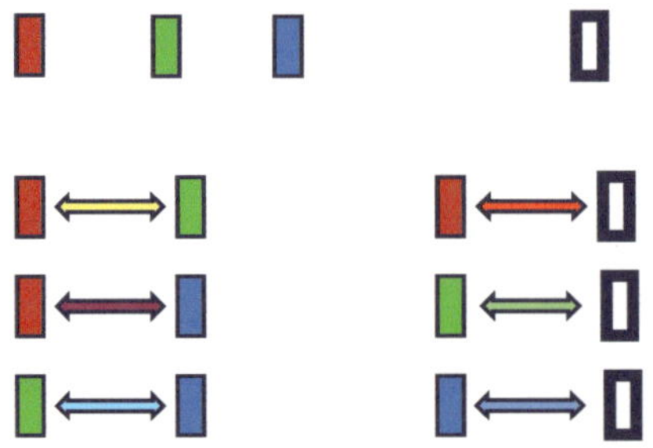

Figure 1.
On top shown is there our four receptors' types and below the six possible interactions types of these receptors between each other, realized by the first 2 layers of a retina.

that wasn't difficult enough, such a potential theory has at least to be converted into numbers if we want to use it in computer vision.

Again, we start simple, define a potential by numbers with its lowers value 0 and maximal value 255. (You know that: that's RGB color theory.) Why we can do so? Now, by taking a look at quantum mechanics we become harmonic oscillators, which only allow certain wavelengths to be stable, and these can only change between it other by a fixed quantum, where in our case this quantum is represented by the integer number 1. You see, sometimes bionic theory is simple.

Now, we have a potential, potential level, which are represented by the different color value of the RGB space, next we need only a symmetry operation, which is near to the opponent color theory [1–13] and must mirror the following items:

- Both colors of the three possible opponent color potentials are modulating each other in the following manner:

- The largest potentials (the largest value of the two opponent colors) defines the color impression of the resulting color. If no opponent color is present, we see the spectral color (red, green, blue).

- In the state of equilibrium of the two opponent colors (when at least none of them is modulating the other one) we get the color, which we call middle-colors. These are the colors (yellow (red-green opponent), purple (red-blue opponent) and turquoise (green-blue opponent). If these colors have the same potential, they form the palette of dark grew to white.

- The modulation range of each color and the white information is in a range of [0–255], the modulation cannot lead to negative values and it has to mirror the following.

Before colors occur in nation, individuum can only divide dark and bright. This change rapidly, when more than one "color-sensor" entered the stage. Suddenly several pieces of information competed, but were not allow to leave the just define range [0, 255] and had to contain gray and white in combination. More physically spoken: in the moment two sensor occur in the eye, there were two different potentials which have to interact. Here and only here the next assumption of classical vision theory has to be deleted: Two different information channels, two different potentials can interact, but they can never represent a common average. For all times the are divided, are solitaires, communicating solitaires but, solitaires. And that this is true, we can see, that the different color and white channels kept be divided on the whole information way from eye to the visual cortex until the identifying structures of the pyramidal cells.

Two small items, describing the "tricky point" for the searched symmetry operation., as now a modulating term or better modulation operation have to solve some weak points in common theories, and most important is has also to define without fixed numbers, what means: larger then, equal or lower than an symmetry in color space, or shorter spoken: it should define under every possible lightning and color-conditions an adequate categorization, which is in the retina realized by the ON-Cells, the OFF-Cells and the Equilibrium-Pathway. And these three pathways do not have negative potentials, no inhibitory or excitatory accessory neurons and a (genetic defined) fixed (not be conditioned) structure.

In 2016 we found such a potential oriented symmetry-operation which more or less is described in [14]. To make a long story short: basis of this theory is a three-compartment model of the information processing of the first 2 layers of the retina, which follows the Lie-Algebra, which (again) we can find in quantum mechanics to describe the different stages of a physical system under varying situations, whereby such a symmetry structure is intrinsic to rapidly varying potential- structures.

Band or better relapsed can such a symmetry operation in 12 lines of common c-code, which opens the door to quick robot vision control and a quick picture analysis, rep. a quick color restauration as now have to be discussed in this paper.

But first, let us summarize what we just discussed in **Figure 2**. Shown are the potentials of the different colors red, green and blue by a value of 255. This announce the maximum value they can modulate the counter color, which then will be zero. If both colors modulate the other one in the same way, we will get the middle colors (yellow, purple and turquoise), which are modulating themselves also. In the equilibrium states, they are producing the colors white as in all cases: (yellow to blue, green to purple and red to turquoise all 3 potentials contribute to the final color. Please note, that so far, we did not take the effect of saturation into account, neither the pastel colors.

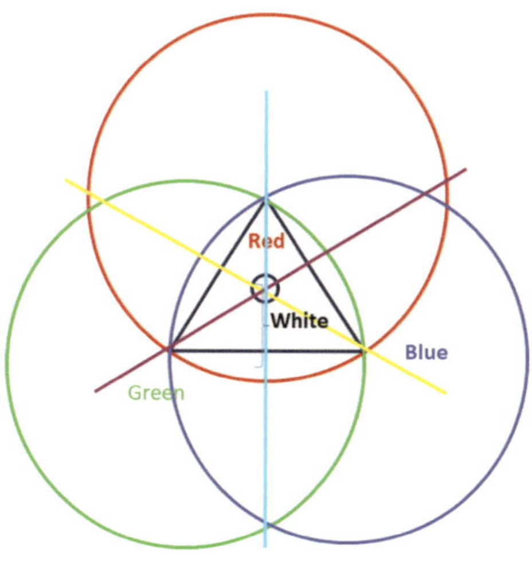

Figure 2.
Potential oriented color model (description see text above).

Also note, that only in the dark triangle the interaction of our three potentials act in the way we can realize colors.

Let us make a short proof, if our potential theory makes sense: We take the middle color yellow. The radius from red is the half of 255, means is 127,5. The radius from green is the half from 255, means is 127,5. If these two contributions are put together, we get 255. So at least (by full illumination) no information (defined by the value 255) is lost.

Our three-compartment model involves an intrinsic feature, which mirrors this example: whatever are the values of both opponent colors, the result for both (modulated) colors, or more physically spoken, the values of the oscillator will never leave the defined range between [0–255]. For that the color space of **Figure 2** is a linear one.

As shown in theory, out of the middle colors the spectral colors are modulated. With this trick nature response to the occurrence of different receptors, acting in different bands of the electromagnetic spectrum. So at least the dominance of one of them leads to a kind of bifurcation out of the middle color. This bifructutation points leads to a categorization, that the dominant color is ON (the on-path neuron in the retina is activated) and the subdominant color is OFF (the off-path neuron in the retina is activated).

That this bifurcation cannot follow a simple plus-minus-calculation now seems clear, as otherwise minus values or values larger than 255 would be possible. The practical result for robot vision at the end is, that the resulting colors of the modulation will be totally different, as in common systems.

Some technical questions:

- What's an edge of contour?
- It's the change from one categorization (ON, OFF, no modulation) to another categorization.
- What's a plane?
- It's the no change of a categorization.
- Is the dimension of the receptive fields are limited?
- No, they are not (except given by the number of neurons the anatomical structures of the retina). Possible will that be, as the gab-junctions produce a short cut of the different receptor potentials (what should not be confused with the calculation of an average potential.)

3. Methods and results

The anatomical structure of the first 3 layers is well investigated. So, we know that in the fovea centralis every sensor has its own ON and OFF bipolar cell where in the periphery of the retina a large number of receptors are innervating single ON and OFF bipolar cells. In the result we can only see really scarf with the fovea centralis.

So at least we have minimum 2 kinds of receptive field dimensions. If we look at the horizonal and amacrine cells we see otherwise, that their receptive field seems some kind of flexible, depending on the momentary illumination, scene vigilance and the presents of accelerated objects.

This on mind we started our experiments with our new model by variating the inner and outer receptive field dimensions (the center and surround dimensions of the receptive fields.)

As expected, for the detection of contours the sharp der contours varies as shown in **Figure 3**. As well come side effect noisy fluctuations in the picture disappears. Both effects, and that's what's really new are totally independent form the illumination of the receptive fields as long as we have a difference on 1 between the opponent receptor potentials in the 3-K-model.

And what happened with the colors of a scene? They are modulated in a manner, that the contours became sharper and colors are restored. What means restored? As we have leaned not the sensor signal itself wears now the information, it wears the power to modulate its opponents only.

So, color can change dramatically. Our camera picture where the moon is silver has now, after filtering, a golden moon - surely only if the moon was golden in the truth. At least that means that the "true colors" are code in the camera picture somewhere and that the 3-k-model can decode them. If you transfer this knowledge to the biological receptors in the retina, it means that they can also be primitive as technical receptors, i.e., largely non-adaptive and with a fixed characteristic curve in terms of the intensity curve.

So at least, the color or receptors detect are not the color we see. And technical spoken even primitive cameras can see the world how we see it. Poor mobile phones which more or less expensive camera equipment, trying to simulate what a bionic symmetry operation does.

But now let us see examples. All pictures shown were taken with cheap cameras from various manufacturers (20–80 €). No lighting conditions were imposed, so all images were taken in natural conditions. On left hand side are shown the original camera picture, on right hand side the processed pictures. The processing time of all pictures are 30 msec. The filter code itself is written in the programming language C and has a size of 389 k. licensed additional libraries were not used because the filter technology is a stand-alone application.

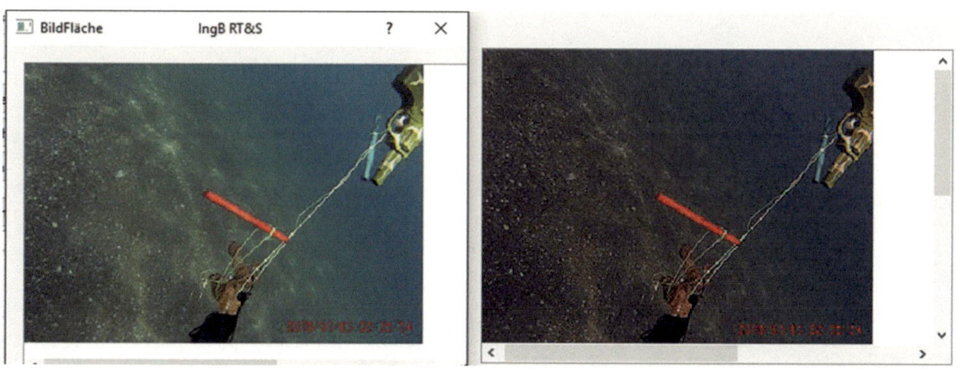

Figure 3.
Sown is here a toy-array in 1.5 m deep. In addition to the considerable increase in contrast, it is noticeable that the colors appear stronger and the seabed is colored completely differently. The image was taken at dusk and the colors correspond to human sensory impressions after filtering.

The first images were taken by a simple underwater camera at different depths. What interested us most here were the different lighting conditions and, above all, suspended matter, which artificial lighting would appear to be rather disturbing (**Figures 4–7**).

Figure 4.
In this image the seabed was photographed at a depth of 2 m during the day. Once again you can see the clear increase in contrast and a brightening of the image, since according to the 3 K model the color modulations lead to an increase in the color components in the RGB space.

Figure 5.
This effect becomes even clearer when there are objects in the room (here the diver at a depth of 3 meters). In addition, the filtering is not significantly disrupted by suspended matter in the sea.

Figure 6.
Shown here is part of a so-called "ghost net" in a dep of 12 m, i.e., a lost fishing net. Unfortunately, these pose an immediate danger, especially to marine mammals, which is why they are on the list of human artifacts that urgently need to be recovered. In order to recover them, it is extremely important to clearly lift them from the ground, even when there is heavy vegetation (like here).

Let us move on to more everyday examples. Below are three pictures from the food industry. The aim of these shots was to achieve the highest possible sharpness as well as the natural colors and color gradients from existing photos (**Figures 8–10**).

As you can see, the bionic filter primarily creates a contrast that not only makes the image itself appear sharper, but also creates a quasi-3-dimensional impression. This also explains why some images appear more plastic to us than others. It is the special representation of edges and color transitions that make objects appear 3-dimensional in our brain.

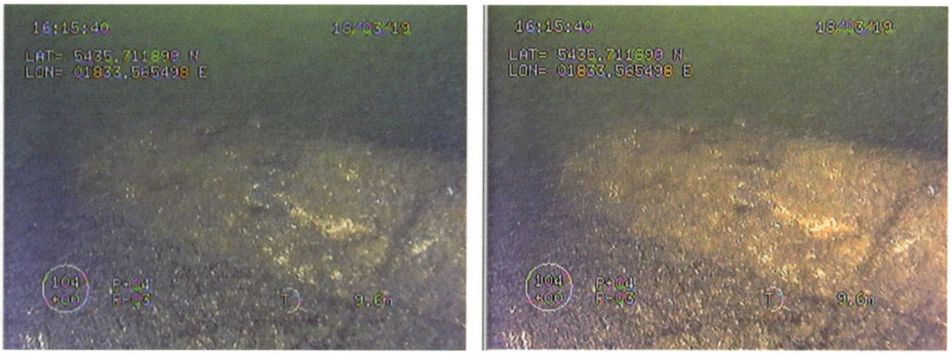

Figure 7.
Here an aircraft bomb from the Second World War is shown at a depth of 40 meters. For these objects, details regarding shape, markings, degree of corrosion and possible damage are of particular interest as they define the immediate threat to the marine habitat. The difference to the previous images is that the bionic filters also enable artificial after-lighting without causing color artifacts.

Figure 8.
Shown here is a typical German dish: Roast pork stewed in onions and in a beer soup. What is noticeable in the original is that at least the bulbs appear unnaturally white for a steaming process. In addition, the reflections on the roast in the original image are rather unnaturally weak. Both points are eliminated by using bionic filters.

Figure 9.
The same effects can be seen in the finished dish. In addition, the potatoes no longer appear raw but actually cooked, as they have taken on the color of boiled potatoes. Due to the three-dimensional highlighting of objects present in the image, you can now easily see in the filtered image that there is a bean fruit at the bottom edge, as it stands out clearly from the pattern on the plate.

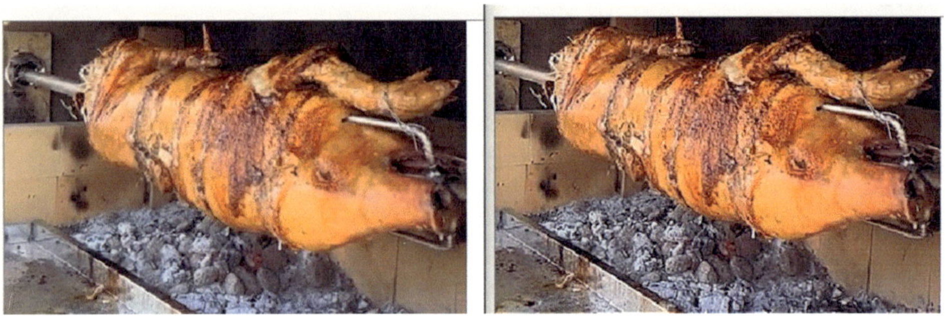

Figure 10.
Lastly, the pork before it was on the plate. Although the coloring is more or less not further optimized here thanks to the good lighting of the original photo through the bionic filters, the details of the pig and the grill - especially the charcoal - are optimized. This makes the image appear more natural and realistic.

4. Conclusions

Using examples, we have shown that if you use a potential-oriented model of the opponent color theory, you can achieve a completely new image processing system that is more similar to the human processing of light senses than was previously known. But the actual insight from this bionic image processing is more profound. It is not complex information steps or those that only take place in the brain areas that lead to a three-dimensional and true-color experience of optical impressions, but rather this information transduction takes place in the first two layers of the retina. In the last few decades, we have already understood that our eye is not just a camera but - in its function as an upstream brain - a kind of supercomputer, but what is new is that this computer uses a completely different way of processing information than we are used to are. He simply follows a different logic, which enables him to work out the optimum from even poor sensory image recordings with just one symmetry operation.

Acknowledgements

Figures 5–7 were collected as part of the EU-funded maritime research project "EROVMUS" and are therefore subject to extra copy rights.

Conflict of interest

The authors declare no conflict of interest.

Author details

Matthias Reuter* and Fenja Ahrens
R&D-Department of IngB RT&S GmbH, Germany

*Address all correspondence to: matthias.reuter@ingb-rts.de

References

[1] Hering E. Outlines of a Theory of the Light Sense. Cambridge, Mass: Harvard University Press; 1964

[2] Conway BR, Malik-Moraleda S, Gibson E. Color appearance and the end of Hering's opponent-colors theory. Cell. 2023;**27**(9):791-804. DOI: 10.1016/j.tics.2023.06.003 [Accessed: August 31, 2023]

[3] Werner JS, Walraven J. Effect of chromatic adaptation on the achromatic locus: The role of contrast, luminance and background color. Vision Research. 1982;**22**(8):929-943

[4] Stockman A, Macleod DI, Ajohnson NE. Spectral sensitivities of the human cones. Journal of the Optical Society of America A. 1993;**10**(12):2491-2521

[5] Shinomori Spillmann K, Werner J. S-cone signals to temporal off-channels: possible asymmetrical connections to postreceptoral chromatic mechanisms. Vision Research. 1998;**39**(1):39-49

[6] Jameson D, Hurvich LM. Some quantitative aspects of an opponent-colors theory. I. Chromatic responses and spectral saturation. Journal of the Optical Society of America. 1955;**45**:546-552

[7] Larimer J, Krantz D, Cicerone C. Opponent process additivity-II. yellow/blue equilibria and non-linear models. Vision Research. 1975;**15**:723-731

[8] Elzinga C, de Weert CMM. Nonlinear codes for the yellow/blue mechanism. Vision Research. 1984;**24**:911-922

[9] Long Z, Qiu X, Chan CLJ, Sun Z, Yuan Z, Poddar S, et al. A neuromorphic bionic eye with filter-free color vision using hemispherical perovskite nanowire array retina. Nature Communications. 2023;**14**(1):1972

[10] Gu L et al. A biomimetic eye with a hemispherical perovskite nanowire array retina. Nature. 2020;**581**:278-282

[11] Sarkar P, Dewangan O, Joshi A. A review on applications of artificial intelligence on bionic eye designing and functioning. Scandinavian Journal of Information Systems. 2023;**35**(1):1119-1127

[12] Paraskevoudi N, Pezaris JS. Eye movement compensation and spatial updating in visual prosthetic mechanisms, limitations and future directions. Frontiers in Systems Neuroscience. 2019;**12**:73

[13] Zhang H, Lee S. Robot bionic vision technologies: A review. Applied Sciences. 2022;**12**(16):7970

[14] Reuter M, Bohlmann S. Biological inspired image analysis for medical applications. Biomimetics and Bionic Applications with Clinical Applications. 2021:211-225

Chapter 10

Perspective Chapter: Simulation and Analysis of Synthetic Aperture Radar Images

Jonathan Blackledge

Abstract

The principal model for an image, generated by the interaction of an incident wave field with an inhomogeneous medium, is based on the 'weak scattering approximation'. This approximation forms the basis for image processing, analysis and image understanding associated with applications over a broad range of frequencies. The physical limitations of such a model are typically overcome by introducing an additional stochastic field term that takes into account those effects that do not conform to the weak scattering approximation, coupled with background 'system noise'. In this chapter, a solution to the scattering problem is presented, which is based on an exact scattering solution. An application of this solution is then considered which focuses on developing a model for a Synthetic Aperture Radar (SAR) image of the earth's surface. By assuming that the surface is a fractal (a Mandelbrot surface), it is shown how an overhead optical image of the surface may be used to simulate a SAR image. The purpose of this is to generate training data for developing computer vision solutions using machine learning for autonomous navigation using SAR and for target detection in cases where only optical image data are available.

Keywords: synthetic aperture radar, strong scattering, mathematical models, simulations from optical images, target detection

1. Introduction

Aperture synthesis is used in a wide range of applications including radar, sonar, diagnostic ultrasound and radio astronomy. The basic principle is very simple. In one form or another, the resolution of an image is determined by the size of the aperture that is used for observation. To improve the resolution, the size of the aperture must be increased. In some cases, to achieve a given resolution, an aperture must be used which is impractical either to build or utilise effectively. However, if a smaller aperture (a real aperture) is used, and its position changed while observations are being made, then, in effect, a much larger aperture can be synthesised.

Although the basic principles of aperture synthesis is the same, the details vary accord to the application. Radar (radio detection and ranging) has been used for many

IntechOpen

years (since the early 1940's) to detect airborne objects using ground based antennas and to image the Earth's surface using airbourne platforms.

Developments in the 1960s paved the way for a new generation of high resolution Radar systems which helped lead to the development of synthetic aperture radar (SAR) in the mid 1970s, although it had been used covertly for military and some space programmes well before that time (e.g. [1, 2]).

SAR was developed to study the surface of the Earth (and other planets) from both spacebourne and airborne platforms. Both systems attempt to classify the inhomogeneous nature of the Earth's surface by repeatedly emitting a frequency modulated (chirped) pulse of microwave (GHz) radiation [3] and recording the back-scattered field. SAR systems essentially provide 'microwave photographs' of the Earth's surface and are normally classified in terms of the wavelength that is used. Typical operational modes include X-band, with a wavelength of 2.8 cm, and L-band, with a wavelength of 24 cm. In addition to different wavelengths, different polarisations are used.

1.1 SAR imaging

A SAR image has a pixel resolution of the order of a metre or less, but the microwave scattering takes place on the scale of a centimetre. The return signals in range at each position of the moving real aperture are demodulated to base-band. Demodulation is coupled with quadrature detection, which provides the imaginary component of the real signal that is recorded, thereby generating the analytic signal [4].

The return (back-scattered) signals, which are generated by emitting a linear frequency modulated or chirped pulse of microwave radiation, are correlated with an identical chirp. This yields an Impulse Response Function (IRF) for the demodulated range signals given by a sinc function ($\text{sinc}(x) \equiv \sin(x)/x$). However, the range at which the system operates is designed to exploit a model of the back-scattered microwave field that is in the Fresnel zone. Thus, the cross range (the direction at right angles to the range) response, is also a chirp function (both a down-chirp, in which the instantaneous frequency decreases, and an up-chirp, meaning that the instantaneous frequency increases). Hence, by correlating the combined return signals in cross range with the appropriate chirp function, the cross range data also becomes characterised by a sinc IRF. In this way, the two-dimensional (complex) data associated with a SAR image is classified by a point spread function (PSF) given by a separable sinc function. A grey scale image is then usually constructed by displaying the Amplitude Modulations associated with the processed data field.

1.2 Original contributions and structure

The principal focus of this work is concerned with the application of an exact scattering solution [5] and its implementation for modelling a SAR. In this respect, the material provide a 'road map' which starts with Maxwell's equations for an Electromagnetic (EM) field and develops a solution that can be cast in terms of a standard model for a SAR image. This 'standard' involves the convolution of a characteristic Point Spread Function with an Object Function whose properties are determined by the scattering associated with the incidence of an EM wave field upon the ground surface.

The structure of the material is as follows: Section 2 provide a review of the EM field equations, casting them in a form that is suitable for generating a model for SAR. Section 3 introduces a scaler field model and the fundamental solution for the electric field. This is coupled with Section 4, which briefly discusses the differences between volume and surface scattering effects, followed by Section 5 which introduces the conventional weak scattering model. In this context, Sections 6 and 7 introduce the exact and strong scattering solutions, respectively; these sections are main components in regard to the most original themes of the material. Section 8 shows how the strong scattering solution can be used to develop a model for SAR and is followed with the introduction of another complementary idea which is concerns the use of a self-affine model for the scattering function. This is provided in Section 9, and is pivotal in the development of the approach presented in Section 10 which explores the basis for the numerical simulation of a SAR image using an optical image. The final components of the work are given in Sections 11 which investigate a vector field model, thereby introducing the effects of polarisation. It is shown how, a cross polarised field can be used to generate quantitative SAR images that differentiate between the dielectric and conductive properties of the ground surface. An Appendix is provided with a MATLAB function deigned to help readers appreciate the relative simplicity of the numerical simulations considered, to repeat the results presented, and provided the basis for further investigations and developments.

2. Electromagnetic field equations

Electromagnetic imaging systems require models to be constructed that are based on the field equations for electric and magnetic fields. These field equations are known as Maxwell's equation, and in this section, we briefly introduce the macroscopic form of these equations for the case of an inhomogeneous conductive dielectric material. This provides a basis for the derivation of an inhomogeneous wave equation in regard to the electric field which forms the basis for the development of an EM imaging systems model.

For a linear, isotropic but inhomogeneous three-dimensional continuum with $\mathbf{r}\in\mathbb{R}^3$, $r \equiv |\mathbf{r}|$, the macroscopic Maxwell's equations are given by (for the International System of Units).

$$\nabla \cdot \varepsilon\mathbf{E} = \rho \tag{1}$$

$$\nabla \cdot \mu\mathbf{H} = 0 \tag{2}$$

$$\nabla \times \mathbf{E} = -\mu\frac{\partial \mathbf{H}}{\partial t} \tag{3}$$

$$\nabla \times \mathbf{H} = \mathbf{J} + \varepsilon\frac{\partial \mathbf{E}}{\partial t} \tag{4}$$

where $\mathbf{E}(\mathbf{r},t)$ is the electric field measured in Volts/metre, $\mathbf{H}(\mathbf{r},t)$ is the magnetic field in Amperes/metre, $\mathbf{J}(\mathbf{r},t)$ is the Current Density (Amperes/metre^2), and $\rho(\mathbf{r},t)$ is the Charge Density (Coulombs/metre^3). These fields are functions of space vector $\mathbf{r}$ and time t and are related to the inhomogeneous (space varying) material parameters quantified by the electrical permittivity $\varepsilon(\mathbf{r})$ (Farads/metre) and the magnetic permeability $\mu(\mathbf{r})$ (Henries/metre). Eqs. (1)–(4) represent (respectively) the differential forms of Coulombs law, the law of no magnetic monopoles, Faraday's law of induction (electricity from magnetism) and Amperes law (magnetism from electricity) coupled with Maxwell's additive displacement current term—the rate of change of an electric field.

The values of ε and μ in a vacuum (denoted by ε_0 and μ_0, respectively) are $\varepsilon_0 = 8.854 \times 10^{-12}$ Farads/metre and $\mu_0 = 4\pi \times 10^{-7}$ Henries/metre. In electromagnetic imaging problems there are two important physical models to consider, based on whether a material is conductive or non-conductive.

For a non-conductive material $\mathbf{J} = 0$. In regard to a conductive material, the induced current depends on the magnitude of the electric field and the conductivity σ (Siemens/metre) of the material. The relationship between the electric field and the current density is given by Ohm's law which can be written in the form

$$\mathbf{J} = \sigma \mathbf{E} \tag{5}$$

Here, the current density is linearly related to the electric field alone, where for a good conductor, $\sigma \gg 1$. However, note that Eq. (5) is strictly only applicable to 'Ohmic materials' such as metals and some relatively poor conductors under specific circumstances. It is not applicable for semi-conductors, a moving Ohmic material in the presence of a magnetic field or for a plasma, for example, where, in the latter case, the generalised Ohm's law for a plasma is required. Nevertheless, for the applications considered in this paper, Eq. (5) is sufficient for near-stationary conductive materials interacting with an EM field.

By taking the divergence of Eq. (4) and noting that

$$\nabla \cdot (\nabla \times \mathbf{H}) = 0$$

then, given Eq. (1) for a constant ε, and Eq. (5) for a constant σ, we can write

$$\frac{\partial \rho}{\partial t} + \frac{\sigma}{\varepsilon}\rho = 0 \;\Rightarrow\; \rho(t) = \rho_0 \exp(-\sigma t/\varepsilon), \quad \rho_0 \equiv \rho(t = 0)$$

This solution for the charge density shows that it decays exponentially with time. For typical values of $\varepsilon \sim 10^{-12} - 10^{-10}$ Farads/metre, then, provided σ is not too small, the dissipation of charge is very rapid. It is therefore physically reasonable to set the charge density to zero and, for problems involving the interaction of EM waves with good conductors, Eq. (1) can be approximated by

$$\nabla \cdot \varepsilon \mathbf{E} = 0 \tag{6}$$

with Eq. (4) becoming

$$\nabla \times \mathbf{H} = \varepsilon \frac{\partial \mathbf{E}}{\partial t} + \sigma \mathbf{E}$$

Note, that in EM imaging systems, the material may not necessarily be conductive throughout, but may be a varying dielectric with distributed conductive elements. For example, when imaging the Earth's surface using microwave radiation, the EM scattering model can be based on a 'ground truth' that is predominantly a dielectric surface with localised conductors, e.g. metallic objects.

2.1 Wave equation

In electromagnetic imaging systems, a primary measurable field is the electric field, which induces a change in the voltage of the field detector. It is therefore appropriate to use a wave equation which describes the behaviour of the electric field. This can be obtained by decoupling Maxwell's equations for the electric field **E**. In regard to Eq. (3), dividing through by μ and taking the curl of the resulting equation yields

$$\nabla \times \left(\frac{1}{\mu} \nabla \times \mathbf{E} \right) = -\frac{\partial}{\partial t} \nabla \times \mathbf{H}.$$

By taking the derivative with respect to time of Eq. (4) and using Ohm's law—Eq. (5)—we obtain

$$\frac{\partial}{\partial t} (\nabla \times \mathbf{H}) = \varepsilon \frac{\partial^2 \mathbf{E}}{\partial t^2} + \sigma \frac{\partial \mathbf{E}}{\partial t}.$$

From the previous equation we can then write

$$\nabla \times \left(\frac{1}{\mu} \nabla \times \mathbf{E} \right) = -\varepsilon \frac{\partial^2 \mathbf{E}}{\partial t^2} - \sigma \frac{\partial \mathbf{E}}{\partial t} \tag{7}$$

Expanding the first term, multiplying through by μ and noting that

$$\mu \nabla \left(\frac{1}{\mu} \right) = -\nabla \ln \mu$$

we obtain

$$\nabla \times \nabla \times \mathbf{E} + \varepsilon \mu \frac{\partial^2 \mathbf{E}}{\partial t^2} + \sigma \mu \frac{\partial \mathbf{E}}{\partial t} = (\nabla \ln \mu) \times \nabla \times \mathbf{E}$$

Further, expanding Eq. (6), we have

$$\varepsilon \nabla \cdot \mathbf{E} + \mathbf{E} \cdot \nabla \varepsilon = 0 \ \Rightarrow \ \nabla \cdot \mathbf{E} = -\mathbf{E} \cdot \nabla \ln \varepsilon$$

and hence, using the vector identity

$$\nabla \times \nabla \times \mathbf{E} = -\nabla^2 \mathbf{E} + \nabla (\nabla \cdot \mathbf{E})$$

we obtain the following wave equation for the electric field

$$\nabla^2 \mathbf{E} - \varepsilon \mu \frac{\partial^2 \mathbf{E}}{\partial t^2} - \sigma \mu \frac{\partial \mathbf{E}}{\partial t} = -\nabla (\mathbf{E} \cdot \nabla \ln \varepsilon) - (\nabla \ln \mu) \times \nabla \times \mathbf{E} \tag{8}$$

This equation is inhomogeneous in ε, μ and σ. Solutions to this equation provide information on the behaviour of the electric field in an inhomogeneous conductive dielectric environment. In electromagnetic imaging problems, interest focuses on the behaviour of the scattered EM field generated by variations in the material parameters ε, μ and σ. The problem is to reconstruct, or to at least interpret these parameters by measuring certain properties of the scattered electric field. This is a three parameter inverse problem which requires us to solve for the electric field $\mathbf{E}$ given ε, μ and σ. In the context of the model considered, a similar type of analysis can be implemented to generate an inhomogeneous wave equation for the magnetic field which is given by

$$\nabla^2\mathbf{H} - \varepsilon\mu\frac{\partial^2\mathbf{H}}{\partial t^2} - \sigma\mu\frac{\partial\mathbf{H}}{\partial t} = -\nabla(\mathbf{H}\cdot\nabla\ln\mu) - (\nabla\ln\varepsilon)\times\nabla\times\mathbf{H} - \varepsilon\mathbf{E}\times\nabla\left(\frac{\sigma}{\varepsilon}\right)$$

Note, that in this case, the equation for $\mathbf{H}$ is coupled to $\mathbf{E}$ through the last term on the right hand side. It is for this reason that the wave equation for the electric field given by Eq. (8) is considered. Moreover, Eq. (8) is consistent with the development of a 'systems model' where the imaging data is based on the detection of the electric wave field; this includes Real and Synthetic Aperture Radar's.

2.2 Inhomogeneous wave equation

In order to solve the wave equation (focusing on the electric field) derived in the last section using the most appropriate analytical methods for imaging science (i.e. the fundamental Green function solution, as discussed later), it is typically re-cast in the form of the (time-independent) Langevin equation

$$\left(\nabla^2 + k^2\right)\mathbf{E} = -\hat{L}\mathbf{E}$$

where $\hat{L}$ is an inhomogeneous differential operator, $\left(\nabla^2 + k^2\right)$ is the Helmholtz operator, and $k = 2\pi/\lambda$ is the wavenumber associated with the wavelength λ.

To achieved this, we first modify the time dependent equation, starting by adding the term

$$\varepsilon_0\frac{\partial^2\mathbf{E}}{\partial t^2} - \frac{1}{\mu_0}\nabla\times\nabla\times\mathbf{E}$$

to both sides of Eq. (7), so that, upon re-arranging, we can write

$$\nabla\times\nabla\times\mathbf{E} + \varepsilon_0\mu_0\frac{\partial^2\mathbf{E}}{\partial t^2} = -\varepsilon_0\mu_0\gamma_\varepsilon\frac{\partial^2\mathbf{E}}{\partial t^2} - \mu_0\sigma\frac{\partial\mathbf{E}}{\partial t} + \nabla\times\left(\gamma_\mu\nabla\times\mathbf{E}\right) \tag{9}$$

where

$$\gamma_\varepsilon = \frac{\varepsilon - \varepsilon_0}{\varepsilon_0} = \varepsilon_r - 1 \text{ and } \gamma_\mu = \frac{\mu - \mu_0}{\mu} = 1 - \frac{1}{\mu_r}$$

Here, $\varepsilon_r \geq 1$ and $\mu_r \geq 1$ are dimensionless variables—the relative permittivity and the relative permeability, respectively. We can then use the result (which is valid for $\rho \sim 0$ in Eq. (1), when $\sigma \gg 1$)

$$\nabla\times\nabla\times\mathbf{E} = -\nabla^2\mathbf{E} + \nabla(\nabla\cdot\mathbf{E}) = -\nabla^2\mathbf{E} - \nabla(\mathbf{E}\cdot\nabla\ln\varepsilon)$$

so that Eq. (9) can now be written as

$$\nabla^2\mathbf{E} - \varepsilon_0\mu_0\frac{\partial^2\mathbf{E}}{\partial t^2} = \mu_0\varepsilon_0\gamma_\varepsilon\frac{\partial^2\mathbf{E}}{\partial t^2} + \mu_0\sigma\frac{\partial\mathbf{E}}{\partial t} - \nabla(\mathbf{E}\cdot\nabla\ln\varepsilon) - \nabla\times\left(\gamma_\mu\nabla\times\mathbf{E}\right) \tag{10}$$

2.3 Time independent wave equation

Construction of a time-independent wave equation can be undertaken by considering the time dependence of the electric field to be harmonic when $\mathbf{E}(\mathbf{r},t) \equiv \mathbf{E}(\mathbf{r},\omega)\exp(i\omega t)$ where ω is a constant angular frequency, thereby allowing Eq. (10) to be cast in the form of the following inhomogeneous Helmholtz equation [6] for a vector field:

$$(\nabla^2 + k^2)\mathbf{E} = -k^2\gamma_\varepsilon\mathbf{E} + ikZ_0\sigma\mathbf{E} - \nabla(\mathbf{E}\cdot\nabla\ln\varepsilon) - \nabla\times(\gamma_\mu\nabla\times\mathbf{E}) \tag{11}$$

where

$$k = 2\pi\lambda = \omega c_0, \quad c_0 = \frac{1}{\sqrt{\varepsilon_0\mu_0}} \text{ and } Z_0 = \mu_0 c_0.$$

The parameter Z_0 is the free space wave impedance and is approximately equal to 377 Ohms. The constant c_0 is the velocity at which EM waves propagate in a perfect vacuum—the speed of light $\simeq 3\times 10^8 \ \text{ms}^{-1}$. In electromagnetic imaging, images are characterised by the spatial variations of the parameters γ_ε, γ_μ and the conductivity σ.

Eq. (11) also applies to the case when the time-dependence of the electric field can be described in terms of a spectrum of frequencies when $\mathbf{E}(\mathbf{r},t)$ is related to the temporal frequency spectrum $\mathbf{E}(\mathbf{r},\omega)$ through the Fourier transform, i.e.

$$\mathbf{E}(\mathbf{r},t) \leftrightarrow \mathbf{E}(\mathbf{r},\omega), \quad \mathbf{E}(\mathbf{r},t) = \frac{1}{2\pi}\int_{-\infty}^{\infty}\mathbf{E}(\mathbf{r},\omega)\exp(i\omega t)d\omega$$

where $\leftrightarrow$ denotes the Fourier transform pair.

Eq. (11) is the wave field model upon which all of the material that follows in this article is based. This material is concerned with two distinct models for a Synthetic Aperture Radar system in association with Eq. (11). The first is a scalar field model when the last two terms on the right hand side of Eq. (11) are neglected. The second model considers a solution to Eq. (11) based on neglecting the last term on the right hand side which is consistent with imposing the condition that $\mu_r = 1$.

3. Scalar field model

In regard to Eq. (11), a scalar wave field model is compounded in the equation

$$(\nabla^2 + k^2)E(\mathbf{r},k) = \gamma(\mathbf{r},k)E(\mathbf{r},k) \tag{12}$$

where

$$\gamma(\mathbf{r},k) = -k^2\gamma_\varepsilon(\mathbf{r}) + ikZ_0\sigma(\mathbf{r}) \tag{13}$$

The field $E(\mathbf{r},k)$ denotes any component of the electric field vector $\mathbf{E}(\mathbf{r},k) = \hat{\mathbf{x}}E_x(\mathbf{r},k) + \hat{\mathbf{y}}E_y(\mathbf{r},k) + \hat{\mathbf{z}}E_z(\mathbf{r},k)$ where $(\hat{\mathbf{x}},\hat{\mathbf{y}},\hat{\mathbf{z}})$ are unit vectors in a Euclidean space and (E_x,E_y,E_z) are the scalar components of the field in that space.

This equation has the fundamental Green's function solution [7].

$$E(\mathbf{r},k) = E_i(\mathbf{r},k) + E_s(\mathbf{r},k) \tag{14}$$

where $E_i(\mathbf{r},k)$ is the incident wave function, taken to be a solution of the homogenous Helmholtz equation

$$(\nabla^2 + k^2)E_i(\mathbf{r},k) = 0 \tag{15}$$

and $E_s(\mathbf{r},k)$ is the scattered field given by

$$E_s(\mathbf{r},k) = g(r,k) \otimes_{\mathbf{r}} \gamma(\mathbf{r},k)E(\mathbf{r},k) \text{ where } g(r,k) = \frac{\exp(ikr)}{4\pi r} \tag{16}$$

The function $g(r,k)$ is the 'out-going free-space Green's function' which is the solution of [7].

$$(\nabla^2 + k^2)g(r,k) = \delta^3(\mathbf{r}) \tag{17}$$

for the three-dimensional delta function $\delta^3(\mathbf{r})$ and the operator $\otimes_{\mathbf{r}}$ denotes the convolution integral, i.e.

$$g(\mathbf{r}) \otimes_{\mathbf{r}} f(\mathbf{r}) \equiv \int_{-\infty}^{\infty} g(\mathbf{r}-\mathbf{s})f(\mathbf{s})d^n\mathbf{s}$$

where $[g(\mathbf{r}),f(\mathbf{r})] \in L^2(\mathbb{R}^3) : \mathbb{C} \to \mathbb{C}$. Thus, we note that

$$g(r,k) \otimes_{\mathbf{r}} \gamma(\mathbf{r},k)E(\mathbf{r},k) \equiv \int_{-\infty}^{\infty} g(\mathbf{r}|\mathbf{s},k)\gamma(\mathbf{s},k)E(\mathbf{s},k)d^3\mathbf{s}$$

where, for notational convenience and clarity, $g(\mathbf{r}|\mathbf{s},k) \equiv g(|\mathbf{r}-\mathbf{s}|,k)$.

A simple proof of the fundamental solution given by Eq. (16) is obtained by noting that

$$\begin{aligned}
\nabla^2 E(\mathbf{r},k) &= \nabla^2 E_i(\mathbf{r},k) + \nabla^2[g(r,k) \otimes_{\mathbf{r}} \gamma(\mathbf{r},k)E(\mathbf{r},k)] \\
&= \nabla^2 E_i(\mathbf{r},k) + \nabla^2[g(r,k)] \otimes_{\mathbf{r}} \gamma(\mathbf{r},k)E(\mathbf{r},k) \\
&= \nabla^2 E_i(\mathbf{r},k) + \left[\delta^3(\mathbf{r}) - k^2 g(r,k)\right] \otimes_{\mathbf{r}} \gamma(\mathbf{r},k)E(\mathbf{r},k) \\
&= \nabla^2 E_i(\mathbf{r},k) + \gamma(\mathbf{r},k)E(\mathbf{r},k) - k^2[E(\mathbf{r},k) - E_i(\mathbf{r},k)] \\
&= -k^2 E(\mathbf{r},k) + \gamma(\mathbf{r},k)E(\mathbf{r},k)
\end{aligned} \tag{18}$$

given Eqs. (15) and (17), and that

$$\delta^3(r) \otimes_{\mathbf{r}} \gamma(\mathbf{r},k)E(\mathbf{r},k) = \gamma(\mathbf{r},k)E(\mathbf{r},k)$$

In the context of Eq. (16), the forward scattering problem is 'Given $\gamma(\mathbf{r},k)$ evaluate $E_s(\mathbf{r},k)$'. The corresponding inverse scattering problem is 'Given $E_s(\mathbf{r},k)$ evaluate $\gamma(\mathbf{r},k)$'. Both problems ideally require unconditional and exact solutions. If the 'scattering function' $\gamma(\mathbf{r},k)$ is taken to be a piecewise continuous function over all space, approaching zero at infinity say, then there are no boundary conditions that need to be taken into account. However, Eq. (14) also applies to the case of a scattering function of compact support with a defined surface for which boundary conditions apply. This is discussed in the following section.

4. Volume and surface scattering effects

Eq. (14) is valid for for $\gamma(\mathbf{r},k) \to 0$ as $r \to \infty$. In the case when $\gamma(\mathbf{r},k)$ is a function of compact support such that $\mathbf{r} \in V$ where V is a finite volume of space, the fundamental solution is [7].

$$E(\mathbf{r},k) = \int\limits_{\mathbf{s}\in V} g(\mathbf{r}|\mathbf{s})\gamma(\mathbf{s},k)E(\mathbf{s},k)d^3\mathbf{s} + \oint\limits_{\mathbf{s}\in S} [g(\mathbf{r}|\mathbf{s}.k)\nabla E(\mathbf{s},k) - E(\mathbf{s},k)\nabla g(\mathbf{r}|\mathbf{s},k)] \cdot \hat{\mathbf{n}}d^2\mathbf{s}$$

where S defines the surface of the scattering function and $\hat{\mathbf{n}}$ is the outward unit normal at each point on S.

If the field does not penetrate into the volume of the scatterer, then the solution is given by the surface integral alone. The solution then depends explicitly on the values of the field (and its gradient) on the boundary of the surface alone, from which the surface integral may then be evaluated. This is a boundary value problem whose solutions describe surface scattering effects and applies to scattering problems when there is no propagation of the incident field into the interior of the scatterer.

When the incident field penetrates into the interior of the scatterer, both volume and surface scattering effects must be taken into account. This is the case when the scatterer is composed on (non-conductive) dielectric materials, for example. Thus, suppose that the field $E_i(\mathbf{r},k)$, which is a solution to Eq. (15), is incident upon the surface of the scatterer. At the point of incidence, the boundary field and its gradient will be $E_i(\mathbf{s},k)$ and $\nabla E_i(\mathbf{s},k)$, respectively. Using these boundary conditions and Green's theorem [7], we have

$$\oint\limits_{\mathbf{s}\in S} [g(\mathbf{r}|\mathbf{s},k)\nabla E_i(\mathbf{s},k) - E_i(\mathbf{s},k)\nabla g(\mathbf{r}|\mathbf{s},k)] \cdot \hat{\mathbf{n}}d^2\mathbf{s}$$

$$= \int\limits_{\mathbf{s}\in V} \left[g(\mathbf{r}|\mathbf{s},k)\nabla^2 E_i(\mathbf{s},k) - E_i(\mathbf{s},k)\nabla^2 g(\mathbf{r}|\mathbf{s},k)\right]d^3\mathbf{s} = \int\limits_{\mathbf{s}\in V} \delta^3(\mathbf{r}-\mathbf{s})E_i(\mathbf{s},k)d^3\mathbf{s} = E_i(\mathbf{r},k)$$

having noted that

$$\nabla^2 E_i(\mathbf{r},k) = -k^2 E_i(\mathbf{r},k) \text{ and } \nabla^2 g(\mathbf{r}|\mathbf{s},k) = -\delta^3(\mathbf{r}-\mathbf{s}) - k^2 g(\mathbf{r}|\mathbf{s},k)$$

Hence, we obtain the same solution as given by Eq. (14) for a scattering function of compact support (or otherwise) with a defined surface upon which the electric field and its gradient are taken to be that of an incident field conforming to Eq. (15). It may be argued that this is also valid for conductive scatterers unless the skin depth, given by $\delta = (2/kZ_0\sigma)^{1/2}$, is taken to be zero (implying that the conductivity is infinite!). In practice, however, the skin depth is finite and thus, Eq. (14) may be applied for a volume that is determined by the surface and the skin depth of the scatterer where, beyond the skin depth, the field is taken to be zero. In this way, a volume scattering model can be applied for cases involving field attenuating scatterers such conductors where $\sigma \gg 0$.

5. Weak scattering model: The born approximation

Eq. (14) is an integral equation obtained through application of the fundamental Green's function solution. However, it is not a solution. This is because the $E(\mathbf{r}, k)$ field is on both the left and right hand sides of the equation. The simplest, and most common solution to this problem, is obtained by applying what is commonly referred to as the Born approximation [8]. This is where it is assumed that the convolution integral for the scattered field can be approximated using the result

$$E_s(\mathbf{r}, k) = g(r, k) \otimes_{\mathbf{r}} \gamma(\mathbf{r}, k) E_i(\mathbf{r}, k) \tag{19}$$

Application of this approximation requires that

$$\frac{\|E_s(\mathbf{r}, k)\|_2}{\|E_i(\mathbf{r}, k)\|_2} \ll 1 \tag{20}$$

where $\|\bullet\|_2$ denotes the Euclidean norm. Essentially, Condition (20) means that the intensity of the field $E_s(\mathbf{r}, k)$ (the scattering cross-section) is small compared to that of $E_i(\mathbf{r}, k)$. The condition implies that the scattering is a 'weak effect', i.e., the scattered field is a small perturbation of the incident field. In physical terms, this means that there are no multiple scattering effects taken to be present. Thus, the Born scattered field is a model for single scattering events alone.

Multiple scattering events can be taken into account through iteration of Eq. (14) which requires that the series converges. This is a formal solution to the (multiple) scattering problem, and is quantified in terms of the series solution to Eq. (14), given by

$$E(\mathbf{r}, k) = E_i(\mathbf{r}, k) + g(r, k) \otimes_{\mathbf{r}} \gamma(\mathbf{r}, k) E_i(\mathbf{r}, k) + g(r, k) \otimes_{\mathbf{r}} \gamma(\mathbf{r}, k)[g(r, k) \otimes_{\mathbf{r}} \gamma(\mathbf{r}, k) E_i(\mathbf{r}, k)] + \ldots$$

The Born approximation is then observed to be the first iteration of a series solution, each higher order term of the series representing the second, third, fourth etc. order scattering effects. In this context, we can analyse the physical limitations that the Born approximation exhibits. To do this, Condition (20) must be investigated further.

The Born approximation requires that $E_s(\mathbf{r}, k)$ is 'small' compared to $E_i(\mathbf{r}, k)$ for all $\mathbf{r} \in \mathbb{R}^3$ and k. To quantify this statement, we use Young's convolution inequality and then Hölder's inequality, respectively. For a Euclidean, this yields the result:

$$\begin{aligned}\|E_s(\mathbf{r}, k)\|_2 = \ & \|g(\mathbf{r}, k) \otimes_{\mathbf{r}} \gamma(\mathbf{r}, k) E_i(\mathbf{r}, k)\|_2 \leq \ \|g(\mathbf{r}, k)\|_2 \|\gamma(\mathbf{r}, k) E_i(\mathbf{r}, k)\|_2 \\ \leq \ & \|E_i(\mathbf{r}, k)\|_2 \|g(\mathbf{r}, k)\|_2 \|\gamma(\mathbf{r}, k)\|_2\end{aligned}$$

It is then clear that the condition for the Born approximation to hold can be written as

$$\|g(\mathbf{r}, k)\|_2 \|\gamma(\mathbf{r}, k)\|_2 \ll 1$$

For a scatterer that is taken to be a sphere of radius R say, we can write the condition as

$$\langle \gamma(\mathbf{r},k) \rangle \ll 1R^2 \quad \text{where} \quad \langle \gamma(\mathbf{r},k) \rangle \equiv \sqrt{\frac{\int |\gamma(\mathbf{r},k)|^2 d^3\mathbf{r}}{\int d^3\mathbf{r}}}$$

Thus, for a dielectric material when $\gamma(\mathbf{r},k) = -k^2\gamma_\varepsilon(\mathbf{r})$ (and $\sigma = 0$), we can write the condition in terms of the wavelength λ as

$$\lambda \gg R\sqrt{\langle \gamma(\mathbf{r},k) \rangle}$$

This 'distillation' of the condition for the Born approximation to be applicable, demonstrates that, for arbitrary values of $\langle \gamma(\mathbf{r},k) \rangle$, Condition (20) holds, provided the physical scale length L say, of the scattering function is small compared to the wavelength. Else, for scale lengths where $L \sim \lambda$, the condition for the Born approximation to apply is $\langle \gamma(\mathbf{r},k) \rangle \ll 1$. This is the condition required for the scatterer to be classified as being 'weak'.

The main point here, is that unless the scattering is taken to be weak, the Born approximation can only be satisfied if $\lambda \gg L$. However, this condition is entirely incompatible with a fundamental reality concerning the structural information associated with any and all images formed from a scattering interaction. This is that information on the structure of a material is determined by the interactions that take place on the scale of a wavelength. It is this dichotomy, at least, for scattering effects that cannot be classified as being 'weak' which is the more common physical reality, that lies at the heart of the problem in using a Born scattering model to processes and analyse images obtained from the scattering of an EM field. For this reason, the approach considered in the following section is now presented.

6. Exact scattering model

For a scalar field, an exact scattering solution to Eq. (12) can be formulated which is compounded in the result [5].

$$E(\mathbf{r},k) = g(r,k) \otimes_{\mathbf{r}} \gamma(\mathbf{r},k) E_i(\mathbf{r},k) \tag{21}$$

where, for spatial frequency vector $\mathbf{u}$,

$$E(\mathbf{r},k) \leftrightarrow \frac{\tilde{E}_i(\mathbf{u},k)\tilde{E}_s(\mathbf{u},k)}{\tilde{E}_i(\mathbf{u},k) + \tilde{E}_s(\mathbf{u},k)},$$

$$\tilde{E}_i(\mathbf{u},k) \leftrightarrow E_i(\mathbf{r},k), \quad \tilde{E}_s(\mathbf{u},k) \leftrightarrow E_s(\mathbf{r},k) \quad \text{and} \quad \tilde{E}(\mathbf{u},k) = \int_{-\infty}^{\infty} E(\mathbf{r},k)\exp(-i\mathbf{u}\cdot\mathbf{r})d^3\mathbf{r} \tag{22}$$

Equation (21) facilitates an exact (near-field) inverse scattering solution given that we can write

$$\gamma(\mathbf{r},k) = \frac{E_i^*(\mathbf{r},k)}{|E_i(\mathbf{r},k)|^2} h(r,k) \otimes_{\mathbf{r}} E(\mathbf{r},k) \;\text{ where }\; h(r,k) \otimes_{\mathbf{r}} g(r,k) = \delta^3(\mathbf{r})$$

However, Eq. (21) is subject to Eq. (15), and, more critically, a further 'conditioning equation' given by [5].

$$\left(\nabla^2 + k^2\right)\gamma(\mathbf{r},k)E_i(\mathbf{r},k) = 0 \tag{23}$$

This is a non-standard condition that requires quantification in terms of the class of scattering functions that are applicable. In this respect, expanding Eq. (23), we can write it in the form

$$\nabla^2\gamma(\mathbf{r},k) + 2\nabla\gamma(\mathbf{r},k) \cdot \nabla \ln E_i(\mathbf{r},k) = 0$$

and thus, for an incident unit plane wave field given by $E_i(\mathbf{r},k) = \exp(-i\mathbf{k}\cdot\mathbf{r}/2)$ say, which is a solution to Eq. (15), we can write Eq. (23) as

$$\nabla^2\gamma(\mathbf{r},k) - i\mathbf{k} \cdot \nabla\gamma(\mathbf{r},k) = 0 \tag{24}$$

Eq. (24) has a solution (for arbitrary constants a and b) given by

$$\gamma(\mathbf{r},k) = a + b\exp(i\mathbf{k}\cdot\mathbf{r})$$

However under the condition that $\mathbf{k}\cdot\mathbf{u} - u^2 = 0$, Eq. (24) has the general solution

$$\gamma(\mathbf{r},k) = \frac{1}{(2\pi)^3} \int_{-\infty}^{\infty} \tilde{\gamma}(\mathbf{u},k)\exp(i\mathbf{u}\cdot\mathbf{r})d^3\mathbf{u}$$

Therefore, Eq. (23) allows Eq. (21) to hold for any scattering function for which a definable frequency spectrum $\tilde{\gamma}(\mathbf{u},k)$ exists, subject to the condition $u \equiv |\mathbf{u}| = k\cos\theta$. An interpretation of this condition can be formulated for the case when $\theta \sim 0$ (i.e. $\mathbf{u} \sim \mathbf{k}$) or $k/u \sim 1$ as follows: Suppose that the temporal frequency is a constant k_0 where $k_0 \gg 1$. Further, let the spatial frequency spectrum of $\gamma(\mathbf{r},k_0)$, over which spectral information is attainable, have a bandwidth K, such that (for the positive frequency half space) $u \in [k_0 \pm K]$ where $K/k_0 \ll 1$. Then, $k_0/u \sim 1$. This condition is compatible with the use of a narrow side-band imaging system such as a SAR, and, in this respect, the exact scattering solution is applicable for modelling such a system. This analysis applies to the case when $E_i(\mathbf{r},k) = P(k)\exp(\pm i\mathbf{k}\cdot\mathbf{r})$ for any amplitude spectrum $P(k)$. In this context, given Eq. (23), we can write Eq. (21) as

$$E(\mathbf{r},k) = -1k^2 g(r,k) \otimes_{\mathbf{r}} \nabla^2[\gamma(\mathbf{r},k)E_i(\mathbf{r},k)] \tag{25}$$

where $k \sim k_0 \gg 1$.

In terms of Eq. (21), it is noted that, subject to the condition,

$$\|\tilde{E}_s(\mathbf{u},k)\|_2 \ll \|\tilde{E}_i(\mathbf{u},k)\|_2 \tag{26}$$

then

$$\frac{\tilde{E}_i(\mathbf{u},k)\tilde{E}_s(\mathbf{u},k)}{\tilde{E}_i(\mathbf{u},k) + \tilde{E}_s(\mathbf{u},k)} = \frac{\tilde{E}_s(\mathbf{u},k)}{1 + \tilde{E}_s(\mathbf{u},k)/\tilde{E}_i(\mathbf{u},k)} \simeq \tilde{E}_s(\mathbf{u},k)$$

In this case, we may consider the approximate relationship

$$E(\mathbf{r},k) \leftrightarrow \tilde{E}_s(\mathbf{u},k)$$

and Eq. (21) reduces to

$$E_s(\mathbf{r},k) = g(r,k) \otimes_{\mathbf{r}} \gamma(\mathbf{r},k) E_i(\mathbf{r},k) \tag{27}$$

This result is equivalent to the Born approximation discussed in Section 5. The exact scattering solution given by Eq. (21) [subject to the condition compounded in Eq. (23)] therefore reduces to the Born approximation under the condition that the spectrum of the scattered field is weaker than the spectrum of the incident field. Note, that Condition (26) is equivalent to Condition (20), given Rayleigh's energy theorem, i.e.

$$\|E(\mathbf{r},k)\|_2^2 = \frac{1}{(2\pi)^3}\|\tilde{E}(\mathbf{u},k)\|_2^2$$

7. Strong scattering model

While Eq. (21) provides an exact scattering solution, subject to Condition (23), it does not provide an expression for the scattered field itself. To achieve this, we consider the following approach: Using a binomial expansion, the scattered field spectrum can be written as

$$\tilde{E}_s(\mathbf{u},k) = \frac{\tilde{E}_i(\mathbf{u},k)\tilde{E}(\mathbf{u},k)}{\tilde{E}_i(\mathbf{u},k) - \tilde{E}(\mathbf{u},k)} = \tilde{E}(\mathbf{u},k)\left(1 + \frac{\tilde{E}(\mathbf{u},k)}{\tilde{E}_i(\mathbf{u},k)} + \dots\right), \quad \left|\frac{\tilde{E}(\mathbf{u},k)}{\tilde{E}_i(\mathbf{u},k)}\right| < 1$$

Given Eq. (25), we observe that the nth term of this binomial series scales as k^{-2n}, and for this reason, we can write

$$\tilde{E}_s(\mathbf{u},k) = \tilde{E}(\mathbf{u},k), \quad |k| \to \infty$$

Thus, we obtain an expression for a high frequency scattered field, given by

$$E_s(\mathbf{r},k) = -\frac{1}{k^2} g(r,k) \otimes_{\mathbf{r}} \nabla^2[\gamma(\mathbf{r},k)E_i(\mathbf{r},k)], \quad |k| \gg 1 \tag{28}$$

Apart from a scaling factor by k^{-2}, the major difference between the weak scattering solution given by Eq. (27) and Eq. (28) is compounded in the Laplacian operator ∇^2. In this context, the scattered field given by Eq. (28) is referred to as a 'strong scattering solution'.

Unlike the Born approximation, this solution is exact and subject only to Eq. (23) for $|k| \gg 1$. The high frequency condition means that Eq. (28) is not suitable for base-band imaging systems where $k \in [-K, K]$ for bandwidth K. However, it is appropriate for sideband systems where (for the positive frequency half-space) $k \in [k_0 \pm K]$ when $k_0 \gg 1$ and $K/k_0 \ll 1$.

A further modification to Eq. (28) can be made by noting that, for a unit plane wave, when $E_i(\mathbf{r}, k) = \exp(i\mathbf{k} \cdot \mathbf{r})$ say, which is a solution to Eq. (15), then

$$\begin{aligned}\nabla^2[\gamma(\mathbf{r}, k)E_i(\mathbf{r}, k)] &= \exp(i\mathbf{k} \cdot \mathbf{r})\left[\nabla^2\gamma(\mathbf{r}, k) + 2i\mathbf{k} \cdot \nabla\gamma(\mathbf{r}, k) - k^2\gamma(\mathbf{r})\right] \\ &\sim \exp(i\mathbf{k} \cdot \mathbf{r})\nabla^2\gamma(\mathbf{r}, k)\end{aligned} \tag{29}$$

This result is based on a further condition which is that the second order gradient of the scattering function dominates (in amplitude) the first order gradient and the scattering function itself, given that the wavelength is taken to be relatively large compared to the scale length over which a gradient occurs. Note, that this is not the same as applying the Born approximation, which is predicated on the wavelength being large compared to the scale length of the scatterer itself (and not its first and second order gradients).

8. Model for a SAR image

As briefly discussed in the introduction, a SAR is based on repeatedly emitting a frequency modulated pulse in range as the radar platform moves cross range, usually at a fixed height. The pulse forms part of an emitted beam that, in regard to the scattering events that take place, has a range that is 'engineered' to be in the Fresnel zone. Thus, the Green's function given in Eq. (28) must be modified to reflect this reality. In terms of the convolution integral given in Eq. (28), and, with a slight change of notation, we consider the following expression for the Green's function as a convolution kernel:

$$g(\mathbf{r}|\mathbf{r}_0, k) \equiv \frac{1}{4\pi|\mathbf{r} - \mathbf{r}_0|}\exp(ik|\mathbf{r} - \mathbf{r}_0|), \quad \mathbf{r}|\mathbf{r}_0 \equiv |\mathbf{r} - \mathbf{r}_0|$$

For a SAR, the vector $\mathbf{r}_0$ denotes the location in space where the incident field is emitted and where the back-scattered field detected. Application of the 'Fresnel zone condition' $r^2/r_0^2 \ll 1$, coupled with a binomial expansion of $|\mathbf{r} - \mathbf{r}_0|$ yields

$$|\mathbf{r} - \mathbf{r}_0| \simeq r_0\left(1 - \frac{\mathbf{r}_0 \cdot \mathbf{r}}{r_0^2} + \frac{r^2}{2r_0^2}\right) = \frac{1}{2r_0}|\mathbf{r}_0 - \mathbf{r}|^2 + \frac{r_0}{2}$$

Thus, the Green's function in the Fresnel zone is reduced to the form

$$g(\mathbf{r}|\mathbf{r}_0, k) \equiv \frac{1}{4\pi\mathbf{r}_0}\exp(ik\mathbf{r}_0/2)\exp[ik|\mathbf{r}_0 - \mathbf{r}|^2/2\mathbf{r}_0]$$

which allows the scattered electric field to be written as

$$E_s(\mathbf{r}_0, k) = -\frac{1}{k^2}\frac{1}{4\pi r_0}\exp(ikr_0/2)A_s(\mathbf{r}_0, k)$$

where

$$A_s(\mathbf{r}_0, k) = \int_{-\infty}^{\infty}\exp\left[ik|\mathbf{r}_0 - \mathbf{r}|^2/2r_0\right]E_i(\mathbf{r}, k)\nabla^2\gamma(\mathbf{r}, k)d^3\mathbf{r} \tag{30}$$

is the 'scattering amplitude'. This model for the scattering amplitude is based on the convolution with a quadratic phase function, where $\mathbf{r}_0$ is the position at which the back-scattering amplitude is recorded.

8.1 Data model

In order to produce a model for SAR, Eq. (30) must be cast in terms of the 'engineering' of a SAR system. This involves having to make some conditional statements relating to the geometry of the system, the characteristics of the incident field that is used and those of the scattering function itself. As with the development of any applied mathematical model, such conditions can be 'challenged'. In the analysis that follows, a governing issue has been to produce a model that is simple enough to be 'mapped' to the processing that is actually undertaken in SAR, while maintaining consistency with, and reference to Eq. (30). In this context, and, using a Euclidean coordinate system we consider the following:

i. The coordinates x_0, y_0 and z_0 are taken to denote the range, cross range and height, respectively.

ii. The range is such that we can consider $r_0 \sim x_0$, implying that $x/x_0 \ll 1$ and $z/x_0 \ll 1$.

iii. The incident field (taken to propagate in range alone) is given by

$$E_i(\mathbf{r}, k) = P(k - k_0) \exp[-i(k - k_0)x] \tag{31}$$

where $P(k - k_0)$ is the spectrum of the (range) pulse and k_0 is the carrier frequency of the system (determined by the operational wavelength). Eq. (31) is a solution to Eq. (15) for the one-dimensional (range) case, which has the more general solution $E_i(\mathbf{r}, k) = P(k \pm k_0) \exp[\pm i(k \pm k_0)x]$. Eq. (31) is chosen for the case of a wave travelling from left to right in the electromagnetism convention [9].

iv. All functions of k given in Eq. (30), except for the incident field, are taken to be functions of k_0, given that the carrier frequency is the dominant frequency component.

v. The scattering function represents a relatively flat surface, whose spatial extent (in range and cross range) is much larger than the 'depth' of the scatterer in terms of relevance to the scattering model. The purpose of this is to introduce a separable scattering function where $\gamma(\mathbf{r}, k_0) = \gamma(x, y, k_0)\gamma(z, k_0)$ thereby facilitating the result

$$\nabla^2\gamma(\mathbf{r}, k_0) = \gamma(z, k_0)\nabla^2\gamma(x, y, k_0) + \gamma(x, y, k_0)\frac{\partial^2}{\partial z^2}\gamma(z, k_0)$$

In regard to points (ii) and (iv), we can now write the convolution kernel in Eq. (30) as

$$\exp\left[ik|\mathbf{r}_0-\mathbf{r}|^2/2r_0\right] = \exp\left[ik_0(x_0-x)^2/2x_0\right]\exp\left[ik_0(y_0-y)^2/2x_0\right]\exp\left[ik_0(z_0-z)^2/2x_0\right]$$
$$\simeq \exp(ik_0x_0/2)\exp\left(ik_0z_0^2/2x_0\right)\exp(-ik_0x)\exp\left[ik_0(y-y_0)^2/2x_0\right]\exp(-ik_0z_0z/x_0)$$

Thus, in regard to points (i)-(v), the scattering amplitude is given by

$$\begin{aligned}A_s(x_0,y_0,z_0,k) &= \exp(ik_0x_0/2)\exp\left(ik_0z_0^2/2x_0\right)P(k-k_0)\\ &\times\int_{-\infty}^{\infty}\int_{-\infty}^{\infty}\int_{-\infty}^{\infty}\exp(-ik_0x)\exp\left[ik_0(y-y_0)^2/2x_0\right]\\ &\exp(-ik_0z_0z/x_0)\exp[-i(k-k_0)x]\left[\gamma(z,k_0)\nabla^2\gamma(x,y,k_0)+\gamma(x,y,k_0)\partial^2\partial z^2\gamma(z,k_0)\right]dxdydz\\ &= \exp(ik_0x_0/2)\exp\left(ik_0z_0^2/2x_0\right)P(k-k_0)\\ &\times\int_{-\infty}^{\infty}\int_{-\infty}^{\infty}\exp(-ikx)\exp\left[ik_0(y-y_0)^2/2x_0\right]\left[C_1\nabla^2\gamma(x,y,k_0)+C_2\gamma(x,y,k_0)\right]dxdy\end{aligned}$$

where

$$C_1=\int_{-\infty}^{\infty}\gamma(z,k_0)\exp(-ik_0z_0z/x_0)dz \tag{32}$$

and

$$C_2=\int_{-\infty}^{\infty}\frac{\partial^2}{\partial z^2}[\gamma(z,k_0)]\exp(-ik_0z_0z/x_0)dz=-\frac{k_0^2z_0^2}{x_0^2}\int_{-\infty}^{\infty}\gamma(z,k_0)\exp(-ik_0z_0z/x_0)dz \tag{33}$$

Since we have considered the case where, $z_0 \ll x_0$, we can further simplify this result, by letting

$$C_1\nabla^2\gamma(x,y,k_0)+C_2\gamma(x,y,k_0)\sim C_1\nabla^2\gamma(x,y,k_0)$$

thereby reducing the scattering amplitude to the form

$$\begin{aligned}A_s(x_0,y_0,z_0,k) &= \exp(ik_0x_0/2)\exp\left(ik_0z_0^2/2x_0\right)P(k-k_0)\\ &\times\int_{-\infty}^{\infty}\int_{-\infty}^{\infty}\exp(-ikx)\exp\left[ik_0(y-y_0)^2/2x_0\right]C_1\nabla^2\gamma(x,y,k_0)dxdy\end{aligned}$$

Application of the inverse Fourier transform, coupled with the convolution theorem and the shift theorem for the frequency domain, then allows us to construct the following result:

$$A_s(x_0,z_0,x,y,k_0) = \exp(ik_0x_0/2)\exp\left(ik_0z_0^2/2x_0\right)S(x,y)$$

where is the SAR signal given by

$$\begin{aligned}S(x,y) &= \exp\left(ik_0y^2/2x_0\right)\otimes_y p(x)\exp(ik_0x)\otimes_x C_1\nabla^2\gamma(x,y,k_0)\\ &= \exp(ik_0x)\left[p(x)\otimes_x q(y)\otimes_y\exp(-ik_0x)C_1\nabla^2\gamma(x,y,k_0)\right]\end{aligned} \tag{34}$$

and

$$q(y) = \exp(i\beta y^2), \quad \beta = k_0/2x_0$$

Here, $\otimes_x$ and $\otimes_y$ denote the convolution integrals over x and y, respectively, and $p(x) \leftrightarrow P(k)$.

In order to complete the model compounded in Eq. (34), the range pulse $p(x)$ needs to be specified and the 'width' of the cross-range response defined. In the latter case, we consider the beam width to be given by Y, so that the cross range response is taken to be specified for $y \in [-Y/2, Y/2]$. In both real and synthetic aperture systems, the range pulse is typically given by a linear frequency modulated 'chirp', i.e. for a unit amplitude pulse, with a 'length' of X,

$$p(x) = \exp(i\alpha x^2), \quad x \in [-X/2, X/2]$$

where α is the 'chirp rate'. It is then clear that the characteristics of a SAR are the same in both range and cross range, i.e. a linear frequency modulation. This is because the instantaneous frequency is defined as the derivative of the instantaneous phase, which varies linearly with the independent variables x and y—the frequency modulations being defined by the modulus of the instantaneous frequency [4].

8.2 Data processing model

The processing of a SAR signal now being modelled by Eq. (34), is based on three principal steps, namely:

i. Demodulation with quadrature detection in range, which yields complex data—the 'analytic signal'—obtained from the detection of a real signal.

ii. Correlation in range with the complex conjugate of the range pulse $p(x)$.

iii. Correlation in cross range with the complex conjugate of the cross range response $q(y)$.

Demodulation essentially eliminates the factor $\exp(ik_0x)$ from Eq. (34). In regard to the correlation processes, we note that

$$p^*(x)\odot_x p(x) = \int_{-X/2}^{X/2} \exp(-i\alpha y^2)\exp\left[i\alpha(x+y)^2\right]dy = \exp(i\alpha x^2)\int_{-X/2}^{X/2} \exp(2i\alpha xy)dy$$
$$= \exp(i\alpha x^2)X\text{sinc}(\alpha Xx) \simeq X\text{sinc}(\alpha Xx), \quad X \gg 1$$

Similarly,

$$q^*(y)\odot_y q(y) \simeq Y\text{sinc}(\alpha Yy), \quad Y \gg 1$$

Thus, following demodulation, the processed data $s(x, y)$ can be modelled as

$$s(x,y) = q^*(y)\odot_y p^*(x)\odot_x S(x,y) = p(x,y)\otimes_x\otimes_y \exp(-ik_0x)C_1\nabla^2\gamma(x,y,k_0)$$

where, after ignoring the scaling factor XY, and with $\alpha \equiv \alpha X$ and $\beta \equiv \beta Y$,

$$p(x,y) = \text{sinc}(\alpha x)\text{sinc}(\beta y)$$

The function $p(x,y)$ is the Point Spread Function (PSF) for the SAR data. A SAR image is typically a display (a grey level image) of the Amplitude Modulations, given by

$$I_{\text{SAR}}(x,y) = |p(x,y) \otimes_x \otimes_y \exp(-ik_0 x) C_1 \nabla^2 \gamma(x,y,k_0)| \tag{35}$$

whose characteristics will depend on the operational wavelength of the system, i.e. $\lambda_0 = 2\pi/k_0$. Note, that Eq. (35) is a strong scattering model for a SAR image and that the equivalent weak scattering model is obtained by replacing the Laplacian of the scattering function with the scattering function alone.

The values of α and β depend on a specific SAR system but typically, a SAR image is based on $\alpha \sim \beta$ so that the range and cross range resolutions are compatible. The coherent nature of such an image (real or simulated) yields a texture that is dominated by a 'speckle pattern'. However, it should be noted, that the model compounded in Eq. (35) does not take into account issues such as the three-dimensional nature of the ground surface and hence, 'shadow effects', for example. It is a scalar field model for the two-dimensional scattering function $\gamma(x,y,k_0)$, designed specifically to provide dimensional compatibility with SAR data.

9. Fractal scattering functions

The evaluation of Eq. (35) is determined by the scattering function $\nabla^2\gamma(\mathbf{r},k_0), \ \mathbf{r}\in\mathbb{R}^2$. This function has a spatial frequency spectrum $-u^2\tilde{\gamma}(\mathbf{u},k_0)$ where $\tilde{\gamma}(\mathbf{u},k_0) \leftrightarrow \gamma(\mathbf{r},k_0)$ and $\mathbf{u} = \hat{\mathbf{x}}u_x + \hat{\mathbf{y}}u_y$. The component of the range spectrum that characterises the scale length over which scattering occurs, is determined by the carrier frequency of the incident field k_0, i.e. the scale of the wavelength. This is because

$$\exp(-ik_0 x)\nabla^2\gamma(\mathbf{r},k_0) \leftrightarrow -\left[(u_x+k_0)^2 + u_y^2\right]\tilde{\gamma}(u_x+k_0,u_y,k_0)$$

In the approach to simulating a SAR image (subject to any scattering model), the variations in space of a scattering function (on the scale of a wavelength) may not necessary be known quantitatively. This is of course, precisely why solutions to the inverse scattering problem are important; in order to estimate the spatial characteristics of the scattering function from measurements of the scattered field.

In the case of a remote sensing system such as SAR, the wavelength scale variations of the scatterer may be required over very large regions of space compared to the wavelength. This is not a practical proposition, i.e. to know relatively precisely the variation in values of the relative permittivity and/or conductivity for a wide variety of surface features on a centimetric scale over an area covering tens of kilometres.

The surface of the earth has of course a wide variety of naturally occurring (and man-made) features. Consequently, we can argue that such features confirm to the 'Fractal Geometry of Nature' [10]. This idea allows us to consider the case when $\gamma(\mathbf{r},k_0), \ \mathbf{r}\in\mathbb{R}^2$ is a fractal surface—a Mandelbrot surface [11].

In this case, the surface features are taken to have the same distribution of amplitudes at all scales. Consequently, the Laplacian of a Mandelbrot surface will also be a self-affine function (at least within a finite level of detail) and therefore exhibit the same distributional characteristics at all scales. In this context, we can consider a random fractal model where

$$\exp(-ik_0x)\nabla^2\gamma(\mathbf{r},k_0) \sim \nabla^2\gamma(\mathbf{r},k_0)$$

given that for any scale length λ (the wavelength of an incident wave field)

$$\Pr[\gamma(\lambda\mathbf{r},k_0)] = \lambda^\alpha \Pr[\gamma(\mathbf{r},k_0)]$$

where Pr denotes the Probability Density Function (PDF) and α is related to the Fractal Dimension D (for $\mathbf{r}\in\mathbb{R}^2$) by $D = 4 - \alpha$ [11]. The 'signature spectrum' for such a self-affine surface is compounded in the result [11].

$$\gamma(\mathbf{r},k_0) \leftrightarrow \frac{S(\mathbf{u})}{|\mathbf{u}|^\alpha}$$

where $S(\mathbf{u})$ is the spectrum of a 'white' stochastic field $s(\mathbf{r})$ with a constant Power Spectral Density Function (PSDF). We may therefore consider a strong self-affine scattering function to be characterised by

$$\nabla^2\gamma(\mathbf{r},k_0) \leftrightarrow -|\mathbf{u}|^{D-2}S(\mathbf{u})$$

which, for $D\in(2,3)$, is a fractional Laplacian according to the Riesz definition [12]. Thus, with reference to Eq. (13) and Eq. (35), by ignoring the scaling factor associated with the coefficient $k_0^2C_1$, this self-affine model for a SAR image yields the equation

$$I_{\text{SAR}}(x,y) = |p(x,y)\otimes_x\otimes_y\nabla^2\gamma(x,y)| \tag{36}$$

where, we redefine $\gamma(x,y)$ as

$$\gamma(x,y) = \gamma_\varepsilon(x,y) - i\frac{Z_0}{k_0}\sigma(x,y) \tag{37}$$

This model presupposes that the analytical signal (in range x) has been obtained. This is because a SAR image is formed from complex data generated by the demodulation and quadrature detection of each (range) signal.

There is an interesting similarity between Eq. (36) and the Marr-Hildreth model for second order edge detection where the PSF $p(x,y)$ is a Gaussian function [13]. This is because, in addition to the algorithm being an edge detector, it is the result of one of the first approaches in pattern recognition to be based on a model for the human visual system where edges associated with different frequency bands are taken to be the basis for object recognition over different scales.

10. SAR image simulation using aerial optical images of the ground

Excepting the limitations associated with the model compounded in Eq. (36), coupled with the scattering function being a self-affine function, let us consider the non-conductive case (so that $\sigma = 0$), where the function $\gamma_\varepsilon(x,y)$ is a fractal surface. The question then remains as to how we can quantify such a surface. One way is through simulation using techniques developed in [11], for example, and references therein, including the applications of stochastic field theory for modelling the sea surface, for example [14]. However, this approach requires significant attention to detail in terms of quantifying variations in the permittivity associated with the 'ground truth'. Instead, suppose we consider an overhead aerial optical (grey level) image of the ground to be a model representation of the function $\gamma_\varepsilon(x,y)$; crucially, in respect of the function being a fractal surface. A SAR image simulation can then very easily be generated on the basis that

$$\gamma_\varepsilon(x,y) \sim I_{\text{Optical}}(x,y)$$

The optical image is taken to be an aerial image of the region over which a SAR simulation is required. The idea associated with this phenomenology, is that the 'ground truth' tends to be composed of self-affine dielectric structures such a trees, grasslands and other natural features that contribute to the fractal geometry of the surface as a whole. Thus, in the context of the fractal model described in Section 9, the scattering characteristics are taken to be invariant of wavelength and an optical image is taken to be a self-affine characterisation for the ground surface.

Assuming that a (grey level) optical image is a scale invariant representation of the ground truth based on dielectric properties of the surface alone is of course not entirely compatible with physical reality. However, given the practical issues associated with obtaining detailed knowledge on the scattering function over the scale of a wavelength, then, in terms of generating a simulation that is texturally compatible with a SAR image, the approach may have value. This 'value' is especially relevant in regard to using optical images to generate training data required for applications in pattern recognition for SAR when SAR data is unavailable *a priori*. In this context, the simulation considered is compounded in a model that is quantified by the simple equation

$$I_{\text{SAR}}(x,y) = |p(x,y) \otimes_x \otimes_y \nabla^2 I_{\text{Optical}}(x,y)| \tag{38}$$

The inclusion of variations in the conductivity in such a model, means that the scattering function becomes a complex function and an optical image is a real only function. In this regard, using a conductive dielectric model is incompatible with a simulation compounded in Eq. (38), even though it can be expected that conductive elements will contribute to features in an optical image of the ground surface. We shall return to this issue later on in the paper.

Figure 1 provides an example simulation of a SAR image using Eq. (38) and the MATLAB code provided in Appendix A. In this example, the optical image is a 1175×1173 (i.e. width×hight) 8-bit grey level image of a predominantly urban area. The PSF is evaluated for sinc functions computed using an array consisting of 10^3 elements with $\alpha = \beta = 1/3$. The Laplacian is computed using the convolution kernel

$$\begin{pmatrix} 0 & 1 & 0 \\ 1 & -4 & 1 \\ 0 & 1 & 1 \end{pmatrix}$$

The optical image is normalised before application of the convolution operations with the Laplacian and PSF (using the MATLAB function conv2). The analytic signals are then computed using a Hilbert Transform (with MATLAB function hilbert) to simulate the quadrature detection process which occurs in range alone (in practice, this is coupled with demodulation). For a real function $f(x)$, the analytic signal is given by [4].

$$s(x) = f(x) + i\pi x \otimes_x f(x) \tag{39}$$

where the imaginary component is, by definition, the Hilbert transform of $f(x)$. However, the MATLAB function hilbert actually computes the analytic signal and not just the Hilbert transform (which is then given by the imaginary component of the function's output).

The range and cross range directions given in **Figure 1** are the vertical and horizontal components of the image, respectively. The simulated SAR image given in **Figure 1** is normalised and histogram equalised [15] (using MATLAB function histeq) in order to enhance the dark field image features (which is a relatively standard practice in SAR image analysis).

The prototype MATLAB function used to generate this simulation—SARSIM—as given in the Appendix A is presented to allow interested readers to repeat the simulation for different input (8-bit grey level) images and control parameters, specifically the array length and the width of the sinc IRF. It provides the basis for further modifications associated with interrogating the processes used, and, as an aid to further improving the simulation based on refinements to the model conceived. This is discussed further in Section 12.1.

Figure 2 shows the IRF in range (and cross range), and a 256-bin histogram of the grey-levels for $I_{SAR}(x, y)$—Eq. (38)—as given in **Figure 1**. The histogram is characteristic of a Rayleigh distribution which is the 'signature distribution' of a SAR image (and coherent images in general). The fact that the distribution of grey levels for $I_{SAR}(x, y)$ is Rayleigh distributed can be quantified using the MATLAB function fitdist, for example, which returns the parameter value $B = 0.0047$ for an assumed (and normalised) Rayleigh distribution given by

$$\Pr[I_{SAR}(x, y)] = xB^2 \exp\left(-\frac{x^2}{2B^2}\right)$$

Figure 1.
A montage providing an example simulation of a SAR image (the amplitude modulations) before (centre) and after (right) histogram equalisation. The simulation is based on the application of an optical image (left) using the .m code provided in Appendix A for size = 1000 and width = 3. The result is predicated on Eq. (38), where the optical image is interpreted to be a map of the self-affine variations in the dielectric properties of the ground surface.

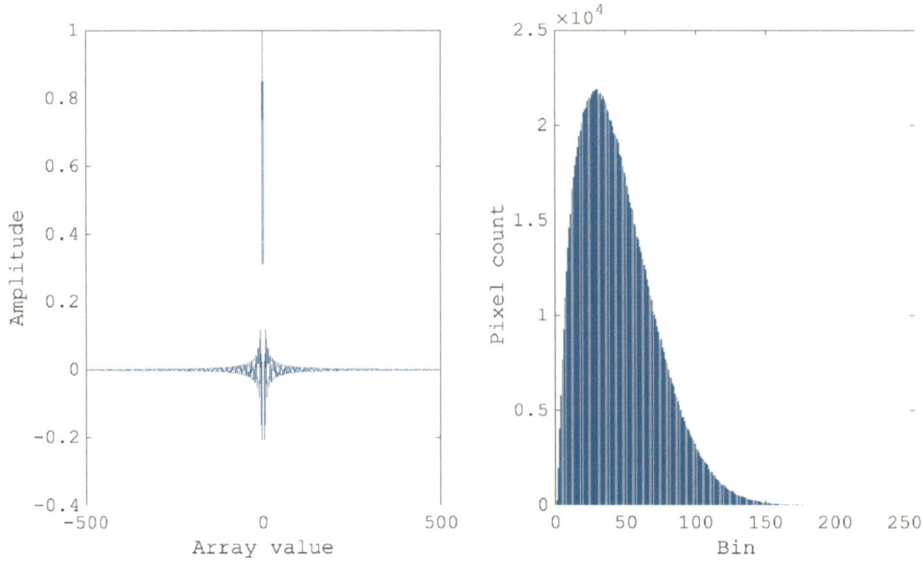

Figure 2.
*The sinc IRF used to generate the SAR image simulation given in **Figure 1** (left) and a 256-bin histogram of the amplitude modulations (normalised to values between 0 and 1) as shown in **Figure 1** (right).*

The simulation produces a result that is statistically compatible with a SAR image but with 'structural features' determined by those associated with the optical image. A simulation of this type must not be expected to provide a detailed resemblance of a real SAR image on a pixel-by-pixel basis. However, the structural and textural properties of the simulation may have similarities with a genuine SAR image, given that the ground surface is taken to be a Mandelbrot surface.

10.1 Texture simulation

A genuine SAR image is the product of a multitude of highly complex three-dimensional interactions (including polarisation effects), that transcend the model given by Eq. (38) based on the application of an areal optical image. However, in the context of assuming a fractal model for the ground surface, the approach considered provides a simulation that is at least texturally compatible with a real SAR image. In this respect, there are a range of texture comparators that can be used to assess the simulated image with respect to genuine data such as those given in [11], for example. It is a 'solution' to the problem of simulating SAR images that goes beyond the conventional approach of generating speckle patterns based on a weak point scattering model, for example [16]. Further, it may also provide value in terms of target detection (e.g. [17, 18]).

10.2 Target detection

Target detection is typically concerned with the interpretation of features in a SAR image that are isolated, but a with high intensities due to increased microwave backscattering from objects that are conductors, for example, with a high Radar Cross Sections (RCS) [19]. In the context of the scalar EM field model considered here, to take into account back-scattering from conductive objects, we are required to consider a conductive dielectric model, and, more specifically, a scattering function where $\sigma(x,y) \neq 0$ for specific locations. In this case, the scattered intensity (the RCS) can be expected to be significantly larger than that generated by variations is the relative permittivity alone [20]. This can be appreciated using an order of magnitude calculation as follows.

Consider a SAR with a wavelength of 1 cm, a relative permittivity for surface features with a Root Mean Square (RMS) value of ~ 10 say, and, an electrical conductivity for isolated metalic objects composed of steel, for example, with a RMS of $\sim 10^6$ Siemens/metre. With reference to the definition of the scattering function given in Eq. (37), then, for a unit area of 1 square metre say, we can write (using the Minkowski inequality for a Euclidean norm)

$$\|\gamma(x,y,k_0)\|_2 \leq \|\gamma_\varepsilon(x,y)\|_2 + \frac{Z_0}{k_0}\|\sigma(x,y)\|_2 \simeq 10 + 0.6 \times 10^6 = 600010$$

which should be compared with ~ 10 for the case of a non-conductive dielectric and the same wavelength for the same unit area. In this respect, the simulation of a SAR image based on Eq. (38), may be used as a texture comparator with a genuine SAR image of the same area (for which an overhead aerial optical image is available) in order to identify conductive agents, should they exist in the a genuine SAR image.

In order to make such a comparator effective, the optical image can be median filtered to eradicate any form of salt-and-pepper noise (impulse noise), that may generate what appears to be isolated back-scattering events from conductive agents. This approach is most relevant to terrain that is relatively flat where conductive agents (such tanks and other military vehicles, for example) may be most likely to operate. Nevertheless, it should be noted that specular reflections from non-conductive dielectric features are capable of generating 'false targets'. In the following section an approach to eradicating false targets is considered using a cross polarisation effect.

11. SAR image modelling with cross polarisation effects

Polarisation effects are compounded in solutions to Eq. (11). In regard to modelling a SAR image, we consider an approach where variations in the permittivity contribute significantly more to the cross polarisation effects of the electric field than do variations in the magnetic permeability. The purpose of this, is that it allows us to consider a reduced model based on the wave equation

$$(\nabla^2 + k^2)\mathbf{E}(\mathbf{r},k) = \gamma(\mathbf{r},k)\mathbf{E}(\mathbf{r},k) - \nabla[\mathbf{E}(\mathbf{r},k) \cdot \nabla \ln \varepsilon(\mathbf{r})]$$

where it is assumed that $\mu_r(\mathbf{r}) \sim 1, \forall \mathbf{r}$. To implement the strong scattering solution to this equation, we note that Eq. (23) is also applicable for a vector field. i.e.

$$(\nabla^2 + k^2)\gamma(\mathbf{r},k)\mathbf{E}_i(\mathbf{r},k) = 0$$

given that this equation is valid for any scalar field component of the electric vector. Thus, we consider an equation for the strong scattering vector field $\mathbf{E}_s(\mathbf{r},k)$ in terms of the incident field $\mathbf{E}_i(\mathbf{r},k)$ given by

$$(\nabla^2 + k^2)\mathbf{E}_s(\mathbf{r}, k) = -1k^2\nabla^2[\gamma(\mathbf{r}, k)\mathbf{E}_i(\mathbf{r}, k)] - \nabla[\mathbf{E}_i(\mathbf{r}, k) \cdot \nabla \ln \varepsilon(\mathbf{r})] \tag{40}$$

This equation only takes into account polarisation effects in the context of the Born approximation, which is, in effect, taken to be a second order effect compounded in the second term on the right hand side of Eq. (40). In this sense, Eq. (40) is a hybrid model for polarisation effects, although it is still possible to consider a solution for $E_s(\mathbf{r}, k)$ with strong polarisation, given that we can write

$$\nabla[\mathbf{E}_i(\mathbf{r}, k) \cdot \nabla \ln \varepsilon_r(\mathbf{r})] = -\frac{1}{k^2}\nabla\left[\frac{\nabla^2[\gamma(\mathbf{r}, k)\mathbf{E}_i(\mathbf{r}, k)]\gamma}{(\mathbf{r}, k)} \cdot \nabla \ln \varepsilon(\mathbf{r})\right]$$

Nevertheless, the analysis that follows is predicated on the hybrid model given by Eq. (40).

Using the same coordinate geometry considered in Section 8.1, we consider an incident vector field given by

$$\mathbf{E}_i(\mathbf{r}, k) = \hat{\mathbf{z}} \cos \phi E_z(\mathbf{r}, k) + \hat{\mathbf{x}} \sin \phi E_x(\mathbf{r}, k) \sim \hat{\mathbf{z}} E_i(x, k)$$

where $E_i(x, k)$ is given by Eq. (31) and $\phi \sim 0$ is the 'Depression Angle'. The condition on the Depression Angle means that the approach that follows is only valid for relatively low Depression Angles which typically occur on military SAR platforms operating at a low altitudes and a long ranges. Moreover, the condition significantly helps to simplify the model in preparation for the analysis that follows, given that, Eq. (40), can now be written in the form

$$(\nabla^2 + k^2)\mathbf{E}_s(\mathbf{r}, k) = -\hat{\mathbf{z}}\frac{1}{k^2}\nabla^2[\gamma(\mathbf{r}, k)E_i(x, k)] - \nabla\left[E_i(x, k)\frac{\partial}{\partial z} \ln \varepsilon(\mathbf{r})\right]$$

In this case, the scattered field that is measured in the same direction of polarisation as the incident field, denoted $E_{sz}(\mathbf{r}, k)$, is given by the solution of

$$(\nabla^2 + k^2)E_{sz}(\mathbf{r}, k) = -\frac{1}{k^2}\nabla^2[\gamma(\mathbf{r}, k)E_i(x, k)] - \partial \partial z\left[E_i(x, k)\frac{\partial}{\partial z} \ln \varepsilon(\mathbf{r})\right] \tag{41}$$

This field are referred to as the VV (Vertical-Vertical) mode field. In addition to this, there is a cross-polarised scattered field, denoted by $E_{sy}(\mathbf{r}, k)$, which is given by the solution of

$$(\nabla^2 + k^2)E_{sy}(\mathbf{r}, k) = -\frac{\partial}{\partial y}\left[E_i(x, k)\frac{\partial}{\partial z} \ln \varepsilon(\mathbf{r})\right] \tag{42}$$

and is referred to as the VH (Vertical-Horizontal) mode field.

11.1 Conditional solution

A condition which is of particular value in solving Eq. (41) and Eq. (42) using the methods presented in Section 8.1 is to consider the case when $\ln \varepsilon(\mathbf{r}) \sim \varepsilon(\mathbf{r}) - 1 = \gamma_\varepsilon(\mathbf{r})$ which is actually only valid for values of $\varepsilon(\mathbf{r}) \sim 1, \quad \forall \mathbf{r}$. Nevertheless, by repeating the analysis given in Section 8.1 (including application of exactly the same conditions), it can be shown that the equivalent solutions to Eq. (41) and Eq. (42) yield the following models for the real component of the processed SAR data (subject to application of a self-affine surface model as discussed in Section 9):

$$s_{VV}(x,y) = p(x,y) \otimes_x \otimes_y C_1 \nabla^2 \gamma(x,y)$$

and

$$s_{VH}(x,y) = p(x,y) \otimes_x \otimes_y C_3 \frac{\partial}{\partial y} \gamma_\varepsilon(x,y)$$

where

$$C_3 = -k_0^2 \int_{-\infty}^{\infty} \frac{\partial}{\partial z}[\gamma_\varepsilon(z)] \exp(-ik_0 z_0 z/x_0) dz = \frac{iz_0 k_0^3}{x_0} \int_{-\infty}^{\infty} \gamma_\varepsilon(z) \exp(-ik_0 z_0 z/x_0) dz \tag{43}$$

Scaling both equations for $s_{VV}(x,y)$ and $s_{VH}(x,y)$ by $C_1 k_0^2$, and redefining the conductivity as $\sigma \equiv Z_0 \sigma / k_0$, we derived the data models

$$s_{VV}(x,y) = p(x,y) \otimes_x \otimes_y \nabla^2[-\gamma_\varepsilon(x,y) + i\sigma(x,y)] \tag{44}$$

and

$$s_{VH}(x,y) = p(x,y) \otimes_x \otimes_y ik_0 \frac{z_0}{x_0} \frac{\partial}{\partial y} \gamma_\varepsilon(x,y) \tag{45}$$

The SAR images associated with these equation are given by

$$I_{VV}(x,y) = |s_{VV}(x,y)| \quad \text{and} \quad I_{VH}(x,y) = |s_{VH}(x,y)|$$

respectively, where, it is again presupposed, that the analytic signals have been generated in range for $s_{VV}(x,y)$ and $s_{VH}(x,y)$ before computation of the SAR images, thereby, providing display's of the Amplitude Modulations.

11.2 Quantitative imaging

For a conductive dielectric, the scattering function is composed of two independent variables, namely $\gamma_\varepsilon(x,y)$ and $\sigma(x,y)$. Consequently, a single VV SAR image is not able to quantitatively differentiate between these variables and can only rely on the expected increase in the RCS associated with a localised conductor in an other non-conductive dielectric environment to identify such a 'target'. However, the VH data model given by Eq. (45) does not include the function $\sigma(x,y)$. In other words, according the model proposed, a SAR image based on the VH mode provides a measure of the variation in permittivity alone. Moreover, the models compounded in Eqs. (44) and (45), provide an option for quantitatively imaging the conductivity of the ground surface. This is important in the military applications of SAR, because isolated targets tend to be conductive agents due to the materials from which they are composed (assuming that stealth technologies have not been implemented).

From Eq. (45), we note that

$$s'_{VH}(x,y) = \left(\frac{\partial^2}{\partial x^2} + \frac{\partial}{\partial y}\right) s_{VH}(x,y) = p(x,y) \otimes_x \otimes_y ik_0 z_0 x_0 \nabla^2 \gamma_\varepsilon(x,y)$$

Thus, using Eq. (44), we can write

$$I^{\sigma}_{\text{SAR}}(x,y) = \left| ik_0 \frac{z_0}{x_0} s_{VV}(x,y) + s'_{VH}(x,y) \right| = |p(x,y) \otimes_x \otimes_y \nabla^2 \sigma(x,y)| \qquad (46)$$

where $\sigma \equiv k_0 z_0 \sigma / x_0$. It should be noted that, for the case when the functions $s_{\text{VV}}(x,y)$ and $s_{\text{VH}}(x,y)$ are taken to be analytic (i.e. analytic signals in range x), then, using Eq. (39), Eq. (46) has the modified form

$$I^{\sigma}_{\text{SAR}}(x,y) = \left| \; p(x,y) \otimes_x \otimes_y \left[\frac{1}{\pi x} \otimes_x \nabla^2 \sigma(x,y) \right] \; \right|$$

A simulation using Eqs. (44) and (45) and the data processing required to yield an image given by Eq. (46) is provided in **Figure 3** for $k_0 z_0 / x_0 = 1$. For this example, an optical image of a port city has been chosen with a defined coastline. The simulated VV image $I_{VV}(x,y)$ is based on using Eq. (44) where

$$\gamma_\varepsilon(x,y) = I_{\text{Optical}}(x,y) + i\sigma(x,y)$$

for $I_{\text{Optical}} \in [0,1]$ and $\sigma \in [0,1]$. In the latter case, the function is taken to be zero except for some random and sparsely located 'targets' (when $\sigma = 1$ for a small cluster of pixels). The simulated VH image $I_{VH}(x,y)$ is based on the application of Eq. (45)

Figure 3.
Simulation of SAR images using the optical image (top left). The VV SAR image $I_{VV}(x,y)$ (top right) includes the effect of scattering from isolated targets. The VH SAR image $I_{VH}(x,y)$ (lower left) is based on the application of Eq. (45). Application of the Eq. (46) then yields the lower right hand image, which provides a quantitative image of the targets.

with $k_0 z_0 / x_0 = 1$. Application of the Eq. (46) then yields an image showing the location of the targets alone.

The simulations provided in **Figure 3** are based on a modification of the code given in Appendix A. The cross range gradient given in Eq. (45) is computed using forward differencing through application of the MATLAB conv2 function; specifically, for image array I say, we apply I = conv2([1 -1], [1], I, 'same'). Thus, for compatibility with this process, the Laplacian is computed by applying the convolution process I = conv2([1 -1], [1 -1], I, 'same') two-fold.

Any application of this quantitative imaging 'solution' using real SAR data requires Eq. (45) to be scaled by the (system specific) value of $z_0 k_0 / x_0$. For a 1 cm wavelength SAR, assuming that $z_0 / x_0 = k_0^{-1}$, as used for the simulation of $s_{VH}(x, y)$, implies a vary shallow depression angle of $\sim 2^o$. An investigation into the use of different digital filters (using Finite Impulse Response and/or Fast Fourier Transform based filters) for computing the (digital) gradients is also necessary to determine an optimum data processing algorithm; research that lies beyond the scope of this work.

12. Summary and conclusions

The main contribution reported in this work is an application of the exact scattering solution developed in [5] to SAR image modelling. This solution cannot be used directly (in a generic sense) for modelling imaging systems (based on recording a scattered field) directly, but must be modified accordingly in relation to the physical configuration of the system, primarily the geometry and frequency of operation. In this regard, the strong scattering solution developed in Section 7 and then implemented for a SAR system in Section 8, provides a very simplified expression for modelling side band systems. In this case, the essential difference between a strong and weak scattering solution is quantified in terms of the use or otherwise of the Laplacian operator, respectively.

A fractal model for the scattering function has been introduced in Section 9. This allows a base band model to be considered, compounded in Eq. (36). An application of this solution has been considered whose aim is to provide a texturally compatible simulation of a SAR image for which a corresponding overhead aerial optical image is available. In this regard, some demonstratives examples have been provided based on the MATLAB code provided in Appendix A. The code is provide as a basis for the reader to repeat the simulations provided, and to further modify, improve and extend the code, subject to further developments of the model as considered in the following section.

12.1 Further developments

The reader will have observed that in evolving the model quantified by Eq. (36), a number of simplifications have been implemented. These are based on conditions that are reasonably compatible with a SAR system, at least, under certain operational conditions. They include, for example, a condition whereby the range is taken to be significantly larger than the operational height of the radar platform (i.e. $z_0 / x_0 \ll 1$). This is the basis for quantifying the relative contributions of terms whose scale is determined by the coefficients C_1, C_2 and C_3 given by Eqs. (32), (33) and (43), respectively. These coefficients are a result of introducing a separation of variables in regard to the scattering function $\gamma(x, y, z, k_0)$ as a function of height. It is key to generating a two-dimensional solution that is designed to be compatible with a SAR data, and relies on a model where $\gamma(z, k_0) \in (-\infty, \infty)$. However, this model can be modified in order to introduce the effect of height variations, for example. Thus, suppose we consider the case where $\gamma(z, k_0) = \gamma_0 \in [0, h(x, y)]$ where γ_0 is a constant and $h(x, y)$ describes the variations in height of the surface at a point (x, y) above a common based line $z = 0$ say. Suppose $h(x, y) \in [0, 1] \ \ \forall (x, y)$, then the integral over $\gamma(z, k_0)$ that is common to Eqs. (32), (33) and (43) is given by

$$\int_0^{h(x,y)} \exp(-ik_0 z_0 z / x_0) dz = h(x, y) - i\frac{k_0 z_0}{2x_0} h^2(x, y) + \ldots \sim h(x, y)$$

Consequently, the strong scattering function $\nabla^2 \gamma(x, y, k_0)$ can be replaced with $h(x, y) \nabla^2 \gamma(x, y, k_0)$. The incorporation of height variations in this way may be served in cases where a stereo optical image of the surface is available, for example.

This is just one example of other developments that can be considered to make the model increasingly more realistic, but necessarily more complicated, e.g. the inclusion of depression angles where $\phi \in (0, \pi/2)$ radians, the inclusion of the second and third terms in Eq. (29), and using an incident field that includes the beam profile. In this respect, and, in addition to further developments of the model as discussed above, the relative simplicity of the result quantified in Eq. (38) can be further investigate through the introduction of additive stochastic fields [21] which are taken to account for the physical limitations of the model as well as 'system noise'.

12.2 Final statement

The goal of attempting to simulate one imaging modality from another is becoming a common theme in imaging science, especially for applications in computer vision. This includes the simulation of one image from another whose physical formation and characteristics are entirely different.

Solutions to this problem can be used to help in the training of deep learning systems, for example [22]. In this context, the strong scattering solution developed in this paper, coupled with a fractal model for the scattering function, may provide an additional tool in the analysis and interpretation of SAR images. More generally, the solution may complement the processing of images formed from strong scattering interactions whose interpretation is undertaken using statistical modelling techniques alone (e.g. [23, 24]).

Acknowledgements

The author acknowledges the Science Foundation Ireland and the Technological University Dublin for supporting the Stokes Professorship program.

Conflict of interest

The author declares no conflict of interest.

Thanks

The author would like to thank Dr. Marek Rebow, Technological University Dublin for his continued support.

Nomenclature

EM	electromagnetic
IRF	impulse response function
PDF	probability density function
PSDF	power spectral density function
PSF	point spread function
RCS	radar cross section
RMS	root mean square
SAR	synthetic aperture radar
VV	vertical-vertical (polarisation)
VH	vertical-horizontal (polarisation)

Appendix: MATLAB function for SAR image simulation

```
function SARSIM(size,width)
%FUNCTION: SAR image simulation using optical images.
%INPUTS: size - array length for computing the IRF.
%width (>1) - width of IRF (sinc function).
%OUTPUT: Display's of three images in Figures 1-3.
%Read optical image (default: 8-bit grey level image),
I = imread('filename'); %covert to double, normalise and show.
I=double(im2gray(I)); I=I./max(max(I)); figure(1), imshow(I);
%Define Laplacian filter and convolve it with the image.
Laplace=[0 1 0; 1 -4 1; 0 1 0]; I=conv2(I, Laplace,'same');
%Compute the sinc function for inputs 'size' and 'width'.
x=round(size/2)-size:round(size/2); p=sinc(x/width);
%Convolve data with the sinc function in range and
%cross range, compute the analytic signals (columns)
%with function hilbert and display Amplitude Modulations.
s = conv2(p,p,I,'same'); s=hilbert(s); I = abs(s);
I=I./max(max(I)); figure(2), imshow(I);
%Display result.figure(3), imshow(histeq(I));%Apply histogram equalisation.
```

Author details

Jonathan Blackledge[1,2,3,4,5,6]

1 School of Electrical and Electronic Engineering, Technological University Dublin, Dublin, Ireland

2 Centre for Advanced Studies, Warsaw University of Technology, Warsaw, Poland

3 Department of Computer Science, University of Western Cape, Cape Town, South Africa

4 Faculty of Arts, Science and Technology, Wrexham Glyndŵr University of Wales, Wrexham, UK

5 School of Mathematics, Statistics and Computer Science, University of KwaZulu-Natal, Durban, South Africa

6 University Campus Barnsley, Barnsley, UK

*Address all correspondence to: jonathan.blackledge@tudublin.ie

References

[1] Harger RO. Synthetic Aperture Radar Systems: Theory and Design. New York: Academic Press; 1971

[2] Kovaly JJ. Synthetic Aperture Radar. London: Artech House; 1976. ISBN: 9780890060568

[3] Blackledge J. On the chirp function, the Chirplet transform and the optimal communication of information. IAENG International Journal of Applied Mathematics. 2020;**50**(2):285-319. Available from: https://arrow.tudublin.ie/engscheleart2/218/ [Accessed: August 22, 2023]

[4] Blackledge JM. Digital Signal Processing (Second Edition). Cambridge: Woodhead Publishing; 2006. ISBN: 1-904275-26-5. Available from: https://arrow.tudublin.ie/engschelebk/4/ [Accessed: June 16, 2023]

[5] Blackledge JM. A solution to the Schrödinger scattering problem. Mathematica Aeterna. 2015;**5**(2): 273-283. Available from: https://www.longdom.org/articles-pdfs/a-solution-to-theschrodinger-scattering-problem.pdf [Accessed: July 3, 2023]

[6] Jean-Claude Nédélec JC. The Helmholtz equation. In: Acoustic and Electromagnetic Equations: Integral Representations for Harmonic Problems. New York: Springer; 2001. pp. 9-109

[7] Evans GA, Blackledge JM, Yardley PD. Analytic Methods for Partial Differential Equations. In: Springer Undergraduate Mathematics Series (SUMS). Springer-Verlag Berlin and Heidelberg GmbH & Co. KG; 1999. ISBN: 9783540761242

[8] Hecht KT. The born approximation. In: Quantum Mechanics, Graduate Texts in Contemporary Physics. New York: Springer; 2000. [Online]. DOI: 10.1007/978-1-4612-1272-0 46 [Accessed: March 17, 2023]

[9] Jones JA. Wave Conventions: The Good, the Bad and the Ugly. 2015. Available from: https://nmr.physics.ox.ac.uk/teaching/wavecon.pdf. [Accessed: September 17, 2023]

[10] Mandelbrot B. The Fractal Geometry of Nature. New York: W. H. Freeman and Co.; 1982. ISBN: 0-7167-1186-9

[11] Turner MJ, Blackledge JM, Andrews P. Fractal Geometry in Digital Imaging. Cambridge, Massachusetts: Academic Press; 1998. ISBN: 0-12-703970-8

[12] Blackledge JM. A new definition, a generalisation and an approximation for a fractional derivative with applications to stochastic time series modelling. IAENG, Engineering Letters. 2021;**29**(1): 138-150. Available from: https://arrow.tudublin.ie/engscheleart2/245/ [Accessed: August 21, 2023]

[13] Marr D, Hildreth E. On the theory of edge detection. Proceedings of the Royal Society of London, Series B, Biological Sciences. 1980;**207**(1167):187-217. Available from: https://www.researchgate.net/publication/17083076_Theory_of_Edge_Detection [Accessed: August 22, 2023]

[14] Blackledge J. A generalised nonlinear model for the evolution of low frequency freak waves. IAENG International Journal of Applied Mathematics. 2011; **41**(1):33-55. Available from: https://arrow.tudublin.ie/engscheleart2/41 [Accessed: August 21, 2023]

[15] Blackledge JM. Digital image processing. Series in Electronic and

Optical Materials. Cambridge: Woodhead Publishing; 2005. ISBN: 1-898563-49-7. Available from: https://arrow.tudublin.ie/engschelebk/3/ [Accessed: August 3, 2023]

[16] Mitchell RL. Radar Signal Simulation. Massachusetts and London: Artech House, Inc.; 1976

[17] Shunjun W et al. HRSID: A high-resolution SAR images dataset for ship detection and instance segmentation. IEEE Access. 2020;**8**:120234-120254. Available from: https://ieeexplore.ieee.org/document/9127939 [Accessed: August 17, 2023]

[18] Wang Y et al. A SAR dataset of ship detection for deep learning under complex backgrounds. Remote Sensing. 2019;**11**:765. DOI: 10.3390/rs11070765

[19] El-Darymli K, McGuire P, Power D, Moloney C. Target detection in synthetic aperture radar imagery: A state-of-the-art survey. Journal of Applied Remote Sensing. 2013;**7**(1):071598. Available from: https://arxiv.org/ftp/arxiv/papers/1804/1804.04719.pdf [Accessed: June 23, 2023]

[20] Guo Q, Wang H, Xu F. Scattering enhanced attention pyramid network for aircraft detection in SAR images. IEEE Transactions on Geoscience and Remote Sensing. 2021;**59**(9):7570-7758. DOI: 10.1109/TGRS.2020.3027762

[21] Barton DK. Radar System Analysis and Modelling. London: Artech House; 2005. ISBN: 9781580536813

[22] Merkle N et al. Exploiting deep matching and SAR data for the geo-localization accuracy improvement of optical satellite images. Journal of Remote Sensing, MDPI. 2017;**9**(6). DOI: 10.3390/rs9060586. Available from: https://www.mdpi.com/2072-4292/9/6/586 [Accessed: June 24, 2023]

[23] Korotkova O. Theoretical Statistical Optics. Singapore: World Scientific; 2021. ISBN-13: 9789811234972

[24] Frery AC, Wu J, Gomez L. SAR Image Analysis—A Computational Statistics Approach: With R Code, Data, and Applications. New Jersey: Wiley-IEEE Press; 2022. ISBN-10:111979529X

Ethanol and Glycerol Chemistry - Production, Modelling, Applications, and Technological Aspects

Edited by Rampal Pandey, Israel Pala-Rosas, José L. Contreras and José Salmones

Published in London, United Kingdom

Ethanol and Glycerol Chemistry - Production, Modelling, Applications, and Technological Aspects
http://dx.doi.org/10.5772/intechopen.102260
Edited by Rampal Pandey, Israel Pala-Rosas, José L. Contreras and José Salmones

Contributors
Patrick U. Okoye, Estefania Duque-Brito, Diego R. Lobata-Peralta, Jude A. Okolie, Dulce M. Arias, Joseph P. Sebastian, Lethiwe D. Mthembu, Anele Sibeko, Rishi Gupta, Nirmala Deenadayalu, Guilherme D. Machado, Jacqueline M. Ortega Bacicheti, Fábio Nishiyama, Vladimir F. Cabral, Donato Aranda, Manikandan Kanagasabai, Babu Elango, Preetha Balakrishnan, Jayachitra Jayabalan, Israel Pala-Rosas, Jose L. Contreras, José Salmones, Ricardo López-Medina, Beatriz Zeifert, Naomi N. González-Hernández, Chakali Ayyanna, Kuppusamy Sujatha, Sujit Kumar Mohanthy, Jayaraman Rajangam, B. Naga Sudha, H. G. Raghavendra, Pietro Salvatori, Ali Amoushahi, Steven W. Stogner

First published in London, United Kingdom, 2023 by IntechOpen
IntechOpen is the global imprint of INTECHOPEN LIMITED, registered in England and Wales, registration number: 11086078, 5 Princes Gate Court, London, SW7 2QJ, United Kingdom

British Library Cataloguing-in-Publication Data
A catalogue record for this book is available from the British Library

Additional hard and PDF copies can be obtained from orders@intechopen.com

Ethanol and Glycerol Chemistry - Production, Modelling, Applications, and Technological Aspects
Edited by Rampal Pandey, Israel Pala-Rosas, José L. Contreras and José Salmones
p. cm.
Print ISBN 978-1-80355-717-5
Online ISBN 978-1-80355-718-2
eBook (PDF) ISBN 978-1-80355-719-9

For EU product safety concerns:
IN TECH d.o.o., Prolaz Marije Krucifikse Kozulić 3, 51000 Rijeka, Croatia,
info@intechopen.com or visit our website at intechopen.com.

Meet the editors

Dr. Rampal Pandey is currently a senior Assistant professor in the Department of Chemistry, National Institute of Technology Uttarakhand. He has been a DST Inspire Faculty member for the Department of Science and Technology (DST) under "Innovation in Science Pursuit for Inspired Research" (INSPIRE) program, a Research Associate, and a junior (JRF) and senior research fellow (SRF). He obtained BSc and MSc degrees from APS University, India, and a Ph.D. from Banaras Hindu University (BHU), India. He has more than 15 years of teaching and research experience. He has research/academic projects worth ~50 Lakhs (INR) and thirteen awards/recognitions/appreciations to his credit, including an Inspired Teacher Award. Dr. Pandey has published more than fifty-five papers and has been granted two patents. He has delivered many invited lectures at national and international seminars/Faculty Development Programmes (FDPs)/Short Term Courses (STCs). Dr. Pandey serves as a coordinator for Massive Open Online Courses (MOOCs) and a content writer for the e-PG-Pathshala programme of the Ministry of Education. He is a member of the American Chemical Society, Royal Society of Chemistry, Society of Material Chemistry, Solar Energy Society of India, and Indian Society of Chemists and Biologists. He is a section and academic editor as well as a reviewer for several journals. He is also a Ph.D. supervisor.

Israel Pala-Rosas is a biochemical engineer. He obtained a master's degree in Chemical Engineering from the Benemérita Universidad Autónoma de Puebla, México, and a Ph.D. in Chemical Engineering Science from the School of Chemical Engineering and Extractive Industries, Instituto Politécnico Nacional, México. Dr. Pala-Rosas has experience in production and quality in the canned food and beverage industry, as well as in the processing of triglycerides for the production of soap and biodiesel. He has been a professor at different universities and a thesis co-director for undergraduate and master's students at Universidad Autónoma Metropolitana, México. His interests include the research and development of catalytic and biotechnological processes for the transformation of biomass-derived molecules to compounds of technological and industrial interest. He focuses his work on the synthesis, characterization, and testing of catalysts, as well as the design and analysis of chemical and biochemical reactors. Areas related to the catalytic processes, such as chemical thermodynamics, unit operations, and economics, are also under his scope. Dr. Pala-Rosas has published research articles on the use of zeolites for the synthesis of pyridine bases from acrolein and ammonia, the catalytic dehydration of glycerol to acrolein, heterogeneous catalysts for biodiesel synthesis, and biomaterials. He is the author of a book chapter dealing with the production of acrolein from glycerol and the editor of the book *Current Drying Processes*.

José Luis Contreras Larios obtained a Ph.D. in Sciences from the Universidad Autónoma Metropolitana- Iztapalapa, México, as well as master's and engineering degrees in Chemical Engineering from the School of Chemical Engineering and Extractive Industries, Instituto Politécnico Nacional, México. Dr. Contreras has more than 40 years of industrial and research experience in heterogeneous catalysis. Currently, he is a research professor and head of the Chemical Industry Processes curriculum of the Chemical Engineering Program, Energy Department, Universidad Autónoma Metropolitana-Azcapotzalco, México, where he teaches undergraduate and postgraduate courses on catalytic materials, chemical reactors, transport phenomena, unit operations, and process engineering. He has also directed undergraduate and postgraduate theses on chemical engineering topics such as chemical reactors, catalysis, and process and environmental engineering. Dr. Contreras is the author of several patents and internationally indexed articles. His research and application areas are focused on the synthesis and characterization of catalysts for processes in chemical and environmental engineering, such as the production of niacinamide from glycerol, hydrogen synthesis by bioethanol and glycerol reforming, fixation of CO2 emissions from thermoelectric power plants using algae, and the design of catalytic converters for diesel and gasoline machines. He is a level I member of the National System of Researchers in Mexico.

José Salmones obtained a master's in Chemical Engineering and a doctorate in Science from the Universidad Autónoma Metropolitana-Iztapalapa, México. He obtained a degree in chemical engineering from the Universidad Veracruzana, México. Dr. Salmones has taught countless courses in the Postgraduate Studies and Research Section of the School of Chemical Engineering and Extractive Industries of the Instituto Politécnico Nacional, México, since 2004. Previously, he held various positions at the Instituto Mexicano del Petróleo and at the Universidad Autónoma Metropolitana. He is the author of sixty-five internationally indexed articles, co-author of a published book, author of two book chapters and twenty-seven registered patents. He has 217 papers in national and international forums to his credit. He has supervised eighteen bachelor's, ten master's, and two doctorate theses. He is a level II member of the National System of Researchers in Mexico. His current research deals with the synthesis and application of catalysts and nanostructured materials for the synthesis and storage of hydrogen and carbon dioxide.

Contents

Preface

In the wake of more stringent health and environment concerns, the world requires more and clearer awareness about the production of valuable chemicals from bio-resources or natural products as well as the use of these natural products in areas of health and environment. With this objective in mind, *Ethanol and Glycerol Chemistry – Production, Modelling, Applications, and Technological Aspects*, discusses the green production of ethanol and glycerol by feasible methods and their possible applications in medical sciences and for environmentally friendly fuel production via a practical approach and appropriate modelling.

The book is organized into three sections and nine chapters contributed by authors from around the globe. Section 1, "Production of Ethanol and Glycerol", is an introductory section that includes three chapters. Chapter 1 by Manikandan Kanagasabai et al., focuses on the production of ethanol from bioresources. Chapter 2 by Chakali Ayyanna et al., discusses the production of bioethanol. Chapter 3 by Lethiwe D. Mthembu et al., illustrates the catalyzed production and applications of glycerol.

Section 2, "Conversion of Glycerol into Aromatic Compounds", focuses on the transformation of glycerol into valuable organic products and includes two chapters. Chapter 4 by Israel Pala-Rosas et al., describes the synthesis of pyridine bases from glycerol using sustainable methods. Chapter 5 by Patrick U. Okoye et al., deals with the preparation of bio-based aromatics via catalytic transformation of glycerol.

Section 3, "Applications", includes four chapters on applications of ethanol in medical sciences. Chapter 6 by Ali Amoushahi et al., illustrates the utility of ethanol inhalation in the treatment and prevention of COVID-19. Chapter 7 by Steven W. Stogner et al., focuses on the use of an old treatment, nebulized ethanol, for a new disease. Chapter 8 by Pietro Salvatori et al., theoretically describes the utility of ethanol inhalation for the disinfection of SARS-COV-2-contaminated airways. Finally, Chapter 9 contributed by Guilherme D. Machado et al., illustrates the modelling of Ethanol to predict the Liquid-Liquid Equilibrium in Food and Fuel Systems.

We congratulate all the authors for providing quality data, research, and analysis and participating in this volume. We would like to thank the staff at IntechOpen, especially Author Service Managers Ms. Marija Nezirovic, Ms. Martina Ivancic, Ms. Nika Karamatic, and Ms. Ana Javor.

Dr. Rampal Pandey
Department of Chemistry,
National Institute of Technology Uttarakhand,
Srinagar (Garhwal), Uttarakhand, India

Israel Pala-Rosas and José Salmones
Higher School of Chemical Engineering and Extractive Industries,
National Polytechnic Institute,
Mexico City, Mexico

José L. Contreras
CBI-Energy,
Autonomous Metropolitan University-Azcapotzalco,
Mexico City, Mexico

Section 1

Production of Ethanol and Glycerol

Chapter 1

Ethanol Production from Bioresources and Its Kinetic Modeling: Optimization Methods

Manikandan Kanagasabai, Babu Elango, Preetha Balakrishnan and Jayachitra Jayabalan

Abstract

Ethanol is viable alternative fuel and it's substitute to fossil fuel has gained importance with rise in fuel prices. The chapter elaborates about methods of production from different types of bio resources like molasses, starch and cellulose commercially. The chapter also details about different methods of pretreatment for cellulisic and starchy raw materials. This also includes hydrolysis using acid and enzymes. The modes of ethanol fermentation using bioreactors like batch fed batch and continuous operation will be discussed. The growth kinetics models like monad logistic model will be elaborated. The product formation growth associated models like Leudiking piret model and parameter estimation methods will be described. Optimization of process variables using response surface methodology and media optimization using PB design will be elaborated. The application of ANN in modeling will be described.

Keywords: ethanol production, growth and product kinetics, optimization response, surface methodology, PB design ANN

1. Introduction

Biomass energy can contribute to sustainable development and plays a significant role in reducing greenhouse gas emissions. In addition, application of agro-industrial residues in bioprocesses not only provide alternative substrates but also helps solve their disposal problem. The transfer of crude oil-based refinery to biomass–based bio refinery has attracted strong scientific interest which focuses on the development of bioethanol as an alternative transportation fuel to petroleum fuels. A huge ethanol demand will come in the near future, forcing the ethanol production to be fast and have high capacity. [1, 2]. Green fuel from bioresources is gaining more importance to meet the increasing demand of fuel supply and reduced emission of pollutant gases like sulfur dioxide [3]. The major biomass resources that can be converted into biofuels are classified into three major types of carbohydrates namely glucose, starch and cellulose [4]. Pre-treatment steps are more vital in conversion of starchy and cellulosic substrates that are cheaper and available in plenty. Optimization techniques like artificial neural network, response surface methodology can be effectively used to improve the yield of biofuel from these substrates.

The biggest challenge of the conversion comes from the recalcitrant structure of lignocellulosic biomass. To improve the biomass digestibility, a pre-treatment step is required to break up the lignocellulosic matrix, thus making the carbohydrate fraction more accessible to hydrolytic enzymes for fermentable sugar production. Pre-treatment of lignocelluloses is intended to disorganize the crystalline structure of macro-and microfibrils, in order to release the polymer chains of cellulose and hemi-cellulose to improve its digestibility and easy access for microbial attack [5] and/or modify the pores in the material to allow the enzymatic hydrolysis [6]. This leads to the fractionation of three components and opening of cellulose structure. It results in enlargement of the inner surface area of substrate particle's, accomplished by partial solubilization and or degradation of hemicellulose and lignin [7].

The bioconversion of starchy substrates like corn, cassava, potatoes, involves pre-treatment with fungal alpha amylase at suitable temperature followed by saccharification and fermentation. The last two steps can also be carried out in a single fermenter by a process called simultaneous saccharification and fermentation using amylotic enzyme and yeast at optimum conditions of pH and temperature. This process reduces substrate inhibition and maximum utilization of glucose formed by amylotic enzymes. Cellulose from different biomass like paper pulp, sulfite waste liquor etc. must undergo pre-treatment with mineral acids or alkali to remove lignin and hemicellulose. Cellulose can be converted into simple sugars by the action of cellulase enzyme and can readily ferment them to ethanol by the action of yeast. [8]. Although lignocellulosic biomass is a very promising alternative feedstock for ethanol production, its conversion to ethanol is more difficult than that of sugar or starch.

Mathematical models are tools that can be applied to biotechnological processes operating at many different levels, from the action of an enzyme within a cell, to the growth of that cell within a commercial scale bioreactor [9]. Unstructured kinetic models give the most fundamental observations concerning microbial metabolic processes and can be considered a good approximation when the cell composition is time dependent or when the substrate concentration is high compared to the saturation constant [10]. In addition to kinetic models describing the behavior of microbiological systems, artificial neural network (ANN) and Response Surface Methodology (RSM) are effectively used for the optimization of process variables for the fermentation of bioethanol [11, 12].

This chapter will focus on the current status of available ethanol production technologies including chemistry, applications, technological aspects and the kinetics and modeling of biotechnological processes and it especially provides essential evidence for the future scale-up conversion studies.

2. Industrial ethanol production

2.1 Ethanol production from corn

Corn is the most viable source for industrial ethanol production as it contains 70% starch. 5% of annual food grins produced can be effectively diverted to ethanol production [13]. The major threat that poses corn as an effective substrate is the horny endosperm that makes it difficult for pretreatment with alpha amylase enzyme with low conversion. Floury endosperm is easy to digest with enzymes and has high swelling when compared with horny endosperm.

The steps involved in the industrial production are

i. Milling of corn grains to remove oil form germs and the hull that reduces the activity of amylase enzyme in pre-treatment step.

ii. Liquefaction of milled corn starch using alpha amylase enzyme at optimum conditions of pH and temperature.

iii. Saccharification of liquified starch using glucoamylase enzyme to convert dextrin to glucose which is primary substrate for ethanol producing yeast.

iv. Fermentation of saccharified starch using *Saccharomyces cerevisiae* yeast at optimum conditions of pH and temperature with suitable initial substrate concentration to yield ethanol.

v. Distillation of the product to yield 95% ethanol which forms an azeotrope with water. Azeotropic distillation is employed to separate water and to form 100% pure industrial alcohol.

2.2 Milling of grains

The two main process that are employed in milling of grains are wet milling and dry milling of corn grains.

2.2.1 Wet milling process

The wet milling of corn grains is very expensive process as it is highly energy consuming. The valuable by products can be obtained in this process and it is generally used in biorefineries. The byproducts obtained from wet milling process are corn oil from germs, hull, fibers and gluten. Gluten along with corn meal is used as high protein content animal feed [14]. The main product starch solution obtained from this process is used as raw material for saccharification and fermentation process. The ethanol yield from this process is about 10 liters per 100 kg of corn used as substrate.

2.2.2 Dry milling

Dry grinding process is currently employed in industries as it is less energy intensive when compared with wet milling process [15]. Corn grains are powdered using hammer mill to pass through 30 mesh screen and mixed with eater to form mash. The mash is first liquefied using alpha amylase enzyme at a initial pH 6 and temperature of 90°C then saccharified with glucoamylase enzyme and fermented with yeast to produce ethanol [16]. The fermented liquid is distilled to produce industrial grade ethanol. The byproduct obtained is distiller's grain used as a animal feed stock and carbon dioxide.

2.3 Liquefaction

Starchy substrates cannot be utilized directly by yeast, and they are to be converted into maltose and dextrin in the first pretreatment step. A thermostable alpha-amylase enzyme is usually employed for converting the starch to dextrin quickly and randomly by hydrolyzing alpha 1–4 bonds of starch molecule. The optimum temperature and pH greatly depends upon the source of alpha amylase enzymes [17]. Microbial sources of alpha amylase includes both bacteria and fungus. Alpha amylase derived from fungi are mostly employed as they are more active at higher temperature in range of 80 to 90°C [18]. The optimum pH is in the range of 5.5- as the activity of the enzyme is maximum. The higher temperature favors the liquefaction of starch by rupturing the molecules and aiding the enzyme molecules to cleave the branching bonds of it. This process is carried out in holding tubes by adding fungal diastase enzyme in excess for a period of 30 minutes.

2.4 Saccharification and fermentation of starch

Liquified starch is converted into simple sugars by saccharification process. Glucoamylase enzyme is generally employed for this process. The optimum temperature is usually 50 to 55°C and pH is 4.5. Glucoamylase attacks the linear chain 1–6 linkages of dextrin and convert them into simple sugars [19]. Saccharified starch is suitable substrate for fermentative production of ethanol by yeast. Thermotolerant yeast can be used for carrying out saccharification and fermentation process in a single step. Optimization of process variables and nutrients is most important to maximize the ethanol yield. Response surface methodology can be employed to carry out optimization statistically by carefully designing the experiments. The RSM yields best combination of pH, temperature, initial starch concentration and enzyme concentration that give maximum ethanol concentration in the fermenter [20]. The interactive effects of process variables can be analyzed very effectively in the single step simultaneous saccharification and fermentation process. Optimization is essential because enzymes are active in a range of temperature and pH that may or may not favor the growth of yeast [21, 22]. Generally, thermotolerant yeast can withstand the temperature that favors optimum activity of glucoamylase enzyme that can produce simple sugars from dextrin and are consumed by yeast to produce ethanol. Optimum pH and temperature for this process are generally pH 5 and 37°C respectively as reported by many researchers [23, 24]. High temperature also favors reduced contamination of fermentation broth. They also reduces the inhibitive effect of high glucose concentration for yeast as it is simultaneously consumed giving 8 to 10% concentration of ethanol in the broth.

2.5 Modes of ethanol fermentation

Three different modes of fermentation that are generally used in commercial production are batch, fed batch and continuous operation. Ethanol production is usually carried out in batch fermenters [25]. The advantages of batch fermentation are mainly effective sterilization of medium and fermenter vessel, reduced contamination risk, maintaining required concentration of microbes for fermentation, effective control of process parameters like pH, temperature agitation speed to maximize the ethanol concentration in the broth. The usual fermentation time for ethanol production using yeast is about 48 hours. The additional feature is simultaneous saccharification and fermentation can be carried out most effectively in a single fermenter in batch mode by controlling the process variables at optimum conditions of pH, temperature and agitation speed. Continuous mode of operation is also employed for production of ethanol using beer still, by maintaining the microbes inside the still using high aspect ratio. The yeast concentration is more at the bottom of the still and the main advantage is that is agitation is not required and continuous production of ethanol is feasible [26].

2.6 Production of absolute alcohol

Distillation is the process of separating the ethanol from the solids and water in the mash. The difference in boiling point of alcohol and water allows water to be separated from ethanol by heating in a distillation column. The maximum ethanol concentration in the top product of distillation column is 95% ethanol and 5% water. Azeotropic extractive distillation using benzene as third component produce absolute alcohol. Modern dry grind ethanol plants use a molecular sieve system to produce absolute (100%, or 200 proof) ethanol.

The bottom product containing fiber, oil, and protein components of the grain, as well as the non-fermented starch is used as feed stock for animals. Bottom product is further processed to remove insoluble solids using centrifuges or extruders. The liquid is decanted and part of it is recycled to the still. The remaining liquor is further concentrated by evaporation and mixed with solids and used ad feed stock. The block diagram for ethanol production from corn is shown in **Figure 1**.

2.7 Ethanol production from molasses

Sugarcane is grown primarily for sucrose and molasses production. The crop may be harvested over an extended period of time due to its long growing season. Black

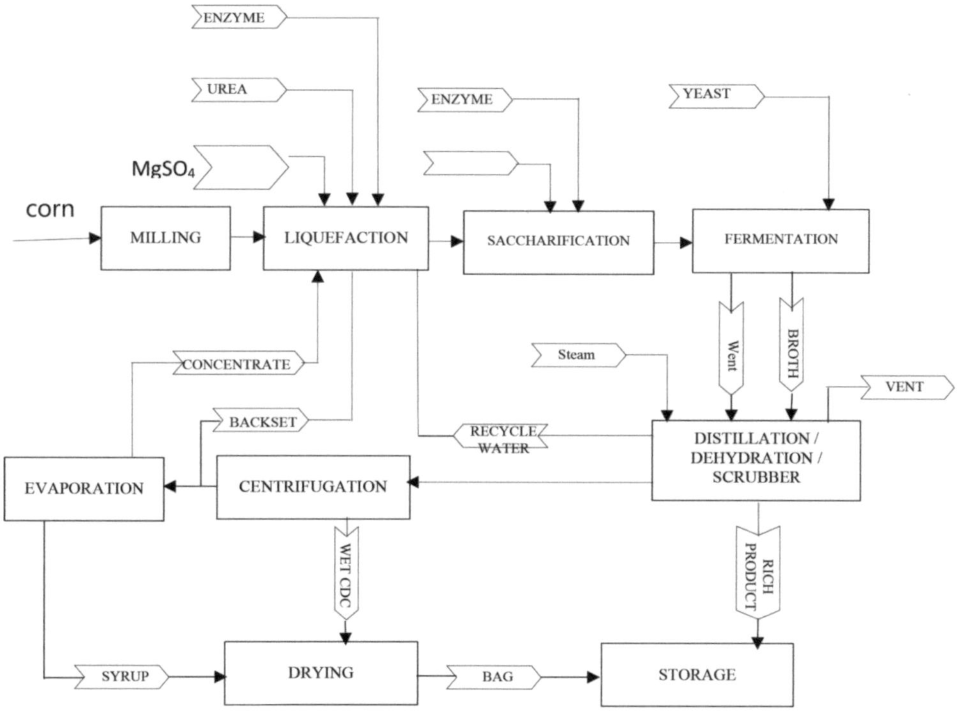

Figure 1.
Ethanol production from corn.

strap molasses is the by- product obtained from sugar mill and can be stored and easily diluted to a concentration of 10% reducing sugars [27]. The total sugar content of molasses is generally in the range of 50 to 60%. The fermentation of diluted molasses is carried out in batch fermenters using yeast as inoculum. The fermentation time is generally 20–24 and rate of ethanol production decreases as sugar utilized by the yeast is about 90–95%. The ethanol concentration in the broth is about 10% and does not increase above it as ethanol inhibits the yeast growth. The additional nitrogen nutrients like ammonium sulphate and micronutrients like magnesium sulfate, potassium hydrogen phosphate is added to favor the growth of yeast [28]. Ethanol production is always growth associated fermentation and hence it is desirable to optimize the process variables like temperature pH and agitation to maximize the yeast concentration and ethanol production. The overall productivity for this process is about 1.8–2.5 kg ethanol produced per m^3 fermenter volume per hour [29]. **Figure 2** illustrates the steps required to produce ethanol from cane juice molasses.

2.8 Ethanol production from cellulose

Cellulose-based ethanol production is attractive as an alternative fuel in the transportation sector. Extensive research in the past 20 years on fuel-grade ethanol fermentation has answered most of the major challenges on the road to commercialization and also open the door for novel technological development [30].

The first step in this process is primarily removal of lignin and hemi cellulose present in the wood wastes by digestion using steam at very high pressure followed by hydrolysis of cellulosic substrate into glucose using sulfuric acid [31]. The final step is fermentation of the reducing sugar solution in a fermenter using yeast. Hydrolysis of

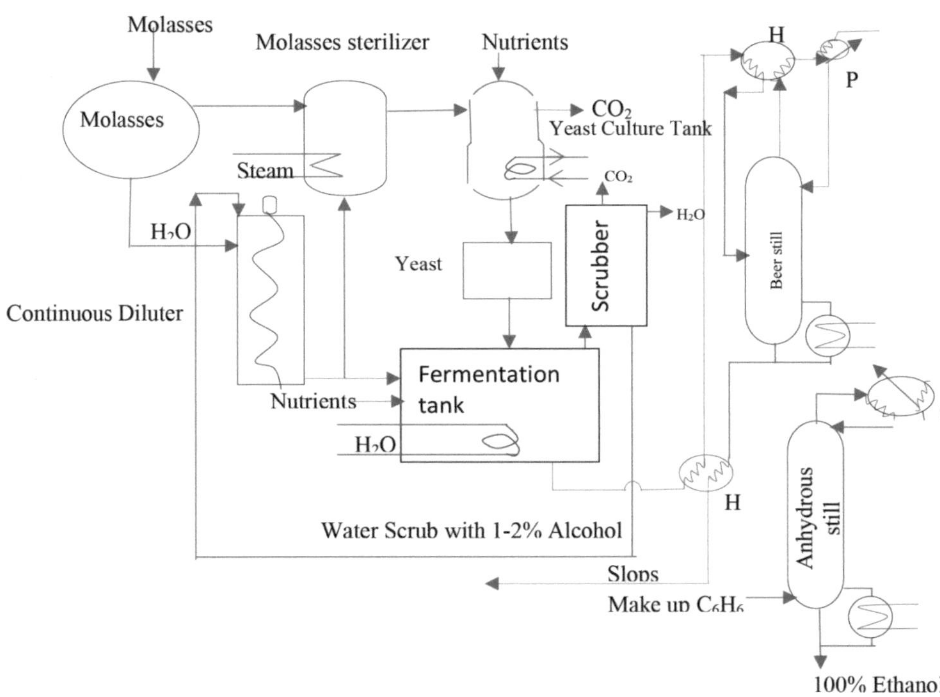

Figure 2.
Ethanol production from cane molasses.

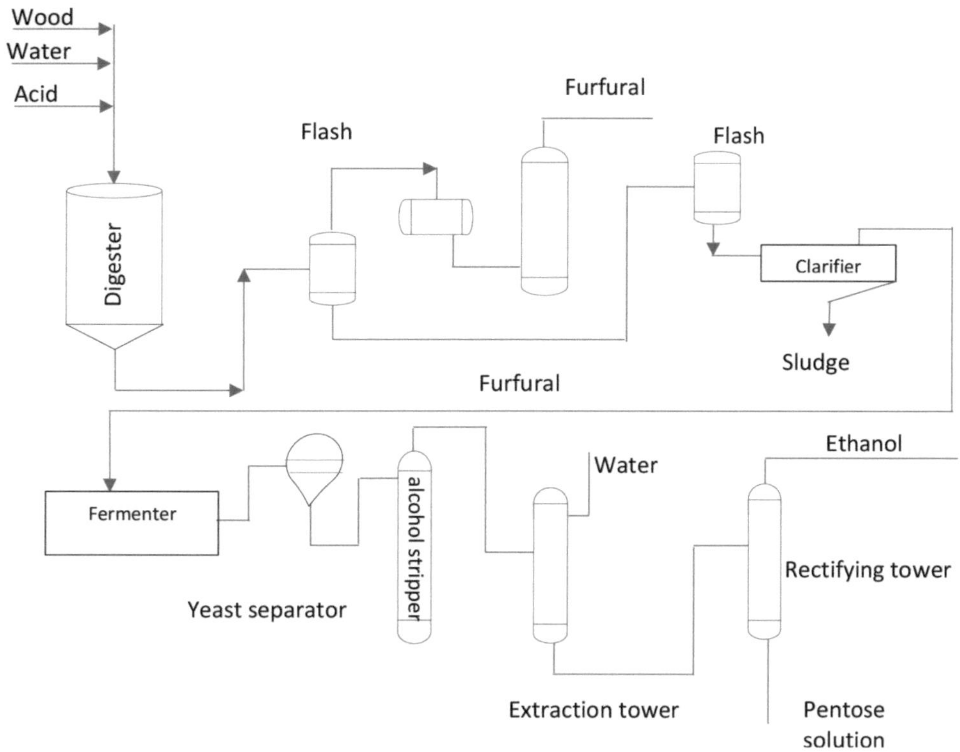

Figure 3.
Ethanol production from cellulose.

wood waste is carried out using sulfuric acid and steam at a temperature of 200°C and at a very high pressure of 1500 kPa. Lignin rich residue is removed as the bottom product and hydrolysate solution containing methanol and furfural is separated from the condenser of the flash vaporization process carried out in two different stages of different operating pressure, i.e., the first stage operating at 456.0 kPa and the second stage is at atmospheric pressure. The underflow of the second stage flash vaporizer is reducing sugar solution and it is diluted to desired concentration and fermented to ethanol using yeast. Methanol and furfural are separated using two stages of distillation.

The sugar rich solution is neutralized using lime and the precipitate is removed as sludge. The clarified liquid is added with additional micronutrients and fermented in a batch fermenter using yeast, The recovered yeast from an earlier fermentation is added to neutralized liquor and sent to fermentation tanks. The fermented liquor is filtered or centrifuged to remove the yeast content. Ethanol is separated from the distillation column as top product containing 95 vol.%. The bottom product contains unfermented pentoses. **Figure 3** shows the flow sheet of industrial ethanol production form cellulose.

3. Modeling

Mathematical models are very much useful to describe the performance of enzymatic and fermentation processes. They can be applied to study the kinetics of enzyme catalyzed reactions, microbial growth in batch fermentation and product formation. These models fit the experimental data and can be modified effectively to find out the inhibiting parameters that affects the growth of microbes or activity of enzymes or rate of product formation [32]. The kinetic models are used in designing the batch fermenter suitable for ethanol production. In addition to kinetic models describing the behavior of microbiological systems, modeling based on combining the effects of various parameters namely time, temperature, and concentration into one single parameter is also used to develop a linear model expressing the relationship between ethanol production and variables like pH, temperature, and initial concentration of substrate. Artificial Neural Network (ANN) and Response Surface Methodology (RSM) are used for the optimization of process variables for the production of bioethanol [33].

3.1 Kinetic models

Kinetic models describing the behavior of microbiological systems can be a highly appreciated tool and can reduce tests to eliminate extreme possibilities. The kinetic parameters are obtained from the concentrations of biomass, products, and substrates consumed during the fermentation.

$$\mu = \frac{\mu_{max} S}{K_s + S} \tag{1}$$

where μ_{max} and K_s are the maximum specific growth rate and the Monod constant respectively.

3.1.1 Logistic growth model

$$x = \frac{x_o e^{kt}}{1 - \beta x_o (1 - e^{kt})} \tag{2}$$

Where x_o is the initial biomass concentration (g/l) and t is time (h).

3.1.2 Leudeking-Piret kinetic model - product formation kinetics

The rate of product formation is well described by an unstructured model. The kinetic expression, Leudeking-Piret equation, does fit the kinetic data of ethanol formation. Ethanol production is a growth associated product kinetics with significant α, the growth associated term [34].

$$p(t) - p_o - \beta\left(\frac{x_s}{k}\right)\left[1 - \frac{x_o}{x_s}\left(1 - e^{kt}\right)\right] = \alpha[x(t) - x_o] \tag{3}$$

3.1.3 Substrate utilization kinetics

$$-\frac{ds}{dt} = \frac{1}{Y_{x/s}}\frac{dx}{dt} + \frac{1}{Y_{p/s}}\frac{dp}{dt} + k_e x \tag{4}$$

where $Y_{x/s}$ and $Y_{p/s}$ are the yield coefficient for the biomass and product, respectively and K_e is the specific maintenance coefficient.

3.1.4 Yield of growth

To evaluate the model parameters and to relate the changes in substrate, cell mass and product concentrations, a Yield coefficient is introduced. The yield coefficients are related by the equation [35].

$$Y_{p/s} = Y_{x/s}\, Y_{p/x} \tag{5}$$

3.2 Experimental design, analysis and optimization using response surface methodology (RSM)

RSM is an empirical statistical technique employed for multiple regression analysis by using quantitative data obtained from properly designed experiments to solve multivariate equations simultaneously. The response surface, which is a two- dimensional graphic representation of the system's behavior, is used to determine the individual and cumulative effects of the variables and the mutual interactions between the variables on the dependent variable [36]. The graphic representations of the regression equation called the response surfaces. The quality of fit of the second order equation is expressed by the coefficient of determination R^2, and its statistical significance is determined by F-test. The significance of each coefficient is determined using Student's t-test.

The application of statistical experimental design techniques in ethanol fermentation process development can result in improved production yields, reduced process variability, closer conformance of the output response (Ethanol yield) to nominal and target requirements and reduced development time and overall costs. The statistical design of experiments using central composite design can be effectively used to optimize the process variables like pH, temperature initial reducing sugar concentration to maximize the ethanol concentration [37]. The chosen independent variables used in this experiment are coded according to the Eq. (6):

$$x_i = \frac{X_i - X_o}{\Delta x} \tag{6}$$

where x_i is the coded value of the ith variable, X_i is the uncoded value of the ith test variable and X_o is the uncoded value of the ith test variable at the centre point. The behavior of the system is explained by the following second- degree polynomial Eq. (7):

$$Y = \beta_o + \sum_{i=1}^{k} \beta_i X_i + \sum_{i=1}^{k} \beta_{ii} {X_i}^2 + \sum_{i=1}^{k-1} \sum_{j=2}^{k} \beta_{ij} X_i X_j \tag{7}$$

where Y is the predicted response, β_o is the offset term, β_i is the coefficient of linear effect, β_{ii} is the coefficient of squared effect and β_{ij} is the coefficient of interaction effect.

3.3 Artificial neural network analysis

Artificial Neural Network (ANN) is another important tool that has also been effectively used in modeling biotechnological process, majorly reduces time and experimental readings required for modeling [38]. It is used to predict the degree of non-linearity and to learn complex analyses in various fields. RSM is used to analyze the data with least experimental data and gives a mathematical relation while ANN is a machine learning statistical approach that can be applied in a wide range of data analysis including optimization thereby estimates the response based on the trained data [39].

3.3.1 Analysis of model predictability in artificial neural network

Eqs. (8) and (9) indicates the Mean Squared Error (MSE) and RMSE, a widespread measure for model predictability in which the ANN output error between the actual and the predicted output can be evaluated [40]:

$$MSE = \frac{1}{n}\sum_{i=1}^{n}(y_i - y_{di})^2 \tag{8}$$

$$RMSE = MSE^{½} \tag{9}$$

where, n is the number of points, y_i is the predicted value obtained from the neural network model, y_{di} is the actual value.

The closer the R^2 value is to 1, the better the model fits to the actual data:

$$R^2 = 1 - \sum_{i=1}^{n}\left(\frac{(y_i - y_{di})^2}{(y_{di} - y_m)^2}\right) \tag{10}$$

where, n is the number of points, y_i is the predicted value from neural network model, y_{di} is the actual value, and y_m is the average of the actual values.

Absolute Average Deviation (AAD) in Eq. (11) is another significant index to evaluate the ANN output error between the actual and the predicted output:

$$Absolute\ Average\ Deviation\ (AAD) = \left\{\left[\sum_{i=1}^{n}\left(|y_i - y_{di}|/y_{di}\right)\right]/n\right\} \times 100 \tag{11}$$

where, y_i and y_{di} are the predicted and actual responses, respectively, and n is the number of the points.

4. Conclusion

Industrial production of ethanol is viable form cheaper substrates like biomass, corn and molasses. The molasses from sugar manufacturing unit can be used as a raw material for ethanol production by fermentation. The starch present in the corn is also used as substrate after liquefaction and saccharification using enzymes. The cellulosic raw materials are cheaper but it is essential to pre-treat the biomass residue by digesting the lignin and hemicellulose using sulfuric acid before fermentation to ethanol. Optimization of process variables like pH, temperature substrate concentration and agitation speed for maximum ethanol production is effectively done using statistical tool response surface methodology and artificial neural network. The modeling and kinetics of ethanol production is the most important to design the suitable bioreactors. Microbial growth kinetics, product formation kinetics and substrate utilization kinetics are enumerated.

Author details

Manikandan Kanagasabai[1*], Babu Elango[1], Preetha Balakrishnan[1]
and Jayachitra Jayabalan[2]

1 Faculty of Engineering and Technology Annamalai University, Department of Chemical Engineering, Bioprocess Laboratory, Annamalainagar, Tamilnadu, India

2 Faculty of Agriculture, Department of Agricultural Microbiology, Annamalai University, Annamalainagar, Tamilnadu, India

*Address all correspondence to: kmchemical_27@yahoo.co.in

References

[1] Lynd LR, Wang MQ. A product nonspecific framework for evaluating the potential of biomass based products to displace fossil fuels. Journal of Industrial Ecology. 2004;7:17-32

[2] Wang PY, Shopsis C, Schneider H. Fermentation of pentose by yeast. Biochemical and Biophysical Research Communications. 1980;**94**:248

[3] Logsdon JE. Ethanol. In: Kirk RE, Othmer DF, et al., editors. Encyclopedia of Chemical Technology. New York: John Wiley & Sons, Inc.; 2006

[4] Lin Y, Tanaka S. Ethanol fermentation from biomass resources: Current State and prospects. Applied Microbiology and Biotechnology. 2006; **69**:627-642

[5] Alani F, Smith JE. Effect of chemical pretreatment on the fermentation and ultimate digestibility of bagasse by *Phanerochaete chrysosporium*. Journal of the Science of Food and Agriculture. 1988;**42**:19-28

[6] Gable M, Zacchi G. A review of the production of ethanol from softwood. Applied Microbiology and Biotechnology. 2002;**59**(6):618-628

[7] Pandey A, Soccol CR, Nigam P, Soccol VT. Biotechnological potential of agro-industrial residues. I Sugarcane bagasse. Bioresource Technology. 2006; **74**:69-80

[8] Adams MR, Little CL, Easter MC. Modelling the effect of pH, acidulant and temperature on the growth rate of *Yersinia enterocolitica*. The Journal of Applied Bacteriology. 1991;**71**:65-71

[9] Anjum MF, Tasadduq I, Al-Sultan K. Response surface methodology: A neural network approach. European Journal of Operational Research. 1997;**101**:65-73

[10] Bailey JE. Kinetics of substrate utilization, product formation and biomass production in cell cultures. In: Bailey JE, editor. Biochemical Engineering Fundamentals. 3rd ed. New York: McGraw Hill Book Company; 1986

[11] Goudar CT, Delvin JF. Nonlinear estimation of microbial and enzyme kinetic parameters from progress curve data. Water Environment Research. 2001;**73**:260-265

[12] Shapouri HJ, Duffield A, Graboski MS. Energy balance of corn ethanol revisited. In: ASAE (ed) Conference proceedings liquid fuel conference. ASAE, St. Joseph. 1996. pp. 253-259

[13] Chandel AK, Es C, Rudravaram R, Narasu ML, Rao LV, Ravindra P. Economics and environmental impact of bioethanol production technologies: An appraisal. Biotechnology and Molecular Biology Reviews. 2007;**2**: 14-32

[14] Duggleby RG, Wood C. Analysis of progress curves for enzyme catalyzed reactions. The Biochemical Journal. 1989;**258**:397

[15] Contois DE. Kinetics of bacterial growth: Relationship between population density and specific growth of continuous culture. Journal of General Microbiology. 1959;**21**:40-50

[16] Chen H, Jin S. Effect of ethanol and yeast on cellulase activity and hydrolysis of crystalline cellulose. Enzyme and Microbial Technology. 2006;**39**: 1430-1432

[17] Egli T. The ecological and physiological significance of the growth of heterotrophic microorganisms with mixture of substrates. In: Jones JG, editor. Advances in Microbial Ecology. Vol. 14. New York: Plenum Press; 1995. pp. 305-386

[18] Gibson AM, Bratchell N, Roberts TA. The effects of sodium chloride and temperature on the rate and extent of growth of Clostridium botulinum type A in pasteurized pork slurry. The Journal of Applied Bacteriology. 1987;**62**: 479-490

[19] Hahn-Hagerdal B, Galbe M, Gorwa-Grauslund MF, Liden G, Zacchi G. Bio-ethanol the fuel of tomorrow from the residues of today. Trends in Biotechnology. 2006;**24**: 549-556

[20] Kanagasabai M, Maruthai K, Thangavelu V. Simultaneous saccharification and fermentation and factors influencing ethanol production in SSF process. In: Alcohol Fuels - Current Technologies and Future Prospect. London, United Kingdom: IntechOpen; 2019 [Online]. Available from: https://www.intechopen.com/chapters/67972. DOI: 10.5772/intechopen.86480

[21] Manikandan K, Rengadurai S, Babu E, Sothivanan S. Optimization studies in simultaneous saccharification and fermentation of wheat bran flour into ethanol. Food and Nutrition Sciences. 2022;**13**:463-470. DOI: 10.4236/fns.2022.135034

[22] Hamelinck CN, van Hooijdonk G, Faaij APC. Ethanol from lignocellulosic biomass: Techno-economic performance in short-middle and long-term. Biomass and Bioenergy. 2005;**28**:384-410

[23] McMeekin TA, Chandler RE, Doe PE, Garland CD, Olley J, Putro S, et al. Model for combined effect of temperature and salt concentration/water activity on the growth rate of *Staphylococcus xylosus*. Journal of Applied Bacteriology. 1987;**62**: 543-550

[24] Keim CR. Technology and economics of fermentation alcohol - An update. Enzyme and Microbial Technology. 1983;**5**:103-114

[25] Haykin S. Neural networks: A comprehensive foundation. New Jersey: Prentice Hall; 1994

[26] Rittmann BE, McCarty PL. Evaluation of steady-state-biofilm kinetics. Biotechnology and Bioengineering. 1980;**22**:2359-2373

[27] Jeffries TW, Jin YS. Ethanol and thermotolerance in the bioconversion of xylose by yeasts. Advances in Applied Microbiology. 2000;**47**:221-268

[28] Kovarova-Kovar K, Egli T. Growth kinetics of suspended microbial cells: From single-substrate-controlled growth to mixed substrate kinetics. Microbiology and Molecular Biology Reviews. 1998;**62**:646-666

[29] Nielson J, Villadsen J. Structured modelling of a microbial system. III. Growth on mixed substrates. Biotechnology and Bioengineering. 1991; **38**:24

[30] Penfold W, Norris D. The relation of concentration of food supply to generation time bacteria. The Journal of Hygiene. 1912;**12**:527-531

[31] Schmidt SK, Alexander M, Shuler ML. Predicting threshold concentrations of organic substrates for bacterial growth. Journal of Theoretical Biology. 1985;**114**:1-8

[32] Simkins S, Alexander M. Nonlinear estimation of the parameters of monod kinetics that best described mineralization of several substrate concentrations by dissimilar bacterial densities. Applied and Environmental Microbiology. 1985;**50**:816-824

[33] Smith MR, Ewing M, Ratledge C. The interactions of various aromatic substrates degraded by *Pseudomonas* sp. NCIB 10643: Synergistic inhibition of growth by two compounds that serve as growth substrates. Applied Microbiology and Biotechnology. 1991;**34**:536-538. DOI: 10.1007/BF00180584

[34] Sutherland JP, Bayliss AJ, Roberts TA. Predictive modelling of growth of *Staphylococcus aureus*: The effects of temperature, pH and sodium chloride. International Journal of Food Microbiology. 1994;**12**:217-236

[35] Tan Y, Wang Z, Marshall KC. Modelling substrate inhibition of microbial growth. Biotechnology and Bioengineering. 1996;**52**:602

[36] Tros ME, Schraa G, Zehnder AJB. Transformation of low concentrations of 3-chlorbenzoate by *Pseudomonas* sp. strain B13: Kinetics and residual concentrations. Applied and Environmental Microbiology. 1996;**62**:437-442

[37] Wang M, Saricks C, Wu M. FUEL-cycle Fossil Energy Use and Greenhouse Gas Emissions of Fuel Ethanol Produced from U.S Midwest Corn. Argonne: Argonne National Laboratory for Illinois Department of Commerce and Community Affairs; 1997. pp. 24-28

[38] Wijtzes T, McClure PJ, Zwietering MH, Roberts TA. Modelling bacterial growth as a function of water activity, pH and temperature. International Journal of Food Microbiology. 1992;**18**:139-149

[39] Overend RP, Chornet E. Fractionation of lignocellulosics by steam-aqueous pretreatments. Philosophical Transactions of the Royal Society of London. 1987;**321**:523-536

[40] Arellano-Plaza M, Herrera-López EJ, Díaz-Montaño DM, Moran A, Ramírez-Córdova JJ. Unstructured kinetic model for tequila batch fermentation. International Journal of Mathematics and Computers in Simulation. 2007; **1**(1):1-6

Chapter 2

Catalysis for Glycerol Production and Its Applications

Anele Sibeko, Lethiwe D. Mthembu, Rishi Gupta and Nirmala Deenadayalu

Abstract

Globally, there is a climate change due to greenhouse gases, hence the production processes for chemicals should comply with green chemistry principles to decrease the impact it has on the climate. This book chapter focuses on the catalytic production of glycerol, which is a platform chemical that is widely used in the manufacture of various industrially important chemicals and derivatives, namely 2,3-dihydroxy-propanal, glycerol ether, glycerol ester, acrolein, 1,2-propanediol and glycidol. The literature reviewed compares the production of glycerol using homogeneous and heterogeneous catalysts, to determine efficient and environmentally benign glycerol catalysts and to study glycerol as a platform chemical and its value in application.

Keywords: catalysis, homogenous catalysts, heterogeneous catalysts, value-added compounds, glycerol production

1. Introduction

The enormous growth in demand for fuels, along with growing environmental concerns and limited raw oil sources has increased the use of renewable energy. Biodiesel is one of the potential alternatives, and renewable fuels, has gained popularity in recent years, and their production capacity have grown significantly.

It is produced through various methods such as the transesterification of non-edible and waste vegetable oils with methanol and efforts are also being made to utilise the glycerol by-product to compensate the production cost of biodiesel to make it commercially viable, yielding quite significant percentage of a glycerol by-product which lowers the production cost and makes it commercially available. For every 4 litres of biodiesel generated [1].

Around 500 grams of glycerol is made, this equates to approximately 11,500 tons of 99.9% pure glycerine produced by a plant with a capacity of 113,562,354 million litres per year. The resulting oversupply of raw glycerol from biodiesel production can influence the purified glycerol market significantly as glycerol is a high-value and commercial chemical with thousands of applications [2].

Although extensive research has been carried out on the use of glycerol for various industrial applications, however, a compilation review on different approaches of glycerol production using homogenous and heterogeneous catalysts is scarce. The present chapter focuses on compiling different state-of-the-art in glycerol manufacturing techniques with a special emphasis on homogeneous and heterogeneous catalysis approaches. Moreover, an attempt has also been made to review the application of glycerol in the production of various platform chemicals preferably using microbial pathways. A section has been dedicated on reviewing the application of glycerol in animal feed.

2. Glycerol production

Glycerol can be manufactured using a variety of chemical synthesis feedstocks. It can be produced, for example, by propylene synthesis by several methods [3], such as oil hydrolysis, or transesterification of fatty acids or oils. The following sections describe briefly about different glycerol production processes.

2.1 Glycerol production by propylene

As previously stated, several methods for producing glycerol from propylene can be used [4, 5]. In **Figure 1**, one of the major processes is shown, which includes the use of chlorination (Cl_2) [6].

2.1.1 Glycerol production via chlorination process

Propylene chlorination (**Figures 1** and **2**) produces allyl chloride at a temperature of 510°C in the presence of hypochlorous acid at 38°C. Glycerine dichlorohydrin is formed when allyl chloride reacts. The glycerol dichlorohydrin is then hydrolysed by sodium carbon oxide in a 6% sodium carbonate solution at 96°C or directly to glycerine, the epichlorohydrin being removed as an overhead in a stripping column. Finally, the epichlorohydrin is hydrated to glycerine using sodium hydroxide [4], resulting in a final glycerol yield of around 90% [6].

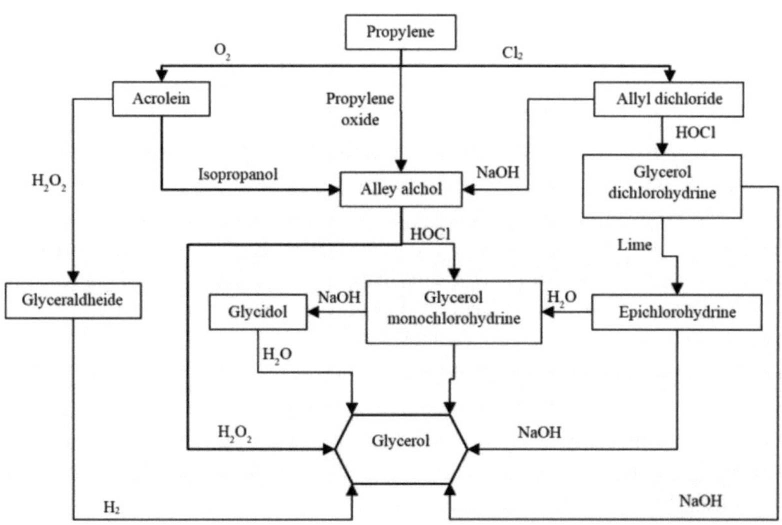

Figure 1.
Flow diagram illustrating the production of glycerol from propylene [6].

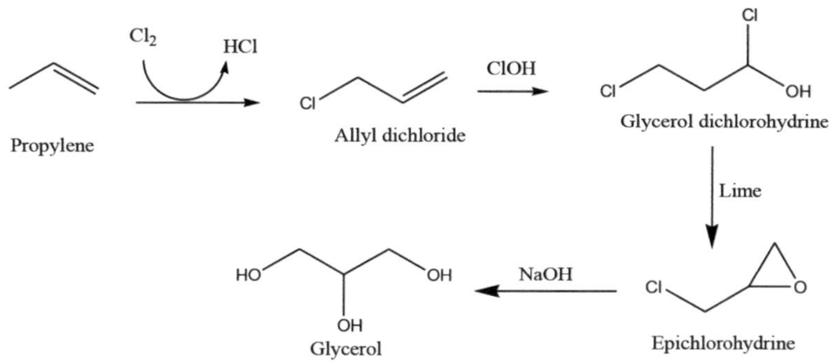

Figure 2.
Reaction of the propylene chlorination process.

2.1.2 Glycerol production via oxygenation process

Figure 3 illustrates two paths to produce glycerol from propylene via oxygenation. Oxygen (O_2) reacts with propylene to produce acrolein, adding an aldehyde (HC=O). Acrolein can be converted to allyl alcohol with a reducing agent sodium borohydride ($NaBH_4$) in a presence of isopropanol as a solvent; peroxide is added to allyl alcohol to produce glycerol. In the other reactions, peroxide is added to acrolein which results in the formation of glyceraldehyde; the glyceraldehyde reacts with hydrogen to produce glycerol.

2.2 Saponification

In this reaction, sodium hydroxide (base) reacts with triglyceride as an ester to form glycerol and soap molecules. This method has been employed since 2800, and the first industrial factory was developed in 1860 [7]. As demonstrated in **Figure 4**, this reaction occurs between triglyceride and sodium hydroxide (caustic soda), producing glycerol and soap [6, 8].

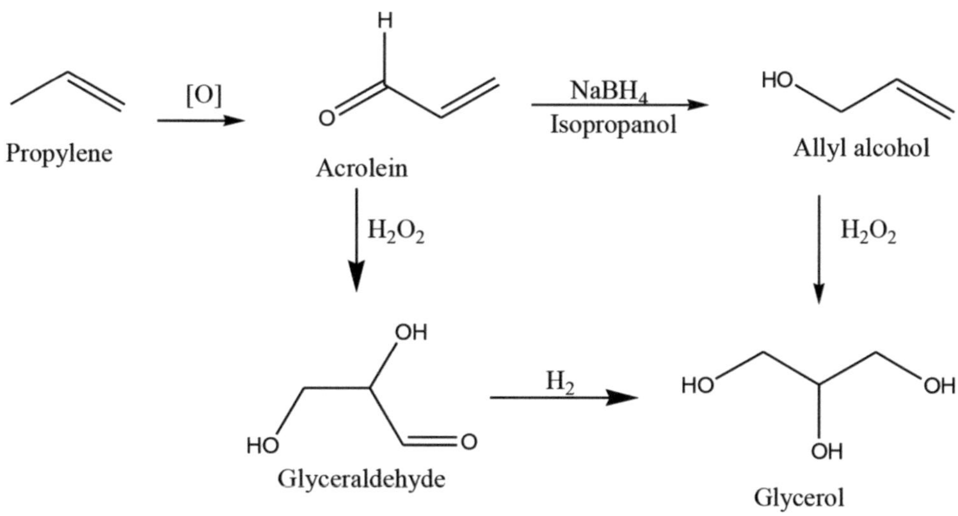

Figure 3.
Production of glycerol from propylene oxygenation reaction.

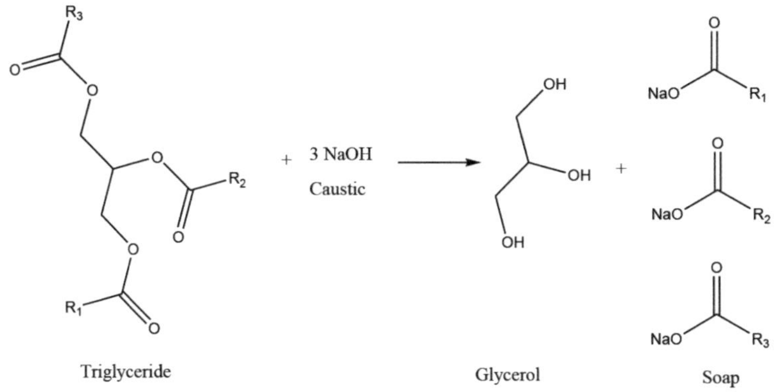

Figure 4.
Illustrates the saponification reaction between triglyceride and sodium hydroxide (caustic soda) for the glycerol production [6].

2.3 Transesterification of the beaver oil

The transesterification reaction of beaver oil with ethanol to produce glycerol was carried out in 1864 [9, 10]. **Figure 5** shows the reaction in which methyl-esters from triglycerides (oils) and methanol (alcohol) combine to form glycerol and fatty esters (or biodiesel) [5, 6, 11, 12].

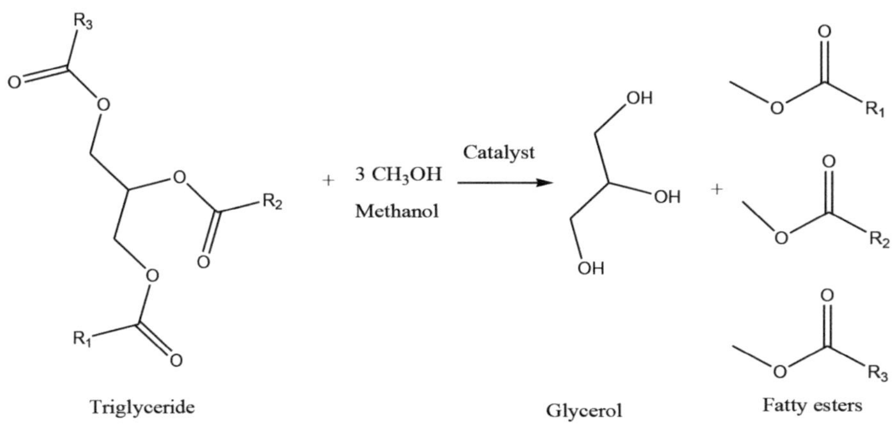

Figure 5.
Glycerol production by a transesterification reaction [6].

Feedstock	Glycerol concentration (w/w %)	Methanol concentration (w/w %)	Soap concentration (w/w %)	Impurities (w/w %)	Ref.
Palm oil waste	87	—	—	6	[13]
Oil of Jatropha	19–22	14.5	29	11–21	[14]
Soybean oil	63	6.2	—	—	[15]
Soybean oil	22	10.9	26.2	23.5	[15]

Feedstock	Glycerol concentration (w/w %)	Methanol concentration (w/w %)	Soap concentration (w/w %)	Impurities (w/w %)	Ref.
Soybean oil	33	12.6	26.1	22.3	[15]
Vegetable oil waste	28	9	21	39	[15]
Palm oil	81	1	—	2.0	[16]
Seed oils	63–77	—	—	—	[17]
Used frying oil	85	—	—	15	[18]

Table 1.
Different glycerol streams depending on initial feedstocks and production reactions.

Interestingly, the glycerol yield from transesterification was not only found to be dependent on different types of processes but also on the different type of oil feedstocks (**Table 1**) [13–18].

3. Glycerol catalysis

Transesterification of oil is accomplished using both homogenous as well as heterogeneous catalysts. **Table 2** depicts glycerol production advantages and disadvantages of using different type of catalysts.

Moreover, depending on the type of catalyst used, the transesterification process can be categorised as homogeneous and heterogeneous catalysis to make biodiesel and subsequently glycerol.

Catalysts group	Type of catalyst	Advantages	Disadvantages
Homogeneous base catalyst	NaOH/KOH	• Fast reaction rate, mild condition and less energy intensity. • Catalysts are widely available and economical.	• If the usage limit for oil is less than 0.5 wt. % free fatty acid. Soap formation occurs as well if the free fatty acid content in the oil is more than 2 wt. %. • Excessive soap formation reduces the glycerol yield and causes problems during product purification.
Heterogeneous base catalyst	CaO/MgO	• Reaction conditions are mild and less energy-intensive, reuse and regenerating of a catalyst. • Mild reaction condition and less energy intensive.	• Sensitive to free fatty acid content in the oil due to its basicity property. • Excessive soap formation decreases the glycerol yield and causes problems during product refining.
Homogenous Acid catalyst	H_2SO_4/HCl	• Affordable than base catalysed process.	• Very slow reaction rate. Not easy to separate the catalyst from products.

Table 2.
Advantages and disadvantages of glycerol catalysts [19].

3.1 Homogeneous catalysis

During homogenous catalysis, the first stage comprises the reaction of vegetable oils with methanol in the presence of a catalyst, and then the separation of glycerol from the resultant mixture using a settler unit follows. The remaining flow is sent to a chamber that uses mineral acids to remove the catalytic component, resulting in two paths: a glycerol recovery chamber and an evaporator that separates biodiesel from the other products. The unit for purifying comprises three output units: the first with 80–95% glycerol; the second one with water, dissolved salts and unreacted methanol (it is then recycled back to the reactor); and one with fatty esters [12]. **Figure 6** depicts the glycerol manufacturing process employing homogeneous catalysts (namely, sodium hydroxide or sodium methylate) [6, 20, 21].

3.2 Heterogeneous catalysis

This type of catalysis procedure envisions two reaction phases to improve vegetable oil conversion; reactor 1 is supplied by vegetable oil and methanol. The product stream is sent through a heat exchanger to evaporate some of the residual methanol, and the remaining stream is directed to a decanter to separate polar and non-polar components such as glycerol and mainly vegetable oil and biodiesel, respectively. While, in reactor 2, the non-polar stream is reacted for the second time to boost biodiesel synthesis and recover methanol. The product stream travels through the heat exchanger, which takes out all unreacted methanol, and the decanter, which separates the biodiesel from polar components.

The polar streams from the first and second polar decanters are directed to another heat exchanger to recover the remaining methanol in the mixture, while the leftover fraction is delivered to a final decanter to separate vegetable oil and residual glycerol. **Figure 7** is a flowchart of triglyceride transesterification using heterogeneous catalysts such as aluminium and zinc oxide [6].

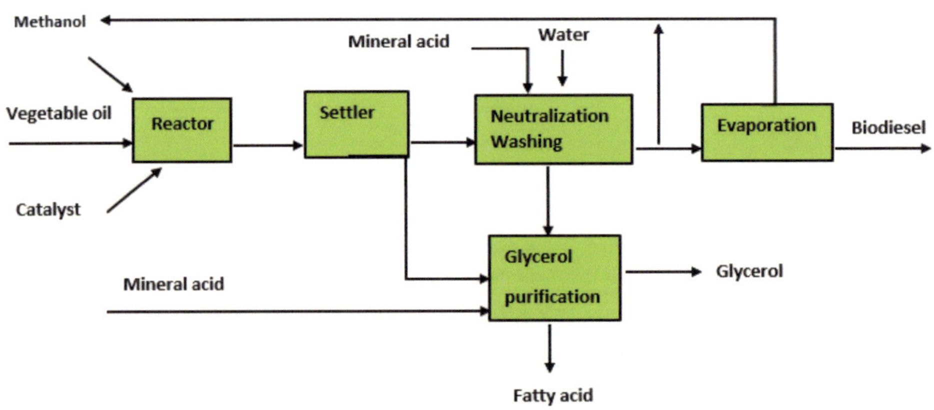

Figure 6.
The production plant for biodiesel is based on a homogenous catalyst.

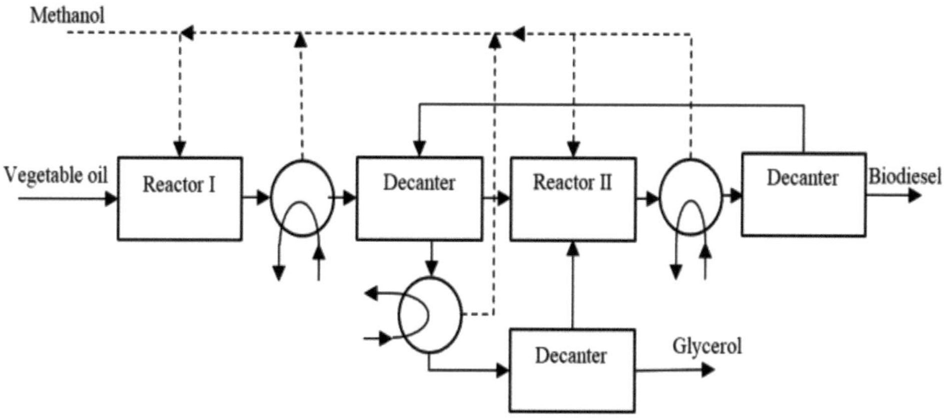

Figure 7.
A heterogeneous catalysis-based production plant flowchart [6].

4. Glycerol: a platform chemical

Synthesis of glycerol following microbial route has been known for over a century, however, new improvements in the biodiesel business have resulted in the production of large amounts of glycerol. During the biodiesel production process, approximately

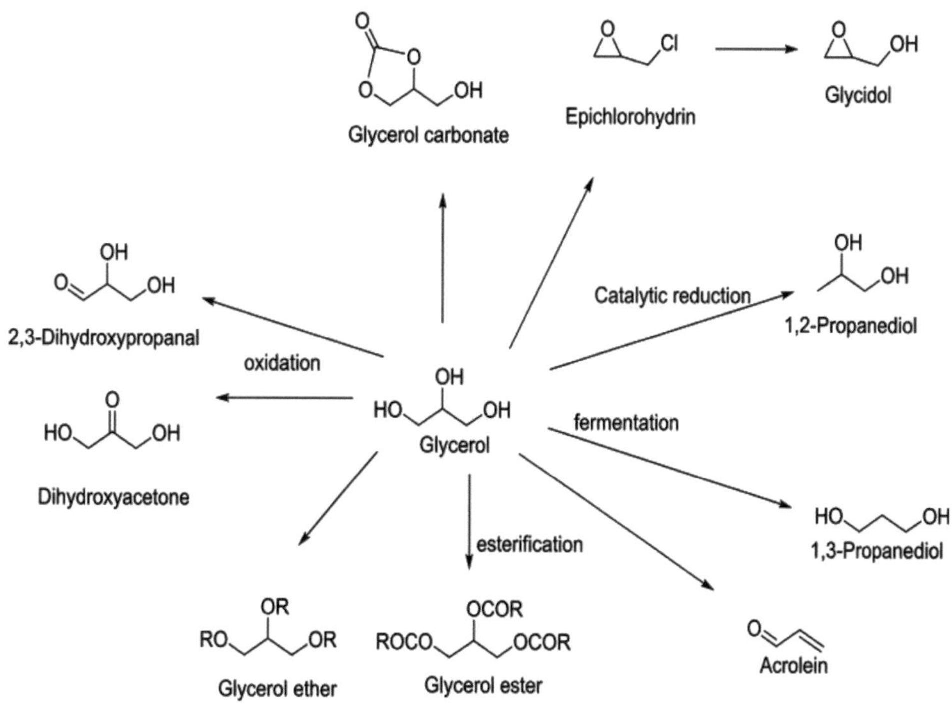

Figure 8.
Glycerol as a platform chemical.

10% of glycerol is produced, accounting for about 90% of total glycerol produced [22]. Glycerol has gathered substantial interest in its conversion to higher value-added compounds due to its availability and potential to operate as a key building block in a biorefinery (**Figure 8**) [23].

Glycerol oxidation produces a wide range of compounds, such as glyceric acid dihydroxyacetone, glyceraldehyde, hydroxy-pyruvic acid, glycolic acid and others. Controlling reaction selectivity is a critical challenge in obtaining the desired molecules.

For example, glyceric acid is a crucial intermediary for more extensively oxidised compounds such as tartronic acid and mesoxalic acid. The catalytic aerobic oxidation of glycerol in a basic media has been extensively studied using monometallic or bimetallic catalysts such as Au, Pt and Pd.

Table 3 lists some of the most prominent catalysts used in this field [24–27, 30, 38–40]. Another approach for producing value-added compounds from glycerol is the reduction process. Lactic acid is produced by a reduction of glycerol in the presence of hydroxide bases [41]. This reaction is frequently carried out at medium to high pressures and temperatures ranging from 100 to 240°C using Cu- and Zn-based catalysts enhanced by sulphide Ru [28].

Glycerol carbonate is another derivative of glycerol that is formed by reaction between glycerol and urea, ethylene or propylene carbonate [22] or carbon dioxide [42]. It is also used in the commercial manufacture of epichlorohydrin. Epichlorohydrin is produced in a similar manner by Solvay and Dow Chemical Company [43]. When the principal hydroxyl groups in glycerol are selectively oxidised, the economically valuable chemicals glyceraldehyde [44], glyceric acid [45] and tartronic acid [46] are formed. Dihydroxyacetone (DHA) is produced by oxidation of the secondary hydroxyl group, whereas ketomalonic acid is produced by oxidation of all three hydroxyl groups [47].

Another glycerol derivative, glycidol, offers immense potential for the synthesis of industrially useful compounds such as epoxy resins, polyurethanes and polyglycerol esters. A bio-based technique for producing glycidol from glycerol was recently published [48]. The manufacture of acrolein from glycerol is an innovative, eco-friendly technology that has several advantages, such as less oil extraction and a minimal environmental impact [31]. In general, acrolein is synthesised from glycerol by acid-catalysed dehydrogenation over synthetic aluminium phosphate ($AlPO_4$), zeolites with varied channel configurations (HY and H-ZSM-5) and SiO_2/Al_2O_3 ratio [31, 49].

A novel synthetic approach for the synthesis of chlorohydrin was proposed, which involved reacting a polyhydroxy aliphatic hydrocarbon with a chlorination agent. Vitiello et al. [33] focused on the activity and selectivity of homologous chlorinated series of catalysts for glycerol halogenation, such as acetic acid, monochloro, dichloro and trichloroacetic acid.

Table 3 also includes information on one of the most significant glycerol conversion processes, esterification with acetic acid, which produces monoacylglycerol, diacylglycerol and glycerol carbonate. These materials are often used in cryogenics, biodegradable polyester and cosmetics [35, 36]. Sulphated-based superacids, heteropoly acid-based catalysts, tin chloride, zeolite, ZrO_2-based solid acids and other significant acid catalysts can be used for glycerol esterification [35–37, 50–52].

Finally, pyrolysis of glycerol to produce syngas is another method of converting glycerol. The pyrolysis of biomass has been extensively studied in the specialist literature, although in most cases, only metal-based catalysts have been used. The microwave-assisted pyrolysis of glycerol over a carbonaceous catalyst is a unique approach

Reaction type	Reactant	Catalyst	Pressure (bar)	Temperature (°C)	Product	Ref.
Glycerol oxidation	O_2	Pd–Ag/C	3	80	Dihydroxyacetone	[24]
	O_2	Pt/NCNT	—	60		[25]
	O_2	Pt/MCN	3	40	Glyceraldehyde	[26]
	O_2	Pt/SiO_2	1	100		[27]
	O_2	Pt/MCN	3	40	Glyceric acid	[26]
	O_2	Pt/SiO_2	1	100		[27]
Glycerol reduction	H_2	Ru/Al_2O_3	25	180	1,2-propanediol	[28]
	H_2	Ru/Al_2O_3	25	200	Ethylene glycol	[29]
	H_2	Ru/ZrO_2	80	240		[30]
Glycerol dehydrogenation	—	$AlPO_4$–450	1	190–230	Acrolein	[31]
	—	HY(5.2)	1	170–230		[31]
	—	12 wt. % V_2O_5, V/P molar ratio of 0.2	1	325		[32]
Glycerol halogenation	HCl	Aspartic acid	4.5	100	1,3-dichloropropanol	[33]
	HCl	Glutamic acid	4.5	100		[33]
Glycerol esterification	Acetic acid	Sb_2O_5	1	80–120	Monoglicerides	[34]
	Palmitic acid	ZrSBA-15	1	160–180	Diacylglicerol	[35]
	Acetic acid	Graphene oxide	1	120		[36]
	Acetic acid	ZSM-5	1	120		[36]
Glycerol pyrolysis	—	Bituminous carbon	1	400–900	Syngas	[37]
	—	Coconut shell	1	400–900		[37]

Table 3.
Compounds derived from traditional glycerol conversion under similar operating conditions.

for syngas generation in which the heating method and operating temperature (between 400 and 900°C) can impact the catalytic action of the activated carbons to optimise syngas production [37]. **Table 3** outlines some of the products derived from glycerol that may be transformed into other compounds with high added value.

5. Value-added products from glycerol via biological conversions

From 2004 to 2008, the global production of crude glycerol from biodiesel conversion increased from 200 thousand tonnes to 1.224 million tonnes [2, 19]. Meanwhile, in 2005, the global market for purified glycerol was anticipated to be over 900,000 tonnes [53]. This provided a chance for scientists to discover new uses for refined and crude glycerol. Multiple publications on the direct use of crude glycerol from biodiesel synthesis have been published.

5.1 1,3-Propanediol

The most promising alternative for the biological conversion of glycerol in anaerobic fermentative production is 1,3-propanediol [54], which indicates that crude glycerol could be employed directly for the manufacture of 1,3-propanediol in fed-batch cultures of *pneumoniae*.

Raw glycerol composition had less influence on the biological conversion and, therefore, a low fermentation cost could be predicted. However, using a response surface approach, the generation of 1,3-propanediol by *Klebsiella pneumoniae* was optimised. The highest concentration of 1,3-propanediol produced However, statistical optimisation along with genetic engineering approaches may be utilised to improve the 1,3-propanediol production [14, 55]. *K. pneumoniae* ATCC 15380 recently improved the synthesis of 1,3-propanediol from crude glycerol from Jatropha biodiesel. The yield, purity and recovery of 1,3-propanediol obtained were 56 g/L, 99.7% and 34%, respectively [14]. In addition, a hollow fibre membrane was used to produce an integrated bioprocess that linked biodiesel generation by lipase with microbial production of 1,3-propanediol by *K. pneumoniae* [56].

5.2 Citric acid

Citric acid synthesis by *Yarrowia lipolytica* ACA-DC 50109 from raw glycerol was not only comparable to that obtained from sugar-based standard media [57] but also single-cell oil and citric acid were produced simultaneously [58, 59]. When acetate-negative mutants of the *Y. lipolytica* Wratislavia AWG7 strain were employed in a fed-batch fermentation to ferment crude glycerol, the final concentration of citric acid was 131.5 g/L, which was similar to that produced from pure glycerol (139 g/L). Similarly, *Y. lipolytica* LGAM S(7)1 has also shown the ability to convert crude glycerol to citric acid [60]. Interestingly, another strain *Y. lipolytica* N15 could produce large levels of citric acid, namely up to 98 g/L of citric acid and 71 g/L of citric acid from pure glycerol medium and crude glycerol medium, respectively [61].

5.3 Hydrogen and other lower molecule fuels

The photo-fermentative conversion of crude glycerol to hydrogen is one of the most fascinating approach to utilise glycerol. Both crude glycerol and pure glycerol can produce up to 6 moles of H_2 per mole of glycerol, representing 75% of the theoretical value. However, significant technological challenges, such as increasing the efficiency of light use by organisms and building effective photobioreactors, must be overcome before a viable method can be developed [62]. When *Enterobacter aerogenes* HU-101 was used, hydrogen and ethanol were synthesised at high yields and rates. However, in order to improve the rate of glycerol use, the crude glycerol should be diluted with a synthetic medium [63]. While Jitrwung and Yargeau [64] modified several media compositions of the *E. aerogenes* ATCC 35029 fermented crude glycerol procedure to maximise hydrogen generation.

5.4 Polyhydroxyalkanoates (PHB)

As an estimate, a biodiesel facility with a capacity of 10 million gallons per year could produce 20.9 tons of PHB [65]. The feasibility of using crude glycerol for PHB manufacture was investigated using *Paracoccus denitrificans* and *Cupriavidus necator* JMP134, and the resultant polymers were shown to be remarkably comparable to those generated from glucose. However, a high osmotic (sodium chloride-contaminated) crude glycerol was found to have harmful impact on PHB synthesis and needs to be taken care of. One way to handle the issue is combining crude glycerol from various producers to reduce the harmful effect of NaCl contamination [66]. In addition, for a large-scale PHB synthesis, a technique based on the *C. necator* DSM 545 fermentation of crude glycerol was developed [67]. Following this in the presence of NaCl, *Zobellella denitrificans* MW1 could use crude glycerol for growth and PHB synthesis at high concentrations. As a result, it was recommended as an appealing alternative for large-scale PHB manufacturing using crude glycerol [68]. Furthermore, when mixed microbial consortia (MMC) were utilised to produce PHA from crude glycerol, it was shown that methanol in the crude glycerol was converted to PHB by MMC.

5.5 Lipids as the sole carbon source

Crude glycerol might be used to manufacture lipids, which could be utilised to make a sustainable biodiesel feedstock. For example, raw glycerol might be used to culture *Schizochytrium limacinum* SR21 and *Cryptococcus curvatus*. However, the glycerol

Product	Reaction	Yield	Ref.
1,3-Propanediol	Fed-batch cultures of *Klebsiella pneumoniae* strain	1.7 g/L/h	[54]
	Maximum 1,3-propanediol production from *K. pneumonia*	13.8 g/L	[55]
Citric acid	*Yarrowia lipolytica* strain ACA-DC 50109 (process modelling)	NA	[57]
	Acetate mutants of *Y. lipolytica* Wratislavia AWG7 strain; fed-batch operation	139 g/L	[74]
	Y. lipolytica strain LGAM S (7)1	35 g/L	[60]
Hydrogen	Photofermentative conversion process; *Rhodopseudomonas palustris* strain	6 mol/mol glycerol	[62]
	Enterobacter aerogenes strain HU-101; continuous culture; porous ceramics as a support material to fix cells	63 mmol/L/h	[63]
Poly(hydroxyalkanoates) (PHAs)	*Pseudomonas oleovorans* NRRL B-14682 and *P. corrugata* 388 grew and synthesised PHB and mcl-PHA, respectively	NA	[75]
	Producing PHB; *Paracoccus denitrificans* and *Cupriavidus necator* JMP 134 strains	48%	[66]
Lipid	*Schizochytrium limacinum* SR21; batch culture	73.3%	[69]
	Cryptococcus curvatus; two-stage fed-batch process	52%	[76]

Table 4.
Biological conversion of crude glycerol.

Product	Reaction	Yield	Ref.
Acrolein	Fluidised bed, tungsten-doped zirconia catalyst	21%	[77]
Monoglyceride	Two-step process, purification of the monoglyceride produced from glycerolysis of palm stearin	~99% purity	[78]
	Glycerolysis of soybean oil	~42%	[79]
Gaseous products	Steam gasification with in situ CO_2 removal	88 vol.% H_2 purity	[80]
	Hydrothermal reforming of crude glycerol	~90 vol.% H_2 purity	[81]

Table 5.
Conventional catalytic conversions of crude glycerol.

content over a certain threshold may prevent the rapid reproduction of cells. The best glycerol content for batch culturing of crude glycerol obtained from yellow grease were 25 and 35 g/L for untreated and treated crude glycerol, respectively, which may subsequently lead to cellular lipid content of approximately 75%. Methanol residues in crude glycerol may cause damage to the development of *S. limacinum* SR21 [69].

For lipid synthesis in *C. curvatus* yeast, fed-batch was preferable to batch; however, the addition of ammonium sulphate and Tween 20 improved the accumulation of lipids and carotenoids Saenge et al. [70] demonstrated that the oleaginous red yeast *Rhodotorula glutinis* TISTR 5159 generated lipids and carotenoids when grown on crude glycerol. *Chlorella protothecoides* was also capable of converting crude glycerol to lipids.

The lipid yield was 0.31 g lipids/g substrate [71]. Similarly, using *C. protothecoides* and crude glycerol (62% purity), Furthermore, Chatzifragkou et al. [72] did research, to investigate the ability of 15 eukaryotic micro-organisms to change crude glycerol to metabolic products. The results showed that yeast accumulated limited lipids (up to 22 wt.% in the case of Rhodotorula), whereas fungi collected greater levels of lipids in their mycelia (range between 18.1 and 42.6 wt.% of dry biomass). Interestingly, Chen and Walker [73] found that a fed-batch operation yielded a maximum lipid productivity of 3 g/L per day, which was greater than that generated by a batch procedure.

Tables 4 and 5 outline an overview of the conversions of crude glycerol to potential chemical through biological and catalytic conversions.

6. Application of crude glycerol in animal feedstock

Glycerol has been used as an animal feed additive since the 1970s [82]. However, the availability of glycerol has limited its application in diets [83], because of the rising corn prices and the oversupply of crude glycerol, the possibility of using crude glycerol from biodiesel in feeds has recently been examined.

6.1 Crude glycerol in non-ruminant diets

Crude glycerol is an excellent energy source due to its high absorption rates for non-ruminants such as broilers. Once ingested, the enzyme glycerol kinase converts it to glucose for energy generation in the liver of mammals [83]. Its samples from various biodiesel manufacturers were tested as energy sources. The digestible energy (DE) values for 85% of the crude glycerol samples ranged from 14.9 to 15.3 MJ/kg, with metabolisable energy (ME) values ranging from 13.9 to 14.7 MJ/kg [84]. Overall, the use of crude glycerol derived from biodiesel process as an animal feed component offers significant potential for replacing maize in diets and is gaining popularity. However, the existence of potentially dangerous contaminants in biodiesel crude glycerol needs to be taken into consideration [85].

6.2 Crude glycerol in ruminant diets

Besides, the non-ruminants, crude glycerol may play a very significant role in the diets of ruminant animals as well. However, to improve its edibility, more emphasis should be placed on the crude glycerol produced by small-scale biodiesel plants that employ basic batch distillation or evaporation processes. There are several reports where use of crude glycerol has shown significant improvement in the overall performance of ruminants. Crude glycerol, at up to 15% dry matter in finishing lamb diets, might increase feedlot performance, particularly during the first 14 days, but had little influence on carcass attributes [86]. Diets for meat goats containing up to 5% crude glycerol were shown to be superior to medium-quality hay [87]. Nursing dairy cows can also be fed up to 15% of their dry matter diet without affecting feed intake, milk output or yield [88, 89]. When crude glycerol was added at 8% or less of dry matter in cow-finishing diets, its weight growth and feed efficiency were increased [90].

7. Summary and conclusions

Glycerol may be produced using various techniques and feedstocks, such as propylene synthesis by various routes, hydrolysis of fatty acid triglycerides, or transesterification of fatty acids or oils. The efficient use of crude glycerol is critical to the commercialisation and advancement of biodiesel synthesis. In the long run, using biomass-derived glycerol will not only help to reduce society's reliance on non-renewable resources, but it will also encourage the development of integrated biorefineries. This review focuses on the value-added prospects for crude glycerol derived from biodiesel production, primarily as a feed ingredient for animal feed and as a feedstock for chemicals.

For example, crude glycerol can be converted into 1,3-propanediol, citric acid, poly(hydroxyalkanoates), butanol, hydrogen, docosahexaenoic acid-rich algae, monoglycerides, lipids and syngas. Though many of the processes discussed have already been employed by the industries, they require additional research to minimise the manufacturing cost and be operationally practical for inclusion into biorefineries.

Furthermore, contaminants in crude glycerol can have a noticeable impact on the conversion of glycerol into other products. Pollutants in crude glycerol hinder cell and fungi's rapid reproduction, resulting in less production rates and product yields in many biological conversion processes (compared with pure or commercial glycerol under the same culture conditions). Contaminants, on the other hand, poison the catalysts in traditional catalytic conversions, boosting char generation and affecting product yield.

Many technologies need to be better understood and refined, such as optimising reaction parameters, production yields and fermentation conditions; generating mutant strains and efficient bioreactors for stable cultures and enhancing the activity and selectivity of catalysts.

Researchers have also obtained promising results on utilisation of crude glycerol as animal feed, particularly with non-ruminant animals such as pigs, laying hens and broilers. But various precautions must be taken before this biomass-derived chemical may be used on a large scale in animal diets. To begin with, animal producers must exercise caution when deciding to incorporate crude glycerol as a component of animal feed diets, since the chemical composition of crude glycerol varies greatly depending on the processes and feedstocks used to manufacture biodiesel. Secondly, contaminants in crude glycerol affect feed performance to some extent. Finally, the amount of crude glycerol in feed formulations must be considered. It is advised that a crude glycerol feed standard be established so that it would be uniform for all producers, the resulting "standard" crude glycerol would have greater value.

There is a need to develop improved processes as well as other important value-added products. For example, among other renewable and bio-derived sources, glycerol has come up as an appealing possibility since it represents a relevant and alternative solution for producing hydrogen via reforming processes that may be carried out in both traditional and novel reactors.

Besides, catalytic process, though it is not yet introduced, the transesterification reaction using supercritical fluids has also gained noticeable attention. As one or two reaction stages are possible in a single-step supercritical fluid transesterification, the reaction occurs only once reactants are heated to critical temperatures and pressures with triglycerides [20, 21]. Triglycerides are initially transformed to free fatty acids and by-products in the hydrolysis reaction during the two-step subcritical-supercritical fluid transesterification. The acquired free fatty acids undergo esterification reaction, yielding fatty acid methyl esters in a supercritical fluid process [91, 92].

Conflict of interest

The authors declare no conflict of interest.

Author details

Anele Sibeko[1], Lethiwe D. Mthembu[1*], Rishi Gupta[2] and Nirmala Deenadayalu[1]

1 Department of Chemistry, Durban University of Technology, Berea, Durban, South Africa

2 Anton Paar India Pvt. Ltd., Gurugram, Haryana, India

*Address all correspondence to: lethiwem@dut.ac.za

References

[1] Yang F, Hanna MA, Sun R. Value-added uses for crude glycerol--a byproduct of biodiesel production. Biotechnology for Biofuels. 2012;**5**(1):1-10

[2] Kerr BJ, Dozier WA III, Bregendahl K. Nutritional value of crude glycerin for nonruminants. In: Proceedings of the 23rd Annual Carolina Swine Nutrition Conference. Journal of Animal Science. Raleigh, NC; 2007. pp. 6-18

[3] Shukla K, Srivastava VC. Synthesis of organic carbonates from alcoholysis of urea: A review. Catalysis Reviews. 2017;**59**(1):1-43

[4] Ciriminna R, Pina CD, Rossi M, Pagliaro M. Understanding the glycerol market. European Journal of Lipid Science and Technology. 2014;**116**(10): 1432-1439

[5] Matar S, Hatch LF. Chemistry of Petrochemical Processes. Elsevier; 2001

[6] Bagnato G, Iulianelli A, Sanna A, Basile A. Glycerol production and transformation: A critical review with particular emphasis on glycerol reforming reaction for producing hydrogen in conventional and membrane reactors. Membranes. 2017;**7**(2):17

[7] Hunt JA. A short history of soap. The Pharmaceutical Journal. 1999;**263**(7076):985-989

[8] Marchetti J, Miguel V, Errazu A. Possible methods for biodiesel production. Renewable and Sustainable Energy Reviews. 2007;**11**(6):1300-1311

[9] Formo M, Jungermann E, Norris F, Sonntag N. In: Swern D, editor. Bailey's Industrial Oil and Fat Products. New York, NY: John Wiley and Sons; 1979

[10] Quispe CA, Coronado CJ, Carvalho JA Jr. Glycerol: Production, consumption, prices, characterization and new trends in combustion. Renewable and Sustainable Energy Reviews. 2013;**27**:475-493

[11] Wang Z, Zhuge J, Fang H, Prior BA. Glycerol production by microbial fermentation: A review. Biotechnology Advances. 2001;**19**(3):201-223

[12] Fukuda H, Kondo A, Noda H. Biodiesel fuel production by transesterification of oils. Journal of Bioscience and Bioengineering. 2001;**92**(5):405-416

[13] Hidawati EN, Sakinah AM. "treatment of glycerin pitch from biodiesel production," international journal of chemical and environmental. Engineering. 2011;**2**(5):309-313

[14] Hiremath A, Kannabiran M, RangaswamyV.1,3-Propanediolproduction from crude glycerol from Jatropha biodiesel process. New Biotechnology. 2011;**28**(1):19-23

[15] Hu S, Luo X, Wan C, Li Y. Characterization of crude glycerol from biodiesel plants. Journal of Agricultural and Food Chemistry. 2012;**60**(23):5915-5921

[16] Liu Y-P, Sun Y, Tan C, Li H, Zheng X-J, Jin K-Q, et al. Efficient production of dihydroxyacetone from biodiesel-derived crude glycerol by newly isolated Gluconobacter frateurii. Bioresource Technology. 2013;**142**:384-389

[17] Tan H, Aziz AA, Aroua M. Glycerol production and its applications as a raw material: A review. Renewable and Sustainable Energy Reviews. 2013;**27**:118-127

[18] Bouaid A, Vázquez R, Martinez M, Aracil J. Effect of free fatty acids contents on biodiesel quality. Pilot plant studies. Fuel. 2016;**174**:54-62

[19] Nomanbhay S, Hussain R, Rahman MM, Palanisamy K. Review paper integration of biodiesel and bioethanol processes: Convertion of low cost waste glycerol to bioethanol. Advances in Natural and Applied Sciences. 2012;**6**(6):802-818

[20] Ilham Z, Saka S. Dimethyl carbonate as potential reactant in non-catalytic biodiesel production by supercritical method. Bioresource Technology. 2009;**100**(5):1793-1796

[21] Goembira F, Saka S. Optimization of biodiesel production by supercritical methyl acetate. Bioresource Technology. 2013;**131**:47-52

[22] Okoye P, Hameed B. Review on recent progress in catalytic carboxylation and acetylation of glycerol as a byproduct of biodiesel production. Renewable and Sustainable Energy Reviews. 2016;**53**:558-574

[23] Schultz EL, de Souza DT, Damaso MCT. The glycerol biorefinery: A purpose for Brazilian biodiesel production. Chemical and Biological Technologies in Agriculture. 2014;**1**(1):1-9

[24] Hirasawa S, Watanabe H, Kizuka T, Nakagawa Y, Tomishige K. Performance, structure and mechanism of Pd–Ag alloy catalyst for selective oxidation of glycerol to dihydroxyacetone. Journal of Catalysis. 2013;**300**:205-216

[25] Ning X, Li Y, Yu H, Peng F, Wang H, Yang Y. Promoting role of bismuth and antimony on Pt catalysts for the selective oxidation of glycerol to dihydroxyacetone. Journal of Catalysis. 2016;**335**:95-104

[26] Wang F-F, Shao S, Liu C-L, Xu C-L, Yang R-Z, Dong W-S. Selective oxidation of glycerol over Pt supported on mesoporous carbon nitride in base-free aqueous solution. Chemical Engineering Journal. 2015;**264**:336-343

[27] Li Y, Zaera F. Sensitivity of the glycerol oxidation reaction to the size and shape of the platinum nanoparticles in Pt/SiO2 catalysts. Journal of Catalysis. 2015;**326**:116-126

[28] Lee S-H, Moon DJ. Studies on the conversion of glycerol to 1, 2-propanediol over Ru-based catalyst under mild conditions. Catalysis Today. 2011;**174**(1):10-16

[29] Soares AV, Salazar JB, Falcone DD, Vasconcellos FA, Davis RJ, Passos FB. A study of glycerol hydrogenolysis over Ru–Cu/Al2O3 and Ru–Cu/ZrO2 catalysts. Journal of Molecular Catalysis A: Chemical. 2016;**415**:27-36

[30] Olmos CM, Chinchilla LE, Rodrigues EG, Delgado JJ, Hungría AB, Blanco G, et al. Synergistic effect of bimetallic Au-Pd supported on ceria-zirconia mixed oxide catalysts for selective oxidation of glycerol. Applied Catalysis B: Environmental. 2016;**197**:222-235

[31] Estevez R, Lopez-Pedrajas S, Blanco-Bonilla F, Luna D, Bautista F. Production of acrolein from glycerol in liquid phase on heterogeneous catalysts. Chemical Engineering Journal. 2015;**282**:179-186

[32] Cecilia J, García-Sancho C, Mérida-Robles J, Santamaría-González J, Moreno-Tost R, Maireles-Torres P. V and V–P containing Zr-SBA-15 catalysts for dehydration of glycerol to acrolein. Catalysis Today. 2015;**254**:43-52

[33] Vitiello R, Russo V, Turco R, Tesser R, Di Serio M, Santacesaria E. Glycerol

chlorination in a gas-liquid semibatch reactor: New catalysts for chlorohydrin production. Chinese Journal of Catalysis. 2014;**35**(5):663-669

[34] Hu W, Zhang Y, Huang Y, Wang J, Gao J, Xu J. Selective esterification of glycerol with acetic acid to diacetin using antimony pentoxide as reusable catalyst. Journal of Energy Chemistry. 2015;**24**(5):632-636

[35] Yusoff MHM, Abdullah AZ. Catalytic behavior of sulfated zirconia supported on SBA-15 as catalyst in selective glycerol esterification with palmitic acid to monopalmitin. Journal of the Taiwan Institute of Chemical Engineers. 2016;**60**:199-204

[36] Gao X, Zhu S, Li Y. Graphene oxide as a facile solid acid catalyst for the production of bioadditives from glycerol esterification. Catalysis Communications. 2015;**62**:48-51

[37] Fernández Y, Arenillas A, Díez M, Pis J, Menéndez J. Pyrolysis of glycerol over activated carbons for syngas production. Journal of Analytical and Applied Pyrolysis. 2009;**84**(2):145-150

[38] Rodrigues EG, Pereira MF, Delgado JJ, Chen X, Órfão JJ. Enhancement of the selectivity to dihydroxyacetone in glycerol oxidation using gold nanoparticles supported on carbon nanotubes. Catalysis Communications. 2011;**16**(1):64-69

[39] Skrzyńska E, Zaid S, Girardon J-S, Capron M, Dumeignil F. Catalytic behaviour of four different supported noble metals in the crude glycerol oxidation. Applied Catalysis A: General. 2015;**499**:89-100

[40] Gil S, Marchena M, Fernández CM, Sánchez-Silva L, Romero A, Valverde JL. Catalytic oxidation of crude glycerol using catalysts based on Au supported on carbonaceous materials. Applied Catalysis A: General. 2013;**450**:189-203

[41] Maris EP, Ketchie WC, Murayama M, Davis RJ. Glycerol hydrogenolysis on carbon-supported PtRu and AuRu bimetallic catalysts. Journal of Catalysis. 2007;**251**(2):281-294

[42] Ma J, Song J, Liu H, Liu J, Zhang Z, Jiang T, et al. One-pot conversion of CO 2 and glycerol to value-added products using propylene oxide as the coupling agent. Green Chemistry. 2012;**14**(6):1743-1748

[43] Bell BM, Briggs JR, Campbell RM, Chambers SM, Gaarenstroom PD, Hippler JG, et al. Glycerin as a renewable feedstock for epichlorohydrin production. The GTE process. CLEAN–Soil, Air, Water. 2008;**36**(8):657-661

[44] Kim HJ, Lee J, Green SK, Huber GW, Kim WB. Selective glycerol oxidation by electrocatalytic dehydrogenation. ChemSusChem. 2014;7(4):1051-1056

[45] Kondamudi N, Misra M, Banerjee S, Mohapatra S, Mohapatra S. Simultaneous production of glyceric acid and hydrogen from the photooxidation of crude glycerol using TiSi2. Applied Catalysis B: Environmental. 2012;**126**:180-185

[46] Behr A, Eilting J, Irawadi K, LeschinskiJ,LindnerF.Improvedutilisation of renewable resources: New important derivatives of glycerol. Green Chemistry. 2008;**10**(1):13-30

[47] Ciriminna R, Pagliaro M. One-pot homogeneous and heterogeneous oxidation of glycerol to ketomalonic acid mediated by TEMPO. Advanced Synthesis & Catalysis. 2003;**345**(3):383-388

[48] Bai R, Zhang H, Mei F, Wang S, Li T, Gu Y, et al. Retraction: One-pot synthesis

of glycidol from glycerol and dimethyl carbonate over a highly efficient and easily available solid catalyst NaAlO 2. Green Chemistry. 2016;**18**(22):6144-6144

[49] Jiang T, Zhou Y, Liang S, Liu H, Han B. Hydrogenolysis of glycerol catalyzed by Ru-Cu bimetallic catalysts supported on clay with the aid of ionic liquids. Green Chemistry. 2009;**11**(7):1000-1006

[50] Ishak ZI, Sairi NA, Alias Y, Aroua MKT, Yusoff R. Production of glycerol carbonate from glycerol with aid of ionic liquid as catalyst. Chemical Engineering Journal. 2016;**297**:128-138

[51] Munshi MK, Biradar PS, Gade SM, Rane VH, Kelkar AA. Efficient synthesis of glycerol carbonate/glycidol using 1,8-diazabicyclo [5.4. 0] undec-7-ene (DBU) based ionic liquids as catalyst. RSC Advances. 2014;**4**(33):17124-17128

[52] Liu J, Li Y, Zhang J, He D. Glycerol carbonylation with CO2 to glycerol carbonate over CeO2 catalyst and the influence of CeO2 preparation methods and reaction parameters. Applied Catalysis A: General. 2016;**513**:9-18

[53] Nilles D. Combating the Glycerin Glut. Biodiesel Magazine; 2006 Available: https://biodieselmagazine.com/articles/1123/combating-the-glycerin-glut/

[54] Mu Y, Teng H, Zhang D-J, Wang W, Xiu Z-L. Microbial production of 1,3-propanediol by Klebsiella pneumoniae using crude glycerol from biodiesel preparations. Biotechnology Letters. 2006;**28**(21):1755-1759

[55] Oh B-R, Seo J-W, Choi MH, Kim CH. Optimization of culture conditions for 1,3-propanediol production from crude glycerol by *Klebsiella pneumoniae* using response surface methodology. Biotechnology and Bioprocess Engineering. 2008;**13**(6):666-670

[56] Mu Y, Xiu Z-L, Zhang D-J. A combined bioprocess of biodiesel production by lipase with microbial production of 1,3-propanediol by *Klebsiella pneumoniae*. Biochemical Engineering Journal. 2008;**40**(3):537-541

[57] Papanikolaou S, Aggelis G. Modelling aspects of the biotechnological valorization of raw glycerol: Production of citric acid by *Yarrowia lipolytica* and 1,3-propanediol by *clostridium butyricum*. Journal of Chemical Technology & Biotechnology: International Research in Process, Environmental & Clean Technology. 2003;**78**(5):542-547

[58] Papanikolaou S, Fakas S, Fick M, Chevalot I, Galiotou-Panayotou M, Komaitis M, et al. Biotechnological valorisation of raw glycerol discharged after bio-diesel (fatty acid methyl esters) manufacturing process: Production of 1, 3-propanediol, citric acid and single cell oil. Biomass and Bioenergy. 2008;**32**(1):60-71

[59] Papanikolaou S, Aggelis G. Biotechnological valorization of biodiesel derived glycerol waste through production of single cell oil and citric acid by Yarrowia lipolytica. Lipid Technology. 2009;**21**(4):83-87

[60] Papanikolaou S, Muniglia L, Chevalot I, Aggelis G, Marc I. *Yarrowia lipolytica* as a potential producer of citric acid from raw glycerol. Journal of Applied Microbiology. 2002;**92**(4):737-744

[61] Kamzolova SV, Fatykhova AR, Dedyukhina EG, Anastassiadis SG, Golovchenko NP, Morgunov IG. Citric acid production by yeast grown on glycerol-containing waste from biodiesel industry. Food Technology and Biotechnology. 2011;**49**(1):65-74

[62] Sabourin-Provost G, Hallenbeck PC. High yield conversion of a crude glycerol fraction from biodiesel production to hydrogen by photofermentation. Bioresource Technology. 2009;**100**(14):3513-3517

[63] Ito T, Nakashimada Y, Senba K, Matsui T, Nishio N. Hydrogen and ethanol production from glycerol-containing wastes discharged after biodiesel manufacturing process. Journal of Bioscience and Bioengineering. 2005;**100**(3):260-265

[64] Jitrwung R, Yargeau V. Optimization of media composition for the production of biohydrogen from waste glycerol. International Journal of Hydrogen Energy. 2011;**36**(16):9602-9611

[65] Dobroth ZT, Hu S, Coats ER, McDonald AG. Polyhydroxybutyrate synthesis on biodiesel wastewater using mixed microbial consortia. Bioresource Technology. 2011;**102**(3):3352-3359

[66] Mothes G, Schnorpfeil C, Ackermann JU. Production of PHB from crude glycerol. Engineering in Life Sciences. 2007;**7**(5):475-479

[67] Cavalheiro JM, de Almeida MCM, Grandfils C, Da Fonseca M. Poly (3-hydroxybutyrate) production by *Cupriavidus necator* using waste glycerol. Process Biochemistry. 2009;**44**(5):509-515

[68] Ibrahim MH, Steinbüchel A. Poly (3-hydroxybutyrate) production from glycerol by *Zobellella denitrificans* MW1 via high-cell-density fed-batch fermentation and simplified solvent extraction. Applied and Environmental Microbiology. 2009;**75**(19):6222-6231

[69] Liang Y, Sarkany N, Cui Y, Blackburn JW. Batch stage study of lipid production from crude glycerol derived from yellow grease or animal fats through microalgal fermentation. Bioresource Technology. 2010;**101**(17):6745-6750

[70] Saenge C, Cheirsilp B, Suksaroge TT, Bourtoom T. Potential use of oleaginous red yeast *Rhodotorula glutinis* for the bioconversion of crude glycerol from biodiesel plant to lipids and carotenoids. Process Biochemistry. 2011;**46**(1):210-218

[71] O'Grady J, Morgan JA. Heterotrophic growth and lipid production of *Chlorella protothecoides* on glycerol. Bioprocess and Biosystems Engineering. 2011;**34**(1):121-125

[72] Chatzifragkou A, Makri A, Belka A, Bellou S, Mavrou M, Mastoridou M, et al. Biotechnological conversions of biodiesel derived waste glycerol by yeast and fungal species. Energy. 2011;**36**(2):1097-1108

[73] Chen Y-H, Walker TH. Biomass and lipid production of heterotrophic microalgae *Chlorella protothecoides* by using biodiesel-derived crude glycerol. Biotechnology Letters. 2011;**33**(10):1973-1983

[74] Rywinska A, Rymowicz W, Zarowska B, Wojtatowicz M. Biosynthesis of citric acid from glycerol by acetate mutants of *Yarrowia lipolytica* in fed-batch fermentation. Food Technology and Biotechnology. 2009;**47**(1):1-6

[75] Ashby RD, Solaiman DK, Foglia TA. Bacterial poly (hydroxyalkanoate) polymer production from the biodiesel co-product stream. Journal of Polymers and the Environment. 2004;**12**(3):105-112

[76] Liang Y, Cui Y, Trushenski J, Blackburn JW. Converting crude glycerol derived from yellow grease to lipids through yeast fermentation. Bioresource Technology. 2010;**101**(19):7581-7586

[77] Sereshki BR, Balan S-J, Patience G, Dubois J-L. Reactive vaporization of crude glycerol in a fluidized bed reactor. Industrial & Engineering Chemistry Research. 2010;**49**(3):1050-1056

[78] Chetpattananondh P, Tongurai C. "synthesis of high purity monoglycerides from crude glycerol and palm stearin," Songklanakarin. Journal of Science & Technology. 2008;**30**(4):515-521

[79] Echeverri DA, Cardeño F, Rios LA. Glycerolysis of soybean oil with crude glycerol c containing residual alkaline catalysts from biodiesel production. Journal of the American Oil Chemists' Society. 2011;**88**(4):551-557

[80] Dou B, Dupont V, Williams PT, Chen H, Ding Y. Thermogravimetric kinetics of crude glycerol. Bioresource Technology. 2009;**100**(9):2613-2620

[81] Dou B, Rickett GL, Dupont V, Williams PT, Chen H, Ding Y, et al. Steam reforming of crude glycerol with in situ CO2 sorption. Bioresource Technology. 2010;**101**(7):2436-2442

[82] Fisher L, Erfle J, Lodge G, Sauer F. Effects of propylene glycol or glycerol supplementation of the diet of dairy cows on feed intake, milk yield and composition, and incidence of ketosis. Canadian Journal of Animal Science. 1973;**53**(2):289-296

[83] Mario Pagliaro MR. Royal Society of Chemistry (Great Britain), the Future of Glycerol: New Uses of a Versatile Raw Material. 2nd ed. Cambridge: Royal Society of Chemistry; 2008

[84] Dasari M. Crude glycerol potential described. Feedstuffs. 2007;**79**(43):1-3

[85] Cerrate S, Yan F, Wang Z, Coto C, Sacakli P, Waldroup P. Evaluation of glycerine from biodiesel production as a feed ingredient for broilers. International Journal of Poultry Science. 2006;**5**(11):1001-1007

[86] Gunn P, Neary M, Lemenager R, Lake S. Effects of crude glycerin on performance and carcass characteristics of finishing wether lambs. Journal of Animal Science. 2010;**88**(5):1771-1776

[87] Hampy K, Kellogg D, Coffey K, Kegley E, Caldwell J, Lee M, et al. Glycerol as a supplemental energy source for meat goats. AAES Research Series. 2008;**553**:63-64

[88] Donkin SS. Glycerol from biodiesel production: The new corn for dairy cattle. Revista Brasileira de Zootecnia. 2008;**37**:280-286

[89] Donkin S, Koser S, White H, Doane P, Cecava M. Feeding value of glycerol as a replacement for corn grain in rations fed to lactating dairy cows. Journal of Dairy Science. 2009;**92**(10):5111-5119

[90] Parsons G, Shelor M, Drouillard J. Performance and carcass traits of finishing heifers fed crude glycerin. Journal of Animal Science. 2009;**87**(2):653-657

[91] Saka S, Isayama Y, Ilham Z, Jiayu X. New process for catalyst-free biodiesel production using subcritical acetic acid and supercritical methanol. Fuel. 2010;**89**(7):1442-1446

[92] Lam MK, Lee KT, Mohamed AR. Homogeneous, heterogeneous and enzymatic catalysis for transesterification of high free fatty acid oil (waste cooking oil) to biodiesel: A review. Biotechnology Advances. 2010;**28**(4):500-518

Chapter 3

Bioethanol Production

Chakali Ayyanna, Kuppusamy Sujatha, Sujit Kumar Mohanthy, Jayaraman Rajangam, B. Naga Sudha and H.G. Raghavendra

Abstract

In recent decades, usage of biofuels as fossil fuel substitutes has increased. One method for lowering both crude oil use and environmental pollution is the production of ethanol (bioethanol) from biomass. This report offers an examination of the existing state of affairs and future prospects for biomass-to-ethanol. We examine different conversion routes from a technological, economic, and environmental standpoint. The main focus of this study is on the yield of ethanol from molasses in relation to the dilution ratio and the quantity of yeast used for fermentation while maintaining a constant fermentation temperature and time. In this investigation, the feedstock is sugarcane molasses. A thick by-product of turning sugar cane into sugar is sugarcane molasses. Consequently, sugarcane molasses and other agricultural byproducts are desirable feedstock for the manufacture of bioethanol. Agricultural wastes are cheap, abundant, and renewable. The least expensive strain for the conversion of biomass substrate is *Saccharomyces cerevisiae*. As a conclusion, it was found that the ethanol yield increased with an increase in yeast quantity, reaching an optimal yeast quantity before ethanol yield started to drop. The ideal ratio of molasses to water was found to be 1:2. The amount of fermentable sugars contained in the biomass has a significant impact on the output of ethanol.

Keywords: bioethanol, fermentation, feedstock, *Saccharomyces cerevisiae*, sugarcane molasses

1. Introduction

The research for alternative energy sources is stimulated by the growth in the nation's renewable sources and the gradual depletion of oil resources [1]. Particularly, biomass is a renewable resource that is currently researched for the utilization of bioethanol as an additive or replacement with gasoline has been driven by concerns about global warming and the need to lower greenhouse gas emissions [2]. Bioethanol can also be used as a raw material in the manufacture of various chemicals, resulting in fully renewable chemical industry. Bioethanol is created by fermenting sugars derived from biomass. Sucrose (e.g., sugarcane, sugar beet) or starch (e.g., corn, wheat), or lignocellulosic material can be used as bioethanol feedstock (e.g., sugarcane bagasse, wood, and straw). The main ethanol producers in the world, the US and Brazil, employ corn and sugarcane as their respective feedstocks. The use of fossil fuels during the processing of sugarcane is far lower than that of corn, making it the most

 IntechOpen

effective raw material for the manufacturing of bioethanol to date [3]. Additionally, there is still room for improvement in the sugarcane-based bioethanol manufacturing process, and large energy savings are conceivable.

Brazil, one of the world's top ethanol producers, has been using sugarcane as a primary input for the production of huge amounts of bioethanol for more than 30 years [4]. Large amounts of sugarcane bagasse are often created during the sugarcane processing (about 240 kg of bagasse with 50% humidity per ton of sugarcane), and this bagasse are presently burned in boilers to produce steam and power. It is now possible to have a surplus of bagasse thanks to improved cogeneration and optimization techniques for the bioethanol production process [5], which can be used as a fuel source for power production or as a raw material for making bioethanol and other biobased products [6]. Although sugarcane bagasse and other lignocellulosic materials have been the subject of intense research over the past few decades, it is still not economically feasible to produce bioethanol on an industrial scale [2]. To make hydrolysis a competitive technique, more research that takes into account process integration, increased fermentation yields, and integration of unit operations is still required [7, 8]. Hemicellulose, a mixture of polysaccharides primarily made of glucose, mannose, xylose, arabinose, lignin, and cellulose makes up the majority of lignocellulosic materials [1]. Sugarcane bagasse needs to be treated to produce fermentable sugars in order to be used as a raw material for bioethanol production [9]. To improve cellulose hydrolysis, lignin and hemicellulose must be separated from cellulose, cellulose crystallinity must be reduced, and the bagasse's porosity must be increased [10]. The Organogold procedure with diluted acid hydrolysis is one approach that might be used to accomplish that [11].

2. Bioethanol production

A gasoline substitute known as bioethanol (grain alcohol; C2H5OH (EtOH)) was used for transportation [12]. Globally, the amount of bioethanol produced has drastically increased [13]. Worldwide production of bioethanol climbed to 51,3 billion liters in 2006 from 45,98 billion liters in 2005 [2, 12]. Biomass-derived ethanol has been shown to be competitive with other liquid fuels on a large scale. The production method was refined and made practical by cellulose's enzymatic hydrolysis [9]. The creation of bioethanol from biomass was one method for lowering oil consumption and environmental contamination [12].

The production use of bioethanol is relevant to major national concerns like permanence, global climate change, biodegradability, municipal contamination, coal sequestration, national security, and the farm economy. It was obvious that production should be assessed in terms of economic factors, including farm-gate prices for biomass, logistic costs (transport and storage of biomass), the direct economic value of feedstocks taking into account byproducts, employment creation or maintenance, water requirements, and water availability [2, 12].

The comparison of the feedstocks for a given production line took into account a number of factors, including the chemical makeup of the biomass, cultivation methods, land availability and land use practices, resource use, energy balance, emission of greenhouse gases, acidifying gases, and ozone-depleting gases, mineral absorption into water and soil, pesticide injection, soil erosion, contribution to biodiversity, and landscape value losses [12]. Agricultural leftovers (such as corn stover and wheat straw), wood, and energy crops were all desirable raw materials for the synthesis of bioethanol [12]. The total amount of bioethanol that might be produced from such biomass was nearly 16 times greater than what is currently produced globally [14].

Arable agricultural starch and sugars were mostly used to make ethanol. Because it was pricey, the quest for other materials that would work for this purpose started [15]. Different processes were utilized depending on the type of biomass used to produce the bioethanol. It was difficult to bio-convert lignocellulosic biomass into fermentable sugars. The bioconversion of starch to sugars for the creation of bioethanol was more efficient and popular [16].

Through the hydrolysis and fermentation of sugars, biomass can be transformed into ethanol. Biomass wastes contain a complex mixture of cellulose, hemicellulose, and lignin, three carbohydrate polymers found in plant cell walls. In order to get sugars from the biomass, the biomass is first pre-treated with acids or enzymes to reduce the size of the feedstock and to open up the plant structure. Enzymes or weak acids hydrolyze the cellulose and hemicellulose components to produce sucrose sugar, which is subsequently fermented to produce ethanol. The biomass, which also contains lignin, is typically burned in the boilers of ethanol manufacturing facilities. The three main techniques for extracting sugars from biomass are as follows.

3. Method of intense acid treatment

The biomass needs to first be dried to a moisture level of 10% before the Alkanol process can begin, which involves adding 70–77% sulfuric acid. The temperature is kept at 50°C and the acid is added at a ratio of 1.25 acid to 1 biomass. The mixture is then heated to 100°C for another hour after the water is added to dilute the acid to 20–30%. The gel that results from this combination is then compressed to produce an acid-sugar mixture, which is purified to use a chromatographic column.

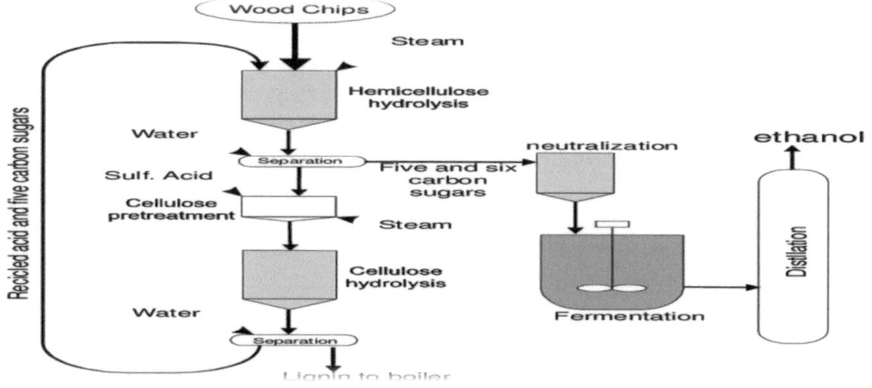

3.1 Acid hydrolysis in dilutes

One of the earliest, simplest, and most effective processes for generating ethanol from biomass is dilute acid hydrolysis. The biomass is hydrolyzed to produce sugar using diluted acid. The hemicellulose included in the biomass is hydrolyzed in the first step using 0.7% sulfuric acid at 190°C. An improved second stage results in a more robust cellulose fraction. By utilizing 0.4% sulfuric acid at 215°C, this is accomplished. Following neutralization, the liquid hydrolases are recovered from the process.

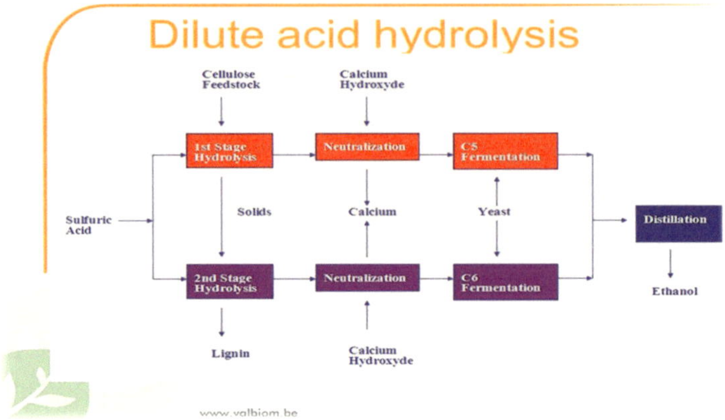

3.2 Enzymatic Hydrolysis

We can similarly break down the biomass using enzymes as opposed to utilizing acid to hydrolyze it into sugar. However, this procedure is still being developed and is highly expensive.

3.3 Wet milling processes

Corn can be processed into ethanol using either the dry milling or the wet milling method. The wet milling procedure involves soaking the maize kernel in warm water. This aids in the breakdown of the corn's proteins, the release of its starch, and softening of the kernel in preparation for milling. Then, the ground maize is used to make products with starch, fiber, and germ. A gluten-wet cake is made from the starch fraction after it has been centrifuged and saccharified; maize oil is then made by removing the germ. The next step is to extract the ethanol using the distillation process. The wet milling method is commonly applied in businesses that generate several hundred million gallons of ethanol annually.

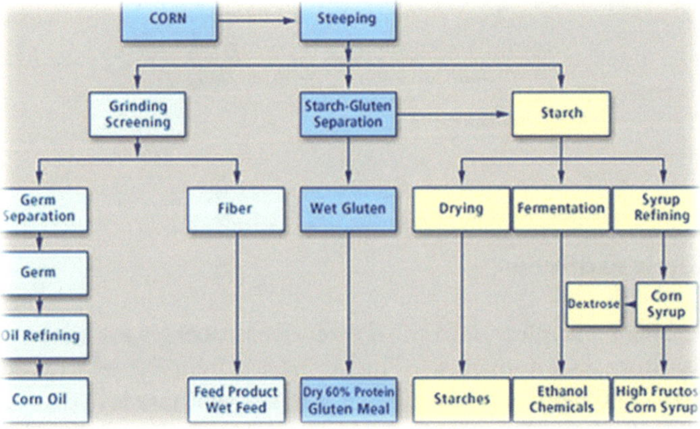

3.4 Dry milling process

Using a hammer mill, the maize kernel is cleaned and reduced to tiny pieces for dry milling. This results in a powder with a consistency similar to a coarse flour. Maize germ, starch, and fiber make up the powder. The combination is hydrolyzed, or changed into sucrose sugars, using enzymes or a moderate acid to create a sugar solution. After cooling, adding yeast causes the mixture to ferment into ethanol. In facilities that annually produce fewer than 50 million gallons of ethanol, dry milling is frequently employed.

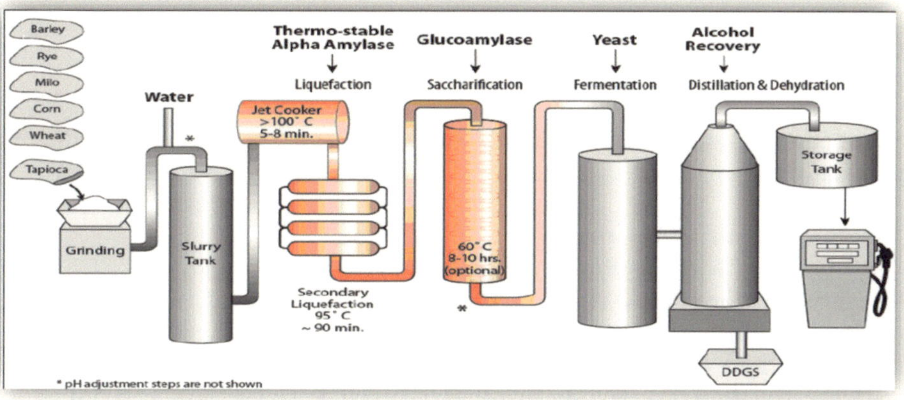

3.5 Sugar fermentation process

The cellulose component of biomass or corn is broken down during the hydrolysis process into sugar solutions, which can subsequently be fermented to produce ethanol. The mixture is heated after adding the yeast. Invertase, an enzyme found in yeast, serves as a catalyst and aids in the breakdown of sucrose carbohydrates into glucose and fructose (both $C_6H_{12}O_6$).

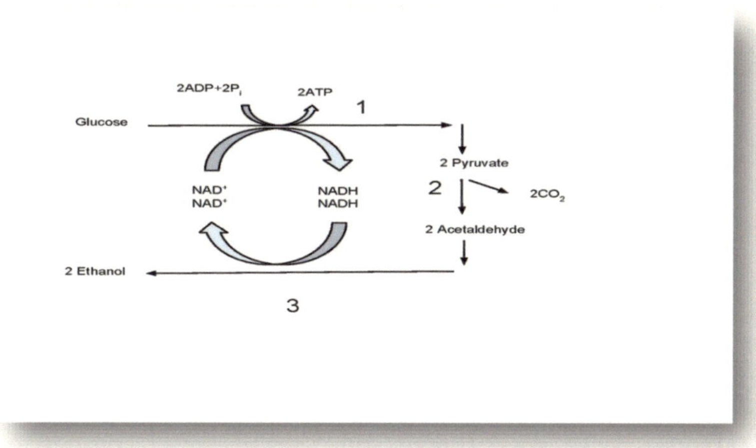

The chemical reaction is shown below

			Invertase			
$C_{12}H_{22}O_{11}$	+	H_2O	→	$C_6H_{12}O_6$	+	$C_6H_{12}O_6$
Sucrose		**Water**	**Catalyst**	**Fructose**		**Glucose**

A second enzyme called zymase, which is also present in yeast, then reacts with the fructose and glucose carbohydrates to create ethanol and carbon dioxide.

The chemical reaction is shown below:

	Zymase			
$C_6H_{12}O_6$	→	$2C_2H_5OH$	+	$2CO_2$
Fructose / Glucose	**Catalyst**	**Ethanol**		

Between 250°C and 300°C, the fermentation process is carried out over the course of around 3 days.

3.6 Fractional distillation process

The fermentation process results in the production of ethanol, but there is still a sizable amount of water present that needs to be removed. Utilizing the fractional distillation method, this is accomplished. The mixture of water and ethanol is heated during the distillation process. The fact that ethanol has a lower boiling point than water (78.3 vs. 100°C) means that it can be separated and condensed before water does.

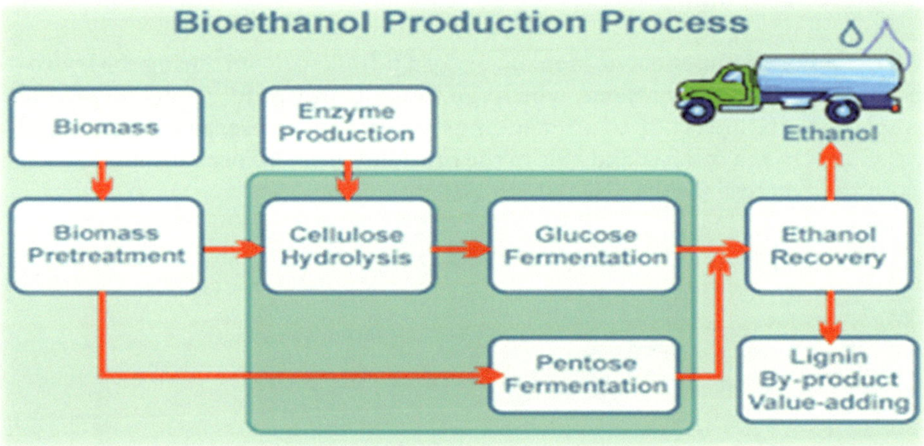

4. The possibility of using bioethanol

The performance of the vehicle would not be affected if bioethanol were used as a pure fuel or in a blend with other fuels in sufficient quantities to replace conventional motor fuels [17]. Without any adjustments, the mixture might be burned in a conventional combustion process. Gasohol was the most popular bioethanol-petrol mixture

(E10). 10% bioethanol and 90% gasoline were combined to create gasohol. Most contemporary automobiles with internal combustion engines (ICEs) were capable of burning E10 [12, 17]. The fuel blend E85, which is composed of 15% gasoline and 85% bioethanol, may also contain bioethanol [18]. About 5% of the ethanol created biologically was water. This blend was azeotropic. Because of this, ordinary distillation was insufficient to clean it. Gasoline and diesel fuel were not entirely blended with hydrated ethanol.

Bioethanol and diesel could be blended together by employing the right emulsifiers. Diesohol is a mixture of hydrated alcohol with diesel oil with an emulsifier. Diesel, hydrated ethanol, and a 0.5 percent emulsifier were used to make diesohol [17]. Ethanol was used as gasohol or clean fuel in Brazil (24% bioethanol and 76% gasoline) [12, 19]. The EN228 standard allows for the use of bioethanol as a 5% blend of gasoline in the European Union [12, 20]. Bioethanol was an oxygenated fuel with 35% oxygen content. Lowering the amount of nitrogen oxide (NOx) and particle pollutants produced during combustion. Utilizing a bioethanol-fuel combination allowed for the decrease in greenhouse gas (GHG) output and oil consumption [12]. It was possible to increase the fuel's oxygen content by adding bioethanol to conventional gasoline, which increased fuel combustion and reduced exhaust pollutants such CO and unburned hydrocarbons [12, 16]. Bioethanol was added to gasoline to reduce environmental pollution and the use of fossil fuels. Because 1 liter of bioethanol could substitute for 0.72 liters of gasoline, using it as a gasoline substitute proved very cost-effective [14].

5. Conclusion

Bioethanol can be employed as a fuel source. Studies are now being done to advance biofuel producing technologies. Bioethanol manufacturing could be carried out using biomass as a raw source. The investigation mainly concentrated on the usage of biomass wastes. With the help of starch and lignocellulosic biomass, bioethanol was formed. Starch was transformed into bioethanol via three sequential steps: hydrolysis, fermentation, and product purification. Hydrolysis, fermentation, pretreatment, and purification were the four steps that were followed in order to produce bioethanol from lignocellulosic biomass. Pretreatment can be done physically, physiochemically, chemically and biologically. Each of these approaches has benefits and drawbacks. It played a crucial role in choosing the best pretreatment strategy. It was crucial to focus on the creation and application of suitable pretreatment techniques in addition to other phases of the synthesis of bioethanol.

Author details

Chakali Ayyanna[1]*, Kuppusamy Sujatha[2], Sujit Kumar Mohanthy[3], Jayaraman Rajangam[4], B. Naga Sudha[5] and H.G. Raghavendra[1]

1 Department of Pharmacology, CES College of Pharmacy, Kurnool, India

2 Department of Pharmaceutical Chemistry, Sri Ramachandra Institute of Higher Education and Research, Chennai, India

3 Department of Pharmaceutical Chemistry, Shri Vishnu College of Pharmacy, Bhimavaram, India

4 Department of Pharmacology, AMITY Institute of Pharmacy, AMITY University, Lucknow, India

5 Department of Pharmaceutical Chemistry, CES College of Pharmacy, Kurnool, India

*Address all correspondence to: ayyannac5@gmail.com

References

[1] Saxena RC, Adhikari DK, Goyal HB. Biomass-based energy fuel through biochemical routes: A review. Renewable and Sustainable Energy Reviews. 2009;**13**:167-178

[2] Balat M, Balat H, Öz C. Progress in bioethanol processing. Progress in Energy and Combustion Science. 2008;**34**(5):551-573

[3] Macedo IC, Seabra JEA, Silva JEAR. Green house gases emissions in the production and use of ethanol from sugarcane in Brazil: the 2005/2006 averages and a prediction for 2020. Biomass and Bioenergy. 2008;**32**(7):582-595

[4] Goldemberg J. Ethanol for a sustainable energy future. Science. 2007;**315**(5813):808-810

[5] Ensinas AV, Nebra SA, Lozano MA, Serra LM. Analysis of process steam demand reduction and electricity generation in sugar and ethanol production from sugarcane. Energy Conversion and Management. 2007;**48**:2978-2987

[6] Buddadee B, Wirojanagud W, Watts DJ, Pitakaso R. The development of multi-objective optimization model for excess bagasse utilization: A case study for Thailand. Environmental Impact Assessment Review. 2008;**28**:380-391

[7] Cardona CA, Sánchez ÓJ. Fuel ethanol production: Process design trends and integration opportunities. Bioresource Technology. 2007;**98**:2415-2457

[8] Zaldivar J, Nielsen J, Olsson L. Fuel ethanol production from lignocellulose: A challenge for metabolic engineering and process integration. Applied Microbiology and Biotechnology. 2001;**56**:17-34

[9] Mosier N, Wyman C, Dale B, Elander R, Lee YY, Holtzapple M, et al. Features of promising technologies for pretreatment of lignocellulosic biomass. Bio/Technology. 2005;**96**:673-686

[10] Kuo C-H, Lee C-K. Enhanced enzymatic hydrolysis of sugarcane bagasse by N-methylmorpholine-N-oxide pretreatment. Bioresource Technology. 2009;**100**:866-871

[11] Rossell CEV, Lahr Filho D, Hilst AGP, Leal MRLV. Saccharification of sugarcane bagasse for ethanol production using the Organosolv process. International Sugar Journal. 2005;**107**:192-195

[12] Balat M, Balat H. Recent trends in global production and utilization of bioethanol fuel. Applied Energy. 2009;**86**:2273-2282

[13] Koh LP, Ghazoul J. Biofuels, biodiversity, and people: Understanding the conflicts and finding opportunities. Biological Conservation. 2008;**141**:2450-2460

[14] Kim S, Dale BE. Global potential bioethanol production from wasted crops and crop residues. Biomass and Bioenergy. 2004;**26**:361-375

[15] Enguídanos M, Soria A, Kavalov B, Jensen P. Techno-economic analysis of Bio-alcohol production in the EU: A short summary for decision-makers. 2002

[16] Maria G, Chisti Y. Biotechnology-a sustainable alternative for chemical industry. Biotechnology Advances. 2005;**23**:471-499

[17] Demirbas A. Biofuels sources, biofuel policy, biofuel economy and global biofuel projections. Energy Conversion and Management. 2008;**49**(8):2106-2116

[18] De Oliviera MED, Vaughan BE, Rykiel EJ Jr. Ethanol as fuel: Energy, carbon dioxide balances, and ecological footprint. Bioscience. 2005;**55**(7):593-602

[19] Demirbas A. Importance of biodiesel as transportation fuel. Energy Policy. 2007;**35**:4661-4670

[20] Malca J, Freire F. Renewability and life-cycle energy efficiency of bioethanol and bio-ethyl tertiary butyl ether (bioETBE): Assessing the implications of allocation. Energy. 2006;**31**:3362-3380

Section 2

Conversion of Glycerol into Aromatic Compounds

Chapter 4

Sustainable Synthesis of Pyridine Bases from Glycerol

Israel Pala-Rosas, José L. Contreras, José Salmones, Ricardo López-Medina, Beatriz Zeifert and Naomi N. González Hernández

Abstract

Catalytic processes have been developed to obtain pyridine bases from glycerol, either by direct conversion or with acrolein as an intermediate. When producing acrolein as an intermediate, the reaction may proceed in a single reactor at temperatures above 400°C in co-feeding with ammonia. A system of two interconnected reactors can also be used: one reactor performs the catalytic dehydration of glycerol to acrolein, while in the second reactor acrolein reacts with ammonia to form pyridine bases. Both processes require the use of solid acid catalysts, for which ZSM-5 zeolite-based catalysts are the most studied. In the direct reaction between glycerol and ammonia, the most active catalysts were Cu/HZSM-5 and the composite zeolite HZSM-5/11. In the two-step systems, the dehydration of glycerol to acrolein over a HZSM-5 zeolite modified by alkali treatment or over a HZSM-22 zeolite modified by an alkali-acid treatment as catalysts in the first reactor, in combination with a Zn impregnated acid-treated-HZSM-5 zeolite have shown to be efficient catalyst pairs for the synthesis of pyridine bases from glycerol in two-step processes. When using acrolein or acrolein diacetals, the most active catalysts were a 4.6%Cu–1.0%Ru/HZSM-5 zeolite in the presence of hydrogen, and a ZnO/HZSM-5-At-acid zeolite.

Keywords: pyridine, picolines, alkylpyridines, lutidines, glycerol, acrolein, zeolite catalyst, ammonia

1. Introduction

Pyridine bases are a family of aromatic heterocyclic compounds of commercial interest since they found applications as solvents in organic reactions, and as precursors of drugs, polymers, insecticides, herbicides, dyes, and adhesives, being pyridine, the series of picolines (α-, β-, and γ-picoline) and some lutidines the most important [1, 2].

The pyridine (azabenzene) structure is defined by a six-membered ring consisting of five carbon atoms and one nitrogen atom (**Figure 1**). It can be considered as an analog of benzene in which one CH group is replaced by a nitrogen atom [3]. On the other hand, the simplest alkyl-substituted pyridines are α-picoline (2-methylpyridine), β-picoline (3-methylpyridine), and γ-picoline (4-methylpyridine), whose structures vary

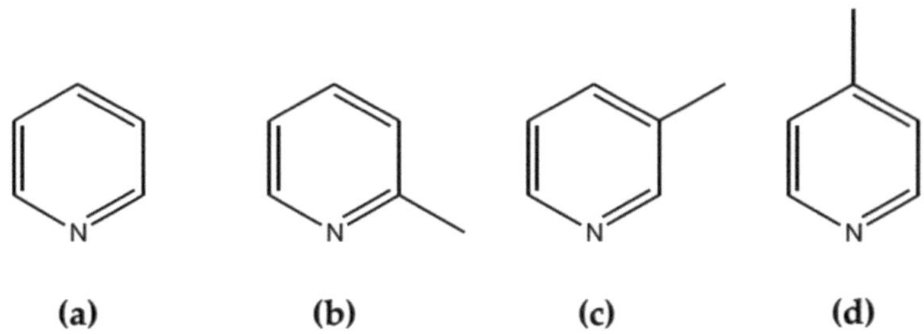

Figure 1.
Chemical structures of (a) pyridine, (b) α-picoline, (c) β-picoline, and (d) γ-picoline.

according to the location where the methyl group is attached to the pyridine ring, either in position 2, 3, or 4 regarding the nitrogen atom. Physically, pyridine and picolines are considered to be dipolar, aprotic solvents, similar to dimethylformamide or dimethyl sulfoxide. They are colorless, flammable, irritating, toxic liquids with an unpleasant odor, and miscible in water and in most organic solvents [2, 3].

The chemical properties of pyridines are related to their structure, that is, ring aromaticity, presence of a basic ring nitrogen atom, π-deficient character of the ring, large permanent dipole moment, easy polarizability of the π-electrons, activation of functional groups attached to the ring, and presence of electron-deficient carbon atom centers at the α- and γ- positions. One or more of these factors can lead to different reactions of pyridine bases, namely electrophilic attack at nitrogen, electrophilic attack at carbon, nucleophilic attack at carbon or hydrogen, and free radical attack at carbon, besides varied substitution reactions of the carbon with N, O, S, halogen, or alkyl groups in the alkylpyridines [2].

The first industrial method for the production of pyridines was by their extraction from fossil sources such as coal tar, oil, and shale. However, it was only possible to obtain yields of less than 0.1% from a mixture of different pyridine bases and other organic compounds. In addition, the products obtained by this process had high sulfur contents, making it impossible to use them in pharmaceutical and agrochemical applications. So that, with a few exceptions, obtaining pyridine compounds by this method was expensive and had not been able to cover the industrial demand [3, 4].

Nowadays, the industrial synthesis of pyridine is based on the aminocyclization reaction (condensation/cyclization) between formaldehyde, acetaldehyde, and ammonia (NH_3) using a ZSM-5 catalyst as shown in Eq. (1). This method generates a mixture of α-, β-, and γ-picoline as byproducts [1].

$2\,CH_3CHO + H_2C{=}O + NH_3 \longrightarrow$ 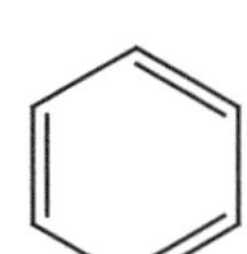 $+\,3\,H_2O + H_2$ (1)

Also, the reaction between acrolein and ammonia has been used for the synthesis of β-picoline and pyridine by means of two parallel reactions, as shown in stoichiometric Eqs. (2a) and (2b). This process allows to modulate the products selectivity, avoiding the formation of α- and γ-picoline, being β-picoline the main reaction product [1].

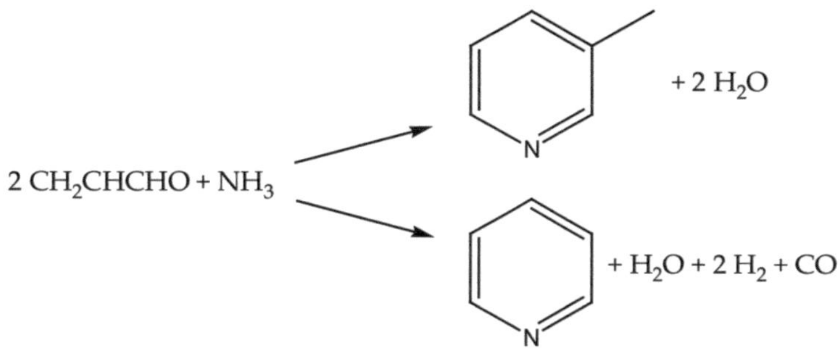

(2a)

(2b)

Despite these synthesis methods, the high demand of pyridine bases has led to research on the use of different raw materials, such as aldehydes, ketones, and alcohols, from renewable sources, to improve the yield of a desired product [5, 6].

On the other hand, glycerol has gained importance as raw material in several catalytic processes, namely hydrogenolysis, dehydration, oxidation, and esterification, since it is industrially obtained as byproduct in the production of biodiesel from vegetable and algae oils [7]. Specifically, the aminocyclization reaction between glycerol and ammonia represents a potential alternative to the current industrial process for the synthesis of pyridine compounds, based on petroleum-derived aldehydes [8–13]. In addition, the acrolein obtained by the catalytic dehydration of glycerol can also be used as feedstock for the production of pyridine bases [14–16].

In this context, this chapter presents the advances on the catalysts and reactor configurations employed for the synthesis of pyridine bases using glycerol and its derivatives, acrolein, and acrolein dialkyl acetals as raw materials.

2. Synthesis of pyridine bases from glycerol in single-step processes

The synthesis of pyridine compounds from glycerol, in batch and continuous one-pot systems, has been reported, under pyrolysis or microwave heating conditions [8]. In the batch pyrolysis, pure glycerol and an ammonium salt, such as $(NH_4)_2HPO_4$, $NH_4H_2PO_4$, $(NH_4)_2SO_4$, NH_4Cl, NH_4OAc, or $H_2NNH_2{\cdot}H_2SO_4$, were packed into a glass tubular reactor. The system was heated to a desired temperature and the reaction was carried out for about 1.5 h. The reason for using ammonium salts was to provide an acidic environment required for the conversion of glycerol to acrolein. Additionally, under thermal conditions, ammonium salts would decompose and release gaseous ammonia for its condensation and cyclization with the acrolein produced from glycerol. A mixture of pyridine and β-picoline was obtained and the highest product yield (36%) was reached when reacting glycerol with $(NH_4)_2HPO_4$ at 450°C. However, glycerol also produced other volatile compounds, which polymerize with acrolein, resulting in tar formation and low product yields.

In the continuous system, an aqueous glycerol solution was fed to a tubular reactor, previously loaded with the ammonium salt and heated at 450°C. The best result (40% product yield) was obtained with $(NH_4)_2HPO_4$ and a mixture of 1 g glycerol and 7.2 ml H_2O. A mixture of pyridine, β-picoline, ethylpyridine, and ethylmethylpyridines was obtained, suggesting that during thermal degradation of glycerol, both acrolein and acetaldehyde were obtained as products. The low yield of pyridines was attributed to the uncontrolled formation and subsequent polymerization of acrolein at the reaction temperature [8].

For the microwave-assisted synthesis, glycerol and the ammonium salt were placed and closed into a glass vial, stirred, and subsequently irradiated by microwave energy to complete the reaction. The authors found that the addition of an organic acid, such as acetic acid, benzoic acid, or *p*-toluenesulfonic acid, improved the formation of pyridine bases [8].

On the other hand, the configuration of the continuous-flow fixed-bed reactor presented in **Figure 2** has been commonly used to evaluate the performance of solid catalysts for the gas-phase synthesis of pyridines from glycerol. The reactor, previously loaded with a certain amount of catalyst and heated at a required temperature, is fed at the top of the reactor with a gaseous stream composed of water, glycerol, and nitrogen (N_2) as carrier gas. At the same time, a flow of preheated ammonia is introduced to react with the glycerol stream by effect of the catalyst. The stream at the reactor outlet contains the pyridine bases and byproducts.

The direct synthesis of pyridine bases from glycerol was performed in a continuous-flow fixed-bed reactor in presence of zeolite catalysts, using ammonia as carrier gas and as the reactive nitrogen source [9]. It was found that the optimal conditions were 550°C, a weight-hourly space-velocity (WHSV) of glycerol of 1 h^{-1}, a NH_3/glycerol molar ratio of 12/1, and HZSM-5 zeolite (Si/Al = 25) as a catalyst. Total conversion of glycerol was reached with a total yield of pyridines around 35.6%. Pyridine was the main reaction product with a selectivity of 70.7%, while α-, β-, and γ-picoline exhibited selectivities of 8.6%, 17.8%, and 2.9%, respectively. Gaseous compounds, such as CH_4, C_2H_4, C_3H_6, and CO, added a yield of 49.3%, and aromatics were produced at around 2.2% yield. After five reaction/regeneration cycles, a slight deactivation of the catalyst was observed.

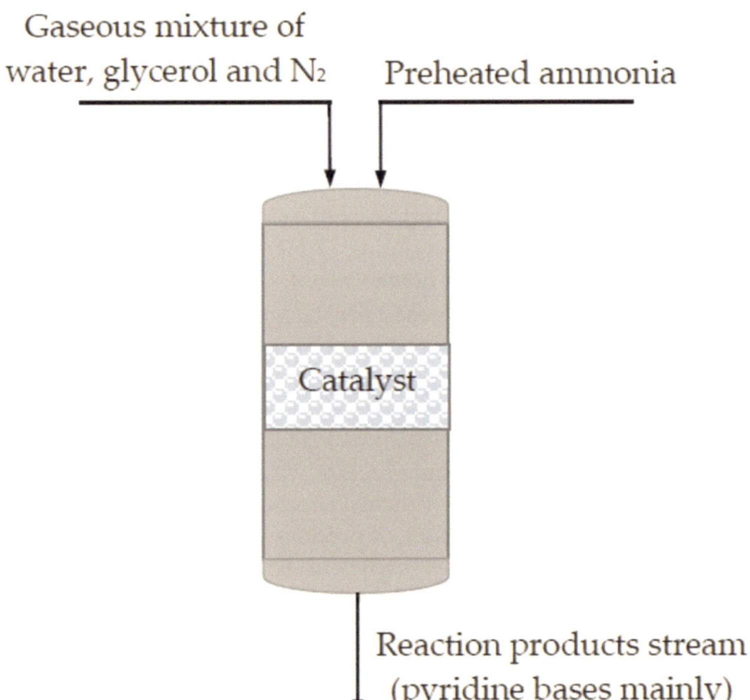

Figure 2.
Continuous-flow fixed-bed reactor for the single-step gas-phase aminocyclization between glycerol and ammonia.

The gas-phase aminocyclization between glycerol and ammonia in presence of a Cu/HZSM-5 catalyst has also been reported [10]. The reaction was performed in a fixed-bed reactor using a catalyst with 4.6% Cu supported on HZSM-5 zeolite with a ratio Si/Al = 38. The identified products were pyridine, α-picoline, β-picoline, acetonitrile, propionitrile, acetaldehyde, propylene, ethylene, and CO_2. The best reaction conditions were 520°C, atmospheric pressure, a NH_3/glycerol molar ratio of 7/1, and a gas-hourly space-velocity (GHSV) of 300 h^{-1}, reaching a total yield of pyridines around 42.8%, 34.9% of pyridine yield, 2.4% of α-picoline, and 5.5% of β-picoline yield, respectively.

The synthesis of pyridine bases from glycerol over a series of modified ZSM-5 zeolites in a continuous fixed-bed reactor was reported [11]. The catalysts tested were a series of metal oxide-impregnated ZSM-5 zeolite (ZnO, La_2O_3, and Fe_2O_3) , an alkali-treated zeolite (HZSM-5-At), and the alkali-acid treated ZSM-5 and ZSM-22 zeolites (HZSM-5-At-acid and HZSM-22-At-acid, respectively). The identified products in this process were pyridine, α-picoline, β-picoline, γ-picoline, small amounts of 3-ethylpyridine, 2-methyl-5-ethylpyridine, 3,5-dimethylpyridine, and benzene derivatives, as well as trace amounts of COx and $C_1 - C_2$ hydrocarbons. At 425°C; LHSV = 0.60 h^{-1}, glycerol concentration of 36 wt%, molar ratio NH_3/glycerol = 4/1, and time on stream (TOS) between 1 and 3 h, the HZSM-5-At-acid catalyst gave the highest total yield of pyridines (28.76%), with yields of pyridine, α-picoline, β-picoline, and γ-picoline around 15.67%, 1.90%, 10.02%, and 1.17%, respectively.

A composite zeolite HZSM-5/11 (SiO_2/Al_2O_3 = 78) has been synthesized and employed as a catalyst in the reaction between an aqueous solution of 20 wt% glycerol and ammonia in a fixed-bed reactor [12]. The products obtained using this catalyst were pyridine, α-picoline, β-picoline, acetonitrile, propionitrile, acetaldehyde, C_2H_4, and C_3H_6. The analysis of the process variables on the synthesis of pyridines revealed that the optimal reaction conditions were a reaction temperature of 520°C, a molar ratio NH_3/glycerol of 12/1, and a GHSV of 300 h^{-1}. At these conditions, glycerol reached total conversion and the total yield of pyridines was 40.8%, with selectivities of pyridine, α-picoline, and β-picoline around 27.7%, 2.6%, and 10.5%, respectively.

3. Synthesis of pyridine bases from glycerol in two-step processes with acrolein as intermediate

The conversion of glycerol to pyridine bases has also been carried out by first producing acrolein, and subsequently reacting it with ammonia [11, 13]. This process can be performed in a system with two coupled reactors. As shown in **Figure 3**, an aqueous solution of glycerol and a N_2 flow are mixed, preheated/vaporized and fed to the first reactor, which was previously loaded with a solid acid catalyst. In this first stage of the process, the catalytic dehydration of glycerol to acrolein takes place at temperatures between 280°C and 350°C.

Subsequently, the stream of dehydration products is introduced to the second reactor, which is simultaneously fed with preheated ammonia to carry out the aminocyclization reaction between acrolein and ammonia to produce pyridine bases in presence of an acid catalyst at temperatures between 375°C and 475°C. Both reactors can be loaded with the same or different acid catalyst. According to literature, this process allows to improve the total yield of pyridines by performing separately the dehydration and aminocyclization reactions at adequate temperatures [11, 13].

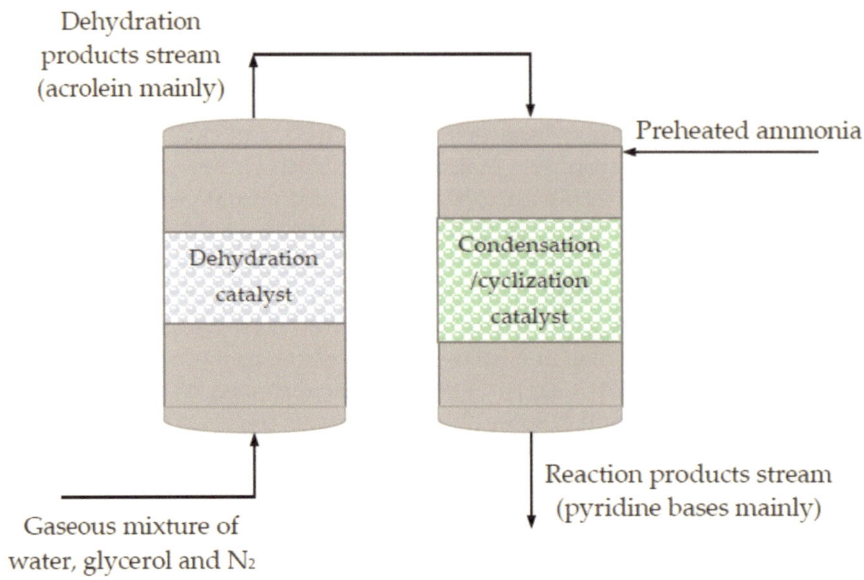

Figure 3.
Continuous flow reaction system for the two-step gas-phase conversion of glycerol and ammonia to pyridine bases. Adapted from ref. [11].

Luo et al. [11] performed the synthesis of pyridines from glycerol in a two-step system comprised of a pair of reactors connected in series with different catalysts, denoted as a catalyst pair. The catalysts tested in the first reactor were the HZSM-5, HZSM-5-At, and HZSM-5-At-acid zeolites, while for the second reactor the HZSM-5-At-acid and the ZnO/HZSM-5-At-acid zeolites were evaluated. The reaction products identified in this process were pyridine, α-picoline, β-picoline, γ-picoline, 3-ethylpyridine, 2-methyl-5-ethylpyridine, 3,5-dimethylpyridine, benzene derivatives, trace amounts of COx, and $C_1 - C_2$ hydrocarbons. The best results were obtained with the catalyst pair (HZSM-5-At + ZnO/HZSM-5-At-acid) at 330°C for the first reactor; 425°C for the second reactor; LHSV = 0.45 h^{-1}; a glycerol concentration of 20 wt %; a molar ratio NH_3/glycerol = 5/1; and TOS between 1 and 3 h, obtaining a total yield of pyridine bases around 62.25%, without the formation of γ-picoline.

Similarly, Zhang et al. [13] performed the conversion of glycerol to pyridine bases in a system of two series-connected reactors. The catalytic dehydration of a 20 wt.% glycerol aqueous solution to acrolein was accomplished at 280°C in the first reactor over an alumina (γ-Al_2O_3) catalyst modified with Fe and P. The output stream from the first reactor was fed to the second one, previously loaded with a $Cu_{4.6}Pr_{0.3}$/HZSM-5 catalyst, which reacted with ammonia to produce pyridine compounds. The identified products were pyridine, α-picoline, β-picoline, 2,4-lutidine, acetonitrile, propionitrile, ethylene, propylene, butylene, and CO_2. At optimal reaction conditions, that is, 420°C in the second reactor, atmospheric pressure, GHSV = 300 h^{-1}, and NH_3/acrolein molar ratio of 7/1; glycerol achieved total conversion and the total yield of pyridines was 60.2%, while pyridine and β-picoline reached 39% and 20% yield, respectively. The impregnation of the zeolite with Cu and Pr resulted in the increase of the Lewis acidity and an improved dehydrogenation activity, enhancing the selectivity toward pyridine bases.

4. Synthesis of pyridine bases from acrolein and acrolein derivatives

Currently, the catalytic dehydration of glycerol, in the presence of a solid acid catalyst, is under research since it is considered a sustainable alternative method to the industrial process based on the partial oxidation of propylene for the synthesis of acrolein [14–16]. The use of acrolein for the synthesis of pyridine bases allows to modulate the products selectivity, enhancing the production of β-picoline and pyridine, without the formation of other pyridine compounds [3].

The synthesis of pyridine bases from acrolein in a batch process has been barely reported. The liquid-phase reaction of acrolein with ammonium acetate (CH_3COONH_4) over a SO_4^{2-}/ZrO_2-FeZSM-5 catalyst was reported [17]. The process requires the addition of a C_2-C_6 carboxylic acid, preferably acetic acid (CH_3COOH), as the reaction medium and solvent of acrolein. It was found that only β-picoline was generated, without the formation of any other pyridine compound. At the optimal conditions of 130°C as reaction temperature, a concentration of 14 wt% acrolein in the solution, a liquid flow of acrolein solution of 12 ml/h, and a catalyst usage of 0.7 g/g acrolein, the yield of β-picoline reached 60%. The presence of a carboxylic acid promoted the formation of β-picoline and retarded the polymerization of acrolein and its intermediate propylene imine.

Schematized in **Figure 4**, the gas-phase reaction between acrolein and ammonia in a continuous-flow fixed-bed reactor has also been reported [18–20]. Similarly, to the continuous single-step process described in Section 2, a preheated gaseous mixture of water, acrolein, and nitrogen is fed to the reactor previously loaded with a solid acid catalyst and heated to the reaction temperature. Simultaneously, a preheated flow of ammonia is introduced at the same end of the reactor as the acrolein stream, to come into contact with the catalytic bed and producing the pyridine bases.

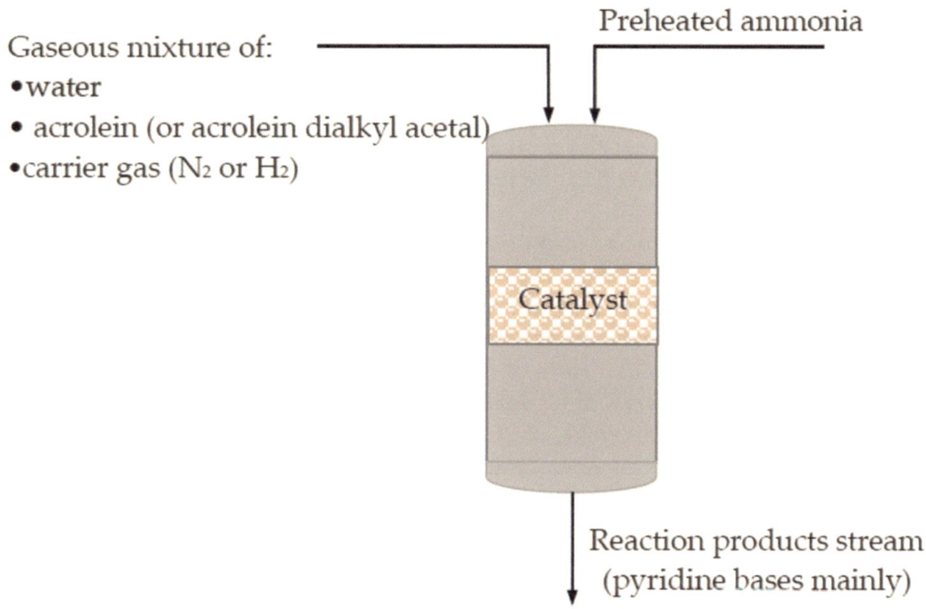

Figure 4.
Continuous-flow fixed-bed reactor for the gas-phase aminocyclization between acrolein and ammonia.

This process has been studied with greater versatility than the direct reaction with glycerol, since the use of hydrogen as carrier gas has been explored, as well as the use of acrolein derivatives as raw material, specifically acrolein dialkyl acetals [21, 22].

The gas-phase reaction between acrolein and ammonia was studied by comparing the activity of a parent H-ZSM-5 catalyst and a series of zeolites modified with magnesium nitrate ($Mg(NO_3)_2$), hydrofluoric acid (HF), or both [18]. The reaction was performed at atmospheric pressure and 425°C in a fixed-bed reactor. When using the HF/MgZSM-5 catalyst, the total yield of pyridines achieved its maximum value (58.86%), with 30.38% being β-picoline and 26.59% being pyridine.

The use of hydrogen as a carrier gas in the synthesis of pyridine bases from acrolein and ammonia has been explored in presence of bimetallic copper-based ZSM-5 catalysts [19]. The identified products in this process were pyridine, α-picoline, β-picoline, 2,4-lutidine, acetonitrile, propionitrile, ethylene, propylene, butylene, and CO_2. Among the tested catalysts, the 4.6%Cu–1.0%Ru/HZSM-5 zeolite produced the highest total yield of pyridines (69.4%) with pyridine and β-picoline yields around 27% and 37%, respectively, performing the reaction at 420°C, acrolein concentration of 20 wt.%, molar ratio NH_3/acrolein = 3.5/1, GHSV = 300 h^{-1}, and H_2 flow of 8.5 ml/min as optimal reaction conditions. The presence of Cu, Ru, and hydrogen enhanced the hydrogenation/dehydrogenation activity of the catalyst, promoting the conversion of acrolein to propionaldehyde, improving thus the formation of pyridine bases, notably of β-picoline. Additionally, the catalyst was stable with TOS, maintaining the total conversion of acrolein during 40 h, and decreasing gradually to 90.5% at 75 h of TOS.

The use of a catalyst other than ZSM-5 zeolite has been scarcely reported for the synthesis of pyridine bases from acrolein. Specifically, Y-type zeolites with different Si/Al composition has been reported as catalysts in the reaction between acrolein and ammonia at 360°C, pure acrolein, molar ratio NH_3/acrolein = 2, and GHSV = 4994 h^{-1} [20]. The best catalytic performance was obtained with the catalyst with an atomic ratio Si/Al = 45. The acrolein conversion was around 93% while the pyridine and β-picoline yields were 15% and 19.1%, respectively. However, formaldehyde and acetaldehyde were also detected as reaction products and the catalysts were rapidly deactivated. It was found that the total acidity of the catalysts was the key factor for the conversion of acrolein and the type of acid sites influenced the products selectivity.

Acrolein dialkyl acetals have also been used as reagents for the synthesis of pyridines [21, 22]. When performing the gas-phase reaction between acrolein diethyl acetal and ammonia in a continuous fixed-bed reactor, the ZnO/HZSM-5 zeolite has shown superior catalytic performance than ZnO/HY and ZnO/α-Al_2O_3 catalysts. At 450°C; LHSV = 0.85 h^{-1}; molar ratio of NH_3/(acrolein diethyl acetal) = 4; TOS between 1 and 3 h; and 1 wt.% of Zn loading, the total yield of pyridines was 61.14%, with pyridine and β-picoline yields of 26.87% and 34.27%, respectively [21].

Similarly, the reaction between acrolein dimethyl acetal and ammonia was performed over a series of ZSM-5 zeolites treated with $Mg(NO_3)_2$, NH_4F-HF, or both [22]. The reaction products were pyridine, α-picoline, β-picoline, and 3,5-dimethylpyridine. At 450°C, LHSV = 0.75 h^{-1}, molar ratio NH_3/(acrolein dimethyl acetal) = 3.5/1, TOS = 1–3 h, and F/Mg-ZSM-5 catalyst with small particle size; the highest total yield of pyridines was 55.4%, with 14.5% for pyridine, 0.9% of α-picoline, 34.2% of β-picoline, and 5.8% yield of 3,5-dimethylpyridine. The catalytic activity of the catalyst was related to an adequate concentration of total acid sites and a ratio B/L < 1.

5. The effect of catalyst acidic properties on the synthesis of pyridine bases from glycerol and acrolein

The reaction conditions and catalytic performance of representative zeolite catalysts reported in the literature for the gas-phase synthesis of pyridine bases from glycerol, acrolein, and acrolein dialkyl acetals in fixed-bed reactors are presented in **Table 1**.

The main features that affect the catalytic performance of these catalysts in the synthesis of pyridine bases are their acidic properties, namely the type and strength of acid sites. In the single-step process, the reaction between glycerol and ammonia takes place through a complex network of simultaneous and subsequent reactions, among which the most relevant for the synthesis of pyridine bases are the catalytic dehydration of glycerol to acrolein, and its subsequent condensation/cyclization with ammonia to produce pyridine bases. Both reactions proceed at the same time in the single

Catalyst	Feedstock composition[a]	T(°C)[b]	Space-velocity (h^{-1})	X (%)[f]	Y (%)[g]	TOS (h)[h]	Coke (wt. %)[i]	Ref.
HZSM-5	Pure gly, NH_3/gly = 12/1	550	1[c]	100	Total = 36 Py = 25.2 αP = 3.1 βP = 6.3 γP = 1.0	—	10	[9]
4.6%Cu/HZSM-5	20 wt% gly aq. soln., NH_3/gly = 7/1	520	300[d]	100	Total = 43 Py = 34.9 αP = 2.4 βP = 5.5	32	27.4	[10]
HZSM-5-At-acid	36 wt% gly aq. soln., NH_3/gly = 4/1	425	0.60[e]	100	Total = 29 Py = 15.7 αP = 1.9 βP = 10.0 γP = 1.2	11	N.R.	[11]
HZSM-5/11	20 wt% gly aq. soln., NH_3/gly = 12/1	520	300[d]	100	Total = 41 Py = 27.7 αP = 2.6 βP = 10.5	2	N.R.	[12]
Two-step process HZSM-5-At + ZnO/HZSM-5-At-acid	20 wt% gly aq. soln., NH_3/gly = 5/1	T_1 = 330 T_2 = 425	0.45[e]	100	Total = 62 Py = 35.8 αP = 0.06 βP = 25.8	11	N.R.	[11]
Two-step process FeP/γ-Al_2O_3 Cu4.6Pr0.3/HZSM-5	20 wt% gly aq. soln., NH_3/gly = 7/1	T_1 = 280 T_2 = 420	300[d]	100	Total = 60 Py = 39 βP = 20.2 2,4-L = 1	10	N.R.	[13]
HF/ MgZSM-5	Molar ratio acr/H_2O/NH_3 = 1/2/2	425	500[d]	100	Total = 59 Py = 26.6 βP = 30.4	12	N.R.	[18]
4.6%Cu-1%Ru/HZSM-5	20 wt% acr. aq. soln., NH_3/acr = 3.5/1	420	300[d]	100	Total = 69 Py = 27 βP = 37 2,4-L = 5.4	75	14	[19]

Catalyst	Feedstock composition[a]	T(°C)[b]	Space-velocity (h^{-1})	X (%)[f]	Y (%)[g]	TOS (h)[h]	Coke (wt. %)[i]	Ref.
Y-45	Pure acr., molar ratio acr/ NH_3= 1/2	360	4994[d]	92.9	Total = 34 Py = 15 βP = 19.1	0.75	22.5	[20]
1%Zn/ HZSM-5	Molar ratio (acr. Diethyl acetal)/ NH_3/H_2O = 1/4/1	450	0.85[e]	100	Total = 61 Py = 26.9 βP = 34.3	11	8	[21]

[a] gly = glycerol, acr = acrolein, [b] T = reaction temperature, [c] WHSV = weight hourly space-velocity, [d] GHSV = gas hourly space-velocity, [e] LHSV = liquid hourly space-velocity, [f] X = feedstock conversion, [g] Y = product yield, Total = total yield of pyridine bases, Py = yield of pyridine, αP = yield of α-picoline, βP = yield of β-picoline, γP = yield of γ-picoline, 2,4-L = yield of 2,4-lutidine, 3,5-DMP = yield of 3,5-dimethyl pyridine, [h] TOS = time on stream, [i] N.R. = not reported.

Table 1.
Reaction conditions and catalytic performance of zeolite catalysts during the synthesis of pyridine bases from glycerol, acrolein, and acrolein dialkyl acetals in continuous systems.

catalytic bed [9–12]. In the two-stage systems, these reactions occurred independently in interconnected reactors [11, 13].

As presented in Eq. (3a), the production of acrolein from glycerol occurs primarily over the Brønsted acid sites (BAS) of the catalyst. However, other dehydration products are obtained, that is, the conversion of glycerol to acetol proceeds over Lewis acid sites (LAS) as in Eq. (3b), while formaldehyde and acetaldehyde can be produced from glycerol (Eq. 3c) or acetol, either over BAS or LAS. Depending on the type of catalyst and the reaction conditions, minor amounts of byproducts, such as aldehydes, ketones, carboxylic acids, and alcohols, in the range of C_1–C_3 may be obtained from the glycerol dehydration reaction [14, 15].

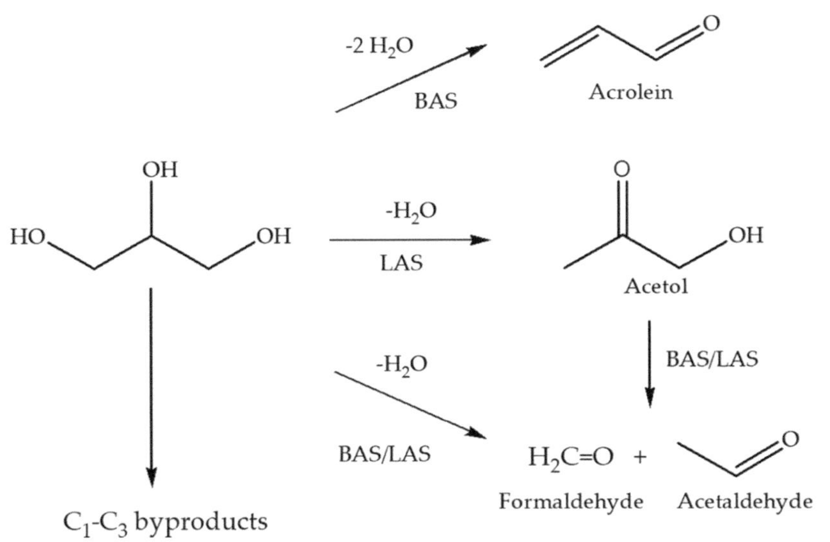

(3a)

(3b)

(3c)

Furthermore, the reaction between acrolein and ammonia proceeds in acid medium, that is, a carboxylic acid in homogeneous reactions or over a solid acid catalyst in heterogeneous systems, mostly a ZSM-5 catalyst. Infrared spectroscopy and theoretical studies have demonstrated that acrolein can react with ammonia over LAS and BAS, producing propylene imine(prop-2-en-1-imine). This compound can undergo a Michael reaction over Brønsted or weak Lewis acid sites, condensing with another propylene imine, closing the ring structure, and producing β-picoline with the liberation of ammonia, as in Eq. (4a) [23, 24].

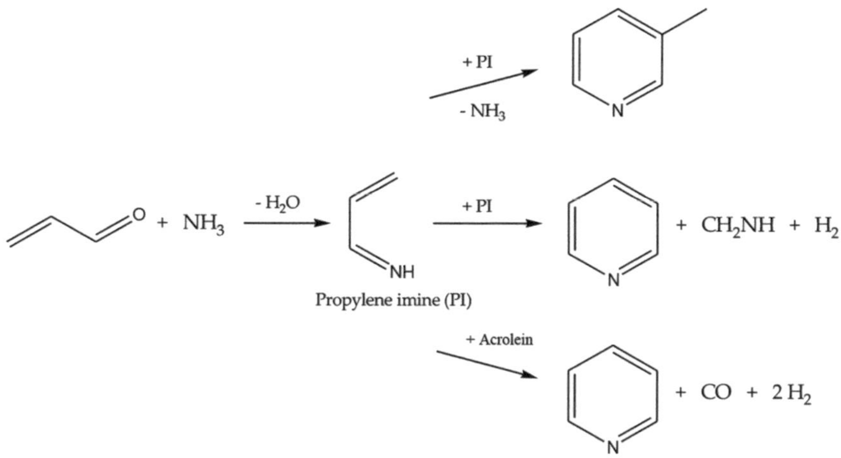

(4a)

(4b)

(4c)

Additionally, as shown in Eqs. (4b) and (4c), the formation of pyridine takes place by a Diels-Alder reaction over strong Lewis sites, in which propylene imine condensates and cyclizes with acrolein or with another propylene imine, releasing CO or CH_2NH, respectively [23, 24]. Similar reaction steps and imine intermediates have been reported in the reaction between formaldehyde, acetaldehyde, and ammonia obtaining pyridine, α-picoline, β-picoline, and γ-picoline as products [24, 25].

Experimental studies have revealed the importance of catalyst acidity on the synthesis of pyridine bases. The effect of the Si/Al molar ratio of HZSM-5 zeolites on the reaction between glycerol and ammonia has been reported [9]. The increase of the Si/Al ratio from 25 to 80 decreased the total acidity from 580.6 to 92.4 μmol/g, resulting in the decrease of the total yield of pyridines with 26%, 22.85%, and 20.9% for Si/Al ratios of 25, 50, and 80, respectively. However, the pyridine selectivity increased from 67.3% to 69.3% and 72.3%, while the selectivity to β-picoline decreased from 21.4% to 17.9% and 16.1% in the same order.

The influence of acidity on the catalytic activity of a series of Cu/HZSM-5 zeolites, with Si/Al molar ratios of 25, 38, 50, 80, and 117, has been explored [10]. The total yield of pyridines increased from 40–43% with the change al Si/Al from 25 to 50. The further increase in the Si/Al ratio resulted in the decrease of the total yield of pyridines and pyridine. It was concluded that an appropriate proportion of BAS and LAS in the catalyst is a key factor for the synthesis of pyridine bases. However, the BAS/LAS ratio is not the only factor affecting the catalytic activity, but also the structure of HZSM-5 and the amount of Cu which enhanced the dehydrogenation/hydrogenation activity of the catalyst.

The acidity of a series of Mg- and HF-modified zeolites affected the gas-phase reaction between acrolein and ammonia [18]. The total yield of pyridines was 8.81%, 52.73%, and 58.86% for the MgZSM-5, HF/ZSM-5, and HF/MgZSM-5 catalysts, respectively. The MgZSM-5 zeolite presented a large quantity of acid sites and a low yield of pyridine bases, while the HF/ZSM-5 and HF/MgZSM-5 exhibited weaker and fewer acid sites and high yields of pyridine compounds. A certain concentration of

Brønsted acid sites and weak Lewis acid sites may promote the formation of β-picoline, while a high concentration of strong acid sites favored the synthesis of pyridine and polymers. It was concluded that the concentration and strength of acid sites promote the formation of pyridine bases, that is, proper amounts of BAS and weak LAS are necessary for the acrolein activation and pyridines formation, as well as the decrease in the formation of polymerization products (coke precursors).

A critical point of these processes is the catalyst deactivation by the deposition of carbonaceous compounds, which are formed by the polymerization of reaction products by the effect of the acid sites of the catalyst. Additionally, pyridine bases are strongly adsorbed on the acidic sites of the catalyst, being decomposed into carbon depositions [18, 20, 21]. In this sense, a proper amount and strength of acid sites can allow to control the polymerization reactions, and thus the catalyst deactivation.

In the direct reaction between glycerol and ammonia over molecular sieves, namely β-zeolite, MCM-41, and ZSM-5, the coke yield of the catalysts were 30.1%, 19.4%, and 13.7%, respectively, in agreement with the total acidity of the catalysts [9], as shown in **Figure 5**.

The comparison of HZSM-5 and ZnO/HZSM-5 catalysts in the reaction of acrolein diethyl acetal with ammonia, showed that both catalysts suffer a rapid deactivation resulting in the decrease of the total yield of pyridines. However, the ZnO/HZSM-5 zeolite, with a minor amount of total acid sites and a higher amount of weak acid sites than the HZSM-5 catalyst, exhibited the highest yield of pyridines even at longer TOS [21].

The characterization of the catalysts after reaction by ^{13}C NMR, FTIR, and Raman spectroscopies has suggested that the coke formed on the zeolites (Y and ZSM-5) was constituted by aliphatic species with alkoxy groups, as well as large polyaromatic compounds, when using formaldehyde, acetaldehyde, acrolein, and acrolein diethyl acetal as reactants for the synthesis of pyridine bases [20, 26, 27].

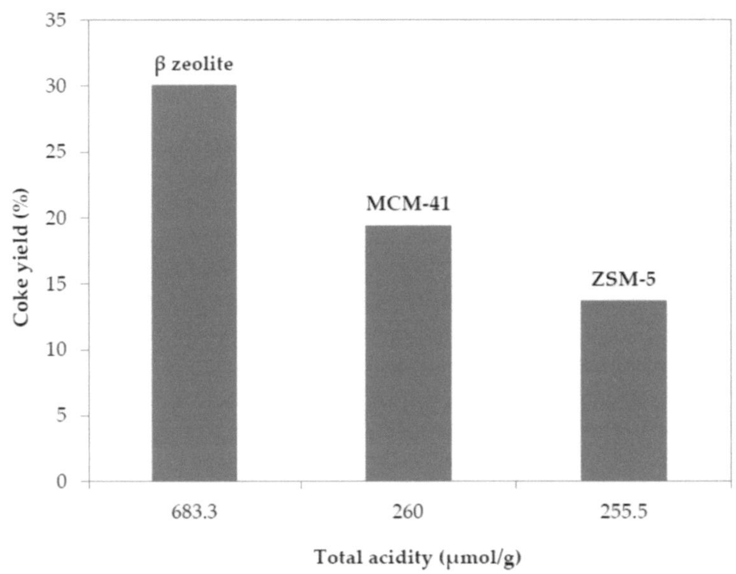

Figure 5.
Effect of the total acidity on the coke yield of molecular sieve catalysts in the reaction between glycerol and ammonia. Adapted from ref. [9].

6. Conclusions

Pyridine bases can be obtained from glycerol and ammonia by an aminocyclization reaction, either in single-step or two-step processes. Glycerol derivatives, such as acrolein and acrolein dialkyl acetals, can also be used as raw materials for this reaction. The main process variables are the reaction temperature, the concentration of a reactant in water, the NH_3/reactant molar ratio, and the space velocity in continuous fixed-bed reactors. When using glycerol as feedstock in the single-step process, the reactors operate usually at temperatures between 450°C and 550°C. The two-step process allows us to improve the total yield of pyridines by performing separately the dehydration and aminocyclization reactions at adequate temperatures, this is 280–350°C and 375–450°C for the first and second reactor, respectively. Single-step processes with acrolein or acrolein dialkyl acetals require reaction temperatures between 420°C and 450°C. The catalysts for the revisited processes are based on ZSM-5 zeolite. The most active catalyst for the direct synthesis from glycerol is Cu/HZSM-5, while for the two-step process, the catalyst pair (HZSM-5-At + ZnO/HZSM-5-At-acid) exhibits higher activity and selectivity. When using acrolein, the most active catalyst is a 4.6%Cu-1%Ru/HZSM-5 zeolite with hydrogen as a carrier gas, while a 1%Zn/HZSM-5 catalyst showed the highest yield of pyridines using acrolein diethyl acetal as raw material.

Acknowledgements

The authors acknowledge the Instituto Politécnico Nacional and the Universidad Autónoma Metropolitana for their support to develop this investigation. I. Pala-Rosas thanks the support of the company Síntesis y Aplicaciones Industriales S.A.

Conflict of interest

The authors declare no conflict of interest.

Author details

Israel Pala-Rosas[1], José L. Contreras[2*], José Salmones[1], Ricardo López-Medina[2], Beatriz Zeifert[1] and Naomi N. González Hernández[2]

1 Higher School of Chemical Engineering and Extractive Industries, National Polytechnic Institute, Mexico City, Mexico

2 CBI-Energy, Autonomous Metropolitan University-Azcapotzalco, Mexico City, Mexico

*Address all correspondence to: jlcl@azc.uam.mx

References

[1] Shimizu S, Watanabe N, Kataoka T, Shoji T, Abe N, Morishita S, et al. Pyridine and pyridine derivatives. In: Ullmann's Encyclopedia of Industrial Chemistry. Weinheim, Germany: Wiley-VCH Verlag GmbH & Co. KGaA; 2012. pp. 557-589. DOI: 10.1002/14356007.a22_399

[2] Scriven EFV, Murugan R. Pyridine and pyridine derivatives. In: Kirk-Othmer Encyclopedia of Chemical Technology. Vol. 21. Hoboken, New Jersey, United States of America: John Wiley & Sons, Inc.; March 2007. ISBN: 978-0-471-48496-7

[3] Yurkanis BP. Organic Chemistry. Mishawaka, IN, USA: Prentice Hall; 2004

[4] Weissberger A, Taylor EC. The Chemistry of Heterocyclic Compounds: Pyridine and its Derivatives, Part 1. Vol. 14. Hoboken, New Jersey, United States of America: John Wiley & Sons, Inc; 1974. Print ISBN: 9780471379133. DOI: 10.1002/9780470186633

[5] Sagitullin RS, Shkil' GP, Nosonova II, Ferber AA. Synthesis of pyridine bases by the Chichibabin method (review). Chemistry of Heterocyclic Compounds. 1996;**32**(2):127-140. DOI: 10.1007/BF01165434

[6] Lazdin'sh IY, Avots AA. Catalytic methods of obtaining pyridine bases (survey). Chemistry of Heterocyclic Compounds. 1979;**15**(8):823-837. DOI: 10.1007/BF00509781

[7] Almena A, Bueno L, Díez M, Martín M. Integrated biodiesel facilities: Review of glycerol based production of fuels and chemicals. Clean Technologies and Environmental Policy. 2018;**20**:1639-1661. DOI: 10.1007/s10098-017-1424-z

[8] Bayramoglu D, Gurel G, Sinag A, Gullu M. Thermal conversion of glycerol to value added chemicals: Pyridine derivatives by one-pot microwave-assisted synthesis. Turkish Journal of Chemistry. 2014;**38**:661-670. DOI: 10.3906/kim-1312-47

[9] Xu L, Han Z, Yao Q, Deng J, Zhang Y, Fu Y, et al. Towards the sustainable production of pyridines via thermo-catalytic conversion of glycerol with ammonia over zeolite catalysts. Green Chemistry. 2015;**17**:2426-2435. DOI: 10.1039/c4gc02235a

[10] Zhang Y, Yan X, Niu B, Zhao J. A study on the conversion of glycerol to pyridine bases over Cu/HZSM-5 catalysts. Green Chemistry. 2016;**18**: 3139-3151. DOI: 10.1039/c6gc00038j

[11] Luo CW, Huang C, Li A, Yi WJ, Feng XY, Xu ZJ, et al. Influence of reaction parameters on the catalytic performance of alkaline-treated zeolites in the novel synthesis of pyridine bases from glycerol and ammonia. Industrial and Engineering Chemistry Research. 2016;**55**:893-911. DOI: 10.1021/ie504934n

[12] Zhang Y, Zhai X, Zhang H, Zhao J. Enhanced selectivity in the conversion of glycerol to pyridine bases over HZSM-5/11 intergrowth zeolite. RSC Advances. 2017;**7**:23647-23656. DOI: 10.1039/c7ra02311a

[13] Zhang Y, Zhang W, Zhang HY, Yin G, Zhao J. Continuous two-step catalytic conversion of glycerol to pyridine bases in high yield. Catalysis Today. 2019;**319**:220-228. DOI: 10.1016/j.cattod.2018.03.035

[14] Galadima A, Muraza O. A review on glycerol valorization to acrolein over solid acid catalysts. Journal of the Taiwan Institute of Chemical Engineers. 2016;**67**: 29-44. DOI: 10.1016/j.jtice.2016.07.019

[15] Pala Rosas I, Contreras Larios JL, Zeifert B, Salmones BJ. Catalytic dehydration of glycerine to Acrolein. In: Frediani M, Bartoli M, Rosi L, editors. Glycerine Production and Transformation - An Innovative Platform for Sustainable Biorefinery and Energy. London, UK, London, UK: IntechOpen; 2019. DOI: 10.5772/intechopen.85751

[16] Liu L, Ye XP, Bozell JJ. A comparative review of petroleum-based and bio-based acrolein production. ChemSusChem. 2012;**5**:1162-1180. DOI: 10.1002/cssc.201100447

[17] Zhang X, Luo CW, Huang C, Chen BH, Huang DG, Pan JG, et al. Synthesis of 3-picoline from acrolein and ammonia through a liquid-phase reaction pathway using SO_4^{2-}/ZrO_2-FeZSM-5 as catalyst. Chemical Engineering Journal. 2014;**253**:544-553. DOI: 10.1016/j.cej.2014.03.072

[18] Zhang X, Wu Z, Liu W, Chao ZS. Preparation of pyridine and 3-picoline from acrolein and ammonia with HF/MgZSM-5 catalyst. Catalysis Communications. 2016;**80**:10-14. DOI: 10.1016/j.catcom.2016.02.011

[19] Zhang W, Duan S, Zhang Y. Enhanced selectivity in the conversion of acrolein to 3-picoline over bimetallic catalyst 4.6%Cu–1.0%Ru/HZSM-5 (38) with hydrogen as carrier gas. Reaction Kinetics, Mechanisms and Catalysis. 2019;**127**:391-411. DOI: 10.1007/s11144-019-01558-0

[20] Pala-Rosas I, Contreras JL, Salmones J, López-Medina R, Angeles-Beltrán D, Zeifert B, et al. Effects of the acidic and textural properties of Y-type zeolites on the synthesis of pyridine and 3-picoline from acrolein and ammonia. Catalysts. 2023;**13**:652. DOI: 10.3390/catal13040652

[21] Luo CW, Li A, An JF, Feng XY, Zhang X, Feng DD, et al. The synthesis of pyridine and 3-picoline from gas-phase acrolein diethyl acetal with ammonia over ZnO/HZSM-5. Chemical Engineering Journal. 2015;**273**:7-18. DOI: 10.1016/j.cej.2015.01.017

[22] Luo CW, Li A. Synthesis of 3-picoline from acrolein dimethyl acetal and ammonia over NH_4F-HF treated ZSM-5. Reaction Kinetics, Mechanisms and Catalysis. 2018;**125**:365-380. DOI: 10.1007/s11144-018-1405-1

[23] Zhang X, Wu Z, Chao Z. Mechanism of pyridine bases prepared from acrolein and ammonia by in situ infrared spectroscopy. Journal of Molecular Catalysis A: Chemical. 2016;**411**:19-26. DOI: 10.1016/j.molcata.2015.08.014

[24] Jiang D, Wang S, Li W, Xu L, Hu X, Barati B, et al. Insight into the mechanism of glycerol dehydration and subsequent pyridine synthesis. ACS Sustainable Chemistry & Engineering. 2021;**9**:3095-3103. DOI: 10.1021/acssuschemeng.0c07460

[25] Calvin JR, Davis RD, McAteer CH. Mechanistic investigation of the catalyzed vapor-phase formation of pyridine and quinoline bases using $^{13}CH_2O$, $^{13}CH_3OH$, and deuterium-labeled aldehydes. Applied Catalysis A: General. 2005;**285**:1-23. DOI: 10.1016/j.apcata.2004.10.021

[26] Jin F, Li Y. The effect of H_2 on Chichibabin condensation catalyzed by pure ZSM-5 and Pt/ZSM-5 for pyridine and 3-picoline synthesis. Catalysis Letters. 2009;**131**:545-551

[27] Luo CW, Feng XY, Liu W, Lia XY, Chao ZS. Deactivation and regeneration on the ZSM-5-based catalyst for the synthesis of pyridine and 3-picoline. Microporous and Mesoporous Materials. 2016;**235**:261-269

Chapter 5

Catalytic Conversion of Glycerol to Bio-Based Aromatics

Patrick U. Okoye, Estefania Duque-Brito, Diego R. Lobata-Peralta, Jude A. Okolie, Dulce M. Arias and Joseph P. Sebastian

Abstract

Green application of biodiesel-derived glycerol will boost biodiesel production in terms of sustainability and economics. The glycerol to liquid fuels is a promising route that provides an additional energy source, which contributes significantly to energy transition besides biodiesel. This pathway could generate alkyl-aromatic hydrocarbons with a yield of ~60%, oxygenates, and gases. MFI Zeolites (H-ZSM-5) catalysts are mainly used to propagate the aromatization pathway. This chapter presents the pathways, challenges, catalytic design, influences of catalyst acidity, metal addition, reaction condition, and catalysts deactivation on glycerol conversion to hydrocarbon fuels and aromatics. Studies revealed that time on stream, temperature, and weight hourly space velocity (range of 0.1–1 h^{-1}) influences the benzene, toluene, and xylene BTX and benzene, toluene, ethylbenzene, and xylene BTEX yield. Acidity of the H-ZSM-5 could be tailored by metals, additives, and binders. Bronsted acidity promotes coke formation which results in reversible deactivation of the H-ZSM-5 catalyst. It is hoped that this study will promote intensified research on the use of glycerol for purposes of fuel generating and valuable products.

Keywords: BTX, BTEX, hydrodeoxygenation, hydrocarbon fuels, glycerol, biodiesel

1. Introduction

To achieve complete decarbonization, there is a need to transition from fossil fuels to renewable and sustainable alternative fuels. This is because fossil fuels are major sources of greenhouse gas emissions, which have contributed to rising earth temperatures and adverse climate change. Transportation sectors still rely heavily on fossil fuels and this trend must be discouraged to minimize the emission of noxious CO_2 emissions [1, 2]. Liquid fuels generated from renewable energy sources, for use in heavy-duty vehicles are a promising option to reduce the impact of fossil fuels. Amongst the commercialized fuels from renewable energy, biodiesel has enjoyed wide acceptability because of lower CO_2 and other greenhouse emissions, can directly be used in the current internal combustion engine without modifying the engine design, and requires facile production processes [3, 4]. More importantly, biodiesel can be obtained from natural sources including waste oil, second-generation non-edible seed oil, third-generation, microalgae and fungus, animal fats, etc. [5, 6].

The transesterification reaction of oils (triglycerides) and alcohol is a widely established route for the synthesis of biodiesel [7]. This route involves the reaction of a triglyceride and 3 mols of alcohol (preferably methanol) to produce 1 mol of fatty acid methyl ester (biodiesel) and glycerol as a byproduct. The glycerol produced in this process is about 10 g for every 100 g of biodiesel produced, which renders it abundant [8, 9]. The produced glycerol is cheap because of impurities of methanol, soap, and catalysts that require energy-intensive steps for purification [10, 11]. However, glycerol is a platform molecule with three hydroxyl groups which can be transformed into fuels and fine chemicals. Many reaction pathways such as acetylation [12], carboxylation [13], etherification [14], oxidation, dehydration, gasification, aromatization [15, 16], etc. have been adopted to valorize glycerol.

Conversion of glycerol to liquid hydrocarbon fuel is a very recent and notable research idea, which will boost the biodiesel process. This is because the hydrodeoxygenation and hydroisomerization of vegetable oils to green diesel is capital intensive. Hydrocarbon fuel is vital in energy transition because of its characteristics which include high density and ease of transportation. This liquid hydrocarbon contains mainly alkyl-aromatic hydrocarbons of cumene, xylene isomers, benzene, toluene, and traces of C9+ compounds [16–18].

The feed has a significant influence on the aromatic product distribution, coke formation, and the type of aromatic products obtained. When the compounds with a H/C ratio is less than 2, for instance, glycerol with 0.67, are used as feed, increasing coke formation on the catalyst is generally observed. Hence, dilution with water or alcohol is employed. The dilution of glycerol with a solvent that has a H/C ratio of 2 increases the H/C ratio and presents improved catalyst stability. This preferred solvent for dilution is methanol with an effective H/C ratio of 2 [19, 20]. The conversion of glycerol and methanol to gasoline has emerged as a promising route to valorize glycerol [21, 22]. Increasing the methanol/glycerol ratio from 10 to 40% favored the production of oxygenated compounds instead of aromatics. Also, when methanol/glycerol are used as feeds, the formation of trimethylbenzenes and xylenes is obvious. These compounds can be transformed into heavy C9 aromatics by dealkylation reaction to xylene and toluene (BTX). The use of higher alcohol like isopropanol and isobutanol for dilution results in the preferential generation of ethylmethylbenzenes, and ethylbenzene with xylenes and trimethylbenzenes (BTEX) from the alkylation of ethylene generated from the cracking of the alcohol or dehydration of ethanol [18].

Notably, benzene, toluene, and xylene (BTX) and/or benzene, toluene, ethylbenzene, and xylene (BTEX) have been the main focus of many researchers in this area of study because of the vast industrial applications of these aromatic compounds including their antiknocking characteristics [23]. In addition to the aromatic compounds, oxygenates such as propanal, hydroxyacetone, and propenal (acrolein) are the product of this process [24, 25]. Also, ethylene, methylene, and propylene gases could be derived from this process. The reaction is usually carried out in a fixed bed reactor at ~400°C under excess hydrogen, alcohols, and/or nitrogen gas flowrate at atmospheric pressure [18, 26, 27].

To promote this reaction, zeolites of ZSM-5 or protonated ZSM-5 have been widely used. However, the yield over these catalysts is generally low. To increase the catalytic activity, noble metals or transition metals have been functionalized on the ZSM-5 and used with remarkable performance [28, 29]. The noble metals of Pt, Pd, and Rh, promote the cleavage of C – O bonds of glycerol, which enhances the formation of hydrocarbons from polyols instead of H_2 and CO_2 gases [24, 30]. Another problem encountered when ZSM-5 or H-ZSM-5 is used is rapid deactivation due to sintering, coking from reaction products, and attrition. This can be minimized by using a binder such as Al_2O_3 [31]. The binder stops irreversible deactivation and prolongs the catalyst life. In all these, control of the reaction conditions such as the temperature, catalyst amount, and sometimes the atmosphere, greatly influence the yield of bio-based aromatics. The operating reaction conditions also determine the operating cost of the process.

In this study, catalytic glycerol conversion to liquid hydrocarbon and bio-based aromatics are investigated with emphasis on the reaction mechanistic pathway and the influence of the reaction conditions such as temperature, time, and catalyst weight. The catalyst design, challenges, and deactivation mechanism are discussed. Prospects on bio-based aromatics are presented to reveal the knowledge gap and provide future guidelines for researchers and industries.

2. Mechanism of glycerol conversion to biobased BTX and BTEX

The mechanism of glycerol to liquid hydrocarbon follows two main routes namely hydrodeoxygenation (HDO), followed by aromatization reaction. Hydrodeoxygenation is an established method of removing oxygen from biomass. Glycerol hydrodeoxygenation is usually carried out to synthesize 1,2-propanediol, which is an oxygenate compound used in pharmaceutical, tobacco, and cryogenic industries. This pathway occurs through simultaneous C-O bond cleavage and hydrogen addition [27]. Usually, hydrogen is added from an external source, however, recent studies have shown that *in situ* hydrogen generation from hydrogen donors such as methanol, formic acid, 2-butanol, ethanol, etc. could eliminate the need for external hydrogen [25]. The hydrodeoxygenation also follows two parts of hydration-hydrogenation and dehydrogenation-hydration-hydrogenation, which is the most common pathway. The dehydration happens on the acid catalyst sites, whereas the hydrogenation is catalyzed by the noble metals or Cu, Zn, Ni, Sn, etc. This is because these metals promote the aqueous phase reforming of glycerol to

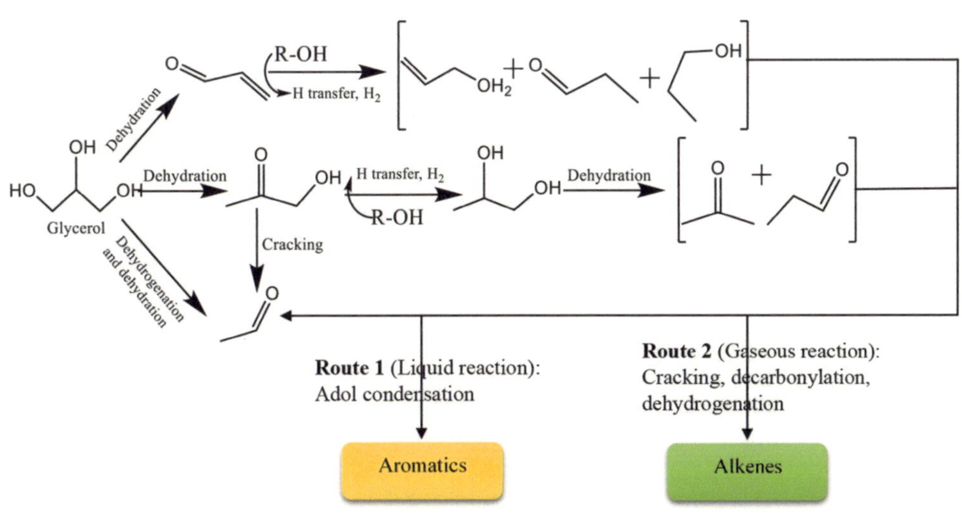

Figure 1.
Reaction pathways for glycerol dehydration-hydrogenation and dehydrogenation-hydration-hydrogenation reaction to produce aromatics [17].

produce hydrogen that is consumed during the hydrogenation stage. **Figure 1** shows the liquid and gaseous steps for glycerol dehydration and dehydrogenation pathways.

Hydroxyacetone can be produced via dehydration or via another route that involves dehydration to obtain glyceraldehyde, followed by hydrogenation to hydroxyacetone [25, 27]. Also, there are other hydrocarbon mixtures of acetone, propenal, alcohols, ketone, paraffins, and olefins of ethylene and propylene. Both liquid and gaseous routes produce a hydrocarbon pool, which in the presence of a catalyst could be upgraded to benzene, toluene, and xylene (BTX) or benzene, toluene, ethylbenzene, and xylene (BTEX) and other oxygenate compounds [17]. Also, the hydrocarbon pool can be further cracked to light paraffin or olefins. Generally, the presence of strong acid sites results in the build up of heavy aromatics such as trimethylbenzene and tetra- methylbenzene, whereas the reduction in the strong catalytic sites that propagates cracking and cyclization reaction, inhibit the gas route. The liquid route however, is unaffected since the aldol condensation reaction requires weak acid sites [16, 17].

3. Effect of HZSM-5 acidity, metals addition, and reaction conditions

The unique three-dimensional cage-like crystalline structure and tunable acid properties of ZSM-5 render it a choice catalyst for many reactions including isomerization reaction, alkylation reaction, and aromatization reaction. Also, this catalyst possesses an appreciably high surface area and has been extensively used successfully to drive the reaction of methanol to aromatics. Studies on the glycerol to aromatics synthesis revealed that protonated ZSM-5 (H-ZSM-5) has been effective for BTX and BTEX production due to its acidity and shape-selective characteristics [32]. The H-ZSM-5 contains sinusoidal channels ($0.51 \times 0.5\, nm$) that are crossed with straight channels of the dimension ($0.53 \times 0.56\, nm$) with intersection channel of 0.9 nm size [33, 34]. However, the relatively large micropores of the catalysts limit the mass transport of large molecules and present a diffusion barrier, which ultimately results in undesired bulkier aromatics and cokes and eventual deactivation of the catalysts [35]. To correct this, hierarchical porous H-ZSM-5 catalysts with macro-meso-and micropores have been developed to ensure hitch-free diffusion of reactants. In the synthesis of hierarchical H-ZSM-5 catalyst, several factors should be considered (see **Figure 2**). These factors are the hydrophobicity of the catalyst since the reaction most times produce water, concentration, and strength of acid sites, presence of mesopores, and shape selectivity of the catalyst. Also, several metals have been added to stabilize the H-ZSM-5 and increase its acidity and efficiency [36]. This section presents the effect of acidity and the effects of metals used to functionalize H-ZSM-5 catalysts. Also, the influence of reaction conditions such as time on stream and reaction temperature was presented.

3.1 Effect of catalyst acidity

The acidity of the ZSM-5 and MFI (H-ZSM-5) is vital to promoting the aromatization or hydrodeoxygenation of glycerol. To determine the influence of the catalyst acidity, several analytical characterizations can be performed. A notable characterization technique employed is temperature desorption programming (TPD) using ammonia as a probe molecule [37]. Ammonia is used because it is basic and can easily interact with acid sites. The TPD can also be used to determine the number of active sites in mmol/g by deconvolution of the peaks using gamma distribution or the gaussian model [12]. The

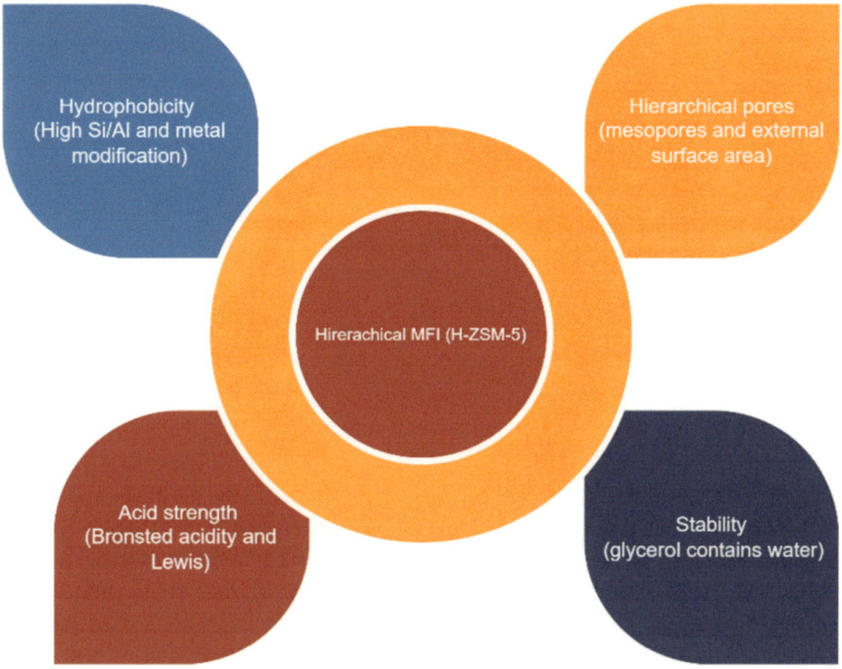

Figure 2.
Considered factors in the application of hierarchical porous H-ZSM-5 [34].

TPD peaks could be classified as weak, moderate, and strong peaks. The weak peak can be appreciated from 150 to 220°C, the moderate acid sites are around 300–350°C and the strong sites are from 400°C and above [38]. For zeolites, only weak and strong acid sites are usually identified [39]. Although weak and moderate peaks contribute to the deoxygenation and aromatization, mainly the strong acidity favors a higher yield of aromatics.

For instance, the yield of aromatics over catalyst of Zn/P/Si/ZSM-5 was lower than Zn/P/ZSM-5 catalyst by about 14.3% because the SiO_2 impregantion reduced the amount of the total acid sites by about 7.02% [38]. Also, the concentration of the surface acid sites is more vital than the total acid sites, because it is largely a surface dominated reaction. A similar study on atomic layer deposition (ALD) of Zn species on Sn/HZSM-5 zeolite revealed that above 20 cycles of ALD of Zn, precisely 40Zn, the interaction between the HZSM-5 and deposited Zn species were limited. Also, the strong acid sites reduced significantly, resulting in a reduction of BTX yield from close to C. 39% (for Sn/HZSM-5@20Zn) to C. 31% (for Sn/HZSM-5@40Zn) based on carbon yield [17]. Dealumination of HZSM-5 by steaming and acid leaching could produced different results. For instance, using 6 M nitric acid to remove extra-framework aluminum from the surface and channels of HZSM-5 and steaming to achieve the same purpose revealed significantly lower Brønsted acidity in steam treated HZSM-5. Whereas the concentration of the strong acid sites for the acid treated HZSM-5 remained almost unchanged. However, the weak acid sites decreased significantly, resulting in reduced total acidity. Likewise, BTX aromatic yield was higher for acid treated HZSM-5 (C. 28.1%) compared to the steam treated zeolite (C. 18.3%) [16].

To evaluate the type and concentration of the acid site, Fourier transforms infrared (FTIR) of adsorbed pyridine are normally used [40]. The pyridine IR is usually conducted by heating a known mass of the catalyst at around 150°C for 3 h, followed by pyridine adsorption for 2 h and subsequent desorption of the pyridine at 200°C under vacuum [41–43].

From pyridine DRIFTS analysis, the types of acid sites normally encountered with ZSM-5 zeolites are Brønsted and Lewis acid sites. Due to high pressure and temperature conditions of the glycerol to liquid fuels and aromatics compounds, high coke selectivity and consequent deactivation often occur for this type of catalyst. Particularly, the strong acid sites, which are mainly Brønsted acids promote the undesired coke formation, because the coke deposits preferentially on these sites through different proton transfer steps that occur on the Brønsted acid sites [26]. It is important to mention that understanding of acidity types of the zeolite catalyst can be appreciated from the Si/Al ratio [44]. Tuning of the acid strength [41] and reduction in the acid density [45] are two notable strategies to reduce coke deposits. The tuning of the acid strength and concentration can be achieved by modifying the zeolite tetrahedral framework Al content of the H-ZSM-5 or exchanging the protons that compensate for the negative charge of the Al sites tetrahedral framework. The strategy adopted over the years to accomplish these are either post-synthesis modification (top-down) or in situ modification during synthesis (bottom-up) [26, 32]. For instance, the synthesis of H-ZSM-5 with different Si/Al ratios is a common bottom-up strategy to evaluate the effect of acidity. For the bottom-up strategy, the total acid sites increase when the Si/Al ratio decreases. Top-down strategies include dealumination by acid extraction or steam treatment and isomorphic substitution of Al or Si atom with Zr, Fe, Ga, In, etc. [21, 46–48], other metals, heteroatoms of phosphorus, sulfur, and alkali metals, and alkaline earth metals [16, 40, 43]. Although these substitution strategies, which focus on the framework tetrahedral sites have been successful, however, they often result in the damage of the framework or defects of the crystalline structure, which adversely impacts the reactants and products diffusion to and from the cage-like zeolite structure. Also, the accurate introduction of these metals could be very problematic and can lead to uncertainty in the pore dimension [26].

Evaluation of the H-ZSM-5 acidity after dealumination via washing with HNO_3 and steaming revealed that the weak acid sites decreased, whereas the strong acid sites were unaffected. It is important to note that ZSM-5 zeolites have amorphous extra framework aluminum, which contributes significantly to the weak acid sites (although it could contribute slightly to the medium and strong acid sites with other silanols (Si-(OH)-Al) species), whereas the framework aluminum species are more related to the strong acid sites. Hence, the reduction in weak acid sites after dealumination can be attributed to the removal of the extra framework aluminum. The steaming treatment, however, resulted in a remarkable reduction of the acid concentration and strength, which shows the dealumination of the framework and extra-framework aluminum [16].

3.2 Effect of metal addition

Metal addition on H-ZSM-5 is bifunctional to provide stability as well as promote the dehydration/dehydrogenation reaction of glycerol to aromatics. A conducted study using only H-ZSM-5 reveal that predominantly oxygenates namely acrolein were obtained with about 11% of C6 – C9 compounds [30]. In this same study, the addition of metals (platinum and palladium), provided bifunctional properties, which promoted the C – O, C – H, O – H, and C – C bonds cleavages to achieve deoxygenation of the oxygenates [24]. Palladium however showed better performance in the conversion of the oxygenates to aromatics because of the higher H/metal ratio.

Notably, noble metals are preferred for fast kinetic activation of hydroxyl groups of glycerol and hydrogen dissociative adsorption [49]. Depending on the operating temperature they generally promote the hydrocarbon formation instead of the CO and H_2 pathway.

Apart from noble metals, which are usually expensive and can impact the overall production cost of liquid hydrocarbon and biobased aromatics from glycerol, other metals have been used with appreciable performance. Binders such as Al_2O_3 have been used to prolong the H-ZSM-5 catalyst life. The mesopores of the Al_2O_3 provided a higher capacity to store coke deposits in amorphous form. Also, the binder promoted a high total BTX yield compared to H-ZSM-5 [31]. Another study investigated the incorporation of tin (Sn) species in ZSM-5 catalysts. The composite catalysts were treated hydrothermally using sodium hydroxide, followed by ion exchange with ammonium chloride. The H[Sn, Al] ZSM-5/0.3AT composite catalysts after ion exchange reaction showed a slight decrease in crystallinity, a decrease in total Bronsted acid sites with an increase in Lewis acid sites [36]. Also, the Sn incorporation replaced some medium and strong acid sites and new acid sites were formed. The addition of the Sn did not destroy the H-ZSM-5 morphology, and the composite catalyst showed intra-mesopores and micropores, which benefits mass transfer of reactants and products. Overall, the catalyst showed a higher carbon yield of BTX (C 32.1%) compared to H-ZSM-5 (C 17.8%). The H[Sn, Al] ZSM-5/0.3AT could sustain about 13 h of time on stream reaction (H-ZSM-5 sustained the reaction for only 3 h with severe deactivation due to coke deposits), which was attributed to the mesopores and tuned Lewis acid and Bronsted acid sites due to alkali post-treatment. Similar studies have demonstrated the effect of binary material of Sn, Zn incorporated on H-ZSM-5 with appreciable BTX yield and longer catalyst life [17]. The Zn has been reported to promote high BTX formation by suppressing H-transfer reactions and light paraffins [29].

3.3 Effect of temperature

Catalytic pyrolysis is employed to achieve glycerol to aromatics and liquid hydrocarbons conversion. The operating temperature is very vital because glycerol to aromatics is a consecutive reaction steps that involves dehydration, oligomerization, cyclization, aldol condensation, cracking, and dehydrogenation. Since these reaction pathways occur simultaneously and parallel, different product distributions could be obtained at different reaction temperatures. An effect of reaction temperature on glycerol to aromatics shows that at a low temperature of ~200°C, O – H and C – H bonds could be easily broken due to their lower activation energy. This activation could be prevented by a possible hydrogenation reaction that is propagated by high H_2 content. An increase in temperature in the range of 300–400°C facilitated the bond cleavages of C – C and C – O species, which could happen simultaneously due to their similar activation energy [24]. However, breaking of the C – C bond at this temperature results in the formation of coke deposits, which could be graphitic or amorphous. Hence, the temperature should be tuned properly with the right amount of catalyst acidity to achieve the breaking of C – O bonds, while minimally avoiding the C – C bond. At 450°C, more of the liquid products are further cracked to gases, and syngas formation and methanation reactions are promoted [30]. Hence, the aromatics yield decreases, whereas the gaseous product increases as shown in **Figure 3** [30]. Most studies adopted 400°C as the optimum temperature to achieve the glycerol to aromatic conversion [18, 32, 50].

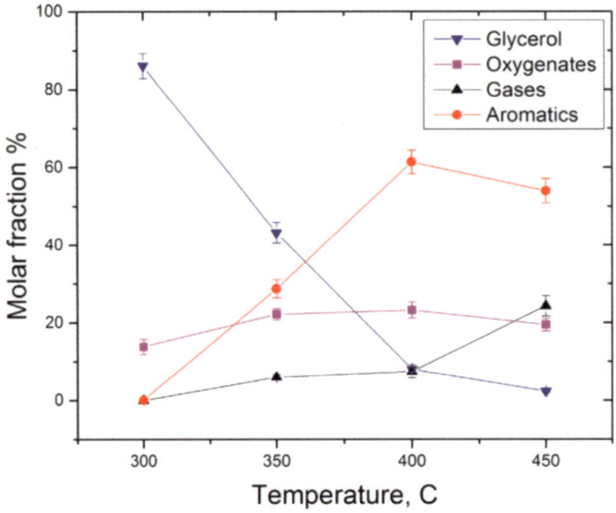

Figure 3.
Effect of pyrolysis temperature using Pd/H-ZSM-5 catalyst. Conditions: 1 atm, H_2/glycerol molar ratio of 10, and 6 g cat·h/g glycerol (copyright obtained https://pubs.acs.org/doi/full/10.1021/acsenergylett.6b00421).

3.4 Effect of time on stream

Time on stream for glycerol conversion to bio-based aromatics could be categorized into induction time, steady-state reaction time, and deactivation time [16]. Selectivity of the products is a clear function of the reaction time on stream; hence, it is important to optimize this factor. This has been generally established based on the yield of the aromatic intermediates in the cage structure of the H-ZSM-5 zeolite during aromatization. A study revealed that polymethyl benzenes and olefines, which is a very vital active hydrocarbon pools, were formed over the H-ZSM-5 cages as a product of the dehydration of the glycerol (oxycarbides) in the induction period [17]. This results in improved aromatic yields with a decrease in oxycarbides. After the induction period in a continuous reaction set-up, aromatization of glycerol proceeds via multiple steps of autocatalytic non-stop reaction of alkylation/dealkylation, oligomerization, and H-transfer. This stage usually has a relatively constant BTX and BTEX yield because the consumed hydrocarbon species are replenished. As the reaction time on stream is prolonged, the dealkylation step is suppressed with a corresponding decrease in lighter aromatic yield (toluene) and a buildup of heavier hydrocarbon species [38]. This was attributed to the coverage of the strong active sites by the heavier autocatalytic species, which suppresses the cracking and cyclization pathways propagated by the strong acid sites [51]. Hence, the gaseous route is mitigated allowing for the liquid synthesis. Further extension of the time on stream for continuous reaction set-up facilitates the conversion of the heavier intermediates (heavier hydrocarbon species) into carbon by a condensation reaction [52]. Eventually, the carbon formed blocks the micropores and the acid sites resulting in the catalyst deactivation. In the deactivation phase, the BTX and BTEX yields drop drastically, however, unconverted glycerol, acetol, acetaldehyde, and acrolein remained in the product [15]. **Table 1** shows the reported catalysts for glycerol conversion to aromatics and reaction conditions with selectivity towards BTX.

Catalyst	Conditions	Glycerol conv. (%)	Selectivity of aromatics (%)	Ref.
Dealuminated H-ZSM-5 (MFI) with initial Si/Al = 25	T = 400°C, glycerol/methanol = 40 wt.%, P = 0.1 MPa, WHSV: 0.71 h^{-1}.	Ca. 98	ca.32 (C% BTX)	[16]
ZSM-5 (SiO_2/Al_2O_3 = 30)	T = 400°C, WHSV = 0.8 h^{-1}.	100	>30 (C% BTX)	[18]
H-ZSM-5 (Si/Al_2 = 200)	T = 400°C, WHSV = 0.9 h^{-1}.	100	18	[36]
Hierarchical Sn-ZSM-5	T = 400°C, WHSV = 0.9 h^{-1}.	100	32 BTX	[36]
H-ZSM-5/Al2O3 (60/40 wt%)	T = 550°C, WHSV = 1 h^{-1}, TOS = 0–12 h.	—	19.5 (C% BTX)	[31]
H-ZSM-5/Al2O3 catalysts (60/40 wt%)	T = 550°C, glycerol/oleic acid = 30/70 wt.%, TOS = 12 h, catalyst = 10 g.	—	26.7 (C% BTX)	[53]
H-ZSM-5 (SiO_2/Al_2O_3 = 23)	T = 400°C, WSHV = 1 h^{-1}, TOS = 5 h, 0–5 mbar.	—	28.1 (C% BTX)	[50]
Nano-sized H-ZSM-5 modified with carboxymethylcellulose sodium, NaCl, and sodium alginate	T = 400°C, WHSV = 0.9 h^{-1}, catalyst = 1.2 g, glycerol/methanol = 40 wt.%.	—	35 (C% BTX)	[33]
Nano-sized H-ZSM-5 produced with sodium alginate (S-HZSM-5–0.75)	T = 400°C, WHSV =0.96 h^{-1}, catalyst =1.2 g, glycerol/methanol = 40 wt.%.	100	35.06 (C% BTX)	[39]
Zn and Sn modified H-ZSM-5 (Si/Al =25)	T = 400°C, WHSV = 0.71 h^{-1}, glycerol/methanol = 40 wt.%, TOS =1.5 ~ 2 h.	—	Ca. 35.7 (C% BTX)	[17]

Table 1.
Reported catalysts for glycerol conversion to aromatics.

4. Deactivation of catalysts

Deactivation of catalyst is the loss of performance over time, and the difference in catalyst life depends on the contaminant and application. There are several mechanisms by which a catalyst can be deactivated including fouling, poisoning, sintering, leaching of active surface, and mechanical attrition. Thermal degradation deactivation could be found with catalysts used in petroleum cracking or polymers [54]. Poisoning is a deactivation mechanism whereby a contaminant is loosely or strongly adsorbed on the active sites of the catalyst, which prevents access to the reactant species. This type of deactivation could be reversible or irreversible. A notable poisoning mechanism is coking, which results in carbon deposits, which could mask the surface of the active sites or even block the catalyst pores (pore mouth-filling). Coke formation can be investigated by temperature gravimetric analysis and visual inspection to observe a color change, usually from off-white to black. In general, catalyst deactivation is inevitable, however, careful catalyst design and operation under mild conditions could prolong the catalyst life in any given application. The design of a suitable shape-selective catalyst with tunable acid properties could increase the peak BTX yield, and total productivity and prolong the catalyst life.

Aromatization reaction occurs through a series of consecutive reaction steps that involves aldol condensation, oligomerization, cracking, cyclization, dehydrogenation, dehydration, aromatization, etc. The strength and concentration of the acid sites influence the yield of BTX and BTEX; specifically, the amount of Bronsted and Lewis acids could propagate the deactivation of the catalysts. The Bronsted acid sites promote cracking, H-transfer, and oligomerization reaction and it is principally responsible for coke generation since it promotes the C – C bond breaking. A Survey of the literature shows that coke deposition is the main deactivation mechanism of the H-ZSM-5. The coking deactivation is considered reversible because the coke can be removed by oxidative treatment. The spent catalyst is subjected to high-temperature recalcination in the air to decompose the coke deposits. For instance, the stability analysis for H-ZSM-5/Al_2O_3 and H-ZSM-5 catalysts used in the synthesis of BTX showed that the Al_2O_3 binder had more coke accommodation capacity than only H-ZSM-5. This was attributed to the mesoporous nature of Al_2O_3. Besides, the coke formation on the H-ZSM-5/Al_2O_3 was amorphous, whereas that of H-ZSM-5 was graphitic [50, 55]. This implies that the decomposition temperature would vary widely and the graphitic coke obviously would result in irreversible deactivation [31].

There are other forms of deactivation of H-ZSM-5 related to the deformation of the structure, reduction of crystallinity, acid strength, and reduction of microporosity. As stated before, this type of structural defect can manifest during the top-down approach. A situation whereby the acidity is reduced by chemical treatment or steaming. In particular, the hydrophobicity and spatial constraints of some chemical agents such as CH_3ONa and NaOH, in high concentrations could promote rapid desilication of the H-ZSM-5, which results in the damage of the catalyst microporous structure, diminished cage-like walls of the H-ZSM-5, and a drastic reduction in the crystallinity [52]. This situation presents a deformed H-ZSM-5 catalyst with low catalytic

Catalyst	Total acidity (μmol NH_3 g^{-1} cat fresh sample)	Total coke content (wt.%)	No. of reuse	catalyst lifetime (h)	Ref.
H-ZSM-5/Al_2O_3 (60/40 wt%)	1051	16.0	5	8.5	[31]
ZSM-5	—	—	—	8	[19]
H-ZSM-5	1466	12	1	4	[15]
3 h 500°C/HZSM-5	413	—	—	8.5	[16]
H-ZSM-5/Al_2O_3	1051	16.8	5	12	[53]
3 h 450°C/0.3 M NaOH/ HZSM-5	615	22.82	—	3	[35]
S-HZSM-5–0.75	1240	1123.90*	3	11.5	[39]
Sn/HZSM-5@20Zn	878	—	3	11	[17]
H-ZSM-5/ Al2O3	1238	15	1	5.3	[56]
H-ZSM-5/SiO2	1286	9	1	3.66	[56]
H-ZSM-5/ Kaolinite	1318	13	1	4	[56]

**is the peak area of the coke determined by the TPO method at 395°C.*

Table 2.
Reported H-ZSM-5-based catalysts, coke content, acidity, and number of reuse.

performance towards the aromatization reaction of glycerol. Another study reported in situ deactivation due to the conditions of the pyrolysis and reaction intermediates. He et al. [56] in their study to produce bio-based aromatics from glycerol revealed that dealumination of H-ZSM-5 occurred, which severely affected the crystallinity and acidity of the catalyst. This dealumination was attributed to catalyst exposure to steam generated by glycerol dehydration and the framework interaction with intermediate oxygenates. These types of deactivation are irreversible and eventually result in the complete deactivation of the catalyst. **Table 2** shows the total acidity of some reported catalysts, total coke content, and catalyst lifetime.

5. Prospects of catalytic glycerol to bio-aromatics

The conversion of glycerol to liquid fuels and aromatics is a notable research effort towards the production of "green" drop-in fuels that can be used as aviation fuel or bio-based chemicals. The glycerol is subjected to pyrolysis and sometimes in situ hydrotreating to reduce the oxygenates under heterogeneous catalysts. Zeolites of MFI (ZSM-5) have been widely applied because of the shape-selective nature, tunable acidity, and structure of the catalyst that promotes dehydration and hydrodeoxygenation reaction to produce hydrocarbon pools. In particular, protonated ZSM-5 (H-ZSM-5) has been synthesized for this synthesis with different modifications to evolve hierarchical pores and moderate the Bronsted acidity. However, there are continuous improvements to this strategy to increase the yield of BTX and BTEX from glycerol pyrolysis.

Notable about this is the modification of the H-ZMS-5 with metals and steaming to dealuminate the catalyst or alkaline treatment. These techniques are deployed to stabilize the zeolite and achieve higher selectivity of BTX. Conducted studies have evidenced that most strategies used to achieve dealumination or functionalization with metals are invasive, i.e., the crystallinity is sometimes affected significantly [44]. Hence, it is pertinent to look for non-invasive methods, such as low-temperature plasma techniques and isomorphous substitution methods [46, 48]. These methods are capable of achieving grafting metals on the H-ZSM-5 with minimal damage to the crystallinity or the framework structure. Also, the synthesis of the zeolite with pore-templating agents to evolve hierarchical pores would benefit the mass transport of reactants and products from the catalyst active sites. Another aspect that needs further insights is the optimization of reaction conditions such as the temperature, time on stream, weight hourly space velocity (WHSV), and methanol/glycerol ratio. Optimization of these reaction influencing parameters will result in minimal operation cost and provide insights into the mechanistic pathways involved.

Wholistic study of the deactivation mechanism of the unmodified H-ZSM-5 based on time and spaced resolved analysis suggested that coke deposit increases with the time on stream. The longer time on stream, the more coke accumulation. The mechanism proposed for this scenario posits that initially, coke is formed at the microporous channel of the H-ZSM-5 catalyst, followed by accumulation on the external surface of the zeolite as the time on stream increases [15]. The primary cause of the coke formation is the strong acid sites of the H-ZSM-5 catalysts, which have been improved by the design of shape-selective catalysts [35], metals, additive addition [33], and dealumination [43]. It is important to search for more binders that are capable of accumulating coke in amorphous form as opposed to the graphitic form, which is energy-intensive to regenerate.

6. Conclusions

Conclusively, the aromatization of glycerol via pyrolysis methods could be promoted using MFI zeolites (HZSM-5 and ZSM-5) catalysts. The acid form of ZSM-5 (H-ZSM-5) possesses appropriate crystallinity and acidity to tailor the reaction to produce benzene, toluene, and xylene (BTX) and/or benzene, toluene, ethylbenzene, and xylene (BTEX) with some oxygenates. The crystalline cage-like structure, acidity, pore size, and channel of the H-ZSM-5 catalysts influence the product's yield and distribution. Also, the reaction conditions such as temperature, time on stream, weight hourly space velocity significantly influence the product distribution and the carbon yield (BTX and BTEX). Also, these factors impact the coke formation mechanism, especially the time on stream and reaction temperature. The addition of metals like Zn, noble metals, Sn, binders (Al_2O_3), and additives (heteroatoms) influence the H-ZSM-5 acid concentration, acid strength, and acid type. These chemical modifications of the H-ZSM-5 catalysts substitute the framework aluminum responsible for high Bronsted acidity, which promotes coke formation and stabilizes the catalysts. Deactivation caused by dealumination techniques and *in situ* reaction conditions destroys the crystalline cage-like zeolite framework and is irreversible. Whereas reversible coke deposition is removed by energy-intensive oxidation that could impact the porosity and crystalline structure of the catalyst.

Hence, it is recommended that further studies should be conducted on the synthesis of shape-selective and hierarchical porous H-ZSM-5 catalyst with moderate Bronsted acidity to minimize coke formation and promote mass transport. Non-invasive modification methods such as plasma techniques should be adopted to achieve metal and heteroatoms incorporation into the cage-like structure of the H-ZSM-5 without damage to the framework. An in-depth study on the techno-economic analysis and life cycle analysis of the aromatization reaction will provide insights on the associated costs for comparison and the environmental impact of this process. Also, machine learning methods should be deployed to optimize the reaction conditions.

Acknowledgements

This work was financially supported by Dirección General de Asuntos del Personal Académico, Mexico under Programa de Apoyo a Proyectos de Investigación e Innovación Tecnológica (DGAPA-PAPIIT) Project Nos: IA102522, IG100217, and IA203320. PhD fellowship was granted to D.R. Lobato-Peralta by Consejo Nacional de Ciencia y Tecnologia, Mexico (CONACYT).

Conflict of interest

The authors declare no conflict of interest.

Author details

Patrick U. Okoye[1*], Estefania Duque-Brito[1], Diego R. Lobata-Peralta[1], Jude A. Okolie[2], Dulce M. Arias[1] and Joseph P. Sebastian[1]

1 Instituto de Energías Renovables, Universidad Nacional Autónoma de México, Temixco, Morelos, Mexico

2 Gallogly College of Engineering, University of Oklahoma, USA

*Address all correspondence to: ugopaok@ier.unam.mx

References

[1] Scrucca F, Rotili A, Presciutti A, Fantozzi F, Bartocci P, Zampilli M. Energy valorization of bio-glycerol: Carbon footprint of Co-pyrolysis process of crude glycerol in a CHP plant. In: Muthu SS, editor. Carbon Footprints: Case Studies from the Energy and Transport Sectors. Singapore: Springer Singapore; 2019. pp. 19-46. DOI: 10.1007/978-981-13-7912-3_2

[2] Li C, Zhang X, Wang K, Su F, Chen CM, Liu F, et al. Recent advances in carbon nanostructures prepared from carbon dioxide for high-performance supercapacitors. Journal of Energy Chemistry. 2021;**54**:352-367

[3] Gouran A, Aghel B, Nasirmanesh F. Biodiesel production from waste cooking oil using wheat bran ash as a sustainable biomass. Fuel. 2021;**295**:120542

[4] Madhuvilakku R, Piraman S. Biodiesel synthesis by TiO2-ZnO mixed oxide nanocatalyst catalyzed palm oil transesterification process. Bioresource Technology. 2013;**150**:55-59

[5] Ilham Z, Haque NF. Quantitative priority estimation model for evaluation of various non-edible plant oils as potential biodiesel feedstock. AIMS Agriculture and Food. 2019;**4**(2):303-319

[6] Ambat I, Srivastava V, Sillanpää M. Recent advancement in biodiesel production methodologies using various feedstock: A review. Renewable and Sustainable Energy Reviews. 2018;**90**:356-369

[7] Ideris F, Shamsuddin AH, Nomanbhay S, Kusumo F, Silitonga AS, Ong MY, et al. Optimization of ultrasound-assisted oil extraction from Canarium odontophyllum kernel as a novel biodiesel feedstock. Journal of Cleaner Production. 2021;**288**:125563. DOI: 10.1016/j.jclepro.2020.125563

[8] Ortiz Olivares RD, Okoye PU, Ituna-Yudonago JF, Njoku CN, Hameed BH, Song W, et al. Valorization of biodiesel byproduct glycerol to glycerol carbonate using highly reusable apatite-like catalyst derived from waste Gastropoda Mollusca. Biomass Convers Biorefinery. Springer; 2020. DOI: 10.1007/s13399-020-01122-0

[9] Aghbashlo M, Tabatabaei M, Rastegari H, Ghaziaskar HS. Exergy-based sustainability analysis of acetins synthesis through continuous esterification of glycerol in acetic acid using Amberlyst®36 as catalyst. Journal of Cleaner Production. 2018;**183**:1265-1275. DOI: 10.1016/j.jclepro.2018.02.218

[10] Das B, Mohanty K. A green and facile production of catalysts from waste red mud for the one-pot synthesis of glycerol carbonate from glycerol. Journal of Environmental Chemical Engineering. 2019;**7**(1):102888. DOI: 10.1016/j.jece.2019.102888

[11] Okoye PU, Abdullah AZ, Hameed BH. A review on recent developments and progress in the kinetics and deactivation of catalytic acetylation of glycerol—A byproduct of biodiesel. Renewable and Sustainable Energy Reviews. 2017;**74**:387-401. DOI: 10.1016/j.rser.2017.02.017

[12] Okoye PU, Abdullah AZ, Hameed BH. Synthesis of oxygenated fuel additives via glycerol esterification with acetic acid over bio-derived carbon catalyst. Fuel. 2017;**209**(July):538-544. DOI: 10.1016/j.fuel.2017.08.024

[13] Aresta M, Dibenedetto A, Nocito F, Pastore C. A study on the

carboxylation of glycerol to glycerol carbonate with carbon dioxide: The role of the catalyst, solvent and reaction conditions. Atmospheric Environment. 2007;**41**(2):407-416

[14] Dominguez CM, Romero A, Santos A. Improved etherification of glycerol with tert-butyl alcohol by the addition of dibutyl ether as solvent. Catalysts. 2019;**9**(4):378. DOI: 10.3390/catal9040378

[15] He S, Goldhoorn HR, Tegudeer Z, Chandel A, Heeres A, Stuart MCA, et al. A time- and space-resolved catalyst deactivation study on the conversion of glycerol to aromatics using H-ZSM-5. Chemical Engineering Journal. 2022;**434**(Jan):134620. DOI: 10.1016/j.cej.2022.134620

[16] Wang F, Chu X, Zhu F, Wu F, Li Q, Liu B, et al. Producing BTX aromatics-enriched oil from biomass derived glycerol using dealuminated HZSM-5 by successive steaming and acid leaching as catalyst: Reactivity, acidity and product distribution. Microporous and Mesoporous Materials. 2019;**277**(November 2018):286-294. DOI: 10.1016/j.micromeso.2018.11.015

[17] Wang F, Kang X, Zhou MX, Yang XH, Gao LJ, Xiao GM. Sn and Zn modified HZSM-5 for one-step catalytic upgrading of glycerol to value-added aromatics: Synergistic combination of impregnated Sn particles, ALD introduced ZnO film and HZSM-5 zeolite. Applied Catalysis A: General. 2017;**539**(April):80-89. DOI: 10.1016/j.apcata.2017.04.005

[18] Jang HS, Bae K, Shin M, Kim SM, Kim CU, Suh YW. Aromatization of glycerol/alcohol mixtures over zeolite H-ZSM-5. Fuel. 2014;**134**(2014):439-447. DOI: 10.1016/j.fuel.2014.05.086

[19] Luo G, McDonald AG. Conversion of methanol and glycerol into gasoline via ZSM-5 catalysis. Energy and Fuels. 2014;**28**(1):600-606

[20] Gayubo AG, Valle B, Aguayo AT, Olazar M, Bilbao J. Attenuation of catalyst deactivation by cofeeding methanol for enhancing the valorisation of crude bio-oil. Energy and Fuels. 2009;**23**(8):4129-4136

[21] Han Z, Zhou F, Liu Y, Qiao K, Ma H, Yu L, et al. Synthesis of gallium-containing ZSM-5 zeolites by the seed-induced method and catalytic performance of GaZSM-5 and AlZSM-5 during the conversion of methanol to olefins. Journal of the Taiwan Institute of Chemical Engineers. 2019;**103**:149-159. DOI: 10.1016/j.jtice.2019.07.005

[22] Valle B, Gayubo AG, Alonso A, Aguayo AT, Bilbao J. Hydrothermally stable HZSM-5 zeolite catalysts for the transformation of crude bio-oil into hydrocarbons. Applied Catalysis B: Environmental. 2010;**100**(1-2):318-327. DOI: 10.1016/j.apcatb.2010.08.008

[23] Lok CM, Van Doorn J, Aranda AG. Promoted ZSM-5 catalysts for the production of bio-aromatics, a review. Renewable and Sustainable Energy Reviews. 2019;**113**(June):109248. DOI: 10.1016/j.rser.2019.109248

[24] Liu B, Greeley J. Decomposition pathways of glycerol via C-H, O-H, and C-C bond scission on Pt(111): A density functional theory study. Journal of Physical Chemistry C. 2011;**115**(40):19702-19709

[25] Yfanti VL, Lemonidou AA. Effect of hydrogen donor on glycerol hydrodeoxygenation to 1,2-propanediol. Catalysis Today. 2020;**355**(May 2019):727-736. DOI: 10.1016/j.cattod.2019.04.080

[26] Xian X, He M, Gao Y, Bi Y, Chu Y, Chen J, et al. Acidity tuning of HZSM-5 zeolite by neutralization titration for coke inhibition in supercritical catalytic cracking of n-dodecane. Applied Catalysis A: General. 2021;**623**(April)

[27] Yfanti VL, Lemonidou AA. Mechanistic study of liquid phase glycerol hydrodeoxygenation with in-situ generated hydrogen. Journal of Catalysis. 2018;**368**:98-111. DOI: 10.1016/j.jcat.2018.09.036

[28] Wang F, Xiao W, Gao L, Xiao G. Enhanced performance of glycerol to aromatics over Sn-containing HZSM-5 zeolites. RSC Advances. 2016;**6**(49):42984-42993

[29] Tamiyakul S, Ubolcharoen W, Tungasmita DN, Jongpatiwut S. Conversion of glycerol to aromatic hydrocarbons over Zn-promoted HZSM-5 catalysts. Catalysis Today. 2015;**256**:325-335

[30] Xiao Y, Varma A. Conversion of glycerol to hydrocarbon fuels via bifunctional catalysts. ACS Energy Letters. 2016;**1**(5):963-968

[31] He S, Kramer TS, Klein FGH, Chandel A, Tegudeer Z, Heeres A, et al. Improved catalyst formulations for the conversion of glycerol to bio-based aromatics. Applied Catalysis A: General. 2022;**629**(September 2021):118393. DOI: 10.1016/j.apcata.2021.118393

[32] Wang F, Li Q, Chu X, Zhu F, Zhao P, Wu F, et al. The synergistic effect of hydroxylated carbon nanotubes and ultrasound treatment on hierarchical HZSM-5 in the selective catalytic upgrading of biomass derived glycerol to aromatics. Catal Letters. 2021;(0123456789). DOI: 10.1007/s10562-021-03823-1

[33] Xu W, Gao L, Xiao G. Effects of additives and metals on crystallization of nano-sized HZSM-5 zeolite for glycerol aromatization. Catalysts. 2019;**9**(11):899. DOI: 10.3390/catal9110899

[34] Muraza O. Peculiarities of glycerol conversion to chemicals over zeolite-based catalysts. Frontiers in Chemistry. 2019;**7**(Apr):1-11

[35] Wang F, Chu X, Zhao P, Zhu F, Li Q, Wu F, et al. Shape selectivity conversion of biomass derived glycerol to aromatics over hierarchical HZSM-5 zeolites prepared by successive steaming and alkaline leaching: Impact of acid properties and pore constraint. Fuel. 2020;**262**(November 2019):116538. DOI: 10.1016/j.fuel.2019.116538

[36] Yang X, Wang F, Wei R, Li S, Wu Y, Shen P, et al. Synergy effect between hierarchical structured and Sn-modified H[Sn, Al]ZSM-5 zeolites on the catalysts for glycerol aromatization. Microporous and Mesoporous Materials. 2018;**257**:154-161. DOI: 10.1016/j.micromeso.2017.08.039

[37] Aptel G, Petrakis D, Jones D, Roziere J, Pomonis P. Mesoporous Al-Fe-P-O solids prepared in non-aqueous medium: Structure and surface acid catalytic behaviour. Studies in Surface Science and Catalysis. 1998;**118**:931-939

[38] Zhang J, Qian W, Kong C, Wei F. Increasing Para-xylene selectivity in making aromatics from methanol with a surface-modified Zn/P/ZSM-5 catalyst. ACS Catalysis. 2015;**5**(5):2982-2988

[39] Xu N, Pan D, Wu Y, Xu S, Gao L, Zhang J, et al. Preparation of nano-sized HZSM-5 zeolite with sodium alginate for glycerol aromatization. Reaction Kinetics, Mechanisms and Catalysis. 2019;**127**(1):449-467. DOI: 10.1007/s11144-019-01566-0

[40] Almutairi SMT, Mezari B, Pidko EA, Magusin PCMM, Hensen EJM. Influence of steaming on the acidity and the methanol conversion reaction of HZSM-5 zeolite. Journal of Catalysis. 2013;**307**:194-203. DOI: 10.1016/j.jcat.2013.07.021

[41] Auepattana-aumrung C, Suriye K, Jongsomjit B, Panpranot J, Praserthdam P. Inhibition effect of Na+ form in ZSM-5 zeolite on hydrogen transfer reaction via 1-butene cracking. Catalysis Today. 2020;**358**(August 2019):237-245. DOI: 10.1016/j.cattod.2019.08.012

[42] Xiao W, Wang F, Xiao G. Performance of hierarchical HZSM-5 zeolites prepared by NaOH treatments in the aromatization of glycerol. RSC Advances. 2015;**5**:63697-63704. Available from: http://xlink.rsc.org/?DOI=C5TC02043C

[43] Fan Y, Bao X, Lin X, Shi G, Liu H. Acidity adjustment of HZSM-5 zeolites by dealumination and realumination with steaming and citric acid treatments. The Journal of Physical Chemistry. B. 2006;**110**(31):15411-15416

[44] Silva DSA, Castelblanco WN, Piva DH, de Macedo V, Carvalho KTG, Urquieta-González EA. Tuning the Brønsted and Lewis acid nature in HZSM-5 zeolites by the generation of intracrystalline mesoporosity—Catalytic behavior for the acylation of anisole. Molecular Catalysis. 2020;**492**(February):111026. DOI: 10.1016/j.mcat.2020.111026

[45] Yabushita M, Kobayashi H, Neya A, Nakaya M, Maki S, Matsubara M, et al. Precise control of density and strength of acid sites of MFI-type zeolite nanoparticles: Via simultaneous isomorphous substitution by Al and Fe. CrystEngComm. 2020;**22**(44):7556-7564

[46] Wloch J. Influence of isomorphous substitution in MFI-type materials on the diffusion of n-hexane: Molecular dynamic studies. Applied Surface Science. 2007;**253**(13 SPEC. ISS):5692-5695

[47] Jin L, Fang Y, Hu H. Selective synthesis of 2,6-dimethylnaphthalene by methylation of 2-methylnaphthalene with methanol on Zr/(Al)ZSM-5. Catalysis Communications. 2006;**7**(5):255-259

[48] Morgan CI, Paredes SP, Flores SO, Alfaro S. Single gel hydrothermal synthesis and characterization of vanadium isomorphously modified silicalite-1 and ZSM-5. Materials Letters. 2017;**209**:513-516. DOI: 10.1016/j.matlet.2017.08.074

[49] Harris J, Andersson S. H2 dissociation at metal surfaces. Physical Review Letters. 1985;**55**(15):1583-1586

[50] He S, Zuur K, Santosa DS, Heeres A, Liu C, Pidko E, et al. Catalytic conversion of pure glycerol over an un-modified H-ZSM-5 zeolite to bio-based aromatics. Applied Catalysis B: Environmental. 2021;**281**(August 2020):119467. DOI: 10.1016/j.apcatb.2020.119467

[51] Hoang TQ, Zhu X, Sooknoi T, Resasco DE, Mallinson RG. A comparison of the reactivities of propanal and propylene on HZSM-5. Journal of Catalysis. 2010;**271**(2):201-208. DOI: 10.1016/j.jcat.2010.01.017

[52] Wang F, Zhou MX, Yang XH, Gao LJ, Xiao GM. The effect of hierarchical pore architecture on one-step catalytic aromatization of glycerol: Reaction routes and catalytic performances. Molecular Catalysis. 2017;**432**:144-154. DOI: 10.1016/j.mcat.2017.01.017

[53] He S, Klein FGH, Kramer TS, Chandel A, Tegudeer Z, Heeres A, et al.

Catalytic co-conversion of glycerol and oleic acid to bio-aromatics: Catalyst deactivation studies for a technical H-ZSM-5/Al2O3 catalyst. Applied Catalysis A: General. 2022;**632**(January)

[54] Okoye PU, Hameed BH. Review on recent progress in catalytic carboxylation and acetylation of glycerol as a byproduct of biodiesel production. Renewable and Sustainable Energy Reviews. 2016;**53**:558-574. DOI: 10.1016/j.rser.2015.08.064

[55] He S, Kramer TS, Santosa DS, Heeres A, Heeres HJ. Catalytic conversion of glycerol and co-feeds (fatty acids, alcohols, and alkanes) to bio-based aromatics: Remarkable and unprecedented synergetic effects on catalyst performance. Green Chemistry. 2022;**24**(2):941-949

[56] He S, Goldhoorn HR, Tegudeer Z, Chandel A, Heeres A, Liu C, et al. Catalytic conversion of glycerol to bio-based aromatics using H-ZSM-5 in combination with various binders. Fuel Processing Technology. 2021;**221**(May):106944. DOI: 10.1016/j.fuproc.2021.106944

Section 3

Applications

Chapter 6

Ethanol Inhalation in Treatment and Prevention of Coronavirus Disease (COVID-19)

Ali Amoushahi

Abstract

The goal of this study was to determine if nebulized ethanol (EtOH) is safe and effective in treating COVID-19. A randomized controlled trial was carried out on 99 symptomatic and RT-PCR-positive patients admitted to a hospital that were given Remdesivir and Dexamethasone. They were randomly given either a 35% EtOH spray (intervention group, IG) or distilled water spray (control group, CG). For a week, each group underwent three nebulizer puffs every 6 hours. Global Symptomatic Score (GSS) comparisons between the two groups at the initial visit and on days 3, 7, and 14. Secondary outcomes include the readmission rate and the Clinical Status Scale (CSS), a seven-point ordinal scale that ranges from death to full recovery. The intervention and control groups, respectively included 44 and 55 patients. The GSS and CSS considerably improved in the IG, despite the fact that there was no difference at admission ($p = 0.016$ and $p = 0.001$, respectively) (Zero vs. 10.9%; $P = 0.02$). The IG readmission rate was much reduced. Inhaled-nebulized EtOH responds well in quickly improving the clinical status and limiting the need for further therapy. Further investigation into the therapeutic and preventative properties of EtOH is advised due to its affordability, availability, and lack of/tolerable side effects.

Keywords: ethanol, inhalation, nebulizer, COVID-19, blood oxygen saturation

1. Introduction

Deaths from cytokine storms are frequently caused by COVID-19. Alcohol has been shown to have in vitro antiviral effects on coronavirus glycoprotein destruction [1] and the breakdown of the fat layer [2]. Ethyl alcohol (EtOH) has been shown to have antiviral effects on extracellular surfaces in the past [3]. Inflammatory factors such TLR, interleukin-6, and TL9, as well as TNF-mRNA protein and mitogen-activated protein kinase, have been proven in immunological investigations to have immunomodulatory effects on the innate immune system and to attenuate cytokine storm [4, 5]. Additionally, it promotes bronchoalveolar macrophages' chemotaxis [6]. Other effects of ethanol include the prevention of viral multiplication through RNA-dependent polymerase inhibition [7], bronchial dilatation by relaxing involuntary smooth muscles [8], patient sedation and relaxation [9], and analgesic effects on muscles [10]. Methanol poisoning [11], fat embolism [12], premature labor prevention [13], preeclampsia [14], and pulmonary edema [15] have all been treated with ethanol-specific treatments in the past. Castro-Balado et al. [16] have shown the histological safety of inhalation ethanol treatment on rats' lungs and respiratory systems. Ethanol was authorized by the Food and Drug Administration. Can ethanol inhalation treatment be beneficial in treating COVID-19? Given the effects of ethanol on virus wall breakdown, proliferation inhibition, and immunological hyperactivity inhibition, the use of inhaled ethanol as a COVID-19 treatment is still unknown. One month following the COVID-19 epidemic in Iran, this concept was initially put forth and published [17, 18]. Later, a paper explaining the justification for ethanol usage in this area was presented [19]. Recent research on the combined administration of dimethyl sulfoxide and ethanol in healthcare professionals, demonstrated positive effects on COVID-19 prevention [20]. We conducted a randomized clinical study to assess the impact of ethanol treatment on the clinical condition and prognosis of a predetermined group of patients in an effort to discover the solution. The Medical University of Isfahan Research and Ethics Committee accepted the study, which was then registered at https://irct.ir/trial/58201.

2. Materials and methods

Study Design and Oversight (**Figure 1**). The Isabn-e-Maryam Hospital (Christian hospital) at the Medical University of Isfahan in Iran, where this study was carried out in September 2021, was the site of a randomized double-blind clinical trial with a control group and parallel design. The patients were matched one to one at random. The study was initially intended to be conducted on hospitalized patients, but because the country's policy had been changed to allow for the establishment of respiratory

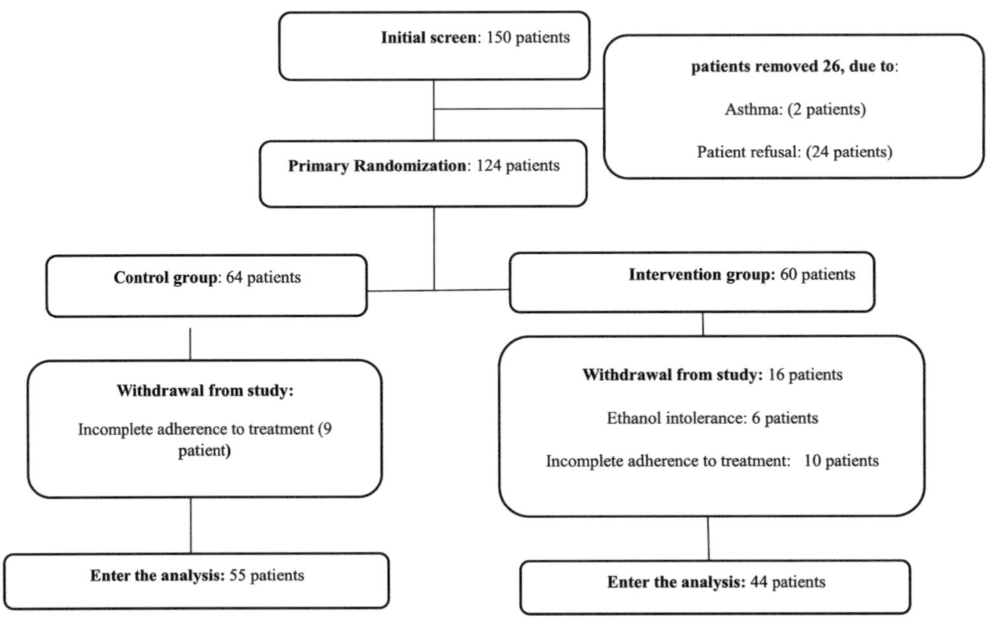

Figure 1.
Flowchart of the study.

clinics in hospitals and the prescription of Remdesivir and Dexamethasone to patients with moderate COVID-19, the study was instead carried out in this clinic. The referral of the patient to the respiratory clinic and this report were shared with the doctors of patients who were being treated in hospitals.

2.1 Patients

Patients who tested positive for SARS-CoV-2-RT-PCR are the foundation of the study population. They were admitted to the hospital's respiratory clinic because they had moderate COVID-19 (based on the national guideline for managing COVID-19, O2Sat 90–94% or lung involvement [21]). The following criteria were required for inclusion: informed consent, age of at least 12 years old, no pregnancy, no history of epilepsy, alcoholism, or asthma, no contraindications to ethanol usage, and no use of ethanol-interacting medications. Intolerance to inhaled ethanol and incomplete or partial therapy were the exclusion criteria. To investigate possible allergies to alcohol, a skin test with ethanol was performed. In this study, the patient's arm was linked to a gauze pad with an ethanol drop on it. Symptoms including skin redness, swelling, or itching were seen after around 7 minutes. These signs may be indicative of an alcohol allergy or intolerance.

2.2 Intervention

According to Iran's national clinical norms, both the control and intervention groups were enrolled in the standard medical treatment [21]. The national standard treatment included intramuscular Dexamethasone, 8 mg/day (5 days), and 200 mg of Remdesivir intravenously on day 1, followed by 100 mg of Remdesivir once daily for 4 days, infused over\s30–60 minutes. Patients received normal care as per routine and were then randomly allocated to either the control group (distilled water spray) or the intervention group (35% ethanol spray). The delivery of two 100 ml sets of spray was done in accordance with randomization. Each patient was told to spray the mask three times per day (every 6 to 8 hours) and inhale deeply. We stressed that, depending on the duration of symptoms, this procedure had to be repeated for 7 days. Patients were guided through the process by nurses until they were able to do it on their own. At each appointment for referrals and follow-up care, patient compliance was evaluated. Failure to follow the protocol (spray not used or used incorrectly) resulted in removal from the trial.

3. Clinical and laboratory monitoring

The demographic and clinical information were separated into different sections on the data collecting sheet. A qualified nurse performed the data-collecting checklist based on clinical symptoms, clinical outcomes, and clinical examination after obtaining demographic data from the patient's records. Up to discharge, information on study variables, such as blood oxygen saturation measured by pulse oximetry, the requirement for supplementary care or hospital readmission, and clinical complaints in both groups, was gathered.

3.1 Study outcomes

Primary outcomes: The global symptomatic score (GSS), which is calculated by adding up the cumulative scores of clinical signs and symptoms like anorexia, fever, headache, body aches, sore throat, runny nose, chills, coughing, and loss of taste and smell, is regarded as a gauge of a patient's clinical condition. This index was created to provide a concise list of clinical symptoms. Using a pulse oximeter, oxygenation status was tracked and documented each day. The patient was not receiving any additional oxygen at the time of the measurement and was breathing room air with a fixed pulse oximeter. Changes in blood C-reactive protein (CRP) levels were used to characterize the presence of inflammation.

Secondary outcomes: On day 14 of the treatment period for the investigation, clinical conditions were evaluated using a modified 7-point ordinal scale [22].

There are seven indicators in this scale:

1. Death.

2. A patient in a hospital receiving invasive mechanical ventilation.

3. High-flow oxygen or non-invasive ventilation systems used in hospitals.

4. Hospitalized and in need of low-flow oxygen.

5. Hospitalized for any cause, requiring continuous medical care (whether linked to COVID-19 or not), and requiring home oxygen supplementation.

6. Continued signs or symptoms of COVID-19 without requiring supplemental oxygen, no longer require ongoing medical care.

7. Both groups reported and dealt with full recovery as well as any potential side effects.

The necessity for critical care unit admission, adverse medication reactions, clinical symptoms, and death in the research samples were noted and tracked in both groups. The last follow-up was scheduled on the day fourteenth of the illness. Physical examinations, history-taking, phone calls, reviews of patient records, and documents from the hospital information system were all used during follow-up. After receiving informed consent, side effects were documented. The main endpoints have undergone some alterations. This was due to the study's implementation restrictions, which coincided with the disease's peak in Iran, and the fact that patients who required hospitalization were followed up on an outpatient basis in the respiratory clinic. We informed the sponsor and institutional review board in great detail of the protocol revisions. The length of stay was the key anticipated result. This index was replaced with a more detailed clinical status since all moderate patients were treated on a 5-day regimen during the surge.

3.2 Sampling

An easy random sample technique was used to do the sampling. Random assignment was performed using a computerized random number table. The order of the random distributions was decided by one nurse. Each participant who was qualified and gave their agreement to participate in the experiment was randomly assigned from a list that she kept confidential. One by one, a different nurse added 100 ml of diluted distilled water or ethanol-35% to the sprays (nebulizers) and labeled them with the numbers from the list. Each spray was given to a participant, who was then instructed on how to use it by their family or companion. Blinding was carried out by analysts, nurses, and clinicians.

4. Statistical analysis

Using a 2-sided significance level of 0.05, we calculated that 88 patients (44 in each group) would offer higher than 90% power to detect an odds ratio of 3 for the ethanol group vs. the placebo group. The analysis was restricted to individuals who, in accordance with the research protocol and inclusion criteria, got full treatments and contributed to the outcomes, as per the "treatment-on" or "per-protocol" method. Means, standard deviations, and percentages (%) were used to report both quantitative and qualitative information. The chi-square test was used to evaluate qualitative characteristics between the two groups, and a mixed model was used to compare SpO2 readings and GSS on days 1, 3, 7, and 14. Repeated-measures analysis was used to calculate the average changes from baseline values. With the use of Mauchly's statistics and the Geisser-Greenhouse adjustment, the sphericity hypothesis was disproved. The cumulative odds ordinal logistic regression with proportional odds was used to compare clinical status between the two groups on day 14, and the two test was used to determine the proportion of patients in each group who required additional medical care after 14 days. These tests were carried out at 0, 3, and 14 days after the intervention. For the intervention group compared to the usual care group, an odds ratio larger than 1 showed changes in clinical status across all categories toward category 7. For clinical status, if a patient recovered, the ordinal score was recorded as 7 on the day of recovery and all subsequent days unless the patient was hospitalized for COVID-19-related reasons or others; all statistical analyses were performed using SPSS software version 22 (SPSS Inc., Chicago, IL, USA), and $p < 0.05$ was considered significant. The outcome markers were adjusted for the patient's gender.

5. Results

Patient Characteristics from September to November 2021, 150 patients from the COVID-19 Respiratory Outpatient Clinic of the Isabn-e-Maryam Hospital of the Isfahan University of Medical Sciences were assessed for participation in the research based on the positive outcome of the RT-CPR test. A total of 24 patients disagreed with the research, and 2 patients did not meet the inclusion requirements. Randomly, 124 more patients were divided into two groups (Intervention and Control). In the next days, 25 participants were removed from the trial due to intolerance to ethanol inhalation (6 patients); their intolerance was mostly caused by hiccups, eye irritation, coughing, shortness of breath, sneezing, and the unpleasant odor of alcohol. On the other hand, 19 patients (9 in the control group and 10 in the intervention group) were disqualified from the trial because of irregularities or failure to adhere to the suggested procedure. Finally, 99 patients entered the analysis: 44 patients in the IG and 55 patients in the CG (**Table 1**).

Table 1 summarizes the baseline characteristics and demographics of the two groups of patients. The male-to-female patient ratio was 43/56 (42.4/56.6%). The patients were 46.4 years old on average. A total of 38 patients had multiple conditions. Diabetes mellitus was the most prevalent underlying condition in both groups, with 6

Index	Control group N = 55	Intervention group N = 44	P value
Age (years) (Mean ± SD)	46.15 ± 13.15	45.91 ± 12.58	0.928
BMI (*Kg/m2*) (Mean ± SD)			
Normal weight	16 (29.1)	9 (20.5)	0.804
Overweight	25 (45.5)	22 (50)	
Obesity	10 (20)	10 (22.7)	
Excessive obesity	3 (5.5)	3 (6.8)	
Gender N (%)			
Female	37 (67.3)	19 (43.2)	0.024
Male	18 (32.7)	25 (56.8)	
Education Level N (%)			
Illiterate and Elementary	3 (5.4)	8 (16.3)	0.251
Secondary	8 (14.3)	7 (14.3)	
Diploma	28 (50)	16 (32.7)	
Bachelor-higher	16 (26.8)	16 (30.6)	
Unknown	2 (3.6)	3 (6.1)	
Risk factors for disease N (%)			
Not any	23 (52.3)	38 (69.1)	0.614
1 risk factor	19 (43.2)	12 (21.8)	
2 risk factors	2 (4.5)	4 (7.3)	
3 risk factors	0	1 (1.8)	

Table 1.
Demographic characteristics in two research groups.

(14.3%) in the intervention group and 4 (7%) in the control group. Seven individuals had high blood pressure and seven others had additional cardiovascular issues. The two groups' mean ages, weights, levels of education, and total number of risk variables did not significantly differ from one another.

5.1 Clinical signs and symptoms at the time of admission

The interval between the onset of symptoms and admission, lung involvement, and early clinical signs and symptoms at baseline did not substantially differ among the patients. The clinical signs and symptoms of the patient's fundamental characteristics are listed in **Table 2**.

Cough, body pains, chills, and headaches were the intervention group's main clinical complaints. The control group had a higher prevalence of anorexia, olfactory disturbance, and cough. There was no discernible change in symptoms. Overall Symptom Score The GSS was evaluated at the start of therapy, 3, 7, and 14 days afterward in two groups. The results are shown in **Figure 2**.

The GSS of the two groups was equal at the start of the research, according to statistical analysis, but in the IG group, clinical symptoms reduced more quickly than in the placebo group. The statistical significance of this difference was ($p = 0.016$).

5.2 Blood oxygen saturation

At the time of the trial, there was no noticeable change in the two groups' blood oxygen saturation levels (92.07 ± 4.6 in the control group vs. 91.56 ± 3.39 in the intervention group). As seen in **Figure 3**.

Characteristic	Control group N = 55	Intervention group N = 44	P value
Distance from onset of symptoms to Start treatment (Mean ± SD)	9.36 ± 5.13	8.50 ± 3.52	0.338
Pulmonary Involvement (CT scan) N (%)			
Less than 30%	22 (40)	19 (43.2)	0.153
30–49%	25 (45.5)	15 (34.1)	
50% and above	2 (3.6)	2 (4.5)	
Unknown	6 (10.9)	8 (18.2)	
Fever N (%)	21 (38.2)	25 (56.8)	0.072
Chills N (%)	35 (63.6)	30 (68.2)	0.675
Cough N (%)	49 (89.1)	41 (95.3)	0.262
Headache N (%)	35 (63.6)	30 (68.2)	0.636
Short Breath N (%)	37 (67.3)	24 (54.5)	0.196
Sore throat N (%)	27 (49)	16 (36.4)	0.204
Rhinorrhea N (%)	18 (32.7)	9 (20.5)	0.173
Body pain N (%)	36 (65.5)	36 (65.5)	0.069
Anorexia N (%)	38 (69.1)	29 (65.9)	0.737
Anosmia N (%)	39 (70.9)	26 (59.1)	0.219
Lack of taste N (%)	32 (58.2)	27 (61.4)	0.749
Global Symptomatic Score (GSS)	6.67 (2.09)	6.72 (2.07)	0.910

Table 2.
Preliminary characteristics of signs and symptoms, risk factors, and laboratory values in baselines.

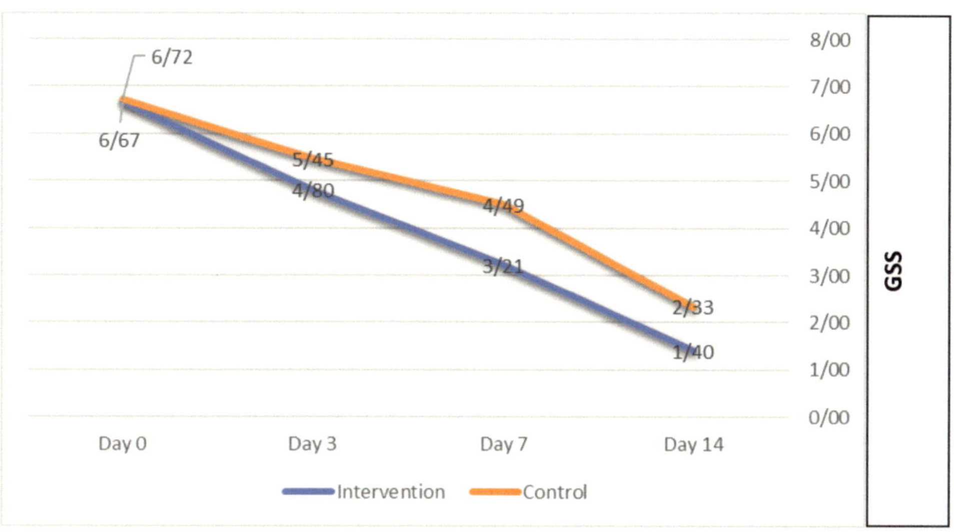

Figure 2.
Comparison of global symptomatic score (GSS) in the intervention and control groups at the beginning of admission, days 3, 7 and 14 after admission.

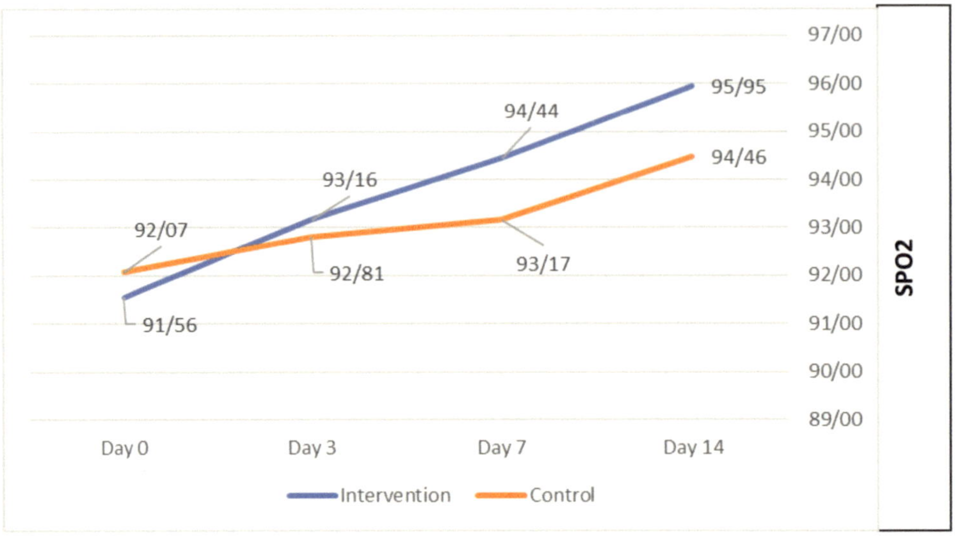

Figure 3.
Comparison of mean blood oxygen saturation (SPO2) in intervention and control groups at the beginning of admission, days 3, 7 and 14 after patient admission.

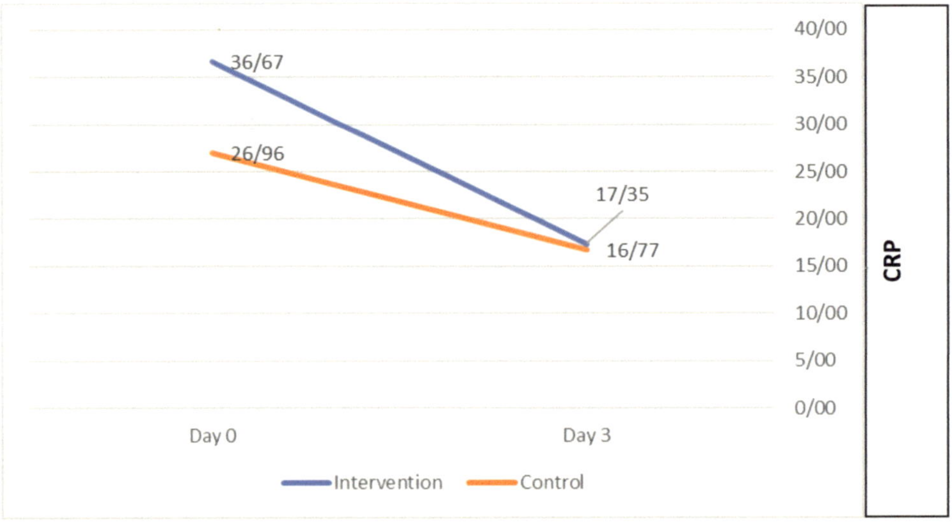

Figure 4.
Comparison of CRP (C-reactive protein) in the intervention and control groups at the beginning of admission and three days after patient admission.

Both groups had an improvement in blood oxygenation, however, the ethanol group's slope of oxygenation was greater. The change is not statistically significant, though ($p = 0.097$) inflammatory factor (CRP) Multiple assessments and statistical comparisons between the two groups revealed a declining trend in CRP (**Figure 4**).

However, the rate of reduction was much faster and more intense in the IG ($p = 0.05$). Two sets of CSS based on the modified 7-point ordinal scale were compared. On day 14, the intervention group had 5.7 times the chance of having superior

Characteristic and Score N (%)	Intervention N = 44	Control N = 55
1. Death	0	0
2. Hospitalized, on invasive mechanical ventilation	0	0
3. Hospitalized, on non-invasive ventilation or high flow oxygen devices	0	0
4. Hospitalizations for any reason and need oxygen	0 (0)	2 (3.63)
5. Requiring ongoing medical care or supplemental oxygen at home	2 (4.54)	10 (18.18)
6. Continue signs or symptoms without requiring supplemental oxygen - no longer requires ongoing medical care	13 (29.54)	29 (52.72)
7. Complete recovery	29 (65.90)	14 (25.45)

Table 3.
Comparison of clinical status scale (CSS) of intervention and control groups on the 14th day of admission.

CSS than the control group (95% CI, 2.47–13.19), which is a statistically significant difference (Wald 2 (1) =16.67, p = 0.001). **Table 3** provides details.

Six patients (10.9%) from the control group were readmitted after the therapy period had ended in order to obtain further care or hospitalization. None of the patients were readmitted to the ethanol group (p = 0.02).

5.3 Adverse events and safety

Six out of 50 patients in the ethanol group (12%) quit taking it due to adverse effects that started as soon as inhalation began, and we eliminated them from the research. Only one instance of each negative effect was noted, and it vanished after ethanol consumption was discontinued. Hiccups, eye discomfort, coughing, shortness of breath, sneezing, and a strong alcohol odor were a few of the undesirable side effects.

6. Discussion

The impact of adding nebulized Ethanol inhalation has been researched in this clinical study on patients having positive RT-PCR test results, mild clinical symptoms, and suitability for Remdesivir and Dexamethasone treatment, according to the Iran Ministry of Health protocol. The rationale for the use of EtOH in COVID-19 has been well discussed [19]. There is no question regarding the ability of ethanol in killing or making SARS-CoV-2 inactive, even at concentrations as low as 30% v/v and for only 30 seconds [23]. The virus's fat layer is broken down by the virucidal effects of EtOH, which then stop the virus from multiplying. EtOH has also been demonstrated to reduce the immune system's hyperactivity during COVID-19. It seems likely that ethanol is ineffective against intracellular viruses. It is crucial to continue ethanol inhalation for at least 3 days since viral multiplication happens within 48–72 hours, followed by cellular death and shedding. Additionally, ethanol is fundamentally effective against all SARS-CoV-2 variants and other "enveloped" viruses due to its non-specificity. The abnormal presence of Mycoplasma salivarium in the lower tract or the lack of Clostridia in the upper tract was linked to worse outcomes in ICU patients [24]. It is interesting to note that ethanol completely inactivates Mycoplasma and SARS-CoV-2 (Eterpi et al.) [25]. Additionally, certain strains of Clostridia synthesize endogenous ethanol [26]. According to a hypothetical scenario, the lack of nasopharyngeal Clostridia would prevent the local generation of ethanol, which would prevent or drastically limit the inactivation of SARS-Cov-2 at this level, allowing the virus to propagate to the lower respiratory tract. A lot of concern has been expressed regarding the potential mucosal harm that breathed ethanol might cause. Castro-Balado et al. careful research [16] appears to have completely dispelled these concerns. It should be noted that spraying into the mask prolongs the action of the nebulized liquid and maintains its efficiency by reducing the dispersion and evaporation of the liquid. The different smells of the two solutions indicate a potential inherent bias. Patients could only recognize that one spray was different from another since they were unaware of the actual ingredient in the spray. To put it differently, the medication may have been in an odorless spray. Dexamethasone and Remdesivir are administered intramuscularly as part of the COVID-19 standard therapy [21]. According to a recent trial, introducing early antibiotic therapy for COVID-19 pneumonia had no positive effects on 30-day mortality [27]. Despite what was predicted [28, 29], the authors [27] did not discover any appreciable vaccination benefit in reducing illness severity and death among patients with COVID-19 pneumonia. The GSS fell more in the Intervention group than in the control group, according to our findings, and these data reached a statistically significant level ($p = 0.016$). Nebulized EtOH inhalation had positive effects on lowering CRP levels, which was a significant advantage ($p = 0.05$). This result supports EtOH's positive immune- modulation effects [3]. On the other hand, blood oxygenation increased more quickly and had a greater slope in the ethanol than it did in the control group. Regarding blood oxygenation, between the two groups, there was, however, no statistically significant difference ($p = 0.097$). In terms of CSS, the intervention responded better than the control since no patient had to be readmitted, as opposed to the control where 6 patients (10.8%) had to repeat the normal therapy or be hospitalized. These results provide credibility to EtOH's virucidal properties.

7. Conclusions

Overall, recovery from moderate COVID-19 is greatly improved by adding EtOH to the conventional therapy (Remdesivir+Dexamethasone). It is advised to do more research and invest more in order to assess ethanol's therapeutic and preventative effects in the early stages of COVID-19 given its accessibility, low cost, and lack of substantial adverse events. The patients in this experiment were far from our rigorous oversight and switched to other treatments, which was one of its shortcomings. The healthcare system is also concerned about unpleasant alcohol consumption and the potential for non-inhaled alcohol intake. This study is constrained by chance (due to the small sample size), confounding factors (due to the imbalance in gender distribution), and low power, among other things. The randomization sequence is broken by a per-protocol analysis, which also introduces bias into the study.

Author details

Ali Amoushahi
Department of Anesthesiology and Intensive Care Unit, Isabn-e-Maryam Hospital, Isfahan University of Medical Sciences, Isfahan, Iran

*Address all correspondence to: aliamoushah@gmail.com

References

[1] Lai MM, Cavanagh D. The molecular biology of coronaviruses. Advances in Virus Research. 1997;**48**:1-100. DOI: 10.1016/S0065-3527(08)60286-9

[2] Singh D, Joshi K, Samuel A, et al. Alcohol-based hand sanitizers as first line of defence against SARS-CoV-2: A review of biology, chemistry and formulations. Epidemiology & Infection. 2020;**148**:e229

[3] Moorer W. Antiviral activity of alcohol for surface disinfection. International Journal of Dental Hygiene. 2003;**1**:1601-5037. DOI: 10.1034/j.1601-5037.2003.00032.x

[4] Mörs K, Hörauf J-A, Kany S, et al. Ethanol decreases inflammatory response in human lung epithelial cells by inhibiting the canonical NF-kB-pathway. Cellular Physiology and Biochemistry. 2017;**43**:17-30

[5] Chandrasekar A, Olde Heuvel F, Palmer A, et al. Acute ethanol administration results in a protective cytokine and neuroinflammatory profile in traumatic brain injury. International Immunopharmacology. 2017;**51**:66-75

[6] Boé DM, Nelson S, Zhang P, et al. Acute ethanol intoxication suppresses lung chemokine production following infection with Streptococcus pneumoniae. The Journal of infectious diseases. 2001;**184**:1134-1142

[7] Berres ME, Garic A, Flentke GR, et al. Transcriptome profiling identifies ribosome biogenesis as a target of alcohol teratogenicity and vulnerability during early embryogenesis. PLoS One. 2017;**12**:0169351

[8] Sakihara C, Jones KA, Lorenz RR, et al. Effects of primary alcohols on airway smooth muscle. The Journal of the American Society of Anesthesiologists. 2002;**96**:428-437. DOI: 10.1097/00000542-200202000-00031

[9] Acevedo SF, Gonzalez DA, Rodan AR, et al. S6 kinase reflects and regulates ethanol-induced sedation. Journal of Neuroscience. 2015;**35**:15396-15402. DOI: 10.1523/JNEUROSCI.1880-15.2015

[10] Arout CA, Perrino AC Jr, Ralevski E, et al. Effect of intravenous ethanol on capsaicin-induced hyperalgesia in human subjects. Alcoholism: Clinical and Experimental Research. 2016;**40**:1425-1429

[11] Ekins BR, Rollins DE, Duffy DP, et al. Standardized treatment of severe methanol poisoning with ethanol and hemodialysis. Western Journal of Medicine. 1985;**142**:337-1306022

[12] Myers R, Taljaard J. Blood alcohol and fat embolism syndrome. The. Journal of bone and joint surgery American volume. 1977;**59**:878-880

[13] Haas DM, Morgan AM, Deans SJ, et al. Ethanol for preventing preterm birth in threatened preterm labor. Cochrane Database of Systematic Reviews. 2015;**2015**:CD011445

[14] Teran E, Racines-Orbe M, Vivero S, et al. Preeclampsia is associated with a decrease in plasma coenzyme Q10 levels. Free Radical Biology and Medicine. 2003;**35**:1453-1456

[15] Gootnick A, Lipson HI, Turbin J. Inhalation of ethyl alcohol for pulmonary edema. New England Journal of Medicine. 1951;**245**:842-843. DOI: 10.1056/NEJM195111292452202

[16] Castro-Balado A, Mondelo-García C, Barbosa-Pereira L, et al. Development and characterization of inhaled ethanol as a novel pharmacological strategy currently evaluated in a phase II clinical trial for early-stage SARS-CoV-2 infection. Pharmaceutics. 2021;**5**:342-317

[17] Amoushahi A. A suggestion on ethanol therapy in COVID-19? EC Anaesthesia. 2020;**6**:1-2

[18] Ezz A, Amoushahi A, Rashad A. Disinfection of SARS-COV-2 (COVID-19) in human respiratory tract by controlled ethanol vapor inhalation combined with Asprin. Journal of Vaccines & Vaccination. 2021;**12**:454

[19] Salvatori P. The rationale of ethanol inhalation for disinfection of the respiratory tract in SARS-CoV-2-positive asymptomatic subjects. The Pan African Medical Journal. 2021;**40**:201

[20] Hosseinzadeh A, Tavakolian A, Kia V, et al. Combined application of dimethyl sulfoxide and ethanol nasal spray during COVID-19 pandemic may protect healthcare workers: A randomized controlled trial. Iranian Red Crescent Medical Journal. 2022;**24**:8. DOI: 10.32592/ircmj.2022.24.8.1640

[21] Rahmanzade R, Rahmanzadeh R, Hashemian SM, et al. Iran's approach to COVID-19: Evolving treatment protocols and ongoing clinical trials. Frontiers in Public Health. 2020;**4**:551889-551810. DOI: 10.3389/fpubh.2020.551889

[22] Spinner C, Gottlieb R, Criner G, et al. Effect of Remdesivir vs standard care on clinical status at 11 days in patients with moderate COVID-19: A randomized clinical trial. JAMA. 2020;**324**:1048

[23] Kratzel A, Todt D, V'kovski P, et al.: Inactivation of severe acute respiratory syndrome coronavirus 2 by WHO-recommended hand rub formulations and alcohols. Emerging Infectious Diseases 2020, 26: 1592-1595. 10.3201/eid2607.200915

[24] Sulaiman I, Chung M, Angel L, et al. Microbial signatures in the lower airways of mechanically ventilated COVID19 patients associated with poor clinical outcome. MedRxiv. 2021;**26**:10-1101. DOI: 10.1038/s41564-021-00961-5

[25] Eterpi M, McDonnell G, Thomas V. Decontamination efficacy against mycoplasma. Letters in Applied Microbiology. 2011;**52**:21198694. DOI: 10.1111/j.1472-765X.2010.02979.x

[26] Ruuskanen MO, Åberg F, Mannistö V, et al. Links between gut microbiome compositon and faty liver disease in a large population sample. Gut Microbes. 2021;**13**:1

[27] Choi YJ, Song JY, Hyun H, et al. Prognostic factors of 30-day mortality in patients with COVID-19 pneumonia under standard remdesivir and dexamethasone treatment. Medicine. 2022;**23**:30474. DOI: 10.1097/MD.00000000000304741

[28] Lopez Bernal J, Andrews N, Gower C, et al. Effectiveness of the Pfizer-BioNTech and Oxford-AstraZeneca vaccines on covid-19 related symptoms, hospital admissions, and mortality in older adults in England: Test negative case-control study. BMJ. 2021;**373**:1088. DOI: 10.1136/bmj.n1088

[29] Tenforde MW, Self WH, Adams K, et al. Association between mRNA vaccination and COVID-19 hospitalization and disease severity. Journal of the American Medical Association. 2021;**326**:54. DOI: 10.1001/jama.2021.19499

Chapter 7

Nebulized Ethanol: An Old Treatment for a New Disease

Steven W. Stogner

Abstract

Ethyl alcohol (ethanol) is known to inactivate SARS-CoV-2, and therefore, direct delivery to the upper and lower respiratory tracts hypothetically would inhibit the progression of COVID-19. After informed consent, nebulized EtOH was given to inpatients admitted with COVID-19, and outcomes were retrospectively compared to randomly selected controls. Benefits of nebulized EtOH included decreased average length of stay, improved inpatient survival, decreased intubation rate and need for transfer to intensive care, improvement in hypoxemia, and decreased need for transfer to another facility for ongoing post-acute care. Also, fewer patients required supplemental home oxygen after discharge to home. Interpretation: Nebulized EtOH is beneficial in the treatment of COVID-19. Further study is warranted.

Keywords: inhaled ethanol, COVID-19, SARS-CoV-2, hypoxemia, virucide

1. Introduction

The virus that causes COVID-19 Disease (designated SARS-CoV-2, Severe Acute Respiratory Syndrome Coronavirus 2) has caused severe morbidity and mortality around the world. In addition to the human toll of disease, the pandemic triggered stark social as well as economic disruption around the world, affecting a global recession [1]. Supply shortages (including food), travel restrictions, business restrictions and closures, workplace hazard controls, quarantines, testing systems, and tracing contacts of the infected has been costly in not only financial terms as governments attempted to control the pandemic but also in societal customs and "norms" as well. Near-global lockdowns of educational institutions and other entities were partially or completely closed in many areas, as well as the postponement of needed surgeries placed major stress on communities across the globe, often resulting in a political uproar. In truth, the world has not experienced a similar pandemic and its results since the 1918 Flu Pandemic (February 1918 until April 1920 in four successive waves affecting 500 million people) [2, 3].

As of August 2022, COVID-19 has infected more than 600 million people and caused almost 6.5 million confirmed deaths worldwide—one of the deadliest in history [3]. First identified in Wuhan, China, in December 2019, the COVID-19 virus outbreak was identified by the World Health Organization (WHO) as a public health emergency of international concern on January 30, 2020, and the astronomical trajectory continued with it being declared a global pandemic only 2 weeks later [4]. In March of that year, hospitals and outpatient clinics alike found themselves overwhelmed with astonishing volumes of patients which stressed healthcare resources to the edge, to the point of having to contemplate the rationing of care [5], including intensive care beds and mechanical ventilators.

In addition to inadequate resources at the onset of the pandemic—other than standard treatment measures for respiratory failure, including ARDS—specific treatment for the COVID-19 virus did not exist. Healthcare workers found themselves having to care for critically ill and dying patients who were most often isolated from their loved ones. Saddled with the grim fact of no specific treatment, the apprehension of becoming infected themselves and transmission of the virus to their own loved ones at home, and the emotional (and *ethical*) nightmarish thoughts which occurred as the potential of rationing healthcare loomed, it is no shock the common *burn-out* of healthcare workers that ensued [6].

2. COVID-19: the disease

The degree of disease caused by COVID-19 ranges from undetectable to lethal, but most commonly includes fever, nonproductive cough, fatigue, and loss of taste and/or smell in 40 percent of cases [7]. While severe illness such as organ failure occurs most frequently in elderly patients, it is also seen in younger patients with certain comorbidities such as chronic obstructive pulmonary disease, heart failure, malignancy, obesity, chronic steroid or immunosuppressive use, etc. [8]. Transmission occurs when people inhale droplets of airborne particles containing the virus, but also when viral-contaminated fluids reach the eyes, nose, mouth, and even contaminated objects (i.e. hands, etc.).

3. Pathogenesis: a clue for an effective treatment

The COVID-19 virus contains genetic material (RNA) packaged in a protein coat which is surrounded by an envelope composed of a lipid bilayer derived from the host cell membrane [9–11]. SARS-CoV-2 affects the upper and lower respiratory tracts, where its entry genes are highly expressed in epithelial cells of the nasal cavity and into the alveolar cells. Thus, the portal of entry of SARS-CoV-2 is the upper respiratory tract where the acute infection begins, then subsequently travels to the alveoli by viral aspiration. A *"cytokine storm"* can then ensue, likely due to an interleukin-6 amplifier resulting in a hyper-activation process that regulates the nuclear factor kappa B (NF-κB) [12–14]. Ultimately, this cascade of events can be fatal in 75% of cases due to the development of ARDS and other acute organ failures including thrombotic complications [15].

4. Nebulized ethanol: potential benefits and risks

Potential benefits: Direct delivery of a drug with viricidal activity against SARS-CoV-2 (or other susceptible respiratory viruses, i.e., influenza) to the epithelial cells of the upper and lower respiratory tracts in an effort to destroy the virus before severe disease can ensue seem advantageous—and is logical. Ethanol/ethyl alcohol/

EtOH suits this purpose. Ethanol is volatile and has long been used as an antiseptic/disinfectant, and constitutes the basis for many hand rubs and disinfectants used in healthcare settings [16, 17] as well as by the general public. Ethanol and other alcohols are known to inactivate many enveloped viruses like SARS-CoV-2 by dissolving the virus' lipid membrane causing its destruction [18–20]. Notably, alcohol-based hand rub solutions have been shown to inactivate SARS-CoV-2 in as little as 30 s [21]. In addition to coronavirus, the effective viricidal activity of ethanol against many other common viruses (i.e., influenza, adenovirus, etc.) as well as Zika and Ebola has been demonstrated [22].

Ethanol is presently used worldwide as a generally nontoxic antiseptic and disinfectant and has been effectively and safely used in medicine for methanol poisoning [23], and as late as the 1950s as an inhalational treatment of pulmonary edema [24, 25] and alcohol withdrawal [26, 27].

Published reports suggest promise for the use of inhaled ethanol in the treatment of ARDS [28]. Ethanol is a well-known efficient surfactant (wetting agent), as it is an amphiphilic chemical compound possessing both hydrophilic and lipophilic properties. Surfactant proteins are critical components of alveolar function, and laboratory studies on animal lungs indicate ethanol has the potential to restore surfactant activity in experimentally-induced non-compliant lungs (produced with nebulized saline) [29]. Notably, analysis of SARS-CoV-2-infected lung tissues has revealed that surfactant proteins are indeed severely downregulated in infected lungs, causing respiratory distress [30].

Ethanol has mediator effects on inflammation [31] and thus could potentially have a beneficial effect on the prevention of cytokine storms [13]. In addition, there may be a possible benefit with ethanol in the prevention of thrombus formation shown by autopsy findings to frequently occur in COVID-19 [15, 32, 33]. Ordinarily, cutting of the fibrin mesh by plasmin enzyme leads to the production of circulating fragments that are cleared by other proteases or by the kidney and liver. Tissue plasminogen activator (t-PA) and urokinase then convert plasminogen to the active plasmin, allowing normal fibrinolysis to occur. Ethanol has been shown to "upregulate" the urokinase receptor in human endothelial cells and thus may be helpful in the elimination of thrombi [34].

Potential risks: Ethanol is flammable and combustible, and if ignited, can cause severe injury or even death. Appropriate cautionary measures are absolutely mandatory with its usage.

The risks and negative health effects on the immune, cardiovascular, pulmonary, gastrointestinal-hepatic, and neurologic systems of chronic oral consumption of ethanol are well-known [35]. Even acute oral consumption of large amounts is known to have the potential for serious health consequences, including even fatal toxicity. Vaporized ethanol used recreationally (*AWOL* = "alcohol without liquid") appears to some extent becoming more prevalent, and serious concerns have appropriately been raised about its acute and unknown long-term health consequences, especially in young adults. However, a review of the literature fails to show any significant acutely negative effects of the short-term intake of small amounts of ethanol on the immune system or other organ systems [36–40].

Inhaled ethanol can irritate the eyes, as well as the nose, throat, and plausibly the lungs [41, 42]. In one small study, a decrease in ventilator flow rates on partial expiratory flow volumes [43] was found up to ninety minutes after inhalation, but no significant change in FEV_1 (forced expiratory volume) occurred compared to placebo (inhaled saline solution). Interestingly, pretreatment with disodium cromoglycate considerably diminished the acute reductions of flow rates caused by ethanol inhalation, suggesting that ethanol in some persons may act, at least partly, through the release of mediators with bronchoconstrictive action.

As with any nebulized treatment, nebulized ethanol poses a risk for aerosolization of respiratory viruses like SARS-CoV-2 and transmission of the disease. Appropriate infection control precautions must be strictly followed when such conditions exist.

In the swarm of patients requiring inpatient care for acute hypoxemic respiratory failure due to SARS-CoV-2 in March 2020, those patients who deteriorated necessitating intubation for adult respiratory distress syndrome (ARDS) were having mortality exceeding 75% [3]. While governments were scrambling to issue emergency-use authorization for experimental treatments as well as civil protections for healthcare providers trying to best care for these patients, patients continued to literally smother ultimately requiring intubation and mechanical ventilation. The situation was not only grim, but it seemed hopeless. The urgency to find an effective treatment for this novel virus had never before been witnessed in the lives of most medical professionals. While some treatments were showing promise (i.e., remdesivir, dexamethasone, etc.), there remained an existential need for an effective readily available treatment. Given its proven viricidal efficacy, history of harmless use in the treatment of other medical conditions, as well as a lack of evidence for acute detrimental health effects when used in mild, non-chronic, non-excessive intake, the reasoning that nebulized ethanol may prove beneficial in the treatment of COVID-19 is rational.

5. Nebulized ethanol for treatment of COVID-19: results of a clinical study

In March 2020, at Forrest General Hospital (a non-profit community hospital in Hattiesburg, Mississippi) due to the emergent onslaught of this lethal and "untreatable" disease, and out of necessity and companionate care, a novel treatment regimen of nebulized ethanol was developed to offer patients with COVID-19 who required inpatient treatment for acute hypoxemia as a sole or supplemental treatment option, at the discretion of their attending physicians. While Shintake [44] had proposed the potential use of inhaled ethanol to eradicate the virus in the respiratory tract, extensive research of the medical literature otherwise revealed no reports of inhaled ethanol for treatment of COVID-19 infection[1] (or any other viral respiratory infection for that matter).

As a sole or additional option, a protocolized order set for the administration of nebulized ethanol was made available to hospital physicians in the electronic medical record beginning in April 2020. Education of all involved healthcare personnel was conducted prior to making the order set available. Administration of all nebulized treatments was performed by respiratory therapists, who in addition to nurses, monitored the patients. Access to and dispensing of the ethanol was meticulously controlled by the hospital pharmacy, which also confirmed that all of the following criteria were met prior to dispensing:

1. Admission for COVID-19 with dyspnea and/or hypoxemia;

2. Non-intensive care unit admission (general medical floor);

---

[1] The results of this study have not been published elsewhere.

3. Positive PCR (polymerase chain reaction test) via nasopharyngeal swab;

4. Pulmonary infiltrates typical of COVID-19 on chest radiographs or chest tomography (CT);

5. No contraindication to the intake of ethanol;

6. Informed consent.

5.1 Dose and administration

Ninety-five percent pure grain ethanol was used for a three-day regimen (3 total doses). Each daily dose was weight-based (actual body weight): female patients = 0.31 g/kg, and males = 0.33 g/kg. An equal volume of sterile water was mixed with the ethanol for a final concentration of 47.5%, and given continuously via face mask over approximately 60–75 min using a standard large-volume nebulizer driven by wall oxygen or air (determined by the patient's pre-treatment supplemental oxygen requirement) at a flow rate of 10 l/min. An anti-viral filter was connected to the exhalation port of the face mask. Respiratory therapists closely observed the patients and monitored SpO2 (oxygen saturation via pulse oximetry) during treatments, and nurses recorded pre-treatment blood pressure, pulse and respiratory rates, and temperature, as well as every 15 min during and for one-hour post-treatment. No other persons were allowed in the room during or post-nebulization except per hospital policy, which included strict adherence to isolation precautions and protection measures such as personal protection equipment.

5.2 Data collection, statistical analysis, and outcomes

Demographic, clinical, and outcomes data were collected by retrospective review of the medical records of three hundred-six patients admitted for COVID-19 with respiratory disease from April through December 2020. Patients who completed the three-day regimen (Ethanol Group) were compared to randomly selected patients (Control Group) who had been admitted to the general medical floor during the same time-period but had received only "standard" therapy for COVID-19 (i.e., no ethanol treatment). Statistical analysis was performed using the T-Test and Fisher's Exact Test, with a statistical significance of p-value < 0.05.

5.3 Demographics

Ninety-one patients received one or more doses of nebulized ethanol, while two hundred twenty-five randomly selected "control" patients were identified. Of the ninety-one patients who received any ethanol treatment, eighty-one (89%) completed the three-day regimen. (*Note: The total number of patients who were offered but refused treatment with alcohol is not known.*)

5.4 Severity of hypoxemia

The severity of hypoxemia was assessed in all patients before receiving any COVID-19 treatment, at 96 h after the first treatment, and again at the time of discharge from the hospital, using the SFR (SpO_2/FiO_2 ratio; "normal" ≥ 4.57) [45–47].

5.5 Outcome metrics

The following data and clinical outcomes of the two groups were collected and compared:

1. Change in level of SFR from admission to discharge;

2. Need for transfer to ICU for progression of disease severity;

3. Need for intubation for invasive mechanical ventilation;

4. Inpatient mortality and survival;

5. The average length of stay (ALOS);

6. Discharge disposition: home, need for supplemental home oxygen, home health services, hospice, or post-hospitalization admission/transfer to another health-care facility, i.e., nursing home, skilled-nursing facility, rehabilitation center, or long-term acute care center.

5.6 Results

Eighty-one patients completed the three-day regimen (Ethanol Group), and were compared to the Control Group (225). Ten patients (11%) who initially gave informed consent to try inhaled ethanol treatment did not complete the three-dose regimen and were not included in the final data analysis. One was in the respiratory extremis prior to starting the first treatment and received an unknown quantity before requiring emergent intubation and immediate transfer to the ICU, and received no further ethanol treatments. This patient subsequently expired after a prolonged hospital stay on mechanical ventilation. The other nine (9.9%) did not complete the first treatment dose or refused the second dose due to a universally reported side effect of immediate mild coughing and / or burning sensation in the naso-oropharynx. Two of these nine patients (22.2%) later required transfer to ICU and intubation for disease progression, and both subsequently expired. Seven of the nine patients (77.8%) improved after prolonged hospital stays and were subsequently discharged from the hospital with home health or to a skilled nursing facility.

As shown in **Table 1**, average age of both groups was similar: 63.6 years (median 64; range 41–96) in the Ethanol Group, compared to 65.5 years (median 62; range 28–99) in the Control Group ($p = 0.50$). Gender distribution was also comparable between the two groups: 42% (34) females and 58% (47) males, 51.6% (116) females and 48.4% (109) males in the Control Group ($p = 0.15$). Average BMI (body mass index = kg/m^2) was similar: 35.3 (median 34), compared to 33.4 (median 34) in the Control Group ($p = 0.06$).

Likewise, the presence of one or more significant co-morbidities was similar in both groups, including diabetes mellitus, chronic obstructive pulmonary disease, drug-induced immunosuppression (i.e., chemotherapy for cancer), obesity, hypertension, end-stage renal disease, and autoimmune disease (i.e., rheumatoid arthritis): 92.5% (75) in the Ethanol Group, and 87.1% (196) in the Control Group, ($p = 0.22$). The average pre-treatment SFR was statistically *worse* ($p < 0.001$) in the Ethanol Group (2.86) compared to the Control Group (3.83).

Demographic	Ethanol group (n = 81)	Control group (n = 225)	p-value*
Average age (years) Median; range	63.6 64; 41–96	65.5 62; 28–99	0.50
Gender M = male; F = female	M = 58% (47) F = 42% (34)	M = 48.4% (109) F = 51.6% (116)	0.15
Average BMI** Median	35.3 34.5	33.4 34	0.06
Comorbidities ≥ 1***	92.6% (75)	87.1% (196)	0.22
Average Pre-treatment SFR**** Range	2.86 2.65–3.07	3.83 3.33–3.93	<0.001

*Statistical significance: $p < 0.05$.
**BMI = body mass index, kg/m^2.
***Comorbidities include diabetes mellitus, chronic obstructive pulmonary disease, drug-induced. immunosuppression (i.e. chemotherapy for cancer), obesity, hypertension, end-stage renal disease, and autoimmune disease (i.e. rheumatoid arthritis).*
****SFR = SpO_2/FiO_2 Ratio (Example: "normal" SFR: SpO_2 0.98/0.21 = 4.67).

Table 1.
Demographic data.

Table 2 shows the use of "standard" (non-ethanol) treatments in both groups were similar, with all patients having received one or more of the following drugs: remdesivir, tocilizumab, azithromycin, intravenous steroids (dexamethasone or methylprednisolone), and convalescent plasma. The most frequent in both groups were remdesivir and intravenous steroids, but no statistical difference was found between both groups for anyone "standard" treatment (p = 0.07–0.86).

Table 3 shows pre-treatment SFR, and average post-treatment SFRs for both groups. In the ethanol group, the average SFR at 96 h (2.89) compared to pre-treatment (2.86) was unremarkable. Notable, the average SFR at 96 h in the Control Group had *decreased* from 3.83 to 3.69, but not statistically significant from the Ethanol Group (p = 0.21). Although not quite statistically significant (p = 0.06), the Ethanol Group had considerable improvement (21.7%) from the average pre-treatment SFR

Medication*	Ethanol group (n = 81)	Control group (n = 225)	p-value**
Remdesivir	45.7% (37)	56.4% (127)	0.22
Tocilizumab	4.9% (4)	8.9% (20)	0.34
Convalescent Plasma	17.3% (14)	16.4% (37)	0.86
Intravenous Steroids***	55.6% (45)	70.2% (158)	0.26
Hydroxychloroquine****	6.2% (5)	53.3% (12)	0.78
Azithromycin	28.4% (23)	14.7% (33)	0.07

All patients in both groups received vitamins C, D3, and zinc.
***Statistical significance: $p < 0.05$; no statistical difference was found between the two groups.*
****Dexamethasone or methylprednisolone.*
*****Removed from hospital "COVID-19 Formulary" in July 2020.*

Table 2.
"Standard" COVID-19 medications received.

Time of SFR*	EtOH group Average SFR (Range)	Control group Average SFR (Range)	p-value
Pre-treatment	2.86 (2.65–3.07)	3.83 (3.33–3.93)	<0.001
96 h post-treatment	2.89	3.69	0.21
Discharge from hospital	3.48 (3.28–3.68)	3.88 (3.87–3.89)	0.13
Δ pre-treatment versus 96 h	+1%	−3.7	0.23
Δ pre-treatment versus discharge	+21.7%	+1.3	0.06

**SFR = SpO_2/FiO_2 ratio; "normal" SFR: SpO^2 0.98/0.21 = 4.67.*

Table 3.
Pre- and post-treatment SPO_2/FIO_2 ratios.

(2.86) to discharge (3.48), compared to the Control Group which had a minor increase (1.3%) from the average pre-treatment SFR (3.83) to discharge (3.88).

Comparison of clinical outcomes is shown in **Table 4**. Progression (e.g., worsening) of COVID-19 disease requiring transfer to the intensive care unit (ICU) occurred less in the Ethanol Group compared to the Control Group: 8.6% (7), and 14.7% (33), respectively (p = 0.18), equating to a 41% less chance of requiring transfer to ICU for disease progression in the Ethanol Group. Intubation was necessary for all seven patients in the Ethanol Group who required transfer to ICU, compared to 82% (27) in

Clinical metric	EtOH group (n = 81)	Control group (n = 225)	p-value
Transfer to ICU	8.6% (7)*	14.7% (33)	0.18
Intubation	8.6% (7)	82% (27)	0.57
ALOS (days)	6.88	9.98	0.03
Median	5.5	8	
Range	4–27	6–33	
Inpatient overall mortality	7.4% (6)	17.8% (40)	0.03
Overall survival	92.6% (75)	82.2% (185)	0.03
ICU mortality	71..4% (5)	48.5% (16)	0.41
Home	81.4% (66)	40.9% (92)	<0.001
Home oxygen	45.7% (37)	64.4% (82)	0.15
Home health	34.6% (28)	28.9% (65)	0.40
DC to another facility**	6.2% (5)	38.2% (86)	<0.001
Hospice	4.9% (4)	3.1% (7)	0.49

**One patient developed hospital-acquired pneumonia and progressive shock due to S. marcescens on day 5. hospitalization; another required intubation for sudden cardiac arrest the day after 3rd EtOH treatment. **Facility = long-term acute care, nursing home, other skilled nursing, or rehabilitation. Abbreviations: ALOS = average length of inpatient stay; DC = discharge from hospital.*

Table 4.
Clinical outcomes.

the Control Group but was not statistically significant ($p = 0.57$). Notably, one of the seven patients in the Ethanol Group who required transfer to ICU had developed progressive respiratory failure and sepsis due to hospital-acquired pneumonia (*Serratia marcescens*) on day five of admission (two days post-third ethanol treatment), requiring intubation and vasopressor support for shock, and subsequently expired in ICU. Another patient expired having required transfer to ICU after emergent intubation for sudden cardiac arrest the day following the third EtOH treatment, although having been stable pre-arrest with no worsening hypoxemia or hemodynamic instability.

ALOS was less in the Ethanol Group (6.88 days, median 5.5, range 4–27) versus the Control Group, (9.98, median 8, range 6–33) and was statistically significant ($p = 0.03$).

Inpatient mortality was also statistically less in the Ethanol Group (6) compared to the Control Group (40): 7.4% and 17.8%, respectively ($p = 0.03$), translating to a significantly improved survival in the Ethanol Group of 92.6% (75) compared to 82.2% (185) in the Control Group ($p = 0.03$). The mortality rates of patients who required transfer to ICU because of disease progression were not statistically different between the two groups ($p = 0.41$), although a larger percentage of patients in the Ethanol Group (71%; $n = 5$) died compared to the Control Group (48.5%; $n = 16$). *Note: Post-discharge mortality rate is not known at this time.*

Interestingly, and statistically significant, 81.4% (66) in the Ethanol Group were able to be discharged to their homes compared to 40.9% (92) in the Control Group ($p < 0.001$), and only five (6.2%) in the Ethanol Group required discharge/transfer and admission to another healthcare facility for ongoing care (i.e. long-term acute care, nursing home, skilled nursing, or rehabilitation) compared to 38.2% (86) in the Control Group ($p < 0.001$). Four survivors (4.9%) in the Ethanol Group were discharged to hospice care, comparable to 7 (3.1%) in the Control Group ($p = 0.49$). The need for home health services post-discharge was similar: 34.6% (28) in the Ethanol Group, and 28.9% (65) in the Control Group ($p = 0.40$). Considerably fewer patients required supplemental home oxygen in the Ethanol Group (45.7%; $n = 37$) versus the Control Group (64.4%; $n = 82$), though not statistically significant ($p = 0.15$).

5.7 Discussion

The results of this study suggest a number of positive benefits of inhaled ethanol in the treatment of COVID-19 in non-ICU patients with acute hypoxemia. Statistically significant benefits included decreased ALOS, improved survival, and increased chance of discharge to home as opposed to requiring post-hospital treatment in long-term acute care, extended care facility (i.e., nursing home), or other skilled nursing facility (i.e. rehabilitation center, etc.). Other benefits included the decreased need for transfer to ICU due to disease progression, decreased need for intubation and decreased need for home oxygen. If such outcomes are confirmed in larger studies, the benefits to patients and healthcare systems worldwide would be incredible.

The science is sound as noted by other researchers [48, 49] regarding the potential use of inhaled ethanol as a treatment for COVID-19. Ethanol is rapidly absorbed in the respiratory tract and then transported via the circulatory system to other tissues. Nebulization into the nares (and mouth) has the benefit of direct deposition and contact with the virus in the upper and lower respiratory tissues, from which it can then circulate to other tissues where the virus has been shown to be present in autopsy findings [12], allowing ethanol to circumvent the "first pass" metabolism by alcohol dehydrogenase in the liver. The hypothesis is logical: direct deposition of ethanol on respiratory tissues may inactivate the virus in the respiratory epithelium thereby inhibiting viral replication and thus decreasing the viral load—and the risk of the inflammatory response (i.e., cytokine storm) which is responsible for organ failure (i.e., ARDS, acute kidney injury, etc.). The clinical results in this study support the hypothesis.

Obviously, while ethanol is known to inactivate SARS-CoV-2 on skin surfaces, the amount needed to inactivate SARS-CoV-2 in the respiratory tract (and other human tissues) is not known. The dose in this regimen was weight-based (0.31 g/kg for females, and 0.33 g/kg for males), estimated to produce a blood alcohol concentration of less than 0.08 mg %. Five ounces or 148 ml of wine is 12% EtOH by volume and contains about 14 g of EtOH, or 0.095 g/ml, whereas 95% EtOH contains 0.75 g/ml. Thus, in this regimen, for example, a 70 kg male would receive a nebulized dose of EtOH of about 23 cc of EtOH or about 17 g of EtOH—3 g more than that in one glass of wine [50]. (Of note, serum EtOH levels were not detectable 1-h post nebulization treatments.) While the dosing of EtOH in this study showed benefits, the optimal dosing and method of administration need further study. Plausibly, different dosing, frequency, and duration of therapy may prove even more beneficial, and it may prove more beneficial if initiated earlier, or within a specified time period of the initial onset of COVID-19 symptoms. (*Note: In this study, the duration of symptoms before seeking treatment is not available.*)

This regimen proved safe and was well tolerated in the great majority (89%) of patients who were known to have been offered the treatment. No severe adverse or untoward events were reported or discovered on review of the medical records. No patient reported a feeling of intoxication, and none became noticeably intoxicated during observance by medical personnel. All patients had onset of a temporary minor cough and/or burning sensation in the nasopharynx and throat, which lasted about 2 min, but these were the reasons given by those who initially gave consent to try the nebulized EtOH but refused subsequent treatments. No patient who received any or all of the three-day regimen was found to have physical evidence of naso-oropharyngeal mucosal inflammation. Likely, dilution of the nebulized weight-based dose with sterile water by one-half is beneficial in reducing the mild cough and/or burning sensation.

6. Where we currently stand

The ability of COVID-19 to cause widespread morbidity, mortality, and profound stress on healthcare systems worldwide has been harrowing. Not only increased costs of healthcare due to COVID-19 on the world economy, but this pandemic has had major negative effects on the entire well-being of society—previously unseen for many decades. No other disease has affected the current generation of medical professionals (or the world) like COVID-19. While other diseases exist for which there is no effective treatment, the mere volume of cases of COVID-19 has made its indelible mark.

From its beginning, the entire world felt the urgent need to find an effective treatment for this novel virus, and the discovery and development of new treatments for SARS-CoV-2 have been remarkable. Published data suggest definite benefits with a variety of medications including antivirals, monoclonal antibodies [51, 52], and high-titer convalescent plasma [51]. Based on COVID-19 pathogenesis, therapies that attack the virus itself are more likely to work *early* in the course of infection, whereas treatments that restrain the immune response (*cytokine storm*) may have more influence later in the disease [13, 14, 53]. Unfortunately, these medications are costly, and the prescriber of such treatments as the antiviral nirmatrelvir-ritonavir must also consider the potential for significant adverse reactions and interactions with a wide variety of other common medications that are highly dependent on *CYP3A* for clearance and for which elevated concentrations are associated with serious and or life-threatening reactions [54].

Obviously, as new COVID-19 variants arise, current therapy guidelines will need to be amended. For example, bebtelovimab has activity against Omicron *BA.2*, but there is a paucity of good clinical data showing an associated reduction in COVID-19 mortality [55, 56]. Monoclonal antibody therapies like sotrovimab, casirivimab-imdevimab, and bamlanivimab-etesevimab have shown a reduction in death and the need for hospitalization in outpatients who have a non-severe disease but at risk for progression [57, 58]. However, these formulations are not appropriate for use in areas where COVID-19 infection is most probably due to SARS-CoV-2 variants that are not susceptible (i.e., Omicron, subvariants, etc.) [59].

Beyond question, prevention of this devastating disease is of utmost importance, and vaccines are very promising. Several COVID-19 vaccines are available globally, but unfortunately, there are areas and populations of people who do not have access to vaccinations [60, 61]. In addition, as with current therapeutic treatments (e.g., anti-virals, monoclonal antibodies, etc.), the existing and future effectiveness of vaccines is a genuine concern given the recurrent mutations already witnessed in the SARS-CoV-2 genome. However, while vaccinations are a mainstay of prevention, *there will always remain a need for efficacious treatment for those who become acutely infected.*

6.1 Final comments

The results of this novel study should not be ignored. Not to downplay the importance of new treatments and vaccines which have been developed since the start of the COVID-19 Pandemic, unfortunately for the foreseeable future as new variants arise, the proclivity of SARS-CoV-2 to mutate and cause widespread infection and wreckage to the health of individuals and society alike remains a global health concern. The world needs an effective, safe, widely-available, and inexpensive treatment for COVID-19—and inhaled ethanol may well be that needed treatment. Extensive studies are needed to confirm and better define the use of inhaled ethanol in combatting this disease—and other susceptible respiratory viruses (i.e. influenza, etc.). If confirmed, inhaled ethanol has the potential to prevent morbidity, and save lives, healthcare resources, and economies the world over. Extensive research is needed to confirm the findings herein, but the results must not be unheeded.[2]

[2] Addendum: Since this writing, data that suggests the benefits of inhaled ethanol in the treatment of COVID-19 has been published, and supports the findings in this study [62].

Author details

Steven W. Stogner
Hattiesburg Clinic Pulmonary Medicine, Hattiesburg, MS, USA

*Address all correspondence to: sstogner@forrestgeneral.com

References

[1] Dong E, Ratcliff J, Goyea TD, Katz A, Lau R, Ng TK, et al. The Johns Hopkins University Center for Systems Science and Engineering COVID-19 Dashboard: data collection process, challenges faced, and lessons learned. The Lancet Infectious Diseases. Dec 2022;**22**(12):e370-e376. DOI: 10.1016/S1473-3099(22)00434-0. Epub 2022 Aug 31. Erratum in: Lancet Infect Dis. 2022 Nov;22(11):e310. PMID: 36057267; PMCID: PMC9432867

[2] Viboud C, Lessler J. The 1918 influenza pandemic: Looking back, looking forward. American Journal of Epidemiology. 2018;**187**(12):2493-2497. DOI: 10.1093/aje/kwy207

[3] COVID-19 surpasses 1918 flu as deadliest pandemic in U.S. history. National Geographic. September 21, 2021

[4] Cucinotta D, Vanelli M. WHO declares COVID-19 a pandemic. Acta Biomedica. 2020;**91**(1):157-160. DOI: 10.23750/abm.v91i1.9397

[5] Rockwood K. Rationing care in COVID-19: If we must do it, can we do better? Age and Ageing. 2021;**50**(1):3-6. DOI: 10.1093/ageing/afaa202

[6] Amanullah S, Ramesh SR. The impact of COVID-19 on physician burnout globally: A review. Healthcare (Basel). 2020;**8**(4):421. DOI: 10.3390/healthcare8040421

[7] Agyeman A et al. Smell and taste dysfunction in patients with COVID-19: A systematic review and meta-analysis. Mayo Clinic Proceedings. 2020;**95**(8):1621-1631

[8] Kompaniyets L, et al. Underlying medical conditions and severe illness among 540,667 adults hospitalized with COVID-19, March 2020–March 2021. Preventing Chronic Disease. Available from: https://www.cdc.gov/pcd/issues/2021/21

[9] Yao H et al. Molecular architecture of the SARS-CoV-2 virus. Cell. 2020;**183**(3):730-738.e13. DOI: 10.1016/j.cell.2020.09.018

[10] Sungnak W, Huang N, Becavin C, et al. SARS-CoV-2 entry factors are highly expressed in nasal epithelial cells together with innate immune genes. Nature Medicine. 2020;**26**:681-687. DOI: 10.1038/s41591-020-0868-6

[11] Severe acute respiratory syndrome-related coronavirus: classifying 2019-nCoV and naming it SARS-CoV-2. Coronaviridae Study Group of the International Committee on Taxonomy of Viruses. Nature Microbiology. 2020;**5**(4):536

[12] Polak SB, Van Gool IC, Cohen D, et al. A systematic review of pathological findings in COVID-19: a pathophysiological timeline and possible mechanisms of disease progression. Modern Pathology. 2020;**33**:2128-2138. DOI: 10.1038/s41379-020-0603-3

[13] Singh E et al. Management of COVID-19-induced cytokine storm by Keap1-Nrf2 system: a review. Inflammopharmacology. 2021;**29**(5):1347-1355. DOI: 10.1007/s10787-021-00860-5

[14] Mousavizadeh L, Ghasemi S. Genotype and phenotype of COVID-19: Their roles in pathogenesis. Journal of Microbiology, Immunology, and Infection. 2021;**54**(2):159-163. DOI: 10.1016/j.jmii.2020.03.022

[15] Alnima T, Mulder MMG, van Bussel BCT, Ten Cate H. COVID-19 Coagulopathy: From Pathogenesis to Treatment. Acta Haematologica. 2022;**145**(3):282-296. DOI: 10.1159/000522498

[16] Kratzel A et al. Efficient inactivation of SARS-CoV-2 by WHO-recommended hand rub formulations and alcohols. bioRxiv. 2020. DOI: 10.1101/2020.03.10.986711

[17] Meyers C et al. Ethanol and isopropanol inactivation of human coronavirus on hard surfaces. The Journal of Hospital Infection. 2021;**107**:45-49. DOI: 10.1016/j.jhin.2020.09.026

[18] Kampf G. Efficacy of ethanol against viruses in hand disinfection. Journal of Hospital Infection. 2018;**98**(4):331-338

[19] Gold NA, Mirza TM, Avva U. Alcohol Sanitizer. [Updated 2022 Jun 21]. In: StatPearls [Internet]. Treasure Island (FL): StatPearls Publishing; 2022. Available from: https://www.ncbi.nlm.nih.gov/books/NBK513254

[20] Singh D, Joshi K, Samuel A, Patra J, Mahindroo N. Alcohol-based hand sanitizers as first line of defense against SARS-CoV-2: a review of biology, chemistry and formulations. Epidemiology and Infection. 2020;(148):e229. DOI: 10.1017/S0950268820002319

[21] Sauerbrei A. Bactericidal and viricidal activity of ethanol and povidone-iodine. Microbiology. 2020;**9**(9):e1097. DOI: 10.1002/mbo3.1097

[22] Siddhartha A et al. Viricidal activity of World Health Organization-recommended formulations against enveloped viruses, including Zika, Ebola, and emerging coronaviruses. The Journal of Infectious Diseases. 2017;**215**:902-906

[23] Barceloux DG et al. American Academy of Clinical Toxicology Ad Hoc Committee on the Treatment Guidelines for Methanol Poisoning. American Academy of Clinical Toxicology practice guidelines on the treatment of methanol poisoning. Journal of Toxicology. Clinical Toxicology. 2002;**40**(4):415-446. DOI: 10.1081/clt-120006745

[24] Gootnick A, Lipson HI, Turbin J. Inhalation of ethyl alcohol for pulmonary edema. New England Journal of Medicine. 1951;**245**:842-843

[25] Luisada A, Ruth W, Goldmann M. Alcohol Vapor by Inhalation in the Treatment of Acute Pulmonary Edema. Circulation. 1952;**5**:363-369. DOI: 10.1161/01.CIR.5.3.363

[26] Zhang P et al. Inhalation of alcohol vapor driven by oxygen is a useful therapeutic method for postoperative alcohol withdrawal syndrome in a patient with esophageal cancer: a case report. Alcohol and Alcoholism. 2011;**46**(4):424-426. DOI: 10.1093/alcalc/agr037

[27] Dillard R et al. Ethanol infusion for alcohol withdrawal prophylaxis does not cause intoxication. The Southwest Respiratory and Critical Care Chronicles. 2016;**4**(16):11-18

[28] Takahashi G, Endo S. Improvement of acute respiratory distress syndrome with ethyl alcohol infusion into the airway: A case report. Pulmonary and Respiratory Medicine. 2018;**8**:464. DOI: 10.4172/2161-105X.1000464

[29] Mcclenahan JB, Mussenden R, Ohlsen JD. Effect of ethanol on surfactant of ventilated lungs. Journal of Applied Physiology. 1969;**27**(1). DOI: 10.1152/jappl.1969.27.1.90

[30] Leng L et al. Pathological features of COVID-19-associated lung injury: a preliminary proteomics report based on clinical samples. Signal Transduction and Targeted Therapy. 2020;**5**:240. DOI: 10.1038/s41392-020-00355-9

[31] Mörs K et al. Ethanol decreases inflammatory response in human lung epithelial cells by inhibiting the canonical NF-kB-pathway. Cellular Physiology and Biochemistry. 2017;**43**:17-30. DOI: 10.1159/000480313

[32] Elsoukkary SS et al. Autopsy findings in 32 patients with COVID-19: A single-institution experience. Pathobiology. 2021;**88**(1):56-68. DOI: 10.1159/000511325

[33] Iba T et al. The unique characteristics of COVID-19 coagulopathy. Critical Care. 2020;**24**(1):360. DOI: 10.1186/s13054-020-03077-0

[34] Tabengwa EM et al. Ethanol-induced up-regulation of candidate plasminogen receptor annexin II in cultured human endothelial cells. Alcoholism, Clinical and Experimental Research. 2000;**24**(6):754-761

[35] Centers for Disease Control and Prevention (CDC). Alcohol and Public Health: Alcohol-Related Disease Impact (ARDI); 2020. Available from: https://nccd.cdc.gov.

[36] Simet SM, Sisson JH. Alcohol's Effects on Lung Health and Immunity. Alcohol Research: Current Reviews. 2015;**37**(2):199-208

[37] Goral J, Karavitis J, Kovacs EJ. Exposure-dependent effects of ethanol on the innate immune system. Alcohol. 2008;**42**(4):237-247. DOI: 10.1016/j.alcohol.2008.02.003

[38] Sarkar D et al. Alcohol and the immune system. Alcohol Research: Current Reviews. 2015;**37**(2):153-155

[39] Watzl B, Bub A, Briviba K, Rechkemmer G. Acute intake of moderate amounts of red wine or alcohol has no effect on the immune system of healthy men. European Journal of Nutrition. 2002;**41**(6):264-270. DOI: 10.1007/s00394-002-0384-0

[40] Jerrells TR. Immunodeficiency Associated with Ethanol Abuse. In: Friedman H, Specter S, Klein TW, editors. Drugs of Abuse, Immunity, and Immunodeficiency, Advances in Experimental Medicine and Biology. Vol. 288. Boston, MA: Springer; 1991. DOI: 10.1007/978-1-4684-5925-8_26

[41] MacLean RR, Valentine GW, Jatlow PI, Sofuoglu M. Inhalation of alcohol vapor: Measurement and implications. Alcoholism, Clinical and Experimental Research. 2017;**41**(2):238-250. DOI: 10.1111/acer.13291

[42] Valentine GW et al. The effects of alcohol-containing e-cigarettes on young adult smokers. Drug and Alcohol Dependence. 2016;**159**:272-276. DOI: 10.1016/j.drugalcdep.2015.12.011

[43] Žuškin E, Bouhuys A, Šari M. Lung function changes by ethanol. Frontiers in Immunology. 1981. DOI: 10.1111/j.1365-2222.1981.tb01590.x

[44] Tsumoru Shintake (2020). "Possibility of Disinfection of SARS-CoV-2 (COVID-19) in Human Respiratory Tract by controlled Ethanol Vapor Inhalation. Available from: https://arxiv.org/abs/2003.12444 (Cornell University).

[45] Boyle AJ, Sweeney RM, McAuley DF. Pharmacological treatments in ARDS; a state-of-the-art update. BMC Medicine. 2013;**11**:166. DOI: 10.1186/1741-7015-11-166

[46] Festic E, Bansal V, Kor DJ, Gajic O. US Critical Illness and Injury Trials

Group: Lung Injury Prevention Study Investigators (USCIITG–LIPS). SpO_2/FiO_2 ratio on hospital admission is an indicator of early acute respiratory distress syndrome development among patients at risk. Journal of Intensive Care Medicine. 2015;**30**(4):209-216. DOI: 10.1177/0885066613516411

[47] Rice TW et al. National Institutes of Health, National Heart, Lung, and Blood Institute ARDS Network. Comparison of the SpO_2/FIO_2 ratio and the PaO_2/FIO_2 ratio in patients with acute lung injury or ARDS. Chest. 2007;**132**(2):410-417

[48] Salvatori P. The rationale of ethanol inhalation for disinfection of the respiratory tract in SARS- CoV-2-positive asymptomatic subjects. The Pan African Medical Journal. 2021;**40**:201. DOI: 10.11604/pamj.2021.40.201.31211

[49] Amoushahi A, Padmos A. A Suggestion on Ethanol Therapy in COVID-19? Available from: https://www.ecronicon.com/ecan/pdf/ECAN-06-00229.pdf

[50] Campbell L, Wilson HK. Blood alcohol concentrations following the inhalation of ethanol vapor under controlled conditions. Journal of the Forensic Science Society. 1986;**26**(2):129-135. DOI: 10.1016/S0015-7368(86)72458-4

[51] Infectious Diseases Society of America Guidelines on the Treatment and Management of Patients with COVID-19. Available from: https://www.idsociety.org/practice-guidelines-and-management.

[52] WHO Solidarity Trial Consortium, Pan H, Peto R, et al. Repurposed antiviral drugs for Covid-19—Interim WHO solidarity trial results. The New England Journal of Medicine. 2021;**384**:497

[53] Libster R et al. Early high-titer plasma therapy to prevent severe Covid-19 in older adults. The New England Journal of Medicine. 2021;**384**(7):610

[54] US FDA. Remdesivir letter of EUA. Available from: https://www.fda.gov/media

[55] National Institutes of Health. The COVID-19 Treatment Guidelines Panel's statement on potential drug-drug interactions between ritonavir-boosted nirmatrelvir (Paxlovid®) and concomitant medications. Available from: https://www.covid19treatmentguidelines.nih.gov/therapies/statement-on-paxlovid-drug-drug-interactions

[56] US Food and Drug Administration. Fact sheet for healthcare providers: Emergency Use Authorization for bebtelovimab. Available from: https://www.fda.gov/media/156152.

[57] O'Brien MP et al. Effect of Subcutaneous Casirivimab and Imdevimab Antibody Combination vs Placebo on Development of Symptomatic COVID-19 in Early Asymptomatic SARS-CoV-2 Infection: A Randomized Clinical Trial. JAMA. 2022;**327**(5):432

[58] US Food and Drug Administration. Coronavirus (COVID-19) update: FDA limits use of certain monoclonal antibodies to treat COVID-19 due to the Omicron variant. January 2022. Available from: https://www.fda.gov/news-events/press-announcements/coronavirus-covid-19-update-fda-limits-use-certain-monoclonal-antibodies-treat-covid-19-due-omicron.

[59] National Institutes of Health. COVID-19 treatment guidelines: What's new in the guidelines. Available from: https://www.covid19treatmentguidelines.nih.gov/about-the-guidelines/whats-new.

[60] Malik JA et al. The SARS-CoV-2 mutations versus vaccine effectiveness: New opportunities to new challenges. DOI: 10.1016/j.jiph.2021.12.014

[61] WHO. Draft landscape of COVID-19 candidate vaccines. Available from: https://www.who.int/publications/m/item/draft-landscape-of-covid-19-candidate-vaccine

[62] Amoushahi A, Moazam E, Tabatabaei A, et al. (December 05, 2022) Efficacy and Safety of Inhalation of Nebulized Ethanol in COVID-19 Treatment: A Randomized Clinical Trial. Cureus 14(12): e32218. doi:10.7759/cureus.32218

Chapter 8

Theoretical Bases for the Disinfection of the SARS-CoV-2-Contaminated Airways by Means of Ethanol Inhalation

Pietro Salvatori

Abstract

Ethyl alcohol, or ethanol (EtOH), is a linear alkyl chain alcohol, whose condensed structural formula is CH_3CH_2OH. Besides the common industrial and recreational uses (spirits, cosmetics, fuelling, etc.), EtOH is considered a medicament and listed in the European and US Pharmacopeias. Medically, EtOH is mainly employed as an antidote in methanol and ethylene glycol poisoning, as an excipient in many medicaments, as a sclerosant agent, and as a powerful disinfectant. Less recently, EtOH was shown to be both effective and safe in the treatment of pulmonary edema and cough. This chapter deals with EtOH use in SARS-CoV-2 infection and COVID-19 treatments.

Keywords: SARS-CoV-2, COVID-19, ethanol, inhalation, public health

1. Introduction

This section resumes and adequately updates as of September 4, 2022 my published article [1].

The SARS-CoV-2 outbreak has hit the global community and we are experiencing the third wave after the first phase—and likely, a fourth one—as well as more aggressive variants surge (Delta and Epsilon, Omicron, Centaurus). To this day, no specific therapy has been identified as effective. While mass immunization campaigns take a long time, and pose questions about their effectiveness against new variants and long-lasting protection, they are very likely to dramatically improve disease control. As consequence, attempts to understand the cold chain and potential active eradication of the virus become of the highest significance and the emphasis on prevention over pandemic control grows. In fact, the main objective still to be achieved for the control of any contagious disease is the individuation and—possibly—treatment of spreading subjects. According to this, research has been done on conjunctival cells, upper respiratory tract goblet cells, type 2 pneumocytes, and enterocytes as the main targets of the virus-binding receptors. Actually, epithelial cells of the nasal cavity and lower respiratory tract, including alveolar cells, are associated with SARS-CoV-2 entry factors, mainly angiotensin-converting enzyme 2 (ACE2) receptors [2] and therefore, COVID-19 infection occurs initially in the epithelial layer of the upper respiratory tract, followed by transfer to the lower respiratory tract [3]. According to Madas et al. [4], pneumonia may be prevented by stopping or significantly limiting the transit of viruses into the acinar airways during the gap between the start of early symptoms and any potential clinical worsening. As a result, even non-specific therapies like disinfecting the mouth, nose, and throat successfully keep the viral load in the upper airways low enough to stop or delay the disease's progression. A very comprehensive study [5] on Wuhan's population (about 10,000,000 individuals) demonstrates that, following a period of isolation, the incidence of symptomatic individuals was reduced to 0.00303%, providing an indication of the success of containment. Many of these infected individuals do not have any clinical manifestations of the disease; they are also known as "asymptomatic positives" or PAS (healthy carriers?). Observations show that PASs have a noticeable SARS-CoV-2 viral load, and this surely draws attention to their contribution to the epidemic's progression. Among a group of students, Nelson et al. [6] recently discovered that, in said group, contacts of people who tested positive returned positive at rates of 10.4 and 4.8% after 3 and 9 days, respectively. One of the latest researches by Atripaldi et al. [7] discovered that asymptomatic patients had a noticeable SARS-CoV-2 viral load. This highlighted the importance of asymptomatic (and pre-symptomatic) individuals in the development of the epidemic.

There still are no established criteria for identifying asymptomatic patients who will spread the infection to other subjects; thus, all of them should be regarded as being suitable for disinfection. Thus, early detection and potential treatment of asymptomatic positive people are of major importance The goal is to terminate the transmission chain and reduce or even end confinement time (and the related financial, social, and psychological costs), and promptly reintroduce recovered patients back in society. The 14-day quarantine is undoubtedly the only option that now is currently given to asymptomatic positive patients. It may be deduced from Liu et al.'s [8] study of SARS-CoV-2 contamination in quarantine rooms that unless the patient lives alone, or each person present in the household has their own private rooms, the strategy is likely to be unsuccessful. The objective is to highlight the extent of the issue, illustrate available solutions, and investigate the effectiveness and toxicological aspects that would support the use of inhaled ethanol (or ethyl alcohol) for airway disinfection in SARS-CoV-2-infected patients who are asymptomatic. For research publications published up to July 29, 2021, databases such as MEDLINE, Embase, Europe PubMed Central, medRxiv, and bioRxiv, as well as the gray literature, have been examined. Key findings were covered in our case reports (with five or more participants), cohort studies, randomized controlled trials, and records of trial registration:

- epidemiological data highlighting the extent of the problem;
- ongoing efforts in disinfection of SARS-CoV-2-positive asymptomatic patients;
- the ability of ethanol to eliminate or inactivate viruses, and SARS-CoV-2 more specifically.
- potentially positive effects of ethanol on the airways.

- ethanol's both local and general harmful effects when ingested or inhaled.
- data allowing the identification of the therapeutic window for ethanol inhalation.

The explanation for the suggested novel technique was supported (or rejected) based on reliable data.

2. Results

2.1 Extension of the problem

As of now (September 4, 2022), the world's active cases are 610,144,519 and total deaths reached 6,503,374 [9]. Thus, lethality accounts for 1.07%. Between 17 and 20% of positives are asymptomatic (healthy carriers) [10]. Within 8 days (mean), 43% of asymptomatic positive patients develop symptoms (of any kind) [11]. As even more nations implement some form of quarantine laws, the effects on the social and economic sectors are extremely detrimental. The mean viral load elimination time for the upper and lower respiratory tracts, respectively is 14 days and 17 days, according to a fairly recent meta-analysis [12]. Interestingly, no live virus has ever been found 9 days after the sickness first appears. Patients who were asymptomatic and those who had symptoms were compared, and the results for the elimination time between the two groups were inconsistent. Among health workers, Bongiovanni [13] reports an average viral load elimination time of 22 days, which may be explained by their propensity to receive a higher viral load in their work environment, compared to the average population.

2.2 Current efforts

Metformin, ivermectin, and fluvoxamine have been studied in less severe COVID-19 infections [14].

Protease inhibitors are currently used in high-risk patients [15].

Highly specialized medications such as monoclonal and polyclonal antibodies are now being studied and used, but their high cost and possibility for effectiveness loss caused by the spread of new variations severely restrict their potential advantages [16].

It is necessary to investigate the potential of nonspecific medications in the absence of particular, well-established therapies for respiratory disinfection. Guenezan et al. [17] made an effort to disinfect positive but asymptomatic individuals. Povidone iodine mouthwash and nasal spray both significantly increased viral titer in a single small-randomized clinical study, although they had no impact on the lower respiratory tract.

According to a recent randomized clinical trial [18], medical professionals could significantly reduce their risk of contracting COVID-19 by using a nasal spray solution composed of dimethyl sulfoxide and ethanol.

2.3 Ethanol efficiency

Ethyl alcohol or ethanol is widely used in disinfection procedures. Additionally, a substantial amount of integrated evidence shows that ethanol does indeed have antiviral properties, which may be related to the solvent's effects on lipids (pericapsid) and the denaturation of proteins (capsid) [19]. The temperature and phase in which the pericapsid is located (which derives from the cell membrane of the infected host) affect the outcome. The effectiveness of ethanol in an aqueous solution of 35.2% by weight (equivalent to 44% by volume) is the highest at about 50°C (crystalline phase) and diminished or rendered ineffective at about 25°C (gel phase) [20]. It is possible to assume an intermediate impact at human body temperature. Human coronaviruses, including Severe Acute Respiratory Syndrome Coronavirus (SARS), Middle East Respiratory Syndrome (MERS), and Human Endemic Coronavirus, have been demonstrated to be significantly affected by ethanol where, on surfaces such as plastic and glass, these viruses can survive for days. Disinfectants, such as EtOH, have been demonstrated to diminish the coronavirus's infectiousness in a short amount of time. The said demonstrations showed a 62–71% effectiveness. Thankfully, SARS-CoV-2 is an enveloped virus that is extremely sensitive to ethanol; current experimental data show that an ethanol concentration of 30% v/v is able to inactivate SARS-CoV-2 in 30 seconds [21].

- The quantity of alcohol required to reduce the SARS-CoV-2 viral load affecting the lungs was determined by Manning et al. [22].
- According to estimates, COVID-19 has a viral load of 20 million copies per milliliter of lung tissue.
- Adult lung tissue contains 120 * 109 (billions) (rounded to 200 * 109 (billions)) virus particles, many of which are infected cells.
- It is estimated that 10 * 106 million molecules of ethanol are required to disinfect or render a virus particle inactive.
- Ethanol has a density of around 0.8 g/ml = 800 g/l = 800,000 mg/l = 80,000 mg/dl = 800 mg/ml. Its molar mass is 46 g/mol. A mole contains N = 6.02252 * 1023 molecules, which is equal to Avogadro's number.
- To remove $200 * 10^9$ (billions) of viruses, $(10 * 10^6) * (200 * 10^9) = 2 * 10^{18}$ molecules of ethanol will be needed (molar mass = 46 g /mol).
- $(2 * 10^{18}$ EtOH$) / (N * 10^{23}$EtOH/mol$) = 3.3 * 10^{-6}$ moles of ethanol
- $(3.3 * 10^{-6}) * (46$ g/mol$) = 0.000153$ gr = 153 μg of ethanol or 191.25 μL

2.4 Effects of ethanol on respiratory cells and microbiota

1. The relationship between alcohol exposure time and dose and the effect it has on respiratory hairy cells is bimodal. Sisson [23] demonstrated (*in vitro*) that ethanol (10 mM concentration = 0.46 mg/ml) caused a 40% increase in beat frequency (6 Hz to 8.5 Hz) after only 10 minutes of treatment. A mechanism that is dependent on nitrogen oxide is responsible for this result. However, the same experiment performed with ethanol at a greater concentration (1 M = 46 mg/ml) resulted in a decrease in the beat frequency, demonstrating that ethanol could a harmful impact by desensitizing ciliary motility, which makes it

stimulation-resistant (a process known as Alcohol-Induced Ciliary Dysfunction mediated by oxidative stress) [24].

2. Up to the 1950s, inhalations of EtOH were proven to be both safe and effective for treating coughs and pulmonary edema [25–28].

3. Up to 9 mg of ethanol per actuation is frequently used as an excipient in inhalation treatment for asthma and chronic obstructive pulmonary disease [29].

It is possible that EtOH might have a harmful effect on the respiratory microbiome, but there is no solid evidence of this in the medical literature. In contrast, some helpful remarks could emerge from this. As a matter of fact, Sulaiman et al. [30] discovered that a poor clinical outcome was connected to an enrichment of the lower respiratory tract's microbiota with an oral commensal (*Mycoplasma salivarium*) and an enhanced SARS-CoV-2 virus load in a group of patients intubated with COVID-19. Intensive care patients with SARS-CoV-2 showed full depletion of *Bifidobacterium* and *Clostridium*, according to Rueca et al.'s [31] study of the nasal/oropharyngeal microbial flora.

2.5 Ethanol toxicity

The toxicity of acute inhalation of ethanol has mostly been researched in four real-world scenarios. From a toxicological perspective, there is a significant difference between ingested and inhaled ethanol, since the latter bypasses the first necessary metabolic step of ingested ethanol and instead travels straight to the left ventricle of the heart and the brain [32].

Surgical disinfection of the hands. Bessonneau [33] has demonstrated that the cumulative dose of ethanol inhaled in 90 seconds while surgically disinfecting hands with a gel containing ethanol at a concentration of 700 g/l is 328.9 mg. The blood alcohol content would be 203.9 mg, giving blood alcohol content (BAC) of 40.6 mg/L because the inhalation/absorption rate (i.e., the amount of ethanol that passes from the alveoli to the bloodstream) is 62%. Hypothetically, even if ethanol absorption was to happen instantly (rather than during 90 seconds), the blood alcohol level would still be well below the limit that is deemed toxic (500 mg/L in Italy and 800 mg/L in the majority of the United States). Healthcare workers may disinfect their hands up to 30 times per day [34], which results in a daily dose of inhaled ethanol of 9.86 grams, depending on the frequency of surgical hand disinfection associated with appropriate care activities with a high risk of contamination (for instance, by washing incontinent patients).

Liquid contained in some "e-cigarettes" (electronic cigarettes) may contain ethanol in various proportions. The usage of electronic cigarettes containing 23.5% ethanol and utilized with various suction mechanisms is reported in the study by More [35] along with statistics on ethanol absorption. The said statistics showed that the absorption of ethanol never exceeded 0.85 mg/l. The calculated blood alcohol content never went over 0.85 mg/l. The estimated blood alcohol level by projecting to triple or quadruple concentrations should be 0.85 mg/lx 3 = 2.55 mg/L in the first hypothesis and 3.4 mg/L in the second, which are both substantially below the toxic limit.

Patients with COVID-19-pneumonia are now being researched to see if ethanol inhalation could be a viable therapy option [36].

Additionally, a phase II clinical trial has been filed to assess the effectiveness and safety of inhaled ethanol in the early stage of COVID-19 therapy. The trial is now actively recruiting new participants [37, 38].

In rodents breathing, 65% v/v ethanol for 15 min every 8 hours (3 times a day), for five consecutive days (flow rate: 2 L/minute), Castro-Balado et al. [38] examined the mucosal or structural damages to EtOH in the lung, trachea, and esophagus. The calculated absorbed dosage was 1.2 g/kg/day. Under the same conditions, this dosage in humans would be equivalent to 151 g per day. Notably, neither the treated animals nor the controls' histology samples showed any signs of damage.

Numerous studies suggest that industrial exposure is not a problem in reproductive medicine (Irvine) [39] nor in oncology (Bevan) [40], despite the toxicity of chronic ethanol inhalation. In Bevan's [40] research, the occupational exposure limit (OEL) for the United Kingdom was examined (1000 ppm of ethanol = 1910 mg/m3 over an 8-hour shift). It was also determined that ingesting 10 g of ethanol (roughly one glass of alcohol) per day would be perfectly in line with the occupational exposure limit (OEL). These numbers are in perfect agreement with Bessonneau's [33] and Boyce's [34] reports.

Chronic ethanol use is not the same as chronic ethanol abuse, which can result in lung damage (alveolar macrophage dysfunction, increased susceptibility to bacterial pneumonia, and tuberculosis) [41].

The greatest amount of ethanol that can be instantly administered to a healthy adult is 2.5 g, given that the blood volume is roughly 5 L and the maximum permissible blood level of ethanol is 500 mg/L.

Elimination of ethanol occurs at a rate of 120 to 300 mg/L/hour [42]. Alcohol dehydrogenase breaks down 95% of EtOH that has been consumed (or breathed), while the remaining 5% is removed—unaltered—by exhaled air, urine, perspiration, saliva, and tears.

2.6 Inhaled ethanol therapeutic window

On this subject, no focused research was found.

The highest permitted ethanol dose or concentration, however, will be determined using previous data from regulatory reports [40].

Each type of inhalation treatment is potentially more effective compared to any other mode of delivery for treating airway diseases [22].

3. Discussion

3.1 Dimension of the problem

The SARS-CoV-2 outbreak pattern exhibits a rather steady trend combined with local upsurges, most likely as result of variant selection and superspreader events [43]. In addition to the immeasurable worth of the suffering and lives lost (4,203,776 to date), the world's lost economic output has tremendously increased to roughly 3.94 trillion U.S. Dollars [44]. These findings logically support the intensive treatment of positive asymptomatic people in an effort to limit or, ideally, stop the spread of the infection.

3.2 Current efforts

In a study evaluating metformin, ivermectin, and fluvoxamine, none of the drugs were effective in avoiding hypoxemia, ER visits, hospital stays, or deaths related to COVID-19 [14].

Protease inhibitors seem to have the potential to cause a rebound infection and appear to be ineffective against some SARS-CoV-2 strains [45, 46].

There is currently no published research on the regular use of monoclonal antibodies to treat SARS-CoV-2 positive and asymptomatic individuals. Furthermore, their high price and the probable loss of efficacy owing to variants seem to substantially restrict any benefit.

In the pharynx and oral cavity, povidone-iodine [17] has demonstrated excellent efficiency in lowering the viral titer. Povidone-iodine gargles, however, does not reach the lower respiratory tract, which is a notable limitation. However, as it focuses on the management of a crucial stage in the chain of viral transmission, this work deserves special attention. Of course, inhaling ethanol removes the previously mentioned limitation.

Actually, the experience of Hosseinzadeh [18] has shown that ethanol (together with dimethyl sulfoxide) can be delivered as a nasal spray in a safe and efficient way. In this randomized clinical trial involving volunteer healthcare providers without a history of SARS-CoV-2 infection or COVID-19, it has been clearly demonstrated that such a prophylactic measure can considerably prevent COVID-19 in the treated group. Namely, the risk of COVID-19 was about eightfold higher in those who used routine care than in those who used dimethyl sulfoxide-ethanol spray.

3.3 Ethanol efficiency

There is no question regarding ethanol's ability to kill or inactivate SARS-CoV-2, even at concentrations as low as 30% v/v in just 30 seconds, according to experimental and clinical data [21].

Alcohol is probably ineffective against intracellular viruses. It is crucial to extend ethanol inhalation by at least 3 days, since viral multiplication happens in 48–72 hours, which is then followed by cellular death and shedding. Additionally, ethanol is fundamentally effective against all SARS-CoV-2 variants and other "enveloped" viruses due to its non-specificity. This particular characteristic broadens the ethanol's range of activity against the SARS-CoV-2 pandemic and suggests its use in potential future viral epidemics.

The determined theoretical lowest dose of ethanol (= 153 μg) required to eradicate the fictitious virus load is relatively low when compared to daily exposure to many different jobs.

3.4 Ethanol effects on respiratory cells and microbiota

Alcohol's impact on respiratory hairy cells has been demonstrated by Sisson [23] to be a bimodal function of both exposure time and dosage. Low concentrations of ethanol (10 mM = 0.46 mg/ml) cause an increase in ciliary clearance, which may help to speed up the viral load's elimination once it has, theoretically, been made inactive by ethanol's own physicochemical features.

There is currently not enough research on how short-term ethanol administration affects respiratory microbiome. On the other hand, certain recommendations can be made in this regard. In fact, patients in the intensive care unit who had abnormally high levels of *M. salivarium* in the lower tract or low levels of clostridia in the upper tract had worse outcomes. It is noteworthy that ethanol totally inactivates SARS-CoV-2, mycoplasma, and SARS-CoV-2 (Eterpi et al.) [47]. Additionally, certain strains of clostridia are known to independently produce ethanol on their own [48]; this ability has been used in commercial ABE fermentation to create acetone, butanol, and ethanol [49]. The lack of nasopharyngeal clostridia may hypothetically result in decreased or nonexistent local ethanol production, which would then let SARS-Cov-2 remain active at this level and move to the lower respiratory tract [3].

3.5 Ethanol toxicity

Rules governing acute ethanol exposure vary by nation or state and are subject to laws. The maximum Blood Alcohol Concentration (BAC) for the general public in the USA is between 500 and 800 mg/L. The regulation also restricts the maximum amount of chronic ethanol exposure in the workplace. For instance, the occupational exposure limit (OEL) for ethanol in the United Kingdom is 1000 parts per million (ppm) of ethanol, or 1910 mg/m3, during an 8-hour shift, which is equivalent to consuming 10 g of ethanol (about one glass of alcohol) daily, according to estimates [40]. These numbers much exceed the amount that would theoretically be needed to reduce the virus load in the respiratory tract. There have been many and vocal concerns made concerning the potential mucosal harm that inhaled ethanol might cause. These worries appear to have been completely dispelled by the thorough study by Castro-Balado et al. [38]. Interestingly, in the RCT from Hosseinzadeh [18], collateral effects are not mentioned, perhaps because were lacking or minimal and tolerable.

3.6 Inhaled ethanol therapeutic window

One must inevitably connect to the current experience because no focused research on this subject was found [33, 40].

Therefore, it appears acceptable and rational to declare that the hazardous risk of such acute inhalation—that is, about 330 mg—may be viewed as negligible [33]. This is because surgical cleaning with 70% ethanol for 90″ is a daily habit and should generally be suggested and implemented. In reality, even if this dose was administered instantaneously to a healthy adult, the amount of ethanol in the air patients would inhale would be 0.078 mg/ml or 330 mg/5 L (airway volume). This quantity is significantly lower than both the legal limit of 500 mg/L (0.5 mg/ml) and the experimentally determined threshold of alcohol-induced ciliary dysfunction, which is 46 mg/ml [23]. Given that the lung and blood volumes are similar, equivalent numbers for the blood's ethanol concentration—which is far lower than the 500 mg/L legal lethal dose— could be derived.

However, this dose is a thousand times greater than the minimal dose of 153 μg needed to inactivate the calculated viral load in the lungs [22].

Each type of inhalation treatment is potentially more successful than any other method of administration for treating airway diseases [22]. Aerosol treatment enables lower doses, access to "hidden" regions, improved targeting of certain cells or compartments, etc., all of which boost the bioavailability of medications.

The size of the particles generated—classified according to the Aerodynamic Median Mass Diameter, or AMMD—well relates to the site to be treated. For the purpose of this chapter, the AMMD of the aerosol particles should be 5 μm.

Because of the relatively fresh technique suggested in this chapter, it is expected that there are little consolidated data in medical literature.

Focusing on the issue's dimension revealed that, in terms of threats to personal and societal health as well as associated economic costs, the disinfection of asymptomatic positive patients is crucial. There are currently no viable or affordable solutions to the issue.

Within a well-defined framework, the review and update of information attest to the high effectiveness and tolerable toxicity of inhaled ethanol. As a result, it is appropriate to administer inhaled ethanol to SARS-CoV-2-positive patients who are asymptomatic. A clinical trial should be carried out to examine its efficacy and tolerance in particular scenarios, as already suggested by Prof. Shintake [50] on March 17, 2020, and Dr. Amoushahi et al. [51] on May 25, 2020. Certainly, the research would be speedy, affordable, and straightforward to carry out.

The Authors post the following propositions:

It must be made clear that ethanol treatment is not believed to be an alternative to vaccination but rather must be considered complementary with it because vaccination appears to not prevent infection and disease from subintrant variants [52]. IF IT IS FOUND THAT THIS TREATMENT IS EFFECTIVE, THE FOLLOWING HEALTH BENEFITS COULD BE EXPECTED:

reduction of the viral load on the respiratory tract, if not elimination, in a period of time much less than the duration of the normal cycle.

lowering the viral pressure on the immune system of the infected person to decrease the disease's course.

decrease in the quantity of virus that is actively released when someone coughs or sneezes.

reduction in the spread of the infection.

Minimal biological/health consequences (lethality, pulmonary fibrosis, psychiatric disorders, etc.).

4. Proposal for a study

4.1 Aim and scope

A study in which ethanol is administered as an inhaled vapor to SARS-CoV-2-positive asymptomatic patients.

The aim is to eradicate or, at the very least, lower the viral load of the respiratory tract, of course, in a span of time much shorter than the natural one.

The predicted health advantages include the following:

- Reduction of the viral pressure on the infected subject's immune system to halt the disease's progression.
- A decrease in the quantity of virus that is actively released when someone coughs or sneezes.
- A reduction in the infection's spread.
- Less biological/health harm (lethality, pulmonary fibrosis, psychiatric disorders, etc.)

4.2 Dosage and timing

Given that the lowest concentration of ethanol that is effective against SARS-CoV-2 is 30% v/v (Kratzel) [20], it is considered reasonable and wise to use a concentration that is between the one mentioned above and the one used for surgical disinfection (70%) [33].

In essence, the following dose is suggested: 1 ml of normal saline solution at 50% v/v (galenic preparation) =390 mg (i.e., 50% by volume = 39% by weight, then 1 ml =390 mg), in 2 at 5 minutes. Although the proposed dose is in absolute terms slightly higher than the dose inhaled during surgical disinfection, it can be assimilated because it is delivered over a longer time.

4.3 Delivery system

Each type of inhalation treatment is potentially more successful than any other method of administration for treating airway illnesses [22]. Aerosol treatment enables lower doses, access to "hidden" areas, improved targeting of certain cells or compartments, etc., all of which boost the bioavailability of medications.

According to the Aerodynamic Median Mass Diameter, or MMAD, the size of the particles produced is closely tied to the area that has to be treated.

1. It is advised that patients utilize a nebulizer, a medical aerosol device, and a mask that covers their mouth and nose. The patient should start nasal inhalation with the mask at a comfortable distance from the face, gradually lowering this distance as much as possible to avoid or reduce the initial (moderate) burning sensation. According to the distillation curve, the ethanol breathed in the beginning is at a higher concentration (approximately 65% v/v) while nearing the ending of the session, in obedience of the distillation curve.

2. The mass median aerodynamic diameter (MMAD) of the aerosol particles should be 5 μm.

4.4 Scheduling

Every 8 hours (6- to 10-hour intervals), for 7 days, there will be one activation (treatment), for a total of 21 administrations. When two-thirds of the solution has been administered, the administration might be terminated, according to the distillation curve.

4.5 Candidates

1. Individuals that turned a positive rapid antigenic test or RT-PCR for COVID-19.

2. Absence of symptoms (fever, anosmia, ageusia, cough, ultrasound, or CT associated with infiltrating/interstitial pneumonia, diarrhea) at the time of testing positive. The potential development of symptoms while undergoing the administration is not a requirement for exclusion.

4.6 Inclusion criteria

Age > 18 years old; ability to give informed consent.

4.7 Exclusion criteria

Alcoholism or a history of adverse reactions to ethanol, drug addiction or previous treatment for alcoholism/drug addiction, currently on disulfiram or cimetidine, non-drinkers of alcohol (no absolute criteria), any liver disease, uncontrolled diabetes, acute or chronic pancreatitis, serious respiratory diseases, tuberculosis or other mycobacterial infections, confirmed or suspected pregnancy, active psychosis, inability to give legally valid informed consent.

4.8 Measures

- After 1 week or at least 10 ethanol doses, nasopharyngeal antigen and molecular swabs (RT-PCR) should be collected. Depending on the current quarantine laws of local, regional, and national health authorities, values are articulated as either positive or negative dichotomies.

- A negative sample must be taken at the conclusion of the quarantine or just before the individual is readmitted in community, all of this, depending on local regulations.

- Determination of viral strain is considered a plus.

4.9 Type of study

Randomized clinical trial.
Arm A: treatment as above, quarantine as prescribed.
Arm B: no treatment, quarantine as prescribed.

4.10 Sample size

This is to be estimated with accuracy using biostatistical knowledge. Although the predicted difference between the two groups (treatment and controls) is projected to be roughly 60%, if we anticipate recruiting 150 participants in total, we are not far from very concrete evidence.

4.11 Primary outcome

Reduction of the mean time to eliminate the viral load (see MEASURES) from 17 to 7 days.

4.12 Secondary outcome

- A decrease in the mean time to viral load eradication (see MEASURES), from 17 to 5 days.

- A decrease in the mean time to viral load eradication (see MEASURES), from 17 to 3 days.

- Reduction in the rate (below 43%, at least) of asymptomatic subjects who will develop symptoms.

- Comparison of the mean timeframes for viral load (see *MEASURES*) decreases in the general population and among medical professionals.

If the proposed treatment were successful in improving health, tremendous benefits could be anticipated:

- Reduction in the financial burden caused by decreased (if not complete interruption) labor productivity (the global GNP (Gross Domestic Product) decline for 2020 is close to 10%) and medical expenses. Savings should be in the number of billions of euros.

- Faster return to normal life (school, work, sports, travel, reduction of measures restricting personal freedom, etc.).

- Ethanol is potentially active no matter the variant in circulation thanks to its nonspecific action mechanism.

- Additionally, it could be effective against "enveloped" viruses that could be the origin of upcoming epidemic outbreaks.

- The pressure on the vaccination campaign can be reduced thanks to the viral circulation's slowing down.

- Even nations with limited financial resources may control the SARS-Cov-2 outbreak effectively thanks to the wide availability and inexpensive cost of ethanol.

Abbreviations

PAS	positive asymptomatic subjects
ACE2	angiotensin-converting enzyme 2
EtOH	ethanol
SARS	Severe Acute Respiratory Syndrome Coronavirus
MERS	Middle East Respiratory Syndrome
HcoV	Human Endemic Coronavirus
OEL	occupational exposure limit
ABE	acetone, butanol, ethanol
BAC	blood alcohol concentration
AMMD	aerodynamic median mass diameter

Author details

Pietro Salvatori
Head & Neck Surgeon, former Head of the ENT Department at the Humanitas San Pio X Hospital, Milan, Italy

*Address all correspondence to: pietro.salvatori@me.com

References

[1] Salvatori P. The rationale of ethanol inhalation for disinfection of the respiratory tract in SARS-CoV-2-positive asymptomatic subjects. The Pan African Medical Journal. 2021;**40**:201. DOI: 10.11604.pamj.2021.40.201.31211

[2] Sungnak W, Huang N, Bécavin C, Berg M, Queen R, Litvinukova M, et al. SARS-CoV-2 entry factors are highly expressed in nasal epithelial cells together with innate immune genes. Nature Medicine. 2020;**26**:681-687. DOI: 10.1038/s41591-020-0868-6

[3] Polak SB, Van Gool IC, Cohen D, von der Thüsen JH, van Paassen J. A systematic review of pathological findings in COVID-19: A pathophysiological timeline and possible mechanisms of disease progression. Modern Pathology. 2020;**33**:2128-2138. DOI: 10.1038/s41379-020-0603-3

[4] Madas BG, Füri P, Farkas A, Nagy A, Czitrovszky A, Balásházy I, et al. Deposition distribution of the new coronavirus (SARS-CoV-2) in the human airways upon exposure to cough-generated droplets and aerosol particles. Scientific Reports. 2020;**10**(1):22430. DOI: 10.1038/s41598-020-79985-6

[5] Cao S, Gan Y, Wang C, Bachmann M, Wei S, Gong J, et al. Post-lockdown SARS-CoV-2 nucleic acid screening in nearly ten million residents of Wuhan, China. Nature Communications. 2020;**11**(1):5917. DOI: 10.1038/s41467-020-19802-w

[6] Nelson EJ, McKune SL, Ryan KA, Lednicky JA, PhD CSR, Myers MJG Jr. SARS-CoV-2 Positvity on or after 9 days among quarantined student contacts of confirmed cases. JAMA. 2021;**325**(15):1561-1562. DOI: 10.1001/jama.2021.2392

[7] Atripaldi L, Sale S, Capone M, Montesarchio V, Parrella R, Bot G, et al. Could asymptomatic carriers spread the SARS-CoV-2 infection? Experience from the Italian second wave. Journal of Translational Medicine. 2021;**19**:93. DOI: 10.1186/s12967-021-02762-0

[8] Liu J, Liu J, He Z, Yang Z, Yuan J, Wu H, et al. The duration of SARS-CoV-2 positive in the environments of quarantine rooms: A perspective analysis. International Journal of Infectious Diseases. 2021;**105**:68-74

[9] Worldometer - real time world statistics [Internet]. COVID Live Update: 234,869,049 Cases and 4,802,852 Deaths from the Coronavirus – Worldometer. Available from: https://www.worldometers.info/coronavirus/ [Accessed: September 17, 2021].

[10] Byambasuren O, Cardona M, Bell K, Clark J, McLaws ML, Glasziou P. Estimating the extent of asymptomatic COVID-19 and its potential for community transmission: Systematic review and meta-analysis. JAMMI. 2020;**5**(4):223-234. DOI: 10.3138/jammi-2020-0030

[11] Yu C, Zhou M, Liu Y, Guo T, Ou C, Yang L, d, et al., Characteristics of asymptomatic COVID-19 infection and progression: A multicenter, retrospective study, Virulence. 2020; 11(1):1006-1014

[12] Cevik M, Tate M, Lloyd O, Maraolo AE, Schafers J, Ho A. SARS-CoV-2, SARS-CoV, and MERS-CoV viral load dynamics, duration of viral shedding, and infectiousness: A

systematic review and meta-analysis. Lancet Microbe. 2021;**2**(1):e13-e22

[13] Bongiovanni M, Marra AM, De Lauretis A, Bini F, Di Carlo D, Manes G, et al. Natural history of SARS-CoV-2 infection in healthcare workers in northern Italy. Journal of Hospital Infection. 2020;**106**:709-712. DOI: 10.1016/j.jhin.2020.08.027

[14] Bramante CT, Huling JH, Tignanelli C, et al. Randomized trial of metformin, Ivermectin, and fluvoxamine for Covid-19. The New England Journal of Medicine. 2022;**387**:599-610. DOI: 10.1056/NEJMoa2201662

[15] Ganatra S, Dani SS, Ahmad J, Kumar A, Shah AGM, DP MQ, et al. Oral Nirmatrelvir and ritonavir in non-hospitalized vaccinated patients with Covid-19. Clinical Infectious Diseases. 2022;**76**:563-572. DOI: 10.1093/cid/ciac673

[16] Chen RE, Zhang X, Case JB, et al. Resistance of SARS-CoV-2 variants to neutralization by monoclonal and serum-derived polyclonal antibodies. Nature Medicine. 2021;**27**(4):717-726. DOI: 10.1038/s41591-021-01294-w

[17] Guenezan J, Garcia M, Strasters D, Jousselin C, Lévêque N, Frasca D, et al. Povidone iodine mouthwash, gargle, and nasal spray to reduce nasopharyngeal viral load in patients with COVID-19: A randomized clinical trial. JAMA Otolaryngology. Head & Neck Surgery. 2021;**147**(4):400-401

[18] Hosseinzadeh A, Tavakolian A, Kia V, Ebrahimi H, Sheibani H, Binesh E, et al. Combined application of dimethyl sulfoxide and ethanol nasal spray during COVID-19 pandemic may protect healthcare workers: A randomized controlled trial. Iranian Red Crescent Medical Journal. 2022;**24**(8):e1640,1-6. DOI: 10.32592/ircmj.2022.24.8.1640

[19] Kampf G. Efficacy of ethanol against viruses in hand disinfection. The Journal of Hospital Infection. 2018;**98**(4):331-338

[20] Eslami H, Das S, Zhou T, Müller-Plathe F. How alcoholic disinfectants affect coronavirus model membranes: Membrane fluidity. Permeability, and Disintegration, J Phys Chem B. 2020;**124**(46):10374-10385

[21] Kratzel A, Todt D, V'kovski P, Steiner S, Gultom M, Nhu Thao TT, et al. Inactivation of severe acute respiratory syndrome coronavirus 2 by WHO-recommended hand rub formulations and alcohols. Emerging Infectious Diseases. 2020;**26**(7):1592-1595

[22] Manning TJ, Thomas-Richardson J, Cowan M, Thomas-Richardson G. Should ethanol be considered a treatment for COVID-19? Revista da Associação Médica Brasileira. 2020;**66**(9):1169-1171

[23] Sisson JH, Pavlik JA, Wyat TA. Alcohol stimulates ciliary motility of isolated airway axonemes through a nitric oxide, cyclase and cyclic nucleotide- dependent kinase mechanism. Alcoholism, Clinical and Experimental Research. 2009;**33**(4):610-616

[24] Simet SM, Pavlik JA, Sisson JH. Dietary antoxidants prevent alcohol-induced ciliary dysfunction. Alcohol. 2013A;**47**:629-635. DOI: 10.1016/j.alcohol.2013.09.004

[25] Gootnick A, Lipson HI, Turbin J. Inhalation of ethyl alcohol for pulmonary edema. New England Journal of Medicine. 1951;**245**:842-843

[26] Luisada AA, Weyl R, Goldmann MA. Treatment of pulmonary edema. Journal

of the American Medical Association. 1954;**1**(154):62. DOI: 10.1001/jama.1954.02940350064019

[27] Calesnick B, Vernick HQ. Antitussive actvity of ethanol. Journal of Studies on Alcohol. 1971;**32**(2):434-441

[28] PJQ B. A new rapid treatment for the useless cough in the postoperative patient. Quarterly Bulletin of the Northwestern University Medical School. 1954;**28**(1):76-78

[29] Available from: https://www.sps.nhs.uk/artcles/ethanol-content-of-inhalers-what-is-the-signifcance/

[30] Sulaiman I, Chung M, Angel L, Tsay JJ, Wu BG, Yeung ST, et al. Microbial signatures in the lower airways of mechanically ventilated COVID19 patients associated with poor clinical outcome. Res. Sq. 29 Mar 2021;**266050**:1-42

[31] Rueca M, Fontana A, Bartolini B, Piselli P, Mazzarelli A, Copeti M, et al. Investigation of nasal/oropharyngeal microbial community of COVID-19 patients by 16S rDNA sequencing. International Journal of Environmental Research and Public Health. 2021;**18**(4):2174. DOI: 10.3390/ijerph18042174

[32] MacLean RR, Valentine GW, Jatlow PI, Sofuoglu M. Inhalation of alcohol vapor: Measurement and implications. Alcoholism, Clinical and Experimental Research. 2017;**41**(2):238-250. DOI: 10.1111/acer.13291

[33] Bessonneau V, Thomas O. Assessment of exposure to alcohol vapor from alcohol-based hand rubs. International Journal of Environmental Research and Public Health. 2012;**9**(3):868-879

[34] Boyce JM, Pitet D. Guideline for hand hygiene in health-care settings. American Journal of Infection Control. 2002;**30**:1-46

[35] More SL, Thornton SA, Maskrey JR, Sharma A, de Gandiaga E, Cheng TJ, et al. PBPK modeling characterization of potential acute impairment effects from inhalation of ethanol during e-cigarete use. Inhalation Toxicology. 2020;**32**(1):14-23

[36] Available from: https://clinicaltrials.gov/ct2/show/NCT04554433

[37] Available from: https://www.clinicaltrialsregister.eu/ctr-search/search?query=2020-001760-29

[38] Castro-Balado A, Mondelo-Garcia C, Barbosa-Pereira L, Varela-Rey I, Novo-Veleiro I, Vázquez Agra N, et al. Development and Characterizaton of inhaled ethanol as a novel pharmacological strategy currently evaluated in a phase II clinical trial for early-stage SARS-CoV-2 infection. Pharmaceutics. 2021;**13**:342. DOI: 10.3390/pharmaceutics13030342

[39] Irvine LFH. Relevance of the developmental toxicity of ethanol in the occupational setting: A review. Journal of Applied Toxicology. 2003;**23**(5):289-299

[40] Bevan RJ, Slack RJ, Holmes P, Levy LS. An assessment of potential cancer risk following occupational exposure to ethanol. Journal of Toxicology and Environmental Health, Part B, Critical Reviews. 2009;**12**(3):188-205

[41] Yeligar SM, Chen MM, Kovacs EJ, Sisson JH, Burnham EL, Brownf LAS. Alcohol and lung injury and immunity. Alcohol. 2016;**55**:51-59. DOI: 10.1016/j.alcohol.2016.08.005

[42] Winek CL, Murphy KL. The rate and kinetic order of ethanol elimination. Forensic Science International. 1984;**25**(3):159-166

[43] Majra D, Benson J, Pitts J, Stebbing J. SARS-CoV-2 (COVID-19) superspreader events. Journal of Infection. 2021;**82**(1):36-40. DOI: 10.1016/j.jinf.2020.11.021

[44] Szmigiera M. Impact of the Coronavirus Pandemic on the Global Economy. Statistics & Facts; 2021. Available from: https://www.statista.com/topics/6139/covid-19-impact-on-the-global-economy/#topicHeader__wrapper

[45] Sai M, Heilmann E, Moraes SN, Kearns FL, von Laer D, Amaro RE, et al. Transmissible SARS-CoV-2 variants with resistance to clinical protease inhibitors. bioRxiv. 26 Dec 2022;**503099**:1-33. DOI: 10.1101/2022.08.07.503099

[46] Wang L, Volkow ND, Davis PB, Berger NA, Kaelber DC, Xu R. COVID-19 rebound after Paxlovid treatment during omicron BA.5 vs BA.2.12.1 subvariant predominance period. MedRxiv. 04 Aug 2022;**2227845**:1-5 DOI: 10.1101/2022.08.04.22278450. PMID: 35794889; PMCID: PMC9258292

[47] Eterpi M, McDonnell G, Thomas V. Decontamination efficacy against mycoplasma. Letters in Applied Microbiology. 2011;**52**(2):150-155

[48] Ruuskanen MO, Åberg F, Mannistö V, Havulinna AS, Méric G, Liuh Y, et al. Links between gut microbiome compositon and faty liver disease in a large populaton sample. Gut Microbes. 2021;**13**(1):e1888673 (22 pages). DOI: 10.1080/19490976.2021.1888673

[49] Seo SO, Lu T, Jin YS, Blaschek HP. A comparative phenotypic and genomic analysis of Clostridium beijerinckii mutant with enhanced solvent production. Journal of Biotechnology. 2021;**329**:49-55

[50] Shintake T. Possibility of disinfection of SARS-CoV-2 (COVID-19) in human respiratory tract by controlled ethanol vapor inhalation. arXiv:2003.12444v1 [physics.med-ph]. 15 Mar 2020:1-12. DOI: 10.48550/arXiv.2003.12444

[51] Amoushahi A, Padmos A. A Suggestion on Ethanol Therapy in COVID-19?. EC Anaesthesia; 2020;**6**(6):1-2

[52] CDC. Laboratory-confirmed COVID-19–associated hospitalizations among adults during SARS-CoV-2 omicron BA.2 variant predominance — COVID-19–associated hospitalization surveillance network, 14 states, June 20, 2021–may 31, 2022. Morbidity and Mortality Weekly Report. 2022;**71**(34):1085-1091

Chapter 9

Ethanol as a Subgroup of the UNIFAC Model in the Prediction of Liquid-Liquid Equilibrium in Food and Fuel Systems

Jacqueline M. Ortega Bacicheti, Guilherme D. Machado, Fábio Nishiyama, Vladimir F. Cabral and Donato Aranda

Abstract

Ethanol has been employed as a solvent in biodiesel production and vegetable oil refining since it is more economically attractive and less toxic than methanol and hexane. Furthermore, ethanol has demonstrated easy recovery, good selectivity, and distribution coefficient for free fatty acids (FFA), which is the primary target in the refining process since high acidity oil can lead to the formation of side products. As the knowledge of phase equilibrium behavior of fatty systems is essential to design and optimize the extraction of FFA, this chapter will present two new UNIFAC subgroups for ethanol: EtOH-B, focused on biodiesel production; and EtOH-D, focused on the deacidification process. Except for ethanol and water subgroups fitted in this study, all remaining UNIFAC parameters were taken from the literature. The new EtOH-B and EtOH-D parameters provide a considerably lower mean square error (1.20% and 0.87%) than the other works available in the literature. The results show that new ethanol subgroups and the developed methodology are valuable tools in predicting liquid-liquid phase equilibrium for ethyl biodiesel and vegetable oil deacidification systems considered, resulting in reduced computational calculations and a relatively small split with the complex dataset established by the UNIFAC-LL model.

Keywords: biodiesel, deacidification, ethanol, liquid-liquid equilibrium, vegetable oil, UNIFAC

1. Introduction

Several studies have introduced ethanol as a solvent for liquid-liquid extraction, resulting in a satisfactory reduction of free fatty acid (FFA) content in oils [1–4]. High acidity level vegetable oils need to be refined either for human consumption or for fuel production. In this way, ethanol can act both as a solvent for oil deacidification by liquid-liquid extraction and as a reagent for transesterification reaction.

Considering edible vegetable oil, high levels of FFA have been associated with digestive problems for consumers, autoimmune disorders, and various types of cancer [5–8]. Besides health problems, the content of pigments, phosphatides, odoriferous molecules, and free fatty acids in edible vegetal oil is detrimental to the oil quality, oxidative stability, and consumer acceptance. Among these impurities, FFA is the most detrimental because they increase the acidity of the oil, inducing an undesirable rancid flavor [9]. In order to reduce neutral oil losses and production of undesired compounds, caused by unwanted chemical reactions [10], liquid-liquid extraction using ethanol as a solvent can replace the conventional physical and chemical refining processes.

Besides deacidification of edible vegetable oils, ethanol can be employed in biodiesel production. The conventional biodiesel production process requires the use of a feedstock with reduced acidity; however, residual oils are characterized by a high FFA content, which promotes soap production with the alkali homogeneous catalysts used in transesterification [11]. Thus, feedstock purification processes, such as oil deacidification, through solvent extraction are needed. Using residual oils for biodiesel production can provide several advantages when compared to the conventional process with refined oils, such as the minimization of environmental impacts related to the disposal of waste oils, a noncompetitive relationship with the food crops, and availability of the feedstock supply, which accounts for over 70% of the refined oil biodiesel production costs [12].

In order to correctly design, operate and optimize extraction columns and the subsequent additional purification or solvent recovery units, liquid-liquid phase equilibrium (LLE) data are necessary to determine the thermodynamic properties of the systems composed of oil, solvent, and FFA [3, 13]. In general, most of the phase equilibrium data for biodiesel systems use methanol as the reacting alcohol [14], studies regarding systems with ethanol are more recent [15]. Some advantages of using ethanol as a solvent are its high affinity for FFAs at ambient temperature, low toxicity when compared to methanol, and its easy removal under mild conditions [16, 17].

Thermodynamic modeling can be used to predict or correlate the experimental behavior of fatty acid systems described through LLE data. The approach using excess Gibbs energy models is widely applied to describe biodiesel and vegetable oil systems through thermodynamic models, such as NRTL [18–22], UNIQUAC [18, 22–24], and UNIFAC [25–28]. Although thermodynamic models, such as UNIQUAC and NRTL, are capable of accurately representing the experimental data, both are restricted to the specificity of the type of vegetable oil used, as the phase equilibrium parameters are adjusted solely for the system described in the experimental data used for the LLE data fitting. Numerous types of refined or residual feedstocks are available for biodiesel production or require deacidification to be safe for human consumption. Thus, the use of a predictive group-contribution method, such as UNIFAC, to describe the phase behavior of the variety of biodiesel reaction systems or deacidification of edible vegetable oil systems is motivated, as larger number of systems would be useful.

In the UNIFAC model, alcohols, such as methanol and propanol, used to be represented by a specific group. As stated by Magnussen et al. [29] in their work, 1-propanol ($CH_3CH_2CH_2OH$) can be represented, in principle, by the CH_3, CH_2, and OH subgroups. However, the fitting of these parameters in the UNIFAC parameter table depends on several other molecules that present these subgroups. An approach that represents molecules by a subgroup of their own, as in the case of methanol (CH_3OH), can provide more accurate property calculations.

On account of the growing tendency of substitution of environmentally damaging chemicals for less impactful compounds, added to its availability and price in the context of biofuels in Brazil and other countries, the use of ethanol as a solvent or reactant is expected to vastly increase. Therefore, the study of the possibility of using ethanol as UNIFAC subgroup must also be evaluated.

In the literature, the thermodynamic modeling of these systems focuses on the UNIQUAC and NRTL models. Reipert et al. [30] correlated the LLE experimental data of refined babassu oil, lauric acid, and hydrated ethanol using the NRTL model. The mass fraction root mean square error (RMSD) between the observed and estimated compositions was 0.85%. Gonçalves et al. [31] applied NRTL and UNIQUAC models to correlate LLE experimental data for corn oil with a hydrated ethanol solvent system at room temperature and atmospheric pressure. The RMSD of 0.89% and 0.92%, respectively. Rodrigues et al. [32] investigated the LLE of Brazil nut oil or Macadamia nut oil + commercial oleic acid + ethanol + water, at 298.2 K. They reported RMSD not higher than 1.5% using the NRTL and UNIQUAC models. Basso et al. [19] determined LLE data for glycerol + ethanol + fatty acid ethyl ester from crambe oil system and adjusted parameters for NRTL model. The RMSD between experimental and calculated values by the NRTL model was less than 0.82%. The authors verified the prediction capacity of the UNIFAC model by testing two different sets of UNIFAC binary interaction parameters and obtained a RMSD of 2.27% and 3.97%, respectively. Da Silva et al. [20] established experimental data for Jatropha curcas oil + oleic acid + ethanol + water systems at (288.15, 298.15, 308.15, and 318.15) K and correlated the experimental data by the nonrandom two-liquid (NRTL) model with temperature-dependent binary parameters. For all systems, the RMSD was lower than 0.96%. Basso et al. [33] obtained LLE experimental data of systems containing glycerol + ethanol + ethyl biodiesel from macauba pulp oil, performed thermodynamic modeling, and simulated the settling step of this biodiesel using simulation software. Binary interaction parameters were adjusted for NRTL and UNIQUAC models and the RMSD between experimental data and calculated values were 0.44%, 1.07%, 3.52%, and 2.82%, respectively, using the NRTL, UNIQUAC, UNIFAC-LLE, and UNIFAC-Dortmund models.

All the aforementioned studies indicate that the NRTL and UNIQUAC models can reproduce the experimental liquid-liquid behavior of the systems involving vegetable oil + fatty acids + ethanol + water and biodiesel + glycerol + ethanol. However, although these thermodynamic models represent satisfactorily the experimental data, the NRTL and UNIQUAC parameters obtained in these studies are specific to these systems, consequently, they are restricted to the specific vegetable oil used in the parameter correlation. Considering the numerous types of vegetable oils that need deacidification, and different triacylglycerides matrices that can be used for biodiesel production, new parameter-fitting procedures are required for other systems, and new experimental databanks are required [9, 17, 30]. However, the new parameter-fitting procedures required for new systems are not mandatory if we consider the group contribution method. UNIFAC (UNIQUAC Functional-group Activity Coefficient) model [34] is a group contribution method established by Fredenslund, Jones e Prausnitz in 1975, that can predict the liquid-liquid behavior of systems containing fatty acids using the activity coefficient calculation, which considers the interaction between the subgroups that form the molecules. Fredenslund et al. [34] proposed a group contribution method that could use experimental data available in the literature to predict the LLE of systems with no disposable experimental data.

Models based in group contribution concept estimate the properties of a mixture considering it as a solution of different functional groups that forms the molecule in the

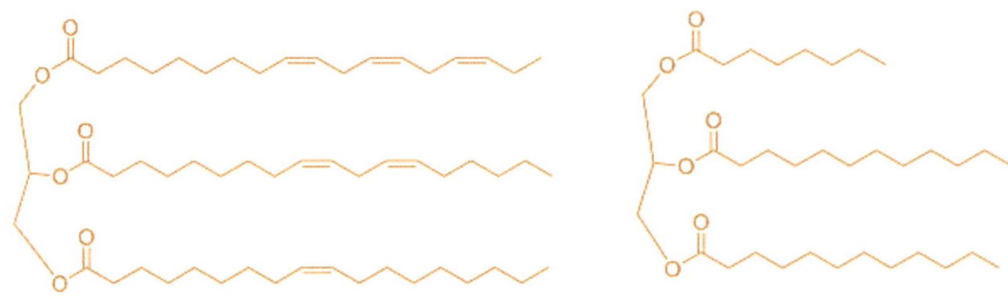

Figure 1.
Soybean oil (left) and coconut oil (right) molecular structures.

mixture. As can be seen in **Figure 1**, soybean and coconut oils are different molecules, but the same chemical compounds are encountered in these molecules. Considering these few functional groups as building blocks, a vast array of vegetable oil can be represented, as all vegetable oils present the same functional groups only differing in quantities.

This type of predictive model applicable to a larger number of systems would be useful and important in the food industry and biofuel industry, respectively, given the diversity of raw materials and the fact that most systems are multicomponent, and the variety of generated biodiesel systems.

Physical and chemical properties are considered as a sum of all contributions made by each one of the functional groups. These contributions are quantified according to the interaction parameters, adjusted by experimental data.

This model was extensively applied to study the liquid-liquid equilibrium of vegetable oils.

Batista et al. [2] applied UNIFAC and ASOG (analytical solution of groups) group contribution methods to correlate interaction parameters of triolein + oleic acid + ethanol and triolein + stearic acid + ethanol systems. The parameters were validated for canola, corn, and Spanish oil and the root mean square deviation between experimental and calculated molar fractions were 1.31% and 1.32% for the UNIFAC and ASOG models, respectively.

Bessa et al. [35] tested the predictive capability of the original UNIFAC model parameters and then modified them in terms of new readjusted binary interaction parameters. Due to inadequate results obtained by UNIFAC model without any changes in its subgroups, the authors introduced a new group ("OHgly") and two matrices of parameters were adjusted. The authors obtained good predictions and a significant improvement in the performance of this group contribution model has been achieved.

Noriega and Narvaez [28] proposed a new set of UNIFAC group interaction parameters to describe the LLE for all the systems involved in biodiesel production. The parameters presented a RMSD up to 2.07%.

In the UNIFAC model, the activity coefficient is given in terms of a combinatorial contribution taking into account entropy effects arising from differences in molecular size and shape, and a residual contribution taking into account energetic interactions between the functional groups in the mixture. To achieve a better description of the experimental data composed by the molecules presented in **Table 1**, the chosen subgroups to represent the studied fatty systems were as follows: CH_3, CH_2, CH, CH=CH, COOH, CH_2COO, OH, H_2O, and the new proposed group EtOH.

Therefore, this chapter proposes the adjustment of thermodynamic parameters of the UNIFAC model considering a new ethanol subgroup in order to predict the LLE for systems containing food or fuel. The fact that vegetable oils present different types

Molecule	Subgroups
Ethanol	1 EtOH
Water	1 H_2O
Glycerol	2 CH_2, 1 CH, 3 OH
Fatty acid	n CH_3, n CH_2, COOH
Triacylglycerol	n CH_3, n CH_2, nCH, nCH=CH, CH_2COO
Biodiesel	n CH_3, n CH_2, nCH, nCH=CH, CH_2COO

Table 1.
Chosen subgroups to represent the studied fatty systems.

of constituent fatty acids but with similarity in their structure makes it possible to use a predictive approach that represents the interactions between groups based on UNIFAC thermodynamic model in the proper representation of the LLE for industrial separation processes. Thus, this study aims to present such methodology in the prediction of food systems containing FFA to be separated as well as systems containing fuels, focusing on biodiesel produced from vegetable oils.

2. Methodology

The isofugacity criterion for phase equilibrium is conventionally used to describe a condition at which the chemical potential of each component is equal in the phases among which this component can distribute. If fugacities are expressed in terms of activity coefficients, the LLE using an excess Gibbs energy model is represented by Eq. (1) [34].

$$\mathrm{x}_{\mathrm{i}}^{\mathrm{AP}}\gamma_i^{AP} = x_i^{OP}\gamma_i^{OP} \tag{1}$$

where x_i^{AP} and x_i^{OP} are the molar fractions of component i in the alcohol and oil phases, respectively, and γ_i^{AP} and γ_i^{OP} are the activity coefficients of component i in the alcohol and oil phases, respectively.

In this chapter, the activity coefficients are calculated through UNIFAC model [34], which considers the combinatorial and residual contributions, Eq. (2).

$$ln\,\gamma_i = ln\,\gamma_i^C + ln\,\gamma_i^R \tag{2}$$

The combinatorial contribution γ_i^C(Eq. (3)) is related to the difference in size and shape of molecules. The volume fraction $\varnothing_i$ and surface fraction θ_i of each molecule i are obtained using Eq. (5) and (6), respectively.

$$ln\,\gamma_i^C(x) = ln\,\frac{\varnothing_i}{x_i} + \frac{Z}{2}q_i\,ln\,\frac{\theta_i}{\varnothing_i} + l_i - \frac{\varnothing_i}{x_i}\sum_{j=1}^{n_c} x_j l_j, \tag{3}$$

$$l_i = \frac{z}{2}(r_i - q_i) - (r_i - 1); Z = 10. \tag{4}$$

$$\varnothing_i = \frac{r_i x_i}{\sum_{j=1}^{n_c} r_j x_j} \quad (5)$$

$$\theta_i = \frac{q_i x_i}{\sum_{j=1}^{n_c} q_j x_j} \quad (6)$$

where x_i is the mole fraction of component i and r_i and q_i are the measures of molecular van der Waals volumes and molecular surface areas, respectively. They are calculated as the sum of the group volume and group area parameters, R_k and Q_k.

$$r_i = \sum_{k=1}^{n_g} \nu_{ki} R_k \quad (7)$$

$$q_i = \sum_{k=1}^{n_g} \nu_{ki} Q_k \quad (8)$$

where ν_{ki} is the number of groups of type k in molecule i. Here, we use the values of R_k *and* Q_k reported by Magnussen *et al.* [29]. Os valores R_k e Q_k são calculados a partir do volume e área superficial dos grupos de Van der Waals (V_{wk} e A_{wk}, respectivamente), retratado por Bondi (1968):

$$R_k = \frac{V_{wk}}{15{,}17} \quad (9)$$

$$Q_k = \frac{A_{wk}}{2{,}5x10^9} \quad (10)$$

The residual contribution γ_i^R, described through Eq. (11), is due to group areas and group interaction parameters. Γ_k and $\Gamma_k^{(i)}$ are the residual activity coefficient from group k in the solution and in a solution containing only molecules of type i, respectively.

$$ln\,\gamma_i^R(T,x) = \sum_k \nu_{ki}\left(ln\,\Gamma_k - ln\,\Gamma_k^{(i)}\right) \quad (11)$$

By Eq. 12 it is possible to calculate the residual activity coefficient.

$$ln\,\Gamma_k = Q_k\left[1 - ln\left(\sum_m^k \theta_m \Psi_{mk}\right) - \sum_m\left(\frac{\theta_{dm}\Psi_{km}}{\sum_n \theta_n \Psi_{nm}}\right)\right] \quad (12)$$

where θ_m is the area fraction of group m given by:

$$\theta_m = \frac{Q_m X_m}{\sum_n Q_n X_n},\# \quad (13)$$

and X_m is the molar fraction of the group m in the mixture.

$$X_m = \frac{\sum_j^n Q_m X_m}{\sum_j \sum_n \nu_{nj} x_j} \# \tag{14}$$

The group interaction parameter ψ_{nm} between groups n and m is given by:

$$\psi_{mn} = exp\left(-\frac{a_{mn}}{T}\right), \# \tag{15}$$

where a_{mn} is an adjustable parameter of the binary interaction between groups m and n, and it has units of kelvins. Each group-group interaction possesses two parameters: a_{nm}, a_{mn}, and $a_{nm} \neq a_{mn}$. These parameters were obtained from a database using a wide range of experimental phase-equilibrium results.

The parameter fitting procedure was applied separately to fit the EtOH interaction parameters for biodiesel separation and deacidification systems. In deacidification process, the presence of water in ethanol solvent increases the polarity of the solution. This feature and the presence of glycerol in biodiesel system makes the behavior of EtOH subgroup different in deacidification systems from that in biodiesel systems, even assuming that the subgroups of both systems were similar (the CH_3, CH_2, CH, CH = CH, COOH, CH_2COO), and accepting that UNIFAC model is a group contribution method that can predict the liquid-liquid behavior considering the interaction between the subgroups that form the molecules.

As the ethanol parameters calculated for the biodiesel system are not adequate for deacidification process, the UNIFAC parameters for new ethanol subgroup were fitted for the biodiesel process separately from deacidification process. As result, this study will present UNIFAC interaction parameters for ethanol subgroup in biodiesel systems (EtOH-B) and in deacidification systems (EtOH-D). The UNIFAC parameters were fitted considering the phase compositions in molar fractions and binary interaction parameters in 1/K.

A data bank containing 56 systems was compiled. We used a total of 88 tie-lines from eight biodiesel types from vegetable oils with ethanol, and 246 tie-lines for the 14 types of vegetable oils with hydrated ethanol, at temperatures ranging from 288.15 to 333.15 K, all systems studied at atmospheric pressure. **Table 2** shows a summary of the equilibrium systems used in the parameter fitting and validation procedure.

For biodiesel separation fitted ethanol-related parameters, the LLE database of seven ethyl systems of vegetable oils (soybean, canola, palm, *jatropha curcas*, cottonseed, crambe, and sunflower) at different temperatures were used to fit the interaction parameters of the ethanol subgroups. The fitted ethanol-related parameters were validated against data for the macauba (*Acrocomia aculeata*) biodiesel system. Lastly, the results obtained are compared with those obtained by the UNIFAC-LL parameters [29] and parameters available from literature work [35].

For deacidification fitted ethanol-related parameters, the LLE database of 13 systems of vegetable oils (brazil nut, corn, cottonseed, garlic, grapeseed, *jatropha curcas*, palm, peanut, rice bran, sesame, soybean, and sunflower) at different temperatures were used to fit the interaction parameters of the ethanol subgroups. The validation procedure was performed using canola oil system and a total of five tie-lines at 303.15 K, and it is worth mentioning that canola oil was not included in the parameter estimation process. Lastly, the results obtained are compared with those obtained by the UNIFAC-LL parameters [29] and parameters available from literature work [26, 28, 43].

The system is composed of biodiesel, ethanol, and glycerol.			
Vegetable oil source	**Tie-lines**	**T (K)**	**References**
Soybean	10	293.15, 323.15	[36]
Canola	5	303.15	[1]
Palm	15	298.15, 323.15	[37]
Jatropha curcas	12	303.15, 318.15, 333.15	[14]
Macauba pulp	6	298.15	[33]
Cottonseed	18	293.15, 313.15, 333.15	[38]
Crambe	18	298.15, 318.15, 338.15	[19]
Sunflower	12	298.15, 313.15	[36]
The system is composed of vegetable oil, free fatty acids (FFA), ethanol, and water.			
Vegetable oil source	Tie-lines	T (K)	References
Brazil nut	6	298.15	[32]
Canola	5	303.15	[18]
Corn	21	298.15	[31]
Cottonseed	21	298.15	[4]
Garlic	21	298.15	[39]
Grapeseed	22	318.15	[39]
J. curcas	40	288.15, 298.15, 308.15, 318.15	[20]
Macadamia	15	298.15	[32]
Palm	10	318.15	[40]
Peanut	7	298.15	[9]
Rice bran	17	298.15	[41]
Sesame	14	298.15	[39]
Soybean	16	323.15	[42]
Sunflower	32	298.15	[3]

Table 2.
LLE database of the systems involved in the correlation process.

The software Microsoft Excel was used in the parameter fitting procedure coupled to XSEOS [44] and SOLVER® add-ins. The XSEOS add-in, an open-source code programmed in visual basic for applications (VBA) with several excess Gibbs energy models and equations of state, was employed to evaluate the activity coefficient of the UNIFAC model, while the SOLVER® add-in with the generalized reduced gradient (GRG) method [45] was used as the numerical calculation tool.

The parameter fitting was performed by minimizing the objective function (Eq. 16) using the generalized reduced gradient (GRG) nonlinear solving method.

$$OF = \sum_{n}^{NLa} \sum_{i}^{NCn} \left(W_{i.n}^{OPexp} - W_{i.n}^{OPcalc}\right)^2 + \left(W_{i.n}^{APexp} - W_{i,n}^{APcalc}\right)^2 \tag{16}$$

where *NLa* and *NCn* represent the total number of tie-lines in each group and the total number of components or pseudo components in tie-line *n*, respectively. $W_{i,n}$ correspond to the mass fraction of the component or pseudo component *i* in the tie-line *n* in the oil phase (*OP*) or alcohol phase (*AP*), while the superscripts *exp* and *calc* the experimental or calculated values, respectively. During the parameter fitting procedure, the minimization of eq. (16) is constrained by the isofugacity condition expressed by Eq. (1), and the calculated mass fraction sum, which must be equal to 1.

In order to evaluate the capability of the ethanol interaction parameters [27, 43] to describe LLE in systems containing FFA accurately, the percentual mass fraction root mean square deviation between the experimental and calculated phase composition values (RMSD), Eq. (17), was compared to the results obtained using parameters available in the literature (UNIFAC-LL from Magnussen et al. [46], Bessa et al. [35], Noriega and Narváez [28], Hirata et al. [26]).

$$RMSD = 100.\sqrt{\frac{\sum_n^{Nla}\sum_i^{NCn}\left(W_{i,n}^{OPexp} - W_{i,n}^{OPcalc}\right)^2 + \left(W_{i,n}^{APexp} - W_{i,n}^{APcalc}\right)^2}{2.NLa.NCn}} \tag{17}$$

The subgroups chosen to represent the fatty acids systems were as follows: CH_3, CH_2, CH, CH = CH, COOH, CH_2COO, H_2O, and ethanol, EtOH. Only the binary interaction parameters corresponding to water and ethanol were estimated in this study.

In order to reduce the number of components considered in the interaction parameter estimation methodology, the pseudo-component approach can be used to characterize a complex mixture as a single component [9]. Several authors had successfully applied this approach assuming the vegetable oil as a single pseudo component with an average molar mass and average physical-chemical properties [4, 9, 17, 19, 20, 26, 28, 30–32, 35, 39–43].

Based on the results of the reported studies, it is assumed that the use of the described methodology does not cause expressive deviations in the thermodynamic modeling of deacidification and biodiesel separation systems. Therefore, each vegetable oil was replaced by a pseudo component, and the same approach was used for commercial fatty acids. The pseudo component is a thermodynamic tool applied to represent the edible oil as a single TAG and FFAs as a unique FFA. A weighted average of the vegetable oil and FFA molar masses and subgroup numbers was applied to each pseudo component, considering the fatty acid profile of each vegetable oil, [2–4, 20, 31, 32, 39–42]. The molar mass data of the components were obtained from the NIST Chemistry WebBook database.

3. Results and discussion

For biodiesel separation system, the methodology was initially applied to fit parameters for the new interaction subgroup representing the ethanol molecule (EtOH-B), while the UNIFAC-LL for the subgroups forming the other components of the system (ethyl biodiesel and glycerol) remained unchanged. The fitting process used seven ethyl biodiesel from soybean, canola, palm, *jatropha curcas*, cottonseed, crambe, and sunflower oils available in the literature. **Table 3** summarizes the UNIFAC-LL parameters [29] used and the interaction parameters fitted for the new EtOH-B subgroup proposed [43].

Subgroup	CH3	CH2	CH	CH=CH	OH	CH2COO	EtOH-B
Rk	0.90	0.67	0.45	1.12	1.00	1.68	**2.11**
Qk	0.85	0.54	0.23	0.87	1.20	1.42	**1.97**
CH3	0.00	0.00	0.00	74.54	644.60	972.40	**3582.81**
CH2	0.00	0.00	0.00	74.54	644.60	972.40	**3582.81**
CH	0.00	0.00	0.00	74.54	644.60	972.40	**3582.81**
CH=CH	292.30	292.30	292.30	0.00	724.40	−577.50	**241.75**
OH	328.20	328.20	328.20	470.70	0.00	195.60	**5299.17**
CH2COO	−320.10	−320.10	−320.10	485.60	180.60	0	**−395.51**
EtOH-B	**−53.92**	**−53.92**	**−53.92**	**−4658.24**	**−550.58**	**106.42**	**0.00**

Table 3.
UNIFAC interaction parameters for CH_3, CH_2, CH, CH = CH, COOH, CH_2COO, H_2O, *and EtOH subgroups.*

The bold numbers are the fitted one.

Figures 2 and **3** show the experimental points and calculated tie-lines obtained using the new interaction parameters summarized in **Table 3** for different types of biodiesel. For all diagrams presented in this chapter, the following classification is valid:

Δ and ▲ for experimental and calculated points, respectively;

□ and ■ for experimental and calculated overall composition, respectively;

- - - and — for experimental and calculated tie-lines;

- .. - for experimental binodal line;

The tie-lines overlapping seen in **Figures 2** and **3** suggest that the fitted UNIFAC parameters for the proposed EtOH subgroup can predict the behavior of the systems considered with high accuracy.

In order to validate these new fitted EtOH parameters, we perform a liquid-liquid equilibrium prediction for ethyl biodiesel from macauba pulp, which was not used during the parameter fitting process.

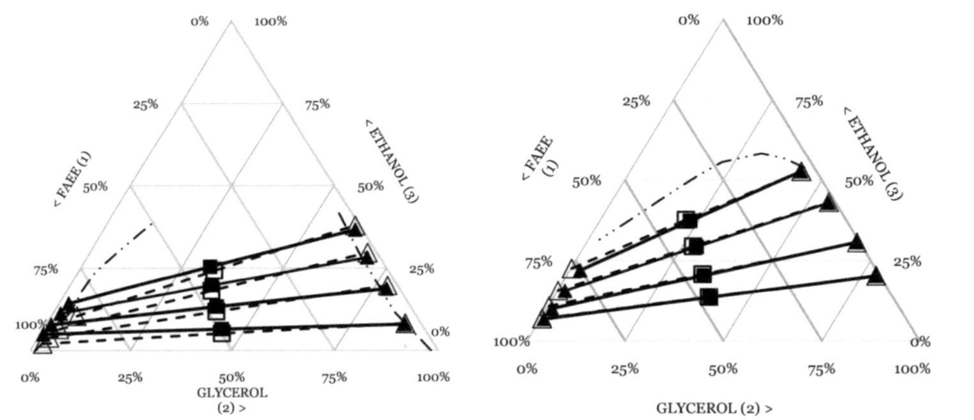

Figure 2.
Ternary LLE diagram for the ethyl biodiesel from soybean oil system at 293.15 K (left) and jatropha curcas *oil at 318.15 K (right). Experimental data from [14, 36], respectively.*

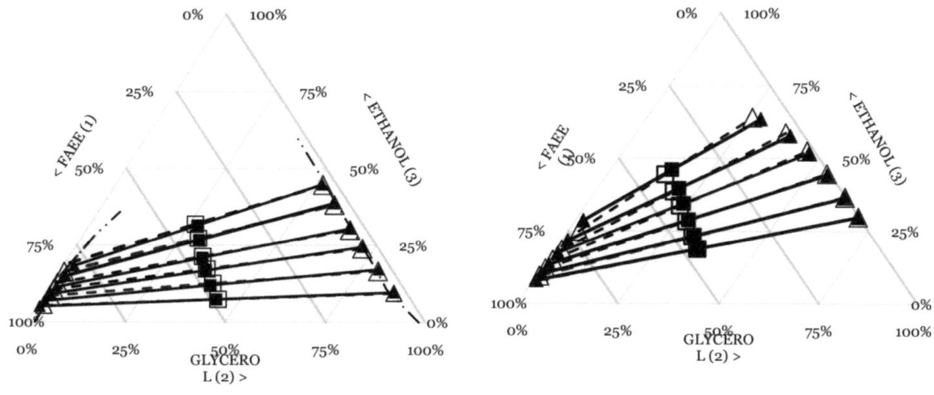

Figure 3.
Ternary LLE diagram for the ethyl biodiesel from cottonseed oil system at 333.15 K (left) and crambe oil at 298.2 K (right). Experimental data from [19, 38], respectively.

Figure 4 shows the results of this prediction in the form of a ternary diagram, which exhibit small deviations from the experimental data, thus validating the methodology used.

The results obtained in the fitting and validation processes were then compared with UNIFAC parameters proposed by Magnussen et al. [29] and Bessa et al. [35]. The UNIFAC-LL database fitted by Magnussen et al. [29] in 1981 is extensively widespread and applied to describe fatty systems equilibrium [47–49]. A more recent research by Bessa and collaborators [35] refitted all interaction parameters of the UNIFAC-LL and proposed a new OH subgroup used to represent uniquely this subgroup present in the glycerol molecule, thus having to fit 42 interaction parameters.

Table 4 shows the percentage mean square error (MSE%). The results using the parameters proposed by Machado et al. [43] are always better than those using the Magnussen et al. [29] and Bessa et al. [35] parameters.

Figure 5 shows ternary LLE diagrams for the ethyl biodiesel from macauba pulp oil system comparison with Bessa et al. [35] fitted parameters (left) and with UNIFAC-LL parameters (right).

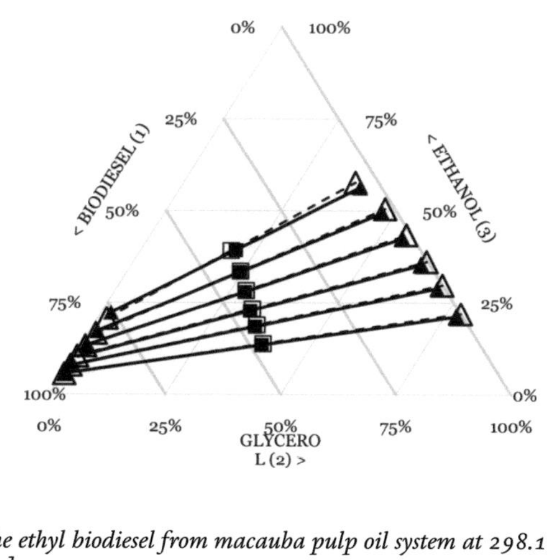

Figure 4.
Ternary LLE diagram for the ethyl biodiesel from macauba pulp oil system at 298.15 K for validation procedure. Experimental data from [33].

Biodiesel	T (K)	MSE (%)		
		UNIFAC-LL [29]	Bessa et al. [35]	Machado et al. [43]
Soybean	293.15	21.07	4.68	0.98
	323.15	30.30	2.77	2.08
Canola	303.15	4.41	2.75	2.13
Palm	298.15	4.62	3.25	0.73
	323.15	4.61	2.54	0.76
Jatropha curcas	303.15	5.62	4.04	1.34
	318.15	5.83	4.01	0.85
	333.15	15.33	5.09	1.55
Macauba pulp	298.15	5.22	3.49	0.87
Cottonseed	293.15	5.16	4.49	1.20
	313.15	5.72	4.45	0.96
	333.15	5.59	4.13	0.87
Crambe	298.15	11.00	4.76	1.50
	318.2	10.07	5.69	1.14
Sunflower	298.15	3.53	2.99	0.92
	313.15	4.17	3.54	1.23
MSE%		8.89	3.92	1.20

Table 4.
Comparative percentage mean square error (MSE%) for this study's fitting and the literature (EtOH).

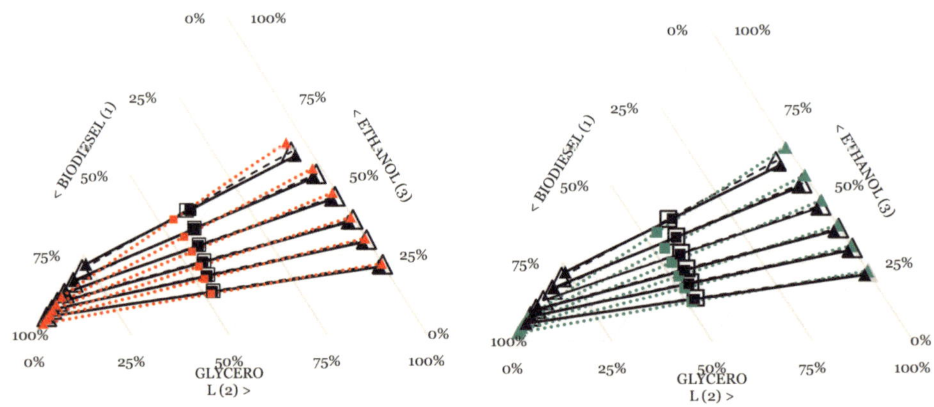

Figure 5.
Ternary LLE diagram for the ethyl biodiesel from macauba pulp oil system at 298.15 K comparison with the Bessa et al. [35] (left, red tie-lines); and with the UNIFAC-LL [29] data (right, green tie-lines). Experimental data from ref. [19].

Figure 5 (right) shows that the UNIFAC-LL results have large deviations and the use of such parameters to predict equilibrium between the glycerol-rich phase and the biodiesel-rich phase for the systems considered by Machado et al. [43] is not recommended. Although the parameters fitted by Bessa et al. [35] could better describe the LLE than the UNIFAC-LL [29] parameters, still there is considerable discrepancy between the predictions and the experimental data. Such observations corroborate the results shown in **Table 4**. **Figure 4** shows that ethanol subgroup fitting tie-lines represent considerably better the equilibrium of the biodiesel-rich phase with the glycerol-rich phase. It is worth mentioning that, only eight parameters were fitted, while Bessa et al. [35] considered 42 adjustable parameters in their study.

For deacidification system, the methodology was initially applied to fit parameters for the new interaction subgroup representing the ethanol molecule (EtOH-D) and H_2O subgroups, while the UNIFAC-LL for the subgroups forming the other components of the system (vegetable oil and free fatty acids—FFA) remained unchanged. The fitting process used experimental LLE data of 17 (Brazil nut, corn, cottonseed, garlic, grapeseed, *jatropha curcas*, macadamia, palm, peanut, rice bran, sesame, soybean, and sunflower) different vegetable oils available in the literature. **Table 5** shows the original UNIFAC-LL [29] parameters used and the interaction parameters fitted for the water (H_2O) and EtOH-D subgroups.

Figures 6 and 7 show the experimental points and calculated tie-lines obtained using the new interaction parameters summarized in **Table 5** for corn and soybean oil. Due to the systems presenting different water contents added to the ethanol solvent, ethanol and water were used as a mixed solvent to represent the pseudo-quaternary systems in a triangular diagram.

Analyzing **Figures 6** and 7 it can be noted an inversion in the tie-line slopes as water is added to the solvent. This phenomenon occurs because water decreases the solubility between oil and ethanol; hence, it increases the two-liquid phase regions [30, 32, 39, 42].

The ternary diagrams presented in **Figures 6** and 7 show that the calculated results are very close to the experimental data. Therefore, the H_2O and EtOH-D adjusted interaction parameters using the UNIFAC model correlated with the high accuracy of the LLE behavior of the considered system containing fatty acids.

Table 6 compares the RMSD from the experimental mass fraction data from the calculated data obtained by UNIFAC modeling using the parameters fitted by Bacicheti et al. [27] for EtOH-D subgroup with those obtained using parameters available in the literature (UNIFAC-LL from Magnussen et al. [29]), Noriega and Narváez [28], Hirata et al. [26]). **Table 6** still presents the RMSD between experimental and calculated data obtained using Machado et al. [43] parameter set.

Subgroup	CH_3, CH_2, CH	CH=CH	H_2O	COOH	CH_2COO	ETOH-D
CH_3, CH_2, CH	0	74.54	962.89	139.40	972.40	624.24
CH=CH	292.30	0	6337.07	1647.00	−577.50	537.49
H_2O	94.39	−134.08	0	363.72	−609.05	−277.75
COOH	1744.00	−48.52	−250.67	0	−117.60	−283.55
CH_2COO	−320.10	485.60	1716.74	1417.00	0	867.81
EtOH-D	−44.17	−61.21	8003.65	1117.01	−493.44	0

Table 5.
UNIFAC-LL [29] parameters and 18 interaction parameters fitted for H_2O *and EtOH-D subgroups.*

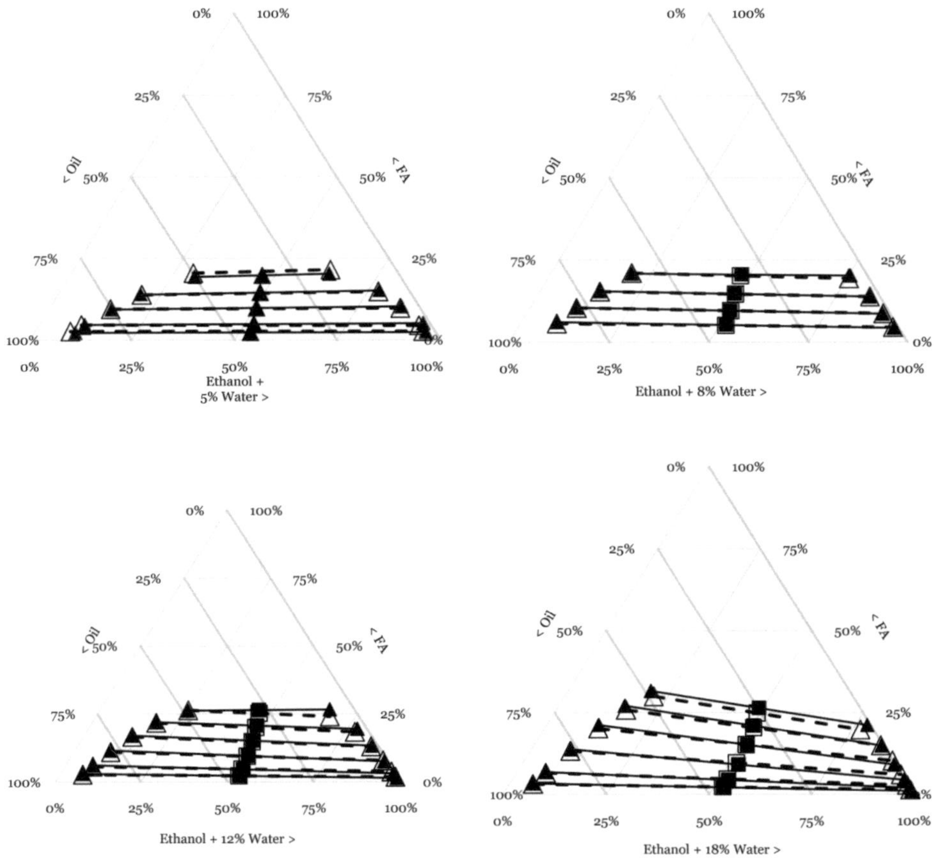

Figure 6.
LLE diagram for corn oil + commercial oleic acid 1 + and solvent (ethanol + %water) system at 298.15 K [31]. All compositions are on a mass basis.

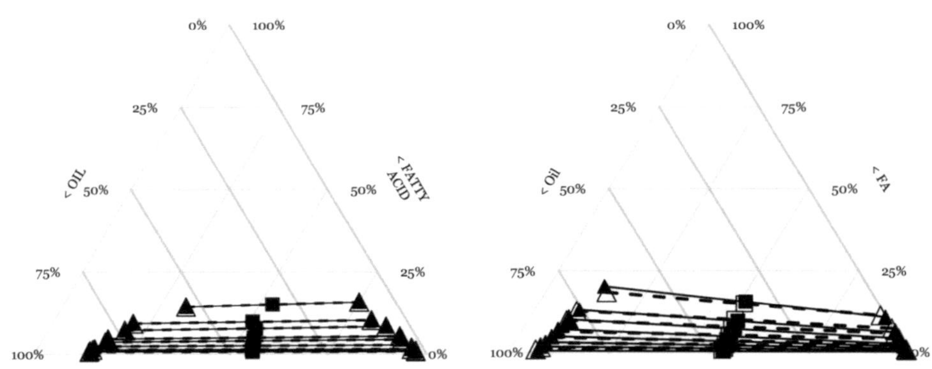

Figure 7.
LLE diagram for soybean oil + commercial linoleic acid 1 + and solvent (ethanol + water) system at 323.15 K [42]. All compositions are on a mass basis.

Oil	T (K)	RMSD (by mass)				
		UNIFAC-LL [29]	Noriega and Narváez [28]	Hirata et al. [26]	Machado et al. [43]	Bacicheti et al. [27]
Brazil nut	298.15	5.95	11.49	0.72	10.90	0.52
Corn	303.15	10.11	14.25	0.93	9.94	0.78
Cottonseed	298.15	9.59	13.63	2.59	12.13	0.90
Garlic	298.15	11.81	12.98	0.63	11.32	0.58
Grapeseed	318.15	7.75	11.90	1.85	12.58	0.77
Jatropha	288.15	9.37	11.05	0.73	11.46	0.89
	298.15	11.99	16.02	0.67	10.31	0.76
	308.15	13.91	16.83	0.64	9.27	0.86
	318.15	15.19	11.49	0.75	8.90	0.59
Macadamia	298.15	5.28	12.11	1.97	10.06	1.77
Palm	318.15	3.74	15.45	0.46	7.19	1.63
Peanut	298.15	11.15	14.04	1.15	11.36	0.72
Rice bran	298.15	10.56	16.46	1.12	11.43	0.59
Sesame	298.15	8.57	12.23	1.42	11.62	0.75
Soybean	323.15	4.74	18.73	1.34	10.18	0.60
Sunflower (O)	298.15	5.53	10.27	2.29	12.27	0.97
Sunflower (L)	298.15	11.63	9.35	2.13	12.72	1.01
Global RMSD%		9.24	13.43	1.27	10.81	0.87

Table 6.
*Root mean square deviation (*RMSD *for fittings in this chapter and the literature.*

As commented previously, Noriega and Narvaez [28] fitted 30 UNIFAC parameters of the subgroups related to pseudo-ternary and pseudo-quaternary systems of biodiesel + alcohol + glycerol and oil + fatty acid + alcohol + water. Hirata et al. [26] used plenty of pseudo-quaternary data available in the literature to fit all the 30 UNIFAC interaction parameters of interest for fatty systems. The present study adjusted only 16 interaction parameters for pseudo-ternary biodiesel systems and adjusted only 18 interaction parameters for pseudo-quaternary deacidification systems.

The global RMSD displayed in **Table 6** shows that the parameters set proposed by UNIFAC-LL [29] and Noriega and Narváez [28] are not suitable to describe the liquid-liquid equilibrium of deacidification and biodiesel-related systems. The global RMSD using UNIFAC-LL and Noriega and Narváez [28] were 9.24 and 13.43, respectively, while using the parameters fitted by Bacicheti et al. [27] resulted in a global RSMD of 0.87.

The considerable difference in RMSD between experimental and calculated data applying Machado et al. [43] parameter set (10.81%) and Bacicheti et al. [27] parameter set (0.87%) subgroup parameters emphasize the difference in ethanol subgroup in biodiesel separation and deacidification systems due to water and glycerol molecules in the system.

It was expected that Noriega and Narváez [28] parameters and Machado et al. [43] parameter set resulted in slightly high deviations (**Table 6**) since they were adjusted to biodiesel systems. But we were expecting that the other UNIFAC subgroups (CH_3, CH_2, CH, CH = CH, COOH, CH_2COO) would be able to represent the liquid-liquid equilibrium behavior, giving a fair and enough performance of UNIFAC model. However, the presence of water is too sharp, turning the hole systems distinct and the deviations significant, despite having similar UNIFAC subgroups.

In contrast to results obtained by the other UNIFAC parameter matrices, the RMSD obtained by using Hirata et al. [26] proposed parameters were closer to this study's parameters performance. It is worthy to quote that, although using a similar databank, this chapter ensues in lower RMSD between experimental and calculated data and, moreover, it has the upgrade of adjusting only 18 interaction parameters, resulting in a considerable faster procedure and relatively lower computational calculations than Hirata et al. [26] that fitted 30 interaction parameters.

The validation procedure of the parameters was taken for canola oil system, which was not used in the parameter fitting process. **Table 7** lists the RMSD between the experimental and calculated molar fractions using Bacicheti et al. [27] parameter set with those obtained using UNIFAC-LL from Magnussen et al. [29]), Noriega and Narváez [28], and Hirata et al. [26]). As previously stated, canola oil [18] data did not take part in this study's parameter fitting, but it was used by Hirata et al. [26] in their parameter fitting procedure, resulting in alike RMSD.

According to **Table 7**, the Bacicheti et al. [27] parameter set exhibits lower RMSD values than those obtained by applying the parameter matrix from the previously cited authors; hence the EtOH-D subgroup can successfully describe the deacidification systems of vegetable oils.

Figure 8 exhibits the ternary diagrams for the validation with canola oil data. Bacicheti et al. [27] parameter set exhibited small deviations from the experimental data than the other parameter matrices. In contrast, the results using the Machado et al. [43] parameter set and the parameters of Noriega and Narváez [28] have a considerable deviation from the experimental data, and thus, they are not recommended for quantitatively predicting the equilibrium of deacidification of vegetable oils.

As shown in **Figure 8**, Machado et al. [43] and Noriega and Narváez [28] parameter set, and UNIFAC-LL [29] present the highest average deviation from the experimental points. The average deviation values between the experimental and calculated data obtained using the interaction parameters from Hirata et al. [26] were close to

Oil	T(K)	RMSD% (by mass)				
		UNIFAC-LL [29]	Noriega and Narváez [28]	Hirata et al. [26]	Machado et al. [43]	Bacicheti et al. [27]
Canola	303.15	8.92	11.16	0.46	9.86	0.40

Table 7.
RMSD between experimental and calculated data mass fraction for the validation system composed of canola oil + commercial oleic acid 3 + ethanol + water at 303.15 K.

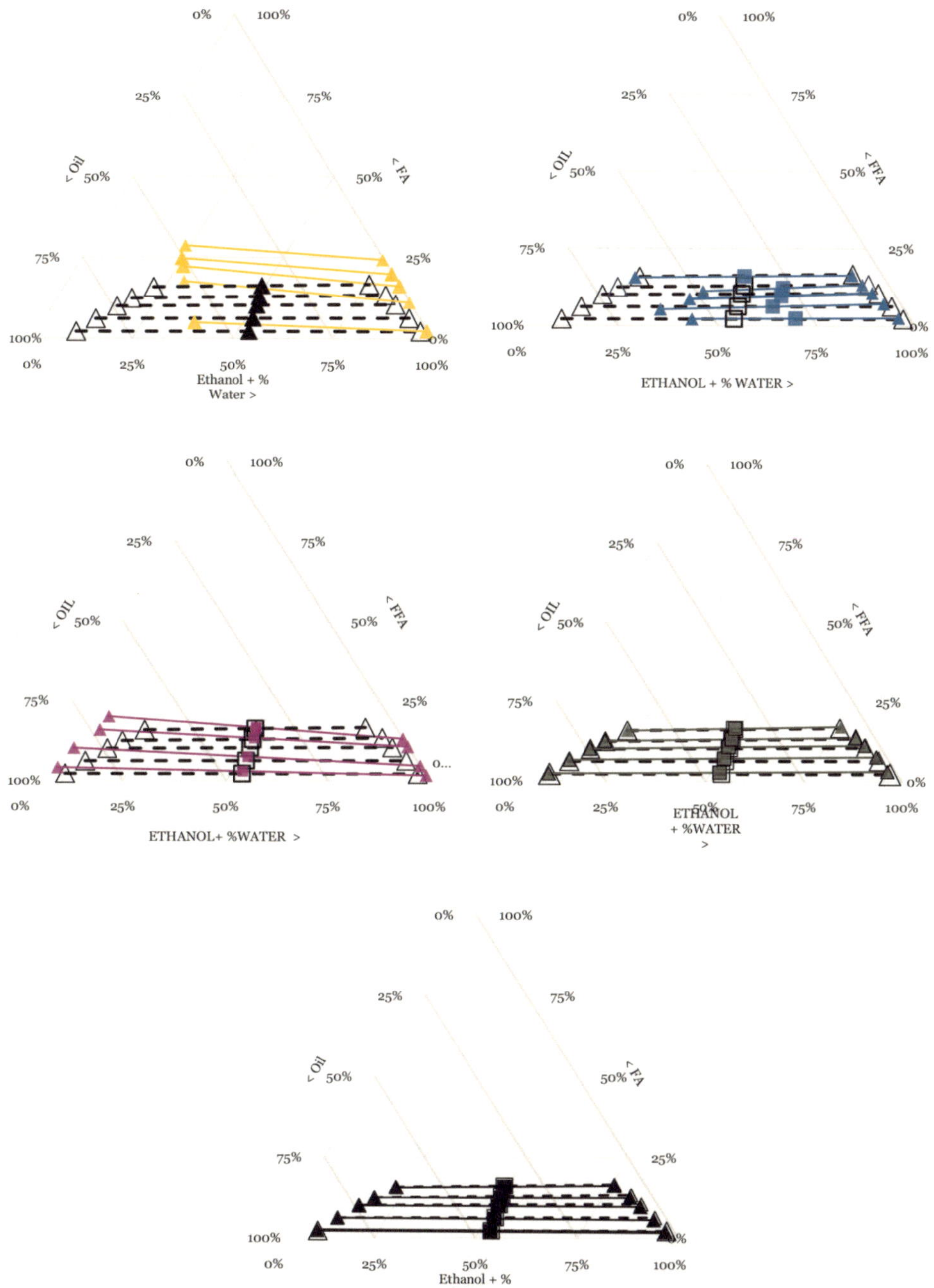

Figure 8.
LLE diagram for validation procedure with canola oil system [18]. Comparison between literature data (traced line) with predictions using parameters from Bacicheti et al. [27] (black lines), Noriega and Narváez [28] (yellow lines), Machado et al. [43] (blue lines), UNIFAC-LL [29] (purple lines), and Hirata et al. [26] (green lines). All compositions are on a mass basis.

those obtained by Bacicheti et al. [27]. However, Bacicheti et al. [27] only refitted 18 parameters, taking fewer computational calculations than those required by Hirata et al. [26], who readjusted all of them.

4. Conclusions

The new ethanol subgroups for the UNIFAC model presented in this chapter could correctly and accurately describe the liquid-liquid phase equilibrium of deacidification and biodiesel systems. The ethanol binary interaction parameters were fitted using a data bank of LLE available in the literature for biodiesel vegetable oil systems.

Using relatively few computational calculations and aiming to result in a relatively small split with the complex data set established by the UNIFAC-LL model, Bacicheti et al. [27] maintain CH_3, CH_2, CH, CH = CH, COOH and CH_2COO subgroups parameters, and refitted just water and ethanol UNIFAC interaction parameters. Ethanol-fitted parameters were then validated with very small deviations in the prediction of macauba pulp oil biodiesel for EtOH-B and canola oil for EtOH-D. The overall deviation calculated in the validation of these new UNIFAC parameters was 1.20% for biodiesel systems and 0.87% for deacidification systems.

When compared to prediction results for biodiesel systems using UNIFAC-LL parameters and those fitted by Bessa et al. [35], Machado et al. [43] had better results for the tie-lines, despite the small number of parameters fitted. The same results were obtained considering deacidification systems of vegetable oils, which ethanol interaction parameters proposed by Bacicheti et al. [27] exhibited small deviations from the experimental data and lower deviations than Noriega and Narváez [28], UNIFAC-LL [29], and Hirata et al. [26].

The method applied can contribute to a better description of the phase behavior of fatty systems involved in the deacidification of vegetable oil using liquid-liquid extraction and biodiesel separation process, as this biofuel is subject to strict composition and purity regulations. Moreover, taking into account the lower root mean square deviation between the experimental and calculated molar fractions obtained here and the relatively low computational calculations for the parameter fitting procedure, this chapter presents an easier and faster alternative approach instead to refitting all UNIFAC parameters.

The results show that the methodology employed is consistent and may be useful in predicting equilibrium when experimental equilibrium data are not available.

Funding

This work was supported by the Brazilian agencies CAPES [88887.486092/2020–2100] and CNPq [grant number 421930/2016–0].

Author details

Jacqueline M. Ortega Bacicheti[1,2], Guilherme D. Machado[2,3*], Fábio Nishiyama[2,3], Vladimir F. Cabral[1,2] and Donato Aranda[3]

1 Food Engineering Program, State University of Maringá, Maringá, PR, Brazil

2 Chemical Engineering Program, State University of Maringá, Maringá, PR, Brazil

3 Department of Chemical Engineering, Federal Tecnologic University of Paraná-UTFPR, Londrina, PR, Brazil

*Address all correspondence to: guilhermed@utfpr.edu.br

References

[1] Sérgio MBO, Soletti BJI, Carvalho SHV, Queimada AJ, Coutinho JAP. Liquid–liquid equilibria for the canola oil biodiesel +ethanol+glycerol system. Fuel. 2011;**90**: 2738-2745. DOI: 10.1016/j.fuel.2011.03.017

[2] Batista E, Monnerat S, Stragevitch L, Pina CG, Gonçalves CB, Meirelles AJA. Prediction of liquid–liquid equilibrium for Systems of Vegetable Oils, fatty acids, and ethanol. Journal of Chemical & Engineering Data. 1999;**44**:1365-1369. DOI: 10.1021/je9900169

[3] Cuevas MS, Rodrigues CEC, Gomes GB, Meirelles AJA. Vegetable oils Deacidification by solvent extraction: Liquid–liquid equilibrium data for systems containing sunflower seed oil at 298.2 K. Journal of Chemical & Engineering Data. 2010;**55**:3859-3862. DOI: 10.1021/je900791w

[4] Rodrigues CEC, Reipert ÉCD, de Souza AF, Filho PAP, Meirelles AJA. Equilibrium data for systems composed by cottonseed oil+commercial linoleic acid+ethanol+water+tocopherols at 298.2K. Fluid Phase Equilibria. 2005;**238**: 193-203. DOI: 10.1016/j.fluid.2005.09.027

[5] Tripathy D, Mohanty P, Dhindsa S, Syed T, Ghanim H, Aljada A, et al. Elevation of free fatty acids induces inflammation and impairs vascular reactivity in healthy subjects. Diabetes. 2003;**52**:2882-2887. DOI: 10.2337/diabetes.52.12.2882

[6] Röhrig F, Schulze A. The multifaceted roles of fatty acid synthesis in cancer. Nature Reviews. Cancer. 2016;**16**: 732-749. DOI: 10.1038/nrc.2016.89

[7] Scoville EA, Allaman MM, Adams DW, Motley AK, Peyton SC, Ferguson SL, et al. Serum polyunsaturated fatty acids correlate with serum cytokines and clinical disease activity in Crohn's disease. Scientific Reports. 2019;**9**:2882. DOI: 10.1038/s41598-019-39232-z

[8] Tsoukalas D, Fragoulakis V, Sarandi E, Docea AO, Papakonstaninou E, Tsilimidos G, et al. Targeted Metabolomic analysis of serum fatty acids for the prediction of autoimmune diseases. Frontiers in Molecular Biosciences. 2019;**6**:120. DOI: 10.3389/fmolb.2019.00120

[9] Rodrigues CEC, Meirelles AJA. Extraction of free fatty acids from Peanut oil and avocado seed oil: Liquid–liquid equilibrium data at 298.2 K. Journal of Chemical & Engineering Data. 2008;**53**:1698-1704. DOI: 10.1021/je7007186

[10] Rodrigues CEC, Gonçalves CB, Marcon EC, Batista EAC, Meirelles AJA. Deacidification of rice bran oil by liquid–liquid extraction using a renewable solvent. Separation and Purification Technology. 2014;**132**:84-92. DOI: 10.1016/j.seppur.2014.05.009

[11] Lu W, Xu Z, Li M, Ma Y, Xiao Z. Deep eutectic solvent (DES) assisted deacidification of acidic oil and retaining catalyst activity: Variables optimization and catalyst characterization. Industrial Crops and Products. 2022;**183**:114990. DOI: 10.1016/j.indcrop.2022.114990

[12] Hajjari M, Tabatabaei M, Aghbashlo M, Ghanavati H. A review on the prospects of sustainable biodiesel production: A global scenario with an emphasis on waste-oil biodiesel utilization. Renewable and Sustainable Energy Reviews. 2017;**72**:445-464. DOI: 10.1016/j.rser.2017.01.034

[13] Mu T, Rarey J, Gmehling J. Group contribution prediction of surface charge density profiles for COSMO-RS(Ol). AIChE Journal. 2007;**53**:3231-3240. DOI: 10.1002/aic.11338

[14] Silva JRF, Mazutti MA, Voll FAP, Cardozo-Filho L, Corazza ML, Lanza M, et al. Thermophysical properties of biodiesel and related systems: (liquid +liquid) equilibrium data for Jatropha curcas biodiesel. The Journal of Chemical Thermodynamics. 2013;**58**:467-475. DOI: 10.1016/j.jct.2012.10.006

[15] Mazutti MA, Voll FAP, Cardozo-Filho L, Corazza ML, Lanza M, Priamo WL, et al. Thermophysical properties of biodiesel and related systems: (liquid+liquid) equilibrium data for soybean biodiesel. The Journal of Chemical Thermodynamics. 2013;**58**: 83-94. DOI: 10.1016/j.jct.2012.10.026

[16] Bou Orm R, Citeau M, Comitis A, Savoire R, Harscoat-Schiavo C, Subra-Paternault P, et al. Walnut oil deacidification by liquid–liquid extraction with ethanol in a single- and multistage crossflow process. OCL. 2020;**27**:35. DOI: 10.1051/ocl/2020029

[17] Mohsen-Nia M, Modarress H, Nabavi HR. Measuring and modeling liquid–liquid equilibria for a soybean oil, oleic acid, ethanol, and water system. Journal of the American Oil Chemists' Society. 2008;**85**:973-978. DOI: 10.1007/s11746-008-1288-9

[18] Batista E, Monnerat S, Kato K, Stragevitch L, Meirelles AJA. Liquid−liquid equilibrium for Systems of Canola oil, oleic acid, and short-chain alcohols. Journal of Chemical & Engineering Data. 1999;**44**:1360-1364. DOI: 10.1021/je990015g

[19] Basso RC, de Almeida Meirelles AJ, Batista EAC. Liquid–liquid equilibrium of pseudoternary systems containing glycerol+ethanol+ethylic biodiesel from crambe oil (Crambe abyssinica) at T/K= (298.2, 318.2, 338.2) and thermodynamic modeling. Fluid Phase Equilibria. 2012; **333**:55-62. DOI: 10.1016/j.fluid.2012.07.018

[20] da Silva CAS, Sanaiotti G, Lanza M, Meirelles AJA, Batista EAC. Liquid−liquid equilibrium data for systems containing Jatropha curcas oil + oleic acid + anhydrous ethanol + water at (288.15 to 318.15) K. Journal of Chemical & Engineering Data. 2010;**55**:2416-2423. DOI: 10.1021/je900831p

[21] da Silva AE, Lanza M, Batista EAC, Rodrigues AMC, Meirelles AJA, da Silva LHM. Liquid−liquid equilibrium data for systems containing palm oil fractions + fatty acids + ethanol + water. Journal of Chemical & Engineering Data. 2011;**56**:1892-1898. DOI: 10.1021/je1009015

[22] Mohsen-Nia M, Dargahi M. Liquid−liquid equilibrium for systems of (corn oil + oleic acid + methanol or ethanol) at (303.15 and 313.15) K, Journal of Chemical & Engineering Data 52 (2007) 910–914. doi:10.1021/je700051j

[23] Serres JDS, Soares D, Corazza ML, Krieger N, Mitchell DA. Liquid–liquid equilibrium data and thermodynamic modeling for systems related to the production of ethyl esters of fatty acids from soybean soapstock acid oil. Fuel. 2015;**147**:147-154. DOI: 10.1016/j.fuel.2015.01.059

[24] Mohsen-Nia M, Khodayari A. De-acidification of sunflower oil by solvent extraction: (liquid+liquid) equilibrium data at T=(303.15 and 313.15) K. The Journal of Chemical Thermodynamics. 2008;**40**:1325-1329. DOI: 10.1016/j.jct.2008.01.029

[25] Ferreira MC, Bessa LCBA, Abreu CRA, Meirelles AJA, Caldas Batista EA. Liquid-liquid equilibrium of systems containing triolein + (fatty acid/partial acylglycerols/ester) + ethanol: Experimental data and UNIFAC modeling. Fluid Phase Equilibria. 2018; **476**:186-192. DOI: 10.1016/j.fluid.2018.07.030

[26] Hirata GF, Abreu CRA, Bessa LCBA, Ferreira MC, Batista EAC, Meirelles AJA. Liquid–liquid equilibrium of fatty systems: A new approach for adjusting UNIFAC interaction parameters. Fluid Phase Equilibria. 2013;**360**:379-391. DOI: 10.1016/j.fluid.2013.10.004

[27] Bacicheti JMO, Machado GD, Cabral VF. Liquid–liquid equilibrium calculations of systems containing vegetable oil + fatty acids + ethanol + water using new parameters for the unifac subgroups of ethanol and water. Fluid Phase Equilibria. 2021; **548**:113182. DOI: 10.1016/j.fluid.2021.113182

[28] Noriega MA, Narváez PC. UNIFAC correlated parameters for liquid-liquid equilibrium prediction of ternary systems related to biodiesel production process. Fuel. 2019;**249**:365-378. DOI: 10.1016/j.fuel.2019.03.124

[29] Magnussen T, Rasmussen P, Fredenslund A. UNIFAC parameter table for prediction of liquid-liquid equilibriums. Industrial & Engineering Chemistry Process Design and Development. 1981;**20**:331-339. DOI: 10.1021/i200013a024

[30] Reipert ÉCD, Rodrigues CEC, Meirelles AJA. Phase equilibria study of systems composed of refined babassu oil, lauric acid, ethanol, and water at 303.2K. The Journal of Chemical Thermodynamics. 2011;**43**:1784-1790. DOI: 10.1016/j.jct.2011.05.039

[31] Gonçalves CB, Batista E, Meirelles AJA. Liquid–liquid equilibrium data for the system corn oil + oleic acid + ethanol + water at 298.15 K. Journal of Chemical & Engineering Data. 2002;**47**: 416-420. DOI: 10.1021/je010273p

[32] Rodrigues CEC, Silva FA, Marsaioli A, Meirelles AJA. Deacidification of Brazil nut and macadamia nut oils by solvent extraction: Liquid–liquid equilibrium data at 298.2 K. Journal of Chemical & Engineering Data. 2005;**50**:517-523. DOI: 10.1021/je049687j

[33] Basso RC, da Silva CAS, de Sousa CO, de Meirelles AJA, Batista EAC. LLE experimental data, thermodynamic modeling and sensitivity analysis in the ethyl biodiesel from macauba pulp oil settling step. Bioresource Technology. 2013;**131**:468-475. DOI: 10.1016/j.biortech.2012.12.190

[34] Fredenslund A, Jones RL, Prausnitz JM. Group-contribution estimation of activity coefficients in nonideal liquid mixtures. AICHE Journal. 1975;**21**:1086-1099. DOI: 10.1002/aic.690210607

[35] Bessa LCBA, Ferreira MC, Abreu CRA, Batista EAC, Meirelles AJA. A new UNIFAC parameterization for the prediction of liquid-liquid equilibrium of biodiesel systems. Fluid Phase Equilibria. 2016;**425**:98-107. DOI: 10.1016/j.fluid.2016.05.020

[36] Mesquita FMR, Feitosa FX, Sombra NE, de Santiago-Aguiar RS, de Sant'Ana HB. Liquid–liquid equilibrium for ternary mixtures of biodiesel (soybean or sunflower) + glycerol + ethanol at different temperatures. Journal of Chemical & Engineering Data. 2011;**56**:4061-4067. DOI: 10.1021/je200340x

[37] de Rocha EGA, Follegatti-Romero LA, Duvoisin S, Aznar M. Liquid–liquid equilibria for ternary systems containing ethylic palm oil biodiesel+ethanol +glycerol/water: Experimental data at 298.15 and 323.15K and thermodynamic modeling. Fuel. 2014;**128**:356-365. DOI: 10.1016/j.fuel.2014.01.074

[38] Mesquita FMR, Bessa AMM, de Lima DD, de Sant'Ana HB, de Santiago-Aguiar RS. Liquid–liquid equilibria of systems containing cottonseed biodiesel +glycerol+ethanol at 293.15, 313.15 and 333.15K. Fluid Phase Equilibria. 2012;**318**: 51-55. DOI: 10.1016/j.fluid.2012.01.016

[39] Rodrigues CEC, Filipini A, Meirelles AJA. Phase equilibrium for systems composed by high unsaturated vegetable oils + linoleic acid + ethanol + water at 298.2 K. Journal of Chemical & Engineering Data. 2006;**51**:15-21. DOI: 10.1021/je0495841

[40] Gonçalves CB, Meirelles AJA. Liquid–liquid equilibrium data for the system palm oil + fatty acids + ethanol + water at 318.2K. Fluid Phase Equilibria. 2004;**221**:139-150. DOI: 10.1016/ j.fluid.2004.05.002

[41] Rodrigues CEC, Antoniassi R, Meirelles AJA. Equilibrium data for the system Rice bran oil + fatty acids + ethanol + water at 298.2 K. Journal of Chemical & Engineering Data. 2003;**48**: 367-373. DOI: 10.1021/je0255978

[42] Rodrigues CEC, Peixoto ECD, Meirelles AJA. Phase equilibrium for systems composed by refined soybean oil +commercial linoleic acid+ethanol +water, at 323.2K. Fluid Phase Equilibria. 2007;**261**:122-128. DOI: 10.1016/ j.fluid.2007.07.021

[43] Machado GD, Castier M, Voll AP, Cabral VF, Cardozo-Filho L, Aranda DAG. Ethanol and methanol Unifac subgroup parameter estimation in the prediction of the liquid-liquid equilibrium of biodiesel systems. Fluid Phase Equilibria. 2019;**488**:79-86. DOI: 10.1016/j.fluid.2019.01.012

[44] Castier M, Amer MM. XSEOS: An evolving tool for teaching chemical engineering thermodynamics. Education for Chemical Engineers. 2011;**6**:e62-e70. DOI: 10.1016/j.ece.2010.12.002

[45] Lasdon LS, Waren AD, Jain A, Ratner M. Design and testing of a generalized reduced gradient code for nonlinear programming. ACM Transactions on Mathematical Software. 1978;**4**:34-50. DOI: 10.1145/355769.355773

[46] Magnussen T, Rasmussen P, Fredenslund A. UNIFAC parameter table for prediction of liquid-liquid equilibria. Industrial & Engineering Chemistry Process Design and Development. 1981; **20**:331-339. DOI: 10.1021/i200013a024

[47] Homrich POB, Ceriani R. Phase equilibria for systems containing refined soybean oil plus Cosolvents at different temperatures. Journal of Chemical & Engineering Data. 2018;**63**:1937-1945. DOI: 10.1021/acs.jced.7b01051

[48] Homrich POB, Dias LG, Mariutti LRB, Bragagnolo N, Ceriani R. Liquid-liquid equilibria and density data for pseudoternary systems of refined soybean oil + (hexanal, or heptanal, or butyric acid, or valeric acid, or caproic acid, or caprylic acid) + dimethyl sulfoxide at 298.15 K. The Journal of Chemical Thermodynamics. 2019;**131**: 149-158. DOI: 10.1016/j.jct.2018.10.030

[49] Kanda LR, Voll FAP, Corazza ML. LLE for the systems ethyl palmitate (palmitic acid)(1)+ethanol(2)+glycerol (water)(3). Fluid Phase Equilibria. 2013; **354**:147-155. DOI: 10.1016/j.fluid.2013. 06.027